MONEY, CAPITAL, AND PRICES

KRANNERT GRADUATE SCHOOL, PURDUE UNIVERSITY MONOGRAPH SERIES

MONEY, CAPITAL, and PRICES

BY GEORGE HORWICH

Professor of Economics
Purdue University

1964
RICHARD D. IRWIN, INC.
HOMEWOOD, ILLINOIS

First Printing, January, 1964

Library of Congress Catalog Card No. 63-22393

PRINTED IN THE UNITED STATES OF AMERICA

TO MY PARENTS

Preface

This is an aggregative monetary study in which the stock of capital is an active variable. Capital is treated as a variable because discrepancies between saving and investment are at the heart of the monetary adjustment process advanced throughout this book. It is a fundamental tenet of the study that the *increment* to capital, whether large or small relative to the existing stock, is always potentially of the greatest magnitude in relation to the other variables of the adjustment process: the *increments* in money, interest, prices, and wealth.

The analysis strives for generality by describing the monetary impact of the central bank, the federal government, and commercial banks within a general-equilibrium framework; by considering the widest range of values for saving and investment ex post, and by viewing ex ante saving and investment in their broadest financial variety within the constraints of the model; by studying multiple-security systems, including a sector of financial intermediaries; by examining stationary and declining economies; by introducing alternative concepts and limiting forms of the demand for money; and by analyzing a wide spectrum of monetary disturbances, including independent changes in the supply and demand for money, in saving, investment, and the demand for nonmonetary assets.

The development of the book began with my Ph.D. dissertation, *Open Market Operations, the Rate of Interest, and the Price Level,* submitted to the University of Chicago in March, 1954. At Chicago Lloyd Mints whetted my initial appetite for monetary theory, and Lloyd Metzler provided the tools and pointed the way to monetary analysis. Mints' *Monetary Policy for a Competitive Society* and Metzler's "Wealth, Saving, and the Rate of Interest" each have had a deep influence on my work. I am indebted to

Milton Friedman, Frank Knight, and H. Gregg Lewis, who taught me the principles of economic analysis; and to Dennis Robertson, who, through continuing correspondence, was most generous in his critique and encouragement of my work, including the present volume.

I was drawn to monetary theory by the great debates between Keynes and his critics. My point of view has thus been shaped by the entire English monetary tradition, as represented by Keynes' *Treatise* and *General Theory*; Robertson's *Banking Policy and the Price Level* and *Essays in Monetary Theory*; Pigou's *Employment and Equilibrium*; and Hicks' *Value and Capital*. I have also been influenced by the Austrian and Swedish writers, particularly by Wicksell in that most perfect of all monetary treatises, Volume II of the *Lectures on Political Economy*. The classic paper by Modigliani, "Liquidity Preference and the Theory of Interest and Money," was always close at hand during my student days, and after.

I have benefited greatly from a collaboration with Vernon L. Smith in an unpublished paper, "A Reconsideration of Aggregate General-Equilibrium Theory," which served to clarify and sharpen the nature of capital and its rate of return, as incorporated in the basic model. Through the years I have received oral and written suggestions, which have vastly improved the manuscript, from Edward Ames, R. W. Clower, J. M. Culbertson, David I. Fand, John G. Gurley, Bert G. Hickman, Walter S. Salant, William H. White, and J. N. Wolfe. My colleague, Frank M. Bass, offered a number of helpful suggestions in regard to the exposition of the appendix to Chapter X, "A Reformulation of the Hicks *IS-LM* Diagram." Finally, but certainly not least, the spirited and able graduate students of Purdue have spotted several errors, improved my documentation, and generally made the teaching and writing of this material a thoroughly enjoyable experience.

The initial financial support for the book was a grant from the Brookings Institution. I am deeply grateful to Ralph J. Watkins, who was unstinting in his moral support of my efforts. The Purdue Research Foundation and the Krannert Graduate School of Industrial Administration provided summer grants from 1959 to 1962. I am especially grateful to John S. Day, Ronald L. Stucky, and E. T. Weiler, of the Krannert School, all of whom saw to it that I had every opportunity to complete this work.

The first draft of the manuscript was typed by Marilyn Schweizer, who, in addition, drew many of the diagrams and rendered valuable editorial assistance. She was indispensable. All of the ink tracings of diagrams were done by Edwin Lippincott.

It is with particular pleasure that I record the constant encouragement and loyal support of my wife, Gerry.

A final word to the reader: the opening chapter, "The Analysis of Monetary Change," is intended to be read piecemeal, as a running commentary on each chapter, in turn, and finally in full as a summary of the entire work.

*　　*　　*

I wish to thank the following publishers for permission to quote from books and journals published by them:

The Econometric Society: F. Modigliani, "Liquidity Preference and the Theory of Interest and Money," *Econometrica*, Vol. XII (January, 1944).

Harcourt, Brace & World, Inc.: J. M. Keynes, *A Treatise on Money*, Vol. I (London, 1930), and *The General Theory of Employment, Interest and Money* (New York, 1936).

Harper & Row, Publishers: D. Patinkin, *Money, Interest, and Prices* (Evanston, 1956).

McGraw-Hill Book Co., Inc.: A. H. Hansen, *Monetary Theory and Fiscal Policy* (New York, 1949).

Macmillan & Co., Ltd., and St Martin's Press, Inc.: A. C. Pigou, *Employment and Equilibrium* (London, 1949).

The Royal Economic Society: J. M. Keynes, "Alternative Theories of the Rate of Interest," *Economic Journal*, Vol. XLVII (June, 1937), and "The 'Ex Ante' Theory of the Rate of Interest," *Economic Journal*, Vol. XLVII (December, 1937); and G. Horwich, "Money, Prices and the Theory of Interest Determination," *Economic Journal*, Vol. LXVII (December, 1957).

University of Chicago Press: L. A. Metzler, "Wealth, Saving, and the Rate of Interest," *Journal of Political Economy*, Vol. LIX (April, 1951); and G. Horwich, "Real Assets and the Theory of Interest," *Journal of Political Economy*, Vol. LXX (April, 1962).

GEORGE HORWICH

West Lafayette, Ind.
July, 1963

Table of Contents

CHAPTER I

The Analysis of Monetary Change

A. AN OVERVIEW

This book sets forth an aggregative model of the closed economy within which the impact and adjustment to monetary change is described. The book is concerned equally with the construction of general framework and the formulation of particular conclusions applicable to policy and prediction. The framework contains both static and dynamic elements. The latter are based upon an integration of stock and flow segments of both the securities market and the supply and demand for cash balances. In a sense, stock-flow analysis and fidelity to stock-flow relationships of the monetary economy are the central themes of this volume.

The theoretical methodology is that of general-equilibrium analysis. Within the range of variables included in the model, a constant effort is made to describe the functioning of the entire system, both in and out of equilibrium. This is not to say that there are a great many variables in the model. On the contrary, the analysis is highly aggregative and contains little more than the minimum number of variables needed for a complete stock-flow system. But even this number creates an analytical network whose inter-relationships are sometimes both numerous and complex.

The flow variables are the supply and demand for current output, which is divided into consumption and investment goods; and the supply and demand for transactions balances. The stock variables are money in its role as an asset, and existing securities, the supply and demand for each of which comprise the existing-asset market. A common-stock (equity) security is used as the representative financial instrument. The flow variables are linked with the securities market through saving—the alternative to consumption—and investment, which in some degree are a demand and supply of new securities, respectively. The variables which equilibrate supply and demand, both within and between the stock and flow markets, are the commodity price level and the yield or rate of interest on securities.

Neither the output of investment goods nor the value of existing securities can legitimately ignore the constant correlative changes in the stock of capital. It is thus a feature of the model that capital also enters as an important short-run variable. There are no restrictions on the time period to which changes in capital are relevant; the economy is assumed to be in a state of continuing growth, in terms of which all monetary disturbances are evaluated.

Not only is capital a variable, but its rate of return is subject to short-run fluctuations, owing to changes in the rate of investment and the marginal cost of capital production. The variability of capital during adjustment processes also gives rise to changes in the capital-security ratio. This, together with changes in the return to capital, causes the income per security—the dividend payment (as opposed to the yield)—itself to become a variable. Accordingly, the simple inverse relation between the rate of interest and the price of securities, commonly assumed in monetary analysis, disappears. This study, therefore, advances independent theories of both of these variables over time.

The analysis of security and money stocks and flows, in which capital and its return are variables, is an effort to close the gap between monetary and growth theory. In this context it is no coincidence that the basic equilibrating force which propels the system from one equilibrium level to another is the interaction of unequal saving and investment flows with the existing-asset market. This interaction provides the mechanism by which the interest rate and the price level are simultaneously carried to their equilibrium values following any disturbance. In disequilibrium, saving and investment react directly on the market rate of interest. Resulting changes in monetary velocity cause movements in the general price level via the consumption-income relation. Under sharply defined circumstances, the price level, through its impact on real balances, supplements saving and investment as an equilibrating variable for the interest rate. But analytically the price level is secondary to saving and investment, which together are the initiating dynamic variables—the *thrust* of the monetary system.

The model contains the basic ingredients for a general theory of wealth: saving, investment, the capital stock, real balances, the return to capital, the rate of interest, and, on occasion, the real price of securities. These variables, properly combined in a wealth equation, are accounted for at all stages of the adjustment process. Total wealth thus supplants real balances as the general asset variable of monetary theory. In this broader framework, "real securities," as determined by the stock of capital, the return to capital, and the rate of interest, are coordinate with real balances in wealth analysis.

After setting forth the elements of the general model in Chapter II, the book analyzes through a sequence of chapters the impact and adjustment to an open-market operation. Chapter III treats the immediate impact of the disturbance. Chapter IV describes the "financial" adjustment process, the interaction of money and security stock and flow variables. Though the process is basically continuous over time, the expositional technique is that of period analysis. Chapter V is an account of the "real" adjustment, in which changes in the capital stock are explicitly considered. Since Chapters IV and V describe the reaction to an open-market purchase, Chapter VI covers the same ground for an open-market sale. Chapter VII introduces a second security, and describes the general features and the impact of an open-market purchase within the resulting system. Chapters VIII and IX generalize the analysis further by considering other kinds of disturbances, altering the form of basic functions of the model, and admitting sectors excluded from the general framework, such as commercial banks and financial intermediaries. Chapter X offers a general summary, an examination of some alternative systems, and several prescriptions for monetary and fiscal policy.

The remainder of this chapter will describe the salient features of the following chapters and their relationship to the general analysis.

B. CHAPTER II: THE MODEL

Chapter II describes in detail the supply and demand variables of the existing-asset and output markets. In the former market, considerable attention is given to the budget restraint on the real demands for money and securities (Part B[4]). The assumption that both demands respond to autonomous wealth changes, though the demand for money responds relatively little, is perhaps the most critical assumption of the book. It serves as a stability condition and as a justification for separating the real and financial analysis of the adjustment process. If only the demand for money reacts to autonomous wealth changes, then, depending on the degree of capital accumulation in an adjustment process, equilibrium may be unattainable (Chapter V-E[4]). But even if stability is guaranteed, a highly responsive demand for money complicates intolerably the purely financial explanation of the adjustment (Chapter IV-B[2]). Neither the movement of the interest rate nor the price level can be described without going at every stage beyond the money-security analysis to the concomitant changes in the capital stock, its rate of return, and total wealth. On the other hand, if the demand for money is relatively stable, a reasonably clean separation can be made between the financial analysis, which accounts adequately for the return to equilibrium, and the real analysis, which supplements rather than qualifies the financial description.

The relative stability of the demand for money may also be a prerequisite for an "effective" open-market operation, in the sense that it succeeds in altering the market rate of interest. One of the requirements of the model, as well as reality, is that the operation can have no direct effect on aggregate private income (Chapter III-B[2]). Thus, following, say, a purchase, the monetary authority must subsidize private incomes by the amount of the earnings on its new securities. If the subsidy is made to security income only, complete variability of the demand for money restores the equilibrium rate of interest instantaneously (Chapter III, note 9). The disturbance is not really a disturbance, and the book ends before it begins!

The account of the existing-asset market in Part B(1) advances the important distinction, retained throughout most of the volume, between idle and active balances. This is the "dichotomized" money supply, which is analytically invaluable in distinguishing between the stock (store-of-value) and flow (medium-of-exchange) functions of money. While it is possible to describe the same phenomena in terms of a non-dichotomized money supply (Chapter IX-D), I have never been under the illusion that I could have done so without first manipulating the dichotomized model. Though simpler, in the sense of employing fewer variables, the non-dichotomized system is extremely subtle, requiring infinite care in sometimes separating, and at other times combining, the stock and flow demand functions for money. By contrast, the idle-active system is an obvious one in which the stock and flow components can invariably be properly drawn upon. Up to a point, the dichotomized and non-dichotomized models are really equivalent structures. A substantive difference emerges only in regard to the price level which, in the dichotomized model only, contributes to the adjustment of the interest rate by an impact on real balances (assuming, once again, that autonomous wealth changes do not fall exclusively on the demand for money). This shows up operationally in a difference between the average and marginal velocity of the total money supply, following changes in transactions balances in the dichotomized model. The question of whether to dichotomize is thus an empirical one, and can only be answered definitively on those grounds. I have entered the dichotomized money supply into the general framework of the book because, in spite of the complicating role of the price level, it is an easier system to handle. Moreover, since dichotomization of the money holdings of just *one* economic unit creates effective specialization of function of the entire money supply (Chapter IX-D[3]), my empirical hunch is that the dichotomy is the more realistic case.

Both the demand for money and total wealth are expressed in real-value units, as is, therefore, the residual existing demand for securities. An important step undertaken in Part B(3) is the conversion of security demand to security-quantity units. This is equivalent to deriving the underlying quantity-demand schedule from a total revenue function. The conversion is made for several reasons. The primary one is that the theory of security prices depends on knowledge of the *number* of securities, which in turn is a function of supply and demand in security-quantity units. Security-quantity schedules are similarly derived for the real-value flow functions, saving and investment (Part C[2]).

One of the tasks of Chapter II is to formulate an investment demand which has the attributes of a true flow function. It is accomplished by utilizing the Keynesian marginal efficiency concept (Part C[2]). This is the foundation for a short-run investment theory in which entrepreneurs endeavor to equate the return to capital to the rate of interest. The resultant demand function varies inversely with the interest rate, and is stable in the face of most of the disturbances analyzed.

Ex ante saving is held to be a positive function of interest and income, and an inverse function of total wealth (Part C[2]). Consumption is thus inverse in interest, but positive in both income and wealth. The positive saving-consumption-income function is the "efficient" cause (in the Aristotelian sense) of household expenditures and saving. Along with the less crucial interest dependency, the consumption-income function is an active behavioral relationship of the entire volume. The saving or consumption-wealth relation is postponed to Chapter VIII-I(1). Growing out of the so-called "Pigou effect" (or, more accurately, the "Scitovsky-Pigou-Haberler effect") of the postwar literature, and referred to nowadays as the "real-balance effect," this relationship in my view has been badly overworked. It has been wrongfully employed as a *deus ex machina* of expenditure theory, where none was required. I consider the time-honored consumption-income function (as modified by modern writers) to be an entirely adequate, logically consistent, and empirically defensible explanation of why economic units spend and save. In general, real balances—or better, real assets—may account for the *division* between saving and consumption, but not for the *aggregate* of the two, as does income. An effort to employ real assets as the determinant of the aggregate of spending and saving (through hoarding and dishoarding) is shown in Chapters VIII-I(1) and X-B to encounter serious logical difficulties. Properly interpreted, the saving-wealth relation is at most a modifying influence on the adjustment and the final equilibrium, both of which are accounted for in principle without it.

One of the most basic (and analytically neglected) attributes of saving and investment is their financial character. Chapter II and most of the book treat them as a demand and supply of securities only (Chapter II-C[2]). If part of saving is instead a demand for additional cash balances, and a part of investment is financed by constantly reducing cash balances, the "equilibrium" is one of a perpetually changing demand for money and price level. The rather global disturbances that occur under these more general (and probably more realistic) circumstances are explored in Chapter VIII-H.

For most of the book, the supply of output is assumed to be constant at a level of full utilization of resources. Variations in output are considered, both in the context of resource unemployment and longer-run growth. But these variations are introduced less for their own sake than to meet the requirements of other analytical interests. For example, a model in which cash balances and claims on financial intermediaries are perfect substitutes avoids overdeterminacy only through output fluctuations (Chapter IX-A[4]c). At the same time variability of the capital stock, which is basic to the entire analysis, must sooner or later take account of the implied changes in output (Chapter VIII-I[2]). However, I have not delved deeply into the determination of output, partly to limit the scope of the book, and partly because I do not believe that the theory of supply is highly relevant to the main issues treated here. The analysis is essentially demand-oriented.

The process of combining stock and flow security markets is one of simply adding the flow demand and supply, saving and invest-ment, to the independently defined existing-demand and supply functions (Part D[2]). This can be done using the security-quantity or the underlying security-value schedules. The latter are more cumbersome, and somewhat unnatural from the viewpoint of traditional price theory. But they have the advantage of allowing total wealth and the supply and demand for money, which are also expressed in value units, to be entered into the process. The result is a more nearly general-equilibrium representation of the system, which is indispensable in the analysis of both equilibrium growth and monetary disturbances.

C. CHAPTERS III–VI: A DISTURBANCE AND THE ADJUSTMENT

Chapter III describes the direct impact of a central-bank pur-chase of securities in the open market. This reduces the market rate of interest. The analysis distinguishes between a "block" pur-chase, in which the securities are bought as a unit at a single price (Part A), and a "sequential" purchase, in which each security is bought individually at the minimum possible price (Part C). The latter purchase is more descriptive of the action of a large buyer, such as the central bank. The sequential operation is also a closer approximation to the continuous security transactions, at gradually rising or falling prices, that characterize adjustment processes (Chapter IV-B[1]).

Chapter III-A sets forth the conditions under which the money directly created (or destroyed) by the central bank is idle or active. In a once-for-all operation of relatively brief duration, the major impact of the bank is likely to be on idle balances. The "funda-mental problem for the analysis of monetary change" (Part F) is accordingly that of relating the impact of the bank on idle balances to one on active balances and the commodity price level.

Chapter III also describes a rotational impact of the operation on the existing-asset demand schedules (Part B[1]). Part B(2) traces the consequences of returning to the community the earnings on securities acquired by the bank. Part D analyzes the error of over-payment, which surely must characterize a goodly portion of open-market activity!

Chapter IV is the analysis of the financial adjustment by which security and money stocks and flows interact to raise both the interest rate and the price level, following an open-market pur-chase. The interest rate is returned to its "natural" level, deter-mined by invariant saving and investment functions, while the price level is brought to its higher equilibrium value, in accordance with the monetary increase. The driving force of the equilibrating proc-ess is the excess investment demand stimulated by the lower market rate. The excess investment takes the form of an excess supply of new securities which, when added to wealth at a higher rate of interest, creates an equal and opposite reduction in the quantity of idle balances demanded. The latter are then activated by invest-ing entrepreneurs. This is the "transfer effect" of the adjustment process. Given the idle-active dichotomy of money, the resulting rise of the price level reduces the real-balance portion of wealth and the existing demand for securities. The interest rate is thus further increased via the "wealth effect."

Parts B(2) and C(2) enumerate the conditions underlying the suc-cessful operation of the transfer and wealth effects. Destabilizing expectations, income leakages, inventory and other changes in the capital stock may cause temporary or permanent offsets to the equilibrating mechanisms. However, as we have noted, relative stability of the demand for money will grant the interest rate and the price level immunity, at least, from autonomous changes in capital and wealth.

Part D of Chapter IV summarizes the monetary disturbance in the framework of the equation of exchange. The analysis of inter-est and prices, money and securities, and capital and wealth is never permitted to stray outside the bounds of that fundamental equa-tion! The appendix provides a quantitative approximation to the relative importance of the transfer and wealth effects in restoring equilibrium.

Chapter V repeats the description of the adjustment process, accounting for the associated changes in capital, wealth, and se-curity prices. Chapter IV left the analysis of the latter variable incomplete, since security prices depend on the capital-security ratio and the return to capital, as well as the rate of interest.

The main portion of Chapter V is divided into two polar cases of capital formation, zero and complete forced saving. In the former case entrepreneurs fail completely to realize ex post investment with funds provided from excess security sales; the rate of growth of capital is determined solely by voluntary saving. In complete forced saving, idle balances tapped by the excess securities are converted fully into physical capital. In both adjustments the wealth of households in the new equilibrium depends critically on the interest elasticities of saving and investment. For example, if saving is completely interest-inelastic, then voluntary saving will not be reduced by the lower interest rates of the adjustment. Any forced saving which occurs in these circumstances is an addition to the pre-disturbance growth rate of capital. At the other extreme, a perfectly interest-inelastic investment schedule implies that complete forced saving is required in order merely to maintain the pre-disturbance rate of growth.

Under the assumption that the monetary authority subsidizes personal income only, following the purchase, wealth in a zero forced-saving adjustment cannot fail to lie below that of an undisturbed economy in the new equilibrium. However, in complete forced saving, wealth may be greater or less than that of the undisturbed system, depending on the flow-schedule interest elasticities.

While in zero forced saving stock watering tends to lower the real security price, voluntary saving tends to raise it. On net, security prices may rise or fall. In complete forced saving security prices invariably fall, owing to the downward tendency in the return to capital. Appendix A establishes that the *mean* security price will always be higher in zero than in complete forced saving.

The algebraic expressions of zero forced saving are, with minor modifications, conveniently applicable to the most general case of partial forced saving. Other sections at the close of the chapter (Part E) treat the circumstances of lagged investment, investment errors, variability of the demand for money, and the subsidization of security income. Appendix B describes a model in which the monetary authority exercises an equity claim to the private stock of capital.

One might suppose that a reverse image of the inflationary process would accurately describe the contractionary adjustment. This would assume, of course, that the same conditions hold, such as full employment and flexible prices. However, Chapter VI, which describes the impact of an open-market sale, demonstrates that the mirror-imagery does not apply. There are indeed elements of symmetry in the movement of idle balances, the interest rate, and the price level (though not in the second difference of prices). But total wealth and security prices behave quite asymmetrically. The basic cause of the asymmetry is that the disturbances are imposed on a growing economy. Whereas the equilibrating inflationary force is an excess security supply, the deflationary mechanism is an excess security demand. The latter originates in the excess of saving over investment stimulated by the higher interest rates of the adjustment. Even in the financial analysis, it is evident that excess security demand does not alter the existing-asset market in a manner opposite and equal to that of the inflationary process (Part B[1]). In the real adjustment, in which forced investment is the analogue of forced saving, total wealth cannot, except in an extreme case, fall below the trend line of the undisturbed economy (Parts D[2] and E[2]). This upward wealth bias of deflation is due partly to the fact that the saving schedule is a uniformly rising function of the interest rate. The inflationary wealth paths, which straddle the trend line, would reappear (invertedly) in deflation only if saving were a *downward* function of interest rates above the natural (Part F[2]).

The practical-minded economist may question the value of a deflationary analysis that assumes price flexibility and full employment of resources. Nevertheless, I consider the analysis of Chapter VI interesting and valuable on its own terms. But I hasten to add that the basic feature of the deflation, an excess of saving over investment, may characterize an inflationary adjustment as well. This rather surprising fact emerges in portions of the following three chapters. In Chapter VII, in which two competing securities are studied, it is entirely possible for one investment component to exceed its saving counterpart, while the opposite is true for the other pair of saving and investment schedules (Parts C[4], D[2], and E). The net effect may be inflationary, but part of the wealth changes that occur are accordingly those of a contractionary process. If a government budgetary deficit raises a dichotomized money supply (Chapter VIII-C[1]*a*), the resulting inflation will be characterized by a rise in the interest rate and an excess of saving over investment. Chapter IX-A describes an inflation, sparked by an increase in the supply of claims on financial intermediaries, in which aggregate saving again exceeds investment. In Chapter IX-B the inflationary adjustment of a *regressive* economy also draws upon the wealth and capital analysis of Chapter VI.

D. CHAPTERS VII–IX: GENERALIZATION

Chapter VII, the two-security model, is an opportunity to study monetary disturbances against the background of the interest structure. The securities are imperfect substitutes, which means that their differences may or may not be those of term-to-maturity. For if the long rate is merely the average of expected short rates, the securities are perfect substitutes. The analysis of Chapter VII would then apply to securities—or, in principle, to all earning assets, including physical capital—whose differences are anything other than those of term-to-maturity.

Chapter VII divides the stock and flow markets into submarkets based on each of the two securities.[1] The submarkets are replicas of the previous markets, except that they contain "financial-substitution" functions, which finance movements between the securities at non-equilibrium interest rates. The existence of independent pairs of stock and flow submarkets underscores the dependence of the interest structure on both stock and flow variables. There are six markets altogether, counting the two combined stock-flow systems. That this makes for a highly complex static and dynamic framework should come as no surprise. The system is reduced to manageable proportions by the use of Hicksian "substitution" functions, adapted from *Value and Capital.*

One of the most worrisome features of Chapter VII is the commodity price level, whose dynamic stability often seems to be in doubt. Even granted the stability conditions of the model, the price level in a two-security system has numerous *a priori* opportunities for oscillating on the way to an equilibrium. This is true even in a purely financial analysis. The fluctuations derive from the possibility, noted above, of simultaneous inflationary and deflationary adjustments in the flow markets for each security. Following, say, an open-market purchase, there is no assurance that the inflationary impulse will always be the predominant one. However, the appendix to the chapter establishes the ultimate attainability of equilibrium in both the price level and the interest structure, given the basic stability conditions.

A once-for-all open-market operation, in all its ramifications, is the prototype for almost all monetary disturbances. There is little in the analysis of other disturbances that has not been encountered,

---

[1] Though I have made no attempt to do so, the sectorization in this chapter should be applicable to the theory of international trade. Each of the submarkets could represent the stock-flow functions of independent trading countries.

directly or indirectly, in the detailed account of Chapters III–VII. This will become apparent in Chapters VIII and IX, which consider other disturbances, or the same disturbance in new contexts. However, in each of the cases analyzed, there is something unique as well as familiar, and this too will emerge in the course of the generalization. One of the implications of Chapters VIII and IX is thus that the earlier analysis, in its totality, is itself unique. The description of open-market activity in a growing economy in which existing-asset demand is interest-elastic cannot be derived as an extension of one of the simpler models or disturbances to be encountered.

Chapter VIII-A analyzes continuing open-market operations. The central bank remains permanently in the money market, pegging the interest rate or injecting a constant nominal or real quantity of money. After reaching the desired interest rate or rate of monetary increase, the bank soon finds itself by-passing the existing-asset market, exercising a direct impact on the income stream. The policy of pegging a lower interest rate is shown to require a constant real quantity, and an increasing *nominal* quantity, of monetary increase over time. The price level thus rises exponentially.

Independent shifts in saving and investment stimulate an adjustment process identical to that of open-market operations (Part B). The only difference is that the natural rate now moves relative to the market rate, rather than conversely.

Government budgetary deficits that create new money are, in a sense, the opposite of open-market operations (Part C). The deficits increase directly active balances and the commodity price level, which, by reducing real idle balances, raises the market rate of interest. Deficits financed by borrowing from the private sector are similar to increases in private investment, except that the rate of growth of the private stock of capital falls instead of rising. Both temporary and permanent deficits and surpluses are considered.

A policy of mutually offsetting open-market and fiscal policy is described in Part D. Other disturbances are shown to involve elements of open-market or fiscal activity or both: independent changes in active velocity, an example of which is an increment in a balanced government budget (Part E); shifts in existing-asset demand (Part F); and autonomous movements between idle and active balances (Part G). When saving and investment are partly a continuing demand and supply of idle balances (Part H), the interest rate gravitates toward the intersection of that part of saving and investment which is a demand and supply, respectively, of securities. The wealth effect, due to a perpetually changing price level, maintains the interest rate above or below that intersection. The rather complex dynamic equilibrium contains elements of both an excess of saving over investment and investment over saving. The capital and wealth changes are a corresponding mixture.

Saving as a function of wealth (Part I[1]) renders the natural rate of interest dependent on both stock and flow variables, including the supply and demand for money. But the impact of monetary changes is highly variable, depending on the degree of capital formation in adjustment processes. Variability of output (Part I[2]) offsets more or less the impact of wealth on saving.

The impact of commercial banks (Part J) on the money supply is the same as that of the central bank. The account of continuing open-market activity (Part A) may thereby describe the secular behavior of commercial banks. Security transactions between households and commercial banks merely involve a redistribution of securities within the private sector. The wealth analysis of Chapters V and VI must accordingly be qualified. Commercial banks also give rise to an interest-elastic money supply.

Chapter IX-A introduces a sector of financial intermediaries, who, in general, are no more than passive brokers in the saving-investment process. However, they are business firms whose marginal costs vary in the short run. Moreover, the claims on intermediaries are demand substitutes for the "primary" security (the direct claim on capital) of the system. This creates a somewhat modified version of a two-security model. Some unexpected results follow from these seemingly innocent assumptions. For example, aggregate saving may now be a downward function of the primary rate of interest, even though the individual saving components (household direct and indirect saving) are rising functions of their respective yields; there is no compelling *a priori* case for the inflationary character of intermediaries, even if they are the initiators of economic disturbances; in the event that claims on intermediaries and money are perfect substitutes owing, say, to governmental insurance on these claims, the system is an extreme "Keynesian" one of the "liquidity-trap" variety.

The stationary state and the declining economy are studied in Chapter IX-B. The latter is a "through-the-looking-glass" version

—a genuine mirror image—of the growing economy. For example, while excess security supply propels the inflationary adjustment of a growth model, an excess entrepreneurial demand to retire existing securities equilibrates the deflationary regressive economy. The classical state (Part C) is the Wicksellian world in which existing-asset demand no longer responds to changes in the interest rate. Various aspects of the adjustment process are telescoped, coinciding with the disturbance itself. Part D recasts the analysis in terms of a money supply, all units of which simultaneously perform the transactions and asset functions of money. Several limiting "Keynesian" cases (Part E) conclude the chapter. These are models in which the demand or supply of money is infinitely elastic, or both saving and investment are completely interest-inelastic. They share a number of characteristics: output and employment enter as variables; once-for-all changes in the money supply, whether through open-market or fiscal policy, can have no effect on income, employment, or the price level; the financial disposition of saving and investment between securities and cash balances is immaterial to equilibrium or the dynamic process of the model.

E. CHAPTER X: SUMMARY AND CRITIQUE

The major alternative theories to the dynamic analysis of this book are to be found in the writings of Patinkin and Keynes. Patinkin's use of the "real-balance effect" is held to involve a blurring of stock and flow concepts. His attack on the "dichotomy" of the real and monetary sectors, as entailing an indeterminate price level, is interpreted as a denial of the medium-of-exchange function of money and the traditional income-expenditures relationship. His claim that a system in which saving and investment are exclusively a demand and supply of securities also has an indeterminate price level is shown to disregard the store-of-value function of money. Patinkin's analysis of monetary change on income account involves interest movements that are shown to result from an inadequate specification of stock and flow variables. His account of bank-credit expansion fails to indicate whether new or old securities are purchased, and to take account of excess new securities in the adjustment process. His use of the real-balance effect in this context lends itself to a variety of interpretations, none of which is both self-consistent and effective in restoring equilibrium.

In the *Treatise* Keynes argued that saving and investment could not react directly on the interest rate because of the overwhelming magnitude of the stock of existing securities. This is shown to lead Keynes and his modern interpreter, Metzler, into difficulties regarding the dynamic forces acting on the interest rate and the price level. It is claimed that the liquidity-preference theory, to which both adhere, is incompatible with the view that saving and investment cannot directly affect the rate of interest. The preponderance-of-existing-securities hypothesis is held to be ambiguous in its implications, depending on whether new-security increments are compared with existing securities or the supply of asset money, both of which are legitimate frames of reference. Finally, the hypothesis is shown to neglect the slope of the existing-security demand schedule, which is also relevant to the interest impact of increments to supply or demand. Empirical evidence indicates that the slope of existing-security demand is relatively very steep.

The liquidity-preference theory of the *General Theory* is interpreted as involving a confusion between the allocation of additional saving to cash balances and the holding of existing cash. Keynes describes all monetary change as invariably operating through the interest rate. This is held to be unexplained and unjustified, since it implies a differential effect on money income of private and public expenditures: only private spending, as stimulated by the interest rate, can have a permanent influence on income and prices. The Keynesian "income theory" attributes interest movements to the impact of a change in income on the demand for money. This appears to rest on an inversion between changes in active balances and in money income. Keynes' "demand for finance," which raises the interest rate prior to new investment, allows old securities to act on interest while denying that an equal volume of new securities can do the same.

Keynes argued that full-employment saving exceeds investment at all positive rates of interest; equilibrium income and employment are accordingly below full employment. Pigou replied that saving-investment equality could be reached at full employment through increases in real balances via deflation. But this ignores the growth in the stock of capital and in capacity output generated during such an adjustment process. Conceivably the Pigovian adjustment might raise, rather than reduce, the deflationary gap. However, Keynes' underemployment equilibrium neglects the continuing hoarding of savers, which he himself stressed, and which prevents saving-investment equality from being established even at low levels of employment.

The appendix to the chapter derives the Hicksian *IS-LM* schedules on the assumption that saving is allocated both to security purchases and the holding of additional cash balances, and investment is financed both by issuing securities and reducing cash balances. The resulting schedules differ substantially from those of the traditional *IS-LM* diagram.

CHAPTER II

The Basic Framework

A. THE ECONOMY

The model employed in this study treats the economy as consisting of three markets and two basic sectors. The markets are the existing-asset, output, and factor. The sectors are households and firms. The existing-asset market consists of all accumulated wealth, which takes the form of money and securities. The output market entails the exchange of money for currently produced consumer and investment goods. The factor market applies labor to the stock of capital to produce the current output. Turning to the sectors, households own all of the wealth of the existing-asset market; they own and supply labor to the factor market; and they receive all of the income from securities and labor which they consume or save. Firms hold and employ (but do not own) capital in combination with labor to produce the output; they pay out income in the form of wages and profits to households; and they carry out investment in new capital by raising funds supplied by households. Firms own no wealth, earn no income, and do not consume or save.

This chapter will describe in detail the existing-asset and output markets, singly and in combined equilibrium. Detailed description of the factor market is not undertaken in this volume. Instead, output is generally assumed to be fixed at a level which fully employs the available resources. Occasionally changes in output are considered, both as a result of unemployment and growth, but no attempt to account for these changes rigorously in terms of the factor market is made. Additional sectors, such as a central bank, the central government, commercial banks, and financial intermediaries are introduced at various stages of the analysis. However, the basic framework is limited to households and firms.

The following account of the existing-asset market describes both the supply and demand for money and securities. Underlying the securities is the stock of capital, whose general characteristics are defined. After describing the demand variables, including various limiting forms and an alternative unit of measurement, the relationship between autonomous supply changes and demand is explored. The output market, described in Part C, is concerned with the role of money as a medium of exchange, and the division of expenditures between consumption or saving and investment. The financial character of saving and investment is defined, along with the technological basis of the investment function. In Part D the two markets are combined, first on the assumption of an infinitesimal and then an unrestricted period of time.

B. THE EXISTING-ASSET MARKET

1. Supply

Discussion of the existing-asset market must be preceded by an important distinction between two components of the money supply: idle and active balances. The total supply of money, M, is the sum of all things usable as a medium of exchange. Since there are no commercial banks, the money supply takes the form of pocket currency which is either full-bodied or, if we may introduce momentarily the central government, a liability of that sector. The active balances, the nominal quantity of which is M_1, perform the exchange function in the output market. Idle balances, whose nominal quantity is M_2, are held in the existing-asset market as a store of real value, an alternative to the holding of securities. Hence M_2 is "idle" only in that it is not currently serving as a medium of exchange, performing instead the function of asset money. M_1 and M_2 are mutually exclusive and exhaust the total money supply:

$$(2B.1) \qquad\qquad M = M_1 + M_2 .$$

Thus a unit of money is in use either as a medium of exchange in the output market, or as a component of wealth in the existing-asset market, but not both. Although in a strict sense M_1 is also part of wealth, it is held only to facilitate transactions in the output market, and is not available as an alternative to existing securities. From the standpoint of wealth, the supply and demand for M_1 are identically equal, and so nothing is lost by excluding it from the existing-asset market. We shall return to M_1 in Part C(1). Our concern with the real value of idle money is made explicit by dividing M_2 by P, the price level of final goods. We let

(2B.2) $$m_2 = \frac{M_2}{P}$$

We designate by W the total value of household wealth, expressed in dollars of constant purchasing power (output units), at an instant of time. If S_{VO} denotes the aggregate real value of existing securities held by households,[1]

(2B.3) $$W = S_{VO} + m_2.$$

Supporting the non-monetary wealth of the economy is the stock of capital, K. The entire analysis will be greatly simplified if we assume that all output units, both consumer and capital goods, consist of identical indivisible units. This provides for a single commodity price (usually referred to as "the price level") and a single process for the production of output. The accumulation of capital entails diverting the completed output unit from consumption to inventories, which constitute the capital stock.[2] In its role as capital, each output unit yields a perpetual income stream, net of depreciation, of x_K dollars per year. When divided by the price of our common capital-consumer good, we obtain both the *rate* of return per unit of capital, in the sense of a ratio of earnings to the price of a capital good, and the *real value* of the return, x_K, since P is also the price of commodities in general:

(2B.4) $$\rho_K = \frac{x_K}{P}.$$

If ρ_K is regarded as the rate of return per unit of capital, its numerator and denominator are both measured in dollars per unit of K,

---

[1] The notation has the following basis: S and D (with various subscripts) refer, respectively, to the supply and demand for securities. The subscript, V, denotes that the schedule is expressed in real-*value* amounts (security-price times security-quantity adjusted for changes in the general price level), while its absence later will indicate that the schedule is expressed in security-quantity units; O has reference to the *old* or existing securities market, and later, N will refer to the *new*, and T, the *total* securities market. At all times, "demand" and "supply" mean demand and supply schedules. If specific quantities are referred to, it is so stated. The use of primes denotes a specific schedule or value of a variable. Symbols without primes are a generic reference to the schedule or variable. The symbol, S, without subscripts (except on pp. 38 and 39 and in Chapter VIII-H, where lower-case subscripts are used) will refer to "saving."

[2] Though capital technically takes the form of inventories only, the latter are intended to be representative of all the varieties of actual capital, including plant and equipment, raw materials, consumers' durables, residential structures, etc.

and ρ_K is a pure number. On the other hand, taking P to be the general price level, ρ_K reduces to a ratio of output to capital units. But since capital and general output are identical, ρ_K again is a pure number.

The entire capital stock is owned by households whose ownership claim is a common-stock (equity) security. Owners do not hold capital directly, and there is no available claim in the form of bonds. Only entrepreneurs, hired by firms, exercise direct control over capital by employing it in cooperation with labor in the production process. The advantage of using common stock as a representative financial claim is that it provides a simple and direct approach to the payment of the aggregate share of capital, a matter of constant concern to this study. A bond model is not an acceptable alternative since it does not account for an ownership claim. An equity claim must be added, requiring that the analysis consider two claims and two rates of return. A common-stock model, on the other hand, is a complete system containing just one security and one rate of return. The question of distribution into bondholder and other component claims, which is not germane to this analysis, is by-passed.[3]

All common-stock holders enjoy a proportionate claim to the total earnings of business firms, $x_K K$, all of which are paid out as dividends. Each share is identical in its claim, regardless of the price or yield at which it was originally sold. Since the number of shares and the number of capital units are not necessarily equal, the annual earnings per share of common stock are

$$(2\text{B}.5) \qquad\qquad x_s = \frac{x_K K}{S_O},$$

---

[3] Metzler is one of the first to recognize the usefulness of the assumption that all securities are common stocks. Cf. his "Wealth, Saving, and the Rate of Interest," *Journal of Political Economy*, Vol. LIX (April, 1951), p. 99, n. 11. A cogent defense of the equities model is advanced by F. Modigliani and M. H. Miller in their paper, "The Cost of Capital, Corporation Finance and the Theory of Investment," *American Economic Review*, Vol. XLVIII (June, 1958), pp. 261–97. While the basic analysis in this volume is carried out with the ease of a single security, Chapter VII describes the framework of a two-security equities system. Chapter IX-A discusses the role of indirect claims issued by financial intermediaries, and Chapter V introduces a constant purchasing-power government bond. Occasional notes in other chapters consider the relevance of corporate bonds. An equities system already implicitly accounts for the direct holding of capital by owners, which is not different in economic principle from the holding of common stocks. Tobin seems implicitly to share this point of view (see his "A Dynamic Aggregative Model," *Journal of Political Economy*, Vol. LXII [April, 1955], pp. 103–15). An equities system also subsumes as a special case internal financing. Since the latter ultimately raises the value of a firm's outstanding shares, it is virtually equivalent to the sale of additional stocks to the existing holders.

where S_O is the total number of shares outstanding. The real earnings or dividends per share, ρ_s, are obtained by dividing both sides of (2B.5) by the price level:

$$(2B.6) \qquad \rho_s = \frac{x_s}{P} = \frac{x_K K}{S_O P} = \frac{\rho_K K}{S_O}.$$

We designate the dollar price of a security by π, and the real price by

$$(2B.7) \qquad p = \frac{\pi}{P},$$

which is the ratio of dollars-per-security to dollars-per-output unit, or the rate of exchange between security and output units. The market rate of interest in an equities system is the ratio of dividends-per-share to the share price:

$$(2B.8) \qquad r_M = \frac{x_s}{\pi},$$

or, dividing numerator and denominator by P,

$$(2B.9) \qquad r_M = \frac{\dfrac{x_s}{P}}{\dfrac{\pi}{P}} = \frac{\rho_s}{p}.$$

r_M, like ρ_K, is a pure number.[4] As a final step, we solve for p in (2B.9), and replace ρ_s by (2B.6):

$$(2B.10) \qquad p = \frac{\rho_s}{r_M} = \frac{\rho_K K}{r_M S_O}.$$

S_{VO}, the aggregate real value of existing securities held by households, may be expressed as the product of the quantity and real price of securities:

$$(2B.11) \qquad S_{VO} = S_O p.$$

---

[4] The payment of dividends on common stocks lacks the obligatory character of interest payments on bonds. But this is mainly a legal rather than an economic difference, for dividends can play an identical role in determining the rate of investment and providing a return to security purchasers. In an informed equities market no firm will be able to obtain finance for investment projects that do not promise to yield a return at least as great as the prevailing dividend rate on shares. Meanwhile, competition among firms will ensure that the return to common-stock holders is no greater than the current dividend rate. At the same time the demand for shares in a rational world will vary with the dividend rate, which is entirely comparable to the interest rate on bonds. Although the firm has more flexibility in timing its dividend payments—a consideration not overlooked by the analysis—a firm that consistently defaults on its implied obligation to stockholders will not long survive. Cf. J. M. Keynes, *The General Theory of Employment, Interest and Money* (New York: Harcourt, Brace & Co., 1936), p. 151, n. 1.

Since p is a ratio of output to security units, S_{VO} itself is measured in output or, equivalently, real-value units. Two S_{VO} functions are plotted in Figure 2–1 as a function of price, with p on the vertical axis and output units, designated by q_c, on the horizontal axis.[5]

FIGURE 2–1
The Value of Existing Securities as a Function of Price

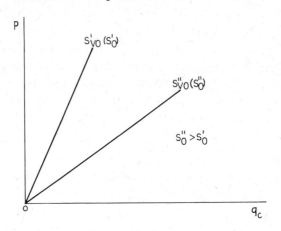

S_{VO} is linear in p, passing through the origin and having a p-axis slope of

(2B.12) $$\frac{\partial S_{VO}}{\partial p} = S_O ,$$

the existing quantity of securities. S_{VO}' is drawn for the given quantity, S_O', while S_{VO}'' is drawn for a greater quantity, S_O''. The effect of raising S_O is thus to rotate S_{VO} clockwise through the origin.

As long as ρ_s is fixed, p and r_M vary inversely ([2B.10]); movements up the vertical axis correspond to reductions in the rate of interest, and conversely for downward movements. However, if ρ_s itself varies, as it frequently will, p is no longer a reliable indicator of the interest rate. In order to preserve the relationship between S_{VO} and r_M independently of ρ_s, we substitute (2B.10) for p in (2B.11):

(2B.13) $$S_{VO} = S_O \rho_s \left(\frac{1}{r_M}\right).$$

---

[5] q_c, the real-value unit of account, is a *quantity* of output units which, in our system, are the identical capital-consumer good. In Section 3 below we employ another unit of account, q_s, a number or *quantity* of securities.

FIGURE 2–2
The Value of Existing Securities as a Function
of the Reciprocal of the Interest Rate

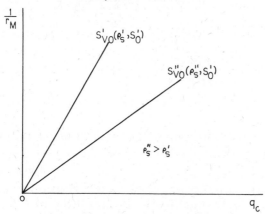

S_{VO}, drawn as a function of $1/r_M$ in Figure 2–2, is again linear and passing through the origin. But now its vertical-axis slope is

$$\frac{\partial S_{VO}}{\partial\left(\dfrac{1}{r_M}\right)} = \rho_s S_O.$$

Thus when ρ_s increases from ρ_s' to ρ_s'', S_O remaining fixed at S_O', S_{VO} swings from S_{VO}' to S_{VO}'' in response to its greater slope.

Rather than draw S_{VO} as a function of just p or $1/r_M$, we shall find it extremely useful to relate S_{VO} simultaneously to both variables. This can be done since, for a given ρ_s, there corresponds to each $1/r_M$ a unique value of $p = \rho_s(1/r_M)$. Since p and $1/r_M$ differ only by the constant, ρ_s, they can be plotted on the same linear scale. However, the $1/r_M$ scale on the vertical axis is held constant. A change in ρ_s thus requires that the entire p-axis be rescaled. But this can be done, while S_{VO} itself rotates. We plot $1/r_M$ as the invariant scale on the vertical axis because of our primary concern with the rate of interest. Adding a sliding implicit price scale provides useful information, while granting S_{VO} a slope with respect to its own price axis of $\partial S_{VO}/\partial p = S_O$. The latter relationship shall prove to be a great convenience.

The reader may find the upward-sloping linear S_{VO} function somewhat unfamiliar. In fact, security values are almost universally expressed as a function of r_M, rather than $1/r_M$ or p.[6] In order

---

[6] Cf. Metzler, *op. cit.*, p. 101.

to do this, we write (2B.13) as

$$(2B.14) \qquad\qquad S_{VO} = \frac{S_O \rho_s}{r_M}.$$

$S_O \rho_s$ is the given total income of securities. S_{VO} as a function of r_M is thus a rectangular hyperbola for which the inscribed rectangular area at any point is $S_O \rho_s$. Total wealth is

$$(2B.15) \qquad\qquad W(r_M) = \frac{S_O \rho_s}{r_M} + m_2,$$

a rectangular hyperbola with its origin at m_2 on the horizontal axis. Manifestly, the advantages of a *linear* S_{VO} and W, expressed as a function of $1/r_M$ and p, are considerable. The only disadvantage is that $1/r_M$ moves opposite to r_M, which is slightly awkward. But this is more than compensated for by the resulting linear relationships among the wealth variables.

Both supply components of the existing-asset market, S_{VO} and m_2, are drawn in Figure 2–3, where $1/r_M$ and p are on the vertical

FIGURE 2–3
Supply Components of the Existing-Asset Market

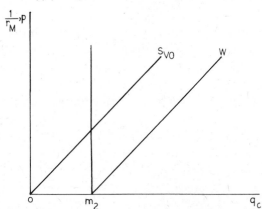

axis, and q_c is on the horizontal. m_2, whose value is independent of r_M or p, is a vertical line, and W, total wealth, is the horizontal sum of S_{VO} and m_2. Thus W has the slope of S_{VO}, but originates on the horizontal axis at the value, m_2.

2. Demand

At each price and rate of interest, asset holders must decide how they wish to divide their existing wealth between securities and money. Such a decision involves both assets simultaneously since, having fixed the demand for one, the demand for the other follows as a residual from the given stock of wealth. Hence if D_{VO} is the number of real dollars households wish to have embodied in securities, and L_2 is the demand for real idle balances,

(2B.16) $$D_{VO} + L_2 = W.$$

It follows from (2B.16) − (2B.3) that

(2B.17) $$D_{VO} - S_{VO} = m_2 - L_2.$$

Verbally, this is to say that the excess demand for securities, in real-value units, equals the excess supply of real idle balances, and equilibrium in the existing market for money implies equilibrium in the market for existing securities.

In accordance with modern interest theory, L_2 is a decreasing function of r_M and an increasing function of $1/r_M$ (see Figure 2–4):[7]

(2B.18) $$\frac{\partial L_2}{\partial r_M} < 0; \qquad \frac{\partial L_2}{\partial \left(\dfrac{1}{r_M}\right)} > 0.$$

This is a sufficient condition for the stability of the existing-asset market, for if r'_M is the equilibrium rate, then at $r_M < r'_M$,

$$m_2 - L_2 = D_{VO} - S_{VO} < 0.$$

FIGURE 2–4
Supply and Demand Components of the Existing-Asset Market

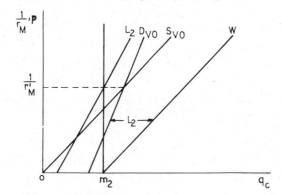

[7] See Keynes, *The General Theory of Employment, Interest and Money,* pp. 172 and 196, for a justification of the $L_2(r_M)$ relationship in terms of interest as the opportunity cost of holding money. For the "speculative" motive see *ibid.,* pp. 196–99. A recent analysis of the demand for money is given by James Tobin in "Liquidity Preference as Behavior toward Risk," *Review of Economic Studies,* Vol. XXV (February, 1958), pp. 65–86.

Households wish to hold less than the value of existing securities; p and $1/r_M$ tend to fall, and r_M to rise. And conversely at $r_M > r_M'$. The relationship between the slopes of D_{VO} and L_2 can be found by rearranging (2B.16) and differentiating it:

$$(2B.19) \quad \frac{\partial D_{VO}}{\partial\left(\dfrac{1}{r_M}\right)} = \frac{\partial W}{\partial\left(\dfrac{1}{r_M}\right)} - \frac{\partial L_2}{\partial\left(\dfrac{1}{r_M}\right)}, \text{ and } \frac{\partial D_{VO}}{\partial\left(\dfrac{1}{r_M}\right)} \gtreqless 0 \text{ when } \frac{\partial L_2}{\partial\left(\dfrac{1}{r_M}\right)} \lesseqgtr \frac{\partial W}{\partial\left(\dfrac{1}{r_M}\right)}.$$

In Figure 2–4,

$$\frac{\partial L_2}{\partial\left(\dfrac{1}{r_M}\right)} < \frac{\partial W}{\partial\left(\dfrac{1}{r_M}\right)}, \text{ and so } \frac{\partial D_{VO}}{\partial\left(\dfrac{1}{r_M}\right)} > 0.$$

The assumption is often made that at some low interest rate and below (or at a high security price and above), the demand schedule for money becomes perfectly flat.[8] This implies that asset holders want to hold all of their wealth in the form of money. This possibility is illustrated in Figure 2–5 where at r_M'', L_2 and D_{VO} are both horizontal. Symbolically,

$$(2B.20) \qquad \frac{\partial L_2}{\partial\left(\dfrac{1}{r_M}\right)} = \frac{\partial D_{VO}}{\partial\left(\dfrac{1}{r_M}\right)} = \infty \qquad \text{when } r_M = r_M''.$$

FIGURE 2–5
Limiting Forms of the Existing-Asset Demand Schedules

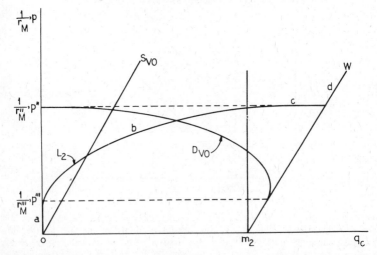

[8] See Modigliani, "Liquidity Preference and the Theory of Interest and Money," *Econometrica*, Vol. XII (January, 1944), pp. 45–88, esp. pp. 53, 55–56, and 74.

However, L_2 cannot exceed total wealth ([2B.16]). While at r_M'', D_{VO} goes to zero, L_2 terminates at its intersection with the total wealth function. At $r_M < r_M''$, the desire to hold wealth exclusively as money means that D_{VO} coincides with the vertical axis and L_2 with W:

(2B.21) $\qquad L_2 = W$ and $D_{VO} = 0$ when $r_M \leq r_M''.$

The assumption is also made that at a sufficiently high interest rate and above (or at a low price and below), households want all of their wealth in the form of non-cash assets.[9] This occurs in Figure 2-5 at $r_M \geq r_M'''$ where D_{VO} achieves a maximum by coinciding with the total wealth function:

(2B.22) $\qquad D_{VO} = W$ and $L_2 = \dfrac{\partial L_2}{\partial \left(\dfrac{1}{r_M}\right)} = 0$ when $r_M \geq r_M'''.$

In Figure 2-6 L_2 is diagramed as a function of r_M. The lettered portions of the curve correspond to those similarly designated in

FIGURE 2-6

The Demand for Idle Money as a Function of the Rate of Interest

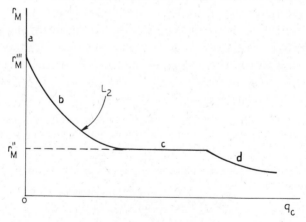

Figure 2-5. $L_2(r_M)$ starts at the vertical axis at a high interest rate, r_M''', and becomes horizontal at r_M''. The implication of the wealth restraint at interest rates below r_M'' is that L_2 (over the range, d) coincides with $W(r_M)$, the rectangular hyperbola representing total wealth ([2B.15]).[10] Superficially, it appears from the diagram that a

[9] *Ibid.*, pp. 52–53, 55, 65–67, and 75.

[10] Cf. D. Patinkin, *Money, Interest, and Prices* (Evanston, Ill.: Row, Peterson & Co., 1956), pp. 146–49 and 245–46.

sufficiently large quantity of m_2 will carry it along L_2 beyond the horizontal segment, c, to the downward-sloping portion, d. But this is effectively impossible. We have seen that m_2 on the horizontal axis is the origin for $W(r_M)$ (see [2B.15]). If m_2 increases without changing the quantity of securities, as through a fiscal deficit, the downward portion, d, itself shifts to the right, always remaining beyond m_2 by the value of securities held. If m_2 increases through open-market purchases, the central bank would have to buy all existing securities in order to drive m_2 to an intersection with d on the wealth function.[11] But even if this should occur, the wealth function at this point would coincide with m_2, taking on a vertical slope. The demand for m_2 would be identically equal to the supply, and perfectly insensitive to the interest rate. Open-market operations on wealth account could not be carried out.[12]

The limiting cases in which asset holders choose to put all of their wealth into money or securities only will not concern us until Chapter IX. Until then we assume that over the relevant range of interest rates L_2 and D_{VO} are both positive quantities, and that the absolute slope of L_2 with respect to the horizontal axis is greater than zero and less than infinity. Except in Appendix A we shall assume at all times that L_2 and D_{VO} are linear functions of $1/r_M$ and p over the effective range.[13] We shall also assume throughout this volume that any shifts in D_{VO} or L_2, not associated with the addition of new saving to the existing-asset market, occur instantaneously.

---

[11] Cf. A. P. Lerner, "A Note on the Rate of Interest and the Value of Assets," *Economic Journal*, Vol. LXXI (September, 1961), p. 543.

[12] The system in which L_2 is zero or completely interest-inelastic is the "classical" model, in which security transactions can be carried out on income account only; i.e., *new* securities only can be purchased, and securities can be sold only to savers. This system is treated in Chapter IX-C.

[13] Linearity of either of the demand schedules is sufficient for linearity of the other. To show this, we differentiate (2B.19):

$$\frac{\partial^2 D_{VO}}{\partial \left(\frac{1}{r_M}\right)^2} = \frac{\partial^2 W}{\partial \left(\frac{1}{r_M}\right)^2} - \frac{\partial^2 L_2}{\partial \left(\frac{1}{r_M}\right)^2}.$$

Since $W = S_{VO} + m_2$,

$$\frac{\partial^2 W}{\partial \left(\frac{1}{r_M}\right)^2} = \frac{\partial^2 S_{VO}}{\partial \left(\frac{1}{r_M}\right)^2} = 0 \text{ , and } \frac{\partial^2 D_{VO}}{\partial \left(\frac{1}{r_M}\right)^2} = - \frac{\partial^2 L_2}{\partial \left(\frac{1}{r_M}\right)^2}.$$

Hence,

$$\frac{\partial^2 D_{VO}}{\partial \left(\frac{1}{r_M}\right)^2} \gtreqless 0 \text{ when } \frac{\partial^2 L_2}{\partial \left(\frac{1}{r_M}\right)^2} \lesseqgtr 0 .$$

Whether the shift entails an independent reshuffling of existing assets, or a dependent response to an autonomous wealth change (see Part B[4]), it is executed in a zero time interval. Finally, we shall simplify our diagram of the wealth market by indicating m_2 to be greater than S_{VO} over the pictured range of interest rates (see Figure 2-5). This may contradict reality, but it will facilitate interpretation of the wealth diagrams by avoiding several intersections between lines, without altering in any way the fundamental relationships discussed.

3. Security Demand in Security-Quantity Units

The next step in the description of the existing-asset market is to derive the security-*quantity* demand schedule that lies beneath D_{VO}. The latter is a relation between price and the real-value amounts that asset holders wish to possess in the form of securities, but does not directly indicate the *number* of securities desired. D_{VO} bears the same relation to a quantity security-demand schedule that S_{VO} does to S_O. D_{VO} is the total revenue curve, expressed in real value; we are seeking the underlying quantity-price demand function. Accordingly, we define the quantity demand for securities, financed out of existing wealth, as

(2B.23)
$$D_O = \frac{D_{VO}}{p}.$$

While D_{VO} is measured in output units, q_c, the unit of account for D_O, as well as S_O, is q_s, a quantity of securities.

The main reason for deriving D_O is that S_O is a variable in the expressions for the income and price of securities ([2B.6] and [2B.10]). Since the analysis describes these variables, along with the rate of interest, knowledge of both security-quantity supply and demand is necessary. A second reason for the derivation is that the markets for securities conform much more to traditional formulation when the schedules are expressed in security-quantity rather

---

Linearity of $L_2(1/r_M)$ does not, of course, imply linearity of $L_2(r_M)$. Consider the following linear function and its derivative with respect to r_M:

$$L_2 = c_O + c_1\left(\frac{1}{r_M}\right), \text{ where } c_1 > 0,$$

$$\frac{\partial L_2}{\partial r_M} = -\frac{c_1}{r_M^2}, \text{ and } \frac{\partial^2 L_2}{\partial r_M^2} = \frac{2c_1}{r_M^3} > 0.$$

$L_2(r_M)$, corresponding to the linear $L_2(1/r_M)$ function, is thus falling and concave upward —as ordinarily drawn.

than real-value units. Though the markets can be described in terms of either unit of account, the presentation is much less cumbersome if security quantities are used. This is particularly true in combining the stock and flow security markets in Part D(2), Chapters III-A, IV-B, and VI-B.[14]

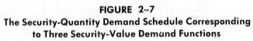

FIGURE 2–7
The Security-Quantity Demand Schedule Corresponding
to Three Security-Value Demand Functions

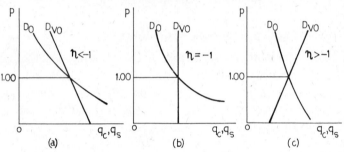

The derivation of D_O is carried out with reference to Figure 2–7. The analysis is restricted to linear D_{VO} schedules consistent with stability of the existing-asset market. The latter requirement implies that if D_{VO} is upward sloping, as in Figure 2–7(c), it must cross the horizontal axis at a positive quantity. Non-linear D_{VO} functions are taken up in Appendix A(1). Though D_O and D_{VO} are measured in different units, they are plotted in each diagram along a common horizontal scale. Since

$$D_O \gtreqless D_{VO} \text{ when } p \lesseqgtr 1 \text{ ([2B.23]),}$$

D_O in each case cuts D_{VO} from the left and above, meeting it at the unity price. Interpreting D_{VO} as a total revenue function, the underlying D_O curve in Figure 2–7(a) has a price elasticity, η, less than -1; i.e., as the security price is lowered, the real monetary outlay on securities, as represented by D_{VO}, increases. D_O is thus a relatively flat downward-sloping schedule. In Figure 2–7(b), D_{VO} is vertical, indicating a constant outlay on securities, and unitary elasticity of D_O. The latter is a rectangular hyperbola. In Figure 2–7(c), D_{VO} is the revenue function either of a downward-sloping

---

[14] A third reason emerges in Chapter V, Appendix B, where the wealth of households depends on their relative holdings of the total *quantity* of securities. The central bank, which is also a holder of the equity securities, competes with households as a claimant to the private stock of capital.

D_O schedule for which $\eta > -1$, or an upward-sloping schedule of $\eta > 0$. In fact, D_O is downward sloping. We establish this by drawing a vector from the origin to any point on D_{VO}. The vertical-axis *slope* of the vector is $D_{VO}/p = D_O$, the security-quantity function itself. As vectors are extended to D_{VO} at successively higher prices, their vertical-axis slope decreases monotonically. D_O is thus an inverse function of price, as drawn. We conclude:

(2B.24) $$\frac{\partial D_O}{\partial p} < 0 \text{ with } \eta \gtreqless -1 \text{ when } \frac{\partial D_{VO}}{\partial p} \gtreqless 0.$$

Security supply and demand in terms of both security-quantity and real-value units are drawn in Figure 2–8. S_{VO} is the usual vector

FIGURE 2–8
Existing-Security Supply and Demand
in Both Security-Quantity and Value Units

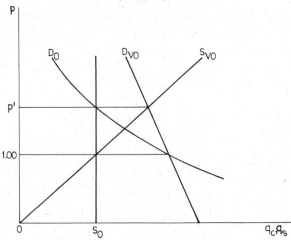

emanating from the origin. The underlying security-quantity schedule is $S_O = S_{VO}/p$ ([2B.11]), measured in q_s units. S_O, the given stock of securities, is independent of price and is drawn as a vertical line intersecting S_{VO} at $p = 1.00$. D_{VO}, which happens to be downward sloping, intersects S_{VO} at p', the equilibrium price.[15] Like S_O and S_{VO}, D_O and D_{VO} meet at $p = 1.00$. In addition, D_O intersects S_O at p'. This follows from the relationship,

(2B.25) $$D_O - S_O = \frac{D_{VO} - S_{VO}}{p};$$

---

[15] There is, of course, no necessary connection between the equilibrium and unity prices. Only by coincidence would p' equal unity.

the excess quantity-demand and value-demand functions differ only by the factor, p. Hence, if at $p = p'$, $D_{VO} - S_{VO} = 0$, then $D_O = S_O$.

4. Autonomous Changes in Wealth

We must now make explicit a major consideration regarding the existing-asset market. This concerns the properties of D_{VO} and L_2 with respect to involuntary changes in wealth. Since the asset-demand schedules are derived from, and conditional upon total wealth (see [2B.16]), an independent change in wealth must impinge on either or both schedules. Those changes that are caused or accompanied by a given shift in D_{VO} or L_2 do not concern us here. In the latter category are the periodic increments to wealth due to current saving; at the going rate of interest the resulting increase in S_{VO} or m_2 is accompanied by an equal increase in D_{VO} or L_2. Nor are we concerned with wealth changes due to movements of the interest rate, since D_{VO} and L_2 are already defined as functions of that variable. Our concern in this section is with changes in m_2 and S_{VO} that occur independently of the demand to hold these assets, and are not due to interest fluctuations. An example would be a capital levy or a revaluation of idle balances due to a price-level movement. The nature of the demand response to such *autonomous* wealth disturbances is clearly an empirical question to which an *a priori* answer cannot be definitive. However, we shall adopt as a working assumption the following: an independent loss or gain of wealth in either component and for any cause leads to a change in the same direction in the demand for both securities and cash. Households are indifferent to the source of the wealth change—i.e., whether in securities or cash—and neither asset is inferior with respect to wealth. Symbolically, our assumption is:

$$(2B.26) \qquad \Delta W = \Delta D_{VO} + \Delta L_2; \text{ when } \Delta W \gtrless 0, \Delta D_{VO} \gtrless 0 \text{ and } \Delta L_2 \gtrless 0,$$

where ΔW is an independent wealth change at a given interest rate, and ΔD_{VO} and ΔL_2 are the increments in the demand schedules. We shall make the further assumption that each demand schedule, expressed in value units, shifts by a fraction of the total change in wealth equal to the ratio of the existing value of the corresponding asset to total wealth. At any rate of interest,

$$(2B.27) \qquad \Delta D_{VO} = \Delta W \left(\frac{S_{VO}}{W}\right), \qquad \Delta L_2 = \Delta W \left(\frac{m_2}{W}\right).$$

Thus, while the nature of the wealth change is immaterial to the general household reaction, as stated by (2B.26), the specific magnitude of the demand responses depends upon the ex post quantities of S_{VO} and m_2.

In a modern industrial society, such as the United States, one would expect the value of securities (representing the entire stock of capital) to be considerably greater than the quantity of real idle or even total money balances. In this event our assumptions imply that security demand will absorb the greater part of any autonomous wealth change. The demand for idle money in such an economy will not move a great deal on this account. An independent change in m_2 or S_{VO} will thus be accompanied by a much smaller shift in the same direction in L_2 and by an almost equal sympathetic movement in D_{VO}. Only if ΔD_{VO} were relatively very small would the common practice of tracing movements in m_2 along a given L_2 schedule be seriously invalidated. For then, if the change in m_2 were autonomous, the accompanying shift in L_2 would largely offset the interest movement. But this is precluded by (2B.27), given the likely magnitude of the wealth components in a modern economy. The limiting case in which $\Delta D_{VO} = 0$ is shown in Chapter V-E(4) to be incompatible with stability for an important variety of adjustment process ("zero forced saving").

The dependence of asset demand on the wealth components violates the usual assumption of independence between supply and demand. But this is not surprising, since the market consists of only two commodities: cash and securities. Ordinarily an uncompensated change in the supply of a single commodity will not alter significantly a total budget or any one of numerous derived demand schedules. This condition is obviously not met in the existing-asset market. But the dependence of demand on supply poses no particular problems, providing that we can specify the relationship between the variables. This we have tried to do.[16]

5. Equation Summary

A summary of the equations of the existing-asset market follows. Real variables are used wherever possible.

$$(2B.28) \qquad W = S_{VO} + m_2,$$

$$(2B.29) \qquad m_2 = \frac{M_2}{P},$$

$$(2B.30) \qquad M_2 = M - M_1,$$

---

[16] Appendix B presents an indifference-curve analysis of the existing-asset market, including this section. The interdependence of supply and demand is akin to the relationship described by F. P. R. Brechling in "A Note on Bond Holding and the Liquidity Preference

(2B.31) $M = \overline{M}$,

(2B.32) $S_{VO} = S_O p$,

(2B.33) $S_O = \overline{S_O}$,

(2B.34) $p = \dfrac{\rho_s}{r_M}$,

(2B.35) $\rho_s = \dfrac{\rho_K K}{S_O}$,

(2B.36) $K = \overline{K}$,

(2B.37) $L_2 = L_2(r_M)$,

(2B.38) $L_2 = \dfrac{M_2}{P}$,

(2B.39) $D_{VO} = W - L_2$,

(2B.40) $D_O = \dfrac{D_{VO}}{p}$.

Most of the above are identities; only five are behavioral equations:

(2B.31), (2B.33), (2B.36), (2B.37), and (2B.38).

(2B.31) is the action of the monetary authority in fixing the nominal quantity of money; (2B.33) and (2B.36) are the accumulated stocks of securities and capital, respectively; (2B.37) is the demand for real idle money expressed as a function of r_M; (2B.38) is the equality of the real supply and demand for idle balances. (2B.28)–

Theory of Interest," *Review of Economic Studies*, Vol. XXIV (June, 1957), pp. 190–97. Cf. also G. Horwich, "Money, Prices and the Theory of Interest Determination," *Economic Journal*, Vol. LXVII (December, 1957), pp. 629–30. However, the analysis should not be confused with that of Boulding. In his important paper, "A Liquidity Preference Theory of Market Prices," *Economica*, N.S., Vol. IX (May, 1944), pp. 55–63, Boulding underscores the interdependence of supply and demand in any market in which the same individuals appear as buyers and sellers. Such interdependence will characterize any stock (i.e., existing-asset) market, since the supply forthcoming at any price can be neither more nor less than the quantity that existing demanders are willing to relinquish. Boulding defines supply and demand as the excess demand function—the algebraic difference between the demand to hold, and the existing (inelastic) supply of a commodity. Excess demand is negative for prices above the equilibrium, indicating that a positive supply is forthcoming. For prices below the equilibrium, excess demand is positive, indicating a desire to add to, rather than to subtract from, existing holdings. Thus an increase in either the demand to hold, or the existing stock of an asset shifts both the "supply" and "demand" portions of the excess demand function. In this very real sense, supply and demand are interdependent. However, our discussion carries the interdependence a step further. When the existing stock of an asset changes, the excess demand function shifts not only on this account, but also because of the derived shift in the same direction in the demand to hold the new stock because of the budget change.

(2B.36) summarize the supply side of the market described in Section 1; (2B.37)–(2B.40) are the demand equations of Sections 2 and 3. As noted on page 25 (cf. [2B.17]), equality between L_2 and M_2/P implies equality of D_{VO} and S_{VO}; hence a separate equation for security-market equilibrium is not written. Equality of D_{VO} and S_{VO} implies, of course, equality of D_O and S_O (cf. [2B.25]). Equations (2B.26) and (2B.27) in Section 4 are a self-contained set describing the demand response to autonomous wealth changes. They are not explicitly included in the above summary, but the W term in (2B.39) implicitly represents them. The role of autonomous wealth changes in the combined stock-flow equilibrium is described in Part D(1).

There are 13 equations and 16 variables:

$$W, S_{VO}, m_2, M_2, P, M, M_1, S_O, p, \rho_s, r_M, \rho_K, K, L_2, D_{VO}, \text{ and } D_O.$$

The output market, described in Part C, will furnish 14 additional equations, but only 11 additional variables. This creates a total system in which the number of equations and variables is the same. The over-all equilibrium will be reflected in the existing-asset market by equality of supply and demand for both securities and idle money at some interest rate and price of securities.

C. THE OUTPUT MARKET

The output market, sometimes referred to as the "income stream," is the circular flow of active money against newly created goods. We begin by describing the monetary variables.

1. Monetary Elements

Aggregate money expenditures per unit of time are the product of the quantity of active money, M_1, and its income velocity, V_1. If y is total output of final goods of the given period, the commodity price level is

(2C.1)
$$P = \frac{M_1 V_1}{y}.$$

Money income, equal to expenditures, is

(2C.2)
$$Y = Py.$$

Expenditures may also be expressed as the product of total money balances and over-all or "total" velocity, V, a weighted average of $V_1 > 0$ and $V_2 = 0$; namely,

(2C.3) $$V = \frac{V_1 M_1 + V_2 M_2}{M_1 + M_2} = \left(\frac{M_1}{M}\right) V_1.$$

Since $M_1 V_1 = MV$,

(2C.4) $$P = \frac{MV}{y}.$$

L_1, the aggregate demand for M_1, depends upon habits of the community and the level, frequency, and regularity of income payments. Since the quantity of M_1 held by households and firms varies over the course of the payment period, L_1 determines the *average* quantity held. L_1 is a demand for a *nominal* quantity of M_1 needed to support a desired volume of money expenditures over time. Hence it is convenient to express L_1 for each economic unit as a desired *ratio* of average nominal active balances to money income or expenditures of a given period. Aggregated for all units,

(2C.5) $$L_1 = k_1 Y,$$

where k_1 is the average of such ratios over all units. Since the average total volume of M_1 held over any period is equal to the *de facto* aggregate quantity, equilibrium in the supply and demand for active money is expressed by

(2C.6) $$L_1 = k_1 Y = M_1.$$

Since $M_1 = (1/V_1) Y$,

(2C.7) $$k_1 = \frac{1}{V_1}.$$

k_1 is thus "Marshallian k," as opposed to Fisher's V, except that both variables apply to active balances only. Assuming that k_1 is independent of the level of M_1, it is useful to draw L_1 as a rectangular hyperbola in $1/Y$ and M_1.[17] This has been done in Figure 2–9 where the area of any rectangle inscribed under L_1 is $M_1/Y = k_1$. If active balances are fixed at $\overline{M}_1$ and k_1 at $\overline{k}_1$, equilibrium money income and expenditures are Y_0, where

$$\frac{\overline{M}_1}{Y_0} = \overline{k}_1 = \frac{L_1(Y_0)}{Y_0}.$$

---

[17] Apropos the discussion on p. 24, L_1 might better be drawn as a *linear* function of Y. However, the more traditional hyperbola is retained for L_1 since this schedule, unlike the wealth function, is referred to rather infrequently. Shifts in L_1 are discussed only in Chapters VIII-E and IX-D.

FIGURE 2-9
The Demand for Active Money as a Function of the Reciprocal of Money Income

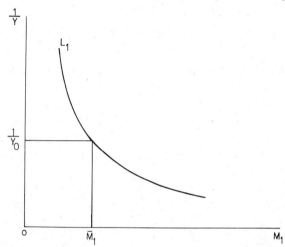

While L_1, like L_2, determines an average stock of money held, the L_1 decision achieves this by *spending* active balances against current output on a continuing basis. The L_2 demand, on the other hand, is basically a stock decision. L_2 reflects the desire of households to hold money indefinitely idle, except insofar as a change in wealth or the interest rate should warrant a movement to or from M_2 with respect to securities. In that event the shift is carried out instantaneously and on a once-for-all basis. But the stock of M_1 held is essentially a byproduct of what is better regarded as a *flow* decision, L_1. While M_1 has the statistical attributes of a stock, its economic role is that of a flow, allocated by its holders to expenditure on a per-unit-time basis.

2. Saving and Investment

Total money expenditures, equal to the money income and the money value of output of any period, are made up of consumption, C, and saving, S:

(2C.8) $$Y = C + S,$$

where in the aggregate all three variables are assumed to flow continuously over the minutest intervals of time. In equilibrium, S is converted into an equal money volume of investment expenditures, I; hence,

(2C.9) $$S = I$$

and

(2C.10) $Y = C + I.$

Both S and I refer to saving and investment net of that required to maintain the stock of capital. Depreciation allowances are assumed taken out of current firm receipts and applied automatically to the repair and replacement of existing equipment. S and I in real terms are independent of movements in money income for which output is constant. It is therefore convenient to express S and I in constant commodity prices or output units. Equations (2C.8) and (2C.10) thereby become

(2C.11) $y = C + S$

and

(2C.12) $y = C + I,$

where C, S, and I are now and hereafter understood to be expressed in output (q_c) units.

We must now specify the financial character of intended saving and investment; i.e., what assets do savers choose to accumulate, and how is investment financed? Within the present framework, the disposition of saving and the sources of investment financing are as follows:

(2C.13) $S = S_s + S_m,$

(2C.14) $I = I_s + I_m,$

where S_s and S_m are ex ante saving constituting a demand for additional securities and idle balances, respectively, and I_s and I_m are ex ante investment financed by the sale of new securities and the drawing down of idle balances, respectively.[18] Since asset holders hold both securities and cash, we might reasonably expect both S_s and S_m to be positive; i.e., the pattern of current accumulation should resemble that of the past.[19] Empirically we know that

---

[18] The existence of an I_m component violates our assumption that idle balances are held only by households. However, $I_m > 0$ is easily handled by the model by simply allowing firms to have idle funds, incorporating their demand attitudes into a community L_2 function. Cf. Chapter VIII-H(2).

[19] G. C. Archibald and R. G. Lipsey ("Monetary and Value Theory: A Critique of Lange and Patinkin," *Review of Economic Studies*, Vol. XXVI [October, 1958], p. 18) criticize Patinkin for failing to identify saving and investment in equilibrium as a demand and supply of securities only. However, I feel that Archibald and Lipsey, while uncovering real weaknesses in Patinkin's model, are defining equilibrium too narrowly. Both on empirical and *a priori* grounds, I would expect households to apply some part of their current saving to idle balances, and firms to finance investment by dishoarding, on a con-

I_s and I_m are both positive. However, for simplicity we assume

(2C.15) $$S_m = I_m = 0;$$

all saving is a demand for securities, and all investment is financed by the issuance of new securities. We let

(2C.16) $$S = S_s = D_{VN}$$

and

(2C.17) $$I = I_s = S_{VN},$$

where D_{VN} is the "new" demand for securities by savers in real-value units,[20] and S_{VN} is the real value of new securities supplied by firms per unit of time, t. If we were to assume positive values for either S_m or I_m, there would be net hoarding or dishoarding in every period, except in the purely coincidental case of $S_m = I_m$. The short-run "equilibrium" of the system would be characterized by a constantly shifting demand schedule for money and a changing price level. These are complications that are neither useful, nor readily amenable to analysis at the present stage. Chapter VIII-H describes the model in which S_m and I_m are positive.

Saving is related to other variables as follows:

(2C.18) $$\frac{\partial S}{\partial r_M} > 0, \quad \frac{\partial S}{\partial \left(\frac{1}{r_M}\right)} < 0,$$

(2C.19) $$\frac{\partial S}{\partial y} > 0,$$

(2C.20) $$\frac{\partial S}{\partial W} < 0.$$

Only (2C.18) and (2C.19), which express desired saving as a positive function of the interest rate and income, respectively, are active assumptions of the model. (2C.20), the inverse relation between saving and wealth, is treated in Chapter VIII-I. Until

---

tinuing basis. As such, net hoarding or dishoarding may characterize the "equilibrium" of a growing economy. This same point is made by R. J. Ball and Ronald Bodkin in "The Real Balance Effect and Orthodox Demand Theory: A Critique of Archibald and Lipsey," *Review of Economic Studies*, Vol. XXVIII (October, 1960), pp. 44–49, and is acknowledged by Archibald and Lipsey in "Monetary and Value Theory: Further Comment," *Review of Economic Studies*, Vol. XXVIII (October, 1960), pp. 54–55.

[20] Notice that saving is a new demand for securities, not a demand for new securities. The demand is defined by its source rather than its particular disposition between new and old securities. Saving is a demand for securities financed out of current income; by contrast, existing-security demand (D_{VO}) is financed out of existing wealth. Either demand may be realized in new or old securities, depending on circumstances.

then we assume

(2C.21)
$$\frac{\partial S}{\partial W} = 0.$$

Of the three independent variables—r_M, y, and W—y is the most fundamental in that it is the general cause and explanation—the *sine qua non*—of household saving and expenditure.

For investment we have

(2C.22)
$$\frac{\partial I}{\partial r_M} < 0;$$

i.e., the volume of real investment expenditures (ex ante investment) is related inversely to the market rate of interest. However, (2C.22) is deducible from a more fundamental relationship,

(2C.23)
$$\rho_K = \rho_K(I), \text{ where } \frac{\partial \rho_K}{\partial I} < 0.$$

$\rho_K(I)$ is an inverse relation between the return to capital and the rate of ex post investment. To explain this we draw upon the concept of the marginal efficiency of investment introduced by Keynes[21] and elaborated by Lerner[22] and Robertson.[23] In the following account we assume that there are no discontinuities of return, and that any existing or additional investment yielding more or less than the prevailing return will be extended or contracted until it yields exactly that amount. Thus ρ_K is the common return to all new and existing investments.

If one looks at the growth of capital in a long-run view, the return to capital declines because of its diminishing marginal product in the production process.[24] The return, $\partial y/\partial K$, falls as capital is increased relative to other factors of production. However, our concern with the growth process in this work applies to a relatively brief period. The direct impact of monetary disturbances and the adjustment process stimulated by them is completely

---

[21] J. M. Keynes, *The General Theory of Employment, Interest and Money*, chap. xi, esp. p. 136.

[22] A. P. Lerner, *The Economics of Control* (New York: The Macmillan Co., 1946), chaps. xxi and xxv.

[23] D. H. Robertson, "Some Notes on the Theory of Interest," *Money, Trade, and Economic Growth: Essays in Honor of John Henry Williams* (New York: The Macmillan Co., 1951), pp. 193–209 (reprinted in *Utility and All That* [London: Allen and Unwin, 1952], pp. 97–115). See also Robertson, *Lectures on Economic Principles*, Vol. II (London: Staples Press, Ltd., 1958), pp. 61–68.

[24] Cf. W. W. Leontief, "Theoretical Note on Time-Preference, Productivity of Capital, Stagnation and Economic Growth," *American Economic Review*, Vol. XLVIII (March, 1958), pp. 105–11.

absorbed by the system within several months at the least, and several years at the most. Within that time the addition to the stock of capital is not likely to depress its marginal physical product perceptibly. How, then, can we argue that the return to capital falls with the rate of investment? Following Lerner, the marginal product of capital is defined as its incremental return when net investment is zero. If ρ_K is plotted on the ordinate axis and investment rates on the abscissa, the marginal product of capital, expressed as a ratio of a future stream of goods to a present quantity given up in exchange, defines the height of the $\rho_K(I)$ schedule at the vertical axis. Investment rates greater than zero yield successively lower returns ("marginal efficiencies") not because capital's marginal physical product falls, but as a result of a decline in the *net value* of that product. The latter declines because of rising short-run marginal costs in capital-goods industries. The greater the *rate* of capital construction, the higher are the cost and supply price of capital. ρ_K, the ratio of net return to cost, falls both because of the increase in the denominator and the decrease in the numerator on account of greater depreciation allowances needed to replace the higher-priced capital.[25] To cite Robertson's example,[26]

---

[25] This account departs from our assumption above that there is only one commodity in the system. However, while two commodities are necessary for defining the short-run investment function, they present complex measurement problems with which we have decided not to encumber the general analysis. Occasional reference will be made to two commodities where the analysis seems to be particularly elucidated by doing so.

In the present account, the existence of two commodities implies a separate return to capital in each of the two commodity industries. Symbolically, where the subscripts K and C refer to the capital and consumer-goods industries, respectively, we have

$$(\rho_K)_K = \frac{\left[\left(\dfrac{\partial y_K}{\partial K_K}\right)P_K - \dfrac{P_K}{L_K}\right]}{P_K},$$

$$(\rho_K)_C = \frac{\left[\left(\dfrac{\partial y_C}{\partial K_C}\right)P_C\left(\dfrac{P_K}{P_C}\right) - \dfrac{P_K}{L_K}\right]}{P_K}.$$

L_K is the life, in years, of a capital good, and (P_K/P_C) in the numerator of $(\rho_K)_C$ is a factor which converts the marginal value product of capital in the consumer-good industry to units of capital-output. Both $(\rho_K)_K$ and $(\rho_K)_C$ are accordingly pure numbers on a per-annum basis. Equilibrium will be characterized by $(\rho_K)_K = (\rho_K)_C = \rho_K$. As labor resources move from one commodity industry to another, both P_K and P_C and $\partial y_K/\partial K_K$ and $\partial y_C/\partial K_C$ are assumed to vary in an offsetting manner. Thus on a first approximation the *average* commodity price and the average marginal physical product of capital are constants. The net return to capital varies only because of movements in P_K, which appears in the numerator and denominator of each expression.

[26] Robertson, *Lectures on Economic Principles*, Vol. II, pp. 64–67. We have altered the illustration by using dollars as the unit of account; Robertson uses "loaves."

suppose that capital's gross marginal product is $9, and the allowance for depreciation $4 when net investment is zero. The net return, x_K, is $5. A positive rate of net investment raises the price of capital goods and increases the depreciation allowance to $5, lowering the net return to $4. While the gross marginal product is constant, and the *quantity* of replacement goods purchased first by a $4, and then a $5 depreciation allowance is the same, the *net* product attributable to capital is lower in both money and real terms.[27]

At any market rate of interest, entrepreneurs will endeavor to finance that rate of investment expenditures which, if realized ex post, will yield a net return, ρ_K, equal to r_M. Given rational and competitive behavior, if $\rho_K > r_M$, the investment rate will rise; if $\rho_K < r_M$, the investment rate will fall. Thus since ρ_K is an inverse function of I, investment also varies inversely with r_M. This completes the transition from $\rho_K(I)$, a technological relation between the return to capital and the rate of ex post investment, and $I(r_M)$, a relation between the rate of interest and the demand schedule for investible funds. We assume, finally, that entrepreneurs know exactly the rate of ex post investment, and hence the quantity of investment funds, that equates ρ_K to a given r_M. $I(r_M)$ thus coincides with $\rho_K(I)$. Chapter V-E(3) explores the alternative assumption that entrepreneurial anticipations as to the $\rho_K(I)$ relationship are in error.[28]

An important characteristic of investment demand, so defined, is its stability. Apart from an independent shift in investment (Chapter VIII-B), none of the monetary disturbances described in this volume will dislodge the I schedule, since they do not affect the marginal physical product of capital. This is true, even though the analysis describes induced changes in the stock of capital and its return, ρ_K, in the Lerner-Robertson sense. As a result, the short-run fluctuations in ρ_K occasioned by movements along the

---

[27] The price level by which the money return is deflated is assumed, on a first approximation, to be constant; the higher cost and price of capital goods is offset by a lower cost and price of consumption goods. The fall in the price of consumption goods is due to a withdrawal of resources and the consequent reduction of marginal costs in that sector as net investment rises (cf. n. 25 above).

[28] This view of the investment function, as depending on the short-run cost of capital, lends strong support to Keynes' repeated emphasis (*The General Theory of Employment, Interest and Money*, pp. 138–39 and 141–44) on the expectational factor in investment demand. Clearly, if the return to capital in an individual enterprise depends on costs of the entire capital-goods industry, the assessment of that return is at best an informed guess

I schedule are reversible, given that the underlying industry cost schedules are themselves stable functions.

Since S and I are the new demand and supply of securities in real-value units, we define their security-quantity counterparts as follows:

(2C.24)
$$S_N = \frac{S_{VN}}{p} = \frac{I}{p},$$

(2C.25)
$$D_N = \frac{D_{VN}}{p} = \frac{S}{p},$$

where S_N is the quantity of new securities supplied by entrepreneurs, and D_N the quantity of securities demanded by savers per unit of time.[29] If we restrict the analysis to S_{VN} and D_{VN} functions that are linear in $1/r_M$ and p, the corresponding S_N and D_N schedules will have the customary positive and negative slopes, respectively, of supply and demand curves.[30] This is the case shown in Figure 2–10, where $S_{VN} = I$ is upward sloping, and $D_{VN} = S$ is downward sloping in $1/r_M$ and p.[31] The reader may verify by constructing vectors from the origin (cf. page 31) that S_N and D_N have the slopes indicated in the diagram. S_N and D_N meet their value counterparts at the zero quantity and unity price (cf. [2C.24] and [2C.25]), the latter of which happens to lie above the equilibrium price, at which S_N and D_N meet each other.

---

[29] Interpreting $S = D_{VN}$ as the revenue demand function, its downward slope in $1/r_M$ and p implies that the security-quantity demand, D_N, is invariably an elastic schedule (i.e., $\eta < -1$).

[30] Non-linear S_{VN} and D_{VN} functions and their underlying security-quantity schedules are discussed in Appendix A(2).

[31] A rising and linear $I(1/r_M)$ function implies that $I(r_M)$ is falling and concave upward; a falling and linear $S(1/r_M)$ function implies that $S(r_M)$ is rising and concave upward. We prove this by defining a function,

$$\chi = c_O + c_1\left(\frac{1}{r_M}\right), \text{ where } c_1 > 0 \text{ if } \chi = I,$$

$$c_1 < 0 \text{ if } \chi = S,$$

and differentiating it:

$$\frac{\partial \chi}{\partial r_M} = -\frac{c_1}{r_M^2} \text{ and } \frac{\partial^2 \chi}{\partial r_M^2} = \frac{2c_1}{r_M^3}.$$

Thus

$$\frac{\partial I}{\partial r_M} < 0, \frac{\partial^2 I}{\partial r_M^2} > 0, \frac{\partial S}{\partial r_M} > 0, \text{ and } \frac{\partial^2 S}{\partial r_M^2} < 0.$$

In diagraming $I(r_M)$ and $S(r_M)$, however, we shall occasionally draw them as linear functions, even though this contradicts our assumption of linearity in $1/r_M$.

FIGURE 2–10
Saving and Investment in Value and Security-Quantity Units

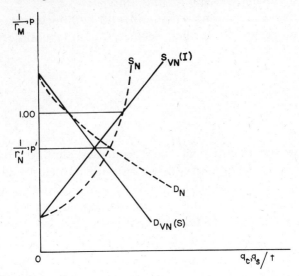

3. Equation Summary

The following equations summarize the output market:

$$(2C.26) \qquad L_1 = k_1 Y,$$

$$(2C.27) \qquad k_1 = \bar{k}_1,$$

$$(2C.28) \qquad Y = Py,$$

$$(2C.29) \qquad y = \bar{y},$$

$$(2C.30) \qquad L_1 = M_1,$$

$$(2C.31) \qquad y = C + S,$$

$$(2C.32) \qquad S = S(y, r_M),$$

$$(2C.33) \qquad S = S_s,$$

$$(2C.34) \qquad \rho_K = \rho_K(I),$$

$$(2C.35) \qquad r_M = \rho_K,$$

$$(2C.36) \qquad I = I_s,$$

$$(2C.37) \qquad S = I,$$

$$(2C.38) \qquad D_N = \frac{S}{p},$$

$$(2C.39) \qquad S_N = \frac{I}{p}.$$

Of the 14 equations, four are identities:

$$(2C.28), (2C.31), (2C.38), \text{ and } (2C.39).$$

(2C.26) is the demand function for active balances; (2C.27) is the household and firm-determined value of k_1; (2C.29) is the fixed level of output given by the factor markets; (2C.30) expresses equality between the supply and demand for M_1; (2C.32) relates saving to output and the rate of interest; (2C.33) is the decision of households to allocate all saving to security purchases; (2C.34) is the relationship between the return to capital and the rate of ex post investment; (2C.35) is the behavior of entrepreneurs in investing to the point where ρ_K and r_M are equal; (2C.36) is the decision to finance all investment by issuing new securities; and (2C.37) is the equality of intended saving and investment. The identities involving V and V_1 ([2C.3] and [2C.7]) are omitted. Altogether there are 14 equations and 16 variables:

$$L_1, k_1, Y, P, y, M_1, C, S, r_M, S_s, I, \rho_K, I_s, D_N, p, \text{ and } S_N.$$

However, five of the variables were present in the equations of the existing-asset market:

$$P, M_1, \rho_K, r_M, \text{ and } p.$$

Thus in combining the output with the existing-asset market, there is a determinate set of 27 equations and 27 variables. The over-all equilibrium will be characterized by equality between saving and investment (and thus the demand and supply of new securities), the demand and supply of idle balances (and thus existing securities), and the demand and supply of active balances. This requires an appropriate interest rate and price level, the latter resulting from a proper division of the money stock between idle and active uses. The determination of variables in the equilibrium is described in Part D in both static and dynamic terms.

D. EQUILIBRIUM

1. Static Equilibrium

In this section we shall describe the way in which the variables are determined in the combined system, (2B.28)–(2B.40) and (2C.26)–(2C.39). While the flow equations of the output market are applicable to any time period, this discussion will be limited to a very brief interval in which the impact of new quantities of saving and investment on the existing-asset market may prudently be ignored. The character of the equilibrium when the stocks and flows merge over unrestricted periods of time is explored in Section 2.

We start with the output market and the allocation of real income between saving and investment. The subset of five equations,

$$(2C.29),\ (2C.32),\ (2C.34),\ (2C.35),\ \text{and}\ (2C.37),$$

determines the five variables,

$$y,\ S,\ I,\ r_M,\ \text{and}\ \rho_K.$$

We can see this by replacing the left side of (2C.37), the saving-investment equality, by (2C.32) in which (2C.29) has been substituted for y: $S(\bar{y}, r_M)$. Next, we replace the right side of (2C.37) by the inverse of (2C.34), in which (2C.35) has been substituted for ρ_K: $I(r_M)$. This gives us a single equation,

$$(2D.1) \qquad\qquad S(\bar{y}, r_M) = I(r_M),$$

in which the single unknown, r_M, is thereby determined.[32] To summarize: The given level of real income determines a saving schedule which, as a function of r_M, determines with $I(r_M)$ an equilibrium level of saving, investment, and the rate of interest; since entrepreneurs equate r_M and ρ_K, the latter is also known. Once y, S, and I are determined, C, S_s, and I_s follow directly from (2C.31), (2C.33), and (2C.36). (2C.38) and (2C.39) will yield values for D_N and S_N as soon as p is determined by the joint action of both markets.

Turning now to the existing-asset market, the latter takes as given the rate of interest—the "natural" rate, r_N—determined by saving and investment. Nothing that can occur subsequently in the system, including the determination of the price level, fluctuations in the level of assets, or the growth of capital (output is assumed fixed), can alter the real saving and investment schedules and their point of equilibrium. Thus, given the existing-asset demand schedules, the *quantities* of existing assets must be adjusted so that supply and demand balance at the pre-determined natural rate of interest. In the brief time interval under consideration, S_O is constant; conceptually, only M_2 may be altered by transfers to or

---

[32]This corresponds essentially to the determination of the interest rate described by Modigliani in the full-employment, liquidity-preference model ("Liquidity Preference and the Theory of Interest and Money," *op. cit.*, pp. 70–72).

from the supply of M_1 balances. The adaptive behavior of the existing-asset market can thus be seen in terms of (2B.38), the equality of demand and supply of real idle money. We replace the left side of (2B.38) by (2B.37), substituting r_N for r_M in the latter equation: $L_2(r_N)$. On the right side of (2B.38) we replace the numerator, M_2, by (2B.30), in which M is replaced by (2B.31): $\overline{M} - M_1$. The denominator, P, is replaced by an expression derived as follows. In the output market, the left side of (2C.30) is altered by substituting (2C.26), in which k_1 has been replaced by (2C.27), and Y by (2C.28) and (2C.29): $L_1 = \overline{k}_1 P \overline{y}$. (2C.30) so adjusted is $\overline{k}_1 P \overline{y} = M_1$, which yields

(2D.2)
$$P = \frac{M_1}{\overline{k}_1 \overline{y}}.$$

Returning to (2B.38), our substitutions for L_2, M_2, and P yield

(2D.3)
$$L_2(r_N) = \frac{(\overline{M} - M_1)\overline{k}_1 \overline{y}}{M_1},$$

a single equation in essentially one unknown, M_1. Writing M_1 as the dependent variable:

(2D.4)
$$M_1 = \frac{\overline{M} \overline{k}_1 \overline{y}}{L_2(r_N) + \overline{k}_1 \overline{y}}.$$

Ignoring for the moment the role of W through its impact on L_2, we now have values for M_1 and thus, M_2 ([2B.30]) and P ([2D.2]), which together determine a value for M_2/P equal to $L_2(r_N)$; i.e., given the natural rate of interest, there is some allocation of $\overline{M}$ between M_1 and M_2 which determines P such that M_2/P equals $L_2(r_N)$.

The real price of securities, p, follows by replacing ρ_s in (2B.34) by (2B.35), in which r_N replaces ρ_K, (2B.33) replaces S_O, and (2B.36) replaces K. The system is now fully accounted for. The determination of p determines S_{VO} ([2B.32] and [2B.33]), the determination of M_2 and P determines m_2 and W ([2B.29] and [2B.28]), the level of W and L_2 determines D_{VO} ([2B.39]), and D_O follows from the values of D_{VO} and p ([2B.40]). p also yields values for D_N and S_N in the output market ([2C.38]) and ([2C.39]).

W is both a determined and a determining variable in arriving at equilibrium in the market for idle balances. Consider any arbitrary allocation of M between M_1 and M_2. This determines a price level, a value of M_2/P, a total wealth function,[33] and an $L_2(r_M)$ schedule. If M_2/P and L_2 meet at $r_M < r_N$, M_2/P is too great, and equilibrium requires a transfer of M_2 balances to M_1. As this occurs, M_2/P falls both because of the decrease in the numerator and the increase in the denominator. But the wealth function shifts equally to the left, causing L_2 to respond sympathetically ([2B.26]). However, if (2B.27) is met, L_2 will not shift to the left as much as does M_2/P, and the movement to equilibrium will be slowed, but not completely inhibited. The equilibrium of $M_2/P = L_2(r_N)$ is thus one in which M_2/P, W, and L_2 are all simultaneously determined.

The over-all equilibrium of the system is shown diagrammatically in Figure 2–11. The saving and investment schedules are drawn in Figure 2–11(a), where ρ_K and r_M are plotted on the vertical axis. The intersection of $S(\bar{y}, r_M)$ and $I(r_M)$ determines an equilibrium interest rate, r'_N, and a rate of saving and investment of OA. Given r'_N, $p' = \rho'_s/r'_N$ is the corresponding equilibrium price.

FIGURE 2–11
**The Combined Equilibrium of the Existing-Asset and Output Markets
in Terms of the Saving, Investment, and Idle-Money Functions**

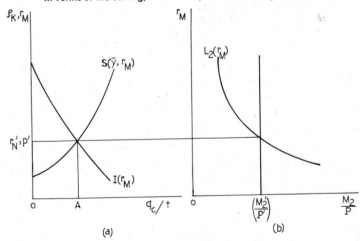

(a)   (b)

---

[33] The wealth component, S_{VO}, is determined as a schedule as soon as $\rho_K = r_N$ is set by saving and investment:

$$S_{VO} = S_O p = S_O\left(\frac{\rho_s}{r_N}\right),$$

which, upon substituting known values, is

$$\overline{S_O}\left(\frac{r_N \overline{K}}{r_N \overline{S_O}}\right) = \overline{K}.$$

When carried over to the existing-asset market, as represented by the market for idle balances in Figure 2-11(b), r'_N determines an equilibrium quantity of real idle money of

$$\frac{M'_2}{P'} = L_2(r'_N), \text{ where } P' = \frac{M'_1}{k_1 \overline{y}} \text{ and } M'_1 = \overline{M} - M'_2.$$

The equilibrium is thus characterized by equality of supply and demand for both idle and active balances, though only the idle component is drawn.

2. Dynamic (Stock-Flow) Equilibrium

We shall now remove the restriction that the time period underlying the equilibrium is a very brief one. With the passage of time, the description of equilibrium must consider the recurring quantities of saving and investment as they flow into the existing-asset market.[34] The following dynamic analysis will enlarge, rather than alter, the static account of the preceding section. The system is assumed to be in static equilibrium, as described in Section 1 and summarized in Figure 2-11.

Saving and investment merge with the existing-asset market by the joining of components of supply and demand for securities. The "new" and the "old" securities market are combined by a process of simple summation. We let

$$2D.5) \qquad\qquad S_{VT} = S_{VO} + S_{VN}$$

be the real value of the "total" supply of securities, and

$$2D.6) \qquad\qquad D_{VT} = D_{VO} + D_{VN},$$

the "total" value demand for securities during any time period, t. Corresponding to these value functions are total security-quantity schedules,

$$2D.7) \qquad\qquad S_T = S_O + S_N,$$

and

$$2D.8) \qquad\qquad D_T = D_O + D_N.$$

---

[34]Cf. R. W. Clower, "The Dynamics of Investment," *American Economic Review,* Vol. XLIV (March, 1954), pp. 64–81; "Productivity, Thrift and the Rate of Interest," *Economic Journal,* Vol. LXIV (March, 1954), pp. 107–15. See also G. Horwich, *Open Market Operations, the Rate of Interest, and the Price Level* (University of Chicago dissertation, March, 1954), chaps. i and iii (summarized in the *Journal of Finance,* Vol. X [December, 1955], pp. 508–9); "Money, Prices and the Theory of Interest Determination," *op. cit.,* pp. 27 and 630.

The summation of markets, using the security-quantity functions, is illustrated for an arbitrary time interval, $t = t_1$, in Figure 2–12. S'_N and D'_N are the quantity of new securities offered by firms, and the quantity of securities demanded by current savers, respectively,

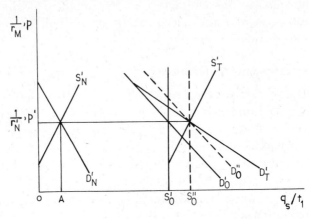

as functions of price. S'_O is the stock of pre-existing securities on hand at the opening of t_1, and D'_O is the demand for securities by existing-asset holders at the same moment in time. S'_N and D'_N are constructed as the smaller pair of schedules, as they are likely to be for most intervals. S'_T is the horizontal sum of S'_N and S'_O, while D'_T is the horizontal sum of D'_N and D'_O. The ruling supply and demand schedules during t_1 are thus S'_T and D'_T, and by the end of the period they determine an equilibrium price, p', at which the rate of interest is r'_N and for which aggregate supply and demand for securities from all sources are in over-all equality. p' is also the price at which S'_N and D'_N and S'_O and D'_O are individually in balance. Thus, at p' the same quantity, OA, is added to both S'_O and D'_O, with the result that there is no tendency to alter the price and yield prevailing at the start of t_1.

By the close of t_1, S'_O has grown by OA to S''_O, which is the stock of securities in existence at the opening of a subsequent period, t_2:

(2D.9) $S''_O = S'_O + S'_N(r'_N)$, where $S'_N(r'_N) = D'_N(r'_N)$.

Assuming that savers desire to hold securities after they have acquired them, one is tempted to say that D'_T represents the demand for the stock of securities at the close of t_1. But this is necessarily true only at p', at which the realized increment to supply is accompanied by an equal ex post increase in demand by current savers. Thus, at p' the new existing-security demand is $D_O'' = D_T'$, which equals the total supply, $S_O'' = S_T'$. However, at all other prices and yields, D_O'' is determined by the new wealth budget. The latter can be identified only by tracing the stock-flow merger in the context of the entire existing-asset market. Since the unit of measurement common to the market for existing securities and idle money is output (real value), the combining of stocks and flows for this purpose is carried out in terms of (2D.5) and (2D.6).

In Figure 2–13, $S_{VN}' = I'$ and $D_{VN}' = S'$ are the value counterparts of S_N' and D_N'; i.e.,

$$S_{VN}' = S_N'p \text{ and } D_{VN}' = D_N'p.$$

S_{VO}' and D_{VO}' correspond similarly to S_O' and D_O'. Separate origins are used for each pair of schedules in order to simplify the diagram. S_{VT}' and D_{VT}', the horizontal sum of S_{VN}' and S_{VO}', and D_{VN}' and D_{VO}', respectively, correspond to S_T' and D_T'. m_2' and L_2' are the supply and demand for idle balances, and total wealth at the opening of t_1 is

(2D.10) $$W' = S_{VO}' + m_2'.$$

Like their security-quantity counterparts, the new, old, and total security-value schedules meet at p', for which $r_M = r_N'$. The closing existing-security value schedule, $S_{VO}'' = S_O''p$, is drawn from the origin through the intersection point of S_{VT}' and D_{VT}'. Relative to S_{VO}', S_{VO}'' represents a clockwise rotation caused by the addition

FIGURE 2–13
The Combining of Security-Market Stocks and Flows in Output (Real-Value) Units

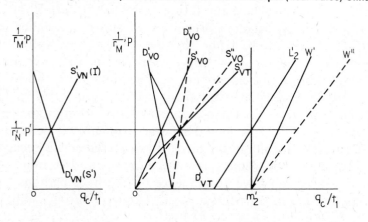

of $S_O'' - S_O'$ to the stock of securities during t_1. The new wealth function is

(2D.11) $$W'' = S_{VO}'' + m_2'.$$

While at p',

$$D_{VO}' = D_{VT}' = S_{VT}' = S_{VO}'',$$

elsewhere D_{VO}'' must be drawn with reference to W'', which exceeds W' by the value of securities added, $S_{VO}'' - S_{VO}'$. Assuming that L_2 is fixed at L_2',

(2D.12) $\quad D_{VO}'' = D_{VO}' + (W'' - W') = D_{VO}' + (S_{VO}'' - S_{VO}'),$

and

$$D_O'' = \frac{D_{VO}''}{p} = \frac{D_{VO}' + S_{VO}'' - S_{VO}'}{p} = \frac{D_O'p + S_O''p - S_O'p}{p}.$$

Hence

(2D.13) $$D_O'' = D_O' + (S_O'' - S_O').$$

Thus D_O'' exceeds D_O' by a constant, $S_O'' - S_O'$, the realized addition to the stock of securities. In Figure 2–12, D_O'' is drawn to the right of and parallel to D_O' by the distance, $S_O'' - S_O' = OA$. D_O'' coincides with D_T' at p', but falls to the right of it at $p > p'$, and to the left at $p < p'$. Whether D_O' is linear, as drawn, or not, the new schedule, D_O'', emerging after an interval of growth lies to the right of and parallel to the original one by the ex post increment to securities. Hence, while its slope is constant, the price elasticity of D_O rises (algebraically) over time.

The process of growth is thus characterized by continuous additions to the stock of securities. For every security added, S_O and D_O, and thus S_T and D_T of any future period, shift parallel and to the right by equal distances. But while S_N and D_N, together with S_O and D_O, determine what the *additions* to securities will be, the new-security schedules are not otherwise relevant to the construction of S_O and D_O at the close of any period. In the case of demand, the underlying budget restraint changes the very moment that security demand by savers is realized in an actual addition to securities held. For while D_N is limited by total income, D_O is determined by total wealth, including the most recent increment to securities due to current saving. Thus quantities along D_N and D_T other than the one realized can have no influence on D_O. It is perhaps more obvious that points on S_N and S_T not realized during t_1 are not relevant to the construction of the new stock-of-securities schedule.

Granted the fixity of L_2, the static equilibrium as presented in Figure 2–11 is also descriptive of the equilibrium over time.[35] Equality between saving and investment at a natural rate of interest at which L_2 and M_2/P and, by (2B.17), D_{VO} and S_{VO} balance, continues to hold as longer periods are considered. In the dynamic process D_{VO} and S_{VO} grow equally by the equilibrium flows of saving and investment, as shown in Figure 2–13. p' and r'_N persist as the equilibrium price and yield of securities. Given the static equilibrium, the growth equilibrium affects only the existing-security market and total wealth, neither of which is pictured in Figure 2–11. In terms of the equation system, we have added two independent equations, (2D.5) and (2D.6) (or [2D.7] and [2D.8], if we choose this formulation), and two variables, S_{VT} and D_{VT} (or S_T and D_T), which determine the course of the security market over time.

Once S_O and S_{VO} are allowed to increase by flotations of new issues, we are logically compelled to follow through the subsequent impact on the stock of capital. However, variations in K are treated in Chapter V in the context of both equilibrium growth and

---

[35] We assume, except in Chapter VIII-H, that L_2 is fixed in response to equal saving and investment additions to wealth. It is, in fact, difficult—though not impossible—to justify movements in L_2 during equilibrium growth, given that saving and investment are a demand and supply of securities only. In the framework of Part B(4), L_2 will shift responsively only as a result of autonomous wealth changes. At p' (see Figure 2–13) the increase in securities is stimulated and accompanied by an equal increase in security demand on the part of savers. Thus the wealth change at the equilibrium price is not autonomous. But how do we interpret the wealth increment at prices other than the equilibrium? Since $W'' - W'$ is the value of the given quantity of securities that savers committed themselves to holding at p', it seems natural to assume that the wealth increase will be absorbed entirely by security demand at all other prices. This is tantamount to arguing that $W'' - W'$ is not an autonomous wealth change at any price. However, one might contend that wealth changes occurring at a given price and yield cannot be allocated exclusively to either demand schedule at other prices and yields. In this event L_2 would be redrawn at the close of each growth interval. There are two possibilities:

1. $W'' - W'$ is viewed as a net wealth increment available for allocation to L_2 at all prices except p'. At the close of t_1 a new (curvilinear) schedule, L_2'', would lie to the right of L_2' at every point except p', at which it would be tangent to L_2'. (A new D_{VO} would replace D_{VO}', as drawn in Figure 2–13, lying to the left of it, except for a tangency point at p'.)
2. The increase in the *value* of securities at p',

$$S_{VO}''(p') - S_{VO}'(p') = W''(p') - W'(p'),$$

   is allocated to D_{VO} at all prices. Thus D_{VO}'' is parallel to D_{VO}', passing through the intersection of S_{VT}' and D_{VT}'. L_2'', as a result, is to the right of L_2' at $p > p'$, and to the left at $p < p'$. In effect, L_2 has *rotated* clockwise through p' ($L_2[r_M]$ will rotate counterclockwise, becoming more interest-elastic).

Both of the foregoing possible movements of L_2 prevent D_O from shifting in the simple parallel manner described. However, the pattern of growth is not changed thereby in any fundamental way.

the adjustment to monetary disturbances. Until then, we shall treat additional securities as self-contained entities, identical to pre-existing ones in the sense of providing the same return per share, ρ_s. K remains fixed at $\overline{K}$.

Variability of S_O and S_{VO} also adds a new dimension to the achievement of equilibrium from a non-equilibrium position. The static account in Section 1 took S_O as a given constant, describing the equilibrium purely as a proper allocation of money between idle and active uses. The equality of supply and demand for idle and active balances is, in fact, a condition of both static and dynamic equilibrium. But the actual dynamic *process* of reaching that equilibrium will involve simultaneous equilibrating changes in S_O, relative to D_O, through an imbalance between saving and invest-ment. The way in which this occurs can best be seen by introducing a monetary disturbance and tracing the adjustment process through to a new equilibrium position. Chapter III will accordingly de-scribe the direct impact of an open-market operation by the central bank. Chapter IV will describe the stock-flow path back to equi-librium.

E. SUMMARY

The framework of this study is limited to two sectors, households and firms, and three markets, the existing-asset, output, and factor. The latter is not explicitly treated in this volume; output is instead generally (but not always) taken to be fixed at a level of full utili-zation of resources. The household sector holds and owns the en-tire wealth of the economy, which consists of money and securities; it supplies labor resources to the factor market; and it receives the entire income which it consumes or saves. Firms organize produc-tive activity and invest in new capital with funds provided by households.

The existing-asset market is made up of real idle balances and common-stock securities. The value of securities derives from the stock of capital, which consists of inventories of a single com-modity that serves both as an investment and consumption good. Each capital unit yields a net return which, when aggregated and divided by the total number of outstanding securities, provides an income per share, all of which is paid out. The rate of interest is the income per share divided by the share price. Both supply com-ponents are represented diagrammatically as linear functions of both the price of securities and the reciprocal of the interest rate. Given total wealth, the real demand for idle money—a downward function of the rate of interest—completely determines security demand in real-value units. The main body of the study is limited to demand functions that are linear in the interest-reciprocal. Extreme cases in which either demand is zero are postponed to Chapter IX. Beneath the security value demand is security demand in security-quantity units. The latter, together with the given stock of securities, is a more traditional, and occasionally more useful, representation of the securities market. For linear and stable security-value demand functions, security-quantity demand is a downward function of security price. Autonomous wealth changes are those, other than interest-rate fluctuations, that are imposed on households from the outside. Both demand functions respond positively to all such changes, the degree of response being proportional to the relative quantity of the corresponding asset. In an economy in which the value of securities (as determined by the capital stock) is considerably greater than the supply of money, the demand for money will thus tend to be relatively stable in the face of autonomous wealth changes.

In the output market the monetary variables are the supply and demand for active balances. The latter, in nominal units, can be expressed as a constant proportion of money income or expenditures. Equilibrium is characterized both by equality between the supply and demand for active money and between desired saving of households and investment undertaken by firms. Saving and investment are, respectively, a demand and supply of securities. Real saving varies positively with the rate of interest and output. The inverse saving-wealth relation is treated only in Chapter VIII. Investment varies inversely with the rate of interest. This derives from the tendency of firms to equate the rate of interest to the return to capital, the latter itself varying inversely with ex post investment because of rising marginal costs in capital-goods industries. The security-quantity unit of measurement is also applied to the saving and investment schedules.

The equilibrium or "natural" rate of interest is determined by the intersection of saving and investment, to which the existing-asset market must adjust. In a very brief interval this requires an allocation of money between idle and active uses so that the resulting value of idle balances is equal to demand at the given natural rate of interest. In any period greater than zero the quantity of securities will also vary in an equilibrating manner. When both markets are in equilibrium at the natural rate of interest, security supply and demand grow equally by the constant saving-investment increments. The supply and demand for idle balances are fixed. In security-quantity units, security supply and demand shift equally and parallel over time.

Appendix A analyzes non-linear security-value functions, for which upward-sloping security-quantity demand schedules, and downward-sloping supply schedules are shown to exist. Appendix B reconsiders the existing-asset market from an indifference-curve approach.

CHAPTER III

Open-Market Operations: The Direct Impact

A. AN OPEN-MARKET PURCHASE EXECUTED

This chapter will describe the immediate effect on the system of an open-market purchase of securities by the central bank. Part E will repeat the analysis for an open-market sale. The central bank is assumed to be the sole monetary authority, combining both monetary and fiscal functions. Since there are no private banks, it is the only institution capable of creating or destroying money. The bank decides to create a fixed amount of money in order to purchase securities from households. It enters the securities market of an economy in dynamic equilibrium, as described in Chapter II-D(2). The rate of interest is

$$(3A.1) \qquad r'_M = r'_N = \rho'_K,$$

and the real price and income of securities are

$$(3A.2) \qquad p' = \frac{\rho'_s}{r'_N} \text{ and } \rho'_s = \frac{\rho'_K K'}{S'_O}, \text{ respectively,}$$

where S'_O is the total quantity of outstanding securities, all of which are held by households, and K' is the total (fixed) number of capital units. The total stock of money, which excludes any central-bank holdings, is M', the supply and demand for real idle balances are m'_2 and L'_2, respectively, the commodity price level is P', and the money price of securities is $\pi' = P'p'$. The bank remains in the market for a period, t_1, during which the total supply and household demand for securities are

$$(3A.3) \qquad S'_T = S'_O + S'_N \text{ and } D'_T = D'_O + D'_N.$$

The bank offers to buy all securities forthcoming at a fixed bid price, $p'' > p'$. The corresponding money price is $\pi'' = P'p''$. Since the purchase can have no direct influence on ρ_s, the increased price entails a reduction in the market rate of interest. The new yield is

$$(3A.4) \qquad\qquad r''_M = \frac{\rho''_s}{p''} < r'_N, \text{ where } \rho''_s = \rho'_s.$$

For simplicity, we assume that the securities are purchased in a single block. In Part C we shall analyze the operation in which the securities are purchased sequentially, one at a time. We assume also that both t_1 and p'' are propitiously selected so as to enable the bank to expend all of its earmarked funds, while at the same time households relinquish an amount of securities just equal to their desires under the terms offered by the bank. If the bank leaves the market without obtaining all the securities offered at its bid price, it has committed an error of overpayment, since a lower price would have been sufficient for the *de facto* purchase. Alternatively, we can imagine that the monetary authority does not succeed in spending all of its earmarked funds or in obtaining a desired number of securities. In this event the impact on the economy depends on the further action of the bank. The analysis of error will be postponed until Part D of this chapter, while continuing open-market activity will be treated in Chapter VIII-A. For the present, we assume that the purchase fully satisfies both buyer and sellers.

Since the monetary authority buys all securities offered at its bid price, p'', its action during t_1 is shown in Figure 3-1, a security-quantity diagram, as a horizontal line—a demand schedule of

FIGURE 3–1
The Direct Impact of an Open-Market Purchase on the Security Markets

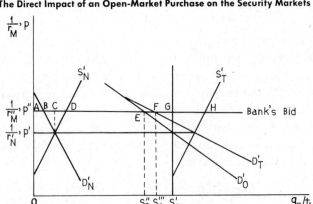

infinite elasticity. At p'' the total excess supply of securities is

$$(3A.5) \qquad S'_T - D'_T = FH,$$

and this is the quantity taken by the bank. The real value of the expenditure on these securities is $p''(FH)$, and this will be known as the "magnitude" of the open-market purchase. The total volume of securities comes from two distinguishable sources, which can be identified by substituting (3A.3) in (3A.5):

$$(3A.6) \qquad S'_T - D'_T = (S'_O - D'_O) + (S'_N - D'_N),$$

which corresponds in Figure 3–1 to the distances,

$$FH = EG + BD.$$

The total excess supply is thus the sum of the excess supply of pre-existing securities and the excess supply of new ones. The EG quantity is obtained by the bank from portfolios at the opening instant of t_1, whereas the BD component accrues to it in increments over the course of the interval. BD is made up of CD, representing an addition to the previous rate of new security supply, plus BC, previously supplied, but now by-passed by savers. The real expenditure of the bank is divided between $p''(EG)$ and $p''(BD)$ on old and new securities, respectively. If the commodity price level is constant, the total money expenditure is $\pi''(FH)$, of which $\pi''(EG)$ is spent on old, and $\pi''(BD)$ on new securities. However, from the viewpoint of money income and commodity prices, funds spent on old securities are held as idle balances, the alternative to securities in the existing-asset market (see [2B.17]). But funds spent on new securities go to entrepreneurs who are committed to spend them without delay on investment projects. This portion of the bank's outlay is thus an immediate addition to factor incomes and the active component of the money supply.[1] The price level rises proportionately. Since P is determined by the interaction of expenditures and the output of our single commodity ([2C.1]), both of which we assume flow continuously over time, prices rise at once in response to additional active money. This means that the dollar price of securities corresponding to p'' must be raised continuously with P. If P_a is the average commodity price during t_1, then the bank's monetary injection to idle and active balances, respectively, is

$$(3A.7) \qquad P'p''(EG) \text{ and } P_a p''(BD).$$

---

[1] Cf. D. H. Robertson, "Some Notes on Mr. Keynes' General Theory of Employment," *Quarterly Journal of Economics,* Vol. LI (November, 1936), pp. 176–78.

The impact of the operation on "income" and "wealth" account can be summarized by excess supply functions,

(3A.8) $\quad E_T' = S_T' - D_T', \qquad E_O' = S_O' - D_O',$ and $E_N' = S_N' - D_N'$.

From (3A.6),

(3A.9) $\qquad\qquad\qquad\qquad E_T' = E_O' + E_N'$.

These E-functions are plotted with respect to $1/r_M$ and p in Figure 3–2. At the equilibrium price, p', no securities are offered to the

FIGURE 3–2
New, Old, and Total Excess Security-Supply Functions

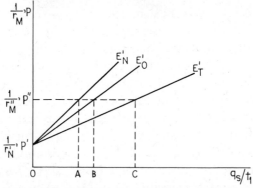

bank. At p'', OC is supplied, of which OA, the gap between saving and investment in security units, comes from entrepreneurs, and OB from the existing stock. E_N' thus measures the ability of the central bank to inject money directly into the income stream. The longer the bank remains in the market, the greater will be the flow security schedules and thus the difference between them, E_N. A huge stock of existing securities or a highly elastic D_O function will tend to enlarge E_O.

At the opening of a subsequent period, t_2, the stock of securities will be S_O''', as indicated in Figure 3–1. The bank's purchase of old securities at the start of t_1 reduced S_O to S_O''. During t_1, S_O increased by the quantity, $EF = AB$, which are new securities purchased by savers and added to the existing stock. The price at the opening of t_2 is p'', at the intersection of S_O''' and D_O''' (not diagramed), the corresponding existing-demand schedule. Any reduction in the *stock* of securities creates a higher price which tends to persist over time. However, S_N and D_N reappear in t_2 without change. They are flow schedules, derived from I and S, and independent of any influence internal to the model. They continue to intersect at p' and r'_N. The way in which S_N and D_N combine with the altered stock schedules during t_2 and future periods is the subject of Chapter IV. But before turning to the stock-flow adjustment, there are other aspects of the direct impact of the disturbance that must be considered. We begin by describing the events of t_1 in terms of the existing-asset *value* market. This will reveal some interesting wealth changes, and enable us to account for the location of D'''_O.

B. THE IMPACT ON WEALTH AND ASSET DEMAND

1. The Rotation of the Wealth Function

To the existing-asset market the open-market purchase is not, as one might suppose, an essentially neutral reshuffling of assets without further repercussions. In fact, the reduced quantity of securities alters not only the total wealth function, but the derived asset-demand schedules as well. This is demonstrated in Figure 3–3, in which solid-line single-primed schedules prevail immediately after

FIGURE 3–3

The Direct Impact of an Open-Market Purchase on the Existing-Asset Value Market

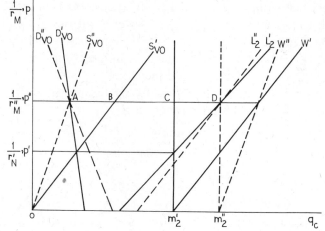

the purchase of existing securities at the start of t_1. The market does not yet reflect the rise in the general price level nor the increase in the value of securities due to new flotations that go to savers during t_1. At p'' the value of the excess supply of existing securities is

$$\text{(3B.1)} \qquad S'_{VO} - D'_{VO} = AB,$$

in exchange for which households demand an equal amount of idle money,

$$(3B.2) \qquad\qquad L_2' - m_2' = CD.$$

A new function,

$$(3B.3) \qquad\qquad S_{VO}'' = S_O''p,$$

is drawn from the origin through A, the security value that asset holders desire at p'' and are, in fact, left with after the purchase. The new value of idle balances is m_2'', as indicated. The new wealth function is W'', drawn from m_2'' on the horizontal axis and parallel to S_{VO}'':

$$(3B.4) \qquad\qquad W'' = S_{VO}'' + m_2''.$$

But W'' can meet the original function, W', at only a single point, the height of which is p''. The wealth functions cross at this point since, as noted, equal-value amounts of cash and securities are exchanged at the purchase price. But at other prices the situation is quite different, because of the smaller number of securities held after the purchase. At $p > p''$ the increase in the aggregate value of securities is less than previously, since fewer securities are available to experience capital gains. Thus W'' rises less rapidly than W', and falls to the left of it. At $p < p''$ fewer securities are on hand to lose value, and so W'' falls less than W', and lies to the right of it.[2] In effect, W rotates *counterclockwise* through p'' in response to the changed quantities of money and securities.

We show the rotation algebraically by taking the difference between the new and old wealth functions:

$$W'' - W' = S_O''p + m_2'' - (S_O'p + m_2')$$
$$= S_O''p - S_O'p + m_2'' - m_2'.$$

Since

$$(3B.5) \qquad m_2'' - m_2' = (S_O' - S_O'')p'',$$

$$W'' - W' = S_O''p - S_O'p + (S_O' - S_O'')p''$$
$$= (S_O'' - S_O')p + (S_O' - S_O'')p''.$$

---

[2]Cf. S. Weintraub, *An Approach to the Theory of Income Distribution* (Philadelphia: Chilton Co.—Book Division, 1958), pp. 156–61, and G. Horwich, "Money, Prices and the Theory of Interest Determination," *Economic Journal*, Vol. LXVII (December, 1957), pp. 633–34. Cf. also R. M. Davis, "Re-Examination of the Speculative Demand for Money," *Quarterly Journal of Economics*, Vol. LXXIII (May, 1959), pp. 326–32, and G. Horwich, "Re-Examination of the Speculative Demand for Money: Comment," *Quarterly Journal of Economics*, Vol. LXXIII (November, 1959), pp. 686–88.

Upon rearrangement,

(3B.6) $\qquad W'' - W' = (S_O' - S_O'')(p'' - p);$ hence
$$(W'' - W') \gtreqless 0 \text{ when } p \lesseqgtr p''.$$

The rotation of the wealth function cannot fail to produce sympathetic movements in the asset-demand schedules. Accordingly, D_{VO}'' and L_2'' are drawn so that

(3B.7) $\qquad (D_{VO}'' - D_{VO}') + (L_2'' - L_2') = W'' - W'.$

The demand schedules also rotate counterclockwise through p''.[3]

The direct impact of the operation on the existing-security market is drawn in Figure 3–4 in terms of both value and security-quantity schedules. The pre-operation equilibrium is characterized

FIGURE 3–4
The Direct Impact of an Open-Market Purchase
on the Existing Security-Value and Quantity Schedules

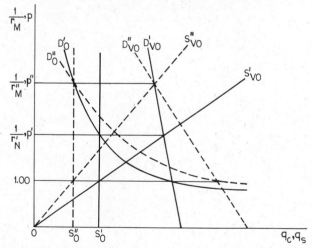

by the intersection of S_{VO}' and D_{VO}' at p'. The security-quantity schedules, S_O' and D_O', also meet at p', and intersect their corresponding value schedules at $p = 1.00$, which happens to be less than p'.

---

[3] The new schedules in Figure 3–3, D_{VO}'' and L_2'', are drawn as linear functions. Strictly speaking, this violates (2B.27), according to which the wealth increment is allocated to each demand schedule in proportion to the relative share of the corresponding asset of total wealth. For at $p = 0$, $S_{VO}'' = 0$ is a zero portion of wealth, and by (2B.27), $\Delta D_{VO} = D_{VO}'' - D_{VO}' = 0$. As a result, D_{VO}'' would meet D_{VO}' both at p'' and at the point where D_{VO}' crosses the horizontal axis. Hence neither D_{VO}'' nor L_2'' can be linear. However, as a practical matter, we shall ignore this implication of the wealth-allocation assumption, leaving the asset-demand schedules in the more convenient linear form. Doing so will not alter the basic analysis.

The purchase at p'' reduces S_O to S_O'' and S_{VO} to S_{VO}''. The resulting wealth rotation causes D_{VO} to rotate counterclockwise through p'', becoming D_{VO}''. D_O, derived from D_{VO}, moves sympathetically to the position of D_O''; i.e., *ceteris paribus*, a movement in D_{VO} will cause a shift in the same direction in D_O. Algebraically,

$$(3B.8) \quad D_O'' = \frac{D_{VO}''}{p} = \frac{D_{VO}' + \phi(W'' - W')}{p} = D_O' + \frac{\phi(W'' - W')}{p} ,$$

where $0 < \phi < 1$ is the fraction of the wealth change, (3B.6), allocated to the security-value demand schedule. In view of (3B.6),

$$D_O'' \gtreqless D_O' \quad \text{when} \quad p \lesseqgtr p''.$$

Thus D_O'' also represents a counterclockwise rotation through p'' relative to the original schedule, D_O'. The wealth rotation flattens

FIGURE 3–5
An Open-Market Purchase in Which
the Security-Demand Schedule Is
Upward Sloping at $p > p'$

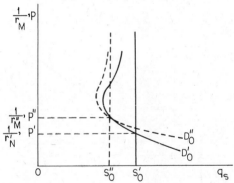

the security-quantity demand function, raising its absolute elasticity. Notice that both D_O'' and D_{VO}'' and S_O'' and S_{VO}'' meet at the unity price.[4]

Thus far we have been describing the events that occur at the

---

[4] Figure 3–5 shows graphically how a D_O schedule, upward sloping at $p > p'$, avoids a double intersection as S_O shifts to the left from S_O' to S_O'' (see Appendix II-A[1]). If D_O remained D_O', there would be a double intersection with S_O'', the reduced quantity of securities. But, since D_O rotates counterclockwise through the purchase price, the portion of the demand curve above p'' moves leftward in the instant following the operation. Since D_O cannot meet S_O a second time (see p. 454), D_O will swing completely clear of S_O'' at $p > p''$, as in the diagram. This will be true no matter where p'' stands relative to p'. If p'' were in the upward-sloping portion of D_O', the segment of D_O' drawn through the point, (S_O'', p''), would be downward sloping. This is because p'' is the new equilibrium price in the existing-asset market, in the vicinity of which $\partial D_O / \partial p < 0$ (see p. 453).

opening instant of t_1. As the interval unfolds, S_{VO} will increase to
(3B.9)
$$S_{VO}''' = S_O'''p,$$

reflecting the purchase of new securities by current savers. The latter acquisition is shown in Figure 3–1 as $AB = EF$, which raises the stock of securities to S_O'''. In Chapter II-D(2) the description of equal saving and investment flows indicated that D_{VO} moves equally with S_{VO} under these circumstances. Thus, if diagramed in Figure 3–4, the *clockwise* rotation from S_{VO}'' to S_{VO}''' would be accompanied by an equal movement of D_{VO} to

(3B.10)
$$D_{VO}''' = D_{VO}'' + (S_{VO}''' - S_{VO}''),$$

the equilibrium price remaining p''. The reflected movement in S_O and D_O is a shift to the right parallel to S_O'' and D_O'', respectively. The final schedules, S_O''' and

(3B.11)
$$D_O''' = D_O'' + (S_O''' - S_O''),$$

continue to meet at p''. In Figure 3–3 the rotation to S_{VO}''' would be accompanied by an equal movement from W'' to

(3B.12)
$$W''' = S_{VO}''' + m_2''.$$

2. Fiscal Action

a) The Problem and the Solution

A serious complication introduced by the open-market operation is that security income formerly going to households will now accrue to the bank. Unless the bank takes some action to return the income on its additional securities to households, total private income and the money supply will fall continuously. Since we have assumed that these variables are constant, apart from specified disturbances, we must require that the bank return its additional earnings.[5] The action taken in this regard will apply only to pre-existing securities purchased by the bank. Since the impact of new securities in raising total income is not considered by the general model, we analyze the bank's offsetting measures only in connection with its purchase of old securities.

One course of action is that the bank consume its additional income. However, this is neither convenient, in terms of the structure of the model, nor realistic. Central banks do not consume or

---

[5] Cf. Metzler, "Wealth, Saving, and the Rate of Interest," *Journal of Political Economy,* Vol. LIX (April, 1951), p. 109, n. 15, and Horwich, "Money, Prices and the Theory of Interest Determination," *op. cit.,* p. 631, n. 2.

expend for any purpose a large portion of their incomes.[6] Nor is the decision to consume income likely to be related to the decision to buy securities and add to the money supply. Hence, viewing the bank as a monetary-fiscal authority, it shall return its earnings to the income stream by an outright subsidy to the incomes of households. An equivalent alternative action of reducing household taxes is not available, since the authority has not previously been introduced as a spender and receiver of income.

The most neutral action that the bank can take is to subsidize personal income. The transfer of earnings from bank-held securities to persons has the desired effect of maintaining total income and the supply of money constant. Active balances received by the bank are simply handed over to households in the form of labor income, and are thereby retained in the expenditures stream. Since the human agent cannot be capitalized, and assuming that household spending is independent of both the distribution and the form of income received, there are no further repercussions on asset values, the rate of interest, the price level, or any other variables of the system. The open-market purchase, as described in the previous sections, remains the only disturbance.[7] We shall, in fact, assume that the bank subsidizes personal income only. Nevertheless, Section *b* describes the impact of the alternative action—the subsidization of security (property) income. This is done for several reasons. First, it contributes to our understanding of reality. One would expect the fiscal authority in practice to apply its earnings to subsidies (or tax reductions) on both types of income. Second, the analysis of security-income subsidization is an account of a change in ρ_s, the real income per share. Changes in ρ_s due to a variety of causes are encountered frequently in the adjustment process. Section *b* is a detailed analysis of a fluctuation in ρ_s which is applicable throughout the volume.

b) Security Income Subsidized: A Change in ρ_s

Following its purchase of $S_O' - S_O''$ in existing securities at the

---

[6] In 1960 the Federal Reserve banks paid $897 million, or 93 percent of their total net earnings to the U.S. Treasury (*Forty-Seventh Annual Report of the Board of Governors of the Federal Reserve System* [covering operations for the year 1960], pp. 120–21). The mechanism of payment is a voluntary tax imposed by the Federal Reserve on its note issues.

[7] However, this course of action has the disadvantage of destroying the equality between the total earnings of the capital stock and the total earnings of securities privately held. But the analysis does not consider such relationships before Chapter V. At that time the model is altered by the introduction of government securities, to which the bank's purchase is limited. Thus in Chapter V households at all times receive the entire earnings of the private capital stock as security income.

opening of t_1, the monetary authority transfers the entire income on its new holdings to the remaining securities held by households. It does so by subsidizing household securities in the instant following the open-market purchase. Assuming that dividends are paid out continuously over time, households will experience a spontaneous increase in ρ_s immediately after the operation. The increase in ρ_s has the effect of restoring *total* security income to its preoperation level; i.e., the smaller number of post-operation securities receives the same aggregate income as the greater number of securities previously held. Thus the capitalized value of security income, including the subsidy, creates a new security-value function, S_{VO}''',[8] equal to S_{VO}', the original one. The combined effect of the purchase and the subsidy is simply to add idle balances of $m_2'' - m_2'$ to household portfolios.

Algebraically, the developments are as follows. Before the open-market operation, we have

$$\rho_s' = \frac{\rho_K' K'}{S_O'}$$

and

(3B.13) $$S_{VO}' = S_O' p = S_O'\left(\frac{\rho_s'}{r_M}\right) = S_O'\left(\frac{\rho_K' K'}{r_M S_O'}\right) = \left(\frac{\rho_K'}{r_M}\right)K'.$$

In Figure 3–6 the initial existing-security market equilibrium is at point A. Immediately after the purchase of existing securities the income per share is unchanged at

$$\rho_s'' = \frac{\rho_K' K'}{S_O'} = \rho_s',$$

and the security value schedule is

(3B.14) $$S_{VO}'' = S_O'' p = S_O''\left(\frac{\rho_s'}{r_M}\right) = \left(\frac{S_O''}{S_O'}\right)\left(\frac{\rho_K'}{r_M}\right)K' < S_{VO}'.$$

In the diagram the equilibrium is at point B. In the next instant the bank's security earnings, $(S_O' - S_O'')\rho_s'$, are added to the earnings of securities still held by households. Thus the same aggregate return,

---

[8] The functions designated by three primes should not be confused with those similarly designated in Parts A and B(1). They are different functions, produced by different circumstances. While single and double-primed functions refer throughout this and other chapters to the pre-operation and immediate post-operation schedules, respectively, higher primes are generally specific to the events of only one or two sections.

FIGURE 3–6
The Impact on the Existing-Asset Market of an Open-Market Purchase
Followed by Security-Income Subsidization

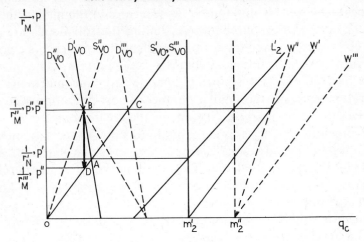

$\rho_K' K'$, is now received by the quantity, S_O'', and ρ_s rises to

$$\rho_s''' = \frac{\rho_K' K'}{S_O''} > \rho_s'.$$

S_{VO} swings rightward from S_{VO}'' to

(3B.15) $S_{VO}''' = S_O'' p = S_O'' \left(\frac{\rho_s'''}{r_M} \right) = S_O'' \left(\frac{\rho_K' K'}{r_M S_O''} \right) = \left(\frac{\rho_K'}{r_M} \right) K' = S_{VO}'.$

W, having rotated counterclockwise through p'' as a direct result of the purchase, now follows S_{VO} in a clockwise rotation through the horizontal intercept, m_2'', from W'' to

(3B.16) $W''' = S_{VO}' + m_2''.$

What happens to the rate of interest and security prices? This depends on the response of the asset-demand schedules to the increase in ρ_s and S_{VO}, which effectively is an autonomous increase in wealth. We assume, for simplicity, that L_2 does not respond, and remains fixed at L_2'. In Figure 3–6 the entire wealth increment is thus absorbed by D_{VO}, which rotates through its horizontal intercept equally with S_{VO} and W, assuming the final position,

(3B.17) $D_{VO}''' = D_{VO}'' + (W''' - W'') = D_{VO}'' + (S_{VO}''' - S_{VO}'').$

The new equilibrium is at point C, which, in view of the equal movements in S_{VO} and D_{VO}, is at the same height and interest rate, r_M''. However, since ρ_s has risen, the implicit price scale has also risen; to each interest rate, the corresponding security price is now higher (see [2B.10]). The new price associated with r_M'' is $p''' > p''$. p''' is brought about by the instantaneous purchase of existing securities implied by the rightward shift of D_{VO}; i.e., as households apply their capital gain to additional securities, they succeed only in raising the price of the fixed stock. Given that S_{VO}''' and D_{VO}''' intersect at $1/r_M''$, p must rise to a level,

(3B.18) p''', such that $\dfrac{\rho_s'''}{p'''} = r_M''$.

If L_2 also responds to the wealth gain, the final price produced by the subsidy will be somewhat below p'''. The interest rate will be above r_M''.[9]

Notice that there can be no increase in the *quantity* of real wealth or security value unless p rises above p''. If, following the subsidy, p is momentarily constant at p'', the immediate impact is to raise the rate of interest. We show this in Figure 3–6 by dropping a vertical line from point B to point D on S_{VO}'''. D is a point on S_{VO}''' at which security value is unchanged at $S_{VO}'(B) = S_O'' p''$. Since the interest-scale is unaltered by ρ_s or any other changes, the yield at point D is read on the vertical axis as r_M''', which is clearly above r_M''.[10] More specifically,

$$r_M''' = \frac{\rho_s'''}{p''} > r_M'' \text{ since } \rho_s''' > \rho_s''.$$

D is not, of course, an equilibrium, since D_{VO}''', incorporating the wealth increment, does not meet S_{VO}''' at that point.

We complete our account of the subsidy to security income by tracing the impact on the security-quantity schedules. This is done with reference to Figure 3–7. We assume once more that the entire wealth gain is allocated to D_{VO}, L_2 remaining fixed at L_2'. The increase in ρ_s due to the subsidy is again shown in the diagram as raising S_{VO} from S_{VO}'' to $S_{VO}''' = S_{VO}'$, and D_{VO} from D_{VO}'' to D_{VO}'''. The equilibrium point moves from A to B, at which the interest rate is unchanged at r_M''. While the increase in ρ_s raises the *value* of securities, it can have no effect on the *number* of securities, which

---

[9] In the extreme case in which only L_2 responded to autonomous wealth changes, D_{VO} would be fixed at D_{VO}'. The final interest rate, produced by the combined action of the purchase and the security-income subsidy would be r_N', at the intersection of D_{VO}' and $S_{VO}''' = S_{VO}'$ (see Figure 3–6). The subsidy has the effect of restoring the interest rate and the system to equilibrium.

[10] In Figure 3–6, $r_M''' > r_N'$. However, this is not a necessary result. The reader may verify that $r_M''' \gtreqless r_N'$ when $\partial D_{VO}'/\partial p \lesseqgtr 0$.

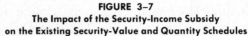

FIGURE 3–7
The Impact of the Security-Income Subsidy
on the Existing Security-Value and Quantity Schedules

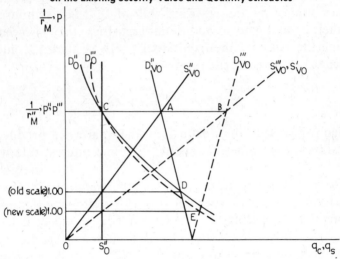

remains S_O'', the post-operation quantity. However, D_O, dependent on the wealth budget, cannot be constant. It will undergo a clockwise rotation through $1/r_M''$. D_O''', the final schedule, must intersect S_O' at that yield, since it is still the equilibrium of the value functions. Thus, at $1/r_M''$, D_O'' and D_O''' coincide. But we can see that they will not coincide elsewhere, by considering the movement of the unity price on the vertical axis. As we have noted, the increase in ρ_s raises the price scale. The unity price is thus lowered. Hence, while D_O'' and D_{VO}'' meet at point D, the height of which is $p = 1.00$, D_O''' and D_{VO}''' meet at E, whose ordinate, $p = 1.00$, is below that of D. Requiring that D_O''' pass through points C and E has the effect of drawing that curve below D_O'' at $r_M > r_M''$, and above at $r_M < r_M''$, as indicated. On net, D_O''' represents a clockwise rotation relative to D_O''. An algebraic proof follows:

$$D_O''' = \frac{D_{VO}'''}{p} = \frac{D_{VO}'' + (S_{VO}''' - S_{VO}')}{\left(\frac{\rho_s'''}{r_M}\right)}$$

$$= \frac{D_O''\left(\frac{\rho_s'}{r_M}\right) + S_O''\left(\frac{\rho_s'''}{r_M}\right) - S_O''\left(\frac{\rho_s'}{r_M}\right)}{\left(\frac{\rho_s'''}{r_M}\right)}$$

$$= D_O''\left(\frac{\rho_s'}{\rho_s'''}\right) + S_O'' - S_O''\left(\frac{\rho_s'}{\rho_s'''}\right).$$

We subtract D_O'' from both sides and collect terms:

$$D_O''' - D_O'' = D_O'' \left(\frac{\rho_s'}{\rho_s'''} - 1 \right) - S_O'' \left(\frac{\rho_s'}{\rho_s'''} - 1 \right)$$

$$= \left(\frac{\rho_s' - \rho_s'''}{\rho_s'''} \right) (D_O'' - S_O'').$$

Since

$$\frac{\rho_s' - \rho_s'''}{\rho_s'''} < 0, (D_O''' - D_O'') \gtreqless 0 \text{ when } (D_O'' - S_O'') \lesseqgtr 0.$$

But

$$(D_O'' - S_O'') \lesseqgtr 0 \text{ when } r_M \gtreqless r_M''.$$

Hence

$$(D_O''' - D_O'') \gtreqless 0 \text{ when } r_M \gtreqless r_M''. \quad [11]$$

---

[11] A *rotation* in D_O, in response to a wealth gain, $S_{VO}''' - S_{VO}''$, which is positive at every price and yield, is rather surprising. But it occurs because the source of the wealth increment is a change in ρ_s. Intuitively, the impact on D_O is this. Since $D_O = D_{VO}/p$, equal relative increases in D_{VO} and p will leave D_O unchanged. At all interest rates, p increases from ρ_s'/r_M to ρ_s'''/r_M, or by

$$\frac{\rho_s'}{r_M} \Big/ \frac{\rho_s'''}{r_M} = \frac{\rho_s'''}{\rho_s'},$$

a given constant. Moreover, the relative increase in S_{VO} is

$$\frac{S_{VO}'''}{S_{VO}''} = \frac{S_O'' \left(\dfrac{\rho_s'''}{r_M} \right)}{S_O'' \left(\dfrac{\rho_s'}{r_M} \right)} = \frac{\rho_s'''}{\rho_s'},$$

which is the relative increase in p. Now the increase in ρ_s raises D_{VO} and S_{VO} by equal absolute amounts; i.e.,

$$D_{VO}''' - D_{VO}'' = S_{VO}''' - S_{VO}''.$$

At $1/r_M'$, the inverse of the equilibrium yield, these absolute changes are also equal relative changes since the initial quantities for each, D_{VO}'' and S_{VO}'', are themselves equal (see Figure 3–7). Thus at $1/r_M'$,

$$\frac{D_{VO}'''}{D_{VO}''} = \frac{S_{VO}'''}{S_{VO}''} = \frac{\rho_s'''}{\rho_s'}.$$

D_{VO}, S_{VO}, and p increase by equal relative amounts, and $D_O''(1/r_M') = D_O''(1/r_M')$. But at $r_M > r_M'$, the situation is different. We have

$$\frac{D_{VO}'''}{D_{VO}''} < \frac{S_{VO}'''}{S_{VO}''} = \frac{\rho_s'''}{\rho_s'},$$

because the initial quantities are $D_{VO}'' > S_{VO}''$, as a condition of stability. Thus the equal absolute increments in D_{VO} and S_{VO} now entail a lower relative change in D_{VO} than in S_{VO} and, equivalently, in p. Hence $D_O''' < D_O''$. By similar reasoning, at $r_M < r_M'$, $D_O''' > D_O''$.

If the increase in D_{VO} is less than the entire capital gain, $S'''_{VO} - S''_{VO}$, the final interest rate is above r''_M. D'''_O will meet S''_O at an ordinate below $1/r''_M$. The reader may verify that D'''_O and D''_O will meet at an ordinate above $1/r''_M$.[12]

C. A SEQUENTIAL PURCHASE

In any market in which supply is an increasing function of price, a large buyer can economize by dividing a block purchase into a sequence of several purchases of smaller units.[13] The price paid for each unit, and the average price, will be less than if the purchase were made in a single transaction. This is equally true of stock or flow markets in which excess supply rises with price, although in a stock market each unit must be bought at successively higher prices. We shall reconsider the open-market purchase on the assumption that the central bank chooses to split its purchase of n securities at a single price into n purchases of one security each at variable prices. This will provide an interesting contrast, in terms of the impact on the existing-asset market, to the analysis of Parts A and B. We shall observe that the magnitude of the operation, the asset-demand schedules confronting a purchaser, and the schedules remaining after his departure, depend not only on the number of securities bought, but on whether the purchase is carried out in one or more stages. Since only the existing-asset market is relevant to all of these considerations, we assume that each of the purchases is made instantaneously. As a result, the output market and new securities are not involved in the operation.

---

[12]An alternative, though unlikely, way for the monetary authority to return the earnings on its securities is to make an outright gift of these issues to randomly selected households. This presents an interesting (and for later purposes, useful) analytic contrast to the method described above. The subsidy to security holdings would raise S_{VO} to $S'''_{VO} = S'_{VO}$, as earlier, but now the functions are identical, rather than merely equal:

$$S'''_{VO} = S'_O p = S'_{VO}.$$

Once again, if D_{VO} alone responds to the wealth gain, r_M remains r''_M. But in the present case, p would also be constant at p''. The wealth gain is no longer dependent on an increase in p stimulated by a rise in ρ_s. It now takes the form of an increase in physical holdings of securities. An equal increase in D_{VO} implies a passive acceptance of the additional holdings, without further movements between assets or changes in r_M or p. In terms of security-quantity schedules, S_O moves to the right of S''_O to $S'''_O = S'_O$, and D_O moves an equal distance to the right, parallel to D''_O. There are no rotations of the demand schedule as a result of the subsidy of securities. Cf. below Chapter V-E(5) and p. 318, n. 43.

[13]Cf. Davis, "Re-Examination of the Speculative Demand for Money," *op. cit.*, and Horwich, "Re-Examination of the Speculative Demand for Money: Comment," *op. cit.*, pp. 686–89.

The sequential purchase is contrasted with a block purchase by reference to the existing-security market in Figure 3–8. The pre-operation equilibrium is p', at the intersection of S'_O and D'_O. If the monetary authority decides to buy two securities in a block purchase, it can do so by offering to pay p'_2 for each of them. This

FIGURE 3–8
A Sequential Purchase Contrasted with a Block Purchase

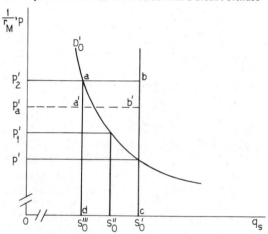

would make the magnitude of the purchase $2p'_2$, represented in Figure 3–8 by the area of the rectangle, *abcd*. Suppose, alternatively, that the authority buys the two securities one at a time, paying the minimum price required for each. It will buy its first security for p'_1, reducing the stock to S''_O. Now, we know that D_O will rotate counterclockwise through the point, (S''_O, p'_1), so that the next purchase is made along a new schedule, nearer to the vertical axis at $p > p'_1$. But, for the moment, let us abstract from this and future rotations, assuming that a sequential purchase is carried out along a fixed schedule, D'_O. Then the second security is bought at p'_2, which again is the market price remaining after the purchase of two securities. But this time the total receipts going to the sellers of securities are

$$(3C.1) \qquad p'_1 + p'_2 < 2p'_2,$$

the receipts netted by the block sale. The sequential receipts are represented in Figure 3–8 by the area of $a'b'cd$, the height of which is the average price paid,

$$(3C.2) \qquad p'_a = \frac{p'_1 + p'_2}{2}.$$

In Figure 3-9, D_O is now permitted to rotate after the purchase of each security. As noted, the initial movement is a counter-clockwise rotation through (S_O'', p_1'). This yields D_O'', along which the second security can be purchased at a price, $p_2'' < p_2'$. A

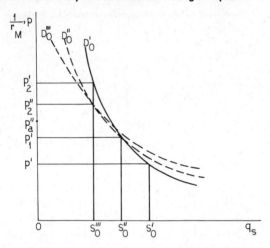

FIGURE 3-9
Rotations of the Security Demand Schedule during a Sequential Purchase

third and final schedule, D_O''', is produced when D_O rotates through (S_O''', p_2''). The average price is now

(3C.3) $$p_a'' = \frac{p_1' + p_2''}{2} < p_a'.$$

The impact on the entire existing-asset market at each stage is shown in Figure 3-10. At p', the pre-operation price,

(3C.4) $$D_{VO}' = D_O'p \text{ and } S_{VO}' = S_O'p$$

intersect, as do L_2' and m_2'. At p_1', the price of the first transaction,

(3C.5) $$S_{VO}' - D_{VO}' = L_2' - m_2' = p_1'.$$

The new security-value function is

(3C.6) $$S_{VO}'' = S_O''p,$$

and idle balances are

(3C.7) $$m_2'', \text{ where } m_2'' - m_2' = p_1'.$$

The new wealth function is

(3C.8) $$W'' = S_{VO}'' + m_2'',$$

which causes sympathetic rotations in the demand schedules, which become D_{VO}'' and L_2''. The second transaction is at p_2'', at which

(3C.9) $$S_{VO}'' - D_{VO}'' = L_2'' - m_2'' = p_2''.$$

The resulting supply schedules are

(3C.10) $$S_{VO}''' = S_0'''p \text{ and } m_2''', \text{ where } m_2''' - m_2'' = p_2''.$$

The wealth function is

(3C.11) $$W''' = S_{VO}''' + m_2''',$$

which induces further rotations in D_{VO} and L_2. However, these are not entered in the diagram, in order to simplify it. If D_{VO}''' were drawn, it would meet D_{VO}'' at p_2'' and D_{VO}' at p_a''. Similarly, L_2''' would intersect L_2'' at p_2'' and L_2' at p_a''. The reason that the final demand schedules meet the initial ones at p_a'' is that total wealth at that price is unaffected by the purchases. This is reflected in Figure 3–10 by the intersection of W''' and W' at p_a''. Since it is an arithmetic mean, p_a'' is the price which, when multiplied by the number of securities sold, equals the total receipts. Symbolically, at p_a''

(3C.12) $$S_{VO}' - S_{VO}''' = (S_0' - S_0''')p_a'' = m_2''' - m_2'.$$

In a word, the reduction in security value is equal to the increase in idle balances, and total wealth is unchanged.

FIGURE 3–10
A Sequential Purchase in the Context of the Entire Existing-Asset Market

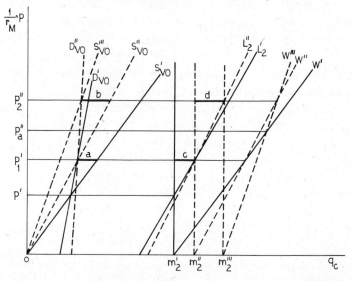

The distinctive feature of the sequential purchase is that the average price paid is less than the final price created by the operation. Thus one cannot measure the magnitude of the purchase by the value of the excess security supply or the excess demand for idle balances at the final market price. At p_2'' in Figure 3–10, for example, neither the excess supply, $S_{VO}' - D_{VO}'$, nor the excess demand, $L_2' - m_2'$, is equal to the magnitude of the purchase. The latter is equal to the sum of the horizontal vectors, a and b, or c and d, which measure the monetary injection at each stage. Alternatively, as noted, the purchase is equal to the difference between the initial and final security-value functions at p_a'', the lower average price. In the sequential purchase the monetary authority takes advantage of the willingness of wealth holders to relinquish securities singly at more favorable terms than in a block sale. In addition, the counterclockwise rotations of the demand schedules, beginning after the purchase of the first security, create even better terms as the operation continues. Having lost just one security, wealth holders experience smaller capital gains than otherwise, as security prices are raised further by the bank. This effect mounts if more and more securities are sold, and the result is that D_{VO} and L_2 are drawn increasingly leftward at higher prices, as compared with their stability when the sale occurs in a block at a single price. This points up a fundamental assumption underlying the construction of the asset-demand schedules: they are drawn on the basis of a fixed stock of securities and idle money. If a movement along D_{VO} or L_2 entails any change in those stocks, then D_{VO} and L_2 will themselves be altered. A sequential purchase of a sufficiently large number of securities might dislodge the demand schedules considerably from the positions they would have held with security holdings intact. As a result, any given number of securities can be bought at lower prices, reducing the magnitude of open-market purchases. At the same time the rotation of L_2 implies that a given reduction in the rate of interest will be accompanied by operations of smaller magnitude. This is illustrated in Figure 3–11, where $L_2(r_M)$ rotates clockwise, first through r_1', corresponding to p_1', and then through r_2'', corresponding to p_2''. At r_2'' the reduction in the possible magnitude of the purchase is $L_2' - L_2''$.[14]

---

[14] If L_2 does not respond to autonomous wealth changes, remaining fixed at L_2', then a given reduction in r_M stimulates a purchase whose magnitude is independent of whether the securities are bought sequentially or in a block. However, if the securities are bought sequentially, a greater number than otherwise must be purchased to create an operation of given magnitude.

FIGURE 3–11
Rotations of the Demand for Idle Money during a Sequential Purchase

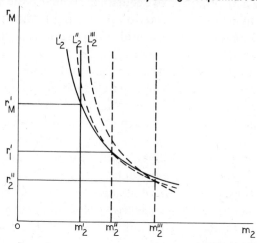

D. OVERPAYMENT

Suppose that in a block purchase the monetary authority fails to buy all securities offered at its bid price. The bank obviously could have acquired the securities by bidding and paying a lower price. Thus it has committed an error of overpayment. How will this affect the stock and flow segments of the economy? We begin with the existing-asset market. In order to simplify the analysis, we assume at this point that the purchase is confined to existing securities; the bank is in the market only for an instant. In Figure 3–12 the initial existing-supply and demand for securities are S'_o

FIGURE 3–12
An Open-Market Purchase Entailing an Error of Overpayment

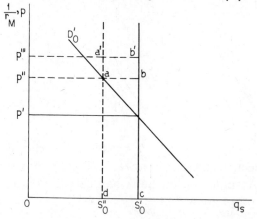

and D_0', respectively, and their equilibrium price is p'. If the bank wanted to buy a dc quantity of securities, reducing the stock to S_0'', it could do so in a single transaction by paying a minimum price of p''. The simultaneous outlay would equal the area of the rectangle, $abcd$. However, if the bank instead paid $p''' > p''$ for the dc quantity of securities, the final market price would again be p'', where D_0' and S_0'' meet, but the real payment would equal the rectangular area, $a'b'cd$, which exceeds $abcd$ by $a'b'ba$. The latter area represents an expenditure in excess of that required by security holders; i.e., it exceeds the value of the excess supply of securities at p'', and constitutes a bounty in cash balances. Since we are involved in instantaneous transactions on wealth account, the latter balances are idle. Overpayment in the existing-asset market may thus be analyzed as the usual purchase supplemented by a gift of idle money. This is done with the aid of Figure 3–13, where the pre-operation schedules are

(3D.1) $S_{VO}' = S_O'p,\ D_{VO}' = D_O'p,\ m_2',\ L_2',$ and $W' = S_{VO}' + m_2'.$

The bank raises p from p' to p''', but obtains a quantity of securities, $(S_{VO}' - S_{VO}'')/p'''$, which is less than the obtainable number

FIGURE 3–13
Overpayment in the Context of the Entire Existing-Asset Market

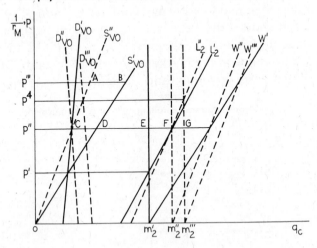

at that price, $(S_{VO}' - D_{VO}')/p'''$. In fact, the number purchased could have been secured at a lower minimum price, p'', at which $D_{VO}' = S_{VO}''$. Assume that the bank had actually paid p''. The magnitude of the purchase is thus

(3D.2) $CD = EF = m_2'' - m_2'.$

p'' is the final market price, and

(3D.3) $$W'' = S_{VO}'' + m_2''$$

is the new wealth function. The asset-demand schedules rotate counterclockwise through p'', assuming the positions of D_{VO}'' and L_2''. But in fact the bank pays p''' and spends $AB > CD$ on the given quantity of securities, raising m_2 by a further amount,

(3D.4) $$FG = AB - CD = m_2''' - m_2''.$$

Hence the final wealth function,

(3D.5) $$W''' = S_{VO}'' + m_2''',$$

exceeds W'' by this additional increment to idle balances. For graphical simplicity, we assume that only D_{VO} responds to the increase in wealth, taking on the position of

(3D.6) $$D_{VO}''' = D_{VO}'' + (m_2''' - m_2'').$$

The final market price, p^4, [15] is at the intersection of D_{VO}''' and S_{VO}''. It is below p''', but above p''. We assume that the purchase price, p''', is the prevailing market price only while the bank is actually purchasing securities. As soon as wealth holders are frustrated in their attempt to sell to the bank, the price drops immediately to p^4, which reflects the *de facto* loss of securities plus the influence on security demand of the bounty on those sold.[16] The final interest rate, corresponding to p^4, is higher than the bank's purchase yield, but less than the loss of securities *per se* would have justified.

In order to discuss overpayment with reference to the output market, we must specify the time period that the monetary authority initially intended to devote to the purchase. Thus if the bank had intended to be in the market for a period, t_1, there is some minimum price that will elicit the desired number of securities, while any higher price would stimulate a greater flow and constitute overpayment for those actually acquired. Suppose, in Figure 3–14,

---

[15] In this and subsequent chapters we simplify our notation by replacing primes above the third order by the equivalent numeral in the superscript position.

[16] In terms of the security-quantity schedules the gift of idle balances appears as an increment at every price to D_O'', the demand curve corresponding to D_{VO}''. In a diagram of price against security quantity, the monetary increment, $m_2''' - m_2''$, is plotted as a rectangular hyperbola,

$$D_O''' - D_O'' = \frac{m_2''' - m_2''}{p},$$

where D_O''' is the quantity counterpart of D_{VO}''', the final value schedule.

FIGURE 3–14
Overpayment in the Purchase of New Securities

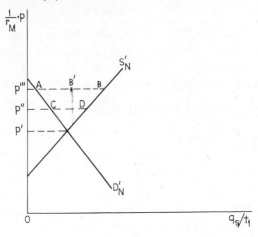

that S_N' and D_N' are drawn for t_1, and that at p'' the excess quantity of new securities is CD, which together with the excess supply furnished by the existing-asset market, exactly satisfies the bank. But the bank erroneously offers p''', at which $AB > CD$ in new securities will be supplied during t_1. At some point before the end of t_1, $AB' = CD$ in new securities will have been received, and the bank departs from the market. At this instant, as any other, the price of securities is determined in the existing-asset market. If S_N and D_N are now re-drawn for a subsequent period, t_2, of the same length as t_1, they will have the same appearance as in Figure 3–14. The excess supply at the opening of t_2 will be determined by the price of the existing-asset market. S_N and D_N, as aggregates, are assumed capable of continuous adjustment over time. The quantity rejected by the bank, $B'B$, does not appear on the market.

E. AN OPEN-MARKET SALE

In an open-market sale the variables move essentially in the opposite direction. The central bank sets a sale price below the prevailing equilibrium price, and offers to provide the market with as large a block of securities as it will take during a period, t_1. The higher yield obtainable on the bank's issues initiates an attempted mass liquidation of existing securities by households, since the new offerings are indistinguishable from existing ones and cannot command a different rate. But as the market moves from old to new securities, the market price falls and the yield rises to conformity with those offered by the bank. At this point, the purchase of securities from the bank proceeds in accordance with the more limited desires of households to add to their holdings at the higher (and now uniform) market rate. If the market is like-minded and perfectly informed, we can expect an instantaneous adjustment of the price to the level determined by the bank—without benefit of trading—prior to the actual operation. Once again, we assume initially that the bank, in providing households with the desired number of securities, fulfills its own intentions with regard to security holdings, and leaves the market at the close of t_1. Thus the sale price and yield prevail at the opening of the next period, t_2.

If we were to diagram the open-market sale, the action of the bank would be represented by a horizontal line indicating an infinitely elastic supply schedule at a price, $p'' < p'$, for which the corresponding interest rates are $r_M'' > r_N'$ (imagine such a line drawn below the equilibrium at p' in Figure 3–1). The securities sold by the bank will go to two sources: the existing-asset market, in which the price is already p'', and the output market. By taking $D_T' - S_T'$ ([3A.3]), we can write excess demand functions:

$$(3E.1) \qquad D_T' - S_T' = (D_O' - S_O') + (D_N' - S_N').$$

In real terms the funds withdrawn from the sale are

$$(3E.2) \qquad p''(D_T' - S_T') = p''(D_O' - S_O') + p''(D_N' - S_N'),$$

and in money terms,

$$(3E.3) \qquad \pi''(D_T' - S_T') = \pi''(D_O' - S_O') + \pi''(D_N' - S_N'),$$

where $\pi'' = P'p''$. Part of the operation, equal to $\pi''(D_O' - S_O')$, thus represents an immediate withdrawal of money from idle balances, and the remaining portion, $\pi''(D_N' - S_N')$, is made up of active money taken from current savers. The higher rate of interest during t_1 creates a gap between intended saving and investment by encouraging thriftiness in the form a demand for securities, while inhibiting the issue of new securities by entrepreneurs. The bank "fills" this deflationary gap by selling directly to savers, whose increased demand for securities in the face of a diminishing supply is thereby met. To this extent, funds are absorbed directly from the income flow and cause the general price level to fall. The money price corresponding to p'' is thus constantly lowered. If $P_a < P'$ is the average commodity price during t_1, the actual withdrawal of funds from the income stream is

$$(3E.4) \qquad P_a p''(D_N' - S_N'),$$

somewhat less than if P were constant. We can summarize the ability of the bank to act on income and wealth account by constructing excess demand functions that slope down and to the right with respect to p and $1/r_M$.

The direct impact of the bank on the existing-asset market at the opening of t_1 is diagramed in Figure 3–15. At p'' the excess value demand for securities is

$$(3E.5) \qquad\qquad D'_{VO} - S'_{VO} = AB,$$

equal to the excess supply of idle balances,

$$(3E.6) \qquad\qquad m'_2 - L'_2 = CD.$$

The sale raises S_{VO} to S''_{VO} and lowers m_2 to m''_2. A new wealth function,

$$(3E.7) \qquad\qquad W'' = S''_{VO} + m''_2,$$

is drawn from m''_2 on the horizontal axis through W' at the height p''. At p'' an equal-value amount of securities and money are exchanged, so total wealth is unchanged; at $p > p''$ more securities are on hand than formerly to enjoy the capital gains, and so $W'' > W'$; at $p < p''$ there are more securities held to experience capital losses, and so $W'' < W'$. Relative to W', W'' thus represents a *clockwise* rotation through p'', the sale price. D_{VO} and L_2 rotate sympathetically:

$$(3E.8) \qquad (D''_{VO} - D'_{VO}) + (L''_2 - L'_2) = W'' - W'.$$

FIGURE 3–15
The Direct Impact of an Open-Market Sale on the Existing-Asset Market

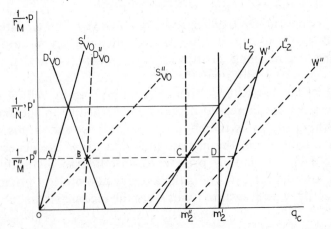

Since the monetary authority is not a recipient or consumer of income in the model, the earnings on all of its securities have previously been returned to households via personal-income subsidies (see Part B[2]a). Thus some counter action must be taken in order that the securities sold by the bank will provide an earnings rate equal to the pre-existing one, ρ_s'. Once again the most neutral policy is to act on personal incomes. Immediately following the open-market sale, we assume that the authority taxes personal incomes, transferring the proceeds to the securities purchased by households. There are no further repercussions on the economy, in general, or the existing-asset market, in particular. The latter remains as diagramed in Figure 3-15. If the authority finances the earnings of the new securities by taxing all existing securities after the sale, then total security income is constant in the face of the disturbances. As a result of the security tax, ρ_s falls to ρ_s''' and S_{VO} swings to $S_{VO}''' = S_{VO}'$. On net, households have failed to gain security value, and have lost $m_2' - m_2''$ in idle balances. If D_{VO} moves equally with S_{VO}, the interest rate remains r_M'', but security prices fall to $p''' = \rho_s'''/r_M''$. If part of the wealth loss is absorbed by L_2, then p will fall less and r_M will be somewhat below r_M''. As for the security-quantity schedules, the sale causes D_O to rotate clockwise through p''. A tax on security income will produce a counterclockwise rotation through $1/r_M \leq 1/r_M''$.

Were the bank to carry out its sale sequentially, it would find that it could sell its securities at an average price above the price of the block sale. This would raise the magnitude (i.e., the revenue) of the sale of any given number of securities. In the absence of demand rotations, however, the price of the last security sold, and thus the final market price would be the same for both types of sale. Taking account of clockwise rotations as each security is received by the community, the bank sells each additional security at lower prices than otherwise. This reduces the proceeds of the sale of any given number of securities, but a given increase in interest rates withdraws a greater quantity of money from asset accounts.

Figure 3-16 illustrates the case of the bank erroneously setting its sale price too low, and failing to provide the existing-asset market with the desired number of securities. The existing-security market is initially in equilibrium at p'. The bank wants to sell a dc quantity of securities, which can be done at a maximum price of p''. The real payment for these securities would be the area bounded by $abcd$. But, instead, the bank asks p'''. Households

FIGURE 3–16
An Open-Market Sale Entailing an Error of Underpricing

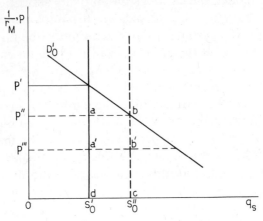

would like a greater number than *dc*, but no more are forthcoming. As a result, the payment going to the bank is only *a'b'cd*, and the difference between this and the maximum amount that households would pay is *abb'a'*. The latter is again a bounty of idle balances which is available for increasing asset demand at all prices. The final market price will be p^4 (between p'' and p'), at which S_O'' meets an augmented D_O schedule. Any underselling below the maximum required price in the output market creates a larger than necessary excess of D_N over S_N. But when the bank ceases its sale, saving and investment adjust immediately to the prevailing market price. Excess savers' demand at p''' not realized in securities offered by the bank is extinguished the moment the bank leaves the market.

F. THE FUNDAMENTAL PROBLEM FOR THE ANALYSIS OF MONETARY CHANGE

In Chapters IV–VI we shall trace the adjustment process by which the system returns to equilibrium following the open-market operation. In doing so, we shall assume that the entire direct impact of the operation, instantaneously carried out, is on the existing-asset market, and that there is no contact between the bank and the components of current saving and investment. Our primary reason for doing this is for analytical ease: it is much easier to isolate the equilibrating forces if the bank has traded in idle money and existing securities only. But this assumption is not unrealistic since a once-for-all purchase or sale of securities by the central bank might very well be executed in an interval so brief that substantial flows of saving and investment cannot accumulate. Meanwhile, a developed economy confronts a trader with a considerable stock of existing securities. Even a small displacement of the interest rate might evoke an excess supply or demand for existing securities sufficient to carry out a given operation. The speed with which suppliers and demanders in each market respond to price changes is also relevant to this consideration. But even if wealth holders react sluggishly, while current savers and entrepreneurs respond rapidly, it would seem unlikely that the initial gap between saving and investment, which determines the impact of an operation on income account, will compare very favorably to the difference between existing supply and demand during a brief sojourn in the market.[17]

Granted, then, that the direct impact of the operation is wholly on wealth account, we are faced with a serious analytical challenge which we designate *the fundamental problem for the analysis of monetary change*: How can money, introduced or withdrawn from the asset accounts of the community, exert an influence on the commodity price level? The operation cannot affect commodity prices unless we demonstrate a mechanism for transferring money between idle and active uses. But such a transfer must be accountable in terms of the model under *ceteris paribus* conditions. We cannot, for example, permit asset holders to dispatch idle money directly to the expenditures stream, or allow a spontaneous change in the velocity of active money to occur. These would be arbitrary, temporizing solutions, not really fundamental in that they are already implied by the basic model. For if the price of securities has moved appropriately, the public will *want* to hold more or less idle money in accordance with the action of the bank, and in the absence of built-in disturbances, will continue to do so. We need,

---

[17] In "Money, Liquidity, and the Valuation of Assets," *Money, Trade, and Economic Growth* (New York: The Macmillan Co., 1951), p. 222, R. A. Musgrave asserts that there is considerable rigidity in existing-asset demand, so that current saving is of considerable importance—more than its size would indicate—in determining total asset demand. Musgrave does not provide any evidence or *a priori* reasoning to substantiate this point, and he does not specify the time interval relevant to his argument. But it seems unlikely that rigidities alone could transfer the impact of the operation from wealth to income account (Musgrave is not, of course, making this claim). Only a small portion of the wealth-holding public, such as professional dealers, needs to be directly involved in an operation, and if such a group is sensitive and informed, then, in effect, the whole market is. However alert, savers are still a small group, unlikely to dominate the money market during the actual period of open-market activity. This need not, of course, be true in an intermediate or long-run period.

instead, a general and automatic link between the operation and commodity prices independent of institutional and behavioral relations not already contained in the system. To this end, Chapters IV–VI will describe the adjustment process, assuming that the operation occurs entirely on wealth account. At the same time the analysis will bring the interest rate back to its joint stock and flow equilibrium level.

G. SUMMARY

The central bank carries out a "block" purchase of securities from households by bidding up security prices and lowering the yield. To the extent that the bank obtains pre-existing securities, the expended funds are held by households in the form of idle balances. Over time the bank obtains newly issued securities, representing the excess of desired investment over intended saving at the lower rate of interest. Funds spent by the bank on new securities are thus channeled directly into active balances by expenditure on capital projects. The commodity price level rises proportionately.

The purchase of existing securities causes a counterclockwise rotation of the wealth function through the purchase price. The asset-demand schedules, including security demand in security units, rotate sympathetically. In order to maintain total income constant, the bank must return to households the earnings on its newly acquired securities. The bank does so by applying these earnings to subsidies on personal incomes. This action is completely neutral with respect to the variables of the system. The alternative action of subsidizing the income of remaining securities held by households is also analyzed. The subsidy to security income raises the value of securities at every yield. If security demand absorbs the entire wealth gain, the price of securities will rise until the rate of interest is again equal to the purchase yield. If security demand rises less than the wealth increment, the rate of interest will also rise. The security-quantity demand schedule rotates counterclockwise.

An alternative to the "block" purchase is a "sequential" purchase, in which the securities are bought individually at the minimum possible price. The latter increases with each purchase. In general, the central bank obtains more securities for any given outlay; any given reduction in the rate of interest can be accomplished by smaller expenditures. This follows from the rotations in the asset-demand schedules that occur during the course of the operation. An error of overpayment occurs when the bank fails to accept all securities forthcoming at its bid price. This is analyzed in the existing-asset market as the errorless purchase plus a subsidy of idle balances. In the output market the purchase, whether in error or not, has no impact on subsequent flow schedules.

The forthcoming analysis of the adjustment process will assume that the impact of the purchase is limited to the existing-asset market; i.e., existing securities only have been sold to the bank in exchange for idle balances. The assumption is made both for analytical ease and realism. However, a fundamental problem results: The analysis must now explain, within the given framework, how a monetary injection to idle balances can raise the commodity price level. The merger of stock-flow security markets will furnish the explanation, while also accounting for the return of the interest rate to the natural level.

The direct impact of an open-market sale is essentially opposite and symmetrical to the impact of the purchase. At a lower price and higher yield, the bank sells securities to both existing-asset holders and current savers, from whom idle and active balances, respectively, are taken. The wealth function and the asset-demand schedules rotate clockwise through the sale price. The bank services the income on securities sold to households by taxing personal incomes. The alternative action of taxing security income would reduce security prices, but not the rate of interest, provided that security demand absorbs the entire wealth loss. A sequential sale will displace the demand schedules during the course of the operation. The sale of any given number of securities will net a smaller revenue; a given increase in the rate of interest requires a greater monetary reduction. A sale entailing an error of underpricing is viewed in the existing-asset market as an errorless operation plus a subsidy of idle balances.

CHAPTER IV

The Adjustment Process: Financial Elements

A. INTRODUCTION

We return now to the open-market purchase and describe the course of events during succeeding periods. We assume that the purchase has been carried out instantaneously in a block at a price satisfying both buyer and sellers. The stock of existing securities held by households has fallen to S_O'', and the real idle money supply has risen to m_2''. The purchase price and yield, p'' and $r_M'' = \rho_s''/p''$, prevail at the opening of the next interval. The asset-demand schedules have rotated counterclockwise through p'', reflecting the new functional relationship between wealth and the rate of interest. The monetary authority has returned the earnings on its additional securities by subsidizing personal incomes. This maintains the money supply and the level of full-employment income constant, and avoids the reverberations on the existing-asset market of a subsidy to security income.

The analysis now has two tasks. One is to relate the direct impact of the bank on existing securities, idle balances, and the rate of interest to a movement in the commodity price level. This, as we noted at the close of Chapter III, must indicate how the increased idle balances of households can be physically channeled into the circulation of active money. The other task is to explain how the rate of interest returns to its equilibrium level at the intersection of saving and investment. An analysis of the co-mingling of the stock and flow markets will reveal how both of these adjustments are accomplished.

The analysis begins in Part B(1), which describes the stock-flow merger and the resulting impact on the rate of interest and the "financial" variables—securities, idle and active balances. Though the supply of active balances and the commodity price level are raised by the adjustment, this portion of the chapter ignores any possible repercussions of these variables on the system. The entire transition to the new equilibrium is treated as the outcome of the interaction of security-market stocks and flows. Part B(2) examines the possible influence of the "real" variables—capital and its rate of return—on the financial adjustment, particularly in regard to the anticipated and *de facto* income per share. Part C(1) describes the impact of the rise in the price level. By reducing the value of idle balances, the movement of the price level is a second force driving the interest rate to its equilibrium value. Part C(2) explores several possible offsets to the inflation—"leakages." Part D summarizes the impact of the adjustment on the variables of the equation of exchange. An appendix assesses the relative quantitative importance of the two equilibrating mechanisms to the adjustment process.

B. FROM STOCKS TO FLOWS: THE TRANSFER EFFECT

1. The Equilibrating Process

The interaction of security markets is studied during a period, t_1, immediately following the open-market purchase. Since the saving and investment components flow continuously over any period of time, there are no necessary restrictions on the length of t_1, other than that it be less than the total time required to reach the new equilibrium. However, for expositional convenience, we take t_1 to be very brief, an infinitesimal fraction of the total adjustment period. If the latter is several months or quarters, then t_1 is several minutes, an hour, or at most a day. In this event the movement of security prices and interest during t_1 is relatively small, and we can assume, without serious error, that all trading occurs at a single price—the equilibrium of the interval. This assumption will greatly simplify our expressions for the variables of the adjustment process.

Figure 4–1 diagrams the securities market during t_1. S_O'' and D_O'' are the existing-asset schedules created directly by the bank's purchase. The opening market price, as determined by these schedules, is p''. S_N' and D_N' are, respectively, the supply of new securities and the demand for securities by savers. Since saving and investment are constant over time, S_N' and D_N' are redrawn without change from any previous period of the same duration as t_1. The total securities

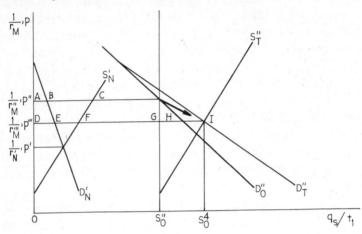

market is obtained, as earlier, by summing the old and new schedules horizontally. Thus

(4B.1) $$S_T'' = S_O'' + S_N' \quad \text{and} \quad D_T'' = D_O'' + D_N'.$$

The equilibrium at the close of t_1 is at the intersection of S_T'' and D_T'' at which the price and yield are $p''' < p''$ and $r_M''' > r_M''$, respectively. Upon substituting, $D_T'' - S_T'' = 0$ yields

(4B.2) $$D_O'' - S_O'' = S_N' - D_N';$$

i.e., the equilibrium at p''' is characterized by equality between the excess existing demand for securities and the excess supply of new securities.

Let us consider the events during t_1 leading to the new equilibrium. At p'' at the start of the interval, savers' security demand proceeds at the rate, $D_N'(p'') = AB$, and entrepreneurial security supply at $S_N'(p'') = AC$. The difference is $AC - AB = BC$, a flow of excess supply of new securities. Since at p'', $S_O'' = D_O''$, BC is a net excess supply that tends to depress security prices. But as p falls in response to each minute increment of excess securities, the rates of flow of S_N and D_N are constantly readjusted. S_N decreases and D_N increases, reducing the rate of excess supply below BC. Simultaneously, the fall in p stimulates a movement down the D_O'' schedule; i.e., the decrease in p and increase in r_M evoke an excess existing demand for securities at the expense of m_2. p continues to fall until at p''' an equilibrium for the interval is reached. Granted that the number of securities sold at prices above p''' is infinitesimal, and that all trading effectively occurs at the equilibrium price, the security quantities realized for the interval are

(4B.3) $$S'_N - D'_N = EF = D''_O - S''_O = GH,$$

at which $D''_T - S''_T = 0$. The quantity of securities purchased by savers is $D'_N(p''') = DE = HI$, reflected in the total market as equal additions to aggregate supply and demand. The closing stock of securities is S^4_O. The course of p and $1/r_M$ during t_1 is shown in the diagram by the downward arrow.

In order to see the impact on all the wealth components, the stock-flow merger of t_1 is drawn in Figure 4–2 in terms of the real-

FIGURE 4–2
The Stock-Flow Merger of the First Adjustment Interval in Real-Value Units

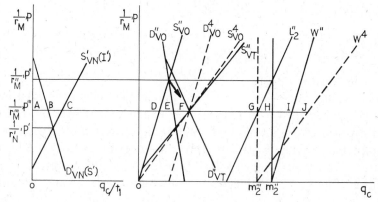

value saving, investment, and existing-asset schedules. In the diagram,

(4B.4) $$S''_{VT} = S''_{VO} + S'_{VN} \quad \text{and} \quad D''_{VT} = D''_{VO} + D'_{VN},$$

where each function is obtained by multiplying the corresponding security-quantity function of Figure 4–1 by the factor, p. A separate origin for the stock and flow markets is used in Figure 4–2 to simplify the geometry. The equilibrium at p''' and r'''_M is one in which

(4B.5) $$S'_{VN} - D'_{VN} = BC = D''_{VO} - S''_{VO} = DE;$$

i.e., the value of the excess supply of new securities equals the excess value demand for existing securities. The equal saving and investment flow is

(4B.6) $$D'_{VN}(p''') = AB,$$

or *EF* in the existing-asset market. The closing security-value function is S_{VO}^4, drawn from the origin through point F, the intersection of S_{VT}'' and D_{VT}''.

Figure 4–2 indicates plainly that the complement of the excess demand for securities is an excess supply of idle balances:

(4B.7) $$D_{VO}''(p''') - S_{VO}''(p''') = m_2'' - L_2''(p'''),$$

corresponding to the distances, $DE = GH$. Asset holders finance their excess demand for securities by drawing down idle funds. These are spent on excess new securities, whose real value is $BC = GH$, and thence transferred to the income stream by expenditure on capital projects.[1] The closing wealth function is thus

(4B.8) $$W^4 = S_{VO}^4 + m_2''', \text{ where } m_2''' = L_2''(p''').$$

The final security-demand schedule is

(4B.9)
$$D_{VO}^4 = D_{VO}'' + (W^4 - W'') = D_{VO}'' + (S_{VO}^4 - S_{VO}'') + (m_2''' - m_2'').$$

L_2 is held constant at L_2''.

The specific influence of the excess new securities on the existing-asset market is shown in Figure 4–3, which reproduces the right-hand portion of Figure 4–2 less the equal saving and investment components. Thus Figure 4–3 is obtained by rotating S_{VO} in Figure 4–2 counterclockwise until it passes through point E. The resulting function is labeled S_{VO}''' in Figure 4–3. m_2 remains m_2'''. W rotates equally with S_{VO} by the distance $IJ = EF$, becoming

(4B.10) $$W''' = S_{VO}''' + m_2'''.$$

D_{VO} moves sympathetically with S_{VO} and W to D_{VO}'''. L_2 is undisturbed at L_2'''. p and r_M remain p''' and r_M''', respectively. The diagram portrays clearly the impact of an excess of investment over saving that takes the form of an excess supply of new securities. Since the excess securities are by-passed by savers, they flow resolutely into the existing-asset market where, at a lower price

---

[1] Keynes' *Treatise on Money*, Vol. I (London: Macmillan & Co., Ltd., 1950), pp. 266–67, contains a reference to new security flotations as the link between banking operations and the price level. See below p. 418 for the complete quotation. D. H. Robertson ("Some Notes on Mr. Keynes' General Theory of Employment," *Quarterly Journal of Economics*, Vol. LI [November, 1936], pp. 176–78) appears also to describe banking policy in these terms. And subsequently in "More Notes on the Rate of Interest," *Review of Economic Studies*, Vol. XXI (1953–54), p. 137, he chided Patinkin for overlooking the rise in the supply of bonds as the mechanism restoring a displaced interest rate.

FIGURE 4–3
The Impact of Excess New Securities on the Existing-Asset Market

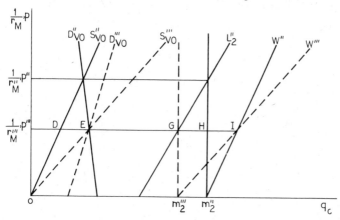

and higher yield, they are purchased in exchange for idle balances. S_{VO} rises from S_{VO}'' to S_{VO}''', m_2 falls from m_2'' to m_2''', and the wealth function rotates clockwise through the exchange price. The resemblance to an open-market sale is striking. The lower yield created by the open-market purchase stimulates an excess supply of new securities which entrepreneurs sell to existing-asset holders at a higher interest rate. However, since entrepreneurs, rather than the bank, sell the excess securities, the idle-money receipts are transferred to the income stream and activated, instead of being removed from the system. Though only D_{VO} in Figure 4–3 has been rotated, in order to simplify the diagram, L_2 will also respond to the clockwise rotation of the wealth function. If D_O''' were to be drawn, it too would exhibit a clockwise rotation relative to the preceding schedule, D_O''. In Figure 4–1, D_O''', so defined, would pass through point H. D_O^4, reflecting the addition of equal saving and investment flows, would pass through point I parallel to D_O'''.

Figure 4–4 is a summary, emphasizing the monetary side of the purchase and the stock-flow adjustment of the first interval (cf. Figure 2–11). Real-value functions are drawn with respect to the interest rate, rather than its reciprocal. In Figure 4–4(a) the more familiar designation, S' and I', replaces D_{VN}' and S_{VN}', the flow security-value schedules of t_{1^*}. In Figure 4–4(b) the supply and demand for idle money represent the entire existing-asset market. The open-market purchase raises m_2 to m_2'' and lowers r_M from $\bar{r}_N'$ to r_M''. L_2 rotates to L_2''. Though not diagramed, there is, of course, a simultaneous decrease in securities held. During the next

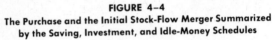

FIGURE 4–4
The Purchase and the Initial Stock-Flow Merger Summarized
by the Saving, Investment, and Idle-Money Schedules

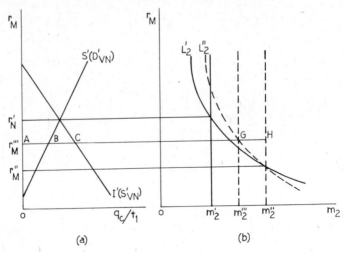

(a)   (b)

interval, t_1, the stock-flow equilibrium occurs when excess investment demand, in the form of an excess supply of new securities, is equal to the excess supply of idle balances. Thus, at r_M''',

(4B.11) $I' - S' = BC = m_2'' - L_2'' = GH$.

Again missing from the diagram is the opposite side of the change in m_2—in this case an increase in security holdings. The resulting counterclockwise rotation of the wealth function (with respect to r_M) will induce a similar movement in L_2 through r_M''', but this is not drawn. The equal saving and investment flows accruing during t_1, AB, are reflected in equal movements in S_{VO}, D_{VO}, and W (see Figure 4–2), and so are not apparent in Figure 4–4.

We shall name the financial process described in this section, by which the conjoining of stock and flow security markets drives the rate of interest toward its equilibrium, the *transfer effect*. In the adjustment to the open-market purchase, the transfer effect is really no more than the process by which excess investment demand raises the market rate of interest by raising the supply of securities in excess of total demand. The subsequent increase in the supply of investible funds is simultaneously a reduction in idle money holdings which are thereby *transferred* to the income stream. The transfer effect is the first, and more fundamental, of two equilibrating mechanisms of the adjustment process. The second, which is due to the resulting rise of the price level, is described in Part C. However, we shall complete our discussion of the transfer effect on the assumption that it is the only equilibrating force. For the present, we abstract from the influence of the price-level movement. It follows that the entire adjustment process adheres to the pattern of the first interval. As long as the market rate of interest is below the natural rate, the combining of stock and flow security markets raises the market rate. Each period excess new securities pour into the existing-asset market where, at a higher yield, they are exchanged for idle balances. Since the adjustment is in fact continuous over time, the interest rate rises and idle balances fall constantly as excess securities flow *sequentially* into the existing-asset market. When r_M is finally equal to r_N', desired saving and investment are also equal, and the merging of stock and flow security markets proceeds in the manner described in Chapter II-D(2).

Figure 4-5 diagrams the approach to equilibrium, as determined by the merger of security markets during the course of

FIGURE 4–5
The Stock-Flow Adjustment during Three Consecutive Intervals

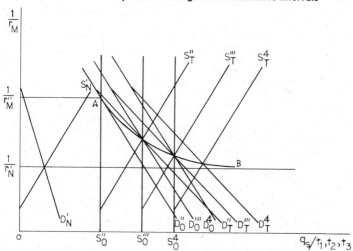

three consecutive intervals. Three pairs of fixed S_N and D_N schedules are added to an existing market in which the rate of interest is initially below the natural rate. After the summation of each pair of schedules, S_O is drawn vertically, and D_O parallel to its original position through each yield at which S_T and D_T intersect. We ignore the clockwise rotations in D_O due to the rising stock of

FIGURE 4–6

The Stock-Flow Adjustment in Terms of Excess Security-Supply and Demand Functions

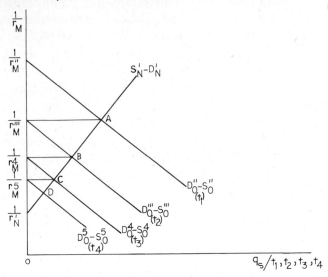

excess new securities. The path of $1/r_M$ with respect to the quantity of securities is approximated by the curve, AB, which approaches $1/r'_N$ asymptotically. In Figure 4–6 the adjustment process is summarized by means of excess supply and demand functions. $S'_N - D'_N$ is constant throughout the adjustment, with a vertical intercept of $1/r'_N$. The equilibrium of the first adjustment period, t_1, is determined by the intersection of $D''_O - S''_O$ with $S'_N - D'_N$, which occurs at point A. The interest rate is r'''_M. In the next interval, $D'''_O - S'''_O$, parallel to $D''_O - S''_O$,[2] has a vertical intercept of $1/r'''_M$, the reciprocal of the previous equilibrium yield. The new equilibrium occurs at point B, the height of which is $1/r^4_M$. In the third period, $D^4_O - S^4_O$ intersects $S'_N - D'_N$ at point C, determining $1/r^5_M$. A fourth period creates an equilibrium at point D, and so on for future periods, until $D_O - S_O$ meets $S'_N - D'_N$ on the vertical axis at $1/r'_N$. Figure 4–6 shows clearly that $1/r_M$ falls by decreasing amounts each period because the excess supply, $S'_N - D'_N$—the source of downward pressure on $1/r_M$—itself declines with $1/r_M$.[3] The information contained in Figure 4–6 can

---

[2] Since both S_O and D_O shift parallel and to the right each period, the excess demand function, $D_O - S_O$, will also undergo a parallel shift.

[3] The reader may verify by a simple sketch that if $S_N - D_N$ increases as $1/r_M$ falls (i.e., is a declining function of $1/r_M$), then $1/r_M$ will fall by *increasing* amounts each period. Unless $S_N - D_N$ reverses its slope at some point, meeting the vertical axis at, say, $1/r'_N$, this is a path for which there is no terminal point.

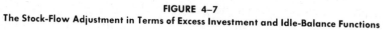

FIGURE 4-7
The Stock-Flow Adjustment in Terms of Excess Investment and Idle-Balance Functions

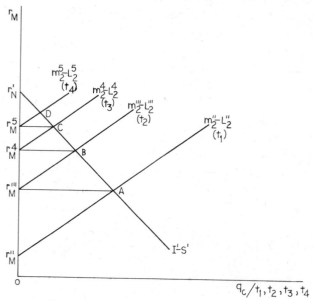

also be expressed in terms of the value functions, $S_{VN} - D_{VN}$ (or $I - S$) and $D_{VO} - S_{VO}$. However, a more useful alternative is to combine $I - S$ with $m_2 - L_2$, plotting both functions with respect to r_M (see Figure 4-4). This has been done in Figure 4-7. In view of the downward slope of $I' - S'$, r_M rises each period by diminishing amounts. The real idle-money transfer, equal to the abscissa of the intersection of the two functions, also declines over time. We can deduce from Figure 4-7, by repeating the type of sketch presented there, that the greater is $I' - S'$, or the less is $m_2 - L_2$, at $r_M < r'_N$, the fewer is the number of intervals required to reach the equilibrium at r'_N.[4]

2. Underlying Assumptions

The foregoing account of the adjustment process is purely "financial" in that it describes the stock-flow interaction of money and securities without considering related changes in the physical stock of capital and its rate of return. The latter "real" variables are of the greatest importance in determining whether securities will

---

[4] The diagram of Figure 4-6 can be used to describe the case in which saving and investment flow at discrete, though closely connected, points in time. Suppose that entrepreneurs supply and savers demand synchronously a quantity of securities at the closing

continue to furnish an income, ρ_s, equal to the pre-operation one.
In this chapter we have simply assumed that all securities, including the excess issues sold to existing-asset holders, automatically
carry the pre-operation earnings, ρ'_s. Thus the clockwise rotation
of S_{VO} from S''_{VO} to S'''_{VO} in Figure 4–3, the resulting impact on
asset demand, and all subsequent increases in security holdings
were premised on the ability of new securities to command a return comparable to that of pre-existing shares. However, there
are several circumstances that tend to change ρ_s during the adjustment process:

1. Increments to the stock of securities and real capital may
easily alter the pre-disturbance ratio of capital to securities,
K'/S'_O, and thereby displace ρ_s from its beginning value,

---

instant of a time period known as a "day." The amounts supplied and demanded are determined by the interest rate prevailing at the opening instant of the day. The resulting
course of the interest rate is shown by Figure 4–8, in which $S'_N - D'_N$ is now the excess
new supply forthcoming at the close of a day. The initial excess existing demand is the same
as previously, $D''_O - S''_O$. The purchase yield, r'_M, prevails during the first day following the
operation, t_1. The excess new supply brought to market at the close of the day is thus
$S'_N(r'_M) - D'_N(r'_M)$, located at point A in Figure 4–8. By extending a vertical vector downward from point A, we see that this *given* excess new supply determines an excess existing demand at point A', where the interest rate is r'''_M and

$$D''_O(r'''_M) - S''_O(r'''_M) = S'_N(r'_M) - D'_N(r'_M).$$

During the next day, t_2, the excess existing demand is $D'''_O - S'''_O$, whose vertical intercept is
$1/r'''_M$. The yield of t_2, r'''_M, stimulates an excess new supply equal to the abscissa of point B.
This quantity, at the close of t_2, evokes an excess existing demand at B', at which $r_M = r^4_M$
and

$$D'''_O(r^4_M) - S'''_O(r^4_M) = S'_N(r'''_M) - D'_N(r'''_M).$$

And so the path to equilibrium continues along the downward step function, $AA'BB'CC'$,
terminating at $1/r'_N$ on the vertical axis. Thus the main difference between the discrete
and continuous case is that a step function replaces the smooth and continuous path along
$S'_N - D'_N$ itself, as drawn in Figure 4–6.

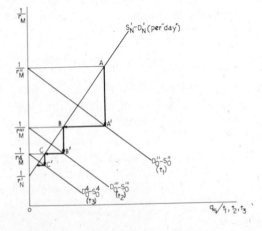

FIGURE 4–8
The Approach to Equilibrium
When Saving and Investment
Are Discontinuous over Time

$\rho_s' = \rho_K' K'/S_O'$. Consider the movement in ρ_s if, following the first adjustment interval, funds raised both from savers and existing-asset holders are realized fully in an addition to the capital stock. We assume for the present that ρ_K is fixed at ρ_K'. If $\Delta S_O'$ is the total number of securities issued, and $\Delta K'$ the capital increment, the relation between the two is

(4B.12)
$$\Delta K' = \Delta S_O' p''',$$

where $p''' = \rho_s'''/r_M'''$ is the real price at which all securities are sold, and $\rho_s''' = \rho_s'$. Hence the ratio of the increments is $\Delta K'/\Delta S_O' = p'''$. But the original ratio of capital to securities is p':

(4B.13)
$$p' = \frac{\rho_s'}{r_N'} = \frac{\rho_K' K'}{r_N' S_O'} = \frac{K'}{S_O'}.$$

Granted that the return to equilibrium is not accomplished in a single interval, $p''' > p'$, and the new value of ρ_s is

(4B.14)
$$\rho_s^4 = \frac{\rho_K'(K' + \Delta K')}{S_O' + \Delta S_O'} > \rho_s''', \text{ since } \frac{\Delta K'}{\Delta S_O'} > \frac{K'}{S_O'}.$$

Of course, entrepreneurs may not be fully successful in their endeavors to create new capital. In general, we must write

(4B.15)
$$\Delta K' = \alpha \Delta S_O' p''', \text{ where } 0 \leq \alpha \leq 1.$$

The ratio of the first-interval increments is thus $\Delta K'/\Delta S_O' = \alpha p'''$. But only by coincidence would $\alpha p''' = p'$ and $\rho_s^4 = \rho_s'''$. This argument applies to all intervals of the adjustment process. Whatever the security price and the degree of capital accumulation, constancy of ρ_s requires constancy in the ratio of the capital-security increments. There is nothing inherent in the adjustment process to meet this requirement.

2. Any change in the rate of realized investment during the adjustment will change ρ_K, and thereby ρ_s. The lower rate of interest created by the purchase sets in motion forces tending to change the rate of investment. Entrepreneurs wish to raise, while savers provide, funds for less investment. But existing-asset holders finance a net excess of investment spending over desired saving. Should ex post investment and thus, realized saving, exceed voluntary saving, we have the phenomenon of "forced saving." In any case, a change in the rate of ex post investment above or below the pre-disturbance rate will change ρ_K and $\rho_s = \rho_K K/S_O$ accordingly. Since, on our assumptions, S', I', and r_N' prevail in the

new as in the old equilibrium, ρ_K eventually returns to its previous level, ρ_K'. The direct effect on ρ_s due to the movement of ρ_K is thus temporary. However, there are indirect effects that remain after ρ_K has been restored to equilibrium. These operate through the changed ratio of capital-security increments described in the preceding paragraph. When ρ_K and ρ_s change, p, corresponding to any given market rate of interest, also changes. As we have seen, the prevailing price of securities determines the ratio of the capital-security increments, and these are permanently incorporated in the factors determining ρ_s, even though ρ_K has ceased to fluctuate.

A complete analysis must account for each of the eventualities affecting the real income and value of securities. This will be done in Chapter V, which is concerned with changes in the capital stock and its rate of return. But nothing that emerges in the "real" analysis will seriously qualify the financial adjustment, provided that the following conditions are met:

1. Firms do not retire existing securities if ρ_s should change because of a failure to equate ex post with ex ante investment.

2. Households purchase new securities in the belief that in due course they will give rise to additional capital which will furnish an income per share equal to that of the current period.

3. Changes in ρ_s, whether anticipated or not, and for any cause, will not materially change the market rate of interest via household reactions.

If firms retire existing securities at their own initiative, this will reverse the adjustment by raising security prices and lowering the rate of interest. If, further, active balances are used to repurchase the shares, the commodity price level will also be reduced, since balances received for existing securities are held idle. However, there is nothing in the nature of success or failure to build *additional* capital that promises to have this reverse effect on the financial adjustment.[5] We have assumed that all funds raised in the securities market are, in fact, spent immediately on capital projects. Hence, whatever the realization on these expenditures, there are no available balances to retire securities. Nor is the motive to such action particularly strong, since all

---

[5] But a change in ρ_s may be due to a reduction in *existing* capital in the form of inventories, rather than a changed ratio of capital-security increments or a change in ρ_K. In this event firms are in a position to carry out a disequilibrating retirement of securities corresponding to the consumed capital. This possibility is discussed in Part C(2)b, where such offsets to the expansionary adjustment are held to be temporary.

financing in our system is by equities. Firms have no legal obligation to asset holders for movements in ρ_s.[6]

Any expectation by households that the income per share will change in the future will stimulate movements in asset demand and the market rate of interest. Since, for a given rate of interest, ρ_s and p are positively related, an expected increase in ρ_s will enhance the attractiveness of securities relative to money. D_{VO} will shift instantaneously to the right and L_2 to the left by equal amounts. This is to say that asset holders apply idle balances to the purchase of securities, raising security prices and lowering the rate of interest. The stock-flow adjustment is prolonged. An expectation that ρ_s will fall induces a movement out of securities into money which lowers security prices and raises the rate of interest. The stock-flow adjustment is truncated.[7]

The assumption in regard to ρ_s, most consistent with the analysis of Section 1, is thus that households expect the current income to prevail in the future.[8] If that expectation is disappointed later owing, say, to inadequate capital formation, the behavior of households can be dealt with at that time. This is where the third

---

[6] If our model were one in which firms held idle (contingency) balances, they might draw upon these balances to retire securities when realized investment falls below the ex ante expenditure. This would reduce the interest rate, prolong the .adjustment, and raise the equilibrium price level. Such measures are more likely to be taken if the relevant securities are bonds, rather than equities. A retirement operation is, of course, limited by the firm's supply of idle balances, and cannot go on indefinitely.

[7] In the extreme case in which ρ_s is expected to fall because new securities will contribute no additional income, simply "watering" outstanding shares, the stock-flow adjustment is unattainable. Consider the reaction of asset holders to a security sale which was avowedly of this character. If the issue of such stock is carried out, it will lower ρ_s and thereby S_{VO}. Only by raising S_O, the number of securities held, can an individual asset holder maintain the value of his securities intact. The practical alternatives are thus to allow the value of securities to fall, or by purchasing additional securities with idle balances, allow the latter to fall by an equal amount. At one extreme, D_{VO} falls equally with the threatened loss of S_{VO}, L_2 remaining fixed. In this event the securities cannot be sold at any price, and the reduction in S_{VO} does not materialize. At the other extreme, L_2 alone responds to the impending loss of security value, and all of the offered securities are purchased with idle balances. S_{VO} and D_{VO} remain intact, while L_2 and m_2 shift equally to the left. In the general case, both D_{VO} and L_2, and thus S_{VO} and m_2, move to the left. But since both members of each pair of asset supply and demand schedules move equally, there can be no impact on the rate of interest. Accordingly, if additional securities are to be salable, or if salable, effective in raising the rate of interest, they must promise some positive marginal income.

[8] We can incorporate some flexibility in regard to expectations by allowing the interest rate to contain a premium (plus or minus) compensating for any anticipated change in ρ_s. For example, investors may have learned through experience to discount the temporary, or even permanent (but not complete) watering of stock that tends to accompany new security issues. The attitudes of asset holders in this regard would be reflected in the slope and elasticity of the asset-demand schedules. If ρ_s is expected to fall, L_2 and D_O would tend to be inelastic; $\partial D_{VO}/\partial p$ would tend to be high.

condition is relevant. Since changes in ρ_s are reflected in spontaneous changes in S_{VO}, an almost equal induced movement in D_{VO}—as we argued would occur in a modern economy (Chapter II-B[4])—will leave the interest rate essentially unmoved. Thus, granted conditions 1, 2, and 3, the equilibrating process stimulated by the sale of excess securities is fundamentally unaltered by subsequent changes in the "real" variables. In the first instance, changes in ρ_s are not expected to occur. If they do, firms take no counter measures. Households respond to the resulting movement of S_{VO} with an approximately equal shift of D_{VO}, and the excess demand functions, $D_{VO} - S_{VO}$ and $m_2 - L_2$, are not seriously affected. Changes in ρ_s are not, of course, reflected in the S and I schedules, measured in real-value units. The adjustment proceeds as described in Section 1 and summarized in Figures 4-6 and 4-7.[9] The character of the adjustment process in which D_{VO} fails to move more or less equally with ρ_s and S_{VO} is described in Chapter V-E(4).[10] Given that changes in ρ_s occur during the adjust-

---

[9] The security-quantity excess demand and supply functions, as drawn in Figure 4-6, are, of course, altered by changes in ρ_s. However, at any interest rate, the functions tend to shift equally in the same direction, so that the equilibrating path of the interest rate is not affected. We can show this by differentiating the functions with respect to ρ_s. Since

$$D_O - S_O = \frac{D_{VO} - S_{VO}}{\dfrac{\rho_s}{r_M}} \quad \text{and} \quad S_N - D_N = \frac{S_{VN} - D_{VN}}{\dfrac{\rho_s}{r_M}},$$

the derivatives are

$$\frac{\partial(D_O - S_O)}{\partial \rho_s} = -\frac{r_M(D_{VO} - S_{VO})}{\rho_s^2}$$

and

$$\frac{\partial(S_N - D_N)}{\partial \rho_s} = -\frac{r_M(S_{VN} - D_{VN})}{\rho_s^2}.$$

At the equilibrium interest rate of any interval, the shifts in $D_O - S_O$ and $S_N - D_N$ in response to a unit change in ρ_s are thus equal, provided that $D_{VO} - S_{VO} = S_{VN} - D_{VN}$. S_{VN} and D_{VN}, measured in real-value units, are not affected by a change in ρ_s; nor will the excess demand, $D_{VO} - S_{VO}$, if D_{VO} moves equally with S_{VO}. Hence, on this assumption, equality between $D_{VO} - S_{VO}$ and $S_{VN} - D_{VN}$ at one level of ρ_s will hold at any other, as will equality between $D_O - S_O$ and $S_N - D_N$.

[10] We can anticipate this analysis by considering the general effect of movements in D_{VO} that are less than those in S_{VO}. If ρ_s rises and D_{VO} and L_2 both respond to the increase in S_{VO}, $D_{VO} - S_{VO}$ and $m_2 - L_2$ both decrease. This raises the prevailing rate of interest and the rate that will equate the excess new supply with the excess existing-security demand (or idle-money supply) at the close of future periods (see Figure 4-6 or 4-7). The upward movement of the interest rate is accelerated. If ρ_s decreases and both D_{VO} and L_2 respond, $D_{VO} - S_{VO}$ and $m_2 - L_2$ increase. This lowers the current market rate of interest, as well as the equilibrium yield of subsequent periods. The upward movement in r_M is retarded.

ment, the relationship between $1/r_M$ and p is altered. Thus the only generalizations that can safely be made are with respect to the interest rate (or its reciprocal), which is plotted alone on the vertical axes of Figures 4–5, 4–6, and 4–7.

C. THE RISE IN THE PRICE LEVEL: THE WEALTH EFFECT

1. The Equilibrating Process

The transfer of idle balances to the income stream via excess new securities creates a proportionate rise in the commodity price level ([2C.1]), since full-employment output is fixed. This section will describe the equilibrating impact of the inflation on the interest rate. But first we shall reconsider briefly the character of the forces raising the quantity of active balances.

The important element in the monetary transfer is that it occurs without a shift in the demand schedule for either active or idle balances. Hence neither the increase in investment demand nor the decrease in desired saving at the lower interest rate entails *in itself* an increase in the supply or velocity of active money. The increase in the quantity of investment funds demanded during t_1 corresponds in Figure 4–1 to the movement along S'_N from the equilibrium at p' to point C at p''. But this is manifested as an increase in the supply of new securities—certainly not a direct source of inflation. Businessmen are not simultaneously dishoarding accumulated funds by any direct, deliberate, or conscious tapping of idle or active balances. On the other hand, the reaction of savers to the lower interest rate during t_1 is shown in Figure 4–1 as the movement along D'_N from the equilibrium at p' to point B at p''. From the monetary viewpoint, this is no more than a rechanneling of existing active balances within the circular income flow. The implication of $\partial S/\partial r_M > 0$ is that savers divert money expenditures from securities to consumption goods. Since in equilibrium at p' saving was going wholly into new securities and thence investment, the response of savers merely converts the purchase of goods for investment to an equivalent purchase of the same goods for consumption. There is no change in total money expenditures or the commodity price level.[11] In terms of our sys-

---

[11] In a two-commodity model we would say that the action of savers causes a decrease in the price of investment goods and an increase in the price of consumption goods. On a first approximation, the average price of commodities remains constant.

tem, the discrepancy between saving and investment raises the price level only when part of the supply of new securities fails to meet an equal demand by savers. Then, if existing-asset holders are willing to finance excess investment by purchasing the excess securities, idle balances are simultaneously transferred to entrepreneurs and activated. The higher interest rate due to the excess securities stimulates a movement *along* the given L_2 schedule, reducing the quantity of idle balances demanded. After the idle money is released through the purchase of excess securities, it is received as factor incomes, inducing an increase in the quantity of active money demanded. The latter takes the form of a movement *along* the given $L_1(Y)$ schedule. In this way, and this way only, the monetary impact of the open-market purchase passes from stocks to flows and raises the general price level.

We assume that entrepreneurs spend balances secured from asset holders at the closing instant of t_1. The price level rises without delay in response to the additional active money.[12] The increase in prices will have no effect on the S, I, and S_{vo} schedules, or on ρ_s, all of which are expressed in output units and are independent of commodity prices. In the first instance, the existing-asset demand schedules, D_{vo} and L_2, and the price and yield of securities, p and r_M, are also invariant in the face of the inflation. But the real value of the money supply is altered. There is no effect on M_1/P, the numerator and denominator of which rise in equal proportions. But M_2/P is reduced. More precisely, the monetary variables before the purchase are:

(4C.1)
$$M_1', V_1', y', P' = \frac{M_1' V_1'}{y'},$$

$$\frac{M_1'}{P'} = \frac{M_1' y'}{M_1' V_1'} = \frac{y'}{V_1'},$$

and

$$\frac{M_2'}{P'} = m_2'.$$

---

[12] We have already observed (p. 59) that P, the product of the flow of money expenditures and the flow of goods, rises immediately in response to a change in the rate of either flow. However, this is based on the assumption of a single commodity, or a continuous flow over time of all commodities if there is more than one in the system. In a multi-commodity model, the price index will continue to rise until each additional unit of money has been turned over against each particular item of output. Any tendency for goods to be traded at concentrated points in time will delay the full recorded rise of the price index.

Directly after the purchase, occurring wholly on wealth account,

(4C.2) $$m_2'' = \frac{M_2''}{P'} > m_2'.$$

Directly after the transfer of t_1, but before the entrepreneurial expenditure of transferred funds,

(4C.3) $$M_2''' = M_2'' - \Delta M_2' \text{ and } m_2''' = \frac{M_2'''}{P'} < m_2'',$$

where $\Delta M_2'$ is the quantity of idle balances secured by entrepreneurs. M_1' and P' still prevail. Following the expenditure of transferred funds,

(4C.4) $$M_1'' = M_1' + \Delta M_2', \ P'' = \frac{(M_1' + \Delta M_2')V_1'}{y'}, \text{ and}$$

$$\frac{M_1''}{P''} = \frac{(M_1' + \Delta M_2')y'}{(M_1' + \Delta M_2')V_1'} = \frac{y'}{V_1'} = \frac{M_1'}{P'}.$$

But

(4C.5) $$m_2^4 = \frac{M_2'''}{P''} < m_2''' = \frac{M_2'''}{P'}, \text{ since } P'' > P'.$$

The impact on the total wealth market of the loss in the value of idle money is drawn in Figure 4–9. The triple-primed schedules and L_2'' prevail following the stock-flow adjustment of t_1, but prior to the inflation. These schedules correspond to those of the

FIGURE 4–9
The Impact of the Rise in the Price Level on the Existing-Asset Market

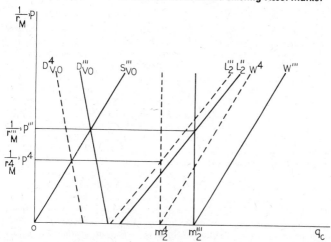

same designation in Figure 4–3. L_2 was held at L_2'', while D_{VO} absorbed the entire clockwise rotation of wealth during t_1, merely for simplicity. At this point we should add to S_{VO}, W, and D_{VO} the securities purchased by savers (see Figure 4–2). But since this would have no effect on m_2, L_2, r_M, or p, it is not done. The latter two variables are r_M''' and $p''' = \rho_s'''/r_M'''$, as created by the transfer effect. The inflation lowers m_2 from m_2''' to m_2^4, and total wealth equally from W''' to

(4C.6) $$W^4 = S_{VO}''' + m_2^4,$$

as shown in the diagram. The demand schedules move responsively to the left:

(4C.7) $$(D_{VO}''' - D_{VO}^4) + (L_2'' - L_2''') = W''' - W^4,$$

creating a lower price and higher yield:

(4C.8) $$p^4 < p''', r_M^4 = \frac{\rho_s'''}{p^4} > r_M'''.$$

Since the loss of real idle balances leads to a diminished demand for both securities and cash, the decline in L_2 is less than the loss of real balances, and there remains a net reduction in the real supply of idle money. At r_M''' asset holders move out of securities into money in an effort to replenish the cash deficiency. The attempted mass liquidation of securities cannot fail to lower security prices and raise the rate of interest until at r_M^4 asset holders are reconciled to the lower quantity of real balances. We designate this additional force on the rate of interest, occurring instantaneously in the wake of the inflation, the *wealth effect*.[13]

---

[13] Since the price level influences the interest rate by changing household wealth, it is important that there are no hidden wealth effects acting in an opposite direction. More specifically, we require that the loss of real balances due to inflation is not accompanied by a simultaneous improvement in the net wealth of the sector to whom the balances may be liabilities; or, if such an improvement occurs, that it not stimulate offsetting actions. See Patinkin, "Price Flexibility and Full Employment," *American Economic Review*, Vol. XXXVIII (September, 1948), pp. 549–50, and Herbert Stein, "Price Flexibility and Full Employment:Comment," *American Economic Review*, Vol. XXXIX (June, 1949), pp. 725–26. We have assumed (p. 18) that the money stock is either full-bodied or a liability of the central government. There are no commercial banks and no bank deposits in our general model. We take as the prototype for our money supply a gold-coin standard or that part of the present-day inconvertible currency backed by gold certificates. In neither case does the inflation increase the government's net worth. The government is clearly not a party to any changes in the value of privately held gold. While changes in the price level will change the real value of its gold-certificate liability, they create equal changes in the real value of its gold-stock asset holdings. The simultaneous asset and liability changes thus prevent a change in government net worth from occurring. Cf. Arnold Collery, "A Note on the Saving-Wealth Relation and the Rate of Interest," *Journal of Political Economy*, Vol.

The return of the interest rate to its equilibrium at r'_N is thus the resultant of two equilibrating forces. In any interval in which the market rate is below the natural, the merging of stock and flow security markets raises r_M directly via the flow of excess new securities. The simultaneous transfer of idle balances to the income stream raises the price level and lowers the value of remaining idle funds. This prompts a shift out of securities into money, and raises the interest rate further. The general effect is to accelerate the adjustment process. In Figure 4-7 the wealth effect is an independent source of additional leftward movements in the excess supply function, $m_2 - L_2$; i.e., after each rise of the price level and reduction of m_2, $m_2 - L_2$ shifts instantaneously to the left, its vertical intercept rising to the new higher rate of interest at which the next stock-flow adjustment interval begins. In Figure 4-6 the wealth effect is reflected in leftward shifts in the excess demand function, $D_O - S_O$. The shifts occur because the reduction in m_2 drives W and thereby D_{VO} leftward. Since ρ_s is unaffected, the movement of D_{VO} causes a similar unambiguous leftward shift in the derived schedule, D_O, at all interest rates and security prices.[14] Finally, in Figure 4-5 D_O again shifts to the left with each inflationary impulse. The net course of $1/r_M$, as a function of the stock of securities, is therefore along downward-shifting curves of the form, AB.

LXVIII (October, 1960), pp. 509-10. These relationships depend, of course, on the fixed dollar price of gold.

The impact of the changed price level on real cash balances and the interest rate should not be confused with the role of a chang*ing* price level. The latter creates expectations about the future value of money and may induce movements between cash and non-cash assets. But any displacement of the interest rate in this event lasts only as long as the price level is expected to be in motion. Cf. Irving Fisher, *The Purchasing Power of Money* (New York: The Macmillan Co., 1925), chap. iv. In the wealth effect on interest, as described above, the movement of the interest rate is a permanent and equilibrating response to a revaluation of money holdings. The wealth effect corresponds to the price level–interest rate relation described by Metzler ("Wealth, Saving, and the Rate of Interest," *Journal of Political Economy*, Vol. LIX [April, 1951], pp. 105 and 110) and Patinkin, *Money, Interest, and Prices* (Evanston, Ill.: Row, Peterson & Co., 1956), pp. 139-40, 160-62, and 177-78. However, I shall argue later (Chapter IX-D) that the failure of both writers to dichotomize money into specialized idle and active components negates the price level–interest rate relation.

[14] While D_{VO}, as pictured in Figure 4-9, shifts parallel to itself, D_O will not. This is because a constant wealth increment, $D'''_{VO} - D^4_{VO}$, is a rectangular hyperbola in p and $D'''_O - D^4_O$:

$$D_O''' - D_O^4 = \frac{D_{VO}''' - D_{VO}^4}{p}.$$

Thus D_O^4 will be farther to the left of D_O''' at lower prices than at higher ones.

2. *Qualifications: Leakages*

The rise in the price level following the transfer of idle balances to the income stream is conditional upon the absence of leakages. Anything tending to return cash to the existing-asset market would curb not only the inflation, but also the associated rise in the interest rate. We shall qualify our description of the adjustment process by discussing briefly several possibilities in regard to leakages.

a) *Movements in Real Saving*

The failure of individuals to consume all their income does not in itself constitute a source of leakages in this system. This follows from our assumption that the whole of savings is a demand for securities. If we compare two positions of equilibrium, one having a higher active money supply and price level than the other, but output is the same for both, we shall find that savers have raised the dollar price of new securities issued by entrepreneurs *pari passu* with the increase in the general price level and money income. Money saving and investment have risen equally, and real saving, investment, and the natural rate of interest are the same for both price levels. But if, in the process of inflation, the rise of the price level lags at all behind the injection of active money,[15] a temporary imbalance between saving and investment on this account may occur. Even though intended real saving is independent of purely inflationary movements in money income, the augmented supply of active balances will initially be "real" enough to their recipients. Savers cannot foresee that their new incomes will eventually be dissipated in higher prices. Hence, until the price level fully reflects the additional money, real saving will increase in response to an apparent rise in real income. In time, when prices have risen proportionately to active balances, and output is unchanged, intended real saving will return to its pre-operation level. But during the first stages of the adjustment process, S must be redrawn to the right, indicating that desired saving is temporarily greater in both real and money terms. Considered by itself—apart from the adjustment process—an increase in saving is an increase in security demand which raises security prices and

---

[15] Cf. n. 12 above. Another factor causing a delay in the rise of the price level is sale out of inventories (see below, Section *b*).

lowers the rate of interest. Since all securities are purchased indiscriminately, new ones will be bought together with existing ones which, in any interval of time, are likely to be more numerous. But active balances expended by savers against existing securities are held by their recipients as idle money, just as in the open-market purchase by the bank. Thus we have leakages from the income stream to the existing-asset market, which tend directly to lower both the rate of interest and the price level. Indirectly, the fall in the price level creates a further reduction in the interest rate via a downward wealth effect (see Chapter VI-B[2]). In the context of the adjustment process, the increase in real saving lowers the saving-investment gap, reducing the magnitude of the transfer in any period. The net effect is to retard the upward movement in the rate of interest and the price level.

As the price level rises, however, the old relationship between real saving and full-employment income is gradually re-established. The change in income becomes more and more a change in prices only, and the previous shifts in S are reversed as the apparent value of income falls. In themselves, the leftward movements create an excess of investment over saving, which is an excess supply of new securities that returns idle balances to the income stream and raises the rate of interest. In the context of the adjustment process, the transfer and the rate of rise in the interest rate and the price level all increase. Since active money and prices rise equally, the shifts of saving in response to each will also be equal. The leakages on account of saving are therefore only temporary, and in equilibrium S occupies its pre-operation position.

b) Inventory Depletion

Leakages, not as readily reversed, may occur if additional expenditures following a transfer stimulate consumption sales out of inventories, which thereby fall below desired levels. The reduction in inventories is a decline in real capital which, in reducing the total stream of property income, waters outstanding shares. But unlike watering that occurs when entrepreneurs lose out in the effort to build additional capital, there are now on hand active balances constituting profits earned from the reduction of inventories. Entrepreneurs can apply these balances to an immediate build-up of inventories, or if they wish, they can use the funds to purchase and retire an equivalent amount of outstanding securities.[16] If the latter course of action is taken, entrepreneurs effectively carry out an open-market purchase aimed at the existing-asset market. They bid up the price of existing securities, lowering the rate of interest, and inducing wealth holders to move out of securities into idle money. The price level follows the tendency of the interest rate to fall, contributing a further impulse to a lower r_M by increasing the value of idle balances. In the context of the adjustment process, the security purchase is merely a partial offset to the impact of the transfer on interest and prices. But if the depletion of inventories, followed by security retirement, were equal to the entire transfer of any period, the net movement of the interest rate and the price level would be nil. However, the reduction of inventories is at most a temporary thing, and eventually merchants must allow prices, rather than quantities, to rise in response to the increase in total expenditures. Later on, moreover, the rebuilding of inventories to normal levels would shift the investment schedule to the right, adding as much upward pressure to the interest rate and the price level as it had removed in an earlier period.

D. MONETARY CHANGES

In this section we shall summarize the impact of the operation and the equilibrating forces on the variables of the equation of exchange. After making a few static comparisons, we shall discuss the basic dynamic pattern.

1. Static Relationships

Prior to the open-market purchase, the total supply of money is

(4D.1) $$M' = M'_1 + M'_2,$$

total velocity is

(4D.2) $$V' = \left(\frac{M'_1}{M'}\right) V'_1,$$

and the commodity price level is

(4D.3) $$P' = \frac{M'_1 V'_1}{y'} = \frac{M' V'}{y'}.$$

---

[16] If the securities corresponding to the consumed inventories were short-term bonds, entrepreneurs would very likely retire the bonds before taking any action toward replenishing the inventories.

The purchase raises the money supply by $\Delta M''$ to M'', the entire increment going to idle balances. Immediately following the operation the variables are

(4D.4)
$$M_1', M_2'' = M_2' + \Delta M'',$$

(4D.5)
$$V'' = \left(\frac{M_1'}{M''}\right) V_1' < V',$$

and

(4D.6)
$$P' = \frac{M'' V''}{y'};$$

i.e., since total expenditures, whether expressed as the product of active or total money balances and velocity, are unchanged, the price level is still P'. Total velocity, however, is reduced. The adjustment process transfers idle money to the active component, raising total velocity and the price level. We can show that if $m_2^n = m_2'$, where m_2^n is the value of m_2 in the new equilibrium, the adjustment process will restore the ratio of idle to active balances and total velocity to their pre-operation values. The restoration of m_2 to m_2' in turn requires that

(4D.7)
$$L_2^n(r_N') = L_2'(r_N') = m_2';$$

i.e., that the final L_2 schedule coincide with the original one at the natural rate of interest. The location of L_2^n depends on numerous rotations and shifts that occur throughout the adjustment process and are summarized in Chapter V-E(4). However, assuming that $m_2^n = m_2'$, we can write $M_2^n/P^n = M_2'/P'$, or upon substitution,

$$\frac{M_2^n y^n}{M_1^n V_1^n} = \frac{M_2' y'}{M_1' V_1'}.$$

But, by assumption, $V_1^n = V_1'$ and $y^n = y'$. Hence

(4D.8)
$$\frac{M_2^n}{M_1^n} = \frac{M_2'}{M_1'}.$$

We show the equality of V^n and V' by substituting for each:

$$\left(\frac{M_1^n}{M^n}\right) V_1^n = \left(\frac{M_1'}{M'}\right) V_1'$$

$$\frac{M_1^n}{M_1^n + M_2^n} = \frac{M_1'}{M_1' + M_2'},$$

which reduces to
$$\frac{M_2'}{M_1'} = \frac{M_2''}{M_1''},$$

which has already been established. With total velocity on net constant, the price level rises proportionately to the change in the total money supply:[17]

(4D.9)
$$\frac{P''}{P'} = \frac{M''}{M'}.$$

We substitute for P'' and P':

$$\frac{M''V''y'}{y''M'V'} = \frac{M''}{M'}$$

$$\frac{V''}{y''} = \frac{V'}{y'}.$$

A final conclusion that we draw is that the total increments to idle and active balances, $\Delta M_2''$ and $\Delta M_1''$, respectively, are in the same ratio as are total idle and active balances:

(4D.10)
$$\frac{\Delta M_2''}{\Delta M_1''} = \frac{M_2''}{M_1''} = \frac{M_2'}{M_1'}.$$

We show this by substituting in the latter (already established) equality:

$$\frac{M_2''}{M_1''} = \frac{M_2'}{M_1'}$$

$$\frac{M_2' + \Delta M_2''}{M_1' + \Delta M_1''} = \frac{M_2'}{M_1'},$$

[17] The recognition that "liquidity preference" (i.e., an interest-elastic demand for money) does not necessarily destroy the proportionality between changes in M and P goes back to Keynes' *Treatise*. In Vol. I, pp. 146–7, he writes:

"This means, indeed, that in equilibrium—*i.e.* when the factors of production are fully employed, when the public is neither bullish nor bearish of securities and is maintaining in the form of savings-deposits neither more nor less than the 'normal' proportion of its total wealth, and when the volume of saving is equal both to the cost and to the value of new investments—there is a unique relationship between the quantity of money and the price levels of consumption-goods and of output as a whole, of such a character that if the quantity of money were double the price-levels would be double also."

A. Smithies ("The Quantity of Money and the Rate of Interest," *Review of Economic Statistics,* Vol. XXV [February, 1943], p. 72), in the wake of the *General Theory,* makes the same point. And the argument is surely implicit in the writings of L. W. Mints (*Monetary Policy for a Competitive Society* [New York: McGraw-Hill Book Co., Inc., 1950], pp. 57–58), who holds that in a liquidity-preference economy, changes in the nominal supply of money do not alter the real value of cash balances (and, one might add, the velocity of money). Patinkin revives the argument in "Keynesian Economics and the Quantity Theory," in K. Kurihara (ed.), *Post-Keynesian Economics* (New Brunswick, N. J.: Rutgers University Press, 1954), pp. 123–52. See also Patinkin, *Money, Interest, and Prices,* p. 180.

which reduces to

$$\frac{\Delta M_2^n}{\Delta M_1^n} = \frac{M_2'}{M_1'}.$$

To summarize: The operation initially raises idle balances. The increase in the total money supply is offset by a proportionate reduction in total velocity, expenditures and the commodity price level remaining constant. The adjustment process activates idle balances, raising total velocity and the price level. If the real value of idle balances is the same in the new as in the pre-disturbance equilibrium, the ratio of idle to active balances and total velocity are also the same. The price level will rise proportionately to the change in total money balances, and the idle and active increments will be in the same ratio as the corresponding total components.

It follows by analogous proofs that if $L_2^n(r_N') > L_2'(r_N')$, $m_2^n > m_2'$ and the ratio of idle to active balances is greater in the new than in the old equilibrium. Total velocity is lower, and the price level rises less than proportionately to the total monetary increment. If $L_2^n(r_N') < L_2'(r_N')$, $m_2^n < m_2'$ and M_2/M_1 is lower as a net result of the disturbance; V is higher and P rises more than in proportion to the change in M.

Consider the following numerical example. Suppose that

$$M' = 150, \ M_1' = 100, \ M_2' = 50, \ V_1' = 2, \ y' = 100,$$

$$P' = \frac{M_1'V_1'}{y'} = \frac{100 \times 2}{100} = 2.$$

The value of idle money is

$$m_2' = \frac{M_2'}{P'} = \frac{50}{2} = 25.00,$$

and total velocity is

$$V' = \left(\frac{M_1'}{M'}\right)V_1' = \left(\frac{100}{150}\right)2 = 1.33.$$

The central bank purchases $\Delta M^n = \$15$ in existing securities only, raising M to $M^n = 165$ and M_2 to $M_2'' = 65$. The real value of idle money is increased from $m_2' = 25.00$ to $m_2'' = 65/2 = 32.50$. Total velocity falls to $(100/165)2 = 1.21$. Assuming that $m_2^n = m_2'$, equilibrium will be restored when the $\$15$ injection has been allocated to both idle and active balances in the ratio,

$$\frac{\Delta M_2^n}{\Delta M_1^n} = \frac{M_2'}{M_1'}, \ \text{or}, \ \frac{\Delta M_2^n}{\Delta M^n - \Delta M_2^n} = \frac{M_2'}{M' - M_2'}.$$

We solve for ΔM_2^n in the latter equality:

$$\Delta M_2^n = \Delta M^n\left(\frac{M_2'}{M'}\right) = 15\left(\frac{50}{150}\right) = 5.$$

Thus the stock-flow merger of security markets must transfer

$$\Delta M_1^n = \Delta M^n - \Delta M_2^n = 15 - 5 = \$10$$

of idle balances to the income stream. When that is accomplished,

$$P^n = \frac{M_1^n V_1'}{y'} = \frac{110 \times 2}{100} = 2.2,$$

and

$$m_2^n = \frac{55}{2.2} = 25.00,$$

the equilibrium value. Total velocity is once again $(100/165)2 = 1.33$. Both P and M rise by 10 percent.[18]

2. Changes Over Time

Since the equilibrium is characterized by zero monetary transfers, the nominal transfer of idle money and the rise of the price level must eventually decrease in successive intervals. We have already established that the real value of the transfer constantly diminishes over time (page 97), but in view of the rising price level, this does not imply that the nominal transfer also declines monotonically. In fact, we can show that over some intervals the number of dollars transferred to the income stream and the *rise* of the price level may increase.

The size of the nominal transfer is discussed with reference to Figure 4–10, in which the excess investment and idle-money functions of Figure 4–7 are drawn in *nominal* units. r_M again appears on the vertical scale, but dollar amounts are measured on the horizontal. During t_1 the functions, expressed in nominal units at the

---

[18] The proportionality of changes in M and P, resting on the net constancy of V, requires that L_2 be a demand for real, not nominal balances. If asset holders are insensitive to the price level, reckoning their cash holdings in nominal units, the wealth effect will be absent, and the return of the interest rate to equilibrium would require that the entire nominal monetary increment be transferred to the income stream. The equilibrium values of M_1/M_2 and V would rise, and P would increase more than proportionately to the increase in M. These results would obtain in models like that of Modigliani ("Liquidity Preference and the Theory of Interest and Money," *Econometrica*, Vol. XII [January, 1944], pp. 49–57, esp. p. 54, equation 12) or Ackley (*Macroeconomic Theory* [New York: The Macmillan Co., 1961], p. 185, equation [4a]), since the price level does not enter into the asset supply or demand for money.

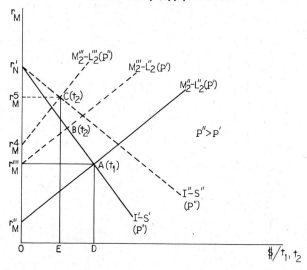

FIGURE 4–10
The Adjustment Process in Terms of Nominal Excess Investment
and Idle-Money Supply Functions

price level, P', are designated $I' - S'$ and $M_2'' - L_2''$. They meet at point A, determining an interest rate of r_M''' and a transfer of OD in M_2 balances. The quantity of idle money remaining after the transfer is M_2'''. If the price level were constant, the adjustment during t_2 would be characterized by the intersection at point B of $I' - S'$ and $M_2''' - L_2''$, whose vertical intercept is r_M'''. We abstract from any rotational tendencies in L_2. However, the transfer raises P to P'' at the closing instant of t_1. Letting $\theta = P''/P'$, the excess investment function becomes

(4D.11) $\qquad I'' - S'' = I'\theta - S'\theta = (I' - S')\theta.$

The new excess idle-money function is

(4D.12) $\qquad M_2''' - L_2'''$, where $L_2''' = \gamma L_2''$ and $1 < \gamma < \theta$;

i.e., L_2, expressed in nominal units, shifts to the right in response to the inflation, but since real wealth is simultaneously reduced, the shift in L_2 is less than proportional to the rise of the price level. $M_2''' - L_2'''$ meets the vertical axis at r_M^4, where $r_M^4 - r_M'''$ is the increase in the interest rate due to the wealth effect.[19] During t_2 the

---

[19] While the wealth effect, as described in Part C(1), results from a reduction in the real supply of idle balances, it is reflected in the present formulation in a rightward shift of the nominal demand schedule, L_2. The latter version is the one generally presented by Patinkin *Money, Interest, and Prices*, p. 146).

stock-flow security-market equilibrium produces r_M^s and a nominal transfer of $OE < OD$. As the final equilibrium is approached, the nominal transfer invariably declines to zero. In earlier intervals such as t_2, the dollar transfer will decline provided that the inflation does not rotate $I - S$ too far to the right, relative to the leftward shift of $M_2 - L_2$. Algebraically, the requirement for $OE < OD$ is

$$[(I'' - S'') - (I' - S')] - [(M_2''' - L_2'') - (M_2'' - L_2''')] < \beta,$$

where $\beta > 0$ is some constant. Upon substitution and rearrangement,

$$(I' - S')\theta - (I' - S')$$
$$- (M_2''' - L_2'' - M_2''' + L_2'' \gamma) < \beta$$
$$(I' - S')(\theta - 1) - L_2''(\gamma - 1) < \beta$$
$$- L_2'' < \frac{\beta - (I' - S')(\theta - 1)}{\gamma - 1}$$

(4D.13)
$$L_2'' > \frac{(I' - S')(\theta - 1) - \beta}{\gamma - 1}.$$

In the limiting case in which the wealth loss due to the inflation is absorbed entirely by D_{VO}, $\gamma = \theta$ and the inequality reduces to

(4D.14) $L_2'' > (I' - S') - \left(\dfrac{\beta}{\theta - 1}\right)$, where $\left(\dfrac{\beta}{\theta - 1}\right) > 0$.

In an economy in which L_2 exceeds the investment-saving gap of the adjustment intervals, the inequality is readily satisfied; the nominal transfer and the rise of the price level decline throughout the course of the adjustment process.

E. SUMMARY

The essence of the stock-flow adjustment process is the "transfer effect." The open-market purchase, instantaneously carried out, has reduced securities and raised idle balances of households by lowering the rate of interest. In the next interval the lower yield stimulates an excess of intended investment over saving in the form of an excess supply of new securities. These securities flow into the existing-asset market where, at a lower price and higher yield, they are purchased in exchange for idle balances. The latter are thereby *transferred* via new investment expenditures to the active circulation, where they raise the commodity price level proportionately.

The increase in the price level lowers the value of idle money further, causing an additional rise in the rate of interest designated the "wealth effect." These two equilibrating mechanisms continue to operate until the interest rate is once more equal to the natural rate at which intended saving equals investment. At this point the flow of excess securities, transfers of idle to active balances, and movements in the interest rate and price level are all zero. The system has returned to equilibrium.

The preceding analysis is based upon the following conditions: (1) firms do not retire securities in response to a change in ρ_s, the real income per share; (2) households expect new securities to bear a real income equal to that of pre-existing shares; (3) changes in the income per share will not cause a significant displacement of the market rate of interest; (4) there are no leakages of active to idle balances. In fact, the adjustment promises almost invariably to alter the income per share. This follows from changes in the capital-security ratio and the rate of return to the capital stock. But given the four conditions, such changes have no bearing on the stock-flow financial adjustment. Firms have neither the incentive nor the means to retire securities should ρ_s fall when ex post investment is below the intended amount. On the other hand, if asset holders expect ρ_s to rise or fall, portfolio adjustments will drive the market rate of interest in an opposite direction, lengthening or shortening the stock-flow adjustment. Any *de facto* change in ρ_s will not seriously affect the market rate of interest, given our earlier assumption that security demand responds almost equally to the induced change in security value.

Since it is a demand for securities only, saving does not constitute a source of leakages when the system is in equilibrium. But during the transition to an equilibrium, any lag of the price level behind additional active balances will cause an apparent rise in real income. Real saving will increase, causing a reduction in the rate of interest and a return transfer of active to idle balances as savers purchase existing securities. However, these non-equilibrating effects are reversed when the price level fully reflects the additional spending. If the lag of the price level is due to inventory depletion, any retirement of securities corresponding to the consumed capital will also lower the rate of interest and rechannel active money to the idle realm. But this, too, is at most a temporary source of leakages.

If the demand for real idle balances remains constant at the natural rate of interest, then in the new equilibrium the value of idle balances, the ratio of idle to active money, and the over-all velocity of money will all be equal to their pre-disturbance values. The price level will have risen proportionately to the total monetary increment. The transfer of idle to active balances and the increase in the price level will decline throughout the adjustment, provided that the demand for idle balances is not less than the investment-saving gap by more than a given constant.

The appendix shows that the fraction of the total movement of the interest rate during the adjustment accomplished by the transfer and wealth effects can be approximated by the ratios, M_1/M and M_2/M, respectively.

CHAPTER V

The Adjustment Process: Real Elements

A. PLAN OF THE CHAPTER

This chapter will extend the financial analysis of a monetary expansion to a consideration of changes in the real stock of capital. Although, on our assumptions, the equilibrating mechanisms are fundamentally independent of induced changes in capital or its rate of return, our purpose here is to study the adjustment process in which changes in capital are allowed to exert an impact. Introducing capital as a variable will greatly increase the range of phenomena handled by our description of the adjustment process. Variables that will enter the analysis in a determinate way are the return to capital, the income per share, the number of securities issued, the real price of securities, and total household wealth. We are particularly interested in tracing the course of the latter two variables, both of which depend critically on the degree of capital accumulation.

Additional capital may be financed by the sale of new securities to savers or existing-asset holders. In the former event the capital is financed by "voluntary" saving; in the latter, by "forced" saving. In general, forced saving refers to any ex post investment, and thus realized saving, that exceeds the intended quantity indicated by the S schedule at the market rate of interest. However, in studying the impact of monetary disturbances, we cannot completely separate forced from voluntary saving. The interaction between them influences the course of variables in a way that cannot be predicted from either one alone. For example, the net impact of forced saving on capital and wealth depends on the interest elasticity of voluntary saving. If $\partial S / \partial r_M = 0$, then voluntary saving is constant throughout the adjustment, and any forced saving is a net addition to the capital that would have been generated in the absence of the disturbance. But when $\partial S/\partial r_M > 0$, forced saving, corresponding to some or all of the excess of I over S, may partially replace intended saving that was curtailed by the reduction in the market rate of interest. In the limiting case when $\partial S/\partial r_M > 0$ and $\partial I/\partial r_M = 0$, forced saving merely maintains the pre-disturbance rate of growth in capital and wealth. The slope and intensity of the S and I schedules, as well as the capital financed by their difference, is thus of crucial importance in determining the net wealth position of households.

We shall begin this chapter by redefining the model for purposes of wealth measurement. This is done in Part B, in which the direct impact of an open-market purchase is also briefly recapitulated. In Part C we shall consider an adjustment process in which there is *zero forced saving*; i.e., excess new securities are not realized in any real capital formation. At any rate of interest, ex post investment lies on the S schedule. Part D will describe the adjustment on the assumption that excess security sales lead fully and immediately to capital accumulation. This is the case of *complete forced saving*, in which ex post investment lies along the I schedule. In both cases the analysis will describe one or two typical adjustment periods, from which the character of the final equilibrium is extrapolated. The analyses of Parts C and D will each proceed by two stages. The adjustment process will be described first in abstraction from, and then in combination with voluntary saving. The initial analysis presents the essential character of the adjustment. The subsequent analysis enables us to describe the movement of variables in the realistic context of a continuously growing economy. In particular, we shall be able to (a) describe without qualification the direction of movement of security prices, (b) compare the total wealth of households at any time following the disturbance, with wealth at a comparable moment in an undisturbed growth process, and (c) generalize our comparisons by altering assumptions as to the interest elasticity of S and I. Part E will relax several of the assumptions underlying Parts C and D, considering degrees of forced saving intermediate between zero and complete, lagged investment, investment errors, variability of L_2, and subsidization of property rather than personal income. Appendix A will derive upper and lower quantitative limits for security prices and quantities of the zero and complete forced-saving adjustment. Appendix B will sketch the adjustment for an alternative model in which the community shares its claim to the stock of capital with an outside agency such as the central bank, the central government, or a foreign power. Chapter VI treats the case of monetary contraction.

Until Part E we shall assume that entrepreneurs spend balances raised in the securities market without lag (except in Part C [2–4], where an assumed lag is merely an analytical aid without significance on its own account); that the balances raised through security sales are, if realized in ex post investment, just sufficient to equate r_M and ρ_K; that L_2 is invariant in the face of autonomous changes in wealth; and that the bank subsidizes the income of persons rather than securities in offsetting additions to its own earnings following the open-market purchase. We continue to assume, as we have hitherto, that output is fixed, as are the real saving and investment schedules and the target or natural rate of interest.

B. THE MODEL AND THE DISTURBANCE

1. The Components of Wealth

Thus far the wealth of households has consisted of idle balances and a single equity-type security, which is also held by the central bank. However, in studying the wealth effects of an open-market operation, we must distinguish between securities issued by private business firms and those supplied by the central government. The former are held only by households, and represent a direct claim on the privately owned stock of capital. The latter securities, held both by households and the central bank, are backed by the general credit standing of the government. The government's ability to service its outstanding securities is partly and indirectly due to the existence of physical capital held by itself and households. But we are not interested in expressing this relationship explicitly at our present level of abstraction. S_O, the total number of securities held by households at a given moment, is thus made up of S_P, issued by the private sector, and S_G, issued by the government. The total number of all existing securities in any instant is

$$(5B.1) \qquad S_\tau = S_O + S_B = S_P + S_G + S_B,$$

where S_B, the quantity held by the central bank, is understood to be of the government variety. The real value of household securities is

$$(5B.2) \qquad S_{VO} = S_P p_P + S_G p_G,$$

where p_P and p_G are, respectively, the real price of private and government issues. By analogy to (2B.10),

(5B.3) $$p_P = \frac{(\rho_s)_P}{(r_M)_P} \quad \text{and} \quad p_G = \frac{(\rho_s)_G}{(r_M)_G},$$

where the numerators are the corresponding incomes per security, and the denominators the yields.

(5B.4) $$(\rho_s)_P = \frac{\rho_K K}{S_P},$$

which is the same as (2B.6), except that S_P replaces S_O in the latter equation. In view of our earlier remarks, $(\rho_s)_G$ cannot be divided into further components.

While private securities are equities, we shall assume that the government issues are perpetual bonds (consols) whose interest payments are tied to the price level by "escalator" clauses. Moreover, the government automatically and immediately equates $(\rho_s)_G$, the income payment adjusted for changes in the general price level, to $(\rho_s)_P$. In spite of possible differences between the securities in regard to risk, etc., households treat the two securities as perfect substitutes. Thus at all times, $(r_M)_P = (r_M)_G$ and, since the incomes are equal, $p_P = p_G$. Accordingly, we may simplify our symbolism by dropping the P and G subscripts, using ρ_s, r_M, and p to refer to the common income, yield, and price. It remains true, of course, that ρ_s can be expressed as a function of other variables only when applied to the private security. On these assumptions the wealth of households is

(5B.5) $$W = S_{VO} + m_2,$$

where

(5B.6) $$S_{VO} = S_P p + S_G p = S_P \left(\frac{\rho_s}{r_M}\right) + S_G \left(\frac{\rho_s}{r_M}\right),$$

and

(5B.7) $$S_P \left(\frac{\rho_s}{r_M}\right) = S_P \left(\frac{\rho_K K}{r_M S_P}\right) = \left(\frac{\rho_K}{r_M}\right) K.$$

Hence,

(5B.8) $$W = \left(\frac{\rho_K}{r_M}\right) K + S_G \left(\frac{\rho_s}{r_M}\right) + m_2.$$

In equilibrium, when $\rho_K = r_M = r_N$,

(5B.9) $$W = K + S_G \left(\frac{\rho_s}{r_M}\right) + m_2.$$

Over time the stock of private securities grows as new investment is undertaken by firms. However, the volume of government securities is a constant, and all household saving is directed to the purchase of private securities only. Finally, we shall assume that the central-bank purchase completely exhausts the holdings of government securities by households. In the subsequent adjustment process,

$$(5B.10) \qquad\qquad S_O = S_P.$$

Limiting the central bank to the purchase of government securities is, of course, a step in the direction of reality. Were we to retain our assumption of a single private security in the system, the central bank would be an equity claimant to the capital stock of the private sector. While this is an immaterial detail in a purely financial analysis, as in Chapter IV, it is generally inappropriate when discussing variability in the capital stock and the resulting impact on household wealth. The appropriate assumption in the present context is that households are the only direct claimants to the earnings of private capital; securities lost to the bank are claims to governmental income, which is not specifically accounted for. There are, perhaps, circumstances in which the central bank, or another sector outside the private domain, might exercise an equity claim to the capital stock. The rather interesting modifications to the adjustment process in this event are explored in Appendix B.

While government bonds are not usually constant purchasing-power instruments, the wealth effects of the typical government bond are adequately represented in our system by the supply of idle money. The real value of idle balances, like that of fixed money-value government bonds, varies inversely with the general price level, without causing offsetting reactions by the government.[1] The

---

[1] We observed on p. 106, n. 13 that governmental net worth is not affected by price-level induced changes in the value of cash balances that are either full-bodied or backed by government holdings of a commodity. However, changes in the value of bonds on account of price-level movements tend to alter the government's net worth. If the government's bond liability is matched by fixed assets, such as buildings or military installations, or by the general power to tax, a change in the price level changes the real bond liability without altering the real value of the corresponding asset (the nominal asset values are assumed to follow the general price movement). The existence of bonds thereby creates an inverse relation between government net worth and the price level. But we assume that the government does not react to changes in its net worth; thus, for practical purposes, the wealth effects of government debt—whether bonds or money—are identical.

assumption that the open-market purchase exhausts the community's government bonds is therefore of no great importance.[2]

Assuming that the income, yield, and price of private and government securities are identical is a stronger condition than the analysis requires or reality justifies. It is a useful simplification, however, and does not qualify the results of this chapter in any major respect. A detailed analysis of a general two-security model is undertaken in Chapter VII. The assumption that the stock of government securities is constant is justified in that neither the monetary disturbance nor the subsequent adjustment is likely to stimulate additional quantities of government debt.

2. Equilibrium Growth

An economy in joint stock and flow equilibrium will follow the pattern of growth described in Chapter II-D(2). Equal flows of intended household saving and private investment are added each period to existing-asset schedules that are in equilibrium at the same interest rate that equates S and I. S_{VO}, D_{VO}, and W rotate equally to the right, while m_2 and L_2 remain fixed. Since saving and investment are equal, as well as constant over time, there is no tendency for the interest rate, the return to capital, security prices, or commodity prices to change.

Let us trace the movement of the wealth components over the course of an interval of equilibrium growth. A "hat," $\hat{\ }$, over a variable will indicate that it is generated by the equilibrium-growth process. Such variables with single primes will occur during the interval, if they are flow variables, or at the close of the interval, if they are stock variables. Variables with single primes, but without the hat, are starting values preceding the interval. The variables are initially:

$$(5\text{B}.11) \quad K', \rho'_K = r'_M = r'_N, S'_O = S'_P + S'_G, \rho'_s = \frac{\rho'_K K'}{S'_P}, p' = \frac{\rho'_s}{r'_N}, m'_2.$$

The value of securities is

$$(5\text{B}.12) \qquad S'_{VO}(\rho'_K, r'_N) = S'_O p' = S'_P p' + S'_G p' = K' + S'_G p',$$

[2]However, since the value of government bonds invariably includes as a factor the price of securities (cf. [5B.8] and [5B.9]), this presents wealth-measurement problems peculiar to government securities. Chapter VI treats these problems in detail in connection with the open-market sale (see, for example, pp. 197–201, 204, 206, 209–11, and 213–14), and refers to them in the context of an inflationary adjustment in Part F(2) (see pp. 218–19).

where the parameters in parentheses are, respectively, the return to capital determining ρ_s and the S_{VO} function, and the rate of interest whose reciprocal determines the point on the function at which security value is measured.[3] Total wealth is

$$(5B.13) \qquad W'(\rho'_K, r'_N) = S'_{VO}(\rho'_K, r'_N) + m'_2 = K' + S'_G p' + m'_2.$$

The wealth parameters are the same as those for S_{VO}; ρ_K determines the underlying S_{VO} function, while the reciprocal of r'_N is the point at which wealth is measured. During an interval of length t_1,

$$(5B.14) \qquad \hat{S}'(r'_N) = \hat{I}'(r'_N) = \hat{\Delta K}';$$

i.e., the equal flows of saving and investment (in real-value units) are realized in an equal increase in the stock of capital. The number of new securities financing the investment is

$$(5B.15) \qquad \hat{\Delta S}'_S = \frac{\hat{\Delta K}'}{\hat{p}'}.$$

Thus, at the close of the interval,

$$(5B.16) \qquad \hat{K}' = K' + \hat{\Delta K}', \hat{S}'_P = S'_P + \hat{\Delta S}'_S,$$

$$\hat{S}'_G = S'_G, \hat{S}'_O = S'_O + \hat{\Delta S}'_S, \text{ and } \hat{m}'_2 = m'_2.$$

Security value is

$$(5B.17) \qquad \hat{S}'_{VO}(\rho'_K, r'_N) = \hat{S}'_O \hat{p}' = \hat{S}'_P \hat{p}' + \hat{S}'_G \hat{p}'$$

$$= (S'_P + \hat{\Delta S}'_S)\hat{p}' + S'_G \hat{p}' = K' + \hat{\Delta K}' + S'_G p',$$

since $\hat{p}' = p'$. The reason that p remains constant at p' is that we add to the numerator and denominator of K'/S'_P, the expression for p when $\rho'_K = r'_M$, increments whose ratio, $\hat{\Delta K}'/\hat{\Delta S}'_S$, is also equal to p'. Total wealth at the close of the interval is

$$(5B.18) \qquad \hat{W}'(\rho'_K, r'_N) = \hat{S}'_{VO}(\rho'_K, r'_N) + \hat{m}'_2 = K' + \hat{\Delta K}' + S'_G p' + m'_2.$$

In subsequent intervals wealth will continue to grow by the increment to capital, which is equal to the constant saving-investment flow. ρ_K, r_M, ρ_s, S_G, and m_2 are all constant at their initial values. After n undisturbed intervals of the same length as t_1, total household wealth is

$$\hat{W}^n(\rho'_K, r'_N) = \hat{S}^n_{VO}(\rho'_K, r'_N) + \hat{m}^n_2$$

$$= \hat{S}^n_P \hat{p}^n + \hat{S}^n_G \hat{p}^n + \hat{m}^n_2.$$

---

[3]Occasionally we shall omit either or both of the parameters in referring to security value if, in the context, the value of the parameter is otherwise apparent. In referring to S_{VO} as a general function of $1/r_M$, the interest parameter is, of course, necessarily omitted. In Part C, ρ_s will generally be used in place of ρ_K as the identifying parameter.

Hence

(5B.19) $\qquad \hat{W}^n(\rho'_K, r'_N) = (S'_P + n\hat{\Delta S'_S})p' + S'_G p' + m'_2,$

where $n\hat{\Delta S'_S} = \sum_n \hat{\Delta S}_S$ is the sum of securities purchased by savers over n intervals of equal length. Since $S'_P = K'/p'$ and $n\hat{\Delta S'_S} = n\hat{\Delta K'}/p'$, a final expression for wealth (see [5B.9]) is

(5B.20)
$$\hat{W}^n(\rho'_K, r'_N) = \hat{K}^n + S'_G p' + m'_2 = K' + n\hat{\Delta K'} + S'_G p' + m'_2.$$

3. An Open-Market Purchase

Let us briefly reconsider the direct impact of an open-market purchase. The initial data given in (5B.11)–(5B.13) are altered by an instantaneous purchase of securities by the central bank. The bank obtains existing government securities only, the quantity, price, and yield of which are

(5B.21) $\qquad S'_B = S'_G, p'' > p', r''_M = \dfrac{\rho''_s}{p''} < r'_N.$

Given our assumptions (Section 1), the new price and yield apply equally to government and private securities. The real magnitude of the purchase is $S'_B p''$, which is taken wholly as an addition to idle balances. If m''_2 is the total real value of idle money after the purchase,

(5B.22) $\qquad\qquad\qquad S'_B p'' = m''_2 - m'_2.$

The remaining quantity of securities held by households is

(5B.23) $\qquad S''_O = S'_O - S'_B = S'_P + S'_G - S'_B = S'_P.$

ρ_s is unchanged at

(5B.24) $\qquad\qquad\qquad \rho''_s = \rho'_s = \dfrac{\rho'_K K'}{S'_P}.$

The value function for securities privately held is

(5B.25) $\qquad S''_{VO}(\rho'_K) = S''_O p = S'_P \left(\dfrac{\rho'_s}{r_M}\right) = \left(\dfrac{\rho'_K}{r_M}\right) K' < S'_{VO}(\rho'_K).$

The total wealth function is

(5B.26) $\qquad W''(\rho'_K) = S''_{VO}(\rho'_K) + m''_2 = \left(\dfrac{\rho'_K}{r_M}\right) K' + m''_2.$

These events are summarized in Figure 5–1, where single and

FIGURE 5–1

**The Existing-Asset Market during the Zero Forced-Saving Adjustment—
Voluntary Saving Excluded**

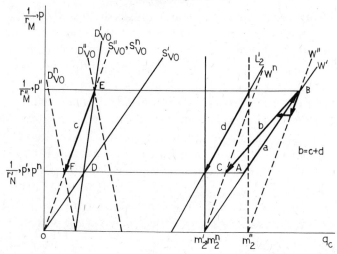

double-primed schedules represent the pre- and post-operation markets, respectively. L_2 is invariant at L_2', D_{VO}'' reflecting the entire rotational tendency in wealth:

$$(5B.27) \qquad D_{VO}'' = D_{VO}' + W''(\rho_K') - W'(\rho_K').$$

The quantity of wealth has increased from $W'(\rho_K', r_N')$ to $W''(\rho_K', r_M'')$, reflecting the capital gains imparted to existing securities by the bank's bid price. In Figure 5–1 the wealth gain is shown as the movement from point A to point B. The magnitude of the gain is

$$
\begin{aligned}
W''(\rho_K', r_M'') &- W'(\rho_K', r_N') \\
&= S_{VO}''(\rho_K', r_M'') + m_2'' - [S_{VO}'(\rho_K', r_N') + m_2'] \\
&= S_O'' p'' + (m_2'' - m_2') - S_O' p' \\
&= S_O'' p'' + S_B' p'' - S_O' p' \\
&= (S_O'' + S_B') p'' - S_O' p' \\
&= S_O' p'' - S_O' p',
\end{aligned}
$$

or

$$(5B.28) \qquad S_O'(p'' - p') > 0.$$

The bank offsets the income on its additional securities by subsidizing personal income. The post-operation existing-asset market remains exactly as indicated in Figure 5–1.

C. ZERO FORCED SAVING

1. Assumptions

The failure to create physical capital during the subsequent adjustment may result from a delay by entrepreneurs in spending funds raised in the securities market, or from a failure of entrepreneurial expenditures to divert resources and goods from consumers. In the latter event the inflation proceeds in spite of the absence of forced saving. However, until Section 5 we shall assume that entrepreneurs are merely hoarding idle-money balances transferred from the existing-asset market, and that the price level is thereby constant. The interest adjustment is accomplished entirely by excess new private securities. We shall also assume for the present that the return to capital is fixed at $\rho'_K = r'_N$. This assumption will be relaxed in Section 4. The adjustment is described in Sections 2–5 in abstraction from the equal saving and investment flows.[4]

2. The First Interval

Whatever the ultimate impact on the stock of capital, the initial interval of the adjustment process proceeds exactly as described in Chapter IV-B(1). Excess new securities are exchanged for idle balances at a lower price, p''', and higher yield,

(5C.1) $r'''_M = \dfrac{\rho'''_s}{p'''} > r''_M$, where $p''' < p''$ and $\rho'''_s = \rho''_s$.

In Figure 4–3 a new security-value function, S'''_{VO}, lies to the right of the post-operation schedule, S''_{VO}, idle balances are $m'''_2 < m''_2$, and both wealth and security demand rotate clockwise to W''' and D'''_{VO}, respectively:

(5C.2) $W''' = S'''_{VO} + m'''_2$,

(5C.3) $D'''_{VO} = D''_{VO} + (W''' - W'')$.

---

[4]Our procedure is to *abstract* from the equal S and I flows—not to assume that they are zero. Thus, while we ignore voluntary saving *per se* in describing the movement of variables, the model does not treat the S schedule as coincident with the vertical axis. S is positive at all interest rates, and may even be interest-elastic. The latter assumption is treated in Section 4 with reference to the movement of ρ_K. But even then the quantity of voluntary saving is itself omitted from the expressions for ρ_s, p, and W. Abstracting from voluntary saving in this sense is analytically convenient; assuming that S is zero throughout its range is both stronger than the analysis requires or reality justifies.

The schedules of the initial adjustment interval are reproduced in Figure 5–2. The equilibrium of the security market at the start of the interval is at point A. The sale of excess securities during the interval moves the equilibrium to point B, where

(5C.4) $$CB = D''_{VO}(r'''_M) - S''_{VO}(r'''_M) = m''_2 - L'_2(r'''_M) = m''_2 - m'''_2.$$

If $\Delta S'_E$ is the quantity of excess new securities taken by asset holders, and

(5C.5) $$S''_P = S'_P + \Delta S'_E,$$

then

(5C.6) $$S'''_{VO}(\rho'''_s) = S''_P \left(\frac{\rho'''_s}{r_M}\right),$$

where ρ'''_s is now used as a parameter defining the S_{VO} function. During the actual transfer, households *value* the new securities as

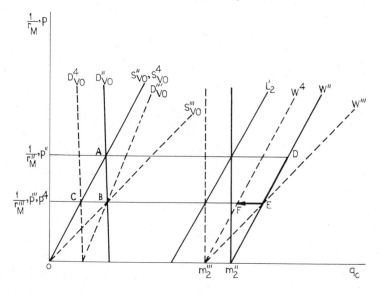

FIGURE 5–2

The Existing-Asset Market during the First Interval of a Zero Forced-Saving Adjustment—Voluntary Saving Excluded

if the earnings, ρ'''_s, were identical to the pre-existing one, $\rho''_s = \rho'_s$ (see pages 101–2). But after a time lag that depends on the dividend-payment period, asset holders discover that the excess issues have failed to materialize in real capital, and have instead simply watered outstanding shares. The same total security income must be divided among a greater number of securities. ρ_s falls to

(5C.7)
$$\rho_s^4 = \frac{\rho_K' K'}{S_P' + \Delta S_E'},$$

creating a reduced schedule, S_{VO}^4, equal to S_{VO}'':

(5C.8)
$$S_{VO}^4(\rho_s^4) = S_P'' \left(\frac{\rho_s^4}{r_M} \right) = \left(\frac{\rho_K'}{r_M} \right) K' = S_{VO}''(\rho_s'').$$

If we assume that dividends are paid continuously over time, the stock watering is recognized in the instant following the transfer, and the final schedules produced by a zero forced-saving interval can be included in Figure 5–2. When S_{VO} rotates to $S_{VO}^4(\rho_s^4)$, wealth moves equally to

(5C.9)
$$W^4(\rho_s^4) = S_{VO}^4(\rho_s^4) + m_2'''.$$

Since L_2 is fixed at L_2', D_{VO} also rotates equally to the left, becoming

(5C.10)
$$D_{VO}^4 = D_{VO}''' + [S_{VO}^4(\rho_s^4) - S_{VO}''(\rho_s''')].$$

Hence D_{VO}^4 and S_{VO}^4 intersect at the same interest rate, r_M'''. The security-market equilibrium moves from point B to C. Though the interest rate is unchanged, the price of securities is lower. The new price is

(5C.11)
$$p^4 = \frac{\rho_s^4}{r_M'''}.$$

Substituting for each price,

(5C.12)
$$p''' - p^4 = \frac{\rho_K' K'}{r_M''' S_P'} \left(\frac{\Delta S_E'}{S_P' + \Delta S_E'} \right) > 0.$$

The reduction to p^4 is brought about by the attempted sale of securities implied by the leftward movement from D_{VO}''' to D_{VO}^4. Since $p''' < p''$, the opening price, the real price of securities falls monotonically throughout the interval.

The course of total wealth is also downward during the interval. Initially the increase in interest lowers wealth along W'' from D to E. This reflects the capital losses on existing securities as p is lowered from p'' to p'''. In response to the stock watering, p declines further to p^4, and wealth falls along the path, EF. Since E is already to the left of D, so is F. A more formal statement of this result is

$$W^4(\rho_s^4, r_M''') < W''(\rho_s'', r_M''),$$
$$S_{VO}^4(\rho_s^4, r_M''') + m_2''' < S_{VO}''(\rho_s'', r_M'') + m_2'',$$

(5C.13)
$$\left(\frac{\rho'_K}{r'''_M}\right)K' + m'''_2 < \left(\frac{\rho'_K}{r''_M}\right)K' + m''_2 .$$

The inequality is established by $r'''_M > r''_M$ and $m'''_2 < m''_2$. On net, households have lost idle balances without gaining security value. The movement of D_{VO} over the entire course of the interval is equal to the net wealth loss:

(5C.14)
$$D''_{VO} - D^4_{VO} = W''(\rho''_s) - W^4(\rho^4_s) = m''_2 - m'''_2 .$$

3. Subsequent Intervals

The events of the first interval are repeated through n intervals of the adjustment process. Each period excess securities are exchanged for idle balances at a lower price and higher yield. But the capital stock is constant, and the excess securities merely water outstanding issues. At the closing instant of every interval, S_{VO} accordingly returns to its pre-interval position. D_{VO} rotates equally with S_{VO}, maintaining the interest rate at its new level, but causing p to fall further. Wealth falls continuously along vectors of the form, DE-EF in Figure 5–2. The final equilibrium is shown in Figure 5–1 by schedules marked with the superscript, n. The interest rate has been raised to r'_N by reducing idle balances from m''_2 to

(5C.15)
$$m^n_2 = m'_2 .$$

The quantities of securities and capital are

(5C.16)
$$S^n_P = S'_P + \sum_n \Delta S_E, K^n = K' ,$$

where $\sum_n \Delta S_E$ is the sum over n intervals of the excess securities floated. The real income per security is

(5C.17)
$$\rho^n_s = \frac{\rho'_K K^n}{S^n_P} = \frac{\rho'_K K'}{S'_P + \sum_n \Delta S_E} < \rho'_s ,$$

the value of securities is

(5C.18)
$$S^n_{VO}(\rho^n_s) = S^n_P\left(\frac{\rho^n_s}{r_M}\right) = \left(\frac{\rho'_K}{r_M}\right)K' = S''_{VO}(\rho''_s),$$

and total wealth is

(5C.19)
$$W^n(\rho^n_s) = S^n_{VO}(\rho^n_s) + m^n_2 = \left(\frac{\rho'_K}{r_M}\right)K' + m'_2 .$$

The value demand for securities may be written in two ways:

(5C.20) $$D_{VO}^n = D_{VO}'' + [W^n(\rho_s^n) - W''(\rho_s'')],$$

$$D_{VO}^n = D_{VO}' + [W^n(\rho_s^n) - W'(\rho_s')].$$

Relative to D_{VO}'', D_{VO}^n is the result of a leftward parallel shift of demand equal to

(5C.21) $$W''(\rho_s'') - W^n(\rho_s^n) = m_2'' - m_2',$$

the net wealth loss of the adjustment process. The zero forced-saving adjustment is thus analogous to a capital levy, payable to entrepreneurs in idle balances. The loss of idle money stimulates an equal reduction in security demand, which causes the necessary rise in the rate of interest. Since the equilibrium is in fact reached by excess securities, rather than a tax, ρ_s is also reduced. Relative to D_{VO}', D_{VO}^n represents a counterclockwise rotation in the amount of

(5C.22) $$W'(\rho_s') - W^n(\rho_s^n) = S_{VO}'(\rho_s') - S_{VO}''(\rho_s'') = (S_O' - S_O'')\left(\frac{\rho_s'}{r_M}\right) = S_B' p,$$

the value of securities sold to the bank. The combined effect of the purchase and the adjustment is thus to remove S_B' from the portfolios of households, security demand falling equally. r_M and m_2 are unchanged, though ρ_s is lower.

The real price of securities in the new equilibrium is

(5C.23) $$p^n = \frac{\rho_s^n}{r_N'} = \frac{K'}{S_P' + \sum_n \Delta S_E} < p'.$$

Figure 5–1 summarizes the movement of wealth from the initial disturbance to the final equilibrium. Starting at point A at $W'(r_N')$, the bank's bid price raises the value of securities, bringing total wealth to point B at $W'(r_M'')$. The equilibrium of the securities market moves simultaneously from D to E. The vector between points A and B is labeled a. The wealth path to equilibrium is represented by the vector, b, connecting point B with C at $W''(r_N')$. b is the locus of end-of-interval wealth totals, incorporating the capital losses due to the rising interest rate and the reduction of idle balances. b is the horizontal sum of the two vectors tracing the individual wealth components:

(5C.24) $$b = c + d.$$

c indicates the value of securities, in the sense of a point on a schedule, at the close of each interval. Since stock watering lowers

S_{VO} to S''_{VO} at the conclusion of every period, the locus of closing security value is along S''_{VO} itself. c terminates at point F, the intersection of S''_{VO} and D^n_{VO}. d is the path of m_2, as a function of r_M. d thus coincides with L'_2 between $L'_2(r''_M)$ and $L'_2(r'_N)$.

If we were to diagram the wealth path during the course of each interval, we would show an initial movement along the opening wealth function. For t_1, this is the path in Figure 5-2, DE, created by capital losses as excess securities are sold at a lower price. In Figure 5-1 a similar path is drawn as an unlabeled vector along W''. When the stock watering is recognized at the close of the interval, a horizontal leftward vector in the diagram links W'' with b. This corresponds to the path in Figure 5-2, EF. The course of wealth over continuous time is thus saw-toothed, moving first along wealth functions that are parallel, but increasingly to the left of W'', and then shifting to a horizontal path that terminates at b.

The difference between pre-disturbance and final wealth corresponds to the distance between A and C. We have already shown ([5C.22]) that this is the value of securities sold to the bank, $S'_B p$, which at r'_N is $S'_B p'$.

Total wealth is drawn as a function of time in Figure 5-3. At t_O, preceding the disturbance, wealth is at point A. The purchase,

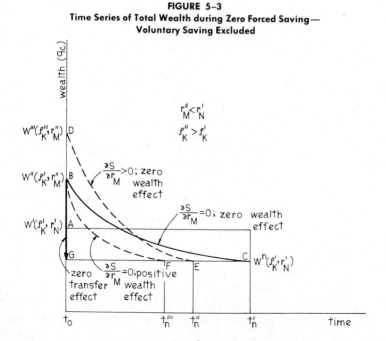

FIGURE 5-3
Time Series of Total Wealth during Zero Forced Saving—
Voluntary Saving Excluded

occurring in the same instant, raises wealth to B, where BA is given by (5B.28). Thereafter, wealth falls monotonically to point C, the new equilibrium at t'_n. The movement from B to C reflects both the rise in the interest rate and the loss of idle balances.

4. Variable ρ_K

The assumption that the return to capital, ρ_K, is constant throughout the adjustment is valid only if $\partial S/\partial r_M$ happens to be zero. This is the case shown in Figure 5-4(a), where S' and I' are the saving and investment schedules that prevail in each interval of length t_1. ρ_K and r_M are on the vertical axis. If at interest rates below r'_N, such as r''_M, only voluntary saving is realized, the rate of growth is unchanged at OA, for which ρ_K is and remains ρ'_K. In the more general case pictured in Figure 5-4(b), desired saving falls with the interest rate. At r''_M the absence of forced saving lowers

FIGURE 5-4
The Saving Schedule in Relation to the Movement of ρ_K

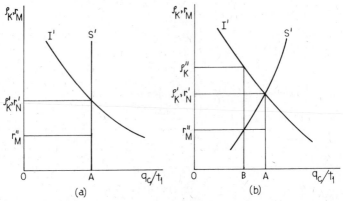

the growth rate from OA to OB, at which the return to investment, read on the marginal efficiency schedule, is $\rho''_K > \rho'_K$. In terms of two commodities, output of capital goods declines, lowering costs and prices, while the opposite occurs with consumer goods. The reduction in the supply price of capital raises ρ_K. As the interest rate and realized saving—equal to voluntary saving—rise during the adjustment, ρ_K falls along I' until, in equilibrium at r'_N, ρ_K is again ρ'_K. The change in ρ_K is thus only temporary; ρ_K rises spontaneously with the reduction in the growth rate at the start of the adjustment process, and falls thereafter to its original value. ρ_s, p, and S_{VO} will all reflect the movement in ρ_K. The derivatives of each with respect to ρ_K are:

$$(5C.25) \qquad \frac{\partial \rho_s}{\partial \rho_K} = \frac{\partial\left(\dfrac{\rho_K K}{S_P}\right)}{\partial \rho_K} = \frac{K}{S_P}.$$

$$(5C.26) \qquad \frac{\partial p}{\partial \rho_K} = \frac{\partial\left(\dfrac{\rho_s}{r_M}\right)}{\partial \rho_K} = \frac{K}{r_M S_P}.$$

$$(5C.27) \qquad \frac{\partial S_{VO}}{\partial \rho_K} = \frac{\partial\left(\dfrac{\rho_K K}{r_M}\right)}{\partial \rho_K} = \frac{K}{r_M}.$$

(5C.27) is the change in S_{VO} per unit change in ρ_K, for given values of K and r_M. ρ_K, a number whose actual magnitude is perhaps .05 or .10, is not likely to change by as much as a unit. But even for changes as small as .01 or .001, the resulting change in K/r_M promises to be considerable. Thus, if ρ_K rises perceptibly during the adjustment period, S_{VO} and W will tend to be well above the value determined by the transfer and stock-watering process. As usual, since D_{VO} rises equally, $D_{VO} - S_{VO}$ will be unaffected by the change in ρ_K, as will be the market rate of interest. But with ρ_K restored to ρ_K', the new equilibrium will be exactly as pictured in Figure 5–1, where total wealth is unchanged at

$$W''(\rho_K', r_N') = S_{VO}''(\rho_K', r_N') + m_2' \quad ([5C.18] \text{ and } [5C.19]).$$

In Figure 5–3 the wealth path would have the appearance of DE. Wealth at D is

$$W'''(\rho_K'', r_M''),$$

where $\rho_K'' > \rho_K'$ is the increased value of ρ_K at the start of the adjustment. Relative to B, the immediate post-operation wealth, we have $D > B$, which is

$$(5C.28) \qquad \left(\frac{\rho_K''}{r_M''}\right)K' + m_2'' > \left(\frac{\rho_K'}{r_M''}\right)K' + m_2'', \text{ where } \rho_K'' > \rho_K' > r_M''.$$

The equilibrium at E occurs at t_n'', an earlier point in time than t_n', since $\partial S/\partial r_M > 0$ raises $I - S$, accelerating the adjustment process (see page 97).

Though the rise in ρ_K is only temporary, its effect on ρ_s and p is more lasting (cf. page 100). Since the increase in ρ_K raises ρ_s directly, the whole family of security prices corresponding to given interest rates also rises. p_a, the average (mean) real security price of the adjustment, is raised, and the *number* of excess securities exchanging for given quantities of idle balances is thereby reduced. With $\sum_n \Delta S_E$ a smaller quantity, ρ_s^n and p^n are increased.

The influence of ρ_K on p_a depends on its magnitude of increase and the timing of its descent during the adjustment process. The factors relevant to the movement of ρ_K are the slopes of the S and I curves. Thus, in Figure 5–5(a), in which $I'(r_M)$ is concave upward and quite elastic, ρ_K rises at the start of the adjustment process to ρ_K'', which is only slightly above ρ_K'. Though ρ_K remains above ρ_K' until equilibrium is restored, its average value, and hence p_a, is not greatly increased. $I'(r_M)$ in Figure 5–5(b) has a completely different

FIGURE 5–5
The Investment Schedule in Relation to the Movement of ρ_K

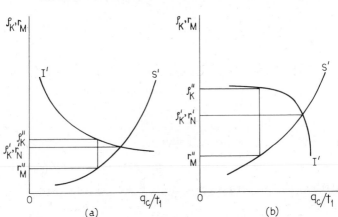

(a)   (b)

configuration. ρ_K rises immediately to ρ_K'', which is well above ρ_K'. Since I' is concave downward, the return movement of ρ_K is confined to the closing intervals of the adjustment period. As a result, ρ_K, ρ_s, and p will be substantially higher than otherwise for most of the interest rates of the adjustment process. p_a is accordingly increased, and $\sum_n \Delta S_E$ reduced. If we take the shape of I as given, then ρ_K and p_a will rise less the more vertical is $S(r_M)$.

5. *Variable P*

Suppose once again that entrepreneurs immediately spend funds obtained in the securities market. Although no capital goods are secured through the expenditures, the money remains in the circular flow where it raises the general price level proportionately. Since all of our behavioral functions are constructed in real-value units and are free of "money-illusion," only the value of idle balances is affected by the inflation (see Chapter IV-C[1]). The increase in P lowers m_2 and stimulates a rise in the rate of interest via the wealth effect. In Figure 5–2 the inflation following the first interval would be reflected in equal parallel and leftward movements in m_2, W, and D_{VO}. The wealth path would move down and to the left of point F.

In the appendix to Chapter IV we indicated that the extent to which the price level lowers the value of idle balances and raises r_M varies directly with the ratio, M_2/M. At one extreme, M_2/M might be so low as almost to eradicate the role of the price level and the wealth effect in restoring the system to equilibrium. At the other limit, M_2/M is so great that the price level produces most of the reduction in idle balances and the increase in r_M. However, in a zero forced-saving adjustment, it is immaterial to households whether real idle balances are lost through transfers or inflation. In either case the interest rate rises along L_2' in accordance with the reduction in m_2, and the security-value function on net is fixed at S_{VO}''. Whatever the contribution of the wealth effect, the final equilibrium is the one indicated in Figure 5–1. In Figure 5–3 the wealth path is BF, where F has the same ordinate as C, but a smaller abscissa, t_n'''. With the wealth effect supplementing the transfer effect, the loss of wealth and the increase in r_M in any interval are both greater. Equilibrium is reached at an earlier point in time.

A positive wealth effect, like the rise in ρ_K, tends to raise the average level of real security prices. The transfer effect not only lowers p as it raises r_M, but it reduces p further via the stock watering ([5C.12]). The wealth effect creates the same reduction in p to achieve any given increase in r_M, but fails, of course, to lower p additionally through the watering of shares. In the extreme case in which the wealth effect accomplishes all of the interest movement instantaneously following an infinitesimal transfer,

(5C.29) $$p^n = \frac{\rho_s^n}{r_N'} = \frac{\rho_K' K'}{r_N' S_P'} = p',$$

the highest possible closing price. The time path of wealth is shown in Figure 5–3 by the movement along the vertical axis from B to G, where G is drawn at the same height as C and F.

In general, the wealth effect reduces $\sum_n \Delta S_E$. This is due both to the increase in p_a and the fact that the inflation leaves a smaller real quantity of idle balances to be exchanged for excess securities.

6. The Total Growth Process

We shall now combine the forces of the adjustment process with the voluntary saving that characterizes a continuously growing economy. For the present, we assume (a) $\partial S/\partial r_M = 0$, causing ρ_K to be constant at $\rho_K' = r_N'$ throughout the adjustment; (b) while entrepreneurs spend idle balances transferred to them and raise the price level, the wealth effect on interest is nil; the rise in the interest rate is accomplished entirely by excess security issues.

a) The First Interval

Let us return to the initial interval following the open-market purchase. The bank has reduced the interest rate to $r_M'' < r_N'$ by raising the price of securities from p' to p''. In Figure 5–6 the security market is in equilibrium at point A. During the interval excess securities are exchanged for idle balances by lowering p to

FIGURE 5–6
The Existing-Asset Market during the First Interval of a Zero Forced-Saving Adjustment—Voluntary Saving Included

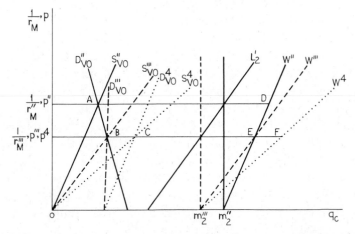

$p''' = \rho_s'''/r_M'''$, where $r_M''' > r_M''$ and $\rho_s''' = \rho_s'$. The schedules produced directly by the transfer are shown with triple primes in Figure 5–6 (they correspond to the functions of the same label in Figure 5–2). The security-market equilibrium is at point B. But simultaneously at the same price and yield savers purchase new securities issued by entrepreneurs. This is reflected in a further rightward movement in S_{VO} to

$$(5C.30) \qquad S_{VO}^4(\rho_s''') = S_P''' p = (S_P' + \Delta S_E' + \Delta S_S')\left(\frac{\rho_s'''}{r_M}\right),$$

where $\Delta S'_S$ is the quantity of securities purchased by savers. The rotation in S_{VO} is accompanied by equal movements in W and D_{VO}:

$$(5C.31) \qquad W^4(\rho'''_s) = S^4_{VO}(\rho'''_s) + m'''_2,$$

$$(5C.32) \qquad D^4_{VO} = D'''_{VO} + [S^4_{VO}(\rho'''_s) - S'''_{VO}(\rho'''_s)].$$

The security schedules intersect at point C. The price and yield of securities remain p''' and r'''_M as determined by the excess issues. At the close of the interval, funds raised from excess securities are dissipated in the income stream; funds acquired from savers lead to an equal and instantaneous increase in the stock of capital,

$$(5C.33) \qquad \Delta K' = \Delta S'_S p'''.$$

The net impact of these events on the existing-asset market depends on the resulting value of ρ_s:

$$(5C.34) \qquad \rho^4_s = \frac{\rho'_K(K' + \Delta K')}{S'_P + \Delta S'_E + \Delta S'_S}.$$

We can show that $\rho^4_s \gtreqless \rho'''_s$:

$$\frac{\rho'_K(K' + \Delta K')}{S'_P + \Delta S'_E + \Delta S'_S} \gtreqless \frac{\rho'_K K'}{S'_P},$$

which reduces to

$$(5C.35) \qquad \Delta K' \gtreqless \frac{K'(\Delta S'_E + \Delta S'_S)}{S'_P}.$$

If $\Delta S'_E = 0$, (5C.35) is

$$\Delta K' > \frac{K'\Delta S'_S}{S'_P} \text{ or } \frac{\Delta K'}{\Delta S'_S} > \frac{K'}{S'_P},$$

which is established by reference to (5C.33):

$$\frac{\Delta K'}{\Delta S'_S} = p''' = \left(\frac{\rho'_K}{r'''_M}\right)\frac{K'}{S'_P} > \frac{K'}{S'_P}, \text{ since } \frac{\rho'_K}{r'''_M} > 1.$$

Intuitively, when $\Delta S'_E = 0$, the movement from ρ'''_s to ρ^4_s entails raising the ratio, K'/S'_P, by increments whose ratio is $p''' > K'/S'_P$ because of the coefficient in p''', $\rho'_K/r'''_M > 1$. $\Delta S'_E$ is not, of course zero, but for sufficiently low values of $\Delta S'_E$ and $\Delta S'_S$, and high values of $\Delta K'$, the left side of (5C.35) will exceed the right. This is the expected result—ρ_s tends to rise at the close of the interval the greater is the capital increment and the less is the added quantity of securities, including excess issues that only water the outstanding stock.

The final schedules produced by the absence of forced saving and the realization of voluntary saving are

$$(5C.36) \qquad S_{VO}^5(\rho_s^4) = (S_P' + \Delta S_E' + \Delta S_S') \left(\frac{\rho_s^4}{r_M} \right),$$

$$(5C.37) \qquad W^5(\rho_s^4) = S_{VO}^5(\rho_s^4) + m_2''',$$

$$(5C.38) \qquad D_{VO}^5 = D_{VO}^4 + [S_{VO}^5(\rho_s^4) - S_{VO}^4(\rho_s''')] \,.$$

If drawn in Figure 5–6 these schedules would lie to the right of, coincide with, or lie to the left of the corresponding fourth-order schedules, depending on whether $\rho_s^4 \gtreqless \rho_s'''$. In all events the interest rate continues at r_M''', since D_{VO} and S_{VO} rotate equally.

With the interest rate constant at r_M''', the movement from ρ_s''' to ρ_s^4 is accompanied by a proportionate movement in the price of securities:

$$(5C.39) \qquad p^4 = \frac{\rho_s^4}{r_M'''} \gtreqless p''' = \frac{\rho_s'''}{r_M'''} \text{ when } \rho_s^4 \gtreqless \rho_s'''.$$

The final price may thus stand above the transfer price, despite the absence of forced saving. In fact, p^4 may even exceed p'', the opening price. $p^4 \gtreqless p''$ reduces to

$$\left(\frac{r_M''}{r_M'''} \right) \left(\frac{K' + \Delta K'}{S_P' + \Delta S_E' + \Delta S_S'} \right) \gtreqless \frac{K'}{S_P'}.$$

In a limiting first interval that takes account of the basically continuous nature of the adjustment, r_M''' is only infinitesimally above r_M'', and r_M''/r_M''' can be approximated by 1.00. On this assumption the inequality is

$$\Delta K' \gtreqless \frac{K'(\Delta S_E' + \Delta S_S')}{S_P'},$$

which is identical to (5C.35).[5]

Though ρ_s may rise or fall, it is invariably above its value in the absence of voluntary saving; i.e.,

$$(5C.40) \qquad \frac{\rho_K'(K' + \Delta K')}{(S_P' + \Delta S_E' + \Delta S_S')} > \frac{\rho_K' K'}{(S_P' + \Delta S_E')},$$

where the left side is the value of ρ_s^4 in the present context

---

[5]However, there are limits to the rise in p. These are described in Appendix A, Section 1(a).

([5C.34]) and the right side is ρ_s^4 when voluntary saving is excluded ([5C.7]). The inequality reduces to

$$\frac{\Delta K'}{\Delta S_S'} > \frac{K'}{S_P' + \Delta S_E'}.$$

Since

$$\frac{\Delta K'}{\Delta S_S'} = p''' = \frac{\rho_s'''}{r_M'''} = \frac{\rho_K' K'}{r_M''' S_P'},$$

(5C.40) is

$$\frac{\rho_K' K'}{r_M''' S_P'} > \frac{K'}{S_P' + \Delta S_E'},$$

$$\frac{\rho_K'}{r_M'''} > \frac{S_P'}{S_P' + \Delta S_E'}.$$

But $\rho_K'/r_M''' > 1$ while $S_P'/(S_P' + \Delta S_E') < 1$. Thus, since voluntary saving raises ρ_s, it also raises the level of real security prices.

The course of total wealth during the interval may be observed in Figure 5-6. As earlier, the initial movement is downward from D to E, owing to the decrease in p as excess securities are exchanged for idle balances. The addition of voluntary saving carries wealth to point F, which lies to the right of E. However, a smaller quantity of $\Delta S_S'$ could bring F to an abscissa midway between D and E. The final wealth change is created by the movement in ρ_s, which may go in either direction. Clearly, wealth over the entire course of the interval may increase, decrease, or remain constant. Symbolically,

$$W^5(\rho_s^4, r_M''') \gtreqless W''(\rho_s'', r_M''),$$

$$S_{VO}^5(\rho_s^4, r_M''') + m_2''' \gtreqless S_{VO}''(\rho_s'', r_M'') + m_2''.$$

Upon substitution and re-arrangement,

$$(5C.41) \qquad \left(\frac{\rho_K'}{r_M'''}\right)(K' + \Delta K') \gtreqless \left(\frac{\rho_K'}{r_M''}\right) K' + (m_2'' - m_2''').$$

$(K' + \Delta K')$ on the left exceeds K' on the right. But appearing on the right are $\rho_K'/r_M'' > \rho_K'/r_M'''$ and $(m_2'' - m_2''') > 0$. Thus wealth will tend to rise the less is the interest movement and the greater is the capital increment financed by voluntary saving relative to the loss of idle balances. But whatever its course, wealth is greater in the presence of voluntary saving than its absence. The difference between wealth in each case, respectively, is

(5C.42)
$$\left(\frac{\rho_K'}{r_M'''}\right)(K' + \Delta K') + m_2''' - \left[\left(\frac{\rho_K'}{r_M'''}\right)K' + m_2'''\right] = \left(\frac{\rho_K'}{r_M'''}\right)\Delta K'.$$

b) The Over-all Adjustment

The events of the first interval are typical of every succeeding interval. The interest rate rises, but the realization of voluntary saving may raise or lower the real income per share. As a result, the closing security price may equal, exceed, or fall below the transfer price or the opening price. Total wealth may increase, decrease, or remain constant. Closing security prices, ρ_s, and wealth are all higher than they were in abstraction from voluntary saving. In the final equilibrium,

(5C.43)
$$S_P^n = S_P' + \sum_n \Delta S_E + \sum_n \Delta S_S,$$

where $\sum_n \Delta S_S$ is the total number of securities purchased by savers, and

(5C.44)
$$K^n = K' + \sum_n \Delta K,$$

where $\sum_n \Delta K$ is the sum over n intervals of the capital financed by savers. Hence

(5C.45)
$$\rho_s^n = \frac{\rho_K' K^n}{S_P^n} = \frac{\rho_K'(K' + \sum_n \Delta K)}{(S_P' + \sum_n \Delta S_E + \sum_n \Delta S_S)} \gtreqless \rho_s',$$

(5C.46)
$$S_{VO}^n(\rho_s^n) = S_P^n\left(\frac{\rho_s^n}{r_M}\right) = \left(\frac{\rho_K'}{r_M}\right)(K' + \sum_n \Delta K),$$

(5C.47)
$$W^n(\rho_s^n) = S_{VO}^n(\rho_s^n) + m_2^n = \left(\frac{\rho_K'}{r_M}\right)(K' + \sum_n \Delta K) + m_2',$$

(5C.48)
$$D_{VO}^n = D_{VO}' + [W^n(\rho_s^n) - W'(\rho_s')] = D_{VO}' + [S_{VO}^n(\rho_s^n) - S_{VO}'(\rho_s')],$$

(5C.49)
$$p^n = \frac{\rho_s^n}{r_N'} = \frac{K' + \sum_n \Delta K}{S_P' + \sum_n \Delta S_E + \sum_n \Delta S_S} \gtreqless p'.$$

Figure 5–7 traces the aggregate wealth of households over time during the zero forced-saving adjustment of the growing economy. A and B are the same points so designated in Figure 5–3. From A we construct an upward-sloping straight line, AC, which represents

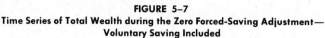

FIGURE 5-7
Time Series of Total Wealth during the Zero Forced-Saving Adjustment—
Voluntary Saving Included

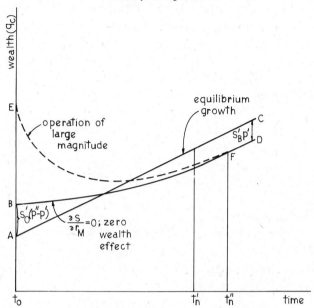

total wealth during an uninterrupted equilibrium-growth sequence (Part B[2]). The slope of AC over an interval of length t_1 is $\hat{\Delta K}'$, the uniform periodic increments to the stock of capital. From point B, created by the direct impact of the purchase, is a curve, BD, representing total wealth following a purchase and a zero forced-saving adjustment. The equilibrium is reached at t_n', after which BD is parallel to AC, since at r_N' the system again grows at the pre-operation rate, $\hat{\Delta K}'$. But at t_n'' and thereafter, BD lies below AC. The distance between the curves is

$$\hat{W}''(\rho_s', r_N') - W''(\rho_s^n, r_N'),$$

which is (5B.20) − (5C.47) evaluated at r_N':

(5C.50) $(n\hat{\Delta K}' - \sum_n \Delta K) + S_G' p'.$

The parenthetical term is the difference between total capital accumulation of the undisturbed and disturbed systems during the period of adjustment. Since $\partial S/\partial r_M = 0$, $\sum_n \Delta K = n\hat{\Delta K}'$ and (5C.50) is

(5C.51) $S_G' p' = S_B' p',$

the bank's purchase valued at the pre-disturbance price. This is exactly the difference between pre-disturbance wealth and the final wealth total that abstracted from voluntary saving (see [5C.22]). The introduction of voluntary saving simply adds a periodic growth factor, $\Delta \hat{K}'$, which is common to the disturbed and undisturbed processes. But while the equilibrium growth rate of capital is maintained throughout the adjustment, securities sold to the central bank in either case are not replaced. Securities sold to savers finance the capital increments, but excess new securities contribute nothing to the wealth total. Since real idle balances are returned to their pre-disturbance level, the net wealth loss is equal to the bank's purchase of securities. The latter are valued at p' because that is the price at which $S'_G = S'_B$ continues to be valued in the undisturbed growth process. Any wealth gain due to the reduction in the market rate of interest at t_O is removed by the gradual restoration of r_M to r'_N. Thus the increment from A to B is completely absent at t'_n.[6]

BD has the characteristic that it is higher in the new equilibrium than at the start of the adjustment; i.e.,

$$W^n(\rho^n_s, r'_N) > W''(\rho''_s, r''_M),$$

which reduces to

(5C.52) $$K' + \sum_n \Delta K > \left(\frac{\rho'_K}{r''_M}\right)K' + (m''_2 - m'_2).$$

The capital stock is greater on the left side than the right, but offsetting this are $\rho'_K / r''_M < 1$ and $(m''_2 - m'_2) > 0$ on the right. Accordingly, the inequality can go either way. But the right side will

---

[6]In Figure 5-7 the distance, BA, by which AC is below BD at t_0, is greater than $S'_B p'$, the distance by which AC is above BD at t'_n and beyond. But this is not invariably the case. Since, by (5B.28),

$$BA = W''(\rho'_K, r''_M) - W'(\rho'_K, r'_N) = S'_O(p'' - p'),$$

the general relation between the two distances is

$$S'_O(p'' - p') \gtreqless S'_B p'$$

$$(S'_P + S'_B)(p'' - p') \gtreqless S'_B p',$$

which reduces to

$$S'_P(p'' - p') \gtreqless S'_B(2p' - p'').$$

The inequality may go in either direction.

exceed the left only for an operation of very considerable magnitude, $m_2'' - m_2'$, with a resulting low purchase yield for which ρ_K'/r_M'' is also a large number. In addition, the growth supported by voluntary saving, $\sum_n \Delta K$, must be small relative to the magnitude of the purchase.[7]

Another characteristic of BD is that its rise is monotonic. This requires that an inequality of the form of (5C.41) be satisfied for every period. Treating (5C.41) as the quantitative relationship between the ending and beginning wealth of *any* interval, it is satisfied if the source of increased wealth, $\Delta K'$, predominates over the wealth-reducing elements, $r_M''' > r_M''$ and $(m_2'' - m_2''') > 0$. The conditions favoring a positive wealth increment right from the start are thus a high voluntary growth rate (which also contributed to [5C.52]), and a small increase in r_M and decrease in m_2 *per interval*. The latter circumstance is brought about by an inelastic I schedule, which reduces $I - S$ and the rise of the interest rate and the magnitude of the transfer of any period. The adjustment is thereby spread over a greater length of time. If the movements of r_M and m_2 are sufficiently small, it is in fact possible for wealth temporarily to increase at a *greater* rate than that of the undisturbed economy. For the typical first interval, we wish to prove

$$W^5(\rho_s^4, r_M''') - W''(\rho_s'', r_M'') > \hat{W}'(\rho_s', r_N') - W'(\rho_s', r_N').$$

Substituting $\hat{\Delta K}'$ for the right side, and the terms given by (5C.41) for the left, the inequality is

$$(5C.53) \quad \left(\frac{\rho_K'}{r_M'''}\right)(K' + \Delta K') - \left(\frac{\rho_K'}{r_M''}\right)K' - (m_2'' - m_2''') > \hat{\Delta K}'.$$

The case most favorable to the wealth of zero forced saving is $\partial S/\partial r_M = 0$, for which $\Delta K' = \hat{\Delta K}'$. In the limiting case in which $r_M''' = r_M''$ and $m_2''' = m_2''$, (5C.53) reduces to

$$\left(\frac{\rho_K'}{r_M''}\right)\hat{\Delta K}' > \hat{\Delta K}',$$

$$\frac{\rho_K'}{r_M''} > 1.$$

---

[7]The conditions favorable to (5C.52) can be classified into those that act on the wealth curve by (*a*) tilting it downward at its starting point at t_0, (*b*) tilting it upward at the equilibrium at t_n', and (*c*) raising its slope at all points in time. In the (*a*) category is a purchase yield, r_M', that is not too low relative to $r_N' = \rho_K'$. In the (*b*) category is a small number of securities purchased, S_B'. Under (*c*) is a large periodic rate of voluntary saving, $\Delta K'$.

Clearly (5C.53) may also be satisfied when $\Delta K' < \hat{\Delta K}'$, $r_M''' > r_M''$, and $m_2''' < m_2''$, provided that $\Delta K'$, ρ_K'/r_M''', and m_2''' are not too low. However, since wealth at the start of the adjustment is above, while the final wealth total is below that of the undisturbed system, (5C.53) cannot be satisfied in every interval of the adjustment. Sooner or later the wealth increment must fall below $\hat{\Delta K}'$, and the wealth total below the AC line of Figure 5–7. In equilibrium when $r_M' = r_N' = \rho_K'$ and r_M and m_2 are constant, (5C.53) reduces to $\hat{\Delta K}' = \hat{\Delta K}'$.

An illustrative alternative path to BD is EF in Figure 5–7. An operation of considerable magnitude and low purchase yield creates a wealth gain at t_o, $EA > BA$. EF declines through most of its course owing to large increases in r_M and decreases in m_2. In equilibrium, wealth is below the immediate post-operation total. Other things equal, an operation of greater magnitude and lower yield will reach equilibrium at a later point in time; for EF, this is t_n''. However, EF coincides with BD at that point and beyond. This assumes that the greater magnitude of the purchase underlying EF is due only to a lower value of r_M'' and higher value of p'', S_B' being the same for both curves. If S_B' is greater for EF, then in equilibrium EF will fall below AC by a greater distance than does BD.

The point in time, t_n', for which the path, BD, reaches equilibrium is determined by the prevailing investment schedule, I'. However, suppose that an I schedule of greater absolute elasticity is combined with the S schedule for which $\partial S/\partial r_M = 0$. In Figure 5–8 we pair S' and I''. The resulting wealth path is labeled BD' in Figure 5–9, which reproduces the AC and BD paths of Figure 5–7. I'' accelerates the adjustment process, creating an equilibrium at t_n'''. I'' causes the interest rate to rise more, and idle balances to fall more in any interval. Since voluntary saving is constant, and forced saving in any case is zero, total wealth is reduced, and BD' lies below BD throughout the adjustment period. But in the equilibrium at t_n''', BD' is the same distance below AC, the undisturbed path, as is BD at t_n'. Given $\partial S/\partial r_M = 0$, L_2', and r_N', the difference between the disturbed and undisturbed paths in equilibrium will always be $S_B'p'$ ([5C.51]), since $n\hat{\Delta K}' = \sum_n \Delta K$ and $m_2^n = m_2'$ for any value of n. By the same reasoning, an investment schedule whose absolute elasticity is less than that of I' will create a path above and tangential to BD.

Let us relax the assumption that $\partial S/\partial r_M = 0$. The saving sched-

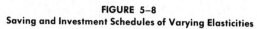

FIGURE 5–8
Saving and Investment Schedules of Varying Elasticities

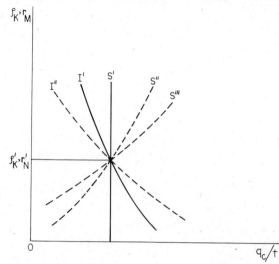

ule takes on the appearance of S'' in Figure 5–8. The investment schedule remains I'. ρ_K rises at the start of the adjustment process (Section 4). This raises the wealth curves at time t_O, but lowers their terminal points in relation to $\hat{W}^n$, even though ρ_K eventually returns to its original level. W^n is less, relative to trend, because the reduction in intended saving at the lower interest rates of the adjustment process lowers $\sum_n \Delta K$, the capital financed by voluntary saving (see 5C.50]). During the adjustment, wealth rises less, or falls more rapidly, to which the return of ρ_K to its original value contributes. An example of such a path is GH in Figure 5–9. The equilibrium is reached at t_n^4, earlier than t_n', since $\partial S / \partial r_M > 0$ speeds the adjustment. The rise in ρ_K will also raise p^n and p_a above the levels they would have otherwise attained.

It is difficult to generalize the effect of still greater elasticity in the saving schedule, I remaining fixed at I'. While the impact of moving from S', the vertical schedule, to S'' is clear, the effect of going to a still more elastic schedule, S''' (see Figure 5–8), is not. For as more elastic S schedules are considered, the speed of the adjustment increases further. The tendency to reduced voluntary saving is offset, more or less, by greater increments each period in the interest rate. The net effect on $\sum_n \Delta K$ and W^n may be plus or minus.

On the other hand, if S'' is combined with a more elastic investment schedule, I'', the resulting wealth path is represented in Figure 5–9 by IJ. Equilibrium is reached at t_n^5, earlier than t_n^4. At time, t_0, point I is below point G. This is because I'' cuts I' from below (see Figure 5–8), with the result that ρ_K and total wealth rise less at the start of the adjustment. But in equilibrium at t_n^5, the IJ path is closer to AC than is GH in its equilibrium at t_n^4. This is due to the greater speed of the adjustment, which raises the average level of the interest rate and thus the voluntary saving of any interval. In view of the absence of forced saving, the investment schedule influences final wealth only indirectly by determining the movement of the interest rate. Unless $\partial S/\partial r_M = 0$, the more elastic investment schedule thereby raises voluntary saving and the equilibrium wealth total. Given S'', the lowest possible wealth total is accordingly produced by the least elastic investment schedule, that for which $\partial I/\partial r_M = 0$.

FIGURE 5–9

Further Time Series of Total Wealth during Zero Forced Saving—Voluntary Saving Included

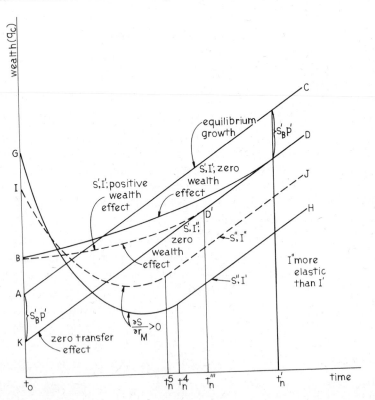

Suppose that the price level again contributes to the rise in the interest rate via the wealth effect. The impact of inflation is the same as in the absence of voluntary saving: the reduction in the value of idle balances and the increase in r_M are both greater in any interval, and equilibrium is reached at an earlier point in time. Since forced saving is nil, and $r'_M = r'_N$ and $m_2 = m'_2$ in equilibrium however it is reached, the influence of the wealth effect on W^n depends on the impact on voluntary saving. If $\partial S/\partial r_M = 0$, $\sum_n \Delta K$ is constant and W^n is the same relative to $\hat{W}^n$ as in the absence of the wealth effect. Thus a positive wealth effect would reduce the slope of a curve, such as BD in Figure 5–9, bringing it to an earlier equilibrium along a tangent drawn to its previous equilibrium point. In fact, the curve, BD', though based on a more elastic I schedule, represents equally well the impact of the wealth effect on the system whose saving and investment schedules are S' and I'. If $\partial S/\partial r_M > 0$, the wealth effect, by raising the average level of r_M and voluntary saving, will raise the terminal points of the wealth curves. In general, the introduction of the wealth effect alters W^n in a manner identical to that caused by a more elastic investment schedule. In the extreme case in which the wealth effect accomplishes the entire interest adjustment, wealth in Figure 5–9 moves at once from B to K, and thence along $KD'D$. The latter lies below AC by the distance, $S'_B p'$.

With fewer excess securities issued during the adjustment, the real security price again tends to be higher if the wealth effect is present (cf. Section 5). If the wealth effect is the only equilibrating mechanism, the adjustment requires an infinitesimal time interval, and p^n will be p', the same as it was under similar circumstances in abstraction from voluntary saving (see [5C.29]).

We conclude that total wealth in all cases is below that of the equilibrium-growth economy. The greatest wealth is produced by the system in which $\partial S/\partial r_M = 0$, since voluntary saving, the only source of increased wealth in the adjustment process, is maximized. Given a non-vertical saving schedule, wealth is minimized when $\partial I/\partial r_M = 0$.

D. COMPLETE FORCED SAVING

. Assumptions

We turn now to an adjustment process diametrically opposed to zero forced saving. In this portion of the chapter we view the adjustment as a series of sequential excess-security flotations, each fully realized in instantaneous increases in the stock of capital immediately following the transfer. This is the *complete* forced-saving adjustment. Sections 2–5 will ignore the equal saving and investment flows, considering only the impact of capital financed by excess securities. Since realized investment and saving now lie along the I rather than the S schedule, no special assumptions need be nor will be made regarding $\partial S/\partial r_M$. Section 6 will discuss alternative assumptions as to $\partial S/\partial r_M$ and $\partial I/\partial r_M$, which, until then, are > 0 and < 0, respectively, as in the general analysis. For the present, the wealth effect on interest is zero. The adjustment process, lasting n intervals, will thus continue until enough excess securities have been issued to reduce real idle balances to $m_2^n = m_2' = L_2'(r_N')$. The total value of the excess security issues will be $m_2'' - m_2'$, which is also the increase in the stock of capital; i.e., abstracting from voluntary saving,

(5D.1) $$K^n = K' + (m_2'' - m_2').$$

Since $m_2'' - m_2' = S_B' p''$ ([5B.22]), we can also write

(5D.2) $$K^n = K' + S_B' p''.$$

The analysis begins with the interval immediately following the open-market purchase, as described in Part B(3).

2. A Limiting First Interval

Our account of the initial adjustment interval, t_1, will stress the continuous character of the saving and investment functions. We emphasize the fact that S and I flow continuously over the minutes interval of time. In the event of complete forced saving, the first small interval following the purchase will thus provide a transfer that raises the rate of ex post investment to $I'(r_M''')$, where r_M''', the transfer yield, is only infinitesimally above r_M'', the purchase yield. But even while the impact on interest is small, and the quantity of money spent on capital goods equally slight, investment at the *rate* of flow of capital expenditures over time rises immediately. If we take the limiting case in which the movement in idle balances, securities, and interest is negligible, then investment will rise to

(5D.3) $$I'(r_M''') = I'(r_M''),$$

and the rate of return to capital will fall at once along the I

schedule from ρ_K' to

(5D.4)
$$\rho_K''' = r_M''' = r_M''.^8$$

Securities, idle balances, and the capital stock are unchanged:

(5D.5)
$$S_P'' = S_P', \quad m_2''' = m_2'', \quad K'' = K'.$$

But the reduction in ρ_K produces reduced values:

(5D.6)
$$\rho_s''' = \frac{\rho_K''' K''}{S_P''} = \frac{r_M'' K'}{S_P'},$$

(5D.7)
$$S_{VO}'''(\rho_K''') = S_P'' \left(\frac{\rho_s'''}{r_M}\right) = \left(\frac{\rho_K'''}{r_M}\right) K',$$

(5D.8)
$$W'''(\rho_K''') = S_{VO}'''(\rho_K''') + m_2'' = \left(\frac{\rho_K'''}{r_M}\right) K' + m_2''.$$

On the usual assumption that D_{VO} follows the movement of S_{VO},

(5D.9)
$$D_{VO}''' = D_{VO}'' + [S_{VO}''(\rho_K') - S_{VO}'''(\rho_K''')],$$

and the change in ρ_K has no effect on the interest rate, which remains r_M''. The price of securities falls accordingly to

(5D.10)
$$p''' = \frac{\rho_s'''}{r_M'''} = \frac{\rho_K''' K''}{r_M''' S_P''} = \frac{K'}{S_P'} = p'.$$

While the reduction in the rate of interest to r_M'' is accomplished initially by raising the price of securities, the lower yield is thus carried forward in the face of complete forced saving by an equal reduction in ρ_K, p on net remaining constant at p'.

The limiting first interval in which ρ_K falls to $\rho_K''' = r_M''$ is analytically convenient because it disposes of the entire tendency in ρ_K and total wealth to decline. Both ρ_K and wealth are at their minimum possible values. In all future periods ρ_K will rise in synchronization with r_M as the rate of investment, both intended and realized, slackens along the I schedule. While wealth will experience temporary declines as r_M rises, it will not fall below the level of the initial interval.

. A Second Interval

The impact of a subsequent and typical interval, t_2, is diagramed in Figure 5–10. The schedules with triple primes prevail at the

---

[8] Strictly speaking, ρ_K at this point should be identified by two rather than three primes, since it is only the second value taken on by that variable. However, we find it convenient to apply identical superscripts to ρ_K and r_M since, during complete forced saving, they tend to equality.

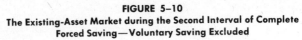

FIGURE 5–10
**The Existing-Asset Market during the Second Interval of Complete
Forced Saving—Voluntary Saving Excluded**

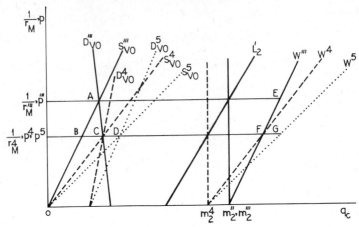

start of the interval, and reflect the fall in ρ_K in the instantaneous first interval. S_{VO}''', D_{VO}''', and W''' are to the left of S_{VO}'', D_{VO}'', and W'' (not in the diagram), respectively, but the interest rate is unchanged at $r_M''' = r_M''$. The quantity of securities is $S_P''' = S_P'$ and the price of securities is $p''' = p'$. The real stock of idle money is $m_2''' = m_2''$. The beginning security-market equilibrium is at point A, and total wealth is equal to the abscissa of point E. During the interval an excess supply of new securities lowers p to p^4 and raises r_M to

$$(5D.11) \qquad r_M^4 = \frac{\rho_s^4}{p^4} > r_M''', \text{ where } p^4 < p''' \text{ and } \rho_s^4 = \rho_s'''.$$

At the higher yield asset holders want

$$(5D.12) \qquad D_{VO}'''(r_M^4) - S_{VO}'''(r_M^4) = BC$$

in additional security value in exchange for idle balances of

$$(5D.13) \qquad m_2''' - L_2'(r_M^4) = m_2''' - m_2^4.$$

The resulting security-value function is

$$(5D.14) \qquad S_{VO}^4(\rho_K''') = S_P'''p = (S_P'' + \Delta S_E'')\left(\frac{\rho_s^4}{r_M}\right),$$

where $\Delta S_E''$ of excess new securities are all presumed to bear a return, ρ_s^4, equal to the pre-existing one, ρ_s'''. The equilibrium of the security market is at point C. A new wealth function,

$$(5D.15) \qquad W^4(\rho_K''') = S_{VO}^4(\rho_K''') + m_2^4,$$

represents a clockwise rotation through point F, whose ordinate is $1/r_M^4$; D_{VO} rotates equally through point C from D_{VO}''' to D_{VO}^4:

(5D.16) $\qquad D_{VO}^4 = D_{VO}''' + [W^4(\rho_K''') - W'''(\rho_K''')]$.

A moment later $m_2''' - m_2^4$ in real idle balances is converted into an equal number of capital units. This occurs at a somewhat reduced *rate* of investment, $I'(r_M^4)$, which is just sufficient to raise ρ_K to

(5D.17) $\qquad \rho_k^4 = r_M^4$.

The resulting stock of capital is

(5D.18) $\qquad K''' = K'' + \Delta K''$, where $K'' = K'$

and

(5D.19) $\qquad \Delta K'' = \Delta S_E'' p^4 = m_2''' - m_2^4$.

The increase in ρ_K and K raises ρ_s to

(5D.20) $\qquad \rho_s^5 = \dfrac{\rho_k^4 K'''}{S_P'''} > \rho_s^4$,

which is proved below. The increase in ρ_s raises the price of securities corresponding to any market rate of interest, and produces

(5D.21) $\qquad S_{VO}^5(\rho_k^4) = S_P''' \left(\dfrac{\rho_s^5}{r_M}\right) = \left(\dfrac{\rho_k^4}{r_M}\right) K''' > S_{VO}^4(\rho_K''')$.

But D_{VO} rotates equally with S_{VO} to

(5D.22) $\qquad D_{VO}^5 = D_{VO}^4 + [S_{VO}^5(\rho_k^4) - S_{VO}^4(\rho_K''')]$,

and the security-market equilibrium at the close of t_2, shown by point D, remains at r_M^4. The closing price is

(5D.23) $\qquad p^5 = \dfrac{\rho_s^5}{r_M^4} = \dfrac{K'''}{S_P'''}$,

and the wealth function is

(5D.24) $\qquad W^5(\rho_k^4) = S_{VO}^5(\rho_k^4) + m_2^4$.

The proof of $\rho_s^5 > \rho_s^4$ follows after substitution of the underlying quantities:

$$\frac{\rho_k^4 K'''}{S_P'''} > \frac{\rho_K''' K''}{S_P''},$$

$$\frac{\rho_k^4 (K'' + \Delta K'')}{S_P'' + \Delta S_E''} > \frac{\rho_K''' K''}{S_P''},$$

which, upon expansion and rearrangement is

$$\rho_K^4 K'' S_P'' > \rho_K''' K'' S_P'' + \rho_K''' K'' \Delta S_E'' - \rho_K^4 \Delta K'' S_P''.$$

For $\Delta K''$ we substitute $\Delta S_E'' p^4$ ([5D.19]), and for p^4, $\rho_K''' K'' / r_M^4 S_P''$. These substitutions convert the last term on the right side of the inequality to

$$\rho_K^4 \Delta S_E'' \left(\frac{\rho_K''' K''}{r_M^4 S_P''} \right) S_P'' = \rho_K''' K'' \Delta S_E''.$$

This expression cancels out against the second term on the right side of the inequality, which reduces to

$$\rho_K^4 K'' S_P'' > \rho_K''' K'' S_P'',$$

$$\rho_K^4 > \rho_K'''.$$

Since ρ_s increases as K and ρ_K rise, while the interest rate is constant, the final price, p^5, exceeds the transfer price, p^4. However, $p^5 < p'''$, the opening price of the interval. Upon substituting, $p^5 < p'''$ is

$$\frac{K'''}{S_P'''} < \frac{K''}{S_P''},$$

$$\frac{K'' + \Delta K''}{S_P'' + \Delta S_E''} < \frac{K''}{S_P''},$$

$$\frac{\Delta K''}{\Delta S_E''} < \frac{K''}{S_P''}.$$

From (5D.19), $\Delta K'' / \Delta S_E'' = p^4$; since $K'' / S_P'' = p'''$, the inequality is $p^4 < p'''$, which is a given fact. Intuitively, in going from $p''' = K'' / S_P''$ to p^5 we add to K'' and S_P'' increments whose ratio, $\Delta K'' / \Delta S_E''$, is $p^4 < K'' / S_P''$. Hence the resulting price is $p^5 < p'''$. During the interval the real security price thus falls, and then makes a *partial* recovery.

In Figure 5–10 total wealth at the close of the interval is shown at point G, which lies directly below point E, the total at the start of the interval. The proof of

(5D.25) $W^5(\rho_K^4, r_M^4) = W'''(\rho_K''', r_M''')$

follows upon substitution:

$$S_{VO}^5(\rho_K^4, r_M^4) + m_2^4 = S_{VO}'''(\rho_K''', r_M''') + m_2''',$$

$$\left(\frac{\rho_K^4}{r_M^4} \right) K''' + m_2^4 = \left(\frac{\rho_K'''}{r_M'''} \right) K'' + m_2''',$$

$$K''' - K'' = m_2''' - m_2^4,$$

$$\Delta K'' = \Delta K''.$$

The loss of real idle balances is matched by an equal increase in the stock of capital. The wealth loss from E to F, due to the increase in r_M, is removed by an equal increase in ρ_K as capital is created.

4. The Over-all Adjustment

Our account of the second interval applies to every succeeding interval of the adjustment process. Each period begins with equality between ρ_K and r_M, and a security price below the opening price of the preceding interval. As a new period unfolds, an excess supply of new securities lowers security prices further, raising the rate of interest and effecting a transfer of idle balances in exchange for the excess issues. In the next instant capital increases, ρ_K rises to the level of r_M, ρ_s and p rise, and households experience a net equality between the gain of security value and the loss of idle funds; total wealth is unchanged. Though p rises, it remains below its starting level. Since L_2 is fixed at L_2' and the wealth effect on interest is absent, the adjustment continues in this manner through a sequence of periods until

$$(5D.26) \qquad r_M' = r_N' = \rho_K', \qquad m_2^n = m_2',$$

and $m_2'' - m_2'$ has been converted into an equal number of capital units. The final values of S_P and K are

$$(5D.27) \quad S_P^n = S_P' + \sum_n \Delta S_E, \quad K^n = K' + (m_2'' - m_2') \, ([5D.1]),$$

where $\sum_n \Delta S_E$ is the total number of excess securities sold to asset holders. The real income per share is

$$(5D.28) \qquad \rho_s^n = \frac{\rho_K' K^n}{S_P^n} = \frac{\rho_K'[K' + (m_2'' - m_2')]}{S_P' + \sum_n \Delta S_E},$$

the value function of securities is

$$(5D.29) \qquad S_{VO}^n(\rho_K') = S_P^n\left(\frac{\rho_s^n}{r_M}\right) = \left(\frac{\rho_K'}{r_M}\right)K^n = \left(\frac{\rho_K'}{r_M}\right)[K' + (m_2'' - m_2')],$$

and total wealth is

$$(5D.30) \qquad W^n(\rho_K') = S_{VO}^n(\rho_K') + m_2^n = \left(\frac{\rho_K'}{r_M}\right)[K' + (m_2'' - m_2')] + m_2',$$

where all variables but the last, m_2', pertain to the stock of capital.

The demand for securities may be written

(5D.31)
$$D_{VO}^n = D_{VO}' + [W^n(\rho_K') - W'(\rho_K')] = D_{VO}' + [S_{VO}^n(\rho_K') - S_{VO}'(\rho_K')].$$

The real price of securities is

(5D.32)
$$p^n = \frac{\rho_s^n}{r_N'} = \frac{K' + (m_2'' - m_2')}{S_P' + \sum_n \Delta S_E} < p'.$$

Since $p^n < p' = \rho_s'/r_N'$, $\rho_s^n < \rho_s'$. Thus, while ρ_s rises each period following its drop to ρ_s''' during t_1, it fails to recover its pre-disturbance value.

Figure 5–11 describes the course of wealth from the initial disturbance to the close of the adjustment process. Single and double-primed schedules prevail immediately before and after the purchase, respectively (except for L_2', which is invariant); those with

FIGURE 5–11
The Existing-Asset Market during the Complete Forced-Saving Adjustment—
Voluntary Saving Excluded

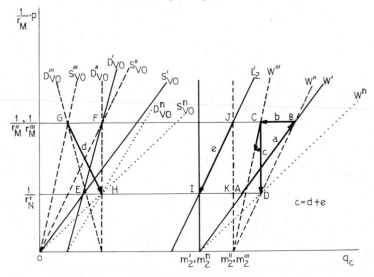

triple primes prevail after the limiting first interval; and those with the superscript, n, in the new equilibrium. The pre-disturbance wealth total is at point A on W'. The corresponding points of equilibrium in the asset markets are E in securities and I in idle balances. The initial movement in wealth is the increase along W' from A to B when the bank bids security prices from p' to p''. The path is labeled a. Following the purchase, the equilibrium of the security market is at point F, and that of the market for idle balances at point J. The purchase rotates wealth to W'', and D_{VO} to D_{VO}''. The next wealth change occurs when ρ_K drops to ρ_K''' following the initial dosage of forced saving during t_1. This entails infinitesimal changes in m_2 and S_P. Hence the resulting wealth function, W''', is produced by a counterclockwise rotation through the point, $m_2''' = m_2''$, on the horizontal axis. Underlying the wealth change is the rotation in S_{VO} from S_{VO}'' to S_{VO}''', in response to which D_{VO} moves equally to D_{VO}'''. The interest rate is assumed to change infinitesimally as a result of the initial transfer. Thus the security-market equilibrium is at point G, and the wealth movement is a horizontal vector, b, connecting the points

$$B = W''(\rho_K', r_M'') \text{ and } C = W'''(\rho_K''', r_M''').$$

In spite of the decline from p'' to $p''' = p'$ as ρ_K falls, wealth at point C remains greater than at A, the pre-operation total. The horizontal distance between C and A is

$$W'''(\rho_K''', r_M''') - W'(\rho_K', r_N'),$$

or, upon evaluating (5D.8) at r_M''' and subtracting (5B.13):

(5D.33) $\quad (m_2'' - m_2') - S_G'p' = S_B'p'' - S_B'p' = S_B'(p'' - p') > 0 .$[9]

During the remainder of the adjustment process, let us value

---

[9]Notice in Figure 5-11 that W^n originates on the horizontal axis at $m_2^n = m_2'$. Thus at $1/r_M = 0$, $W^n = W'$. Relative to W'', W^n has evolved by clockwise rotations (a) through the reciprocal of each transfer yield, as idle balances are given up for securities, and (b) through the intersection point of W and the horizontal axis, as ρ_K and K increase. W^n intersects W'' at point D:

$$W^n(\rho_K', r_N') = W''(\rho_K', r_N')$$
$$S_{VO}^n(\rho_K', r_N') + m_2^n = S_{VQ}''(\rho_K', r_N') + m_2''$$
$$K^n + m_2' = K' + m_2''$$
$$K' + (m_2'' - m_2') + m_2' = K' + m_2''$$
$$K' + m_2'' = K' + m_2'' .$$

D_{VO} follows exactly the movements in W. Thus D_{VO}^n, which meets S_{VO}^n at $1/r_N$, has evolved from D_{VO}'' by the same rotations experienced by W. Since $W^n(r_N') = W''(r_N')$, $D_{VO}^n(r_N') = D_{VO}''(r_N')$. Also, at $1/r_M = 0$, $D_{VO}^n = D_{VO}'$.

Another interesting feature of the diagram is the location of S_{VO}^n relative to S_{VO}'. S_{VO}^n is not only to the right of S_{VO}'', but S_{VO}' as well:

$$S_{VO}^n(\rho_K', r_N') > S_{VO}'(\rho_K', r_N')$$
$$K^n > K' + S_G'p'$$
$$K' + (m_2'' - m_2') > K' + S_G'p'$$
$$S_B'p'' > S_B'p'$$
$$p'' > p' .$$

wealth at the level reached after each transfer, incorporating the impact of the associated increase in K and ρ_K due to forced saving. The locus of wealth so defined is constant. Its path is described by the vertical vector, c, connecting points C and D, where D is at $W''(\rho_K', r_N')$. c is simply an extension of the path in Figure 5-10 between points E and G. The proof to (5D.25) established that in the latter diagram G is directly below E. Since the events of Figure 5-10 are typical of every forced-saving interval, following the limiting first period, we draw a fixed locus of end-of-interval wealth totals leading to the final equilibrium. Underlying the total-wealth movement along c is the locus of total security value, d, and the vector tracing the value of idle balances, e:

$$(5D.34) \qquad\qquad c = d + e.$$

d indicates the value of securities, in the sense of points on constantly rotating S_{VO} functions. d connects point G, created during t_1, with H, the intersection of S_{VO}^n and D_{VO}^n. The e vector connects J at $L_2'(r_M''')$ with I at $L_2'(r_N')$.

While c represents the course of wealth following each round of forced saving, the initial impact of any transfer is to reduce wealth. Like an open-market sale, the flow of excess new securities creates capital losses as it raises the rate of interest by lowering security prices. In Figure 5-10 the initial movement in wealth is downward along W''' from E to F. The corresponding movement in Figure 5-11 is the solid-line downward path along W''' from point C. But when capital increases and ρ_K rises to the interest level, wealth moves horizontally at the height of the transfer yield. This is the movement from F to G in Figure 5-10, and along the horizontal vector in Figure 5-11 connecting W''' with c. The actual path of wealth during the adjustment process is thus saw-toothed, moving down along positively sloping, rotating wealth functions during the transfers, and then veering horizontally rightward to an intersection with the vector, c, as ρ_K rises and capital is created.

Since C, the initial point on the vector, c, in Figure 5-11, is to the right of A, it is clear that every point on c, including its terminus, D, is also to the right of A. In fact, since c is vertical, AD is equal to (5D.33):

$$(5D.35) \qquad W''(\rho_K', r_N') - W'(\rho_K', r_N') = S_B'(p'' - p') > 0 .$$

5. A Positive Wealth Effect

Suppose that the price level creates an upward wealth effect on interest. Following any transfer, the resulting inflation creates equal parallel leftward shifts in m_2, W, and D_{VO}, the latter being the direct cause of the increase in r_M. In Figure 5–11 wealth at the close of any interval falls to the left of the vector, c. In the limiting case in which M_2/M is so great that the wealth effect accomplishes the entire interest adjustment following an infinitesimal transfer, there are no additional securities or capital to match the loss of idle balances;

$$(5D.36) \qquad W''(\rho_K', r_N') = S_{VO}''(\rho_K', r_N') + m_2' = K' + m_2',$$

which is exactly equal to total wealth following a zero forced-saving adjustment (cf. [5C.19]). In Figure 5–11 wealth is at point K, which is to the left of point A by (5B.13) − (5D.36) or:

$$(5D.37) \qquad W'(\rho_K', r_N') - W''(\rho_K', r_N') = S_G' p' \text{ (cf. [5C.22])}.$$

For the general case in which the wealth effect produces less than the entire interest movement, the final wealth total will lie between K and D on either side of A. Thus the wealth effect does not necessarily prevent W'' from exceeding W'. The wealth effect will, of course, reduce the time required to reach equilibrium.

The wealth effect tends to raise the average real security price, as it did during zero forced saving, though in the present case the reason is entirely different. In complete forced saving, ρ_s and p increase following the interest movement, whether caused by the transfer or wealth effect, but the increase is greater following the wealth effect. After the transfer of the second interval, ρ_s rose from

$$\rho_s^4 = \frac{\rho_K''' K''}{S_P''} \text{ to } \rho_s^5 = \frac{\rho_K^4 K'''}{S_P'''}.$$

But if the same interest movement had been accomplished by the wealth effect, we would observe at the close of the interval

$$(5D.38) \qquad \rho_s^5 = \frac{\rho_K^4 K''}{S_P''},$$

where K and S_P are now constant, and the increase from ρ_s^4 to ρ_s^5 is due wholly to the rise in ρ_K. The latter movement results from a slackening of the investment pace as the inflation raises r_M. We assume that the reduction in investment occurs instantaneously without discernible changes in the quantity of securities or capital. Comparing ρ_s^5, following the wealth and transfer effect, respectively, we have (5D.20) < (5D.38):

$$\frac{\rho_K^4 K'''}{S_P'''} < \frac{\rho_K^4 K''}{S_P''},$$

$$p^5 < p'''.$$

The last inequality, which is obtained by cancelling ρ_K^4, has already been proved. Thus the closing values of ρ_s and p are higher if a given interest rise has been accomplished by the wealth rather than the transfer effect. We can show further that while the rise in ρ_s after a transfer leaves $p^5 < p'''$, after the wealth effect it produces $p^5 = p'''$. Upon substituting for p^5, as produced by the wealth effect, and p''', respectively:

$$\frac{\rho_K^4 K''}{r_M^4 S_P''} = \frac{\rho_K''' K''}{r_M''' S_P''},$$

$$\frac{K''}{S_P''} = \frac{K''}{S_P''}.$$

We conclude that ρ_s and p are both higher following a given interest movement due to the wealth effect than to the transfer effect, and that the fall in p due to the inflation is completely offset by the subsequent rise in ρ_K.[10] In the limiting case in which a single application of the wealth effect creates the entire interest adjustment, the inflation lowers security prices from p''' to

(5D.39) $$p^4 = \frac{\rho_s^4}{r_N'} = \frac{\rho_K''' K''}{r_N' S_P''},$$

after which the increase in ρ_K to $\rho_K' = r_N'$ raises p to

(5D.40) $$p^n = \frac{\rho_K' K''}{r_N' S_P''} = p''' = p',$$

the price at which the adjustment process effectively begins.

6. The Total Growth Process

We shall now add the equal saving and investment flows to the excess investment described in Sections 2–5. We revert to the assumption of a zero wealth effect on interest, the adjustment consisting entirely of excess security issues followed immediately by equal increases in the stock of capital. A positive wealth effect will be considered later, along with alternative assumptions as to $\partial S/\partial r_M$ and $\partial I/\partial r_M$.

a) The First and Second Intervals

The limiting first interval described in Section 2 is applicable in the present context. The first infinitesimal sale of securities both to

---

[10]The loss of wealth in any interval on account of the inflation is thus limited to the reduction in the value of idle balances. The wealth loss due to the increase in r_M is offset by the induced increase in ρ_K, p on net remaining constant.

existing-asset holders and current savers raises the rate of ex post investment to $I'(r_M''')$, where $r_M''' = r_M''$, and the resulting return to investment is $\rho_K''' = r_M'''$. As indicated in Section 2, ρ_s, S_{VO}, D_{VO}, and p fall immediately to ρ_s''', $S_{VO}'''(\rho_K''')$, D_{VO}''', and $p''' = p'$, respectively. Total wealth is $W'''(\rho_K''')$.

The second interval proceeds as described in Section 3, except that at p^4 and r_M^4, the transfer price and yield, we add to S_{VO}^4 the value of securities purchased by savers. This produces an S_{VO} function,

$$(5D.41) \qquad S_{VO}^5(\rho_K''') = S_P'''p = (S_P'' + \Delta S_E'' + \Delta S_S'')\left(\frac{\rho_s^4}{r_M}\right),$$

where $\Delta S_S''$ is the quantity of securities acquired by savers, and $\rho_s^4 = \rho_s'''$. In Figure 5–10, S_{VO}^5, so defined, would lie to the right of S_{VO}^4 by the amount of voluntary saving. Though the schedule labeled S_{VO}^5 in that diagram is in fact due to the subsequent increase in ρ_s, it can be used equally well to represent $S_{VO}^5(\rho_K''')$, our present function. However, the distance from C to D now equals voluntary saving, which may be any amount. The corresponding wealth function is

$$(5D.42) \qquad W^5(\rho_K''') = S_{VO}^5(\rho_K''') + m_2^4,$$

and D_{VO} is

$$(5D.43) \qquad D_{VO}^5 = D_{VO}^4 + [S_{VO}^5(\rho_K''') - S_{VO}^4(\rho_K''')],$$

as drawn. At the close of the interval the stock of capital rises to

$$(5D.44) \qquad K''' = K'' + \Delta K'',$$

where $\Delta K''$ is now

$$(5D.45) \qquad \Delta K'' = (\Delta S_E'' + \Delta S_S'')p^4.$$

In the same instant, ρ_K increases to $\rho_K^4 = r_M^4$. Once again we can show that the resulting security income is

$$(5D.46) \qquad \rho_s^5 = \frac{\rho_K^4 K'''}{S_P'''} > \rho_s^4.$$

The final security-value schedule of the interval is

$$(5D.47) \qquad S_{VO}^6(\rho_K^4) = S_P'''\left(\frac{\rho_s^5}{r_M}\right) = \left(\frac{\rho_K^4}{r_M}\right)K''' > S_{VO}^5(\rho_K''').$$

Closing total wealth is

$$(5D.48) \qquad W^6(\rho_K^4) = S_{VO}^6(\rho_K^4) + m_2^4,$$

and D_{VO}, following the movements of S_{VO} and W, is

(5D.49) $$D_{VO}^6 = D_{VO}^5 + [S_{VO}^6(\rho_K^4) - S_{VO}^5(\rho_K''')].$$

The interest rate remains r_M^4.

The proof of $\rho_s^5 > \rho_s^4$ on pages 153 and 154 is applicable to the growing economy if in ρ_s^5, $\Delta S_S''$ is added to the denominator, and after analogous transpositions, (5D.45) is substituted for $\Delta K''$. The inequality will again reduce to $\rho_K^4 > \rho_K'''$.

While ρ_s rises following complete forced saving, we can show that it rises *less* than it did in abstraction from voluntary saving. We wish to prove

$$\frac{\rho_K^4(K'' + \Delta S_E'' p^4 + \Delta S_S'' p^4)}{S_P'' + \Delta S_E'' + \Delta S_S''} < \frac{\rho_K^4(K'' + \Delta S_E'' p^4)}{S_P'' + \Delta S_E''},$$

where the left side of the inequality is ρ_s^5 in the present context ([5D.46]), and the right side is ρ_s^5 when voluntary saving was excluded ([5D.20]). Expansion and rearrangement yield

$$p^4 < \frac{K''}{S_P''},$$

$$p^4 < p'''.$$

Hence p rises to $p^5 = \rho_s^5/r_M^4 > p^4 = \rho_s^4/r_M^4$, as earlier, but the extent of the increase is reduced. The proof of $p^5 < p'''$ on page 154 is thereby strengthened.[11]

Since the transfer alone maintains total wealth constant, the addition of any voluntary saving during t_2 causes a net increase in wealth. More formally,

(5D.50) $$W^6(\rho_K^4, r_M^4) > W'''(\rho_K''', r_M'''),$$

which is

$$S_{VO}^6(\rho_K^4, r_M^4) + m_2^4 > S_{VO}'''(\rho_K''', r_M''') + m_2''',$$

$$K''' - K'' > m_2''' - m_2^4,$$

$$(\Delta S_E'' + \Delta S_S'') p^4 > \Delta S_E'' p^4,$$

$$\Delta S_S'' p^4 > 0.$$

---

[11]The same intuitive reasoning in abstraction from voluntary saving is applicable to the present case. The addition of voluntary saving simply means that the increments added to $p''' = K''/S_P''$ are greater than otherwise. The ratio of the increments is still $p^4 < p'''$, but now their increased magnitude enables them to depress p^5 to a greater extent.

b) The Over-all Adjustment

In any future interval of the adjustment process the events of the second interval are repeated. Initially p falls and r_M rises; at the close of the interval voluntary and forced saving together create a net wealth increment equal to the voluntary component. ρ_s and p rise, but p remains below its opening value. Equilibrium is reached when $r'_M = r'_N = \rho'_K$. The total quantity of privately held securities is

$$(5D.51) \qquad S^n_P = S'_P + \sum_n \Delta S_E + \sum_n \Delta S_S,$$

where $\sum_n \Delta S_S$ is the total number purchased by savers during the adjustment process. The stock of capital is

$$(5D.52) \qquad K^n = K' + \sum_n \Delta K + (m''_2 - m'_2),$$

where $\sum_n \Delta K$ is financed by voluntary saving. The income per share is

$$(5D.53) \qquad \rho^n_s = \frac{\rho'_K K^n}{S^n_P} = \frac{\rho'_K [K' + \sum_n \Delta K + (m''_2 - m'_2)]}{S'_P + \sum_n \Delta S_E + \sum_n \Delta S_S},$$

the value of securities is

$$(5D.54)$$
$$S^n_{VO}(\rho'_K) = S^n_P \left(\frac{\rho^n_s}{r_M}\right) = \left(\frac{\rho'_K}{r_M}\right) K^n = \left(\frac{\rho'_K}{r_M}\right)[K' + \sum_n \Delta K + (m''_2 - m'_2)],$$

and the wealth function is

$$(5D.55)$$
$$W^n(\rho'_K) = S^n_{VO}(\rho'_K) + m^n_2 = \left(\frac{\rho'_K}{r_M}\right)[K' + \sum_n \Delta K + (m''_2 - m'_2)] + m'_2,$$

where every variable but the last, m'_2, applies to the capital stock. An expression for security demand is

$$(5D.56)$$
$$D^n_{VO} = D'_{VO} + [W^n(\rho'_K) - W'(\rho'_K)] = D'_{VO} + [S^n_{VO}(\rho'_K) - S'_{VO}(\rho'_K)].$$

The price of securities is

$$(5D.57) \qquad p^n = \frac{\rho^n_s}{r'_N} = \frac{K' + \sum_n \Delta K + (m''_2 - m'_2)}{S'_P + \sum_n \Delta S_E + \sum_n \Delta S_S} < p'.$$

Once again, since $p^n < p'$, $\rho^n_s < \rho'_s$.

Time series of total household wealth are plotted in Figure 5–12. Points A, B, and C correspond to the points of the same designation in Figure 5–11. Point C is the wealth total produced by the drop in ρ_K to $\rho_K''' = r_M'''$ during the limiting first interval. Point C lies above A by $S_B'(p'' - p')$ ([5D.33]). AD is the wealth line of an undisturbed economy growing at the uniform rate, $\hat{\Delta} K'$. The difference between total wealth of the disturbed and undisturbed systems in the new equilibrium is

$$W''(\rho_K', r_N') - \hat{W}''(\rho_K', r_N').$$

This is (5D.55) evaluated at r_N', less (5B.20):

$$(5D.58) \qquad \left(\sum_n \Delta K - n\hat{\Delta} K' \right) + (m_2'' - m_2') - S_G' p'.$$

The first parenthetical term is the difference between the growth of capital financed by voluntary saving in the two systems. The second parenthetical term is the additional capital due to forced saving in the disturbed economy.

Suppose that $\partial S / \partial r_M = 0$. In this event $\sum_n \Delta K = n\hat{\Delta} K'$ and (5D.58) reduces to

$$(5D.59) \quad (m_2'' - m_2') - S_G' p' = S_B' p'' - S_B' p' = S_B'(p'' - p'),$$

FIGURE 5–12

Time Series of Total Wealth during the Complete Forced-Saving Adjustment—Voluntary Saving Included

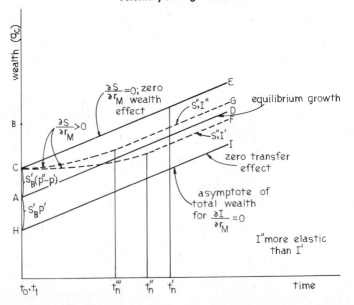

which is exactly the difference between wealth of the two systems at t_1 ([5D.33]). The wealth line produced on this assumption is CE, which lies above AD in the equilibrium at t'_n by the same distance that separates the lines at t_1. But CE is in fact parallel to AD at all points. We have seen that the adjustment itself maintains total wealth constant; the loss of idle balances is offset by an equal increase in capital, and the increase in r_M by an equal increase in ρ_K. Thus the slope of the wealth line is equal to the rate of voluntary saving. When $\partial S/\partial r_M = 0$, the growth of wealth is $\Delta K' = \widehat{\Delta K}'$ in every interval. However, while the difference between CE and AD is constant, at t_1 it is due to an excess of $m''_2 - m'_1$ in *idle balances*, while at t'_n it represents an excess of $m''_2 - m'_2$ in units of the *capital stock* of the disturbed over the undisturbed economy. In each case $m''_2 - m'_2 = S'_G p''$ more than compensates for the loss of $S'_G p'$ in government securities sold to the central bank.

The equilibrium on CE at time, t'_n, is determined by the prevailing investment schedule, I'. But equilibrium wealth would lie on CE to the left or right of t'_n for an investment function of greater or less absolute elasticity, respectively. For any investment schedule, $\partial S/\partial r_M = 0$, and a zero wealth effect on interest, (5D.59) is the net increase in wealth as a result of the disturbance, since $\sum_n \Delta K = n\widehat{\Delta K}'$ and $m''_2 - m'_2$ is total forced saving for any value of n. CE, moreover, represents the upper bound of wealth for all systems, since voluntary saving, which is the only variable component, is maximized.

A saving schedule such as S'' in Figure 5–8, for which $\partial S/\partial r_M > 0$, reduces $\sum_n \Delta K$ in (5D.55) and (5D.58), the other terms remaining constant. The wealth line resulting from S'' and I' is labeled CF in Figure 5–12. In equilibrium, which occurs earlier than t'_n at t''_n, wealth lies below the CE line because of the reduction in voluntary saving. Forced saving, equal to $m''_2 - m'_2$, is, of course, unaffected. The equilibrium wealth total is also below AD, though this depends on the degree of interest elasticity of S'', and might not be true of another non-vertical saving schedule. The conditions underlying

$$W^n - \widehat{W}^n < 0$$

are, upon adding < 0 to (5D.58), transposing terms, and substituting $S'_B p''$ for $m''_2 - m'_2$,

(5D.60) $$S'_B p'' - S'_B p' < n\widehat{\Delta K}' - \sum_n \Delta K.$$

The left side of the inequality is the excess of capital due to forced saving, $S'_B p''$, over the value of securities sold to the central bank, $S'_B p'$. The right side is the absolute reduction in the capital stock due to $\partial S / \partial r_M > 0$.

Combining I' with still more elastic saving schedules, such as S''', creates still earlier equilibrium points. But the impact on the wealth path, including the terminal point, can be in either direction. The tendency to reduced voluntary saving is counterbalanced by greater increments each period in the interest rate. Only if the more elastic S schedules are combined with less elastic I schedules, $I - S$ remaining constant, will greater elasticity in S lower wealth unambiguously at every point in time, including the equilibrium.

If we take the non-vertical S schedule, such as S'', as given, and combine it with a more elastic I schedule, such as I'', the adjustment again is accelerated. Wealth is increased, since the accelerated rise of the interest rate increases voluntary saving. The wealth line produced by S'' and I'' is labeled CG in Figure 5–12. It lies above CF, reaching equilibrium at an earlier point, t'''_n. CG also lies above AD. This assumes that the elasticity of I'', and thus the magnitude of $\sum_n \Delta K$, is great enough for the left side of (5D.60) to exceed the right. As S'' is combined with increasingly *in*elastic I schedules, the wealth lines accordingly drop. The limiting case occurs when $\partial I / \partial r_M = 0$. *Total* capital accumulation, including forced saving, is the same as in equilibrium growth or zero forced saving and $\partial S / \partial r_M = 0$:

$$(5D.61) \qquad \sum_n \Delta K + (m''_2 - m'_2) = n \hat{\Delta K}',$$

and (5D.58) collapses to $-S'_G p'$. In equilibrium the wealth curve would thus be tangent to HI, which lies below AD in Figure 5–12 by $S'_B p'$. These conclusions regarding the vertical I schedule hold for any saving schedule, changes in the latter merely altering the point along HI at which equilibrium is reached.

We can show that HI, to which the wealth curves are tangent when $\partial I / \partial r_M = 0$, constitutes a lower bound to wealth of the complete forced-saving adjustment. For this purpose we view W'' as determined solely by capital accumulation owing to the movement along the I schedule from r''_M to r'_N. We ignore the breakdown between voluntary and forced saving; the changes in r_M and ρ_K, which are only temporary; and the value of idle balances, which is

m_2' in any equilibrium. From this perspective the lowest level of wealth for any value of n will be generated by the investment schedule having the minimum average distance from the vertical axis. Given the equilibrium rate of growth at r_N', $\Delta \hat{K}'$, the investment schedule least productive of wealth is thus the vertical one. We have already seen that CE, corresponding to $\partial S/\partial r_M = 0$, is the upper bound of wealth for any I schedule.

A positive wealth effect reduces the extent to which idle balances are converted into physical capital; the inflation simply causes an uncompensated loss in the value of idle money. The adjustment process also proceeds more rapidly. If $\partial S/\partial r_M = 0$, the slope of the wealth line is reduced. Since the excess of W^n over $\hat{W}^n$ depends on forced saving, any reduction in the latter may create $W^n \lesseqgtr \hat{W}^n$. If $\partial S/\partial r_M > 0$, the decrease in forced saving is accompanied by an increase in voluntary saving owing to the faster movement of the interest rate. The net effect on wealth may be plus or minus. In the limiting case in which only the wealth effect is operative, wealth falls immediately from C to H on the vertical axis of Figure 5–12, where AH is $S_B'p'$ (cf. [5D.37]). Wealth then proceeds along HI at the equilibrium rate, $\Delta \hat{K}'$, but the wealth total remains permanently below the undisturbed amount by $S_B'p'$.[12] The wealth effect again tends to leave the real security price unchanged; the reduction in p, by which r_M is raised, is followed by an equal increase as ρ_K rises to the level of r_M.

E. ALTERNATIVE ASSUMPTIONS

1. Partial Forced Saving

If entrepreneurs succeed in converting only a portion of transferred idle balances into capital, realized investment will lie between the S and I schedules. This is the case of *partial forced saving*. Since realized investment falls short of the intended amount at each rate of interest, the adjustment process is characterized by $\rho_K > r_M$, or $\rho_K/r_M > 1$, as in the case of zero forced saving. In fact, the latter adjustment, as developed for the growing economy in Part C(6), may be viewed as a general analysis of which partial forced saving—also for the growing economy—is a special case.

---

[12]This is the same result that occurred in zero forced saving when the wealth effect accomplished the entire adjustment (see p. 149), or when the transfer effect was the only equilibrating force and $\partial S/\partial r_M = 0$ (see [5C.51]).

The only qualification is that while $\rho_K/r_M > 1$, it will tend to be less than under zero forced saving. Moreover, ΔK, realized investment of any interval, is greater than voluntary saving, and may even exceed $\Delta \hat{K}'$, the rate of voluntary saving when $\partial S/\partial r_M = 0$. However, there are still some excess securities that water the stock, though the quantity is now less than the total number of excess issues, ΔS_E. (5C.33) is rewritten,

(5E.1) $\Delta K' = \Delta S'_S p''' + \alpha \Delta S'_E p'''$, where $0 < \alpha < 1$.

Clearly these are not serious qualifications in the expressions of the typical first interval for ρ_s^4, S_{VO}^5, W^5, and p^4. The tendency of ρ_s, S_{VO}, W, and p either to rise or fall during the interval still holds. Insofar as partial forced saving raises the effective amount of ΔK in these formulas, while reducing the effective quantity of ΔS_E, the variables, ρ_s, S_{VO}, W, and p will fall less or rise more than otherwise. Insofar as partial forced saving reduces the general level of ρ_K/r_M, the variables will tend to fall more or rise less. But if the rate of partial forced saving falls as r_M increases, ρ_K and ρ_K/r_M will tend to rise at the close of each interval, providing a direct stimulus to increased ρ_s, S_{VO}, W, and p.[13]   Interpreting W^n in (5C.47) as equilibrium wealth in the case of partial forced saving of the growing economy, it cannot fail to be greater than previously, since $\sum_n \Delta K$ now represents the sum of both voluntary and partial forced saving. In fact, where formerly, $W^n < \hat{W}^n$, we now have $W^n \gtreqless \hat{W}^n$. Substituting (5C.47), evaluated at r'_N, and (5B.20), the latter inequality reduces to

(5E.2) $\sum_n \Delta K \gtreqless n\Delta \hat{K}' + S'_G p'$.

Thus $W^n > \hat{W}^n$ requires that $\sum_n \Delta K$ incorporate a degree of forced saving that more than compensates for (*a*) the loss of $S'_G p'$ to the central bank, plus (*b*) any tendency of voluntary saving to fall below $n\Delta \hat{K}'$ due to $\partial S/\partial r_M > 0$. As partial converges to complete forced saving, $W^n - \hat{W}^n$ approaches a maximum value, $S'_B(p'' - p')$ ([5D.35]).

The expressions for ρ_s, S_{VO}, W, and p given in Part C(6) may also be used to describe partial forced saving in *abstraction* from

---

[13]The actual movement of ρ_K depends, of course, on total realized saving, which is the sum of voluntary and partial forced saving. ρ_K will rise, fall, or remain constant during the typical adjustment interval when total ex post saving falls along a downward-sloping, vertical, or upward-sloping path, respectively.

voluntary saving. The only necessary adjustments to the formulas are to remove the security quantities going to savers, and to allow for a possible upward or downward movement in ρ_K. We must also specify that for the typical first interval,

(5E.3) $\qquad\qquad \Delta K' = \omega \Delta S'_E p''', \quad \text{where} \quad 0 < \omega < 1 .$

For the over-all adjustment,

(5E.4) $\qquad\qquad \sum_n \Delta K = \omega_a \sum_n \Delta S_E p_a ,$

where ω_a is the average of ω over n intervals. Once again the changes do not alter the tendency of ρ_s, S_{VO}, W, and p either to rise or fall during any interval. Consider the movement of ρ_s in the first interval. Taking ρ_K to be constant at ρ'_K, ρ_s rises if the left side of (5C.35) is greater than the right. With $\Delta S'_S$ now absent, (5C.35) reduces to

$$\frac{\Delta K'}{\Delta S'_E} \gtreqless \frac{K'}{S'_P} ,$$

where $\Delta K'$ represents partial forced saving ([5E.3]). The inequality,

$$\frac{\Delta K'}{\Delta S'_E} > \frac{K'}{S'_P} ,$$

is satisfied if

$$\omega p''' > \frac{K'}{S'_P} ,$$

or, upon substituting for p''',

$$\omega \left(\frac{\rho'_K}{r'''_M}\right) \frac{K'}{S'_P} > \frac{K'}{S'_P} ,$$

$$\omega > \frac{r'''_M}{\rho'_K} .$$

Any tendency of ρ_K to rise or fall as partial forced saving proceeds, would, of course, raise or lower ρ_s proportionately. With r_M constant at r'''_M, p follows the movement of ρ_s. (5C.41) expresses the relation between beginning and ending wealth of the interval. Even though $\Delta K'$ now represents partial forced saving only, and is less than $m''_2 - m'''_2$, there is some level of $\Delta K'$ for which the left side of (5C.41) exceeds the right. This is because $\Delta K'$ on the left is multiplied by $\rho'_K / r'''_M > 1$, while $m''_2 - m'''_2$ on the right is not. This is paradoxical—while wealth in abstraction from voluntary saving falls during zero forced saving, and is constant or decreasing for complete forced saving, it may *rise* during partial forced saving. The key to the paradox is the presence in (5C.41) of $\Delta K > 0$ and $\rho_K / r_M > 1$. For zero forced saving, $\Delta K = 0$; for complete forced saving, $\rho_K / r_M = 1$. However, the wealth gain in partial forced saving due to $\rho_K / r_M > 1$ is only temporary. In equilibrium, $\rho_K / r_M = 1$ and only $\sum_n \Delta K < (m_2'' - m_2')$ remains in W^n in (5C.47).[14] Thus, while W^n will be higher for partial than zero forced saving, it will be less than final wealth of complete forced saving.

The empirical question of the likely degree of forced saving is, of course, outside the scope of this volume. However, one may speculate *a priori* that forced saving will vary directly with the ratio of the increment in investment expenditures to that of consumption. Since the slopes of the I and S schedules represent the respective incremental expenditures, the schedule whose absolute slope is greatest would dominate the movement of resources. However, even if entrepreneurs fail completely to increase the rate of growth, forced saving is not necessarily zero. For if their failure is due to all-around resource immobility, then at the least, the pre-disturbance growth will be maintained. Meanwhile, if desired saving falls, as reflected in $\partial S / \partial r_M > 0$, there will be an immediate rate of forced saving equal to the pre-disturbance growth rate less the reduced rate of voluntary saving. In Figure 5–4(b) at r_M'', forced saving under these assumptions would proceed at the rate, BA.

On purely *a priori* grounds, it is tempting to conclude that the general empirical case is partial forced saving representing some increase in the pre-disturbance growth rate of capital. As such, the account of zero forced saving in the growing economy is the general analysis, as modified in the preceding pages. Complete forced saving represents an ideal limiting case of the expansionary adjustment which the economy may on occasion approach.

2. Lagged Investment

Suppose that entrepreneurs do not immediately spend idle balances transferred to them. A time period customarily elapses before the funds are released. The price level tends to rise more slowly, though its total increase is ultimately the same. Such

---

[14]However, the influence of $\rho_K / r_M > 1$ on ρ_s and p is permanent. This is because $\rho_K / r_M > 1$ determines the ratio of the increments, $\Delta K'$ and $\Delta S_E'$, that are added to and *retained* in the numerator and denominator of ρ_s (cf. p. 100).

lagged investment spending has several consequences: (1) The total reduction in m_2 on account of the transfers is increased, while the reduction in m_2 due to the inflation is decreased. This is because the sooner an equilibrating mechanism operates, the greater is its net impact on m_2 (see the appendix to Chapter IV). The longer the inflation is delayed, the greater will be the real balances acquired by entrepreneurs, and the possible degree of forced saving. (2) Security prices are more likely to fall during the adjustment. This is because the investment delay does not prevent the interest rate from rising via the continuing transfers. The expenditure of any period will therefore exceed the amount justified by the prevailing rate of interest. For a sufficient degree of forced saving, ρ_K will be driven below r_M, creating $\rho_K/r_M < 1$. By analogy to the argument on pages 139–40, this will tend to reduce security prices. (3) If the lag is not the same for all entrepreneurs, then clearly those for whom it is less than average will face a lower price level than otherwise, and enjoy a greater real expenditure at the expense of others.

3. Investment Errors

Throughout this volume we have assumed that entrepreneurs correctly anticipate the real return on each level of investment. At any interest rate the funds raised through security flotations are assumed to be the amount exactly required to equate ρ_K and r_M (cf. Chapter II-C[2]). Such an assumption is unlikely to characterize the actual world, particularly since ρ_K in our system is the outcome of the *collective* demand for capital goods. No individual entrepreneur can anticipate the impact of aggregate entrepreneurial behavior, except by the crudest reference to past experience. *A priori,* it would be surprising if financial behavior were entirely consistent with the technological relationship embodied in the $\rho_K(I)$ function. Taking the I schedule as the $\rho_K(I)$ relationship, it is thus possible for the value of new security issues to lie off the curve, and realized investment to lie outside the vertical angle defined by the S and I curves together. This constitutes a qualification to all of our previous analysis of wealth and security-price movements. If we continue defining as forced saving any accumulation beyond the S schedule, aggregate forced saving may range from a minus quantity to an amount in excess of $m_2'' - m_2'$.[15] Moreover, ρ_K may deviate

---

[15] However, given L_2', the aggregate transfer of funds from the existing-asset market cannot exceed $m_2'' - m_2' = L_2'(r_M'') - L_2'(r_N')$. If forced saving exceeds $m_2'' - m_2'$, this results from defining forced saving as any ex post investment in excess of voluntary saving.

from r_M for reasons of miscalculation, as well as incomplete forced saving. But while the latter creates $\rho_K/r_M > 1$, the former produces $\rho_K/r_M \gtrless 1$ when ex post investment falls below or above the amount called for by the $\rho_K(I)$ schedule. While $\rho_K/r_M > 1$ tends to raise, $\rho_K/r_M < 1$ serves to lower wealth and security prices.

The case of complete and immediate forced saving is the only one in which investment errors may be assumed to be negligible. The tendency of ρ_K and r_M to be equated throughout the adjustment gives entrepreneurs a gauge by which to judge the correctness of their financial behavior. If investment is continuous over the minutest intervals of time, any discrepancy between ρ_K and r_M can be eliminated by rapid adjustments in the *rates* of security issuance and investment expenditure.[16]

4. Variable L_2

Suppose that L_2, along with D_{VO}, responds to autonomous changes in wealth. What are the implications of this for the adjustment process and the new equilibrium? An autonomous change in wealth (cf. Chapter II-B[4]) is one over which households have no direct control, other than capital gains or losses due to changes in the market rate of interest (both L_2 and D_{VO} are defined as functions of r_M, and do not shift in response to movements in that variable). The typical autonomous wealth change is a change in m_2 due to inflation, or a movement in S_{VO} due to variation of ρ_s. In both cases the disturbances to wealth are neither anticipated nor directly controllable by households. On the other hand, if a change in S_{VO} or m_2 originates in voluntary saving, we assume that it is accompanied by an equal planned movement in D_{VO} or L_2, respectively. Such shifts in D_{VO} or L_2 are outside our present consideration.[17]

If an autonomous wealth change is positive, L_2 shifts to the right. This raises the value of idle balances in equilibrium, $m_2^n = L_2^n(r_N')$, and accelerates the adjustment process by reducing the excess sup-

---

[16]If partial forced saving is the general empirical case, and is known to be by entrepreneurs, the latter might, as a matter of course, raise more funds than complete forced saving would justify. The resulting less-than-complete forced saving would then tend to equate ρ_K and r_M. Under these circumstances the financial I-schedule, showing the value of new security issues as a function of r_M, would lie permanently to the right of the real schedule, relating ex post investment to ρ_K. The I–S gap, relevant to the financial adjustment, would be greater than otherwise. This would have the effect only of accelerating the adjustment process. The total transfers are in any case limited to $m_2'' - m_2'$—the distance between $L_2'(r_M'')$ and $L_2'(r_N')$.

[17]See, however, Chapters II-D(2), where D_{VO}, and VIII-H, where both D_{VO} and L_2 shift constantly as part of the equilibrium-growth process.

ply of idle balances, $m_2 - L_2$, in any interval (see Figure 4–7). If an autonomous wealth change is negative, L_2 shifts to the left. This lowers the equilibrium m_2, and retards the speed of the adjustment by increasing $m_2 - L_2$ of any interval. An increased equilibrium level of m_2 implies that the over-all velocity of money is lower, and that the price level has increased less than proportionately to the increase in M. A reduced equilibrium m_2 implies that V is higher, and P has risen more than proportionately to the monetary increment.

The direct impact of a purchase is shown in Figure 5–1 to raise wealth by the horizontal distance between points A and B. If the ensuing adjustment is one of zero forced saving and excludes voluntary saving, the wealth path is BC, where W^n at C is to the left of W' at A. Part of the leftward movement from B to C is due to the restoration of the interest rate to r_N', offsetting the earlier capital gain. But the *net* wealth loss, CA, reflects *unanticipated* wealth changes during the course of the adjustment process in S_{VO} (due to stock watering) and m_2 (due to inflation). Hence households experience a net autonomous loss of wealth. In response, L_2 will undergo a net leftward shift at the equilibrium interest rate, r_N', becoming $L_2^n(r_N') < L_2'(r_N')$. This will produce

$$(5E.5) \qquad m_2^n = L_2^n(r_N') < m_2',$$

and reduce the speed of the adjustment. Since $S_{VO}^n = S_{VO}''$ in any case,

$$(5E.6) \qquad W^n = S_{VO}'' + m_2^n$$

is also reduced. In Figure 5–3 the wealth curves will decline less rapidly, but to a lower terminal level. In the extreme case in which L_2 absorbs the entire wealth change, D_{VO} remaining fixed at D_{VO}', the equilibrium will be unattainable (see Figure 5–1). This is because all of the wealth changes, after the direct impact of the purchase, take the form of a net reduction in m_2. During the transfer, idle balances initially are replaced by securities. But the subsequent stock watering, reflected in a leftward shift in S_{VO}, leaves households with a net loss of idle money. When the wealth effect is operative, the increase in the price level causes a direct uncompensated reduction in m_2. If, in each case, L_2 shifts equally with the loss of m_2, the interest rate will remain constant at r_M''.

The conclusions are the same if voluntary saving is accounted for. The autonomous wealth changes are still the net loss of m_2 on account of stock watering and the inflation. L_2 shifts to the left of $L'_2(r'_N)$, producing $m^n_2 < m'_2$. The adjustment is prolonged and wealth in equilibrium is reduced. If L_2 again is the only demand schedule responding to autonomous wealth changes, m_2 and L_2 move equally to the left indefinitely. The interest rate remains r''_M.

Consider the complete forced-saving adjustment. After the gain created by the direct impact of the operation, wealth falls during the first interval as ρ_K goes to ρ'''_K. In Figure 5–11 this is the movement from B to C, in response to which L_2 will shift to the left. However, C is to the right of A, and at $1/r'_N$, L_2, shifting proportionally to all wealth changes, will remain to the right of L'_2; i.e., the leftward shift will not completely offset the rightward movement at $1/r'_N$ due to the counterclockwise rotation through $1/r''_M$.[18] If, during the adjustment, voluntary saving is ignored and the wealth effect is absent, total wealth is constant along the CD path. L_2 remains to the right of $L'_2(r'_N)$, and $m^n_2 > m'_2$. Though total wealth in equilibrium is unchanged, it consists of more idle money and fewer securities. The capital stock financed by excess securities is also reduced. If the wealth effect is positive, the c vector will slope down and to the left (Part D[5]). If the terminal point is to the right of A, $L^n_2(r'_N)$ and m^n_2 are still to the right of $L'_2(r'_N)$ and m'_2, respectively, though by a smaller distance than previously. If the terminal point is to the left of A, L_2 will undergo a net leftward shift at $1/r'_N$, producing $m^n_2 < m'_2$. But in either case the total reduction in m_2 during the adjustment is greater than in the absence of the wealth effect. The total flotation of excess securities, the increase in capital, and the final wealth total cannot, therefore, be predicted without knowing the relative contributions of the transfer and wealth effects. The addition of voluntary saving does not alter our conclusions.

5. Property Income Subsidized

Suppose that the monetary authority returns the income on its newly acquired securities by subsidizing security or property rather than personal income. This effectively "returns" the purchased securities to households by an upward revaluation of remaining ones (Chapter III-B[2]b). ρ_s and p increase, and S_{VO} swings from

---

[18]Although the rotation of L_2 has no direct effect on r_M, the leftward shift during the first interval will tend to reduce r_M below r''_M. In Figure 5–11 point C will move up and to the left, reflecting the lower level of r_M and the greater induced reduction in ρ_K and wealth.

S''_{VO} back to equality with S'_{VO}. At r''_M at the start of the adjustment, the wealth gain is

$$S'_{VO}(r''_M) - S''_{VO}(r''_M) = S'_B p''.$$

Thereafter the movement of ρ_s, p, and W is the same as previously. The wealth lines in Figures 5-7, 5-9, and 5-12 are all raised by the quantity, $S'_B p$, where p is the same as it was in the case of personal-income subsidization; i.e., the wealth impact of security-income subsidization is equivalent to restoring the securities purchased by the bank, with no change in price (see page 72, note 12). In the new equilibrium the wealth gain attributable to the subsidization of security income is thus $S'_B p''$. In the case of zero forced saving with $\partial S/\partial r_M = 0$, no wealth effect, and personal-income subsidization, $\hat{W}'' - W'' = S'_B p'$ ([5C.51]). Thus, subsidizing property income will create

(5E.7) $$W'' \gtreqless \hat{W}'' \text{ when } p'' \gtreqless p'.[19]$$

F. SUMMARY

The system is modified by the introduction of a government security, to which open-market operations are confined; i.e., households hold private and government securities, while the central bank holds only the government issue. The latter is identical to the private security in regard to income, price, and yield, but represents a claim to governmental income, rather than the earnings of the private stock of capital.

A re-examination of the model over time reveals that in equilibrium, household wealth grows by capital increments equal to the balanced saving-investment flow. Security income and prices, the rate of interest, the return to capital, and the commodity price level are all constant.

The system is once more disturbed by an instantaneous open-market purchase. In a zero forced-saving adjustment, excluding voluntary saving and with $\partial S/\partial r_M = 0$, ρ_s, p, and W fall monotonically. In equilibrium, wealth has decreased by the value of securities sold to the bank. A positive wealth effect and $\partial S/\partial r_M > 0$ speed the adjustment and mitigate the fall in p, but have no effect on the final wealth total. However, $\partial S/\partial r_M > 0$ causes wealth temporarily to increase via the movement of ρ_K. Voluntary saving raises the

---

[19]See Appendix A for the derivation of upper and lower limits for p'' in both zero and complete forced saving.

level of ρ_s, p, and W to the point where they may rise in any interval. W must eventually turn upward to the equilibrium-growth rate, though it may actually rise temporarily at a greater rate before equilibrium is reached. In the context of voluntary saving, total wealth in equilibrium is invariably below that of the undisturbed economy. The minimum difference between final wealth and that of the undisturbed system, which occurs when $\partial S/\partial r_M = 0$, is equal to the value of securities sold to the bank. Given the vertical S schedule, greater absolute elasticity in the investment schedule speeds the adjustment, but does not alter the wealth total relative to trend. Given the investment schedule, $\partial S/\partial r_M > 0$ also accelerates the adjustment, but lowers equilibrium wealth below that of $\partial S/\partial r_M = 0$. However, with I fixed, the impact on final wealth of varying degrees of elasticity of the non-vertical saving schedule is unclear. Given a saving schedule for which $\partial S/\partial r_M > 0$, additional elasticity in the investment function raises equilibrium wealth. The wealth effect on interest again creates an earlier equilibrium, while tending to raise security prices. It has no impact on equilibrium wealth if $\partial S/\partial r_M = 0$; it raises equilibrium wealth by accelerating the rise of the interest rate, if $\partial S/\partial r_M > 0$.

During the limiting first interval of complete forced saving, ρ_K falls to equality with the lower market rate of interest. ρ_s, S_{VO}, W, and p decrease sympathetically. W remains above, though p falls exactly to its pre-disturbance level. Thereafter, without a wealth effect and abstracting from voluntary saving, ρ_s rises and p undergoes a net decline each interval, though total wealth is constant. A positive wealth effect accelerates the adjustment and reduces wealth, while tending to leave p constant. Voluntary saving causes ρ_s to rise less and p to fall even further, but creates a net increase in wealth. If the wealth effect is absent, the wealth increment is equal to the rate of voluntary saving. The maximum increase in wealth is therefore equal to the growth rate of the undisturbed economy. With voluntary saving, $\partial S/\partial r_M = 0$, and a zero wealth effect, total wealth in equilibrium exceeds that of the undisturbed economy by the maximum possible amount. The latter quantity is the securities sold to the bank valued by the difference between the purchase and pre-disturbance price. Greater elasticity in the investment schedule speeds the adjustment, but has no impact on the wealth total relative to trend. Given the investment function, $\partial S/\partial r_M > 0$ creates an earlier equilibrium, but one in which wealth is less, relative to trend, than in the case of $\partial S/\partial r_M = 0$. With I

given, the effect on wealth of more or less elasticity in the non-vertical saving schedule may be in either direction. Given a non-vertical saving schedule, wealth varies directly with the absolute elasticity of the investment schedule. Minimum wealth, which is independent of the saving schedule, occurs when $\partial I/\partial r_M = 0$. In this case wealth is below trend by the value of securities sold to the bank. The wealth effect on interest reduces the quantity of forced saving; but if $\partial S/\partial r_M > 0$, the greater speed of the adjustment due to the wealth effect raises voluntary saving. On net, the final wealth total may be greater or less. Security prices are again constant in the face of the wealth effect.

Appendix A establishes that the mean real security price is invariably higher for zero than complete forced saving, though this is not necessarily true for the terminal prices. Security quantities tend to be, but are not invariably lower for zero than complete forced saving. Appendix B studies the single-security model in which the central bank exercises an equity claim to the capital stock. The general effect is to raise the wealth increments in adjustment processes, but not in equilibrium growth. ρ_s and p are not affected.

The expressions developed for zero forced saving in the growing economy turn out to be completely applicable to the more general case of partial forced saving—both inclusive and exclusive of voluntary saving. A lag in investment spending raises the possible degree of forced saving and tends to reduce security prices. If entrepreneurial financial activity fails to conform in the $\rho_K(I)$ technological relationship, forced saving may be less than zero or more than $m_2'' - m_2'$, the real magnitude of the bank's purchase. If aggregate security issues and ex post investment exceed the amount called for by the $\rho_K(I)$ schedule, p tends to fall; otherwise to rise. In zero forced saving, variability of L_2 reduces m_2 and W in equilibrium. If L_2 is the only demand schedule responding to autonomous wealth changes, the equilibrium is unattainable. In complete forced saving with a zero wealth effect, the movement of L_2 raises m_2 and lowers capital, but leaves total wealth unchanged. Finally, if the monetary authority subsidizes security rather than personal income, households enjoy a wealth gain equal to the value of the securities purchased by the bank.

CHAPTER VI

Monetary Contraction

A. INTRODUCTION

This chapter will survey the financial and real adjustment to an open-market sale. This is necessary because the deflationary process is not a simple inverted image of the inflationary adjustment. The asymmetry follows from the fact that the monetary disturbance is imposed on a constantly growing economy. While the financial adjustment to the purchase takes the form of an excess security supply, the sale stimulates excess security demand. This makes for asymmetrical tendencies in the movement of security prices, the asset-demand schedules, and the final wealth position of households. But even where the deflationary adjustment is opposite and symmetrical to the inflationary, it is incumbent on the analysis to establish this. The following pages will accordingly telescope, for deflationary purposes, the presentation of the previous two chapters. Part B is the stock-flow analysis of securities and money—the financial adjustment—showing the deflationary counterpart of the transfer and wealth effects. Part C introduces the "real" analysis by entering explicitly into the model the stock of capital and its rate of return. These are the variables that underlie the movement of real security prices and household wealth. The deflationary analogue of forced saving is "forced investment," in which realized investment, drawn toward the S schedule, is greater than the amount intended by firms. Parts D and E consider zero and complete forced investment in turn. Part F is a summary of the chapter, and an intercomparison of the real inflationary and deflationary adjustments.

The direct impact of an open-market sale is described in Chapter III-E. The sale, instantaneously executed at a reduced price, p'' and higher yield, r_M'', adds securities to the existing-asset market and withdraws idle balances. The wealth function and the asset-demand schedules rotate clockwise through p''. By analogy to the inflationary adjustment, the interaction of stock and flow security markets in subsequent periods will simultaneously lower the interest rate to the natural level and transfer active to idle balances. We turn now to the adjustment process. Part B(1) describes the transfer effect, abstracting from the impact of the falling price level. Part B(2) considers the deflationary wealth effect.

B. THE FINANCIAL ADJUSTMENT

1. The Transfer Effect

The merger of stock-flow security markets during the first (and relatively brief) adjustment interval, t_1, is diagramed in Figure 6-1. The total schedules are derived as in Chapter IV-B(1):

$$(6B.1) \qquad S_T'' = S_O'' + S_N' \quad \text{and} \quad D_T'' = D_O'' + D_N'.$$

The opening security price, p'', is determined by the intersection of the post-operation schedules, S_O'' and D_O''. The closing price, at which $S_T'' = D_T''$, is $p''' > p''$, for which the interest rate is $r_M''' < r_M''$. The equilibrium condition, $D_T'' - S_T'' = 0$, implies

$$(6B.2) \qquad D_N' - S_N' = S_O'' - D_O'',$$

corresponding to the distances $EF = GH$. The equilibrium is thus characterized by equality between excess savers' demand and an ex-

FIGURE 6–1

The Combining of Stock and Flow Security Markets during the First Deflationary Adjustment Interval

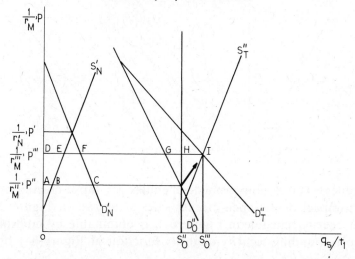

cess supply of existing securities. The latter is identical to an excess demand for idle money.

The events over time are as follows. At the opening instant of t_l, p'' and r_M'' stimulate an excess of intended saving over investment in the form of an excess demand for securities, shown in the diagram as the quantity, $D_N' - S_N' = BC$. Since the existing market is in equilibrium at p'', BC is a net excess demand which tends to raise security prices. During the course of the interval savers, confronted by an inadequate new supply, bid up the prices of new and old securities alike. The increase in price reduces the rate of excess new demand, but simultaneously stimulates an offering of securities by existing holders. The price continues to rise until at p''', the excess demand of savers is exactly equal to the excess existing supply. The movement of p and $1/r_M$ is shown by the upward arrow. Assuming that all securities are purchased at the price, p''', the ex post quantities are EF of excess savers' demand and GH of excess existing supply. The quantity of new securities purchased by savers is $S_N'(p''') = DE$, corresponding to HI in the total market. S_O''' is the closing stock of securities.

The events of the first adjustment interval are drawn in Figure 6–2 in terms of the saving, investment, and existing-asset value

FIGURE 6–2
The Stock-Flow Merger of the First Deflationary Adjustment Interval in Value Units

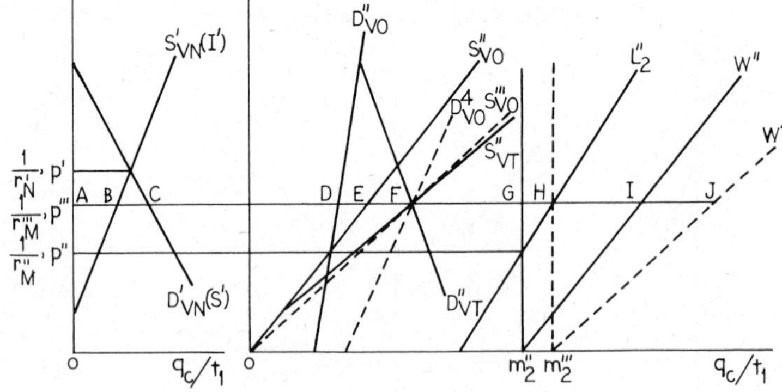

schedules. The double-primed schedules are those created by the direct impact of the open-market sale, as shown in Figure 3–15. Each security schedule in Figure 6–2 is obtainable by multiplying the corresponding security-quantity function of Figure 6–1 by the factor, p. The total value-schedules during t_1 are

(6B.3) $\qquad S''_{VT} = S''_{VO} + S'_{VN}$ and $D''_{VT} = D''_{VO} + D'_{VN}$.

At p''', $D''_{VT} - S''_{VT} = 0$ implies

(6B.4) $\qquad D'_{VN} - S'_{VN} = S''_{VO} - D''_{VO}$,

for which the corresponding distances are $BC = DE$. Figure 6–2 indicates plainly that the value of the excess supply of existing securities is accompanied by an equal excess demand for idle balances:

(6B.5) $\qquad S''_{VO}(p''') - D''_{VO}(p''') = L''_2(p''') - m''_2$,

corresponding to the distances, $DE = GH$. The ex post increase in idle balances, $m'''_2 - m''_2$, where $m'''_2 = L''_2(p''')$, materializes when existing-asset holders apply the proceeds of their security sales to savers, $DE = BC$, to the idle holdings. Since current saving entails the turnover of active balances received as current income, $m'''_2 - m''_2$ represents a *transfer* of funds from the active to the idle realm. The security-value function at the close of t_1 is S'''_{VO}, drawn from the origin through point F, the intersection of the total schedules. The closing wealth and security-demand functions are, respectively:

(6B.6) $\qquad W^4 = S'''_{VO} + m'''_2$,

$\qquad D^4_{VO} = D''_{VO} + (W^4 - W'') = D''_{VO} + (S'''_{VO} - S''_{VO}) + (m'''_2 - m''_2)$.

The specific character of the equilibrating process is more discernible if we subtract from the existing-asset market the equal components of saving and investment. The latter are reflected in Figure 6–2 as the quantities,

(6B.7) $\qquad S'_{VN}(p''') = AB = S'''_{VO}(p''') - S''_{VO}(p''') = EF$.

Thus Figure 6–3 is obtained by rotating S_{VO} in Figure 6–2 counterclockwise until it passes through point E. The resulting function coincides with S''_{VO}. D_{VO} moves equally with S_{VO}, rotating about the horizontal intercept of D^4_{VO} until the final schedule, D'''_{VO}, also passes through point E. The yield and price of securities remain r'''_M and p''', respectively. The supply and demand for idle balances are constant at m'''_2 and L''_2. The final wealth function, W'''', is obtained by rotations equal to those of S_{VO} and D_{VO}:

(6B.8) $\qquad W'''' = S''_{VO} + m'''_2$.

FIGURE 6–3
The Impact of Excess Savers' Demand on the Existing-Asset Market

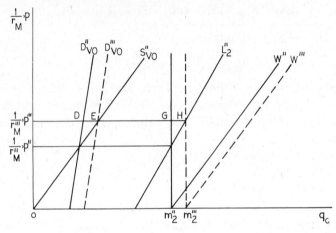

In Figure 6–3 the triple-primed schedules thus reflect the addition of excess savers' demand. The latter creates equal movements in existing-security demand and idle balances:

$$(6B.9) \qquad D'''_{VO}(p''') - D''_{VO}(p''') = DE = m'''_2 - m''_2 = GH.$$

The wealth function shifts equally with the increase in m_2. D'''_{VO} is drawn *parallel* to D''_{VO} since the value of the underlying wealth change, $m'''_2 - m''_2$, is independent of the rate of interest. Unlike the financial adjustment to the open-market purchase, there are thus no counter-rotations in the wealth function.[1] If the security-quantity schedule, D'''_O, created directly by the transfer, were drawn in Figure 6–1, it would pass through point H, lying to the right of D''_O by the variable distance, $(D'''_{VO} - D''_{VO})/p$. D^4_O, incorporating the equal saving and investment increments, would pass through point I parallel to D'''_O.

Figure 6–4 summarizes the open-market sale and the first adjustment interval in terms of the S, I, L_2, and m_2 functions, all of which are drawn with respect to r_M. The sale creates m''_2 and r''_M, through which L_2 rotates counterclockwise. During t_1 equilibrium is

---

[1] The rotations of the wealth function depend upon simultaneous and opposite changes in the stock of securities and the quantity of idle balances. Thus, in the inflationary adjustment, the open-market purchase is succeeded by reverse changes in both variables, causing offsetting rotations of the wealth function. We compared the adjustment to an open-market sale. However, in the deflationary process, savers buy existing securities, all of which continue to be held by households. We cannot compare this to an open-market purchase, since the securities are not actually removed from household portfolios. Unless the securities are removed, the wealth function cannot, of course, rotate.

achieved at r_M''' at which

(6B.10) $$S' - I' = BC = L_2'' - m_2'' = GH.$$

There are no further rotations in W or L_2.

The adjustment proceeds in the manner of the first interval. In any period in which r_M is above r_N', excess saving bids up security

FIGURE 6–4
The Sale and the Initial Stock-Flow Merger Summarized by the Saving, Investment, and Idle-Money Schedules

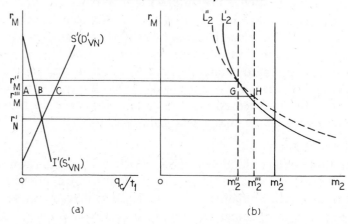

prices and pours into the existing-asset market where, at the lower yield, savers obtain existing securities. Active balances furnished by savers are transferred to the sellers of existing securities, who take the proceeds as idle balances. The price level falls proportionately. Diagrams analogous to Figures 4–5, 4–6, and 4–7 can be drawn to describe the entire stock-flow path to equilibrium. The deflationary path corresponding to AB in Figure 4–5 would be rising and concave downward. In Figure 4–6, $S_N' - D_N'$ would be replaced by a downward function, $D_N' - S_N'$, and $D_O - S_O$ by $S_O - D_O$, a family of upward-sloping functions. Similarly inverted schedules would replace those of Figure 4–7.

When we go beyond the financial variables to the capital stock, we can again expect changes in ρ_s to occur. Initially security prices are below p', the pre-disturbance price. Capital-security increments, whose ratio equals the lower price, will reduce ρ_s. Changes in ρ_K may drive ρ_s on net in either direction. However, the changes in ρ_s will be of no consequence to the financial adjustment if (a) firms refrain from issuing additional securities when ρ_s changes because capital rises in excess of the intended amount, (b) households do not expect changes in ρ_s to occur, and (c) changes in S_{VO}

on account of ρ_s are met by approximately equal changes in D_{VO}. If firms sell additional securities at their own initiative, this will tend to reverse the adjustment by raising the rate of interest and rechanneling idle money to the income stream. But if, at the going commodity price level, entrepreneurial expenditures are realized in more capital units than were originally sought, there is no necessity or likelihood that additional securities will be floated. The unexpected and essentially gratuitous capital increment will simply be employed as profitably as possible, without further recourse to the financial markets.[2] The behavior of households consistent with the contractionary adjustment is the same as it was in the expansionary process. For in either case the interest rate will be moved—up or down—if ρ_s is expected to change, or if D_{VO} fails to respond equally to S_{VO} when a change in ρ_s materializes. Accordingly, if (a), (b), and (c) are met, the induced changes in capital will have no repercussions on the stock-flow financial adjustment.

2. The Wealth Effect

In discussing the reduction in the price level, it is again important to stress that there is no correlative movement in the demand schedule for idle or active balances. The decrease in investment demand at the higher rate of interest is simply a decrease in the supply of new securities. The increase in desired saving is a diversion of active balances from expenditure on consumption goods to securities. Neither the investment nor the saving response in itself has a direct effect on total spending and the price level. Rather, it is the discrepancy between saving and investment which, inadvertently and automatically, leads to a purchase of existing securities by savers and a transfer of active to idle balances.

Since full-employment output continues, the price level falls proportionately to the loss of active money. The deflation occurs without delay and raises the value of idle money.[3] Granted that the

---

[2] We must, of course, distinguish the above from undesired capital increments in the form of inventories, which accumulate when sales fall below production. Unintended capital of this variety will indeed stimulate financial adjustments that tend to reverse the stock-flow equilibrating process. See p. 185, where this is discussed as a possible but temporary offset.

[3] The fall in the price level is simultaneous with the transfer of active to idle balances by excess savers. Thus all idle balances, including those in the process of transfer, gain in value. But it is only the increase in the value of *pre-existing* idle balances that is relevant to the wealth effect. This latter increment is an addition to the increase directly effected by savers. Symbolically, the pre-transfer idle balances are $m_2'' - M_2''/P'$. Excess savers add $\Delta M_1'$ to M_2, causing P to drop simultaneously to P''. The final value of m_2 is $m_2'' = (M_2'' + \Delta M_1')/P''$. Savers are responsible for raising m_2 by $\Delta M_1'/P''$, valuing their increment at the new price level. The wealth effect is attributable to the increase of m_2 from M_2''/P' to M_2''/P''.

wealth gain is divided between the existing demand for both securities and idle money, there is a net increase in m_2 which is spent instantaneously on existing securities. The price of securities rises and the rate of interest falls. Though Figure 6–3 diagrams the transfer effect on interest, it can be used almost as well to show the "negative" wealth effect. To do so, we attribute the increase from m_2'' to m_2''' to the fall in commodity prices. Total wealth moves responsively from W'' to W'''. We would like to shift both D_{VO} and L_2 to the right, but the diagramed movement in D_{VO} indicates adequately the resulting increase in p and decrease in r_M.

In the contractionary adjustment, both equilibrating mechanisms thus take the form of a net increase in security demand. The additive influence of the wealth effect on security prices and interest accelerates the return to equilibrium, at which excess saving is zero. If we abstract from the equal saving and investment flows and any movement in S_{VO} due to changes in ρ_s, the equilibrium would be characterized in Figure 6–3 by the intersection of a demand schedule, D_{VO}^n, with S_{VO}'' at r_N'. If $L_2^n(r_N') = m_2'$, the total rightward shift in D_{VO} is

(6B.11) $$D_{VO}^n - D_{VO}'' = m_2' - m_2''.$$

The total wealth function shifts parallel and to the right by the same distance.

If, during the adjustment, the price level lags behind the loss of active balances, real income will apparently be less, reducing saving. This reduces the excess of saving over investment and retards the downward movement in r_M and P. If entrepreneurs fail to lower commodity prices proportionately to the fall in money expenditures, sales will decline and a portion of current output will flow into inventories. To this extent, firms will lack receipts with which to meet production costs, and will be forced to issue new securities to finance the additional inventories. Such security sales will tend to lower security prices, raise the rate of interest, and tap idle balances from the existing-asset market. The new flotations effectively offset the impact of excess savers' demand on all of these variables, including the price level. But in time, entrepreneurs will reduce product prices, preventing further inventory accretions. And at some future date, the entrepreneurial demand for investment goods will shift to the left, neutralizing the growth in inventories and their earlier impact on the system.

The monetary summary of the inflationary process in Chapter IV-D(1) is applicable to the downward adjustment if we simply reverse the direction of the changes. The reduction in money, coming entirely out of idle balances, raises over-all velocity. The gradual transfer of M_1 to M_2 lowers P and V. If L_2 is on net constant at r_N', V and M_1/M_2 will return to their pre-disturbance values, and P will fall proportionately to the decrease in M. The numerical example on page 113 can be altered by letting the bank sell $\Delta M'' =$ \$15 in securities to existing-asset holders. M falls to $M'' = 135$ and M_2 to $M_2'' = 35$. $m_2'' = 35/2 = 17.50$. After transferring \$10 from active to idle balances, we have

$$P'' = \frac{M_1'' V_1'}{y'} = \frac{90 \times 2}{100} = \$1.80 ,$$

and

$$m_2'' = \frac{45}{1.80} = 25.00 = m_2' .$$

Figure 6–5 diagrams the excess saving and idle-money demand functions in nominal units, with a view to determining the change in

FIGURE 6–5

The Deflationary Adjustment in Terms of Nominal Excess Saving and Idle-Money Demand Functions

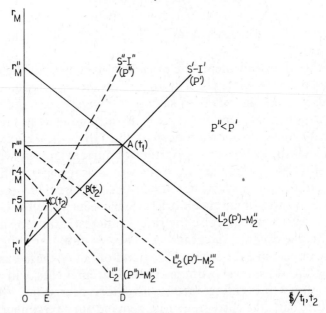

the nominal transfer between two intervals. During t_1, the first adjustment interval, $S' - I'$ and $L_2'' - M_2''$, based on P', meet at point A. The equilibrium interest rate of the interval is r_M''' and the nominal transfer is OD to the idle balances, which increase thereby to M_2'''. If P were fixed, the equilibrium during t_2 would be at point B, where $L_2'' - M_2'''$ and $S' - I'$ meet. However, the loss of active balances reduces P to P''. Money saving and investment decrease proportionately, as does their difference, excess money saving. $S'' - I''$, based on P'', is thus to the left of $S' - I'$. L_2 also shifts to the left as P falls, becoming L_2''' and producing $L_2''' - M_2'''$, which is to the left of $L_2'' - M_2'''$. $L_2''' - M_2'''$ cuts the vertical axis at r_M^4, where $r_M''' - r_M^4$ is the decrease in interest due to the wealth effect. The equilibrium for t_2 is at point C, for which the yield is r_M^5 and the transfer is $OE < OD$. Since in going from A to C all functions move unambiguously to the left, their intersection points also drift leftward, and the decline in the nominal transfer is inevitable. The price level thus falls by diminishing amounts over time.[4]

C. THE REAL ADJUSTMENT: THE MODEL AND THE SALE

In describing the impact of capital we revert to the system as modified in Chapter V-B(1). Households hold two securities, one issued by private business firms and the other by the central government. The securities are identical in regard to income, price, and yield, but only the income on the private security can be related to the capital stock, as in (2B.6). Security income, though identical for all issues, is in fact determined by events in the private sector; the government automatically and immediately equates the income on its securities to that of the private share. Apart from specified disturbances, the quantity of government securities is fixed, all saving and investment entailing transactions in the private security. The

---

[4] The derivation of the relative quantitative importance of the transfer and wealth effects in the appendix to Chapter IV is relevant to the deflationary adjustment, but with qualifications. In that appendix the impact of each of the equilibrating mechanisms on the interest rate was measured by the impact on the value of idle balances. During the inflation each mechanism was shown to have its maximum impact on m_2 when it led the alternative mechanism. But in deflation an equilibrating force maximizes its impact on m_2 by *lagging* behind the alternative one. This can be seen by reference to (4A.1)' and (4A.2)'. The former equation states that the change in M_2/P due to a change in M_2 varies inversely with P. Thus during the deflation the transfers to M_2 will have their greatest impact on M_2/P *after* the price level has fallen. The latter equation indicates that the absolute response of M_2/P to a change in P varies directly with M_2 and inversely with P. Hence the change in P creates the maximum change in M_2/P *after* the transfers to M_2 have occurred. Accordingly, while (4A.9)' and (4A.14)' are maximum and minimum contributions of the transfers to the change in m_2 during the inflation, they are the minimum and maximum contributions, respectively, during the deflation. Similarly, (4A.10)' and (4A.15)', the minimum and maximum changes in m_2 attributable to the price level during inflation, are the maximum and minimum changes, respectively, in deflation. In all four equations the increments, ΔM_1^n and ΔM_2^n, are, of course, negative for deflation.

process of equilibrium growth, described in Chapter V-B(2), serves as a frame of reference for deflationary as well as inflationary disturbances. Assumptions comparable to those in Chapter V-A also underlie the deflationary analysis: excess savers' demand is added without lag to idle balances; $I(r_M)$, the investment demand schedule, coincides with $\rho_K(I)$, the technological relationship; output, S, I, and the natural rate of interest are fixed; L_2 does not respond to autonomous wealth changes; and the securities sold to households are serviced by a tax on personal incomes.

The variables of the system prior to the disturbance are given by (5B.11)–(5B.13). The general equations for total household wealth are (5B.5)–(5B.9). The central bank, which holds government securities only, sells to households a quantity, S'_B, at a price

$$(6C.1) \qquad p'' = \frac{\rho''_s}{r''_M} < p', \text{ where } \rho''_s = \rho'_s .$$

The funds withdrawn by the sale are entirely idle balances:

$$(6C.2) \qquad S'_B p'' = m'_2 - m''_2 ,$$

which is analogous to (5B.22). The increased quantity of government securities held by households is

$$(6C.3) \qquad S''_G = S'_G + S'_B ,$$

and total holdings of private and government securities are

$$(6C.4) \qquad S''_O = S'_O + S'_B = S'_P + S'_G + S'_B = S'_P + S''_G .$$

The security-value function is

$$(6C.5) \qquad S''_{VO}(\rho'_K) = S''_O p = S'_P \left(\frac{\rho'_s}{r_M}\right) + S''_G \left(\frac{\rho'_s}{r_M}\right)$$

$$= \left(\frac{\rho'_K}{r_M}\right) K' + S''_G \left(\frac{\rho'_s}{r_M}\right) > S'_{VO}(\rho'_K) .$$

Total wealth is

$$(6C.6) \quad W''(\rho'_K) = S''_{VO}(\rho'_K) + m''_2 = \left(\frac{\rho'_K}{r_M}\right) K' + S''_G \left(\frac{\rho'_s}{r_M}\right) + m''_2 .$$

The wealth loss (see the derivation to [5B.28]) is

$$(6C.7) \qquad S'_O(p' - p'') = (S'_P + S'_G)(p' - p'') > 0 .$$

Figure 3–15 remains an accurate representation of the direct impact of the sale, except that L_2 is now held constant at L'_2. Hence

$$(6C.8) \qquad D''_{VO} = D'_{VO} + [W''(\rho'_K) - W'(\rho'_K)] .$$

D. ZERO FORCED INVESTMENT

The zero forced-investment adjustment is one in which ex post and ex ante investment are equal throughout the transition to equilibrium; i.e., realized investment lies on the I schedule. This is the deflationary analogue of complete forced saving in the inflationary case. We shall seek—but not always find—in the analysis of the latter process elements that are symmetrical to the following account. In Section 1 we exclude components of desired or voluntary investment from the expressions for all variables. This enables us to study the specific impact of the excess saving. There are no restrictions on the interest elasticities of I and S, which are simply < 0 and > 0, respectively. The wealth effect on interest is initially zero. In Section 2 voluntary investment is added to the analysis.

1. Voluntary Investment Excluded

As in the inflationary adjustment, a limiting first interval, t_1, is characterized by an instantaneous adaptation in the rate of investment to the new market rate of interest. Both desired and ex post investment fall at once to $I'(r_M''')$, where r_M''' is infinitesimally below r_M'', the sale yield. The return to investment rises accordingly to

$$(6D.1) \qquad \rho_K''' = r_M''' = r_M''.$$

ρ_s, S_{VO}, and W increase to the following values:

$$(6D.2) \qquad \rho_s''' = \frac{r_M''' K'}{S_P'} = \frac{r_M'' K'}{S_P'},$$

$$(6D.3) \qquad S_{VO}'''(\rho_K''') = (S_P' + S_G'')\left(\frac{\rho_s'''}{r_M}\right) = \left(\frac{\rho_K'''}{r_M}\right)K' + S_G''\left(\frac{\rho_s'''}{r_M}\right),$$

$$(6D.4) \qquad W'''(\rho_K''') = S_{VO}'''(\rho_K''') + m_2''' = \left(\frac{\rho_K'''}{r_M}\right)K' + S_G''\left(\frac{\rho_s'''}{r_M}\right) + m_2''.$$

D_{VO} is assumed to shift equally with S_{VO} and W:

$$(6D.5) \qquad D_{VO}''' = D_{VO}'' + [S_{VO}'''(\rho_K''') - S_{VO}''(\rho_K'')].$$

The interest rate is maintained at r_M''', and p increases to its predisturbance value:

$$(6D.6) \qquad p''' = \frac{\rho_s'''}{r_M'''} = \frac{K'}{S_P'} = p'.$$

Thus, at r_M''' the wealth total is

$$(6D.7) \qquad W'''(\rho_K''', r_M''') = S_{VO}'''(\rho_K''', r_M''') + m_2'' = K' + S_G''p' + m_2''.$$

ρ_K has now risen to its maximum value, and will fall hereafter in synchronization with r_M. However, we cannot, by analogy to the inflationary adjustment, assert that total wealth is also at its maximum. Wealth will, in fact, increase in subsequent intervals.

The events of a succeeding period, i_2, are drawn in Figure 6–6. Point A is the security-market equilibrium at the start of the interval, as determined by S_{VO}''' and D_{VO}'''. Both schedules are to the right

FIGURE 6–6

The Existing-Asset Market during the Second Interval of Zero Forced Investment—Voluntary Investment Excluded

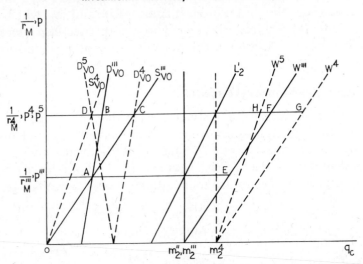

of the post-operation functions, S_{VO}'' and D_{VO}'' (not in the diagram). The quantity of securities is still S_O'', their price is $p''' = p'$, and their yield is $r_M''' = r_M''$. The volume of real idle balances is $m_2''' = m_2''$, and the wealth function is W'''. The merger of stock-flow security markets during the interval generates excess savers' demand which raises p and lowers r_M, respectively, to

$$(6D.8) \qquad p^4 > p''' \quad \text{and} \quad r_M^4 = \frac{\rho_s^4}{p^4} < r_M''', \text{ where } \rho_s^4 = \rho_s'''.$$

The value of the excess supply of existing securities is

$$(6D.9) \qquad\qquad S_{VO}'''(r_M^4) - D_{VO}'''(r_M^4) = BC,$$

in exchange for which asset holders demand

$$(6D.10) \qquad\qquad L_2'(r_M^4) - m_2''' = m_2^4 - m_2'''$$

in additional idle balances. As savers purchase the existing shares,

m_2, D_{VO}, and W shift simultaneously to

(6D.11) $$m_2^4, D_{VO}^4 = D_{VO}''' + (m_2^4 - m_2'''),$$

and

(6D.12) $$W^4(\rho_K''') = S_{VO}'''(\rho_K''') + m_2^4,$$

respectively. The security-market equilibrium is at point C. In the following instant the rate of intended and ex post investment increases in response to the lower interest rate. This reduces ρ_K to

(6D.13) $$\rho_K^4 = r_M^4.$$

ρ_s, S_{VO}, D_{VO}, and W fall proportionately:

(6D.14) $$\rho_s^5 = \frac{\rho_K^4 K'}{S_P'} < \rho_s''',$$

(6D.15) $$S_{VO}^4(\rho_K^4) = S_O'' p = \left(\frac{\rho_K^4}{r_M}\right) K' + S_G''\left(\frac{\rho_s^5}{r_M}\right),$$

(6D.16) $$D_{VO}^5 = D_{VO}^4 + [S_{VO}^4(\rho_K^4) - S_{VO}'''(\rho_K''')],$$

(6D.17) $$W^5(\rho_K^4) = S_{VO}^4(\rho_K^4) + m_2^4.$$

Since S_{VO} and D_{VO} move equally, r_M continues at r_M^4, and the closing price is

(6D.18) $$p^5 = \frac{\rho_s^5}{r_M^4} = \frac{K'}{S_P'} = p'.$$

The security-market equilibrium is at point D. Though S_{VO} has moved leftward, the value of securities, in the sense of a point on a schedule, is unchanged from the starting amount:

(6D.19) $$S_{VO}^4(\rho_K^4, r_M^4) = S_O'' p^5 = S_O'' p' = S_O'' p''' = S_{VO}'''(\rho_K''', r_M''').$$

In the diagram point D accordingly is directly above point A.

While total wealth falls with ρ_s and S_{VO} at the close of t_2, it remains above its value at the start of the interval. This is because security value is on net constant, and idle balances are greater. In Figure 6–6 wealth is initially at point E, as given by (6D.7). As a result of the transfer, wealth increases to point G. This entails a movement along W''' from E to F, reflecting the capital gains due to $p^4 > p'''$, followed by a shift from F on W''' to G on W^4 as idle balances are increased. The reduction in ρ_K carries wealth to point H, at which it is

(6D.20)

$$W^5(\rho_K^4, r_M^4) = S_{VO}^4(\rho_K^4, r_M^4) + m_2^4 = S_O'' p' + m_2^4 = K' + S_G'' p' + m_2^4.$$

The difference between beginning and ending wealth of the interval is the horizontal difference between H and E, or (6D.20) − (6D.7):

$$(6D.21) \qquad W^s(\rho_K^4, r_M^4) - W'''(\rho_K''', r_M''') = m_2^4 - m_2'',$$

the increase in idle balances. The reduction in ρ_K removes the wealth gain due to the reduction in r_M, and only the additional idle balances remain to augment the wealth total.

The pattern of the second interval is repeated for n intervals until

$$(6D.22) \qquad r_M' = r_N' = \rho_K' \text{ and } m_2^n = m_2'.$$

In every interval after the first, excess savers' demand raises p, whose opening price is always p'. This lowers r_M and raises idle balances. ρ_K falls to the level of r_M, reducing ρ_s and p, the latter returning to p'. Households are left with a net wealth gain equal to the increase in idle balances. In the final equilibrium,

$$(6D.23) \qquad \rho_s^n = \frac{\rho_K' K'}{S_P'} = \rho_s',$$

$$(6D.24) \qquad S_{VO}^n(\rho_K') = S_{OP}'' p = \left(\frac{\rho_K'}{r_M}\right) K' + S_G'' \left(\frac{\rho_s'}{r_M}\right) = S_{VO}''(\rho_K'),$$

$$(6D.25) \qquad W^n(\rho_K') = S_{VO}^n(\rho_K') + m_2^n = \left(\frac{\rho_K'}{r_M}\right) K' + S_G'' \left(\frac{\rho_s'}{r_M}\right) + m_2',$$

(6D.26)
$$D_{VO}^n = D_{VO}' + [W^n(\rho_K') - W'(\rho_K')] = D_{VO}' + [S_{VO}^n(\rho_K') - S_{VO}'(\rho_K')],$$

$$(6D.27) \qquad p^n = \frac{\rho_s^n}{r_N'} = p'.$$

At the equilibrium interest rate, total wealth is

$$(6D.28) \qquad W^n(\rho_K', r_N') = (S_P' + S_G'')p' + m_2' = K' + S_G'' p' + m_2'.$$

ρ_s has fallen from ρ_s''', created by the limiting first interval, to ρ_s', its pre-disturbance value. Apart from temporary increases during each transfer, p is p' following the initial adjustment interval. Since both the quantity and the income of securities are at their immediate post-operation values, S_{VO} has fallen from S_{VO}''' in the first interval to $S_{VO}^n = S_{VO}''$.

The over-all movement of wealth is described with the aid of Figure 6–7, which presents the existing-asset market prior to the disturbance, directly afterwards, during t_1, and in the new equilibrium. Total wealth before the open-market sale is on W' at

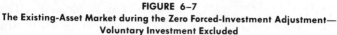

FIGURE 6-7

The Existing-Asset Market during the Zero Forced-Investment Adjustment—
Voluntary Investment Excluded

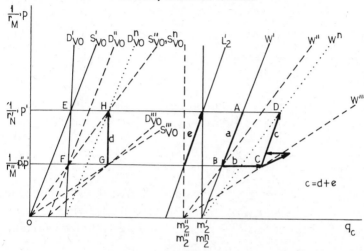

point A. The equilibrium of the security market is at point E. The sale of securities lowers wealth along the vector, a, from A to B, and moves the equilibrium of the security market to F. The wealth loss is given by (6C.7). The wealth function rotates clockwise to W'', and D_{VO} to D''_{VO}. In the limiting first interval ρ_K rises to equality with r''_M, raising S_{VO} and W to S'''_{VO} and W''', respectively. D_{VO} moves with S_{VO} to D'''_{VO}, carrying the security-market equilibrium to G, at which r_M is still r''_M. The movement of wealth is along the horizontal vector, b, from B to C. We can show that wealth at point C is greater than at point A:

$$(6D.29) \quad CA = W'''(\rho'''_K, r'''_M) - W'(\rho'_K, r'_N)$$
$$= (6D.7) - (5B.13) = S'_B(p' - p'') > 0,$$

which is obtained by substituting $S'_B p''$ for $m'_2 - m''_2$.

In subsequent intervals S_{VO} falls with ρ_K and ρ_s until it coincides with S''_{VO}. But the point on any closing S_{VO} schedule corresponding to the market rate of interest has a constant abscissa value. Thus the locus of points on the rotating S_{VO} schedules is along the vertical vector, d, from G to H. This is merely an extension of the path in Figure 6-6 from A to D. Point H at the terminus of d is the final security-market equilibrium, as determined by S^n_{VO} and D^n_{VO}. Total closing wealth, meanwhile, increases each interval by the addition of idle balances. This is shown in the movement along c, which connects point C at $W'''(\rho_K''', r_M''')$ with D at $W''(\rho_K', r_N')$.[5] The horizontal distance between C and D is the total increase in idle balances,

$$(6D.30) \qquad m_2^n - m_2''' = m_2' - m_2''.$$

The relationship between the vectors is

$$(6D.31) \qquad c = d + e,$$

the latter being the locus of $r_M - m_2$ points as determined by L_2'.[6]

The net increase in wealth between the two equilibrium positions is AD, or

$$(6D.32) \quad W''(\rho_K', r_N') - W'(\rho_K', r_N') = (6D.28) - (5B.13) = S_B'p',$$

the securities sold by the bank valued at the pre-disturbance price. The reader will recall that in the zero forced-saving inflationary adjustment, the net *loss* of wealth, excluding voluntary saving, was also $S_B'p'$ ([5C.22]).

The operation of the wealth effect on interest does not alter the equilibrium values of the variables. The analysis is effectively the same whether the equilibrating force is an increase in security demand due to excess saving or a decrease in the price level. In either case p is raised and r_M is lowered by a simultaneous increase in D_{VO} and m_2. Investment responds to the reduction in r_M, lowering ρ_K and restoring p to p'. The course of ρ_s, S_{VO}, W, and p is the same, whether, and in whatever degree, the price level contributes to the

---

[5] While c indicates wealth at the close of each interval, when $\rho_K = r_M$ and $p = p'$, p rises during the course of the interval, creating capital gains. This is shown as the movement in Figure 6–6 from E to F. In that diagram a vector incorporating both the capital gain and the increase in m_2 would extend from E to G. A similar (unlabeled) vector is drawn in Figure 6–7, starting at point C and extending to the right of W'''. When ρ_K falls at the close of the interval, wealth moves along a horizontal vector that terminates at c. This corresponds to the movement in Figure 6–6 from G to H. Over continuous time, wealth thus follows a saw-toothed pattern.

[6] The wealth vectors form three sides of what may appear to be a parallelogram, $ABCD$. However, while the two sides, a and c, must be equal, the other two, AD and BC, need not be. $AD \gtreqless BC$ is, upon substitution and rearrangement,

$$W''(\rho_K', r_N') - W'(\rho_K', r_N') \gtreqless W'''(\rho_K''', r_M''') - W''(\rho_K', r_M''),$$

$$S_B'p' \gtreqless S_P'(p' - p'') + (S_G' + S_B')(p' - p''),$$

which reduces to

$$S_B'p' \gtreqless S_O'(p' - p'').$$

Notice also in Figure 6–7 that W^n is parallel to W'' and greater by the increase in idle balances, $m_2' - m_2''$. The same is true of D_{VO}^n in relation to D_{VO}'. Further, W^n and W' meet on the horizontal axis, where they are both equal to m_2'. Thus D_{VO}^n and D_{VO}' likewise meet at $p = 0$.

equilibrating process. The only impact of the wealth effect is to speed the movement to equilibrium. In the inflationary case of zero forced saving, the wealth effect also failed to influence household wealth, though it tended to raise ρ_s and p.

2. Voluntary Investment Included

The analysis will now be enlarged by consideration of the equal saving and investment flows. The wealth effect on interest is again absent.

The limiting first interval proceeds as described on page 189, except that now the variables must reflect the infinitesimal changes in capital and securities. Thus, while the variables have the same values for t_1 previously written, we would express, say, ρ_s as

$$(6D.33) \qquad \rho_s''' = \frac{r_M''' K''}{S_P''} = \frac{r_M'' K'}{S_P'}, \text{ since } K'' = K' \text{ and } S_P'' = S_P'.$$

During the second interval S_{VO}, D_{VO}, and W will all be greater by the quantity of voluntary investment. The greater value-function of securities is

$$(6D.34) \qquad S_{VO}^4(\rho_K''') = (S_O'' + \Delta S_I'')\left(\frac{\rho_s^4}{r_M}\right), \text{ where } \rho_s^4 = \rho_s'''$$

and $\Delta S_I''$ is the quantity of new securities issued by entrepreneurs and added by savers to household wealth. In a diagram such as Figure 6–6, S_{VO}^4, so defined, would lie to the right of the indicated schedule, S_{VO}'''. The security-market equilibrium would be at the same height and to the right of point C, where an augmented D_{VO} schedule intersects the new S_{VO}^4 function:

$$(6D.35) \qquad D_{VO}^5 = D_{VO}^4 + [S_{VO}^4(\rho_K''') - S_{VO}'''(\rho_K''')].$$

The supply and demand for idle balances remain m_2^4 and L_2', respectively. Total wealth would be to the right of point G on a schedule,

$$(6D.36) \qquad W^5(\rho_K''') = S_{VO}^4(\rho_K''') + m_2^4.$$

Once again at the close of the interval, investment, ex ante and ex post, increases, and ρ_K falls to $\rho_K^4 = r_M^4$. The increase in the capital stock is

$$(6D.37) \qquad \Delta K'' = \Delta S_I'' p^4,$$

where p^4 is the transfer price of the interval. The value of ρ_s, incorporating the changes in ρ_K, K, and S_P, is

$$(6D.38) \qquad \rho_s^5 = \frac{\rho_K^4 K'''}{S_P'''} = \frac{\rho_K^4(K'' + \Delta K'')}{S_P'' + \Delta S_I''}.$$

We can show that $\rho_s^5 < \rho_s^4$:

$$\frac{\rho_K^4(K'' + \Delta K'')}{S_P'' + \Delta S_I''} < \frac{\rho_K''' K''}{S_P''},$$

$$\rho_K^4 K'' S_P'' < \rho_K''' K'' S_P'' + \rho_K''' K'' \Delta S_I'' - \rho_K^4 \Delta K'' S_P''.$$

$\Delta K''$ is replaced by (6D.37), in which p^4 is replaced by

$$\frac{\rho_s^4}{r_M^4} = \frac{\rho_K''' K''}{r_M^4 S_P''}.$$

This reduces the inequality to

$$\rho_K^4 K'' S_P'' < \rho_K''' K'' S_P'',$$

$$\rho_K^4 < \rho_K'''.$$

However, ρ_s^5 is higher than it was in abstraction from voluntary investment. We compare (6D.38) with (6D.14):

$$\frac{\rho_K^4(K'' + \Delta K'')}{S_P'' + \Delta S_I''} > \frac{\rho_K^4 K'}{S_P'}.$$

Since $K'' = K'$ and $S_P'' = S_P'$, the inequality becomes

$$\frac{\Delta K''}{\Delta S_I''} > \frac{K'}{S_P'},$$

$$p^4 > p'.$$

The reduction from ρ_s^4 to ρ_s^5 in the present context lowers S_{VO}, W, and D_{VO}:

(6D.39) $$S_{VO}^5(\rho_K^4) = (S_O'' + \Delta S_I'')\left(\frac{\rho_s^5}{r_M}\right) < S_{VO}^4(\rho_K'''),$$

(6D.40) $$W^6(\rho_K^4) = S_{VO}^5(\rho_K^4) + m_2^4,$$

(6D.41) $$D_{VO}^6 = D_{VO}^5 + [S_{VO}^5(\rho_K^4) - S_{VO}^4(\rho_K''')].$$

The interest rate is still r_M^4, and p falls from p^4 to

(6D.42) $$p^5 = \frac{\rho_s^5}{r_M^4}.$$

But $p^5 > p'''$, the opening price:

$$\frac{K'''}{S_P''} > \frac{K''}{S_P''},$$

$$\frac{K'' + \Delta K''}{S_P'' + \Delta S_I''} > \frac{K''}{S_P''},$$

which is established by the inequality, $\Delta K''/\Delta S_I'' > K''/S_P''$, or equivalently, $p^4 > p'''$.

The quantity of total wealth at the close of t_2 is

$$(6D.43) \quad W^6(\rho_K^4, r_M^4) = S_{VO}^5(\rho_K^4, r_M^4) + m_2^4 = K''' + S_G'' p^5 + m_2^4.$$

This represents an increase over wealth at the start of the interval of

$$(6D.44) \quad W^6(\rho_K^4, r_M^4) - W'''(\rho_K''', r_M''')$$
$$= (K''' - K'') + S_G''(p^5 - p''') + (m_2^4 - m_2'''),$$

where all of the parenthetical terms are positive. Since the wealth gain was $m_2^4 - m_2'''$, excluding voluntary investment ([6D.21]), the inclusion of the latter contributes

$$(6D.45) \quad (K''' - K'') + S_G''(p^5 - p''')$$

to total wealth.

In succeeding intervals security income continues to fall, while security prices and total wealth rise. If we let $\sum_n \Delta K$ be total voluntary investment, and $\sum_n \Delta S_I$ the total quantity of securities issued, the variables in the final equilibrium are

$$(6D.46) \quad K^n = K' + \sum_n \Delta K, \qquad S_P^n = S_P' + \sum_n \Delta S_I,$$

$$(6D.47) \quad \rho_s^n = \frac{\rho_K' K^n}{S_P^n} = \frac{\rho_K'(K' + \sum_n \Delta K)}{S_P' + \sum_n \Delta S_I},$$

$$(6D.48) \quad S_{VO}^n(\rho_K') = (S_P^n + S_G'')\left(\frac{\rho_s^n}{r_M}\right) = \left(\frac{\rho_K'}{r_M}\right)(K' + \sum_n \Delta K) + S_G''\left(\frac{\rho_s^n}{r_M}\right),$$

$(6D.49)$

$$W^n(\rho_K') = S_{VO}^n(\rho_K') + m_2^n = \left(\frac{\rho_K'}{r_M}\right)(K' + \sum_n \Delta K) + S_G''\left(\frac{\rho_s^n}{r_M}\right) + m_2',$$

$(6D.50)$

$$D_{VO}^n = D_{VO}' + [W^n(\rho_K') - W'(\rho_K')] = D_{VO}' + [S_{VO}^n(\rho_K') - S_{VO}'(\rho_K')],$$

$$(6D.51) \quad p^n = \frac{\rho_s^n}{r_N'} = \frac{K' + \sum_n \Delta K}{S_P' + \sum_n \Delta S_I} > p'.$$

Since $p' = \rho_s'/r_N'$, $\rho_s^n > \rho_s'$ even though ρ_s falls constantly after its increase to ρ_s''' during t_1. At r_N' the wealth total is

$$(6D.52) \quad W^n(\rho_K', r_N') = (K' + \sum_n \Delta K) + (S_G' + S_B')p^n + m_2'.$$

A more useful formulation of (6D.52) is to write the term, $(S'_G + S'_B)p^n$, as follows:

(6D.53) $(S'_G + S'_B)p^n = S'_G p' + S'_G(p^n - p') + S'_B p'' + S'_B(p^n - p'')$.

We let

(6D.54) $\mu = S'_G(p^n - p')$ and $\nu = S'_B(p^n - p'')$.

The wealth total is thus

(6D.55) $W^n(\rho'_K, r'_N) = (K' + \sum_n \Delta K) + S'_G p' + S'_B p'' + \mu + \nu + m'_2$.

The pattern of wealth over time is drawn in Figure 6-8. Points

FIGURE 6-8
Time Series of Total Wealth during the Zero Forced-Investment Adjustment—
Voluntary Investment Included

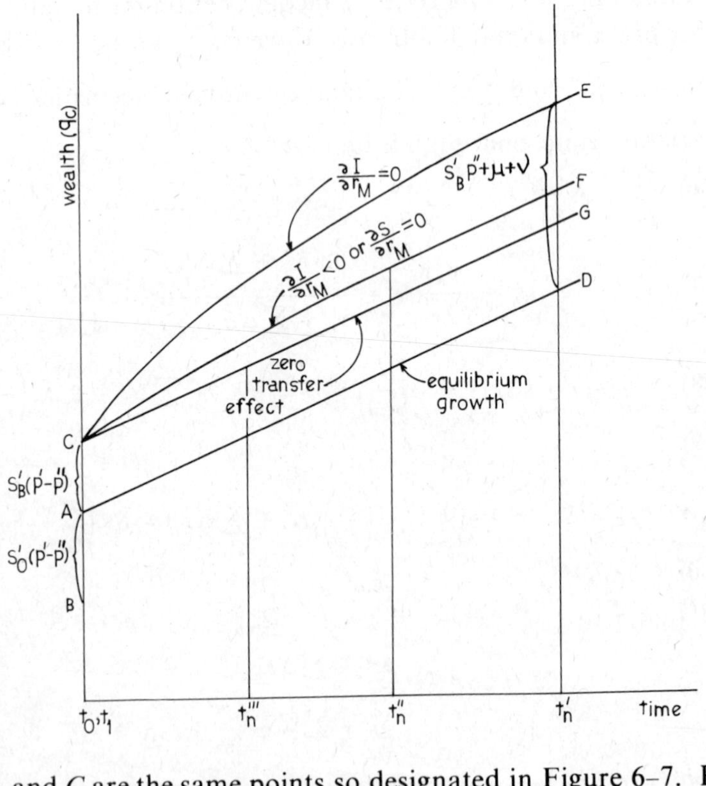

A, B, and C are the same points so designated in Figure 6-7. Point C, which is the wealth total produced by the limiting first interval, is above point A by $S'_B(p' - p'')([6D.29])$. The line, AD, is total wealth of the undisturbed equilibrium-growth system. The general

difference between equilibrium wealth of the disturbed and un-disturbed economies is (6D.55) − (5B.20):

$$(6D.56) \qquad \left(\sum_n \Delta K - n \hat{\Delta K}' \right) + S_B' p'' + \mu + \nu.$$

The first parenthetical term is the difference between the growth of capital in the two systems, the second term is the increase in securities due to the open-market sale, and μ and ν are the capital gains on government securities due to $p'' - p'$ in the case of pre-disturbance holdings, and $p'' - p''$ with reference to S_B'. Suppose that $\partial I / \partial r_M = 0$. Then capital accumulation due to voluntary investment is independent of the disturbance; $\sum_n \Delta K = n \hat{\Delta K}'$ and (6D.56) reduces to

$$(6D.57) \qquad S_B' p'' + \mu + \nu.$$

The wealth curve generated on this assumption is CE, rising and concave downward. The downward concavity results from the fact that the terminal distance, ED, exceeds the beginning distance, CA. This is readily apparent when we consider that just one of the components, $\nu = S_B'(p'' - p'')$, in the distance, ED, is greater than $CA = S_B'(p' - p'')$, since $p'' > p'$.

Given the vertical I schedule, a more elastic S curve will speed the adjustment and lower total wealth relative to trend. Though in (6D.56) the parenthetical term and $S_B' p''$ are unaffected, a briefer adjustment and growth of capital reduce p'' in μ and ν. In general, since forced investment is zero and $m_2 = m_2'$ in any equilibrium, total wealth is maximized when voluntary investment and the capital gains on government securities are also at a maximum. The former condition is met when I is vertical. The latter condition requires the *slowest* possible adjustment, which is produced by a saving schedule which is only infinitesimally greater than I at $r_N' < r_M < r_M''$.

Let I resume its general slope of $\partial I / \partial r_M < 0$. The given S schedule is non-vertical. The adjustment is accelerated and $\sum_n \Delta K$ and total wealth are reduced absolutely and relative to the AD line. μ and ν are also reduced since p'' is lower for a more rapid adjustment and a reduced level of voluntary investment. An example of such a wealth path is CF, which reaches equilibrium at t_n''. The impact of additional degrees of absolute elasticity in the I schedule cannot be anticipated. Though a flatter I schedule lowers ΔK at any interest rate, it also accelerates the adjustment process and lowers the interest rate of any point in time. The latter tendency raises ΔK. The net effect on $\sum_n \Delta K$ and total wealth, including the p^n coefficient, may be in either direction.

Given the non-vertical I schedule, additional elasticity in the S function raises ΔK per period by speeding the adjustment and lowering the average interest rate. However, the impact on μ and ν may be plus or minus, since the p^n component varies directly with the absolute value of $\sum_n \Delta K$. For example, an increased periodic ΔK, lasting a shorter period of time, may raise p^n less than a lower periodic ΔK of a longer duration. This can occur even though the difference, $\left(\sum_n \Delta K - n\hat{\Delta K}'\right)$, is increased by the more elastic S schedule. The net effect on wealth cannot, therefore, be specified without more detailed information.

Though passing from the vertical to a non-vertical I schedule lowers the wealth curve, the latter cannot cross nor lie below AD, given that $\partial S/\partial r_M \geq 0$. Consider the least favorable case in which $\partial S/\partial r_M = 0$. In this system the growth rate of capital and idle balances together, as given by a point on the S schedule, is constant and equal to $\Delta K'$. In equilibrium,

$$(6D.58) \qquad \sum_n \Delta K + (m_2' - m_2'') = n\hat{\Delta K}',$$

and, since $m_2' - m_2'' = S_B' p''$, (6D.56) reduces to

$$(6D.59) \qquad \mu + \nu > 0.$$

As a general expression, (6D.59) holds for any I schedule, changes in which merely alter the time of equilibrium. However, the numerical values of μ and ν are lower for more rapid adjustments. (6D.59) is thus minimized when the vertical S schedule is combined with the horizontal I function. This produces the most rapid possible adjustment period,

$$(6D.60) \quad \sum_n \Delta K = 0, \; n\hat{\Delta K}' = (m_2' - m_2''), \; p^n = p', \text{ and } \mu = 0.$$

(6D.56) and (6D.59) both reduce to

$$(6D.61) \qquad \nu = S_B'(p' - p'') > 0.$$

In Figure 6–8 wealth proceeds along CG, parallel to AD. The equilibrium is reached at t_n'''. The reader will notice that (6D.61) i analogous to (5D.59), which is the *maximum* by which wealth may exceed trend in the inflationary adjustment.[7]

In the context of voluntary investment, the wealth effect on interest again accelerates the adjustment process. Since real idle balances increase by $m_2' - m_2''$, whether caused by excess saving or deflation, the wealth effect can influence wealth only by altering the rate of voluntary investment and p^n. The introduction of the wealth effect will, in fact, alter wealth just as would a more elastic saving schedule. If I is vertical, the wealth effect reduces wealth by reducing p^n. If I is non-vertical, the wealth effect may raise or lower wealth depending on the net impact of counterbalancing forces on p^n, relative to the positive effect on ΔK of each period. In the limiting case in which the wealth effect accomplishes the entire adjustment during t_2 instantaneously, following an infinitesimal dosage of excess saving, $p^n = p'$ and wealth is again above trend by the minimum quantity, (6D.61). The wealth path is CG.

E. COMPLETE FORCED INVESTMENT

We reconsider the contractionary adjustment on the assumption that savers determine the level of ex post investment. This is the same assumption underlying the inflationary analysis of zero forced saving. Section 1 describes the adjustment process in abstraction from voluntary investment. In order to simplify the analysis, we assume initially that $\partial S/\partial r_M = 0$ and the wealth effect on interest is absent. The former assumption is made in order to maintain ρ_K constant at ρ_K'. In Section 2 voluntary investment is re-introduced. The first adjustment period follows the open-market sale, as described in Part C.

1. Voluntary Investment Excluded

The initial adjustment interval, t_1, as described in Part B(1), is relevant in the present circumstances. The specific impact of the excess saving, as summarized in Figure 6–3, is reproduced in Figure 6–9. The security-market equilibrium at the opening of t_1 is at point A, the intersection of $S_{VO}''(\rho_s'')$ and D_{VO}'' (see Part C). The rate of interest is $r_M'' = \rho_s''/p''$, where $\rho_s'' = \rho_s'$. Real idle money

---

[7] However, (5D.59), which is generated by complete forced saving, measures a change in the capital stock, while (6D.61) is literally a change in the value of government securities.

FIGURE 6–9
The Existing-Asset Market during the First Interval of Complete Forced
Investment—Voluntary Investment Excluded

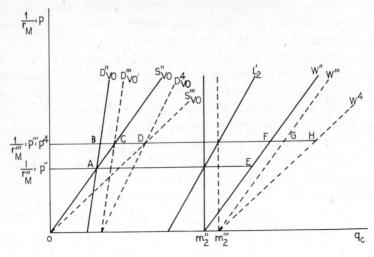

is m_2''. The demand for m_2 is now L_2', instead of L_2'', incorporating the assumption that L_2 does not respond to autonomous wealth changes. Total wealth is $W'' = S_{VO}'' + m_2''$. During t_1 excess saving raises p and lowers r_M:

(6E.1) $$p''' = \frac{\rho_s'''}{r_M'''} > p'', \quad \text{where} \quad r_M''' < r_M'' \quad \text{and} \quad \rho_s''' = \rho_s''.$$

At r_M''' existing-security supply of

(6E.2) $$S_{VO}'' - D_{VO}'' = BC$$

goes to excess savers who raise existing-security demand and idle balances equally to

(6E.3) $D_{VO}''' = D_{VO}'' + BC$ and $m_2''' = m_2'' + [L_2'(r_M''') - m_2'']$,

respectively. The equilibrium of the security market is at point C, and the total wealth function is

(6E.4) $$W'''(\rho_s''') = S_{VO}'' + m_2'''.$$

At the closing instant of t_1 excess saving is realized in an equal increase in the stock of capital:

(6E.5) $$\Delta K' = D_{VO}''' - D_{VO}'' = m_2''' - m_2'' = \Delta m_2''.$$

(6E.5) is based on our assumption that the locus of realized investment is the saving schedule. The resulting forced investment reflects the failure of entrepreneurs to lose resources to consumers during the deflationary adjustment. Thus, while the increment in idle balances, $\Delta m_2''$, measures the level of forced investment, it is not a financing component in the investment process. The only financial relevance of $\Delta m_2''$ is as a sum of money that households have successfully withheld from real consumption. In the face of full employment of resources, ex post investment rises residually over the intended amount to equality with desired saving.

Since $\partial S / \partial r_M = 0$, the growth of capital does not alter ρ_K, which remains ρ_K'. But $\Delta K'$ has an effect on security income and value opposite to that of stock watering. ρ_s rises to

$$(6E.6) \qquad \rho_s^4 = \frac{\rho_K'(K' + \Delta m_2'')}{S_P'} > \rho_s''' = \frac{\rho_K' K'}{S_P'}.$$

S_{VO} becomes

$$(6E.7) \quad S_{VO}'''(\rho_s^4) = S_O''\left(\frac{\rho_s^4}{r_M}\right) = \left(\frac{\rho_K'}{r_M}\right)(K' + \Delta K') + S_G''\left(\frac{\rho_s^4}{r_M}\right) > S_{VO}''(\rho_s''').$$

W and D_{VO} follow the rightward shift of S_{VO}:

$$(6E.8) \qquad W^4(\rho_s^4) = S_{VO}'''(\rho_s^4) + m_2''',$$

$$(6E.9)$$
$$D_{VO}^4 = D_{VO}''' + [W^4(\rho_s^4) - W'''(\rho_s''')] = D_{VO}''' + [S_{VO}'''(\rho_s^4) - S_{VO}''(\rho_s''')].$$

The equilibrium of the security market is at point D, at which the interest rate is still r_M'''. The increase in ρ_s, while r_M is constant, raises the price of securities to

$$(6E.10) \qquad p^4 = \frac{\rho_s^4}{r_M'''}.$$

The difference between the prices is

$$(6E.11) \qquad p^4 - p''' = \frac{\rho_K'}{r_M'''}\left(\frac{\Delta K'}{S_P'}\right) > 0.$$

The rise in p is brought about by the purchase of securities implicit in the shift of D_{VO} from D_{VO}''' to D_{VO}^4. Since the excess saving also raises p, the price of securities rises throughout the course of the interval.

Wealth, like prices, rises monotonically during t_1. First, there are the gains on securities as r_M is lowered and p raised from p'' to p'''. This is the movement along W'' from E to F. The interest adjustment is accompanied by an increase in idle balances, raising the wealth function from W'' to W''' and the quantity of wealth from F to G. Then forced investment creates a further round of price increases and shifts wealth to W^4. The final wealth total is at H. The symbolic relation between ending and beginning wealth is

$$W^4(\rho_s^4, r_M''') > W''(\rho_s'', r_M''),$$

$$S_{VO}'''(\rho_s^4, r_M''') + m_2''' > S_{VO}''(\rho_s'', r_M'') + m_2'',$$

(6E.12) $\left(\dfrac{\rho_K'}{r_M'''}\right)(K' + \Delta K') + S_G'' p^4 + m_2''' > \left(\dfrac{\rho_K'}{r_M''}\right)K' + S_G'' p'' + m_2'',$

where $r_M''' < r_M''$, $\Delta K' > 0$, $p^4 > p''$, and $m_2''' > m_2''$. Since L_2 is fixed at L_2', the movements of D_{VO} and W are equal during the interval:

(6E.13) $\quad D_{VO}^4 - D_{VO}'' = W^4(\rho_s^4) - W''(\rho_s'')$

$$= K'\left(\frac{\rho_K'}{r_M'''} - \frac{\rho_K'}{r_M''}\right) + (m_2''' - m_2'')\left(\frac{\rho_K'}{r_M'''} + 1\right) + S_G''(p^4 - p'').$$

The final expression, in which all parenthetical terms are positive, is obtained by substituting $m_2''' - m_2''$ for $\Delta K'$ (see [6E.5]) in the expression for $W^4(\rho_s^4)$ ([6E.7] and [6E.8]).

The first interval is typical of all future intervals. As long as $r_M > r_N'$, excess saving raises p and lowers r_M. Idle balances and security demand shift equally to the right. At the close of each interval excess saving is realized in an equal increase in the stock of capital. ρ_s and S_{VO} both increase. Since D_{VO} rotates equally with S_{VO}, the interest rate remains at its new lower level. But the increase in ρ_s raises p further. Wealth rises in response to the initial increase in p, the increase in idle balances, and the secondary increase in p as the unintended capital increment is realized. Equilibrium is reached after n intervals. Since excess saving does not entail a change in the quantity of securities,

(6E.14) $\qquad\qquad\qquad S_O^n = S_O'' = S_P' + S_G''.$

But the new capital stock is

(6E.15) $\qquad\quad K^n = K' + (m_2^n - m_2'') = K' + (m_2' - m_2''),$

$$\text{since } m_2^n = m_2'.$$

$m_2^n - m_2''$ is the total capital imposed on firms by excess savers. Since total excess saving is equal to the total required increment in idle balances, $m_2^n - m_2'' = m_2' - m_2''$. The other variables are as follows:

(6E.16) $\qquad \rho_s^n = \dfrac{\rho_K' K^n}{S_P'} = \dfrac{\rho_K'[K' + (m_2' - m_2'')]}{S_P'} > \rho_s',$

(6E.17)

$$S_{VO}^n(\rho_s^n) = S_O^n\left(\frac{\rho_s^n}{r_M}\right) = \left(\frac{\rho_K'}{r_M}\right)[K' + (m_2' - m_2'')] + S_G''\left(\frac{\rho_s^n}{r_M}\right) > S_{VO}''(\rho_s''),$$

(6E.18) $W^n = S_{VO}^n(\rho_s^n) + m_2^n = \left(\dfrac{\rho_K'}{r_M}\right)[K' + (m_2' - m_2'')] + S_G''\left(\dfrac{\rho_s^n}{r_M}\right) + m_2',$

(6E.19) $D_{VO}^n = D_{VO}' + [W^n(\rho_s^n) - W'(\rho_s')] = D_{VO}' + [S_{VO}^n(\rho_s^n) - S_{VO}'(\rho_s')],$

(6E.20) $\qquad p^n = \dfrac{\rho_s^n}{r_N'} = \dfrac{K' + (m_2' - m_2'')}{S_P'} > p'.$

At r_N' total wealth is

(6E.21) $\qquad W^n(\rho_s^n, r_N') = K' + (m_2' - m_2'') + S_G'' p^n + m_2'.$

Figure 6–10 summarizes the course of the existing-asset market during the over-all adjustment. Prior to the disturbance, wealth is at point A on W', and the security market is in equilibrium at point D. The open-market sale lowers security prices, reducing wealth along the vector, a, to point B. The security schedules intersect at E. The exchange of money for securities produces W'' and D_{VO}'', which have rotated clockwise relative to their original posi-

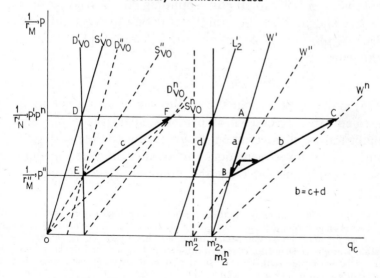

FIGURE 6–10
The Existing-Asset Market during the Complete Forced-Investment Adjustment—Voluntary Investment Excluded

tions. Thereafter during the adjustment process security value, idle balances, and total wealth rise along northeast vectors $c, d,$ and

$$(6E.22) \qquad\qquad b = c + d,$$

respectively. The vectors are merely extensions of the diagonal paths in Figure 6–9: AD, $L_2'(r_M'')$ to $L_2'(r_M''')$, and EH. The vector c, in Figure 6–10, connects E with F, the intersection of S_{VO}^n and D_{VO}^n. At r_N' the increase in S_{VO} during the adjustment process is

$$(6E.23) \quad S_{VO}^n(\rho_s^n, r_N') - S_{VO}''(\rho_s'', r_N') = m_2' - m_2'' + S_G''(p^n - p').$$

The d vector, tracing the movement of m_2 as a function of r_M, coincides, as usual, with L_2'. The b vector connects point B with C at $W^n(\rho_s^n, r_N')$. W^n exceeds W'' at r_N' by

$$S_{VO}^n(\rho_s^n, r_N') + m_2^n - [S_{VO}''(\rho_s'', r_N') + m_2''],$$

which is

$$(6E.24) \qquad\qquad 2(m_2' - m_2'') + S_G''(p^n - p').$$

The difference between the new equilibrium and pre-disturbance wealth is

$$AC = W^n(\rho_s^n, r_N') - W'(\rho_s', r_N'),$$

which is (6E.21) − (5B.13):

$$(6E.25) \qquad\qquad (m_2' - m_2'') + S_G'' p^n - S_G' p',$$

where $(m_2' - m_2'')$ is capital corresponding to forced investment, $S_G'' > S_G'$, and $p^n > p'$. A more useful way to write (6E.25) is to replace $S_G'' p^n = (S_G' + S_B')p^n$ by (6D.53) and (6D.54). The net wealth gain is thus

$$(6E.26) \qquad\qquad (m_2' - m_2'') + S_B' p'' + \mu + \nu.$$

(6E.26) makes explicit that the wealth increment is due to forced investment, the increase in securities sold by the bank, and the capital gains on all government securities due to the rise of p.[8]

Since forced investment does not require financing in the usual sense, resulting instead from the dominance of consumers over

---

[8] While the b vector represents wealth at the end of each interval, the path during the interval is shown in Figure 6–9 to consist of two segments. The initial increase in p raises wealth along EF on the pre-existing wealth function. The increase in idle balances and the capital stock produces the horizontal movement, FH. In Figure 6–10 a similar movement is shown by the unlabeled vector on W'' starting at B, followed by the horizontal vector moving rightward to an intersection with b.

entrepreneurs in curtailing real expenditures, it is immaterial to wealth whether the adjustment is accomplished by the transfer or wealth effect. In either case the interest rate falls, real balances and security demand rise, and ex post investment moves along the S schedule. Though the wealth effect speeds the adjustment, it has no effect on the variables in the new equilibrium. Typically the wealth effect will influence ρ_s and p by altering the ratio of the capital-security increments. But in the present adjustment the quantity of securities is constant, and the stock of capital rises by $(m_2' - m_2'')$ in any event.

If $\partial S / \partial r_M > 0$, ρ_K will fall at the start of the adjustment to

$$(6E.27) \qquad \rho_K'' < \rho_K', \text{ where } I(\rho_K'') = S(r_M'').$$

ρ_K will rise thereafter along the I schedule until it is again ρ_K'. ρ_s, p, S_{VO}, and W move sympathetically. But with D_{VO} following the movement of S_{VO}, the course of r_M is not affected, nor are any of the variables in the new equilibrium. ρ_s^n and p^n, for example, are based on a fixed quantity of securities, S_P', and forced investment, $m_2' - m_2''$, neither of which is influenced by the variability of ρ_K.

2. Voluntary Investment Included

We consider now the total growth process, in which voluntary investment is accounted for. For the present, the wealth effect on interest is again absent and ρ_K is constant at ρ_K'. The latter assumption derives from $\partial S / \partial r_M = 0$.

The first interval, t_1, proceeds exactly as before, except that S_{VO} now incorporates the quantity of securities sold by entrepreneurs to savers, $\Delta S_I'$:

$$(6E.28) \qquad S_{VO}'''(\rho_s''') = (S_O'' + \Delta S_I') \left(\frac{\rho_s'''}{r_M} \right).$$

Wealth and security demand reflect the increased S_{VO} function:

$$(6E.29) \qquad W^4(\rho_s''') = S_{VO}'''(\rho_s''') + m_2''',$$

$$(6E.30) \qquad D_{VO}^4 = D_{VO}'' + [W^4(\rho_s''') - W''(\rho_s'')].$$

In Figure 6–9 $S_{VO}'''(\rho_s''')$ would lie to the right of S_{VO}'', $W^4(\rho_s''')$ to the right of W''', and D_{VO}^4, as defined above, would be to the right of D_{VO}'''. The supply and demand for idle balances remain as indicated in the diagram, as do the price and yield of securities. At the close of t_1 the capital stock increases by both forced and voluntary investment:

(6E.31) $\Delta K' = \Delta m_2'' + \Delta S_I' p'''$.

ρ_s becomes

(6E.32) $\rho_s^4 = \dfrac{\rho_K' K''}{S_P''} = \dfrac{\rho_K'(K' + \Delta m_2'' + \Delta S_I' p''')}{S_P' + \Delta S_I'}$.

While forced investment tended to raise ρ_s, the addition of voluntary investment may drive ρ_s in either direction:

$$\rho_s^4 \gtreqless \rho_s''' ,$$

$$\frac{\rho_K'(K' + \Delta m_2'' + \Delta S_I' p''')}{S_P' + \Delta S_I'} \gtreqless \frac{\rho_K' K'}{S_P'} .$$

Since

$$p''' = \frac{\rho_s'''}{r_M'''} = \frac{\rho_K' K'}{r_M''' S_P'} ,$$

the inequality expands and reduces to

(6E.33) $\dfrac{\Delta m_2''}{K'} \gtreqless \left(1 - \dfrac{\rho_K'}{r_M'''}\right) \dfrac{\Delta S_I'}{S_P'}$,

where the parenthetical term is > 0. Clearly there is no necessary
relation between the relative magnitude of forced investment,
$\Delta m_2''/K'$, and the relative number of securities purchased by
savers, $\Delta S_I'/S_P'$. The depressive influence of voluntary investment on ρ_s is shown explicitly by comparing (6E.32) with
(6E.6):[9]

$$\frac{\rho_K'(K' + \Delta m_2'' + \Delta S_I' p''')}{S_P' + \Delta S_I'} < \frac{\rho_K'(K' + \Delta m_2'')}{S_P'} .$$

Upon substituting for p''' and transposing,

$$0 < K' \left(1 - \frac{\rho_K'}{r_M'''}\right) + \Delta m_2'' .$$

The closing S_{VO} schedule produced by the change in ρ_s is

(6E.34) $S_{VO}^4(\rho_s^4) = (S_O'' + \Delta S_I')\left(\dfrac{\rho_s^4}{r_M}\right) = \left(\dfrac{\rho_K'}{r_M}\right)(K' + \Delta K') + S_G''\left(\dfrac{\rho_s^4}{r_M}\right).$

---

[9] Intuitively, forced investment raises ρ_s since it increases the numerator only:

$$\rho_s^4 = \frac{\rho_K'(K' + \Delta m_2'')}{S_P'} > \rho_s''' = \frac{\rho_K' K'}{S_P'} .$$

Voluntary investment raises both numerator and denominator by increments whose ratio,
$\Delta S_I' p'''/\Delta S_I'$, is $p''' < p' = K'/S_P'$.

$S_{VO}^4(\rho_s^4)$, as given by (6E.34), will coincide with or lie on either side of $S_{VO}'''(\rho_s''')$, as given by (6E.28), depending on whether $\rho_s^4 \gtreqless \rho_s'''$. W and D_{VO} follow S_{VO}:

(6E.35) $$W^5(\rho_s^4) = S_{VO}^4(\rho_s^4) + m_2''',$$

(6E.36) $$D_{VO}^5 = D_{VO}^4 + [S_{VO}^4(\rho_s^4) - S_{VO}'''(\rho_s''')].$$

The equal movements of S_{VO} and D_{VO} maintain the interest rate at r_M'''.

Since r_M remains at r_M''', security prices move with ρ_s:

(6E.37) $$p^4 = \frac{\rho_s^4}{r_M'''} \gtreqless p''' = \frac{\rho_s'''}{r_M'''} \quad \text{when} \quad \rho_s^4 \gtreqless \rho_s'''.$$

Thus the closing price may fall below the transfer price, despite the increase in investment. In fact, p^4 may fall below p'', the opening price. Letting $r_M''' = r_M''$, which is approximated by a sufficiently brief interval, $p^4 \gtreqless p''$ reduces to (6E.33).[10] But whatever its course, p^4 will be less than in the absence of voluntary investment, since ρ_s^4 is lower.

The net wealth relationship over the interval is

$$W^5(\rho_s^4, r_M''') \gtreqless W''(\rho_s'', r_M''),$$

$$S_{VO}^4(\rho_s^4, r_M''') + m_2''' \gtreqless S_{VO}''(\rho_s'', r_M'') + m_2'',$$

(6E.38) $$\left(\frac{\rho_K'}{r_M'''}\right)(K' + \Delta m_2'' + \Delta S_I' p''') + S_G'' p^4 + m_2''' \gtreqless \left(\frac{\rho_K'}{r_M''}\right)K'$$
$$+ S_G'' p'' + m_2''.$$

The inequality is handled more easily if we transfer all terms to the left side and consolidate:

(6E.39)
$$\left(\frac{\rho_K'}{r_M'''} - \frac{\rho_K'}{r_M''}\right)K' + \left(1 + \frac{\rho_K'}{r_M'''}\right)\Delta m_2'' + \left(\frac{\rho_K'}{r_M'''}\right)\Delta S_I' p''' + S_G''(p^4 - p'') \gtreqless 0.$$

---

[10] The minimum possible value of p^4 is

$$\lim_{\substack{\Delta m_2' \to 0 \\ \Delta S_I' \to \infty \\ p''' \to p''}} \left(\frac{\rho_s^4}{r_M'''}\right) = \lim \frac{\rho_K'(K' + \Delta m_2'' + \Delta S_I' p''')}{r_M'''(S_P + \Delta S_I)} = \left(\frac{\rho_K'}{r_M'''}\right)p''.$$

The limit is taken for $\Delta m_2' = 0$ since forced investment tends to raise ρ_s^4 and p^4. Since voluntary investment lowers security income and prices, we let $\Delta S_I' = \infty$. However, we maximize the depressive effect of voluntary investment by minimizing p''', the ratio of the voluntary investment-security increments. The lower limit of p''', the transfer price, is p'', the opening price.

All terms but $(p^4 - p'')$ are invariably positive. The conditions underlying (6E.39) < 0 are derived by letting $r_M''' = r_M''$ and $\Delta m_2'' = 0$. On these assumptions (6E.39) < 0 reduces to

$$(6\text{E}.40) \qquad\qquad S_G'' > \frac{S_P' + \Delta S_I'}{1 - \dfrac{\rho_K'}{r_M''}},$$

where the denominator is < 1, and quite possibly close to zero. A wealth decline during t_1 will thus generally require that total government securities be considerably greater than private securities, and that ρ_K'/r_M'' be small. Entering $r_M''' < r_M''$ and $\Delta m_2'' > 0$ into (6E.39) < 0 makes the inequality even more difficult to satisfy, since these terms raise wealth by raising the coefficients of the capital increments and p^4.

As the interest rate falls toward the equilibrium, the pattern of the first interval is repeated. Security income and prices may rise or fall. However, total wealth will rise, except under very extreme assumptions. In the new equilibrium,

$$(6\text{E}.41) \qquad\qquad K^n = K' + \sum_n \Delta K + (m_2' - m_2''),$$

where $\sum_n \Delta K$ and $(m_2' - m_2'')$ are voluntary and forced investment, respectively. Also,

$$(6\text{E}.42) \qquad\qquad S_P^n = S_P' + \sum_n \Delta S_I,$$

where $\sum_n \Delta S_I$ is the total number of securities sold by entrepreneurs to savers. The other variables are:

$$(6\text{E}.43) \qquad \rho_s^n = \frac{\rho_K' K^n}{S_P^n} = \frac{\rho_K'[K' + \sum_n \Delta K + (m_2' - m_2'')]}{S_P' + \sum_n \Delta S_I} \gtreqless \rho_s',$$

$$(6\text{E}.44) \qquad S_{VO}^n(\rho_s^n) = (S_P^n + S_G'')\left(\frac{\rho_s^n}{r_M}\right)$$

$$= \left(\frac{\rho_K'}{r_M}\right)[K' + \sum_n \Delta K + (m_2' - m_2'')] + S_G''\left(\frac{\rho_s^n}{r_M}\right),$$

$$(6\text{E}.45) \qquad W^n(\rho_s^n) = S_{VO}^n(\rho_s^n) + m_2^n$$

$$= \left(\frac{\rho_K'}{r_M}\right)[K' + \sum_n \Delta K + (m_2' - m_2'')] + S_G''\left(\frac{\rho_s^n}{r_M}\right) + m_2'$$

(6E.46)
$$D_{VO}^n = D_{VO}' + [W''(\rho_s^n) - W'(\rho_s')] = D_{VO}' + [S_{VO}^n(\rho_s^n) - S_{VO}'(\rho_s')],$$

(6E.47)
$$p^n = \frac{\rho_s^n}{r_N'} = \frac{K' + \sum_n \Delta K + (m_2' - m_2'')}{S_P' + \sum_n \Delta S_I} \gtreqless p'.$$

ρ_s^n may stand above or below ρ_s', the beginning value, since forced investment in the absence of voluntary investment raises ρ_s, while voluntary investment lowers it. There are clearly combinations of forced and voluntary investment for which $\rho_s^n \gtreqless \rho_s'$ and consequently, $p^n \gtreqless p'$.

The quantity of wealth in the final equilibrium, using the μ and ν substitutions, (6D.54), is

(6E.48)
$$W''(\rho_K', r_N') = (K' + \sum_n \Delta K + m_2' - m_2'')$$
$$+ S_G'p' + S_B'p'' + \mu + \nu + m_2',$$

where μ and ν are now $\gtreqless 0$.[11]

The wealth time series are plotted in Figure 6–11. Point A is the pre-disturbance wealth total at time t_0, and B is produced in the same instant by the open-market sale. The distance, AB, is $S_O'(p' - p'')([6C.7])$. AC is the wealth path of the undisturbed equilibrium-growth economy. In equilibrium the difference between wealth of the disturbed and undisturbed systems is (6E.48) − (5B.20):

(6E.50)
$$\left(\sum_n \Delta K - n\hat{\Delta}K'\right) + (m_2' - m_2'') + S_B'p'' + \mu + \nu.$$

The first parenthetical term is the difference between the growth of capital due to voluntary investment in the two systems, the second parenthetical term is the additional capital due to forced investment in the disturbed economy, $S_B'p''$ is the value of securities sold by the bank, and μ and ν are capital gains or losses on government securities. Let us assume for the present that $\mu = \nu = 0$.

When $\partial S/\partial r_M = 0$ (as we have been assuming), the periodic sum of voluntary investment and the increment in idle balances, as determined by a point on the S schedule, is constant and at a

---

[11] Since *partial* forced investment is characterized by $\Delta K > 0$, $\Delta S_I > 0$, and $\rho_K/r_M < 1$, the expressions developed in this section for complete forced investment of the growing economy are applicable to *any* adjustment in which forced investment is not zero. In the general case of partial forced investment, (6E.31) is written

(6E.49)
$$\Delta K' = \alpha \Delta m_2'' + \Delta S_I' p''', \text{ where } 0 < \alpha < 1.$$

Thus ρ_s and p again may rise or fall in any interval, though the reduction in the $\Delta m_2''$ term of $\Delta K'$ contributes to a downward movement. Cf. Chapter V-E(1).

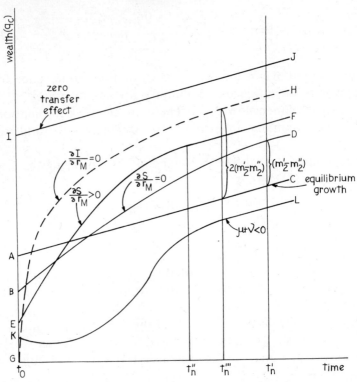

minimum, $\hat{\Delta} K'$. In equilibrium at t_n',

$$\text{(6E.51)} \qquad \sum_n \Delta K + (m_2' - m_2'') = n\hat{\Delta} K',$$

and, replacing $(m_2' - m_2'')$ by $S_B' p''$, (6E.50) reduces to

$$\text{(6E.52)} \qquad (m_2' - m_2'') > 0,$$

which represents forced investment. The corresponding wealth curve is BD, rising and concave downward. The downward concavity results from the fact that at t_0, BD is below AC, while at t_n', BD is above and parallel to AC. (6E.52) is independent of the I schedule, greater elasticity of which merely creates an earlier equilibrium.

Let S pass from a vertical to a rising schedule, I remaining fixed. At r_M'' and time t_0, ρ_K falls to $\rho_K'' < \rho_K'$, where $I(\rho_K'') = S(r_M'')$. ρ_s, p, and W fall with ρ_K, the wealth total moving to a point below B, such as E. The movements in ρ_K and those in W attributable to ρ_K are gradually reversed during the adjustment, but in equilibrium, which is prior to t'_n, wealth exceeds trend by more than (6E.52). This is because the upward slope of S accelerates the adjustment and reduces the interest rate at any point in time. Voluntary investment of each interval is increased, as is $\left(\sum_n \Delta K - n\hat{\Delta K'} \right)$ in (6E.50), the other terms of which are constant. EF, which reaches equilibrium at t''_n, is an example of the resulting path. A still flatter S schedule will further reduce wealth at t_0 and raise it in the equilibrium, which occurs to the left of t''_n.

The maximum equilibrium wealth total, relative to trend, occurs when $\partial I / \partial r_M = 0$. In this case the rate of voluntary investment is a maximum and equal to $\hat{\Delta K'}$. Hence, $\sum_n \Delta K = n\hat{\Delta K'}$, and (6E.50) becomes

$$(6E.53) \qquad (m'_2 - m''_2) + S'_B p'' = 2(m'_2 - m''_2).$$

The wealth curve is GH, the equilibrium of which happens to be t'''_n. The initial point, G, coincides with the origin, reflecting the implied reduction of ρ_K and W to zero when I is vertical. Given a rising S function, the transition from the vertical to a downward-sloping I schedule accordingly lowers (6E.50) by reducing $\left(\sum_n \Delta K - n\hat{\Delta K'} \right)$. However, a still flatter I schedule may raise or lower the wealth line.

The wealth effect will again speed the adjustment. Though this has no effect on the degree of forced investment, the more rapid decline of the interest rate will raise the rate of voluntary investment, given $\partial I / \partial r_M < 0$. The impact of introducing the wealth effect is comparable to that of additional elasticity of the saving function. If the wealth effect were the only effective equilibrating force, the value of idle balances would rise at once to m'_2, followed by an equal increment of forced investment. Since the adjustment is instantaneous, total wealth is given by (6E.21), which abstracts from voluntary investment. The p'' term of (6E.21) is given by (6E.20), and wealth is above trend by (6E.25) or (6E.26). The corresponding wealth curve is IJ, parallel to AC.

Since $p'' > p'$, both μ and ν are > 0 and (6E.26) exceeds (6E.53), which we have just identified as the maximum by which wealth exceeds trend. But (6E.53) incorporates the arbitrary assumption that $\mu = \nu = 0$. If this is relaxed, the preceding analysis must be qualified. We have seen that forced investment tends to raise security prices, and voluntary investment to lower them. (6E.20), which includes forced investment only, is thus the maximum attainable p^n, and (6E.26), produced by the exclusive operation of the wealth effect, is indeed the maximum by which wealth can exceed trend. In general, the adjustment is not instantaneous, and the transfer effect is also operative, if not actually dominant. Positive voluntary investment will therefore reduce p^n below (6E.20), and the wealth difference below (6E.26).

The general effect of re-introducing μ and $\nu \gtrless 0$ is to raise or lower the wealth curves, depending on whether $p^n \gtrless p'$ in the case of μ, and whether $p^n \gtrless p''$ in the case of ν. Though the requisite conditions are extreme (see [6E.40]), it is conceivable that a sufficiently large negative value of $\mu + \nu$ might reduce a wealth curve to the point of falling below AC in equilibrium, and even turning downward at an earlier point. An example is the path, KL. The reduction of ρ_K during the adjustment reinforces the net downward tendency in wealth by lowering the average real security price and thus the ratio of the voluntary investment-security increments. However, the return movement of ρ_K tends to raise the wealth increments on the way to equilibrium.

F. SUMMARY AND INTERPRETATION

1. Summary of Monetary Contraction

The contractionary disturbance is an open-market sale instantaneously carried out by the central bank. At a higher rate of interest, securities are increased and idle balances reduced. In the following period the higher yield evokes an excess of intended saving over investment in the form of an excess demand for securities. Savers inadvertently purchase existing securities at a higher price and lower yield. Active balances, of which all current saving consists, are thereby transferred to the holders of existing securities and held idle. The loss of active money reduces the commodity price level proportionately. The deflation raises the value of idle money further, and produces a downward wealth effect on interest. The combined effect of the "transfer" of excess saving and the wealth effect, both of which materialize in an increase in existing-security demand, eventually reduces the interest rate to the natural level at which saving and investment are again equal. Unlike the inflationary process, the contractionary adjustment does not create rotations in the asset-demand schedules counter to those produced by the central bank.

The adjustment again promises to cause changes in the income per share, ρ_s, but the financial adjustment is not affected if (a) firms do not issue securities when ρ_s is altered by an unintended capital increment (there is no inherent inducement for firms to issue securities in this event), (b) households expect the current income of securities to continue (expectations of change in ρ_s will shorten or lengthen the adjustment process), (c) changes in security value due to ρ_s stimulate equal changes in security demand. A return flow of idle money to the income stream will occur if the downward movement of prices is delayed. Apparent real income is reduced, as are saving and the investment-saving gap. The lag of the price level may be due to inventory accretion. But sooner or later prices are assumed to respond fully to the loss of active balances, reversing any earlier offset to the adjustment process.

With L_2 fixed at the natural rate of interest, the value of idle balances, the ratio of active to idle money, and the total velocity of money are the same in the new equilibrium as in the old. Given the form of our functions, the transfer of active to idle balances and the decline of the price level invariably fall over time.

If the real adjustment is one of zero forced investment, a limiting first interval raises ρ_K to the level of the higher rate of interest. ρ_s, S_{VO}, W, and p increase, the latter returning to its pre-disturbance value. In each subsequent interval, abstracting from voluntary investment and the wealth effect, ρ_s falls but p is on net constant. Wealth rises by the increment to idle balances. From one equilibrium to another, the net wealth gain is the total increase in m_2, which is equal to the value of securities sold by the bank. The wealth effect on interest accelerates the adjustment, but has no effect on the variables in the new equilibrium. Voluntary investment mitigates the fall in ρ_s and creates a net increase in p over the course of a typical interval. The net wealth increment is the sum of voluntary investment, the increase in idle balances, and capital gains on government securities due to the rise of p. In the new equilibrium, wealth is above trend by the maximum amount when $\partial I/\partial r_M = 0$ and $\partial S/\partial r_M$ is only infinitesimally above zero. The former condition maximizes voluntary investment, while the latter condition creates the slowest possible adjustment and thereby the maximum increase in p. The excess of wealth over trend can be expressed as the value of securities sold by the bank plus the capital gains due to the rise of p. Given $\partial I/\partial r_M = 0$, more elastic saving schedules speed the adjustment and lower wealth relative to trend by reducing the increase in p. Given a non-vertical S function, the passage of I from a vertical to a downward-sloping function produces an earlier equilibrium in which wealth is lower. A still flatter I schedule will have counterbalancing effects on wealth. The minimum wealth total is produced by the vertical S schedule in combination with a horizontal I schedule. The former minimizes the periodic growth of capital and idle balances, while the latter creates the fastest possible adjustment and the minimum increase in p. However, even in the least favorable case, wealth exceeds trend by the securities sold by the bank valued at the difference between the pre-disturbance and sale price. The wealth effect influences the adjustment in a manner identical to that of a more elastic saving schedule.

When forced investment is complete, $\partial S/\partial r_M = 0$, and voluntary investment is excluded, ρ_s, p, and W rise monotonically throughout the adjustment. In equilibrium, wealth has increased by the value of securities sold by the bank, the capital gains on government securities due to the rise of p, and total forced investment, which is equal to the increase in the value of idle balances. The wealth effect again accelerates the adjustment without altering the values of variables in the new equilibrium. $\partial S/\partial r_M > 0$ causes a temporary decrease in ρ_K and thereby ρ_s, p, and W. Voluntary investment tends to reduce ρ_s and p to the point where they may fall in any interval. The wealth change is the sum of voluntary investment, forced investment, and the capital gains or losses on government securities. Apart from extreme values of the variables, creating a substantial security-price reduction, the wealth change is positive. For the moment, we abstract from changes in the value of government securities and the wealth effect. $\partial S/\partial r_M = 0$ then creates the minimum possible wealth total, which is above trend by the total increase in real idle balances. This result is independent of the I schedule. Given a non-vertical I function, $\partial S/\partial r_M > 0$ lowers ρ_K and W at the start of the adjustment, but raises wealth in the equilibrium over that produced by $\partial S/\partial r_M = 0$. Still greater elasticity of S raises W further. The maximum wealth is produced by the vertical I schedule, for which wealth exceeds trend by the increase in the value of idle balances (which measures forced investment) plus the value of securities sold by the bank. The wealth effect again duplicates the impact of greater elasticity of the saving function. Allowance for capital gains or losses on government securities raises or lowers the wealth curves. Maximum wealth in relation to trend occurs when voluntary investment is zero, which maximizes p. This can be brought about in the growing economy if the wealth effect is the only equilibrating mechanism. The adjustment period is then infinitesimal and wealth exceeds trend by the increase in idle balances, the value of securities sold by the bank, plus capital gains on all government securities. At the other extreme, capital losses may reduce equilibrium wealth below trend.

2. Inflation and Deflation Compared

The behavior of real security prices and total wealth for both the expansionary and contractionary adjustment is summarized in Table 6-1. There and in the following discussion we let ZFS denote zero forced saving; CFS, complete forced saving; ZFI, zero forced investment; CFI, complete forced investment; VS, voluntary saving; and VI, voluntary investment. A sum, such as $CFS + VS$,

TABLE 6-1
SECURITY-PRICE AND WEALTH CHANGES IN INFLATION AND DEFLATION

| | | p | W | $+ VS$ or VI | |
				p	W at Equilibrium in Relation to Trend
Inflation	ZFS	↓	↓	↑ or ↓	< (or >)*
	CFS	↓	κ (or ↓)*	↓	> or <
Deflation	ZFI	κ	↑	↑	>
	CFI	↑	↑	↑ or ↓	> or <

*The wealth change or inequality in parentheses refers to an inflationary adjustment in which government-security holdings of households are not zero.

denotes a complete forced-saving adjustment in the context of voluntary saving. In the table an upward or downward arrow indicates that the variable rises or falls, respectively, during the adjustment; the letter, κ, that it is constant. The last two columns refer to the adjustment with voluntary saving, in the case of inflation, and voluntary investment, in deflation. We begin by abstracting from both VS and VI. When the voluntary components are introduced, the reader will find that Figures 5–9, 5–12, 6–8, and 6–11 are helpful references.

The ZFI deflationary adjustment exhibits features that parallel both CFS and ZFS of the expansion. In both ZFI and CFS, ex post investment lies along the I schedule, maintaining equality between ρ_K and r_M. But while wealth is constant for CFS, the loss of idle balances being offset by an equal gain of capital, wealth rises during ZFI by the increment in idle balances. In this respect ZFI is, apart from the movement of ρ_K, equal and opposite to ZFS, in which wealth falls by the loss of idle balances. However, the constancy of real security prices during ZFI is unique, since prices fall both for CFS and ZFS. Notice that had we not assumed that the open-market purchase exhausts private holdings of government securities, the decline of security prices during the inflation would have created capital losses on these issues. For ZFS wealth would fall more; for CFS wealth would decline instead of remaining constant.

CFI without VI exhibits fewer similarities to either expansionary adjustment. Since ex post investment lies along the S schedule, ρ_K moves opposite to that of ZFS. But wealth rises during CFI by the increase in idle balances, forced investment (which is equal to the increase in idle money), plus capital gains on government securities because of the rise of prices. This is a wealth change which is considerably greater than the absolute wealth change of any other adjustment.

$ZFI + VI$ results in wealth curves that are uniformly above trend in equilibrium. The parallel that comes to mind is $ZFS + VS$, for which equilibrium wealth is invariably below trend. However, while security prices rise for $ZFI + VI$, they may rise or fall for $ZFS + VS$. Hence, if we modify the latter adjustment by allowing households to hold government securities, there is doubtless some limiting security-price rise for which equilibrium wealth is drawn above trend. There are, perhaps, more similarities between $ZFI + VI$ and $CFS + VS$. While security prices rise in the former case, they fall in the latter. Though the wealth curves of $CFS + VS$ straddle the trend line, the highest attainable line is also the minimum line for $ZFI + VI$. Moreover, the maximum by which a line of $CFS + VS$ falls below trend is the value of securities purchased by the bank. If households held other government securities, this quantity would be increased by capital losses due to the decline of security prices. The resulting sum is exactly equal to the maximum distance by which a line of $ZFI + VI$ lies *above* trend.

$CFI + VI$ produces wealth paths that are above and below trend, though the maximum above trend is considerably greater than that of $ZFI + VI$. The parallel inflationary case is probably $ZFS + VS$, for which security prices may also rise or fall, and for which

the conditions underlying an equilibrium wealth total above trend
are doubtless as extreme as they are for one below trend in the case
of $CFI + VI$.

The most apparent anomaly that emerges from this comparison
is that some of the wealth totals of $CFS + VS$ lie above trend. For
if this were not true, we might summarize our results by saying that
equilibrium wealth is invariably above trend in the case of deflation,
and below for inflation, except in extreme cases of a security-price
decline during $CFI + VI$, and a security-price rise during $ZFS +
VS$. However, in spite of the exception, wealth gains certainly
seem to be more characteristic of deflation, and wealth losses, of
inflation. In spite of some overlap, deflationary cases occupy most
of the attainable area above the trend line, inflationary cases below.
Why is this so? One relevant consideration is that the monetary
changes produced by the central bank are, in real terms, ultimately
neutralized. Thus, in inflation the increase in real idle balances is
reduced by the adjustment, and conversely in deflation. These
changes in real balances, together with the open-market security
transactions, are in fact the only wealth movements, apart from
the temporary interest fluctuations, that are bound to occur. The
inflationary process *reduces* real balances, but may or may not replace the securities *lost* to the bank; deflation *increases* real balances, but may or may not offset the *gain* of securities sold by the
bank. Clearly the balance of wealth tends downward in inflation,
upward in deflation. A second consideration is the non-sym-
metrical form of the saving function. In inflation the least favorable case of the growing economy is zero forced saving, for which
the net periodic wealth gain is the difference between voluntary
saving and the loss of idle balances. Since the saving schedule
slopes upward, voluntary saving and the total wealth gain are reduced below the growth rate of the undisturbed economy. In deflation the least favorable case is zero forced investment, for which
the net periodic wealth gain—the sum of voluntary investment plus
the growth of idle balances—is provided by a point on the S schedule.[12] Since saving cannot have an interest elasticity below zero,

---

[12] The wealth gain, as described in this sentence and the preceding two, abstracts from
any change in the value of government securities due to security-price movements. The
only wealth components that change during either the inflationary or deflationary adjustments are idle balances and the capital stock. A more detailed treatment of the wealth
changes of the contractionary adjustment in which government securities are excluded is
given in Chapter VIII-H(1).

the minimum increase in wealth, determined by a vertical S function, is equal to the growth rate of the undisturbed system. Only a saving schedule that sloped *downward* for interest rates above the natural would duplicate the wealth-reducing powers of the inflationary adjustment.[13]

---

[13] Insofar as the deflationary adjustment tends to raise wealth, variability of the L_2 function will result in a net rightward shift of that schedule (see Chapter V-E[4]). This will slow the adjustment, raise m_2 in equilibrium, reduce over-all velocity, and cause price-level declines that are more than proportional to the monetary contraction.

The conclusions of the inflation-deflation wealth comparison are generally favorable to Metzler's thesis that an open-market purchase reduces wealth and, via a saving-wealth relation, stimulates saving and the rate of growth (Metzler, "Wealth, Saving, and the Rate of Interest," *Journal of Political Economy,* Vol. LIX [April, 1951]). I have criticized Metzler for treating what is basically a dynamic problem in static terms (Horwich, "Real Assets and the Theory of Interest," *Journal of Political Economy,* Vol. LXX [April, 1962], pp. 157–69). Metzler completely ignores changes in securities and capital during the adjustment process. However, if we can sweep aside the task of assigning empirical probabilities to the net wealth impact of a disturbance, Metzler's hypothesis gains some support from the dynamic analysis of Chapters V and VI.

Once questions of empirical relevance are raised, the likelihood that short-run deflation in modern economies is accompanied by unemployment of labor and capital must be considered. If such unemployment occurs, there will be a reduction in total security income and thus the value of securities and total wealth. The tendency of wealth to rise during deflation must accordingly be qualified.

CHAPTER VII

Two Securities: Macroeconomics of the Interest Structure

A. A NEW SECURITY

In this chapter we introduce an additional security to compete with the one already present in the system. This will replace our single security price and rate of interest by a "structure" of two prices and interest rates. Such a generalization will provide useful knowledge of the analysis of monetary change under conditions more nearly approximated in the empirical world. The particular qualities of the new security that distinguish it in the minds of asset holders from the old one are immaterial to this analysis. We shall only require that it, too, be a common-stock, equity-type security, the issuance of which has created a given number of the identical capital units. The new security might be the obligation of non-corporate as opposed to corporate business, small as opposed to large enterprise, or riskier as compared with safer investment undertakings. It is only important that the new security be a less-than-perfect substitute for the old one over a wide and continuous range of interest rates for both wealth holders and current savers.[1]

---

[1] The analysis of this chapter is applicable to securities of differing maturity only if they are less than perfect substitutes. If expectations are the dominant influence acting on the term structure, then such securities are in effect perfect substitutes. If long and short-term securities are imperfect substitutes owing, say, to differences in liquidity, then they are covered by the framework of this chapter. For a detailed discussion of the expectations hypothesis see Friedrich A. Lutz, "The Structure of Interest Rates," *Quarterly Journal of Economics,* Vol. LV (November, 1940), pp. 36–63, esp. pp. 36–37 (reprinted in William Fellner and B. F. Haley [eds.], *Readings in the Theory of Income Distribution* [Philadelphia: The Blakiston Co., 1946], pp. 499–529). A significant empirical study by David Meiselman tends to support the expectations hypothesis: *The Term Structure of Interest Rates* (Englewood Cliffs, N.J.: Prentice-Hall, Inc., 1962). A more recent work by John Wood, *The Term Structure of Interest Rates: A Theoretical and Empirical Study* (unpublished dissertation; Purdue University, June, 1962), finds that expectations may explain the yield differentials between securities of relatively short maturity, but not of the entire range of maturities. For an analysis of the imperfect-substitute theory, based on liquidity considerations, see J. M. Culbertson, "The Term Structure of Interest Rates," *Quarterly Journal of Economics,* Vol. LXXI (November, 1957), pp. 485–517.

For each class of security purchaser we are thus providing an additional margin of substitution—between securities—as well as between each security and idle balances for wealth holders, and between each security and consumption for current savers. In keeping with our separation of stock and flow decisions, we assume that the rates of substitution are in general not the same for asset holders as they are for savers. But we shall assume that the coefficients of supply and demand have the same sign with respect to their individual interest rates and prices as did the previous functions with respect to their interest rate and price. s_1 will denote the type 1 security, whose price is p_1, s_2 the type 2 security, having a price of p_2. K_1 is the number of capital units financed by the issuance of s_1 securities, and K_2 the number financed by s_2 securities. The total capital stock is

$$(7A.1) \qquad\qquad K = K_1 + K_2 .$$

ρ_{K_1} is the rate of return on the K_1 capital units, and ρ_{K_2} the return on the K_2 units. The income on type 1 and type 2 securities, respectively, is

$$(7A.2) \qquad\qquad \rho_{s_1} = \frac{\rho_{K_1} K_1}{S_{10}} \quad \text{and} \quad \rho_{s_2} = \frac{\rho_{K_2} K_2}{S_{20}} ,$$

where S_{10} and S_{20} are the existing quantities of s_1 and s_2, respectively. The corresponding interest rates are

$$(7A.3) \qquad\qquad r_1 = \frac{\rho_{s_1}}{p_1} \quad \text{and} \quad r_2 = \frac{\rho_{s_2}}{p_2} .$$

Although all capital units are physically identical, ρ_{K_1} and ρ_{K_2} differ because of differences in the marginal product of capital financed by the two types of securities.[2] The over-all return to investment is ρ_K, the mean of ρ_{K_1} and ρ_{K_2}, weighted by K_1 and K_2, respectively.

In Part B we shall specify the relation between every supply and demand function and the yield and price of each security. In doing so we shall "sector" the stock and flow markets into two components each, one in which the s_1 security, and the other, the s_2 security is held or traded. Included in the budget of all markets will be a "financial-substitution function," which finances movements be-

---

[2] Since all capital is physically identical, there is a single process and cost of capital production. Hence differences in the return to capital cannot be based on differences in the rate of build-up and cost, or "marginal efficiency," of the K_1 and K_2 units. Instead, we must assume that capital is employed in the several uses corresponding to the two types of finance more and less intensively with labor. In this way differences in the marginal product of capital will provide the basis for the difference between ρ_{K_1} and ρ_{K_2} (see pp. 40–42).

tween the substitute securities at all prices and yields other than the equilibrium. Part C considers the direct impact of an open-market purchase, first on the isolated stock and flow markets, and then on the combined system. Part D reconstructs the model in terms of Hicksian "substitution functions," each of which is the locus of r_1–r_2 combinations that constitute equilibrium for a given market or submarket. Using this framework Part E outlines the entire financial adjustment to the open-market purchase. Specific paths to the new equilibrium are described in the appendix.

B. THE MODEL REDEFINED

The two-security system is described for the existing-asset, output, and total markets in turn. We shall specify the sign of the supply and demand yield-price coefficients initially in terms of the security-quantity, rather than the security-value functions. This appears to be a more natural course in discussing related securities.

1. The Existing-Asset Markets

Since S_{10} and S_{20} are the given existing-security quantities, they are independent not only of their own yield and price, but also that of the alternative security:

(7B.1) $$\frac{\partial S_{10}}{\partial\left(\frac{1}{r_1}\right)} = \frac{\partial S_{10}}{\partial p_1} = 0, \qquad \frac{\partial S_{10}}{\partial\left(\frac{1}{r_2}\right)} = \frac{\partial S_{10}}{\partial p_2} = 0;$$

(7B.2) $$\frac{\partial S_{20}}{\partial\left(\frac{1}{r_2}\right)} = \frac{\partial S_{20}}{\partial p_2} = 0, \qquad \frac{\partial S_{20}}{\partial\left(\frac{1}{r_1}\right)} = \frac{\partial S_{20}}{\partial p_1} = 0.$$

D_{10} is the quantity demand for s_1 securities, financed out of existing wealth. It is assumed to be an inverse function of its own interest-reciprocal and price, but a positive function of the interest-reciprocal and price of the substitute s_2 security:

(7B.3) $$\frac{\partial D_{10}}{\partial\left(\frac{1}{r_1}\right)} \text{ and } \frac{\partial D_{10}}{\partial p_1} < 0, \qquad \frac{\partial D_{10}}{\partial\left(\frac{1}{r_2}\right)} \text{ and } \frac{\partial D_{10}}{\partial p_2} > 0.$$

D_{20} is the existing demand for s_2 securities. It responds to interest and price analogously:

(7B.4) $$\frac{\partial D_{20}}{\partial\left(\frac{1}{r_2}\right)} \text{ and } \frac{\partial D_{20}}{\partial p_2} < 0, \qquad \frac{\partial D_{20}}{\partial\left(\frac{1}{r_1}\right)} \text{ and } \frac{\partial D_{20}}{\partial p_1} > 0.$$

The corresponding security-value functions are:

(7B.5) $$S_{1VO} = S_{1O}p_1 = S_{1O}\left(\frac{\rho_{s_1}}{r_1}\right), \qquad S_{2VO} = S_{2O}p_2 = S_{2O}\left(\frac{\rho_{s_2}}{r_2}\right);$$

(7B.6) $$D_{1VO} = D_{1O}p_1 = D_{1O}\left(\frac{\rho_{s_1}}{r_1}\right), \qquad D_{2VO} = D_{2O}p_2 = D_{2O}\left(\frac{\rho_{s_2}}{r_2}\right).$$

In diagrams of the wealth market S_{1VO} and S_{2VO} will emanate from the origin, as did the previous single-security function, S_{VO}; D_{1VO} and D_{2VO} will be rising, falling, or vertical, depending on the elasticity of the underlying security-quantity demand schedule (see Chapter II-B[3]).

Next we divide total wealth into two components, W_1 and W_2, where

(7B.7) $$W = W_1 + W_2.$$

Included in W_1 are S_{1VO} and m_{12}, a portion of real idle balances held as an alternative to s_1 securities. W_2 contains S_{2VO} and m_{22}, an alternative to s_2 securities. Hence

(7B.8) $$W_1 = S_{1VO} + m_{12},$$

(7B.9) $$W_2 = S_{2VO} + m_{22}.$$

L_{12} and L_{22} are the demands, respectively, for m_{12} and m_{22}, where

(7B.10) $$\frac{\partial L_{12}}{\partial\left(\frac{1}{r_1}\right)} > 0, \qquad \frac{\partial L_{22}}{\partial\left(\frac{1}{r_2}\right)} > 0.$$

The idle-balance aggregates are:

(7B.11) $$m_2 = m_{12} + m_{22}, \qquad L_2 = L_{12} + L_{22}.$$

The dichotomy of m_2 and total wealth is a natural step following the introduction of an additional security. It is a convenient device for tracing the process of substitution between securities, but has no other significance. The dichotomy simplifies the analysis without altering the total variables in any way. Any household with a diversified portfolio will, of course, own both W_1 and W_2 components.

At all interest rates other than the equilibrium, there is in each sector of the wealth market a desired movement between the given security and the alternative one. Each wealth budget accordingly must include a demand component that reflects this desire to substitute between securities. We let r_1' and r_2' be the prevailing equilibrium yields of s_1 and s_2, respectively, and define two security "financial-substitution functions":

(7B.12) $\Delta D_{2VO} \gtreqless 0$ when $r_1 \lesseqgtr r_1'$,

(7B.13) $\Delta D_{1VO} \gtreqless 0$ when $r_2 \lesseqgtr r_2'$.

ΔD_{2VO} is the demand for s_2 securities by s_1 holders, and ΔD_{1VO} is the demand for s_1 securities by s_2 holders, both in real-value units. The asset-demand equations are thus:

(7B.14) $D_{1VO} + L_{12} + \Delta D_{2VO} = W_1$,

(7B.15) $D_{2VO} + L_{22} + \Delta D_{1VO} = W_2$.

We assume that in general all three demand components of each equation respond sympathetically to autonomous wealth changes. Since each wealth total, the demand for securities, and the demand for idle balances is a linear monotonic function of its interest-reciprocal, ΔD_{2VO} and ΔD_{1VO} are also linear and monotonic in $1/r_1$ and $1/r_2$, respectively. Hence (7B.12) and (7B.13) imply

(7B.16) $$\frac{\partial \Delta D_{2VO}}{\partial \left(\dfrac{1}{r_1}\right)} > 0,$$

(7B.17) $$\frac{\partial \Delta D_{1VO}}{\partial \left(\dfrac{1}{r_2}\right)} > 0.$$

This is to say that the real balances wealth holders commit to the purchase of substitute securities varies directly with the interest-reciprocal and inversely with the interest rate.

The W_1 existing-asset market is illustrated in Figure 7–1. D_{1VO} is constructed on the basis of the given yield of the alternative

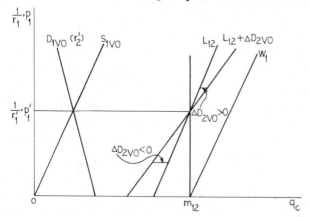

FIGURE 7–1
The W_1 Existing-Asset Market, Including the s_2 Financial-Substitution Function

security, r_2'. L_{12} and ΔD_{2VO} are both rising functions. The latter is the horizontal difference between L_{12} and $L_{12} + \Delta D_{2VO}$. The difference, (7B.8) − (7B.14), is

(7B.18) $$S_{1VO} - D_{1VO} = L_{12} - m_{12} + \Delta D_{2VO},$$

which states that the excess value supply of (or demand for) s_1 securities is equal to the excess demand for (or supply of) m_{12} balances plus the incremental value demand for s_2 securities. In equilibrium at r_1' and p_1', $\Delta D_{2VO} = 0$ and holders of the W_1 component are willing to allocate their wealth entirely between s_1 and m_{12}. But at $r_1 < r_1'$ and $p_1 > p_1'$, the *quantity* demanded of s_1 securities drops (although the value demand, D_{1VO}, will increase, decrease, or remain constant depending on the elasticity of D_{1O}), and W_1 holders choose to replace s_1 not only with m_{12}, as measured by the movement along L_{12}, but also by additional s_2 securities, as indicated by $\Delta D_{2VO} > 0$. At $r_1 > r_1'$ and $p_1 < p_1'$, the quantity demanded of s_1 securities increases at the expense of both m_{12} and s_2 securities, as indicated by the movement down L_{12} and $\Delta D_{2VO} < 0$, respectively. The presence of ΔD_{2VO} has the general effect of rotating L_{12} counterclockwise through $1/r_1'$. For at $r_1 < r_1'$, s_2 securities compete with m_{12} balances as the alternative to s_1; hence L_{12} is farther to the left than it would otherwise be. At $r_1 > r_1'$, the additional demand for s_1 securities is financed both by drawing down m_{12} and by transferring demand from s_2 securities; this enables L_{12} to be farther to the right.

The W_2 market has analogous characteristics. The equation corresponding to (7B.18) is:

(7B.19) $$S_{2VO} - D_{2VO} = L_{22} - m_{22} + \Delta D_{1VO}.$$

The latter expression is (7B.9) − (7B.15).

The equilibria of the individual wealth markets are replicas of the single existing-asset market summarized in Chapter II-B(5). The equations, (2B.28)–(2B.40), are replaced by a corresponding set in which each component variable and equation is subdivided into two. In the following summary the only equations that do not correspond accordingly to an equation in (2B.28)–(2B.40) are (7B.21), (7B.25), (7B.26), (7B.32), and (7B.35), which are merely identity aggregates, and (7B.38), which are equilibrium conditions for the financial-substitution functions:

(7B.20) $$W_1 = S_{1VO} + m_{12}, \quad W_2 = S_{2VO} + m_{22},$$

(7B.21) $$W = W_1 + W_2,$$

(7B.22)
$$m_{12} = \frac{M_{12}}{P}, \quad m_{22} = \frac{M_{22}}{P},$$

(7B.23)
$$M_{12} = M - M_1 - M_{22},$$

(7B.24)
$$M = \overline{M},$$

(7B.25)
$$M_2 = M_{12} + M_{22},$$

(7B.26)
$$m_2 = \frac{M_2}{P},$$

(7B.27)
$$S_{1VO} = S_{1O}p_1, \quad S_{2VO} = S_{2O}p_2,$$

(7B.28)
$$S_{1O} = \overline{S}_{1O}, \quad S_{2O} = \overline{S}_{2O},$$

(7B.29)
$$p_1 = \frac{\rho_{s_1}}{r_1}, \quad p_2 = \frac{\rho_{s_2}}{r_2},$$

(7B.30)
$$\rho_{s_1} = \frac{\rho_{K_1}K_1}{S_{1O}}, \quad \rho_{s_2} = \frac{\rho_{K_2}K_2}{S_{2O}},$$

(7B.31)
$$K_1 = \overline{K}_1, \quad K_2 = \overline{K}_2,$$

(7B.32)
$$K = K_1 + K_2,$$

(7B.33)
$$L_{12} = L_{12}(r_1), \quad L_{22} = L_{22}(r_2),$$

(7B.34)
$$L_{12} = \frac{M_{12}}{P}, \quad L_{22} = \frac{M_{22}}{P},$$

(7B.35)
$$L_2 = L_{12} + L_{22},$$

(7B.36)
$$D_{1VO}(r_1, r_2) = W_1 - L_{12} - \Delta D_{2VO}, \quad D_{2VO}(r_1, r_2) = W_2 - L_{22} - \Delta D_{1VO},$$

(7B.37)
$$D_{1O} = \frac{D_{1VO}}{p_1}, \quad D_{2O} = \frac{D_{2VO}}{p_2},$$

(7B.38)
$$\Delta D_{2VO} = 0, \quad \Delta D_{1VO} = 0.$$

(7B.36) makes explicit the dependence of both D_{1VO} and D_{2VO} on r_1 and r_2, as derived from (7B.3) and (7B.4). Altogether there are 31 independent equations and 36 variables:

$$W_1, W_2, W, S_{1VO}, S_{2VO}, m_{12}, m_{22}, m_2, M_{12}, M_{22}, M_2,$$
$$M_1, M, P, S_{1O}, S_{2O}, p_1, p_2, \rho_{s_1}, \rho_{s_2}, r_1, r_2, \rho_{K_1}, \rho_{K_2},$$
$$K_1, K_2, K, L_{12}, L_{22}, L_2, D_{1VO}, D_{2VO}, \Delta D_{2VO}, \Delta D_{1VO},$$
$$D_{1O}, D_{2O}.$$

The output markets in Section 2 will provide 30 additional equations and 25 variables, creating a total system of 61 equations and 61 variables. In the existing-asset markets, equilibrium will be characterized by a unique combination of r_1 and r_2 and p_1 and p_2 and an allocation of cash between M_1, M_{12}, and M_{22} at which supply and demand for all assets are equal.

2. The Output Markets

We let S_{1N} be the new supply of s_1 securities per unit of time, and S_{2N}, that of s_2 securities. We assume:

(7B.39) $$\frac{\partial S_{1N}}{\partial \left(\frac{1}{r_1}\right)} \text{ and } \frac{\partial S_{1N}}{\partial p_1} > 0, \quad \frac{\partial S_{1N}}{\partial \left(\frac{1}{r_2}\right)} = \frac{\partial S_{1N}}{\partial p_2} = 0;$$

(7B.40) $$\frac{\partial S_{2N}}{\partial \left(\frac{1}{r_2}\right)} \text{ and } \frac{\partial S_{2N}}{\partial p_2} > 0, \quad \frac{\partial S_{2N}}{\partial \left(\frac{1}{r_1}\right)} = \frac{\partial S_{2N}}{\partial p_1} = 0.$$

Verbally, the new supply of each security varies directly with its own interest-reciprocal and price, but is independent of the yield and price of the competing security; there is no substitution between securities on the part of new suppliers. We define D_{1N} as the quantity-demand over time by current savers for s_1 securities, and D_{2N}, the demand for s_2 securities. As in the case of existing-security demand:

(7B.41) $$\frac{\partial D_{1N}}{\partial \left(\frac{1}{r_1}\right)} \text{ and } \frac{\partial D_{1N}}{\partial p_1} < 0, \quad \frac{\partial D_{1N}}{\partial \left(\frac{1}{r_2}\right)} \text{ and } \frac{\partial D_{1N}}{\partial p_2} > 0;$$

(7B.42) $$\frac{\partial D_{2N}}{\partial \left(\frac{1}{r_2}\right)} \text{ and } \frac{\partial D_{2N}}{\partial p_2} < 0, \quad \frac{\partial D_{2N}}{\partial \left(\frac{1}{r_1}\right)} \text{ and } \frac{\partial D_{2N}}{\partial p_1} > 0.$$

The value counterparts for the new supply and demand are:

(7B.43) $$S_{1VN} = I_1 = S_{1N}p_1 = S_{1N}\left(\frac{\rho_{s_1}}{r_1}\right),$$

$$S_{2VN} = I_2 = S_{2N}p_2 = S_{2N}\left(\frac{\rho_{s_2}}{r_2}\right);$$

(7B.44) $$D_{1VN} = S_1 = D_{1N}p_1 = D_{1N}\left(\frac{\rho_{s_1}}{r_1}\right),$$

$$D_{2VN} = S_2 = D_{2N}p_2 = D_{2N}\left(\frac{\rho_{s_2}}{r_2}\right).$$

Thus all investment is a supply of new securities, and all saving is a demand for securities. More precisely,

(7B.45) $I_1 = I_{s_1}, \quad I_2 = I_{s_2}, \quad S_1 = S_{s_1}, \quad S_2 = S_{s_2}.$

In accordance with (2C.18),

(7B.46) $\dfrac{\partial S_1}{\partial\left(\dfrac{1}{r_1}\right)}$ and $\dfrac{\partial S_2}{\partial\left(\dfrac{1}{r_2}\right)} < 0,$

which implies that D_{1N} and D_{2N} are elastic schedules.[3]   The technological investment functions are

(7B.47) $\rho_{K_1} = \rho_{K_1}(I_1), \quad \rho_{K_2}(I_2), \quad$ where $\dfrac{\partial \rho_{K_1}}{\partial I_1}$ and $\dfrac{\partial \rho_{K_2}}{\partial I_2} < 0.$

Entrepreneurial profit-maximizing behavior results in

(7B.48) $r_1 = \rho_{K_1}, \quad r_2 = \rho_{K_2}, \quad \dfrac{\partial I_1}{\partial\left(\dfrac{1}{r_1}\right)}$ and $\dfrac{\partial I_2}{\partial\left(\dfrac{1}{r_2}\right)} > 0.$

Equilibrium exists when

(7B.49) $S_1 = I_1$ and $S_2 = I_2.$

Total real income, like wealth, is divided into two portions, y_1 and y_2:

(7B.50) $y = y_1 + y_2.$

Included in y_1 are S_1 and its own consumption alternative, C_1, plus a financial-substitution function:

(7B.51) $\Delta S_2 = \Delta D_{2VN} \gtreqless 0$ when $r_1 \lesseqgtr r_1',$

which is the value demand for additional s_2 securities by y_1 savers to replace s_1. r_1' is the prevailing equilibrium interest rate in the y_1 market. The sum of the demand components is

(7B.52) $S_1 + C_1 + \Delta S_2 = y_1.$

In order to preserve the relationships of the single-security model, we assume

(7B.53) $\dfrac{\partial C_1}{\partial\left(\dfrac{1}{r_1}\right)} > 0.$

Assuming that S_1 and C_1 are linear and monotonic in $1/r_1$, so is

---

[3] See p. 43, n. 29.

ΔS_2 $(\partial y_1 / \partial [1/r_1]$ is, of course, zero). Hence (7B.51) implies

(7B.54)
$$\frac{\partial \Delta S_2}{\partial \left(\dfrac{1}{r_1}\right)} > 0.$$

For the y_2 income component:

(7B.55) $\Delta S_1 = \Delta D_{1VN} \gtreqless 0$ when $r_2 \lesseqgtr r_2'$,

(7B.56) $S_2 + C_2 + \Delta S_1 = y_2$,

(7B.57)
$$\frac{\partial C_2}{\partial \left(\dfrac{1}{r_2}\right)} > 0,$$

(7B.58)
$$\frac{\partial \Delta S_1}{\partial \left(\dfrac{1}{r_2}\right)} > 0,$$

where r_2' is the equilibrium yield, C_2 the consumption alternative to S_2, and ΔS_1 the demand for s_1 substitute securities. The saving, consumption, and investment aggregates are:

(7B.59) $S = S_1 + S_2$,

(7B.60) $C = C_1 + C_2$,

(7B.61) $I = I_1 + I_2$.

The y_1 output market of an interval, t, is drawn in Figure 7–2. The total budget, y_1, is a vertical line, while S_1 is falling in $1/r_1$

FIGURE 7–2
The y_1 Output Market, Including the s_2 Financial-Substitution Function

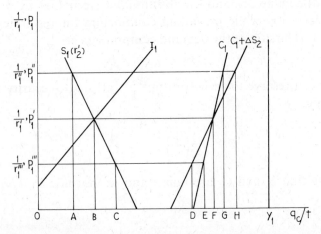

and p_1 in accordance with (7B.46). C_1 is a rising schedule ([7B.53]). $S_1 = D_{1VN}$ is drawn for a given value of the alternative yield, r_2'. ΔS_2, the horizontal difference between C_1 and $C_1 + \Delta S_2$, increases with $1/r_1$ ([7B.54]). Finally, I_1, together with S_1, determines the equilibrium at r_1' and p_1'. At r_1', $\Delta S_2 = 0$ and y_1 is exhausted between saving directed at s_1 securities and consumption. At $r_1'' < r_1'$ the quantity of s_1 securities demanded by savers falls and the value demand, S_1, falls from OB to OA. In the absence of a substitute security, consumption would rise by an equal amount, $OB - OA = AB$. But now both consumption and the value demand for s_2 rise by $FH = AB$, of which FG is the addition to consumption expenditures, and $GH = \Delta S_2$ are the funds transferred to the market for s_2. At $r_1''' > r_1'$ the quantity of s_1 securities demanded increases, and the corresponding value expenditure, S_1, rises from OB to OC, a net increment of BC. Consumption and the value demand for s_2 securities together drop by $DF = BC$, C_1 accounting for EF and ΔS_2 for DE of the total decline; i.e., when the yield rises to r_1''' expenditures of DE are diverted from the y_2 market to increase the purchase of s_1 securities.

The output markets are summarized by an equation set corresponding to that of Chapter II-C(3). Two variables and two equations correspond to each of those in (2C.26)–(2C.39), with the following exceptions: (1) The equations representing the supply and demand for active balances, (2C.26)–(2C.30), are repeated without change. It is neither necessary nor conceptually possible to restrict the use of active balances between either of the output markets. Active money will flow indiscriminately between y_1 and y_2 over time. (2) An additional equation, (7B.71), representing an independent consumption function, $C_1 = C_1(y_1)$, is present. This is necessary, as is evident in Section 3, to prevent the underdeterminacy of the system. It has no particular economic significance, since aggregate consumption, C, retains its residual character, given the saving functions. (3) Several identity aggregates are included: (7B.68) and (7B.78)–(7B.80). (4) Equations (7B.67) contain the financial-substitution functions, and (7B.81) expresses the accompanying equilibrium conditions. The equation system follows:

(7B.62) $$L_1 = k_1 Y,$$

(7B.63) $$k_1 = k_1,$$

(7B.64) $$Y = Py,$$

$$(7B.65) \qquad\qquad y = \bar{y},$$

$$(7B.66) \qquad\qquad L_1 = M_1,$$

$$(7B.67) \qquad y_1 = S_1 + C_1 + \Delta S_2, \quad y_2 = S_2 + C_2 + \Delta S_1,$$

$$(7B.68) \qquad\qquad y = y_1 + y_2,$$

$$(7B.69) \qquad S_1 = S_1(y_1, r_1, r_2), \quad S_2 = S_2(y_2, r_1, r_2),$$

$$(7B.70) \qquad\qquad S_1 = S_{s_1}, \quad S_2 = S_{s_2},$$

$$(7B.71) \qquad\qquad C_1 = C_1(y_1),$$

$$(7B.72) \qquad \rho_{K_1} = \rho_{K_1}(I_1), \quad \rho_{K_2} = \rho_{K_2}(I_2),$$

$$(7B.73) \qquad\qquad r_1 = \rho_{K_1}, \quad r_2 = \rho_{K_2},$$

$$(7B.74) \qquad\qquad I_1 = I_{s_1}, \quad I_2 = I_{s_2},$$

$$(7B.75) \qquad\qquad S_1 = I_1, \quad S_2 = I_2,$$

$$(7B.76) \qquad\qquad D_{1N} = \frac{S_1}{p_1}, \quad D_{2N} = \frac{S_2}{p_2},$$

$$(7B.77) \qquad\qquad S_{1N} = \frac{I_1}{p_1}, \quad S_{2N} = \frac{I_2}{p_2},$$

$$(7B.78) \qquad\qquad C = C_1 + C_2,$$

$$(7B.79) \qquad\qquad S = S_1 + S_2,$$

$$(7B.80) \qquad\qquad I = I_1 + I_2,$$

$$(7B.81) \qquad\qquad \Delta S_2 = 0, \quad \Delta S_1 = 0.$$

(7B.69) incorporates the dependence of S_1 and S_2 on both r_1 and r_2, as derived from (7B.39) and (7B.40). There are 30 equations in the above subset and 33 variables:

$$L_1, k_1, Y, P, y, M_1, y_1, y_2, S_1, S_2, C_1, C_2, \Delta S_1, \Delta S_2,$$
$$r_1, r_2, S_{s_1}, S_{s_2}, I_1, I_2, \rho_{K_1}, \rho_{K_2}, I_{s_1}, I_{s_2},$$
$$D_{1N}, D_{2N}, p_1, p_2, S_{1N}, S_{2N}, C, S, I.$$

Eight of these variables were encountered in the existing-asset markets:

$$P, M_1, r_1, r_2, \rho_{K_1}, \rho_{K_2}, p_1, p_2.$$

Hence the combined system contains 61 equations and 61 variables. The over-all equilibrium is one of equality between each pair of saving and investment components, each pair of idle-balance supply and demand functions, and the supply and demand for active balances. The equilibrium requires an appropriate combination of interest rates and a price level as determined by the allocation of money between active and both idle uses.

3. The Markets Combined

The equilibrium of the combined stock and flow two-security system is roughly comparable to that of the single-security model as described in Chapter II-D. We begin by taking the total system, (7B.20)–(7B.38) and (7B.62)–(7B.81), as stated; i.e., the impact of saving and investment on each of the existing-asset markets is, for the moment, ignored.

The output markets will independently determine the following variables:

$$y, y_1, y_2, S_1, S_2, I_1, I_2, r_1, r_2, \rho_{K_1}, \rho_{K_2},$$

and related identities. We can see this by reference to four derived equations:

$$(7B.82) \qquad S_1(y_1, r_1, r_2) = I_1(r_1),$$
$$S_2(y_2, r_1, r_2) = I_2(r_2),$$
$$\overline{y} = y_1 + y_2,$$
$$y_1 - S_1 = C_1(y_1).$$

The first two equations are the equilibrium conditions, (7B.75), the left sides of which have been replaced by (7B.69), and the right sides by (7B.72) and (7B.73). The third equation is (7B.68), the left side of which is replaced by (7B.65). The fourth and final equation is (7B.71), in which the left side is replaced by a combination of the initial equations of (7B.67) and (7B.81). The four equations determine four unknowns, r_1, r_2, y_1, y_2, and simultaneously the values of S_1, S_2, I_1, and I_2. Thus are the two natural rates of interest determined, along with the individual levels of saving and investment. The values of ρ_{K_1} and ρ_{K_2} follow from (7B.73), and S_{s_1}, S_{s_2}, I_{s_1}, I_{s_2}, S, and I are given by the identities, (7B.70), (7B.74), (7B.79), and (7B.80). In (7B.67) C_1, C_2, ΔS_2, ΔS_1 follow by substitution of the known values of y_1, y_2, S_1, S_2, and the conditions, (7B.81). C is given by the identity, (7B.78).

The existing-asset markets must adapt to the given natural rates of interest, which we designate r_1' and r_2'. The way in which this is done is described by consolidating all of the supply and demand equations for money:

$$(7B.83) \qquad PL_{12}(r_1') = M_{12},$$

$$PL_{22}(r_2') = M_{22},$$

$$\overline{k}_1\, P\overline{y} = \overline{M} - [PL_{12}(r_1') + PL_{22}(r_2')].$$

The first two summary equations are (7B.34), in which the left sides are replaced by (7B.33) and the given values, r_1' and r_2', and P, the denominator of the right sides, is transferred to the left. The third equation is (7B.66), with (7B.62)–(7B.65) entered on the left and (7B.23) on the right, the latter equation being replaced by (7B.24) and the two summary equations above. The third equation has one unknown,

$$P = \frac{\overline{M}}{\overline{k}_1\,\overline{y} + L_{12}(r_1') + L_{22}(r_2')}.$$

The equilibrium of the monetary variables is thus characterized by a price level and allocation of cash balances at which $L_1 = M_1$, $L_{12}(r_1') = M_{12}/P$, and $L_{22}(r_2') = M_{22}/P$.[4]

The real security prices, p_1 and p_2, were determined as soon as r_1, r_2, $\rho_{K_1^-}$, and ρ_{K_2} were set by the output markets. In (7B.29) we replace the denominators by r_1' and r_2', and the numerators by (7B.30). In the latter equation we substitute r_1' and r_2' for ρ_{K_1} and ρ_{K_2}, and (7B.28) and (7B.31) for the remaining variables. The system is now fully determined. The values of p_1 and p_2, together with (7B.28), determine S_{1VO} and S_{2VO} ([7B.27]), and the latter, together with the monetary equilibrium and (7B.22), determine total wealth ([7B.20] and [7B.21]). D_{1VO} and D_{2VO} in (7B.36) are determined by the values of W_1, W_2, L_{12}, L_{22}, ΔD_{2VO}, ΔD_{1VO}, and the conditions, (7B.38). D_{1VO} and D_{2VO}, in combination with p_1 and p_2, determine D_{1O} and D_{2O} ([7B.37]), and D_{1N}, D_{2N}, S_{1N}, and S_{2N} ([7B.76] and [7B.77]) follow from S_1, S_2, I_1, I_2, p_1, and p_2.

(7B.71), the independent consumption function, is an "accidental" result of the sectoring of the output markets. For if the markets were not divided, the equations, (7B.82), would be replaced by a comparable set,

(7B.84) $$S_1(\overline{y}, r_1, r_2) = I_1(r_1),$$

$$S_2(\overline{y}, r_1, r_2) = I_2(r_2),$$

---

[4] The determination of the price level, as described above, determines the real idle-money totals and thereby the individual wealth totals. The latter in turn react reciprocally on the demand-for-money schedules. This is implicit in the equation system, by virtue of (7B.36), although it is not explicit in (7B.83). However, granted that all demands respond to wealth changes (p. 225), there is no danger that this reciprocal influence between the supply and demand for money will prevent the equilibrium from being achieved. Cf. pp. 47–48.

which determines the two unknowns, r_1 and r_2, output being given by (7B.65). However, we noted earlier that (7B.71) does not deprive aggregate consumption, which is the only meaningful consumption variable, of its expected residual character, given independent saving functions. Nothing is essentially changed by introducing (7B.71), while the convenience attached to sectoring remains.

While the equilibrium of two securities is not unlike that of a single-security model, we have ignored a number of problems associated with a multiple-security system. We have not explicitly shown the way in which a combination of the two interest rates and security prices, compatible with the desires of each class of security demander of both the stock and flow markets, is obtained, nor have we discussed the stability of any equilibrium combination. This will be done in Part D, where the entire system is represented by the Hicksian substitution functions. The latter framework is particularly useful in tracing the financial adjustment to a monetary disturbance beyond the first or second impact interval.

The combined equilibrium of the system is summarized in Figure 7–3 by saving, investment, and idle-money schedules, all drawn as functions of the interest rates. The variables with primes are equilibrium values.

Over time the individual existing-asset markets grow by the corresponding saving-investment components. We write equations comparable to those of Chapter II-D(2):

(7B.85) $S_{1VT} = S_{1VO} + S_{1VN}, \quad S_{2VT} = S_{2VO} + S_{2VN},$

(7B.86) $D_{1VT} = D_{1VO} + D_{1VN}, \quad D_{2VT} = D_{2VO} + D_{2VN},$

where the total functions are the ruling dynamic supply and demand schedules. In security-quantity units:

(7B.87) $S_{1T} = S_{1O} + S_{1N}, \quad S_{2T} = S_{2O} + S_{2N},$

(7B.88) $D_{1T} = D_{1O} + D_{1N}, \quad D_{2T} = D_{2O} + D_{2N}.$

The dynamic equilibrium, as defined by (7B.87) and (7B.88), is diagramed in Figure 7–6 in connection with an open-market purchase. In any equilibrium interval S_{1O} and D_{1O} shift equally to the right and parallel by the equal saving-investment increment. S_{2O} and D_{2O} move analogously. We again abstract at this level of analysis from changes in the capital stock, treating new securities as self-contained entities whose return is the same as that of pre-

FIGURE 7–3
The Combined Equilibrium of Stock and Flow Markets in the Two-Security System

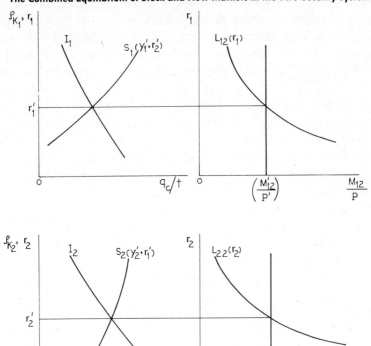

existing shares. The equilibrium, as pictured in Figure 7–3, remains intact.

Our procedure is once more to impose a disturbance in the form of an open-market purchase. The equilibrating mechanisms now will operate against a background of constant substitution between the two securities, for only in equilibrium are demanders in each market of each sector willing to hold and purchase their own security exclusively. Not only do two securities increase the complexity of the adjustment process by increasing the number of variables, but also by introducing diverse tendencies to the economy. One stock-flow sector may be undergoing an inflationary adjustment while simultaneously the other, a deflationary. Variables, such as the interest rates and price level, that formerly pursued a monotonic path to equilibrium, may undergo oscillations and cyclical movements. All of this will be discussed in Parts C, D, and E. Part C treats the direct impact of the purchase, showing how the substitution process is carried out during a typical first interval. Part D derives the Hicksian substitution functions, and Part E describes the general character of the over-all financial adjustment.

C. AN OPEN-MARKET PURCHASE: THE DIRECT IMPACT

1. General Plan

We turn now to the direct impact of the open-market purchase. We begin from a position of equilibrium in both the stock and flow markets for both securities as described in Part B(3). A unique structure and level of interest rates agreeable to wealth holders, investing entrepreneurs, and current savers prevail without change over time. The central bank enters the market for a period, t_1, and offers to purchase a block of one of the two securities—say, s_1—at a price above the market. The bank secures both old and new securities at the higher price, which generates a movement by savers and wealth holders into the several alternatives now available. In order to trace the substitution process, while taking full account of the required financing and money transfers, we shall describe the direct impact on the existing-asset and output markets separately. After doing so, we shall consider the impact on the combined stock and flow system. We assume that the bank returns the income on its additional securities by subsidizing personal incomes. Thus, during the brief intervals considered, ρ_{s_1} and ρ_{s_2} are fixed, and there is a unique relationship between each interest rate and the corresponding price of securities. This will be true until the equilibrating mechanisms are explicitly introduced into the analysis in Part E.

2. The Existing-Asset Markets

In the following analysis of the wealth markets we assume that the given existing-asset schedules are the sole determinants of security prices and interest rates. There are no flow schedules of the supply and demand for securities, and the bank can purchase existing securities only. On this assumption we can describe the essence of the substitution process among wealth holders, free of outside influences.

The W_1 and W_2 sectors of the existing-asset market are pre-

sented in Figures 7–4(a) and (b), respectively. D'_{1VO}, drawn for
the prevailing alternative yield, r'_2, is the value function of an
inelastic D_{10} schedule, while D'_{2VO}, based on r'_1, corresponds to
a D_{20} schedule of unitary price elasticity. Δ'_2 in the W_1 market is
an abbreviation for $\Delta D'_{2VO}$, the substitution demand for s_2, and
Δ'_1 in the lower diagram denotes $\Delta D'_{1VO}$, the substitution demand
for s_1. The bank's bid price, shown in the W_1 market, is $p''_1 > p'_1$
corresponding to $r''_1 < r'_1$. The operation evokes an excess value
supply of

(7C.1) $$S'_{1VO}(r''_1) - D'_{1VO}(r''_1),$$

FIGURE 7–4
The Direct Impact of an Open-Market Purchase on the Existing-Asset Markets

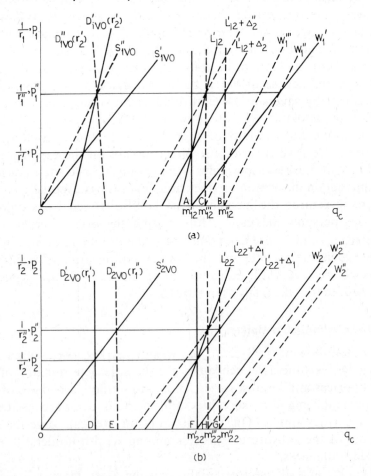

(a)

(b)

reducing security value to S''_{1VO}. The offsetting excess demand,

$$(7C.2) \qquad L'_{12}(r''_1) + \Delta'_2(r''_1) - m'_{12},$$

is a desire both for money and s_2 securities. But suppose that the bank's monetary injection is accepted initially as an increase in m_{12} only. This will enable us to trace the substitution process step by step. Hence m_{12} increases from m'_{12} to m''_{12}, equal to the distance, AB. W_1 rotates counterclockwise to W''_1, and D_{1VO} moves sympathetically to D''_{1VO}. For simplicity, L_{12} and Δ_2 are assumed not to respond to the wealth rotation.

Thus far, the W_2 market has remained in equilibrium at p'_2 and r'_2. But only AC of the AB addition to m_{12} balances is a desired increase, and we now transfer the remainder, $CB = \Delta'_2(r''_1)$, to the W_2 market where it is added to the demand for s_2 securities. By this act W_1 holders reduce both the supply and the temporary component of the demand for m_{12}. m_{12} and $L_{12} + \Delta_2$ shift leftward by the distance, CB, leaving idle balances of m'''_{12} and a demand function, $L'_{12} + \Delta''_2$. Δ''_2 differs from Δ'_2 only in intersecting L'_{12} at r''_1 and p''_1 instead of r'_1 and p'_1. At r''_1 and p''_1, $\Delta''_2 = 0$ since at that yield and price asset holders have now transferred to s_2 securities the portion of wealth—$\Delta'_2(r''_1)$—that they were unwilling to allocate to s_1 or m_{12}. The remaining W_1 wealth total, $W'''_1 = W''_1 - CB$, is thus exhausted by the demand for s_1 securities and m_{12} balances.

In Figure 7–4(b) the value increment to the demand for s_2, financed by the transfer of m_{12}, is shown as equal rightward and parallel shifts in D_{2VO} and m_{22}, respectively, of DE and FG, both equal to CB. The new schedules are:

$$(7C.3) \qquad D''_{2VO}, \text{ based on } r''_1; m''_{22}; \text{ and } W''_2 = S'_{2VO} + m''_{22}.$$

However, the s_2 substitute securities are obtained from the fixed supply only by bidding up their price. The desired excess supply,

$$(7C.4) \qquad S'_{2VO} - D'_{2VO} = DE = CB,$$

is sold by pre-existing holders at p''_2 and r''_2. But once again the offsetting demand for alternative assets is directed only partly at idle balances. W_2 holders want

$$(7C.5) \qquad L'_{22}(r''_2) - m'_{22} = FH$$

in m_{22}, and $\Delta'_1(r''_2) = HG$ in s_1 securities. The increase in m_{22} balances to m''_{22} is thus only temporary, pending a retransfer of

$HG < FG$ in funds to the W_1 market in the form of demand for s_1. This is the same kind of transfer as the movement from W_1 to W_2 just described. m_{22} and $L_{22} + \Delta_1$ drop equally by $\Delta_1'(r_2'') = HG$, leaving new functions of

(7C.6) m_{22}''', $L_{22}' + \Delta_1''$, and $W_2''' = S_{2VO}' + m_{22}'''$.

The resulting changes in the W_1 market (not entered in Figure 7-4[a]) are rightward shifts in D_{1VO}, m_{12}, and W_1, equal to the HG reduction in m_{22}. This creates D_{1VO}''', based on r_2'', plus m_{12}^4 and W^4, both of which originate on the horizontal axis at a point between C and B. The purchase of s_1 substitute securities is accomplished by bidding p_1 to $p_1''' > p_1''$, but once more the proceeds of security sales are taken only in part as m_{12} balances. There is a further rechanneling of funds to the W_2 market, raising p_2 to $p_2''' > p_2''$, and then a movement back to W_1, and so on. At each stage a portion of the funds spent on substitute securities is withdrawn to the idle balances; the transfers between markets thus grow smaller until a point is reached at which all of the bank's monetary injection is held willingly as idle money in either the W_1 or W_2 market. Both p_1 and p_2 are higher, and r_1 and r_2 lower than they were before the operation and immediately after the bank's purchase of s_1 securities.

3. The Output Markets

The substitution process in the new securities market will be described on the assumption that it is the only market for securities. Moreover, the bank's purchase will be shown as a rightward and parallel shift in the demand for s_1 securities, which persists as long as the substitution operation is in progress. If the bank's bid were an infinitely elastic demand, diagramed as a horizontal line, p_1 would be fixed at the bid price, p_1'', and could not increase further as the substitution is carried out. In reality, the prices of securities are determined over time by the bank, the stock, and the flow markets. But on our present assumptions the new securities market will complete the substitution process on its own terms. Part E is concerned with the combined stock and flow dynamic analysis.

In Figure 7-5(a), S_1', based on r_2', and I_1' are the s_1 saving and investment schedules, C_1' is the consumption alternative, and $C_1' + \Delta S_2'$ is consumption plus the value demand of y_1 savers for s_2. y_1' is total real income during t_1 applied to s_1 securities, C_1, and ΔS_2. In the lower diagram S_2', based on r_1', and I_2' are the saving and invest-

FIGURE 7–5
The Direct Impact of an Open-Market Purchase on the Output Markets

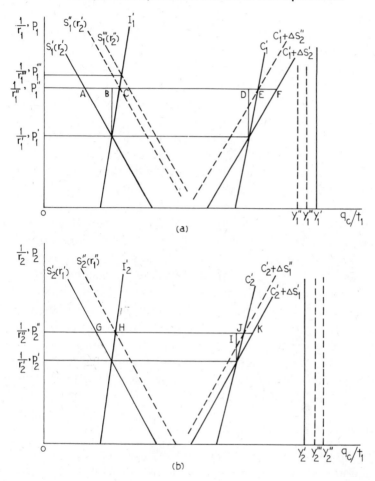

(a)

(b)

ment schedules for s_2 securities; C_2' is the consumption alternative, and $C_2' + \Delta S_1'$ is consumption plus the value demand of y_2 savers for s_1. y_2' is the portion of income allocated during t_1 to s_2, C_2, and ΔS_1. The bank's demand is shown in Figure 7–5(a) as an increase in S_1 to S_1'', raising p_1 to p_1'' and lowering r_1 to r_1''. This creates an excess value supply of

(7C.7) $$I_1'(r_1'') - S_1'(r_1'') = AC$$

in new s_1 securities, the proceeds of which are added to the active circulation. The decline in saving is

(7C.8) $$S_1'(r_1') - S_1'(r_1'') = AB,$$

which is offset by a movement up the schedule, $C_1' + \Delta S_2'$, of

(7C.9) $$DF = DE + EF = AB.$$

DE is the desired increase in real consumption expenditures, and EF is the value of the demand for substitute s_2 securities. y_1 savers execute the substitution demand by transferring an EF portion of y_1 expenditures to the y_2 market. Hence in Figure 7–5(a), $C_1 + \Delta S_2$ and y_1 shift leftward and parallel by an equal distance, EF, producing $C_1' + \Delta S_2''$ and y_1'', respectively. In Figure 7–5(b), S_2 shifts to the right by $GH = EF$, and y_2 increases by the same amount, reflecting the greater flow of expenditures against y_2 components. The new schedules are S_2'', based on r_1'', and y_2''. However, savers secure substitute s_2 securities by raising their price to p_2'' and lowering their yield to r_2'', at which a sufficient excess supply is forthcoming. In response to r_2'', y_2 income earners increase C_2 consumption by $IJ < GH$ and increase their demand for s_1 securities by JK. $C_2 + \Delta S_1$ shifts leftward to $C_2' + \Delta S_1''$, and y_2 to y_2''', by the distance JK. In the y_1 market S_1 increases by JK, becoming S_1''', based on r_2'', and y_1 shifts equally to y_1'''. p_1 increases further to p_1''', stimulating both consumption and the desire for s_2 securities. A portion of y_1 expenditures $< JK$ is returned to y_2, raising S_2, y_2, and p_2. And so the substitution continues by diminishing degrees until p_1 and p_2 are at higher levels, and r_1 and r_2 at lower levels, at which y_1 and y_2 are exhausted by expenditures on their own securities and consumption.

4. Stocks and Flows Combined

The direct impact of an open-market purchase on the combined stock and flow security markets is shown in Figure 7–6, where all schedules are drawn in security-quantity units. The total s_1 market is in the upper diagram, where q_{s_1} on the horizontal axis denotes quantity of s_1 securities. In the lower diagram is the total s_2 market, where q_{s_2} is quantity of s_2 securities. Both markets are drawn for a time period, t_1, during which the bank is in the market purchasing s_1 securities, and simultaneously one round of substitution expenditures for s_2 by y_1 income recipients and W_1 asset holders is carried out. In Figure 7–6(a) the prevailing supply schedules are S_{1N}', S_{1O}', and S_{1T}'. The demand schedules are D_{1N}', D_{1O}', and D_{1T}', all based on r_2'. The equilibrium price for both the stock and flow markets is p_1', corresponding to r_1', the initial natural rate of interest in the s_1 market. In Figure 7–6(b) the prevailing schedules are S_{2N}', S_{2O}', S_{2T}',

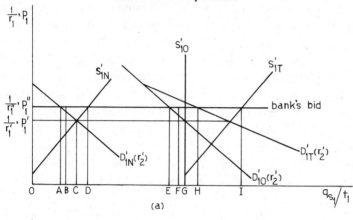

(a)

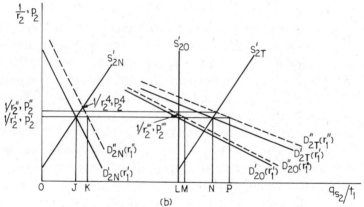

(b)

D'_{2N}, D'_{2O}, and D'_{2T}, the latter three of which are based on r'_1. The equilibrium price and yield are p'_2 and r'_2, respectively.

The bank's bid is p''_1, shown in Figure 7–6(a) as a solid-line schedule of infinite elasticity. At p''_1 the total offerings of s_1 securities are

$$(7C.10) \qquad (S'_{1T} - D'_{1T}) = (S'_{1O} - D'_{1O}) + (S'_{1N} - D'_{1N}),$$

indicated in the diagram as the distances,

$$(7C.11) \qquad\qquad HI = EG + AD.$$

The value of the EG security sales by asset holders, $(EG)p''_1$, consists of a component, designated arbitrarily as EF, the value of which is added directly to m_{12} balances, plus $FG = EG - EF$, the proceeds of which are earmarked for expenditure on s_2 securities (see Section

2). In the output market the proceeds of AD in security sales go wholly to entrepreneurs who promptly send the money into the income stream. Hence none of $(AD)p_1''$ is available to y_1 earners to finance the desired increase in consumption and the purchase of s_2 substitute securities. Instead, we have seen that additional C_1 and ΔS_2 are financed by a reduction in S_1 (see Section 3). The movement from C to A along D_{1N}', an elastic schedule, thus represents a releasing of funds from expenditure on s_1 for additional consumption and expenditure on s_2. We divide AC arbitrarily into AB and BC, the value of which goes into consumption and additional s_2 securities, respectively.

The impact of the purchase of substitute s_2 securities during t_1 is shown in Figure 7-6(b). The aggregate rise in the demand for s_2 is

$$(7C.12) \qquad\qquad NP = BC + FG,$$

creating a total schedule, $D_{2T}''(r_1'')$. The increment in the s_2 flow demand is shown separately as $JK = BC$. The increase in existing-asset demand for s_2 is $LM = FG$.[5] At the close of t_1 the s_2 price and yield are p_2'' and r_2'', at the intersection of D_{2T}'' and S_{2T}'. The path of p_2 and r_2 during t_1 is determined by the relative timing of the stock and flow substitution transfers. We assume that asset holders sell their securities to the bank at the opening instant of t_1 and then move immediately into s_2 securities. p_2 is thus raised initially to p_2''', and r_2 reduced to r_2''', the point of intersection of S_{2O}' and the augmented demand schedule,

$$(7C.13) \qquad\qquad D_{2O}''(r_1'') = D_{2O}'(r_1') + LM.$$

Then as y_1 savers purchase s_2 securities during the course of t_1, the price rises further to p_2''. However, p_2 can also fall or remain constant following the initial boost by the shift of asset demand. $p_2'' > p_2'''$ and $r_2'' < r_2'''$ tends to occur when: (a) existing-asset substitution demand (FG) is small relative to that of savers (BC),[6] and (b) the absolute vertical-axis slopes of S_{2N} and D_{2N} are small and that of D_{2O} is large.

In subsequent periods when the bank has left the market, security

---

[5] Each of the demand increments should be drawn as a rectangular hyperbola, relative to the schedule to which it is added. In Sections 2 and 3, Figures 7-4 and 7-5, the substitution demand transfers were shown as parallel movements in the value schedules; hence, they are rectangular hyperbolae in a diagram of security price and quantity (cf. p. 107, n. 14). However, the geometry is greatly simplified by representing the increments as parallel shifts in the security-quantity demand schedules.

[6] A large substitution demand by y_1 savers, BC, requires that C_1 be relatively vertical, and that S_1, and hence D_{1N}, be relatively flat (elastic) (see Figure 7-2).

prices are determined jointly by the continuing transfer of funds for substitution purchases and by the equilibrating mechanisms. To describe the movement of security prices and interest rates over time, taking account of all forces at work, we shall replace the diagrams of Figure 7–6 by a geometrical device better suited for this purpose. Developed by Hicks in his discussion of related commodities in *Value and Capital*,[7] the new diagram extracts from each sector of the stock, flow, and total markets a functional relation between r_1 and r_2. The diagram will also provide explicit information about the movement of the general price level. This is particularly important, since in a two-security system the direction of movement in commodity prices is not unambiguous. In this connection notice in Figure 7–6(b) that the intersection of S'_{2N} with the augmented schedule, $D''_{2N}(r''_1)$, is at a price, $p^4_2 > p''_2$, and yield, $r^4_2 < r''_2$; i.e., the interest rate that equates s_2 saving and investment is below the s_2 market rate determined by total supply and demand. This is not an inevitable result, and may not be true in later periods of the adjustment. The conditions favorable to this outcome are the same as those that produced $p''_2 > p'''_2$ (see [a] and [b] above). The significance of $r^4_2 < r''_2$ for the general price level is that saving exceeds investment at the market rate of interest and cash will be transferred from income to wealth account as part of a deflationary adjustment in the s_2 market. While the bank's purchase has driven the s_1 market yield below its natural rate, will this inflationary tendency always offset the deflationary impetus in s_2? The discrepancy between r''_2 and r^4_2 is not likely to be as great, initially, as that between r'_1 and r''_1, but will this continue to be true? Moreover, even though the initial tendency in the s_1 market is inflationary, will the return flow of demand from s_2, as r_2 falls, maintain the s_1 market yield below the natural? The answer to these questions will be furnished by an appropriate function on the Hicksian diagram, which we derive in Part D.

D. SUBSTITUTION FUNCTIONS

1. Derivation

The Hicksian "substitution functions" are general relationships between r_1 and r_2 derived from each sector of the existing-asset,

---

[7] J. R. Hicks, *Value and Capital* (London: Oxford University Press, 1946), chap. v, pp. 62–77. To my knowledge the first application of the Hicksian diagram to an analysis of security holding was made by William Dunaway in an unpublished paper, "A Liquidity Theory of Interest Rates Unfettered by 'Constant' Structure," presented before Economics 432, the seminar in Monetary Dynamics, conducted by Professor Milton Friedman at the University of Chicago, spring quarter, 1951.

output, and total securities markets. More specifically, the functions are the equilibrium values of the interest-reciprocal and price of a given market expressed as a function of the alternative interest-reciprocal and price. We begin by deriving the substitution function for the s_1 existing-asset market.

In Figure 7–7 the wealth components are initially S'_{1VO}, m'_{12}, and W'_1. The demand functions are D'_{1VO}, based on r'_2, L'_{12}, and $L'_{12} + \Delta'_2$. The equilibrium is at r'_1 and p'_1. Suppose that r_2 is reduced to

FIGURE 7–7
The Effect of Different Yields of the Alternative Security on the s_1 Existing-Asset Market

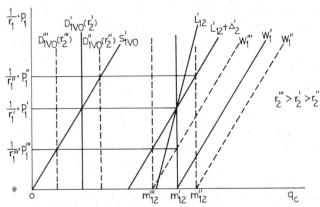

r''_2 by raising p_2 to p''_2. In response, wealth holders move out of s_2 into the substitute s_1 security. This shifts D_{1VO} rightward to $D''_{1VO}(r''_2)$, m_{12} to m''_{12}, and W_1 to W''_1, where each of the shifts is equal to $\Delta'_1(r''_2)$. p rises responsively to p''_1, and r_1 falls to r''_1. We know that p''_1 and r''_1 will stimulate a partial return expenditure of m_{12} on s_2, but as long as $r_2 = r''_2$, the s_1 existing-asset market is in equilibrium at p''_1 and r''_1. Suppose that r_2 is raised to $r'''_2 > r'_2$ by lowering p_2 to $p'''_2 < p'_2$. D_{1VO}, m_{12}, and W_1 shift leftward to $D'''_{1VO}(r'''_2)$, m'''_{12}, and W'''_1, respectively. The s_1 equilibrium is now at r'''_1 and p'''_1. The functional relation between the two interest rates, derived from the s_1 wealth market, is thus drawn as an upward-sloping line, s_{1O}, in Figure 7–8, where $1/r_1$ and p_1 are on the vertical axis, and $1/r_2$ and p_2 on the horizontal.[8] A similar rising

---

[8] Granted linearity in the underlying functions, s_{1O} will itself be linear, as drawn. More specifically, if Δ_1, the substitution value demand for s_1 by W_2 holders, is linear and increasing in $1/r_2$, then D_{1VO} will increase by equal amounts with equal increments in $1/r_2$. Since D_{1VO} moves along a linear S_{1VO} function, $1/r_1$ will also increase by constant amounts for equal increases in $1/r_2$.

FIGURE 7–8
The Hicksian Substitution Functions Derived
from the Existing-Asset Markets

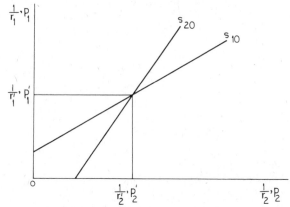

function, s_{2O}, the locus of equilibrium values of $1/r_2$, given $1/r_1$, can be derived from the W_2 market, and is also plotted in Figure 7–8. A unique pair of prices and yields, p_1' and p_2', and r_1' and r_2', located at the intersection of s_{1O} and s_{2O}, is an equilibrium solution for the W_1 and W_2 markets simultaneously.

The equilibrium of Figure 7–8 is stable only if $\partial s_{2O}/\partial p_2 > \partial s_{1O}/\partial p_2$, as drawn. In order to see why this is a stability requirement, we shall repeat the description of the direct impact of a purchase (Part C[2]) in terms of the s_{1O} and s_{2O} functions—first with and then without the stability condition. In Figure 7–9 stable s_{1O} and s_{2O} functions are shown directly before and after an instantaneous open-market purchase of s_1 securities. The pre-disturbance equilibrium is at point A, the intersection of s_{1O}' and s_{2O}'. The bank's purchase shifts s_{1O} upward to s_{1O}'', since the reduced quantity of s_1 securities raises the equilibrium price, p_1, and lowers the yield, r_1, corresponding to any given value of r_2 (see Figure 7–4[a]).[9] The bank's bid price, p_1'', is located on s_{1O}'' at point B, which combines the new equilibrium price in the s_1 market and the still unchanged price and yield in the s_2 market, p_2' and r_2'. The direct impact of the purchase will also produce a movement in the s_{2O} function, for in general Δ_2 will rotate counterclockwise along with W_1 through p_1''

---

[9]The shift of s_{1O} in Figure 7–9 is not drawn as a parallel movement. This is because the purchase creates a counterclockwise rotation in D_{1VO}, reducing its p_1-axis slope (see Figure 7–4[a]). Thus, as p_2 rises, increments are added to a flatter security-demand schedule, and p_1 rises less than formerly. Hence $\partial s_{1O}/\partial p_2$ is reduced, as indicated by the diminished slope of s_{1O}'' relative to s_{1O}'.

FIGURE 7–9
The Direct Impact of an Open-Market Purchase in Terms of Stable Existing-Asset Substitution Functions

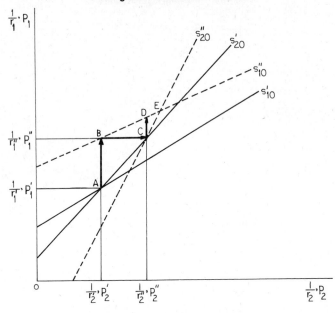

(see Figure 7–4[a], where W_1 rotates, but Δ_2 is held constant). Hence only at p_1'' is the same amount of money forthcoming for substitute movements in and out of existing s_1 securities. At $p_1 > p_1''$, less money is available from the W_1 market to add to D_{2VO}, and p_2 increases less than formerly; a new function, s_{20}'', lies to the left of s_{20}'. At $p_1 < p_1''$, a greater amount is transferred from s_2 to s_1 securities, and p_2 falls more than formerly; s_{20}'' is to the right of s_{20}'. On net, s_{20} rotates counterclockwise through the ordinate, p_1'', located at point C. Returning to point B, created by the direct impact, p_1'' stimulates a substitution expenditure on s_2, raising its price and lowering its yield to p_2'' and r_2''. This is shown as the horizontal movement terminating at s_{20}'', B to C, the coordinates of which are p_1'' and p_2''. The latter price evokes a return flow into s_1 securities, raising p_1 further to the height of point D on s_{10}''. And so the process continues along a rising and diminishing step-path until the security prices and yields reach their new joint equilibrium at E, the intersection of s_{10}'' and s_{20}''.

The case of unstable equilibrium, in which $\partial s_{20}/\partial p_2 < \partial s_{10}/\partial p_2$, is diagramed in Figure 7–10. The bank's purchase creates the same shifts in s_{10} and s_{20} described above, but now the new equilibrium is at point E, at which both prices are *below* their starting level at point A. Meanwhile, the bank's bid is again located *above* A at B. The initial substitution purchase carries the prices to C, and so on along a path that moves explosively away from both the new and the old equilibria. The essential difference between the convergent and divergent paths is that successive increments in either of the security prices decrease in the former case, increase in the latter. Granted that $\Delta_1(p_2)$ and $\Delta_2(p_1)$ are monotonic increasing functions, divergence occurs if only the first round of s_1 substitution demand, $\Delta_1'(p_2'')$, is sufficiently large to raise p_1 by a greater amount than did the bank (see Figure 7–4). This in turn would raise the quantity of s_2 substitution demand, $\Delta_2''(p_1''')$, above its previous level, creating a correspondingly greater increase in p_2, which would increase the quantity of Δ_1, etc. The process is self-reinforcing. The conditions for divergence can be expressed symbolically if, on a first approximation, we assume that the price movements are proportional to the magnitude of the monetary increments to security demand. Then, with reference to Figure 7–4, the instability requirement is simply $HG > AB$ or, upon substitution,

(7D.1) $$\Delta_1'(p_2'') > \Delta_2'(p_1'') + [L_{12}'(p_1'') - m_{12}'].$$

Additional positive relationships between $1/r_1$ and $1/r_2$ can be derived from the independent substitution reactions of current savers during a given period. In the y_1 market an increase in p_2 and $1/r_2$ shifts S_1 and y_1 rightward by equal amounts. Given the I_1

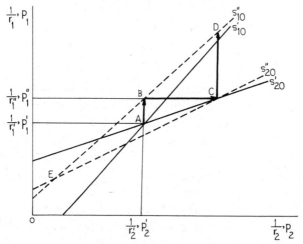

FIGURE 7–10
The Direct Impact of an Open-Market Purchase in Terms of Unstable Existing-Asset Substitution Functions

schedule, the equilibrium values of p_1 and $1/r_1$ also rise. And conversely if p_2 and $1/r_2$ are lowered. A similar relationship emerges from the y_2 sector as p_1 and r_1 are altered. We shall name the new substitution functions s_{1N} and s_{2N}, respectively. Stability requires $\partial s_{2N}/\partial p_2 > \partial s_{1N}/\partial p_2$. Finally, an over-all or resultant pair of substitution functions, s_{1T} and s_{2T}, is derived from the combined responses of the old and the new securities markets. In Figure 7–6(b), for example, the first round of total substitution expenditure for s_2 raised the market price to p_2'', while the equilibrium price for savers at this stage was $p_2^4 > p_2''$, and that for wealth holders, $p_2''' < p_2''$. In Figure 7–11, where all three pairs of functions—the old, the new, and the aggregate—are drawn, the price corresponding to p_1'' on the s_{2O} function is thus p_2''', on s_{2T}, p_2'', and on s_{2N}, p_2^4.

FIGURE 7–11
Substitution Functions Derived from the Existing-Asset, Output, and Total Markets

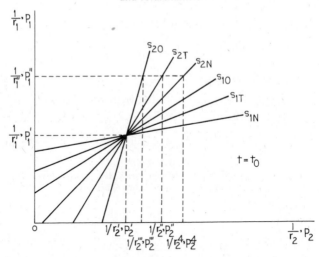

Except at intersection points, s_{1T} and s_{2T} will lie between their respective new and old substitution functions, with the new and the old placed on either side. The total functions will lie nearer the new ones the greater is the substitution demand of savers per unit of time, and the greater the time interval considered. For zero time, the new functions are non-existent and the total functions coincide with the old. The aggregate stability condition is $\partial s_{2T}/\partial p_2 > \partial s_{1T}/\partial p_2$. In Figure 7–11 any s_2 function has a greater slope than that of any s_1 function. But this is not a requirement, and the schedules could also be arranged as follows, reading clockwise from the top:

(7D.2) $$s_{2N}, s_{1N}, s_{2T}, s_{2O}, s_{1T}, s_{1O}.$$

The output, existing-asset, and total markets are all stable, and each total function lies appropriately between its corresponding new and old functions. The fact that $\partial s_{1N}/\partial p_2 > \partial s_{2T}/\partial p_2$ and $\partial s_{2O}/\partial p_2$ has no significance. However, stability of both the new and the old markets is neither necessary nor sufficient for stability of the total market. Consider this pattern:

(7D.3) $$s_{2O}, s_{1O}, s_{1T}, s_{2T}, s_{2N}, s_{1N}.$$

We have stability in both the new and the old markets, but instability of the total system, as indicated by $\partial s_{2T}/\partial p_2 < \partial s_{1T}/\partial p_2$. In the next example, there is instability in both the new and the old markets, but stability in the total market:

(7D.4) $$s_{1N}, s_{2N}, s_{2T}, s_{1T}, s_{1O}, s_{2O}.$$

Hence stability in the component markets is not a prerequisite for total stability. But it seems unlikely that a system in which the existing-asset market is unstable would remain long in equilibrium, owing to the possibility of instantaneous adjustments by wealth holders; the system might explode before the neutralizing impact of savers's substitution demand accrued in sufficient quantity over time. But if only the market for savings is unstable, with security prices determined instantaneously by the existing-asset market, and over time by the total market—both of which are now stable—then the instability of the new market is effectively neutralized.[10] An example of such a system is the following:

(7D.5) $$s_{1N}, s_{2N}, s_{2T}, s_{2O}, s_{1T}, s_{1O}.$$

---

[10] While an individually unstable pair of s_{1N} and s_{2N} functions does not necessarily prevent the interest rates from moving convergently to the intersection of s_{1T} and s_{2T}, the system is nevertheless unstable. This is shown in the appendix, Section 2(b), in connection with the over-all adjustment process. Unstable s_{1N} and s_{2N}, in particular, create serious problems for the movement of the general price level. See n. 13 below.

The behavioral circumstances underlying instability of s_{1N} and s_{2N} can be derived by analogy to the argument on p. 249 (see [7D.1]). The first round of savers' substitution expenditure following an open-market purchase must raise p_1 more than did the bank. We assume, as a first approximation, that the price movements are proportional to the magnitude of the substitution expenditures. With reference to Figure 7-5, instability occurs when $JK > DF$, or

$$\Delta S_1'(p_2'') > \Delta S_2'(p_1'') + [C_1'(p_1'') - C_1'(p_1')].$$

The bracketed term on the right is positive, and measures the increase in desired consumption when p_1 rises from p_1' to p_1''.

All three markets in Figure 7–11—the new, the old, and the aggregate—yield the same pair of equilibrium interest rates, r_1' and r_2'. The static derivation of such an equilibrium was set forth in Part B(3). The *process* by which the equilibrium is reached following a disturbance is described in Part E. But first we shall develop the implications of the diagram for the commodity price level, which so far has been ignored in a discussion involving only security supply and demand. We have already observed (Part C[4]) that in a two-security system the price level may be subject to diverse forces, even though the outside disturbance is a "purely" inflationary monetary increase. Section 2 accordingly investigates the properties of the Hicksian diagram with regard to the dynamic tendency of the price level.

2. The Stable Price-Level Line

We begin by subdividing the area of the Hicksian space with reference to the induced movement of the price level. From this apportionment we shall derive a function along which commodity prices are constant. This function, known as the "stable price-level line," will enable the analysis to specify unambiguously the directional tendency of prices at any time during the adjustment process. To obtain the function, it is sufficient to consider only the output markets and their derived s_{1N} and s_{2N} functions, which are reproduced in Figure 7–12. s_{1N} and s_{2N} are assumed to be an individually stable pair of functions.

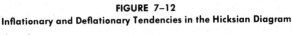

FIGURE 7–12
Inflationary and Deflationary Tendencies in the Hicksian Diagram

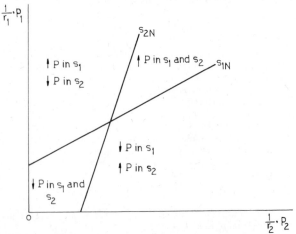

Every point on either s_{1N} or s_{2N} is a contribution to a stable price level, since it implies equilibrium in either of the output markets and equality between its components of intended saving and investment. But only at the intersection of s_{1N} and s_{2N} do we secure equality of S and I in both markets and actual stability of the price level. Every point in the diagram above s_{1N} corresponds to an inflationary condition in the s_1 securities market, since the values of r_1 are below equilibrium and produce an excess of I_1 over S_1. Similarly, every point to the right of s_{2N} represents an inflationary combination of interest rates in s_2, since r_2 in that area is below its equilibrium and stimulates $I_2 > S_2$. All points below s_{1N} are deflationary, since r_1 is above equilibrium and $I_1 < S_1$. Finally, all points to the left of s_{2N} are deflationary, because r_2 is above the y_2 equilibrium and $I_2 < S_2$. This information is summarized in Figure 7–12, where an arrow before the symbol, P, indicates the upward or downward tendency to commodity prices provided in each market over the given area of the diagram. The space enclosed by the vertical angles of s_{1N} and s_{2N} emerges as the only area of pure inflation or deflation; elsewhere each market contributes an opposite tendency to the movement of the price level. Fortunately, it is possible to ascertain which of the tendencies predominates, and thus to allocate the doubtful region entirely between areas of net inflation or deflation.

Instead of regarding s_{1N} and s_{2N} as unique functions, let us consider them as special cases of a family of isoquants that indicate for each interest rate of the alternative security the yield at which $I - S$ in the given market is equal to any constant. Thus s_{1N} and s_{2N} in Figure 7–12 are, for each alternative yield, the loci of yields at which new security supply and demand in the given market are equal, and hence $I - S = 0$. s_{1N} and s_{2N} are the *natural* rates of interest of each market. But in addition to these functions, let us plot the interest rates which produce any given *inequality* between a market's new-security supply and demand (in real-value units). This is done for several cases in Figure 7–13, where s_{1N} and s_{2N} of Figure 7–12 are reproduced as solid-line schedules for which $I_1 - S_1 = 0$ and $I_2 - S_2 = 0$, respectively. Now, for each value of $1/r_2$, we plot the value of $1/r_1$ at which $I_1 - S_1 = c_1 > 0$. Clearly, at any $1/r_2$ (or r_2), this inflationary condition requires a higher $1/r_1$ (or lower r_1) than that at which $I_1 - S_1 = 0$. s_{1N}, drawn for $I_1 - S_1 = c_1$, therefore lies above the solid-line schedule.[11] Alternatively, we

---

[11] All of the schedules of Figure 7–13 are linear. This assumes linearity of the underlying supply and demand functions (cf. n. 8 above).

plot the value of $1/r_1$ which, at each $1/r_2$, creates $I_1 - S_1 = -c_1$, a deflationary excess of saving over investment. The required class of $1/r_1$ values is uniformly smaller than the natural rates of the y_1 market, and $s_{1N}(I_1 - S_1 = -c_1)$ accordingly lies below $s_{1N}(I_1 - S_1 = 0)$. The saving-minus-investment isoquants for the y_2 market, based on the same constants, c_1 and $-c_1$, lie analogously to the right and left, respectively, of the solid-line s_{2N} function. Next we connect the points of intersection between s_{1N} and s_{2N} schedules for which the saving-investment gap is equal, but opposite in sign. In Figure 7–13 there are three such points, counting the intersection of the two solid-line schedules, and they are circled. The resulting

FIGURE 7–13
Derivation of the Stable Price-Level Line

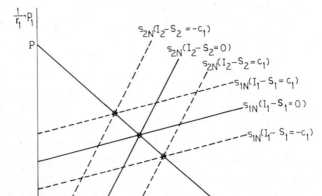

straight line is extended to the axes and labeled PP'. This is the stable price-level line, which has the property that every point on it is a combination of interest rates for which the inflationary excess of I over S in one market is exactly offset by a deflationary excess of S over I in the other market. Every point on PP' thus provides for stability of the general price level by equating *aggregate* saving and investment. Only one point on PP', the intersection of the two solid-line schedules, produces stable prices by equating the individual components of S and I in each market. PP' is drawn as a downward-sloping line, and will be so regarded for the moment. However, it may also be an increasing function; the underlying conditions are described below.

PP' performs the useful function of dividing the total space into

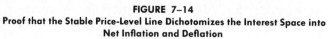

FIGURE 7–14

Proof that the Stable Price-Level Line Dichotomizes the Interest Space into
Net Inflation and Deflation

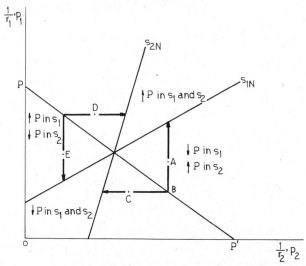

two clearly defined areas of net inflation and deflation—inflation above the line, deflation below. The proof is given with reference to Figure 7–14, a reproduction of Figure 7–12 with PP' super-imposed. Starting at an arbitrary point, A, in the doubtful region above PP' and below s_{1N}, a straight line is drawn through A and intersecting both PP' and s_{1N}. A vertical line through A, meeting PP' at B, will fulfill this requirement. In moving from B to A, we go from a combination of interest rates at which the price level is stable to one at which there is deflation in the s_1 market and infla-tion in s_2. The net impact on the price level seems to be in doubt. Assume, for the sake of argument, that the deflationary tendency in s_1 predominates, and the price level falls. If we continue moving up the vertical line beyond A, we must eventually meet s_{1N} and enter the area of pure inflation enclosed by s_{2N} and s_{1N}. But this implies that we have passed from deflation to inflation, experiencing an intermediate point of stability. However, PP' is the unique locus of interest rates producing a stable price level, and we cannot simul-taneously move up and away from it and also intersect it. We are involved in a contradiction; point A must have been an inflationary one in the first place. By analogous reasoning, any point, C, in the doubtful region below PP' and to the right of s_{2N}, lies on a line, which can be horizontal, leading into the area of pure deflation; thus, all points on the line must themselves be deflationary. Any point, D, in the doubtful area above PP' and to the left of s_{2N}, is on an inflationary horizontal path; any point, E, in the doubtful region below PP' and above s_{1N}, is on a deflationary vertical path. In summary, all points above PP' are inflationary, all points below are deflationary.

When PP' is downward sloping, as we have been drawing it, we shall find that the price level tends to react in the expected manner, generally rising after open-market purchases. But the downward slope of PP' is not inevitable. In Figure 7–15(a) and (b) three parallel schedules each of s_{1N} and s_{2N} are drawn, as in Figure 7–13, for the same three values of $I - S$. The intersections between schedules of equal but algebraically opposite gaps are again connected to form PP'. In Figure 7–15(a) the vertical shifts in s_{1N} are so much greater than the horizontal movements of s_{2N} that PP' has a positive slope. In Figure 7–15(b) the horizontal shifts in s_{2N} exceed the vertical movement of s_{1N} to the point where PP' is again rising, though its horizontal-axis slope is much less than in Figure 7–15(a). The shifts in s_{1N} and s_{2N} must be quite unequal before PP' loses its downward slope, but the possibility cannot be precluded.

The conditions underlying the rising stable price-level line are best understood by considering those responsible for the downward PP' function. In the latter case the excess investment functions, $I_1 - S_1$ and $I_2 - S_2$, are roughly similar in slope and magnitude as functions of $1/r_1$ and $1/r_2$, respectively. Hence a given saving-investment gap requires approximately equal displacements of the interest rate in each market. For example, given r_2, which determines

FIGURE 7–15
Derivation of Two Rising Stable Price-Level Lines

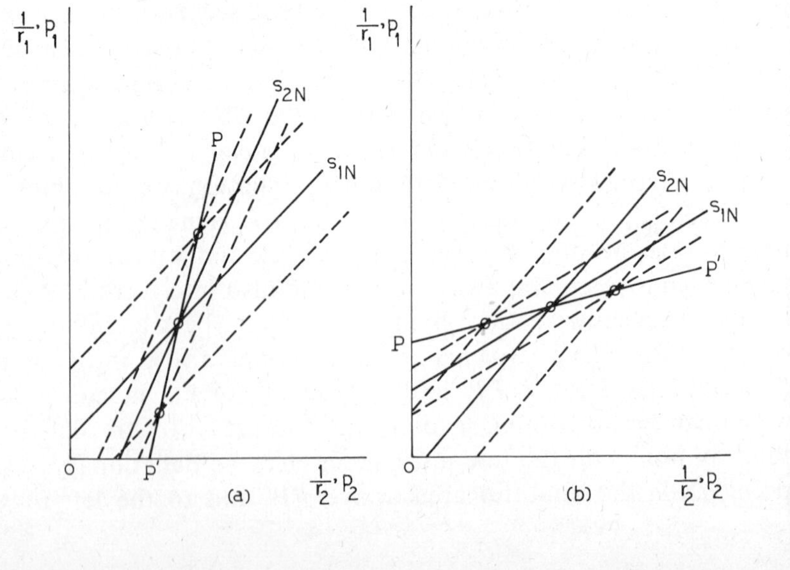

S_1, the value of $1/r_1$ that produces $I_1 - S_1(r_2) = c_1$ is about as far removed from the natural y_1 rate as the value of $1/r_2$, given r_1, that produces $I_2 - S_2(r_1) = -c_1$ is removed from the natural y_2 rate. This is equivalent to saying that s_{1N} moves vertically and s_{2N} moves horizontally by comparable distances, as in Figure 7–13, when constructing the family of saving-minus-investment isoquants. Alternatively, suppose that I_1 were very horizontal in $1/r_1$, creating a relatively horizontal $I_1 - S_1$ function.[12] Then, in constructing the isoquants, s_{1N} would shift by comparatively small amounts, reflecting the small changes in $1/r_1$ required to produce any value of $I_1 - S_1$. If, at the same time I_2 were quite vertical in $1/r_2$, $I_2 - S_2$ would itself tend to be vertical. As a result, s_{2N} will undergo considerable shifts, reflecting the substantial changes in $1/r_2$ that produce the required values of $I_2 - S_2$. There is some point at which the functions, $I_1 - S_1$ and $I_2 - S_2$, are so dissimilar—whether due to extreme forms of I_1, S_1, I_2 or S_2—that PP' emerges as a positively sloping line.

Though a rising function, PP' still divides the total space into areas of net inflation and deflation. Thus in Figure 7–15(a) the area to the right of PP' is inflationary; to the left, it is deflationary. In Figure 7–15(b) the area above PP' is inflationary; below, it is deflationary. The proof is the same as in the case of downward-sloping PP', except that the lines through points in the doubtful region, connecting PP' with s_{1N} or s_{2N}, may not be vertical or horizontal. However, a non-vertical or non-horizontal connecting line can always be drawn to establish the proof.[13]

E. THE ADJUSTMENT PROCESS

The open-market purchase will be carried forward in this section from the initial impact into the process of adjustment. The dia-

---

[12] Given that I_1 is relatively horizontal in $1/r_1$, $s_{1N}(1/r_1)$ will also tend to be, for as r_2 varies, the induced movements in S_1 tend to create small changes in the equilibrium value of $1/r_1$. But insofar as the slope of s_{1N} is determined by the strength of the substitutability response of S_1, this is not relevant to the slope of PP'. It is, rather, the movement in the entire s_{1N} schedule required to generate the given values of $I_1 - S_1$ that bears on PP'.

[13] Another limiting or "pathological" case occurs when s_{1N} and s_{2N} are individually unstable; i.e., $\partial s_{2N}/\partial p_2 < \partial s_{1N}/\partial p_2$. We have seen that this does not necessarily imply instability of the market rates of interest, as determined by total security supply and demand (see p. 251 and [7D.5]). However, the reader may verify that for unstable s_{1N} and s_{2N}, the upper vertical angle determined by the two schedules is an area of pure deflation; the lower vertical angle, an area of pure inflation (cf. Figure 7-12). The area to the right of PP' is accordingly one of net deflation; to the left, net inflation. This circumstance causes instability of the system. See the appendix, Section 2(b).

grammatical framework will be the system of substitution functions derived in Part D, henceforth referred to simply as "s-functions." The economy is in stock-flow equilibrium, as indicated by the joint intersection of the six s-functions in Figure 7–11. Each pair of new, old, and total functions is individually stable.

The impact of the purchase on the three s-functions derived from the s_1 markets is drawn in Figure 7–16. The functions with single

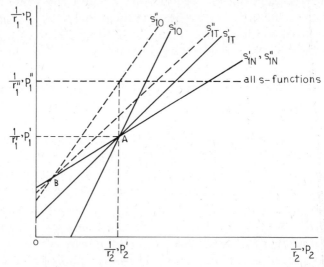

FIGURE 7–16
The Direct Impact of an Open-Market Purchase on the s_1 Substitution Functions

primes prevail for a non-zero interval before the purchase, t_0; they intersect at point A. The purchase of s_1 securities is executed during a period, t_1, equal in duration to t_0, at a price and yield of p_1'' and r_1''. During t_1 the bank's infinitely elastic demand reduces all three s-functions to a horizontal line at the height of the bid price, p_1''. In a succeeding interval, t_2, equal in length to t_1 and t_0, the functions, now denoted by double primes, are redrawn incorporating the impact of the purchase only; i.e., we abstract for the present from the influence of the equilibrating mechanisms. Only s_{1N}, the product of invariant flows, recovers its original position; hence, $s_{1N}'' = s_{1N}'$. As earlier, s_{1O} shifts upward to s_{1O}'' (see Figure 7–9), reflecting the loss of securities to the bank. s_{1T}'', the resultant of s_{1O}'' and s_{1N}'', mirrors, to a lesser extent, the changes in s_{1O}. Thus s_{1T}'' is above s_{1T}'.[14] s_{1T}''

---

[14] We have seen (n. 9 above) that s_{1O} shifts upward with diminished slope, owing to the rotation of wealth and security demand. Thus in Figure 7–16 the slope of s_{1T}'' will itself be somewhat less than that of s_{1T}'.

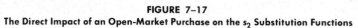

FIGURE 7–17
The Direct Impact of an Open-Market Purchase on the s_2 Substitution Functions

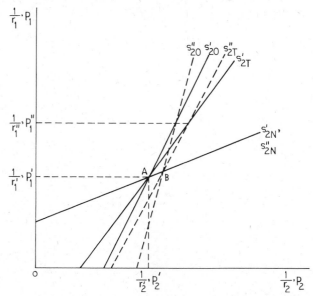

must also pass through point B, the intersection of s_{1O}'' and s_{1N}''. Point B is a combination of security prices and yields at which both the new and the old markets are in equilibrium. The total market must itself be in equilibrium at B.

The changes occurring simultaneously in the s_2 s-functions are shown in Figure 7–17. The single-primed functions, which meet at point A, prevail during t_0, while those with double primes apply to both t_1 and t_2, again abstracting in the latter period from the equilibrating mechanisms. The basic change in Figure 7–17 is the counterclockwise rotation of s_{2O} through p_1'' during t_1. This is the response to the rotation of W_1 and Δ_2 (see pages 247–48). s_{2T} reflects the movement of s_{2O} by itself rotating somewhat less at the height, p_1''. The new function, s_{2T}'', meets $s_{2N}'' = s_{2N}'$ and s_{2O}'' at B, the point common to the new and the old markets.

All of these developments are incorporated in Figure 7–18, which reproduces the six double-primed s-functions of t_2. PP', a downward-sloping stable price-level line, is also in the diagram. Point 1 is the pre-disturbance equilibrium, and point 2 is the bank's bid price in combination with the still constant price and yield, p_2' and r_2'; i.e., the substitution purchases are assumed to begin during t_2. By inspection of the diagram it is apparent that subsequent movements from point 2 must lie within an upper right quadrant projected from point 1. This is because the intersections of all possible

FIGURE 7–18
The Impact of an Open-Market Purchase on the Entire System
of Substitution Functions

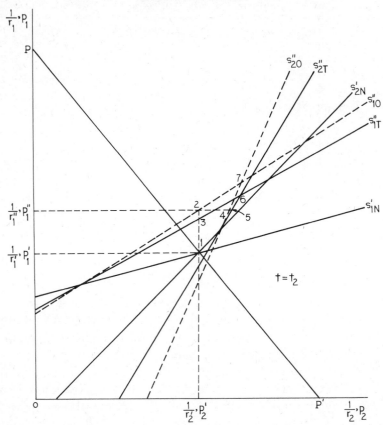

combinations of s_1 and s_2 s-functions—all of which are upward sloping—lie within that area. Hence we are assured for the present, at least, that the interest rates will pursue a course that lies above any downward-sloping line passing through point 1. Such a line is PP', and it follows that the shorter-run impact of the operation must be inflationary, even though the path of r_1 and r_2 does not happen to lie within the upper vertical angle of s_{1N} and s_{2N}, the area of "pure" inflation.[15]

---

[15] If PP' were drawn with positive slope, close to s'_{2N} (see Figure 7–15[a]), it is entirely possible that the substitution process should carry the system into a deflationary movement. If PP' were rising, but close to s'_{1N} (as in Figure 7–15[b]), the purchase and substitution process do not hold any immediate danger of stimulating deflation. Rising PP' functions are treated in the appendix, Section 2(a).

The precise movement from point 2 depends on the relative speed with which stock and flow demanders in each market respond to changing interest rates. Suppose that existing-asset holders carry out an instantaneous substitution operation at the opening of t_2. The initial reaction following the purchase is a reduction in r_2, corresponding to the movement from point 2 to point 4 on s''_{2O}. Thereafter the interest rates fall along a rising step-path between s''_{1O} and s''_{2O}, ending at the intersection at point 7. As the flow schedules accrue during t_2, the interest rates are gradually drawn upward toward the intersection of s''_{1T} and s''_{2T} at point 6. Whether the initial movement from point 7 is rightward to s''_{1T}, downward to s''_{2T}, or on a resultant southeast vector, depends on the relative timing of substitution reactions of savers in the two markets.[16] But as soon as the interest rates reach either s''_{1T} or s''_{2T}, they proceed stepwise between those schedules to point 6. If existing-asset holders executed their substitution purchases over time at the same rate as do current savers, then the interest path would be a direct one from point 2 to point 3 or 5 on either of the total schedules, and thence stepwise between them to point 6.[17]

---

[16] Even though we abstract from the equilibrating mechanisms, s''_{1T} and s''_{2T} are not really fixed functions during t_2. The total schedules of any interval are drawn continuously over time toward their respective new functions (see p. 250). Hence during the course of t_2 point 7 drifts away from point 6, the opening equilibrium.

[17] In the unlikely, but not impossible event that savers carry out their entire substitution operation ahead of existing-asset holders, the functions of Figure 7-18 are not relevant to describing the interest movement. s_{1N} and s_{2N} were constructed on the assumption that output was the only market for securities, while s_{1T} and s_{2T} assume that both savers and existing-asset holders are responding simultaneously. What is required if wealth holders are present, but not participating in the substitution operation, is a new set of s-functions indicating the more limited extent to which savers are able to change security prices when their shifting demand is added to given existing-demand schedules. This would be illustrated by Figure 7-6 if the initial shift of BC from s_1 to s_2 by current savers—the only demand response—were added to $D'_{2O}(r'_1)$, and the return flow from s_2 to s_1 added to $D'_{1O}(r'_2)$. In each case the impact of savers' demand on price would be determined in the context of a total market containing new-security supply schedules, savers' demand, plus constant existing-security supply and demand components. The relevant s-functions for current savers would therefore be constructed on the assumption of given existing-security supply and demand schedules of each market. For time intervals of less than a year or two, the s-function of y_1 savers is likely to be nearly horizontal, while that of y_2 savers is almost vertical. In the case of an open-market purchase of s_1 securities, s_1 existing supply is reduced, and the whole locus of s_1 prices determined by savers at each alternative price is raised. The modified s_{1N} schedule accordingly shifts upward. Following the initial increase in p_1 to p''_1, savers respond by raising p_2 by some small amount, p_1 in turn is raised further, and so on along the usual step-path to a temporary equilibrium. Given the likely slopes of the new s-functions, the equilibrium will not be too far removed from point 2 in Figure 7-18. When existing-asset holders are finally aroused to substitution action, the interest rates will be drawn to the total schedules of Figure 7-18 and the intersection at point 6.

Thus far in t_2 we have been abstracting from the equilibrating mechanisms, studying the substitution process in terms of stable s-functions. But in fact the equilibrating forces begin operating immediately following the purchase, and the substitutability movements should accordingly be described in a context of constantly shifting s_O and s_T s-functions. We shall introduce the adjustment process, approaching it on the level of abstraction of Chapter IV; i.e., the adjustment is an interaction of money and security-market stocks and flows, without explicit consideration of changes in the stock of capital or its rate of return. On the assumptions of Chapter IV-B(2), the latter variables can have no significant effect on the financial adjustment and the market rate of interest. At most, the real adjustment causes changes in ρ_s, movements of the security schedules, and rotations of the s-functions about or near the prevailing rate of interest. The transfer and wealth effects together restore equilibrium with considerable detachment from developments in the real sector.

The transfer effect in either market entails increments of security supply and demand to the existing-security schedules, tending to bring the market rate to the level of the natural rate. Thus, in the s_1 existing-asset market, any r_2 corresponds to an r_1 whose level is nearer to the natural s_1 rate. In terms of the s-functions s_{1O} and the derived schedule, s_{1T}, move toward s_{1N} along a vertical line drawn through the prevailing yield on s_2 securities. By the same token, s_{2O} and s_{2T} shift toward s_{2N} along a horizontal line passing through the current value of r_1. In Figure 7–18 the post-operation interest rates lie in a region in which the s_1 market undergoes an inflationary adjustment; r_1 increases as excess new s_1 securities are added to existing wealth. Assuming that the initial substitution carries the interest rates instantaneously to point 6, the beginning s_1 adjustment causes s_{1O} and s_{1T} to shift downward along a vertical line drawn through point 6. The adjustment in s_2 is deflationary, and excess savers' demand in that market raises p_2 and lowers r_2. s_{2O} and s_{2T} shift horizontally to the right along a line passing through point 6.

As long as the interest rates remain to the right of PP', the decrease of idle balances in s_1 exceeds the increase in s_2, and the price level will rise. The inflation creates a loss in the value of idle balances and a decrease in existing-security demand in *both* markets, causing an upward wealth effect on each interest rate. Thus in Figure 7–18, s_{1O} and s_{1T} shift further downward, while s_{2O} and

s_{2T} shift to the left in opposition to the rightward impulse of the s_2 transfer effect. In general, we can isolate three possible cases with regard to the character of the adjustment in each market, occurring at some time following an open-market purchase. We continue to assume that the net impact of the operation is inflationary:

1. The market rates of interest lie within the upper vertical angle of s_{1N} and s_{2N}, and there is an inflationary adjustment in both markets (see Figure 7A–1 or 7A–4). The transfer and wealth effects shift s_{1O} and s_{1T} downward, and s_{2O} and s_{2T} leftward.

2. The market rates of interest lie to the left of the upper vertical angle of s_{1N} and s_{2N}, as in Figure 7–18. The adjustment is toward inflation in s_1, deflation in s_2. The transfer and wealth effects shift s_{1O} and s_{1T} downward, while the transfer effect shifts s_{2O} and s_{2T} rightward and the wealth effect shifts s_{2O} and s_{2T} leftward.

3. The market rates of interest lie to the right of the upper vertical angle of s_{1N} and s_{2N} (see Figure 7A–6). There is a deflationary adjustment in s_1 and an inflationary one in s_2. The transfer effect shifts s_{1O} and s_{1T} upward, while the wealth effect shifts them downward. The transfer and wealth effects shift s_{2O} and s_{2T} leftward.[18]

The net course of the interest rates is determined, thus, by the simultaneous influence of substitution and adjustment-process tendencies. In the absence of the equilibrating forces, the rates are carried step-wise to the intersection of either the old or the aggregate s-functions, depending on whether the time interval under consideration is equal to or greater than zero. But the emergence of the total schedules over time coincides with the first installment of the transfer effect, and after any finite interval the whole set of

---

[18] The impact on wealth in Cases 2 and 3 is thus a combination of inflationary (Chapter V) and deflationary (Chapter VI) paths. In Case 2, pictured in Figure 7–18, the s_1 market produces wealth series that vary with the degree of forced saving; the s_2 market generates series that depend on the extent of forced investment. However, the fact that the price level is rising means that the s_2 wealth series are all reduced by a factor representing the net loss of m_{22} on account of the inflation; the increases in m_{22} via transfers, of course, remain. At the same time, the deflationary force of the s_2 market is an offset to the decrease in both m_{12} and m_{22} that would otherwise occur. We must also qualify the wealth series by pointing out that the m_{12} balances are reduced from their immediate post-operation level by the subsequent substitution operation. This will lower the general level of the s_1 wealth paths. Moreover, the initiating disturbance to the s_2 market is the internal substitution operation, rather than an open-market sale, which underlies the analysis of Chapter VI. The disturbance in s_2 is a combination of an increase in the saving schedule and a smaller increase—in terms of the interest impact—of both the supply of m_{22} balances and s_2 existing-security demand. The adjustment must reduce r_2 from the decreased market level to the still lower natural level. The disturbance effectively is a *net* increase in saving. Chapter VIII-B(1) describes this disturbance and indicates how the real analysis of Chapter VI can be applied to it.

s_O and s_T s-functions must be reconstructed in the light of new existing-security supply or demand schedules. Before long the price level rises, and this, too, is reflected in movements of the s-schedules, contributing new pushes and pulls to the path of the interest rates. However, the adjustment process must eventually bring the old and total s-functions back to the common intersection they held with s_{1N} and s_{2N} before the operation. Apart from any temporary changes in the schedules of saving and investment, s_{1N} and s_{2N} are invariant throughout the entire process, and the equilibrium of the system continues to be the pair of interest rates at their intersection. In view of the manifold dynamic tendencies, can we predict the course of the interest rates and the price level to such an equilibrium?

An exact account of the path of the interest rates can only be based on knowledge of the numerical values of the parameters of the system. Short of that, however, we can indicate the *possibility* of reaching equilibrium by surveying and classifying the whole range of paths that the interest rates conceivably may follow. This is done in the appendix. But first we must define an "equilibrating" movement of an s-function.

The approach of the market to the natural rate of interest does not necessarily mean that the simultaneous movements in s_O and s_T are also equilibrating. Thus in Figure 7–18 the initial deflationary transfer in s_2 shifts s_{2O} and s_{2T} rightward, bringing them closer to s'_{2N} in the vicinity of point 6, but driving them farther to the right of point 1, the intersection of s'_{1N} and s'_{2N}. However, if s_{2O} and s_{2T} were less steeply inclined, lying to the left of point 1, the transfer-induced rightward movement would instead bring them nearer the equilibrium at point 1. At the same time the inflation-produced wealth effect in the s_2 market is disequilibrating, because it raises r_2 even farther above the intersection of S_2 and I_2. In response, s_{2O} and s_{2T} move leftward, away from s'_{2N} in the area of point 6. But in the vicinity of point 1, the leftward movement is actually equilibrating, since it brings s_{2O} and s_{2T} closer to the intersection of s'_{1N} and s'_{2N}. In general, the equilibrating mechanisms will be evaluated in the two-security model in terms of whether they bring the old and aggregate s-functions nearer to the intersection of s'_{1N} and s'_{2N}. A movement of an s-function will be considered equilibrating if its vertical distance, in the case of s_{1O} and s_{1T}, and its horizontal distance, in the case of s_{2O} and s_{2T}, from the intersection of s'_{1N} and s'_{2N} is reduced.

In each of the three cases summarized above, the increase in the price level creates downward shifts in s_{1O} and s_{1T}, and leftward shifts in s_{2O} and s_{2T}. As long as the equilibrium rates at point 1 lie within the lower vertical angle of s_{1T} and s_{2T} (as in Figure 7–18), such movements will be equilibrating for both pairs of schedules; moreover, the resulting market rates of interest at the intersection of s_{1T} and s_{2T} will be nearer to the equilibrium pair at point 1. On the other hand, the transfer effect will be equilibrating with respect to both sets of schedules when point 1 lies inside the lower vertical angle of s_{1T} and s_{2T}, *and* the intersection of s_{1T} and s_{2T} lies inside the upper vertical angle of s_{1N} and s_{2N}; or whenever *neither* of these conditions is fulfilled. In this event the transfer effect will carry both pairs of schedules nearer to point 1—s_{1T} shifting vertically, and s_{2T} shifting horizontally toward it. It is this tendency of the transfer effect, together with the possibility of reaching a temporary equilibrium on PP', where the price level is stable, that establishes the equilibrating character of the dynamic process.

In the appendix we shall isolate seven distinguishable cases with regard to the action of both equilibrating mechanisms on the s-functions. We may anticipate these results by noting that the wealth and transfer effects can be disequilibrating at one time or another with respect to one or both sets of s-schedules. However, if the stability conditions are met, we are assured of eventually reaching a pair of market rates which lie on PP'—at, above, or below the equilibrium at the intersection of s_{1N}' and s_{2N}'. Since the equilibrium rates are only one combination out of many on PP' toward which the system tends, the initial intersection of the s-schedules on PP' very possibly will not coincide with the point of equilibrium. As such, the independent contribution of the price level—with or without the assistance of the transfer effect—may be characterized as bringing the interest rates to their *average* equilibrium level; i.e., if PP' is negatively sloped, it may not be far removed from a downward function along which the average of the two interest-reciprocals is constant and equal to the equilibrium average. Once on PP', however, the price level has exhausted its role in the adjustment process, and it devolves upon the transfer effect to establish the appropriate differential between the interest rates by way of further adjustments in the existing supply and demand for securities. Thus, when the price level, which is essentially a blunt instrument in the adjustment process, has worked itself out, the more sensitive action of the transfer effect—now entirely equilibrating—completes the movement along PP' to equilibrium. It is possible that the price level will itself undergo slight oscillations as the final increments of security supply and demand are brought onto the markets. But if at r_1' and r_2', L_{12} and L_{22}, respectively, are fixed (or vary in an offsetting manner), then $m_2 = m_{12} + m_{22}$ will be the same in the new as in the old equilibrium, and the price level on net will have risen proportionately to the monetary injection.

F. SUMMARY

A second security, which is a less-than-perfect substitute for demanders of the initial one, is introduced into the system. The existing-asset, output, and total markets are divided into submarkets in which each of the securities is held or traded. The submarkets are essentially replicas of the markets previously described. For example, the type 1 or s_1 security has in its existing-asset market its own idle-balance supply and demand and total-wealth components. Each existing-security demand and saving function varies inversely with the interest rate of the alternative security. This requires that in each submarket a portion of the wealth or income budget be reserved to finance the desired shifts between securities at non-equilibrium interest rates. The portion of the budget so allocated is named the "financial-substitution function."

The natural rates of interest and the returns to capital are determined by the two pairs of new-security supply and demand schedules, interacting separately and together in accordance with the substitution coefficients. These rates are imposed on the existing-asset markets, which adapt to them when the money stock is properly divided between the two idle uses and the active circulation. Over time the existing-asset market for each security grows by the constant and equal saving-investment increments.

An open-market purchase of s_1 securities is carried out. The direct impact on the existing-asset and output markets, separately considered, is shown to involve repeated substitution transfers, causing the interest rates to fall to a level below that created directly by the central bank. In the combined stock-flow system, an initial round of substitution purchases is seen to generate a possible diversity in the direction of movement of the price level. Security demanders may drive the s_2 natural rate below the level of the market rate, stimulating a deflationary adjustment in the s_2 submarkets. The analysis of the price level, as well as further rounds of substitution expenditures, is handled more elegantly by the framework of Hicksian substitution functions.

The substitution functions are six rising linear relationships between the two interest rates derived from each submarket, including the combined stock-flow market for each security. In the s_1 existing-asset market, for example, the substitution or s-function is the set of equilibrium values of r_1 (the yield on s_1 securities) as related to different values of r_2; the latter interest rate determines r_1 by determining the s_1 existing-security demand schedule. Stability for each pair of s-functions derived from the existing-asset, output, or total markets requires that the derivative with respect to $1/r_2$ of the s_2 function exceed that of the corresponding s_1 function. Instability is shown to result from a sufficient degree of diversity between the financial-substitution functions of the submarkets of a given market. Stability of each pair of existing-asset and output s-functions is neither necessary nor sufficient for stability of the total s-functions. However, because of possible instantaneous explosive movements, stability of the existing-asset functions is assumed. The appendix demonstrates that instability in the output-market functions, even though the total functions are stable, prevents the system from reaching equilibrium following a disturbance. Thus stability of all pairs of s-functions is assumed.

The Hicksian space also carries implications for the commodity price level. Superficially, there appear to be diverse tendencies acting on the price level, except in the vertical angles defined by the output-market substitution functions. However, a downward function of the two interest rates, labeled PP' and designated the "stable price-level line," is shown to divide the total space unambiguously into areas of net inflation on the right, and net deflation on the left. PP' is the locus of interest-rate combinations along which the price level is stable. There are infinitely many such combinations, obtained by pairing a rate which creates an excess of, say, investment over saving in one submarket, with a rate that creates an equal and offsetting excess of saving over investment in the other submarket. There is some degree of dissimilarity in the slope and magnitude of the excess investment functions for each security that causes PP' to be upward sloping. In the appendix this is shown to be a possible, but not inevitable cause of (a) deflation in the early stages following a monetary increase, and (b) instability of the total system.

In stock-flow equilibrium the six s-functions meet at a common point, the equilibrium natural rates of interest. An open-market purchase dislodges the s-functions derived from the existing-asset and total markets of the purchased security. The induced rotations of wealth and the underlying demand components cause sympathetic rotations in the s-functions of the alternative security. The burden of the adjustment process is to return the displaced schedules to the common intersection still shared by the output-market functions. The equilibrating mechanisms, the transfer and wealth effects, cause movements of the s-functions which do not necessarily bring them nearer to an intersection at the equilibrium point. However, the appendix establishes that if the stability conditions are met, the displaced schedules must sooner or later meet on PP', from which they proceed to the equilibrium. The price level may oscillate during this final transition to equilibrium.

CHAPTER VIII

The Analysis Generalized

The preceding chapters have described the response stimulated by a once-for-all purchase and sale of securities by the central bank. This and the next chapter will generalize the analysis by describing the response to additional kinds of disturbances, and by relaxing a number of the assumptions made in the basic model as set forth in Chapter II. To some extent the original assumptions have already been relaxed, as in Chapter VII, where two securities are handled, and Chapter V-E(2) and (3), where lagged investment and investment errors are introduced. Chapters VIII and IX will extend the generalization.

We begin this chapter by analyzing a continuing open-market operation; i.e., the central bank remains permanently in the market, buying or selling securities in pursuit of given objectives. Following this we describe independent shifts in saving and investment, the impact of government fiscal policy, a combination of monetary and fiscal action, a change in active velocity, independent shifts in existing-asset demand, and autonomous movements between idle and active balances. We continue with an account of the system in which saving and investment are partly a demand and supply, respectively, of idle balances. Saving as a function of both wealth and income is described, and the chapter concludes by adding a new sector, a system of commercial banks. Chapter IX introduces a sector of financial intermediaries, analyzes stationary and regressive economies and the so-called "classical" model, and relaxes the assumption that money is dichotomized into idle and active portions. A final section considers three "Keynesian" cases.

With the exceptions noted, the model remains as summarized in Chapter II-D. There are two sectors, households and firms, and two markets explicitly treated, the existing-asset and output. There is a single equity-type security, any central-bank purchase or sale of which results in subsidies or taxes on personal income, maintaining total private income constant. Output is generally, but not always, fixed at full employment. The demand for idle balances, L_2, will be invariant in the face of autonomous wealth changes. Since the equilibrium and adjustment of the system have already been described in considerable detail, the following presentation will focus on the novel elements of each section. Previously offered supporting analysis will not be repeated. Unless specifically referred to, the assumptions and disturbances of one section are not carried over to another.

A. PERPETUAL OPERATIONS IN THE OPEN MARKET

Suppose that the central bank remains indefinitely in the market, continuing to buy or sell securities after an initial transaction. The bank enters a market which is in dynamic stock-flow equilibrium at a market rate of interest, $r'_M = r'_N = \rho'_K$. In Section 1 continuing purchases are carried out at discrete intervals, and in Section 2, continuously over time. Section 3 considers open-market sales.

1. A Repeated Purchase

The bank begins by executing an instantaneous purchase at the start of a period, t_1. It obtains existing securities only and increases the stock of idle balances. The impact is shown in Figure 8–1(b), where the interest rate is lowered to r''_M and real idle money raised from m'_2 to m''_2. The saving and investment schedules that prevail during t_1 are drawn in Figure 8–1(a). In the absence of further disturbances, the period produces an investment-saving gap of AB, equal to CD, the excess supply of idle balances. The transfer thus raises the interest rate to r'''_M as it lowers m_2 to m'''_2. Assuming, for simplicity, that the increase in the price level lowers m_2 only after the transfer is completed, the inflation creates m^4_2 and a final increase in r_M to r^4_M via the wealth effect. Now, the bank wishes to maintain the interest rate at r''_M by a compensating purchase at the opening of the next period, t_2. It can do so by buying instantaneously securities equal to $m''_2 - m^4_2$ in aggregate value; i.e., the bank must add to real idle balances an amount equal to the reduction caused by both equilibrating forces

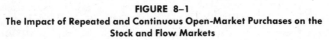

FIGURE 8–1
**The Impact of Repeated and Continuous Open-Market Purchases on the
Stock and Flow Markets**

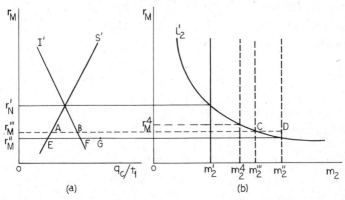

in the preceding period. When this is done, m_2 returns to m_2''. In
every period the interest rate rises thus above r_M'', and falls again
to r_M'' at the start of the following period. The price level rises in
proportion to the monetary transfer. Since neither S, I, nor L_2 are
altered by the inflation, the periodic real transfer to the active balances (AB) is constant. Thus the nominal transfer rises with the
price level, which in turn rises by increasing periodic amounts.
Since the real injection of the bank cannot be less than the real
transfer ($m_2'' - m_2'''$), the total quantity of money also increases
at an increasing rate. As m_2 returns to m_2'' at the opening of each
period, M_1/M_2 and total velocity return to the corresponding
levels, which are below those of the pre-disturbance equilibrium.[1]

It is clear that the periodic transfer will always lower m_2 to m_2'''
and raise r_M to r_M'''. But will the impact of the price level and
thereby, the wealth effect, on m_2 and r_M also be constant over time;
i.e., will the increase in the price level, following a given real transfer, always lower idle balances by the same real amount? In order
to show that this is in fact so, we consider a typical period following t_1. We let M_2' be the nominal quantity of money at the start,
and $\Delta M_1'$ the nominal transfer to the income stream during the

---

[1] The constancy of the real injection and the increase in the nominal injection applies to
the third period, relative to the second, and in all subsequent periods relative to the preceding. We have assumed that the real injection by the bank at the opening of the second
period, $m_2'' - m_2^4$, is less than the initial injection, $m_2'' - m_2'$, since the duration of the first
period was not great enough for the equilibrating mechanisms to restore the system to equilibrium. However, there is no necessary relation between the relative magnitudes of the first
and second *nominal* injections. In the numerical example of Table 8–1 below, the second
injection is only $11, while the first is $20. But examples showing an opposite relation can
be constructed.

period. The real transfer is $\Delta m_1' = \Delta M_1'/P'$, where P' is the price level preceding and during the course of the transfer. The price level following the transfer is P''. Active velocity and output are constant at V_1' and y', respectively. The value of idle balances after the inflation is

$$(8A.1) \qquad\qquad m_2^4 = \frac{M_2' - \Delta M_1'}{P''}.$$

For P'' we substitute $P' + \Delta M_1'(V_1'/y')$, and for $\Delta M_1'$, $\Delta m_1' P'$. (8A.1) becomes

$$m_2^4 = \frac{M_2' - \Delta m_1' P'}{P' + \Delta m_1' P' \left(\dfrac{V_1'}{y'}\right)},$$

$$= \frac{M_2' - \Delta m_1' P'}{P' \left[1 + \Delta m_1' \left(\dfrac{V_1'}{y'}\right)\right]},$$

$$= \frac{m_2'' - \Delta m_1'}{1 + \Delta m_1' \left(\dfrac{V_1'}{y'}\right)}.$$

We have noted that the real transfer, $\Delta m_1'$, is constant over time. Since the bank restores m_2 to m_2'' at the beginning of every period, all terms in the final expression are constants, as is, therefore, m_2^4 and the corresponding interest rate, r_M^4.

Data derived from a hypothetical numerical case of a repeated purchase are entered in Table 8–1. In the second column is the pre-disturbance value of idle balances, m_2', prevailing at the start of t_1; the corresponding interest rate, r_N', is entered in the caption in parentheses. In the next three columns are the succeeding values of m_2 during the course of t_1 and two subsequent periods. The caption of each column again indicates parenthetically the interest rate corresponding to the values of m_2. The numerator and denominator of each numerical entry for m_2 are given separately. On the basis of this information the last two columns present for the three periods the nominal value of the bank's injection and the transfer of idle to active balances. The initial data for the economy are

$$M_1' = M_2' = \$100,\ V_1' = 2,\ y' = 200,\ \text{and}\ P' = M_1' V_1'/y' = \$1.00.$$

The value of idle balances is $m_2' = M_2'/P' = \$100/\$1.00 = 100$. At the start of t_1 the bank lowers r_M to r_M'' and raises idle balances by \$20, producing $m_2'' = 120/1.00 = 120$. The initial transfer is

TABLE 8–1

A NUMERICAL EXAMPLE OF A REPEATED OPEN-MARKET PURCHASE

Period	$m_2'(r_N')$	$m_2''(r_M'')$	$m_2'''(r_M''')$	$m_2^4(r_M^4)$	Nominal Changes	
					Bank's Injection	Transfer
t_1	$\dfrac{100}{1.00}$ $= 100$	$\dfrac{120}{1.00}$ $= 120$	$\dfrac{115}{1.00}$ $= 115$	$\dfrac{115}{1.05}$ $= 109.52$	\$20	\$5
t_2		$\dfrac{126}{1.05}$ $= 120$	$\dfrac{120.75}{1.05}$ $= 115$	$\dfrac{120.75}{1.1025}$ $= 109.52$	\$11	\$5.25
t_3		$\dfrac{132.30}{1.1025}$ $= 120$	$\dfrac{126.7875}{1.1025}$ $= 115$	$\dfrac{126.7875}{1.1576}$ $= 109.52$	\$11.55	\$5.525

assumed to be 5, in both monetary and real units. This leaves real idle balances of $m_2''' = 115/1.00 = 115$. The transfer of \$5 from M_2 to M_1 raises P to $105 \times 2/200 = \$1.05$, and lowers m_2 to $m_2^4 = 115/1.05 = 109.52$, entered in the fifth column. At the opening of t_2 the bank restores r_M to r_M'' and m_2 to m_2'' by adding \$11 to idle balances. Thus at the start of t_2, $m_2'' = 126/1.05 = 120$. The remaining data in the table are computed on the assumption that the changes in m_2 on account of the transfer, the relative increase in the price level, and the bank's real injection are constant. The corresponding nominal values are thus greater by the increase in the price level of the previous period.

Suppose that the bank pursues an alternative policy of a constant increase in the *nominal* stock of money each period. It is clear from the foregoing analysis that it cannot prevent some increase in the rate of interest from occurring; i.e., we have seen that a constant *real* injection, and a rising nominal increase, is necessary to peg the rate of interest. The bank's purchase loses potency, since a fixed nominal increase is a declining relative increase in the stock of money, reducing thereby the impact on both m_2 and r_M. r_M rises each period and approaches r_N' asymptotically.[2] The magnitude of

---

[2] In the initial stages a constant nominal injection may constitute a greater increase in *real* idle balances than the decrease caused by the equilibrating mechanisms. This would be the case in the numerical example of Table 8–1 if the injection of t_2 were the same as that of t_1, \$20. For then m_2 at the start of t_2 would be \$135/\$1.05 > 120. As such, r_M will fall below r_M''. But the continued decline in r_M will itself contribute to the growth of the forces tending to reduce m_2 and raise r_M: the saving-investment gap and the rise of the price level. Eventually, the latter will more than counter the impact of the bank on m_2 and r_M.

the real transfer thus falls. The rate of increase of the price level depends on the increase in M_1, which cannot be predicted *a priori*. We noted in Chapter IV-D(2) that a declining real transfer is not incompatible with a rising nominal transfer over time.

2. A Continuous Purchase

Let the bank be more ambitious, insisting that r_M be constant at r_M'' throughout the period. This requires that the bank remain in the market continuously. After its initial purchase of $m_2'' - m_2'$, it must be willing to buy a quantity of securities not less than $EF = I'(r_M') - S'(r_M')$ in real value (see Figure 8–1[a]); i.e., the bank must be prepared to buy at least every excess new security floated at r_M'' during the period. This will prevent the transfer of a single dollar of idle balances and nullify any upward pressure on the rate of interest on that account. However, the purchase of excess new securities sends money directly into the income stream, raising commodity prices and lowering m_2. This raises r_M via the wealth effect. To prevent this, the bank must extend its purchase beyond EF to, say, EG. The component, $FG = EG - EF$, is in excess of the investment-saving gap, and represents a purchase of existing securities and an addition to idle money replacing the value loss due to the inflation. The interest rate will be perfectly constant at r_M'' if the bank synchronizes its purchase with the flotation of excess new securities and the loss of real balances occasioned by the rise in the price level. As in the previous case, the bank's real monetary injection will be constant, offsetting the constant real transfer and wealth effects. But the real monetary injection, EG, is greater for this operation than for that of the discontinuous case, $m_2^4 - m_2''$, since the I–S gap and the associated inflation is greater at r_M'' than it is at r_M'''.

The significance of continuous open-market operations is that the bank is brought into direct contact with the income stream. If the wealth effect were zero, then after an initial purchase on wealth account, the policy of maintaining r_M at a low level requires that the bank buy new securities only. This raises active balances and the price level directly. A positive wealth effect on interest forces the bank to purchase existing securities also, but the bank will continue to raise money incomes to the extent of the I–S gap at the lower rate of interest. As in the repeated purchase, a constant rate of real monetary increase implies that the increase in the nominal stock of money and the rise of the price level increase over time. The velocity of money remains constant at the lower level associated with the greater value of m_2; i.e., the monetary injection is allocated directly between idle and active balances in accordance with the greater desired ratio of M_2/M_1 at r_M''. In general, the policy of continuous injections can be regarded as the limiting instance of repeated compensating purchases when the interval between the latter goes to zero.

The equilibrium real price of securities in the face of continuous purchases that fix the interest rate depends on the degree of forced saving. If the latter is complete and immediate, p will approach p'. The initial movement is from the pre-disturbance to the bid price:

$$(8A.2) \qquad p' = \frac{\rho_s'}{r_N'} \text{ to } p'' = \frac{\rho_s''}{r_M''}, \text{ where } \rho_s'' = \rho_s'.$$

But the rate of realized investment rises at once to $I'(r_M'')$, reducing ρ_K to $\rho_K'' = r_M''$, and ρ_s to $\rho_s''' < \rho_s'$ (see Chapter V-D[2]). At r_M'', p is equal to p', and the bank's interest-rate policy requires that it pay this price. Thereafter capital increases relative to securities in the ratio, p', thereby perpetuating that price.[3] If forced saving is less than complete, the policy of fixing a lower interest rate results in rising, falling, or constant security prices, depending on the movement of ρ_s in response to stock watering, voluntary saving, and changes in ρ_K.[4] In general, the appropriate price to pay for securities is simply the one at which the bank's real outlay is constant and the yield remains r_M''.

The analysis of this and the preceding section assumes that the stock and flow schedules remain fixed, as indicated. However, over the longer periods of time consumed by continuous disturbances, this assumption is difficult to justify. The saving schedule will shift on net to the right or left, depending on the elasticity of response to income and wealth, respectively (see Part I). Any forced saving created by the bank's purchases of new securities will accelerate this tendency.[5] I tends to fall with reductions in the marginal product of capital, though increases in labor and tech-

---

[3] In complete forced saving security prices tend to fall (p. 154). But this results from the lower transfer price of each interval. However, if the bank is in the market continuously, all security transactions occur at the price, p', at which $r_M = r_M''$. Since neither r_M nor the terms underlying $\rho_s - \rho_K$ and K/S_P tend to change, p persists at p'.

[4] Though the bank prevents the reductions in p that would occur if the interest rate were allowed to seek its natural level, the bank obviously cannot control the movements of ρ_K and K/S_P underlying variations in ρ_s.

[5] In the case of complete forced saving the wealth increment is constant and equal to the growth of capital, $I'(r_M'')$.

nological advance will raise the schedule. In the face of continuing and predictable inflation, households may reduce the demand for idle balances each period, lowering the rate of interest. The equity securities are, of course, more attractive under these circumstances. In any case, the real and nominal monetary injection that maintains the lower interest rate varies with the shifts in S, I, and L_2. The reader may verify that any reduction in $I - S$ or increase in $m_2 - L_2$ will lighten the burden of the bank.

3. Perpetual Sales

A repeated or continuous open-market sale is simply the converse of the corresponding purchases. After an initial sale on wealth account, the bank can restore the higher rate of interest by removing the increase in real idle balances that occurred during the period. If the bank wants to maintain a higher interest rate continuously, then it must constantly offer securities equal in real value to the sum of excess saving and the increase in m_2 on account of the deflation. Since its real monetary withdrawal is constant, while the price level falls, the required nominal decrease diminishes. Thus M, M_1, and P fall by decreasing amounts. At the higher interest rate, V is higher. Were the bank to withdraw a fixed quantity of money, the real reduction in m_2 would increase each period. This would create successively higher interest rates. But as the interest rate rises, excess saving and the negative wealth effect on r_M is built up. Depending on the stock and flow excess demand functions, the equilibrating mechanisms may counter or even exceed the increased impact of the bank. Without knowing the actual parameters of the system, the net course of r_M and P cannot be predicted.

B. CHANGES IN SAVING AND INVESTMENT

The schedules of saving and investment have figured prominently as given variables in the analysis. In the general equilibrium they determine the natural rate of interest. In the process of adjustment, movements along them and discrepancies between them have constituted a mechanism for channeling funds in and out of the income stream, creating direct and indirect movements in the market rate of interest, and determining changes in the stock of capital and total wealth. It will be a short but significant step to place the source of disturbance in the schedules themselves. We shall analyze an independent shift in saving and then investment. The model remains as summarized in Chapter II-D. Saving and investment continue to be a demand and supply of securities, the supply and demand for money being fixed.

1. Saving

Suppose that the saving schedule shifts independently to the left, as in Figure 8–2(a) where S, drawn for a period, t_1, moves from S' to S''. The natural rate of interest increases from r'_N to r''_N, at which $L'_2 (r''_N) < L'_2 (r'_N)$. Given the schedules in the diagram, it is thus clear that r''_N can be imposed on the existing-asset market

FIGURE 8–2
A Decrease in the Saving Schedule

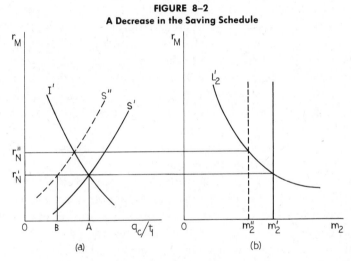

only by reducing real idle balances via transfers to the income stream. The equilibrium value of M_1, as given by (2D.4), and hence P, as given by (2D.2), is accordingly raised. Other changes are immediately discernible in the combined system, (2B.28)–(2B.40) and (2C.26)–(2C.39). ρ_K will rise to $\rho''_K = r''_N$. Since any transition to a new equilibrium entails changes in securities and capital, along with idle balances, there will tend to be new values for almost every other variable. The (post-shift) S, I, and L_1 *functions* are constant. But we may expect changes in S_O, K, W, ρ_s, and p—to name a few variables. The general impact of the disturbance is readily seen by sketching the adjustment process.

The reduction in saving is simultaneously a reduction in security demand originating in current income, and an equal increase in consumption expenditures. The increase in consumption spending is not directly inflationary, since it is financed by a withdrawal of savings formerly going into investment expenditures. However, as an initial period, t_1, unfolds, a discrepancy between intended saving and investment appears. At r'_N, which prevails at the start of the period, the supply and demand for existing securities are equal. Moreover, entrepreneurs continue to issue new securities at the rate, OA (see Figure 8–2[a]). But the demand for securities by savers proceeds at the rate, $OB < OA$. This excess of new supply causes a fall in security prices and a rise in the market rate of interest. As r_M rises, the rate of excess supply falls, and the excess security demand of wealth holders increases until, at the close of the period, the two are equal. The counterpart of this is a reduction in idle balances, which are transferred to entrepreneurs via the excess securities. Active balances thereby increase, raising the price level and the interest rate further via the wealth effect. This process continues through a number of periods until the transfers and increases in the price level have reduced the value of idle balances to m''_2. For when $m_2 = m''_2$, the existing-asset market is in equilibrium at r''_N, the new natural rate of interest at which $S'' = I'$. The reduction in saving has increased active balances at the expense of idle, thus raising the velocity of the total money supply. The price level rises proportionately.

The adjustment process stimulated by the shift in saving is identical with that following an open-market purchase. In both cases the adjustment must raise the prevailing market rate of interest to the level of the higher natural rate. In the purchase the market rate is driven below the natural; when saving falls, the natural rises above the unchanged market rate. But in each case the ensuing adjustment is the same. All of the analysis in Chapters IV and V pertaining to financial and real elements of the adjustment process apply to the decrease in saving.[6] However, while the processes are identical, the points of origin and the final equilibria differ for the two disturbances. For example, each may follow a complete forced-saving wealth path, such as c in Figure 5–11. But this downward vector originates at point C for the purchase, and point A for the shift of saving. In Figure 5–12 the point of origin is again at A for the decrease in saving. This is because there is no

---

[6] In terms of the stock-flow security-quantity schedules, the decrease in saving is a downward shift in D_N, tracing a path similar to that of Figure 4–5. In terms of the diagram of Figure 4–7, the initiating disturbance is a rightward shift in the excess investment function, $I - S$.

security transaction with the central bank, creating capital gains, and, since $\rho'_K = r'_N = r'_M$ initially, there is no limiting first interval following the decrease in saving. Moreover, the maximum wealth time series of the adjustment is now AD, the former equilibrium-growth path. This is generated when $\partial I / \partial r_M = 0$ and the wealth effect is absent. All other paths are drawn below AD, since the reduction in saving tends to lower the growth rate. A typical path might be rising and concave downward, reaching in equilibrium a linear trend whose slope is less than previously. Finally, while the price level rises both for the purchase and the decrease in saving, the adjustment tends to restore total velocity to its pre-disturbance value in the former case, and to raise it in the latter.[7]

When saving increases, the S schedule shifts to the right, driving the natural below the market rate of interest. The increase in saving is a diversion of consumption expenditures to securities. At the prevailing interest rate, the security demand of savers exceeds the new supply. Since existing-security supply and demand are equal, the excess demand of savers raises security prices and lowers the market rate of interest. The decline in r_M reduces somewhat the excess new demand and stimulates an excess supply of existing securities. In any period, r_M will fall until enough existing securities are forthcoming to meet the excess demand of savers. In this way, active balances of savers are expended against existing securities, after which they are held idle as an alternative to securities in the existing-asset market. This drain of active money lowers the price level, which provides a further downward impulse to the interest rate via the wealth effect. The adjustment continues until m_2 is raised by nominal transfers and by the fall in the price level to the larger quantity demanded at the lower natural rate of interest. In the new equilibrium real saving has increased, the price level has fallen, and the over-all velocity of money is less.

The adjustment following an increase in saving is the same as that created by an open-market sale. But the wealth paths tend to be greater when an increase in voluntary saving is the source of the disturbance. And while velocity tends to recover its pre-disturbance value following the sale, the increase in saving lowers V by increasing m_2.

---

[7] We have shown in Chapter V-E(4) that if L_2 responds to autonomous wealth changes, it may well be displaced from its original position during an adjustment process. Thus, at the natural rate of interest, m_2 and V will differ somewhat from their pre-disturbance values. We might speculate that it is probably unusual for L_2 and V to recover exactly their previous values following any disturbance.

2. Investment

A rightward shift in the investment schedule is caused by an increase in the marginal product of capital. This will increase the return to investment by raising total output. But we shall retain our working assumption that output is fixed. The disturbance is shown in Figure 8–3(a) as an increase in I from I' to I''. ρ_K rises spontaneously to ρ_K'', the return now corresponding to the prevailing growth rate, OA. The increase in I also raises the natural rate of interest to r_N'', to which the existing-asset market adapts by reducing m_2 from m_2' to m_2''. At r_N', the still prevailing market rate of interest, I exceeds S, and the excess supply of securities sets in motion the usual stock-flow financial adjustment. It is identical with that following a reduction in saving, except that the equilibrium rate of growth tends to increase in this case instead of falling.[8] If forced saving is complete and immediate, ρ_K will fall along I'' from ρ_K'' to $\rho_K' = r_N'$ and rise thereafter with r_M to the new equilibrium, r_N''. Thus, following a limiting first interval, the wealth path originates at point A in Figures 5–11 and 5–12, as it did in the decrease of saving. But in the present case AD represents, in the absence of the wealth effect, a lower rather than an upper limit to the wealth time series. AD is the path when $\partial S/\partial r_M = 0$. Since the equilibrium value of m_2 falls, velocity and the price level again rise.

FIGURE 8–3
An Increase in the Investment Schedule

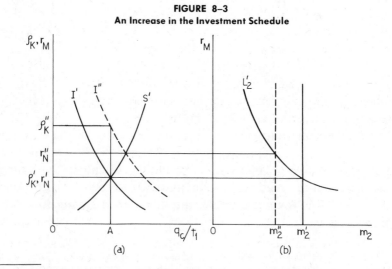

(a)   (b)

---

[8] In the framework of security-quantity schedules, the increase in I is an independent rightward shift of S_N.

A decrease in investment lowers the natural rate of interest and inflicts a deflationary adjustment on the system. At the beginning market rate of interest, the reduced supply of new securities creates an excess demand by savers, who inadvertently purchase existing securities. The rate of interest is simultaneously lowered and active balances, received from the sale of existing securities, are held idle. When the price level falls, the interest rate is driven lower still.

C. GOVERNMENT BUDGETARY POLICY

In this section we shall examine the monetary impact of fiscal deficits and surpluses. Since the federal budget has previously been assigned only a very passive, non-interfering role (Chapter III-B[2]), the government is assumed to enter the economy as a taxer and spender for the first time. In each case, expenditures and revenues are initially zero. We shall analyze both deficits and surpluses on a once-for-all and continuing basis. Initially, deficits will be financed by borrowing from the central bank, and surpluses will be applied to the retirement of debt held by the bank. Thus the fiscal disturbance will be accompanied by changes in the money supply. Later the budgetary imbalance will add to or subtract from the security holdings of households, leaving the money supply unchanged. An analysis of the non-zero balanced budget is given in Part E.

1. A Variable Money Supply

a) A Deficit

We begin by considering a fiscal deficit, lasting one period only, and financed by interest-free loans from the central bank. The government in effect prints new money which is injected into the economy during a finite interval. Like any once-for-all monetary increase, our assumptions lead us to expect that in the resulting equilibrium the natural rate of interest, the real value of idle balances, and the over-all velocity of money will be the same as in the beginning equilibrium. The price level will have risen proportionately to the increase in M. Security and capital changes, associated with an adjustment process, may, however, alter other variables in the system. Let us consider the transitional process.

The money created by the government is introduced as a subsidy to personal incomes. The deficit thus produces a direct increase in the supply of active balances. The new money is spent forthwith on consumption goods and additional saving. Since output is constant, the price level rises proportionately, thereby preventing real consumption and saving from changing. Thus far, the existing-asset market is not a party to these events. The increase in money saving is matched by an equal increase in the money value of new securities supplied, reflecting the general increase in prices and costs. As long as real saving is unchanged, it is met by the same quantity of real investment, and there are no leakages from the income stream. However, the increase in the price level reduces the real value of idle balances below the equilibrium, m_2', causing the interest rate to rise above r_N' via the wealth effect. The increase in r_M creates an excess of real saving over investment, forcing savers to purchase existing securities. In this way money is transferred from the income stream to idle balances, and the price level is lowered. The interest rate is reduced both by the transfer and the resulting fall in the price level. This process continues until r_M has been restored to the natural rate, and idle balances are increased to m_2'. With L_2 and output fixed, the price level on net will have risen proportionately to the over-all monetary injection, and the ratio of idle to active balances, and thus V, will be unchanged. Depending on the timing of the injection, the price level may rise continuously during the adjustment, its rate of increase moderated by the transfer of money to the existing-asset market.

The fiscal deficit provides an interesting contrast to the open-market purchase. In both cases the money supply is increased, but the purchase initially raises idle balances, and the deficit, active balances. In each case, with constant S, I, and L_2 schedules, the equilibrium interest rate and the ratio of idle to active money are invariant. Thus the adjustment process following the purchase transfers some of the additional idle balances to the income stream, while the deficit requires an opposite movement. In one case the interest rate temporarily falls, in the other it rises. The inflation caused by the purchase is characterized by $I > S$, that of the deficit, by $I < S$. The wealth changes described for the inflationary process (Chapter V) are relevant to the purchase, while those of the contraction (Chapter VI) apply to the deficit.[9] The

---

[9] Notice that wealth is altered only by the adjustment to the deficit, not by the deficit itself, since the government expenditure is received as an addition to personal incomes. Also, the wealth impact of the deficit differs from the open-market sale of Chapter VI in that the initiating disturbance is not an addition to the stock of securities. Hence the wealth curves of Figure 6–8 and 6–11, if generated by a deficit, would all be lower in equilibrium by the value of securities sold by the bank.

initial (positive) wealth effect on interest is of crucial importance in the adjustment to the deficit; it is the initiating force in stimulating the necessary transfer of active money to the existing-asset market. But in the open-market purchase the wealth effect is never more than a supplement to the transfer effect, which provides the beginning stimulus to the movement in the interest rate and the transfer of idle balances.

Let the deficit of the federal government be repeated each period. We assume that the same *real* quantity of money is added periodically to the incomes of households. Since the price level rises, the nominal injection also rises, and P increases by increasing amounts. In response the value of idle balances falls, raising the interest rate above r'_N via the wealth effect. As r_M rises, an excess of S over I appears, sending active balances to the existing-asset market. As a security purchase, the excess saving counters the upward tendency in r_M directly; at the same time the reduction in M_1 effected by $S > I$ reduces the increase in the price level and lowers the magnitude of the wealth effect on r_M. m_2 will thus fall and r_M will continue to rise until the force of excess saving on these variables is exactly equal to the opposite impact of the price level. m_2 and r_M thereafter are constant. In any period of such a "moving equilibrium" the price level rises in response to the total deficit less the transfer to the idle balances. Since both the deficit and the transfer are constant in real terms, the net real addition to the income stream is also constant, implying an increasing nominal increment in active balances. We have already seen (pages 271–72) that a rise in the price level in response to a constant real monetary injection produces a constant reduction in m_2 and increase in r_M. In equilibrium this counters the constant increase in m_2 on account of excess saving, stabilizing m_2 below its pre-disturbance value. Thus V is higher, r_M is constant at some level above the natural rate, and there is a continuing excess of S over I. The price level rises exponentially as the additions to M_1 increase over time.

If the deficit were constant in nominal units, the price level would rise by constant amounts, and the real deficit would approach zero. Since only a price level increasing by increasing amounts can produce a constant reduction in m_2, the price level in the present case would create successively smaller reductions in real balances. The wealth effect on interest thus goes to zero, and the long-run equilibrium is one in which m_2 and r_M are equal to their pre-disturbance values and $S = I$, in spite of the rising price level.

b) A Surplus

In the event of a once-for-all surplus, accomplished by a single-period income tax the proceeds of which retire bank-held government debt, M_1 and P fall, and the interest rate is lowered by a negative wealth effect. The decrease in r_M stimulates $I > S$ and a transfer of idle balances to the income stream, raising the price level. In the new equilibrium, M_1/M_2, V, and r_M are unaltered, and P has fallen proportionately to the loss of money. If the same real surplus continues perpetually, the interest rate will reach an equilibrium below the natural rate with I greater than S, m_2 higher, V lower, and M_1 and P falling by decreasing amounts. A continuing surplus constant in nominal units would create an increasing relative reduction in the money supply. This would augment the negative wealth effect on r_M by producing increasing increments in m_2. Whether r_M would fall continuously depends on the excess saving function relative to the excess supply of existing securities.[10]

2. A Fixed Money Supply

a) A Deficit

Suppose that the government borrows from households rather than from the central bank. The budgetary imbalance will therefore not alter the money supply. Consider a temporary deficit, in which government commodity expenditures are financed by borrowing for one period from households. We assume, as in Chapter V-B(1), that asset holders view government securities as perfect substitutes for private securities. Thus the action of the government is described as an addition to the prevailing financial I schedule, accompanied by an increase in government spending on goods. The borrowing operation, lasting for one period, t_1, is diagramed in Figure 8–4(a) as the movement from I' to $I' + G'$. During t_1 the interest rate rises from r'_N to r''_M at which the excess supply of securities, $I' + G' - S' = BC$, is equal to the excess demand of wealth holders, $m'_2 - L'_2 = DE$. The total real funds raised by the government is thus AC, of which BC is idle balances and AB, active balances. The AB component represents current saving not taken by private entrepreneurs. AB is created partly by an increase in saving (at the expense of consumption) in response to the higher

---

[10] Gold movements, in response to balance-of-payments surpluses and deficits, will produce monetary and wealth effects identical to those described in this section for government deficits and surpluses, respectively.

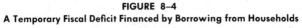

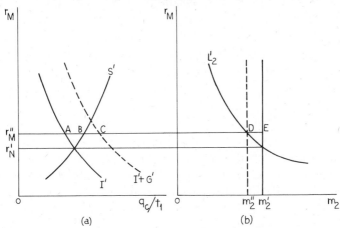

(a) (b)

interest rate, and partly by a diversion of saving from private investment due to the downward slope of I'. The government simultaneously spends the funds obtained from the securities market. Since part of its expenditure is drawn from idle balances, there is a net increase in M_1 and the price level. We assume that the price rise occurs at the closing instant of t_1. The inflation reduces m_2 below m_2'' and increases r_M above r_M'' via the wealth effect. At this point the government withdraws from the scene, allowing the internal forces of adjustment to bring on a new equilibrium. I' is again the ruling new-security supply schedule. Since the market rate is above the natural rate, there exists $S > I$, followed by a transfer of active to idle balances until m_2 is again m_2' and $r_M = r_N'$. The money supply is constant, and so all of the balances activated by the government must be returned to the existing-asset market. The price level returns to its pre-disturbance level, as do M_1/M_2 and V.

The wealth changes are those associated with an open-market sale and an excess of private saving over private investment. The exchange of government securities for idle balances during t_1 produces a direct wealth impact identical to that of a sale. At r_M'' the private sector releases $S' - I' = AB$ in goods to the government, of which $I'(r_N') - I'(r_M'')$ represents a decrease in investment, and $S'(r_M'') - S'(r_N')$ is a voluntary reduction in consumption. But the government competes with households for an additional quantity of goods, $I' + G' - S' = BC$. If the government obtains the BC

increment, private consumption is reduced further by that amount; but the corresponding increase in realized government spending is not forced saving, since we define the latter as an increase in the private stock of capital. Rather, the BC component is simply an addition to government consumption. The net wealth effect of the interval may thus be summarized as an open-market sale in conjunction with *zero* forced investment (i.e., realized investment lies on the I schedule), except that the price level rises instead of falling. At the close of t_1 the price level raises r_M above r_M'', and the government leaves the market. In subsequent intervals the real adjustment is entirely analogous to that of a monetary contraction, except that the increase in interest is due both to a security sale and an increase in the price level. In the absence of the government, forced investment will again be zero, complete, or intermediate between the extremes.

Were the government to carry out a perpetual real deficit by borrowing from households, the new equilibrium would resemble that of an increase in I. The interest rate would rise and remain at the intersection of S' and $I' + G'$, m_2 would be permanently lower, V higher, and P constant at a proportionally greater level. Wealth follows a contractionary zero forced-investment path during the adjustment, and the new equilibrium is characterized by a reduced rate of private investment.[11] If the deficit were fixed in nominal units, $I + G$ in Figure 8-4(a) would shift to the left of $I' + G'$ during the adjustment process, reflecting the smaller real government deficit due to the rising price level. This in turn would reduce the transfer, the inflation of each succeeding period, and the resulting leftward shift of $I + G$. An equilibrium would be reached with $I + G$ to the left of its initial position, but to the right of I', and $r_M > r_N'$, $m_2 < m_2'$, and V and P fixed at a higher level.

b) A Surplus

A government surplus, financed by a personal-income tax and applied to the retirement of privately held government debt, does not alter the quantity of money. The surplus is limited to a single period, during which it lowers money incomes, M_1, and P. Simultaneously the government repurchases a portion of its previously

---

[11]Cf. F. Modigliani, "Long-Run Implications of Alternative Fiscal Policies and the Burden of the National Debt," *Economic Journal,* Vol. LXXI (December, 1961), pp. 730–55.

issued debt, now held in the existing-asset market. Thus the balances withdrawn from the income stream are transferred to the idle realm as the government bids up security prices and lowers r_M below r_N'. Meanwhile, the deflation raises m_2 and lowers r_M further by a negative wealth effect. At the close of the period the government departs. At $r_M < r_N'$, I exceeds S and idle money is transferred to the income stream. The new equilibrium is identical to the old one in respect to r_M, M_1/M_2, V, and P. A lack of symmetry between this and the one-period deficit is that the government borrows both active and idle balances, but in retiring outstanding debt it increases idle balances only. The wealth effects of the disturbance can be divided into those sparked by the increase in m_2 attributable to the retirement operation and to the deflation, respectively. That part of the increase in m_2 and decrease in r_M due to the retirement of government debt produces wealth changes identical to those of an open-market purchase. The further increase in m_2 on account of the deflation again generates the wealth effects of an open-market purchase, except that there is not an initial loss of securities.[12]

A continuing real surplus applied to the retirement of existing debt will produce a reduction in M_1 and P each period. At the same time the interest rate will be lowered below r_N' as both the wealth effect and the repurchase of government debt raise m_2 above m_2'. This will stimulate an excess of I over S which tends to raise the interest rate by reducing m_2. If we consider just the wealth effect on interest, r_M will fall until $I - S$ in any period is sufficiently great to reduce m_2 by the same amount that the fall in the price level raises it. The interest rate at that point is constant. If we add to the wealth effect the impact on r_M of the government's continuing retirement operation, then equilibrium will be characterized by a lower (but constant) rate of interest, a greater excess of I over S, and a reduced rate of decline in the price level. P falls by diminishing amounts. A surplus constant in nominal terms will produce

---

[12]The surplus itself, originating in a tax on personal income, does not change wealth directly. The tax lowers money income and prices equally, leaving real income and expenditures of households intact. However, if the surplus were created by a reduction in government commodity expenditures, goods would be released for either private consumption or investment, which accordingly would increase. This assumption is actually more consistent with our view of the deficit in Section a as caused by an increase in government commodity expenditures. We attribute the surplus to an increase in taxes, rather than a reduction in commodity expenditures, because of our assumption that the budget is initially zero. Reality, of course, may involve any of these cases.

an increasing impact on m_2 and r_M via the wealth effect and the repurchase operation. The investment-saving gap may or may not counter the downward tendency in the rate of interest.

D. COMBINED MONETARY AND FISCAL POLICY

An interesting application of our system is to the analysis of a simultaneous open-market and fiscal operation. Specifically, a common proposal[13] is that the monetary authority stimulate growth by lowering the interest rate through perpetual open-market purchases, while countering the inflationary impact of such a policy through a continuing budgetary surplus. The surplus is applied to the retirement of debt held by the central bank, so that on net the money supply is constant. In Part A(2), the policy of fixing the interest rate below the natural rate through open-market purchases was seen to entail a constant real monetary injection, equal to the $S-I$ gap plus the decrease in m_2 on account of the inflation. The required nominal increase, ΔM, rose with the price level. Now, if each period the government raised its tax revenues by the added active balances, ΔM_1, the price level would be stabilized. A fixed price level would prevent a decrease in m_2 and enable the bank to maintain the lower interest rate with a purchase of smaller magnitude, all of which goes directly to the income stream (i.e., $\Delta M = \Delta M_1$). With the price level constant, the nominal purchase would also be constant. The surplus thus removes periodically the same increment to the active balances provided by the bank. Money and real income of households are unchanged, the interest rate is lower, I exceeds S, and M, V, and P are constant at their pre-disturbance values. Were the bank to sell securities perpetually while financing a continuing government deficit, the interest rate would lie above the natural, S would exceed I, and M, V, and P would again be fixed at their earlier values.

In terms of our framework, simultaneous but offsetting monetary and fiscal policy is a perfectly feasible goal of national policy. However, we are led to question whether the desired impact on the rate of growth is necessarily attainable. In the combined purchase and fiscal surplus, any increase in ex post investment takes the form of forced saving. The analysis of Chapter V has indicated clearly

---

[13]Cf. Dean A. Worcester, Jr., "Monetary versus Fiscal Policy at Full Employment," *Journal of Finance*, Vol. XII (March, 1957), pp. 1–15. This proposal has been associated with the position of the Democratic Party in policy statements of the late 1950's and early 1960's.

that there are an infinity of possible outcomes, depending on the success of entrepreneurs in obtaining resources through the forced-saving process. The resulting growth rate may lie above or considerably below that of the pre-disturbance economy.

E. A CHANGE IN ACTIVE VELOCITY

1. The Analysis

Suppose that households reduce the demand for active money in relation to income. This occurs spontaneously or in response, say, to a shortening of the average payments period. Symbolically, there is a shift from

(8E.1) $\qquad L_1' = k_1' Y$ to $L_1'' = k_1'' Y$, where $k_1'' < k_1'$.

Hence active velocity, $V_1 = 1/k_1$, rises. The equilibrium price level will also rise. We show this by reference to the monetary summary equation, (2D.4):

(8E.2) $$M_1 = \frac{\overline{M} k_1 \bar{y}}{L_2'(r_N') + k_1 \bar{y}},$$

where primes have been added to L_2 and r_N, which are fixed, and the crossbar removed from k_1, which is now variable. Both the natural rate of interest and the real quantity of idle money demanded are, of course, unaltered by a shift of active demand. The derivative of M_1 with respect to k_1 is positive:

(8E.3) $$\frac{\partial M_1}{\partial k_1} = \frac{L_2'(r_N') \overline{M} \bar{y}}{[L_2'(r_N') + k_1 \bar{y}]^2} > 0 .$$

The decrease in k_1 is thus accompanied by a *decrease* in M_1. But the latter change cannot offset the former in terms of the impact on the price level. In the present circumstances total real balances are

$$\frac{\overline{M}}{P} = \frac{M_1}{P} + m_2', \text{ where } m_2' = L_2'(r_N') .$$

Hence

(8E.4) $$P = \frac{\overline{M} - M_1}{m_2'} .$$

A decrease in M_1, while M and m_2 are constant, clearly raises P.

Let us trace the adjustment process caused by an increase in V_1. The initial effect is a rise in the price level in response to the increase in the rate of expenditures. Real idle balances fall below m_2' and

r_M increases above r'_N via the wealth effect. The higher interest rate stimulates $S > I$, which lowers the price level by converting active into idle balances until r_M is again r'_N and m_2 is m'_2. We know from (8E.4) that P, and hence V, remain above their pre-disturbance values. We can show this in the dynamic context as follows. m_2 falls and then rises to its earlier value, m'_2. But M_1/P is lowered by the initial increase in V_1 and P; the subsequent transfers of M_1 to M_2 reduce P proportionately, leaving M_1/P intact at its new lower level. On net, m_2 is constant and M_1/P is lower; hence M/P is lower and V must be higher.

The reader will notice the similarity between the foregoing adjustment and that of a one-period government deficit financed by new money (Part C[1]a). Though changes in active and total velocity occur in one case, while a change in the money supply occurs in the other, the changes in the price level and in wealth, via a common adjustment process, are the same for both disturbances.

An increase in the transactions demand—a decrease in V_1—will lower V and P, while raising M_1 via an $I > S$ adjustment process.

2. An Application: The Balanced-Budget Multiplier

Assume that a continuing increase in government spending is matched by an equal increase in personal tax revenues, creating a balanced budget. Assume also that the government spends additional tax receipts, paid out of current household income, without delay.[14] The disposable money income of households is thus constant—what is removed through taxes reappears promptly as new income generated by additional government spending. Accordingly, household money saving and consumption are also constant. But total money income of the economy has increased by the government expenditure. This occurs because the government has given some active balances an additional turnover against current output.[15] This is a net addition to the number of

---

[14] It is quite conceivable that even though the government's holdings of cash balances are not zero, an *increment* to the balanced budget would not appreciably add to these holdings. On this point, and for an elegant treatment of this entire subject, see Thomas Mayer, "The Quantity Theory and the Balanced Budget Theorem," *Review of Economics and Statistics,* Vol. XLIII (February, 1961), pp. 88–90.

[15] We assume that a tax on income is paid entirely out of current income—hence with active balances. But this is not a necessary assumption. If, for any reason, the demand for idle balances varied with disposable money income, the tax would be paid in part with idle balances. But when disposable income is restored by the government's expenditure, such activated funds would be returned to the idle holdings. There would be no net change in the quantities of idle and active money. The expenditure of a previously idle dollar is, of course, equivalent in its inflationary effects to an additional turnover of an active dollar.

turnovers that these balances would have otherwise received, since households are not themselves deprived of these funds for any finite period. In effect the government merely intercepts a portion of the income stream, securing active balances through its power to tax. But it maintains the flow of income and restores the balances by an immediate expenditure on output. On net, there is an increase in the average velocity of active money. This raises the price level and interest rate in the manner already described, tending to create a new equilibrium in which V and P are higher, though less than by the initial impact. At the same time the inflation reduces the disposable real income of households; income is constant only in money terms.[16] Thus real saving shifts to the left along the fixed I schedule, raising r_N. This reduces the necessary downward adjustment in r_M and P in response to the wealth effect.

The above analysis is a monetary explanation of the so-called "balanced-budget multiplier," which holds that a balanced budget is inherently inflationary.[17] The resulting increase in money income is said to equal the magnitude of the budget, if the interest rate is constant.[18] In this analysis the initial increase in money income is indeed equal to the budgetary increment, but the net increase in P and V is dependent on the secondary reactions. One such reaction is deflationary: the adjustment to restore real idle balances to their equilibrium, m_2', after their reduction by the increase in the price level. The other repercussion is inflationary: the reduction in saving in response to the loss of household real income. But the balanced budget is in any case inflationary, the secondary reactions merely increasing or decreasing somewhat the extent of the price rise (cf. Section 1).[19]

Assume now that there is in fact a delay between the inflow and

---

[16] When the increase in V_1 is due to the action of households, as in Section 1, household money income rises proportionally with the price level, and real income is unchanged. In the present case the increase in money income is an increase in disposable income of the government only, the money income of households remaining constant. Since total output is fixed, the exercise of the government's claim to output raises the price level and reduces the real share of households.

[17] See P. A. Samuelson, "The Simple Mathematics of Income Determination," in *Income, Employment and Public Policy, Essays in Honor of Alvin H. Hansen* (New York: W. W. Norton & Co., Inc., 1948), pp. 133–55. See in particular Part III and the references cited on p. 140, n. 5.

[18] See Davidson, Smith, and Wiley, *Economics: An Analytical Approach* (Homewood, Ill.: Richard D. Irwin, Inc., 1958), p. 220.

[19] The secondary deflationary adjustment, described in Section 1, depends in part on the slope of the L_2 schedule. Given the strength of the wealth effect on interest, the more steeply inclined is $L_2(r_M)$ the less is the subsequent transfer from active to idle balances and the resulting deflation needed to restore m_2'. The secondary inflationary adjustment varies directly with the responsiveness of saving to changes in income.

outflow of balances through the government sector, and this delay is equal to that of the private sector. In this event the balanced budget increment has no direct effect on velocity or aggregate money income. However, since a portion of the given income now accrues to the government, private disposable income is less, and household saving falls. The decrease in saving raises the natural rate, causing a transfer of idle to active balances and a rise of the price level. In the new equilibrium, total velocity and money income are at a higher level, which is determined by the income response of saving and the interest elasticity of the S, I, and L_2 schedules.[20]

Granted that the balanced-budget multiplier is positive, a useful application of these results is to the analysis of a fiscal deficit created by reducing taxes, while holding expenditures constant. The deficit is financed by borrowing from households, as in Part C(2)a. Such a deficit is almost invariably regarded in the literature as being inflationary. But it must be analyzed in two stages. Assume first that the reduction in tax receipts is accompanied by an equal reduction in expenditures. The balanced-budget multiplier is applicable here, and, whether it alters velocity directly or indirectly, has the effect of reducing it. Assume next that expenditures return to their previous level, and are financed by borrowing from the private sector. Given our interest-elastic demand for money, the second stage raises velocity. Whether the *net* effect on velocity and the price level is positive or negative depends on the interest elasticities of L_2, S, and I, and the income response of saving.[21]

---

[20] As Mayer notes (*op. cit.*, p. 89), the case in which the government turnover rate is equal to the private rate underlies the traditional Keynesian case, for which the multiplier is unity. The Keynesian model is described below in Chapter IX-E. In a common formulation of that model the interest rate is fixed by an infinitely elastic L_2 schedule, and real income assumes a unique level which equates S to I at the given interest rate. When taxes, imposed for the balanced budget, reduce private disposable income, S falls below I, as in the analysis above. But the inflationary gap persists until real disposable income has returned exactly to its pre-tax level, which is the only level at which S and I can be equal. The net effect of the balanced budget increment is thus to raise aggregate income by the disposable income of the government, while leaving private disposable income constant.

[21] It is instructive to compare the inflationary effects of a continuing fiscal expenditure financed by (a) borrowing from the central bank, (b) borrowing from households, and (c) additional taxes. Eventually the most inflationary is (a), since the money supply rises perpetually and must at some point overtake the inflated, but stable price levels created by (b) and (c). Assume that the balanced budget, (c), raises active velocity. Then (c) would tend to raise prices more immediately than the privately financed deficit, (b), since (c) raises the rate of expenditures instantaneously, while (b) stimulates a time-consuming adjustment process. Ignoring secondary effects, the ultimate inflationary impact of (c) de-

F. SHIFTS IN EXISTING-ASSET DEMAND

Equal and offsetting shifts in the existing-asset demand schedules change the equilibrium price level. For example, if wealth holders move from idle balances to securities, this would be a simultaneous leftward shift in L_2 and an equal rightward shift in D_{VO}. With S, I, and the natural rate of interest unchanged, equilibrium requires that m_2 be lowered from, say, $L_2'(r_N')$ to $L_2''(r_N')$. This is accomplished by transferring idle to active balances by the familiar expansionary adjustment process. Since the demand shifts are instantaneous, the security purchase is confined to existing issues, whose price accordingly rises. At the lower yield, $I > S$

---

pends on M_1 and y $(\partial P/\partial V_1 = M_1/y)$. The inflationary effect of (b) depends on the interest elasticities of S, I, and L_2, and on V_1 and y $(\partial P/\partial M_1 = V_1/y)$. Consider a numerical example:

$$M_1' = 100, M_2' = 50, V_1' = 6, y' = 600,$$

$$S = 1{,}000\, r_M - 20, I = \frac{1.5}{r_M}, L_2 = 100 - 1{,}000\, r_M,$$

$$r_N' = .05, L_2(.05) = m_2' = 50, P' = M_2'\left(\frac{1}{m_2'}\right) = \$1.00,$$

$$S(.05) = I(.05) = 30.$$

The equations for S, I, and L_2 are in real terms. Suppose that the government raises expenditures by \$6 and spends the money, upon receipt, without delay. If the money is raised through taxes, \$6 of active balances are given an additional turnover. This raises the overall velocity of M_1 to

$$V_1'' = \frac{6 \times 94 + 7 \times 6}{100} = \frac{606}{100} = 6.06,$$

a weighted average of 6 and 7, with weights of 94 and 6, respectively. The price level rises to

$$P'' = \frac{100 \times 6.06}{600} = \$1.01.$$

Now, if the expenditure, G, is raised through borrowing from the public, we substitute in the equation, $I + G = S$:

$$\frac{1.5}{r_M} + 6 = 1{,}000\, r_M - 20,$$

for which the solution is $r_M = .0538$, $S = 33.8603$, and $I = 27.8603$. $L_2(.0538) = 46.1600 = m_2''$, and since $P'' = (M' - P''m_2'')\,V_1'/y'$,

$$P'' = \frac{\left(\dfrac{V_1'}{y'}\right)M'}{1 + \left(\dfrac{V_1'}{y'}\right)m_2''} = \$1.03.$$

Taking the percentage increments with respect to the relative interest movement, the arc elasticity of real investment is $-.66$, of real saving, 1.19, and of liquidity preference, $-.71$. Empirically the saving elasticity is probably high, but this is offset more or less by the L_2 elasticity, which is probably also high (cf. p. 426, n. 43). Given these results, the deficit in which taxes are reduced and expenditures remain constant is clearly inflationary.

transfers M_2 to M_1 and restores r_M to r'_N by the transfer and wealth effects. In the new equilibrium M_1/M_2, V, and P are higher. The disturbance is thus entirely comparable to an open-market purchase, except that a change in total velocity replaces the change in the money supply. The wealth changes described in Chapter V apply to the shift of L_2, except that there is no initial loss of securities to the central bank.[22]

A shift from securities to idle balances is a simultaneous reduction in D_{VO} and an increase in L_2. The sale of securities lowers their price and raises their yield, which stimulates a contractionary process identical with that following an open-market sale.

G. AUTONOMOUS MOVEMENTS BETWEEN IDLE AND ACTIVE BALANCES

The analysis has thus far shown how the interaction of stock and flow markets transfers money between idle and active uses by an essentially automatic process; i.e., the transfer is "built" into the stock and flow schedules, as defined, and does not require a shift in any of them. But let us consider now the impact of a deliberate decision to reallocate funds between idle and active uses, independently of any outside disturbance or movement of the market or natural rate of interest. Such a decision will involve simultaneously the permanently desired level of liquid wealth and the temporary level of consumption expenditures.

Consider a once-for-all expenditure of idle balances on consumers goods. This is shown in Figure 8–5(a) as equal leftward movements in L_2 and m_2 to L''_2 and m''_2, respectively. The idle-money equilibrium moves from A to B. There is no direct effect on the market rate of interest since the reduction in L_2 is offset by a reduction in total wealth held, rather than by an increase in security demand. There is no change in the natural rate of interest since real saving and investment are not a party to these events. Since the shift of L_2 is permanent, the new equilibrium will be one of lower real balances and a higher price level. The direct effect of the dishoarding is comparable to that of a government deficit financed

---

[22] The wealth changes stimulated by the decrease of L_2 are exactly the same as those of the open-market purchase in which the monetary authority returns its additional security earnings by subsidizing security income. In the latter case, there is no effective loss of securities, though the lower interest rate created by the purchase remains. See Chapters III-B(2) and V-E(5).

FIGURE 8–5
An Autonomous Shift from Idle to Active Balances

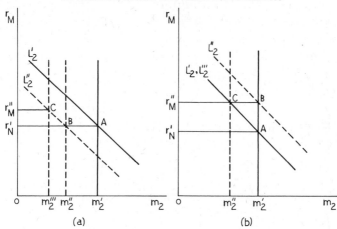

(a)   (b)

by the central bank. The increase in consumption expenditures raises active balances, prices, and money saving and investment equally. There is accordingly no change in real saving and investment. But the increase in P lowers m_2 further to, say, m_2''', and raises r_M to r_M'' by the wealth effect. The equilibrium, for the moment, is at point C. At r_M'' $S > I$ sends active balances to the idle realm and reduces r_M and P until $r_M = r_N'$ and m_2 is again m_2''. In the final equilibrium at B, $m_2'' < m_2'$ implies that M_1, P, and V are still above their previous equilibrium values. In addition to the loss of idle balances, the wealth effects of the disturbance are (a) those associated with the temporary increase in consumption which, in competing with investment for resources, is equivalent to $I > S$, and (b) those identified with $S > I$ during the restoration of m_2 to m_2'' following its reduction by the inflation. There is no necessary relation between the magnitudes involved in (a) and (b).[23]

---

[23] In the event that the dishoarded balances are applied to current saving, rather than consumption, the final equilibrium is the same, but the adjustment process may be altered. Initially L_2 and m_2 again shift equally to the left. But let the new active balances be turned over at the rate, V_1, against securities. Effectively this constitutes a constant increase in saving from S' to S'' during a non-zero interval, t_1. Security prices rise and a temporary equilibrium for t_1 is reached at $r_M''' < r_N'$ at which $S'' - I' = L_2'' - m_2'''$. Both sides measure the addition to idle balances. The quantity of active balances remaining is $I'(r_N') - I'(r_M''')$, the portion of $S'' - S'$ going into *additional* investment expenditures. This raises the price level and causes m_2 to fall below $L_2'(r_M''')$ and r_M to rise above r_M'''. In a succeeding period S' is again the ruling saving schedule. If m_2 happens to be m_2', and r_M, r_N', the system is in equilibrium. Otherwise an inflationary or deflationary adjustment ensues.

An autonomous transfer of active to idle balances, financed by a temporary reduction of consumption, is an implied increase in desired total wealth. Prices fall, lowering r_M and returning some of these balances to the income stream.

A movement from idle to active balances might be financed by an initial shift out of securities. In this event D_{VO} would shift to the left and L_2 to the right, raising the market rate of interest. This is shown in Figure 8–5(*b*) as the movement from L_2' to L_2'', raising r_M to r_M''. The equilibrium point moves from *A* to *B*. At r_M'' the difference between the new and old demand for money is

$$(8G.1) \qquad L_2''(r_M'') - L_2'(r_M'') = m_2' - m_2'',$$

and this is the real value of idle balances obtained by the sellers of securities. Then, when $m_2' - m_2''$ is applied to the expenditures stream, L_2 and m_2 move equally to the left to $L_2''' = L_2'$ and m_2'', respectively. In the diagram the shift is from *B* to *C*. At this point the adjustment is identical with that following a direct movement from idle to active balances. The subsequent rise in the price level raises r_M via the wealth effect. But, since r_M is already $r_M'' > r_N'$, the yield is driven higher than in the previous case. This stimulates a proportionately greater deflationary transfer of M_1 to M_2 via $S > I$. Since the final schedule, L_2''', coincides with L_2', the equilibrium at r_N' will restore m_2 to m_2', the pre-disturbance value. With the total supply of money constant, $m_2 = m_2'$ implies that the price level is the same as it was before the disturbance—the deflationary adjustment has completely replaced the dishoarded idle balances. The activation of idle money obtained through a movement out of securities is thus completely self-defeating. The monetary variables, M_1/M_2, V, and P, recover their pre-disturbance values.

H. SAVING AND INVESTMENT: A DEMAND AND SUPPLY OF BOTH SECURITIES AND IDLE BALANCES

We modify our basic assumption that saving and investment are exclusively a demand and supply of securities by extending the analysis of the preceding section. Specifically, we allow a portion of saving to be a demand for idle balances, and a part of investment to be financed out of idle money. This will provide for a deliberate and continuing transfer of funds between idle and active uses. We apply the dual financial character to saving and investment in turn, and then to both simultaneously.[24]

1. Saving: A Demand for Both Securities and Money

Households are assumed to apply their savings both to the purchase of additional securities and to idle balances. Thus

$$(8H.1) \qquad\qquad S = S_s + S_m,$$

where $S_s > 0$ is the portion of saving constituting a demand for securities, and $S_m > 0$ is that portion which is a demand for additional idle balances. Given total saving, only one of the two components can be independent. The impact of $S_m > 0$ on the total economy is seen most readily by treating it as a continuing disturbance suddenly imposed on the system in which $S = S_s$. I is and continues to be wholly a supply of new securities; i.e., $I = I_s$.

In Figure 8–6 stock-flow equilibrium at the opening instant of t_1 is at r'_N, the intersection of S' and I' and L'_2 and m'_2. Until this moment S' is a demand for securities only. But during

FIGURE 8–6
Saving: A Demand for Both Securities and Idle Balances

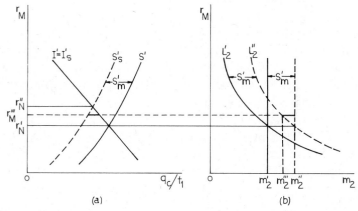

(a)   (b)

---

[24] Cf. pp. 38–39. Investment financed by drawing down the firm's idle balances should not be confused with internal financing out of current profits. In the latter case the firm is simply by-passing the securities market, tapping active balances that would ordinarily be paid out as current dividends and presumably re-invested by household savers. In principle, this is not different than the issuance of additional securities, since the new capital so financed will eventually raise the value of the firm's outstanding shares by an equal amount (cf. p. 20, n. 3). Internal financing in this sense has no effect on the demand for money or the price level. For a succinct statement of the financial varieties of saving, as well as investment, see H. G. Johnson, "The Matrix Multiplier and an Ambiguity in the Keynesian Concept of Saving," *Economic Journal*, Vol. LXII (March, 1952), pp. 197–200.

t_1 savers decide to allocate their funds both to securities and idle balances. Savers' demand for securities is accordingly represented by S_s', which is parallel and to the left of S'. The distance between the curves is S_m', the household demand for additional idle balances. This is reflected simultaneously in Figure 8–6(b) as equal parallel movements in L_2 and m_2:

(8H.2) $$L_2'' = L_2' + S_m',$$

$$m_2'' = m_2' + S_m'.$$

As S_m accrues during t_1, L_2 and m_2 shift equally to the right, occupying the position of the double-primed schedules at the close of the interval. Since the additional demand for idle money is financed by a portion of current saving earmarked for that purpose, it has no direct effect on the market rate of interest; S_m' is an equal addition to L_2' and m_2' at all interest rates. S_m' is also a *constant* addition at all interest rates, but this is not inevitable. S_m' may very well be an inverse function of r_M, causing S' and S_s', L_2' and L_2'', and m_2' and m_2'' all to converge at higher interest rates. But L_2 and m_2 will in any case increase equally at all points, so that there can be no direct effect of S_m' on the rate of interest.

Since saving is financed out of current income and thus active balances, the transfer of saving to idle balances is a withdrawal of active money from the stream of spending. The price level falls proportionately. As long as households continue to add to hoards, prices in fact fall constantly over time. Let us assume for the present that there is no wealth effect on interest. The market rate will thus climb gradually via the transfer effect to an equilibrium at r_N'', the intersection of the new-security schedules, I' and S_s'. During t_1 the transfer specifically raises r_M from r_N' to r_M''', at which

(8H.3) $$I' - S_s' = m_2'' - L_2''$$

(corresponding to the bold-face horizontal segments in the diagram).[25] m_2 falls to $m_2''' = L_2''(r_M''')$, and the *net* withdrawal of active money, in real terms, is

(8H.4) $$m_2''' - m_2' = S'(r_M''') - I'(r_M''') < S_m'.$$

---

[25] Though L_2 and m_2 are shifting continuously to the right throughout t_1, they do so by equal amounts. Thus their difference, $m_2 - L_2$, which together with $I' - S_s'$ determines the rise in r_M, is constant. Hence it is immaterial whether the excess supply of idle money is taken to be $m_2'' - L_2''$, $m_2' - L_2'$, or the difference between any of the intermediate m_2 and L_2 schedules prevailing during t_1.

When r_M is finally r_N'', the interest rate is constant and the net reduction of active money is equal to all of S_m':

(8H.5) $\quad S'(r_N'') - I'(r_N'') = S'(r_N'') - S_s'(r_N'')$, since $I'(r_N'') = S_s'(r_N'')$.

Since the active real withdrawal is constant, the nominal withdrawal declines, and the price level falls by diminishing amounts over time.

With total saving greater than total investment at r_N'', the periodic wealth changes are those of a deflationary adjustment (Chapter VI), except that excess saving is added directly and deliberately to idle balances, rather than indirectly and inadvertently through a purchase of existing securities. The minimum total wealth gain of each period is $S'(r_N'')$ which, in view of $\partial S/\partial r_M > 0$, exceeds that of the system for which $S_m = 0$.[26] The minimum wealth increase may be written

(8H.6) $\quad S'(r_N'') = I'(r_N'') + [S'(r_N'') - I'(r_N'')]$, where $I'(r_N'') = S_s'(r_N'')$.

The term, $I'(r_N'')$, is voluntary investment, which is equal to savers' purchases of securities. The bracketed term, the hoarding of savers, is the increase in idle balances. It also represents the maximum possible forced investment of any period. Hence, depending on the success of savers in determining the allocation of resources, total wealth can increase by a maximum of

(8H.7) $\quad I'(r_N'') + 2S_m'$, where $S_m' = S'(r_N'') - I'(r_N'')$.

$I'(r_N'')$ is again the voluntary increase in capital, and the two S_m' terms are the increase in real idle balances and the possible additional increase in capital, respectively. Thus in equilibrium all of saving directed at securities is channeled into investment. The portion which is hoarded raises idle balances but may or may not be realized in capital formation. The higher equilibrium interest rate implies that total saving and the maximum possible growth of capital and wealth tend to be greater than otherwise.[27]

Let us now acknowledge that the fall in prices raises the value of idle money and tends to lower r_M via the wealth effect. We can show that the transfer and wealth effects, acting in opposite

---

[26] The present model contains, of course, a single equity security. Hence the wealth analysis of Chapter VI pertaining to government securities, whose value depended on the real price of securities, is not relevant here.

[27] Forced investment is reflected in a spontaneous increase in ρ_s, rotating S_{VO}, W, and D_{VO} equally to the right (cf. Chapter VI-E). Notice that in view of $\partial I/\partial r_M < 0$, the growth of capital cannot equal or exceed that of the previous equilibrium, $I'(r_N')$, unless *some* forced investment is realized.

directions, will counterbalance each other at an interest rate between r'_N and r''_N, which remains the market rate thereafter. There are two possibilities regarding the influence of the price level on the events of t_1:

1. Suppose, at the close of t_1, that prices raise m_2 *less* than the transfer has lowered it. r_M rises to a point between r'_N and r'''_M. But if this pattern recurs in future intervals, r_M rising on net, the opposing forces will gradually be brought into balance. At higher values of r_M the magnitude of the transfer, as determined by $I' - S'_s$, diminishes, while the net deflationary force, equal to

$$(8H.8) \qquad S'_m - (I' - S'_s) = S' - I',$$

increases. Notice that r''_N cannot be the "equilibrium" market rate, since at that point the transfer effect on interest is zero, while the negative wealth effect is at its maximum. A stable rate of interest must have been reached below r''_N.

2. Suppose, at the close of t_1, that the price level raises m_2 *more* than the transfer has lowered it. r_M falls below r'_N. But at such a yield the inflationary transfer of any future interval, $I' - S'_s$, exceeds the deflationary transfer, S'_m, and there is an increase in the price level. Both the transfer and wealth effects under these conditions serve to *raise* r_M. This continues until, at an interest rate above r'_N, the price level again is decreasing and the upward transfer effect exactly balances the downward wealth effect. r'_N cannot be the point of stability since at this yield, there is no net movement between active and idle balances, and the price level is stable. The transfer effect will continue to raise r_M to a level above r'_N.

The dynamic equilibrium is thus one in which there is a constant market rate of interest above the rate at which total saving and investment are equal, and below the rate at which investment and saving directed at securities are equal. At the market rate total saving exceeds total investment, though by a lesser amount than in the absence of the wealth effect. At the same time total investment exceeds saving applied to security purchases. There is a net addition to idle balances each period by the difference between savers' hoarding and the excess of investment over savers' security purchases. Assuming that real saving and its components are independent of the price level, there is a constant real withdrawal from the active balances, but in view of the declining price level, a decreasing *nominal* withdrawal. Hence P again falls by diminishing amounts, though less than at r_N''. We have already seen that the change in P, in response to a constant *real* transfer, changes m_2 and r_M by constant amounts, maintaining the "moving" equilibrium (see pages 271–72).

The wealth changes are a mixture of those generated during an inflationary and deflationary process. At the market rate $S' - I'$ again represents the net addition of savings to the idle balances, and the possible increase in capital via forced investment. But $I' - S_s'$ is now a withdrawal of idle funds by excess new securities, and the potential increase in capital via forced saving. At the "equilibrium" market rate the minimum total wealth gain of each period is

$$(8H.9) \qquad [S_s' - (I' - S_s')] + (S' - I'),$$

where S_s' is saving applied to securities, $I' - S_s'$ measures the reduction in real idle balances due to excess new securities, and $S' - I'$ is the net increase in idle balances by savers' hoarding. The loss of idle balances is uncompensated by an increase in capital via forced saving, and savers' hoarding is not accompanied by forced investment. More succinctly, both zero forced saving and zero forced investment obtain. Both terms of (8H.9), and hence the minimum wealth gain, are less than the corresponding terms in the absence of the wealth effect (cf. [8H.6]). The maximum wealth increase is characterized both by complete forced saving and complete forced investment:

$$(8H.10) \quad [I' - (I' - S_s')] + 2[S_m' - (I' - S_s')], \text{ or } S_s' + 2(S' - I').$$

I' is *de facto* investment inclusive of forced saving, $I' - S_s'$ is again the loss of idle balances, and the second bracketed term is the net increase in savers' hoarding and forced investment. A moment's inspection will indicate that (8H.10) is less than (8H.7), the maximum wealth increment when the wealth effect is not operative.

2. Investment: A Supply of Both Securities and Money

We continue to generalize our system by assuming that entrepreneurs finance investment expenditures partly by issuing new securities, and partly by drawing down idle balances each period. Symbolically,

$$(8H.11) \qquad I = I_s + I_m,$$

where $I_s > 0$ is the component financed by the issuance of new securities, and $I_m > 0$ is financed by dishoarding idle money. Dishoarding by entrepreneurs violates our assumption that idle balances are held only by households.[28] But we shall relax that assumption now and allow m_2 to be divided between households and firms. L_2 is understood to be a demand function incorporating the attitudes of both sectors. It has the same essential characteristics as previously. All of saving is once again a demand for securities only; i.e., $S = S_s$.

Investment financed by dishoarding will modify the financial system in a manner exactly opposite to that of hoarding out of current saving. New security supply shifts leftward from I' to I'_s, where $I' - I'_s = I'_m$. $I_m > 0$ corresponds to equal leftward shifts in L_2 and m_2 each period. The price level rises. In the absence of a wealth effect on interest, r_M *falls* from r'_N, the intersection of I' and S', to r''_N, the intersection of I'_s and S'. In equilibrium, dishoarding is equal to all of I'_m which, since it is fixed in real terms, raises active balances and the price level by increasing amounts over time. At r''_N total investment exceeds total saving, corresponding to a reduction in idle balances. This resembles the usual inflationary adjustment, except that m_2 falls directly through entrepreneurial withdrawals, rather than indirectly through excess new securities. Zero forced saving produces the minimum wealth gain:

$$(8H.12) \qquad S'(r''_N) - [I'(r''_N) - S'(r''_N)] = S'(r''_N) - I'_m,$$

$$\text{since } S'(r''_N) = I'_s(r''_N).$$

Complete forced saving creates the maximum increase in wealth:

$$(8H.13) \qquad S'(r''_N) = I'(r''_N) - [I'(r''_N) - S'(r''_N)].$$

Taking account of the positive wealth effect, the interest rate is stabilized at a level between r'_N and r''_N. In dynamic equilibrium total investment exceeds total saving, but total saving exceeds investment representing a supply of new securities. Net dishoarding is equal to

$$(8H.14) \qquad I' - S' = (I' - I'_s) - (S' - I'_s) < I'_m,$$

since $S' - I'_s$ represents a transfer of active to idle balances. Since the rate of dishoarding is constant in real terms, active money and prices rise by increasing amounts over time. The periodic

---

[28] Cf. p. 38, n. 18.

wealth change, a combination of inflationary and deflationary elements, is minimized when forced saving and forced investment are nil. The wealth increment is then

$$(8H.15) \qquad [I'_s + (S' - I'_s)] - (I' - S') = S' - (I' - S'),$$

which exceeds (8H.12) because of $\partial S / \partial r_M > 0$ and $\partial I / \partial r_M < 0$. When forced saving and forced investment are complete, wealth increases by

$$(8H.16) \qquad I'_s + 2(S' - I'_s) = S' + (S' - I'_s),$$

which is greater than (8H.13). Thus, while in the case of $S_m > 0$ the wealth effect tended to lower the market rate and lower the wealth increments, in the event of $I_m > 0$ it raises the market rate and raises the wealth increments.

3. Saving: A Demand for Securities and Money; Investment: A Supply of Securities and Money

Let us consider the most general system in which S_s, S_m, I_s, and I_m are all positive. There are three distinguishable cases, corresponding to $S_m \gtrless I_m$, which are diagramed in Figure 8–7(a,b,c).

The simplest case is $S'_m = I'_m$, presented in Figure 8–7(a). The hoarding of savers is exactly offset by the dishoarding of entrepreneurs, leaving L_2 and m_2, total saving, total investment, the natural rate, the market rate, and the price level unchanged. Though a portion of investment, I'_m, is financed outside of the securities market, the growth rate, equal to voluntary saving, is unaffected by the dual financial character of the functions.

The case of $S'_m > I'_m$ is drawn in Figure 8–7(b). This resembles the model in which $S_m > 0$ and $I_m = 0$, described in Section 1. The natural rate, determined by S'_s and I'_s, is r''_N, which is above r'_N, the intersection of S' and I'. If, in the absence of a wealth effect, r''_N were also the market rate, net hoarding would be

$$(8H.17) \qquad S'(r''_N) - I'(r''_N) = S'_m - I'_m,$$

in response to which P falls at a declining rate. The minimum and maximum wealth gains, produced by zero and complete forced investment, respectively, are:

$$(8H.18) \quad I'_s(r''_N) + [S'(r''_N) - I'(r''_N)] = I'_s(r''_N) + (S'_m - I'_m),$$

$$\text{where } I'_s(r''_N) = S'_s(r''_N);$$

$$(8H.19) \qquad I'_s(r''_N) + 2(S'_m - I'_m).$$

FIGURE 8–7
Both Saving and Investment with a Dual Financial Character

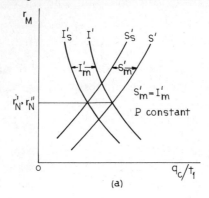

(a)

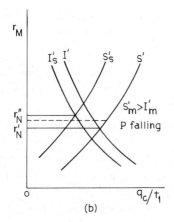

(b)

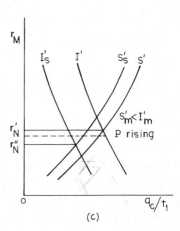

(c)

A negative wealth effect on interest lowers the market rate to a point between r_N'' and r_N' (at the height of the dashed line). The reader may verify that this reduces the rate of net hoarding, and creates minimum and maximum wealth expressions identical to (8H.9) and (8H.10), respectively. In relation to the system in which $S_m > 0$ and $I_m = 0$ (Section 1), the addition of $I_m > 0$, where $I_m < S_m$, lowers the equilibrium interest rate, the rate of deflation, and the possible range of increase in capital and wealth.

The final possibility, $S_m' < I_m'$, is presented in Figure 8–7(c). This case is analogous to $I_m > 0$ and $S_m = 0$, described in Section 2. The natural rate, given by the new-security schedules, is $r_N'' < r_N'$. Net dishoarding is

$$(8H.20) \qquad I'(r_N'') - S'(r_N'') = I_m' - S_m',$$

which causes the price level to rise by increasing amounts. The least and greatest possible wealth gains, corresponding to zero and complete forced saving, are:

$$(8H.21) \quad S_s'(r_N'') - [I'(r_N'') - S'(r_N'')] = S_s'(r_N'') - (I_m' - S_m'),$$
$$\text{where } S_s'(r_N'') = I_s'(r_N'');$$
$$(8H.22) \quad S_s'(r_N'') = I'(r_N'') - [I'(r_N'') - S_s'(r_N'')].$$

A positive wealth effect raises the market rate (see dashed line), at which net dishoarding is lower, and the lower and upper wealth gains are equal to (8H.15) and (8H.16), respectively. Comparing this system with that in which $I_m > 0$ and $S_m = 0$ (Section 2), the presence of $S_m > 0$, where $S_m < I_m$, raises the equilibrium interest rate and the possible range of the rate of growth of capital and wealth.[29]

I. SAVING: A FUNCTION OF WEALTH AND INCOME

Saving will now be assumed to be a variable in relation to wealth and income. The inverse saving-wealth relation is essentially a generalization of the so-called "Scitovsky-Pigou-Haberler effect." The positive saving-income relation, the complement of the Keynesian "consumption function," has been an active assumption throughout this volume.[30] Our purpose here is merely to indicate the impact of permanent changes in the level of income and output.

1. The Saving-Wealth Relation

A popular assumption in contemporary theory is that saving is an inverse function of total assets held.[31] If saving and wealth are

---

[29] An extreme model in which all of saving is a demand for idle balances, and all of investment is financed directly out of idle balances, is referred to in Chapter IX-E(3). If no part of either saving or investment is mediated through the securities market, it is difficult to justify any relation between these functions and the rate of interest: savers clearly cannot be concerned with the price and yield of securities; while it may be argued that investing entrepreneurs treat the rate of interest as an opportunity cost for their idle balances, this is tantamount to saying that some portion of the flow of saving (furnished by firms) is responsive to the rate of interest—but this is precluded by the assumption that $S_s = 0$. Thus the case in which $S = S_m$ and $I = I_m$ is subsumed under the "Keynesian" model in which S and I are both perfectly interest-inelastic.

[30] Cf. p. 39.

[31] See A. C. Pigou, "The Classical Stationary State," *Economic Journal,* Vol. LIII (December, 1943), pp. 342–51; "Economic Progress in a Stable Environment," *Economica,* N.S., Vol. XIV (August, 1947), pp. 180–88 (reprinted in *Readings in Monetary Theory,* pp. 241–51). See also Patinkin, "Price Flexibility and Full Employment," *American Economic Review,* Vol. XXXVIII (September, 1948), pp. 543–64 (reprinted in *Readings in Monetary Theory,* pp. 252–83).

in fact related, then both the static and dynamic equilibrium and the analysis of monetary disturbances must be qualified for the possible impact on wealth, saving, and the natural rate of interest. This section will accordingly indicate the way in which the basic system is modified by the relation,

(8I.1)
$$\frac{\partial S}{\partial W} < 0 .$$

The timeless saving-investment equilibrium, expressed by (2D.1), is now written

(8I.2) $S(\bar{y}, r_M, W) = I(r_M)$,   where $W = S_{VO} + m_2$.

Where previously the determination of existing-asset values had no repercussion on the saving-investment equilibrium, the W term in (8I.2) introduces a reciprocal relation between the stock and flow equilibria. The natural rate of interest will thus be determined jointly by the output and existing-asset markets. In the static equilibrium the latter market exercises its influence on saving and the natural rate by the determination of m_2; S_{VO} is effectively a constant. In the very short run (see Chapter II-D[1]) total wealth is thus

$$W\left(\frac{1}{r_M}\right) = \bar{S}_O p + \frac{M_2}{P}$$

$$= \bar{S}_O\left(\frac{\rho_s}{r_M}\right) + \frac{M_2}{P} , \quad \text{where} \quad \rho_s = \frac{\rho_K \bar{K}}{S_O} .$$

Since in equilibrium, $\rho_K = r_M$ ([2C.35]), wealth is

(8I.3)
$$W\left(\frac{1}{r_M}\right) = \bar{K} + \frac{M_2}{P} .$$

The natural rate of interest, the allocation of money between M_1 and M_2, and the price level are determined simultaneously by the two summary equations:

(8I.4)
$$S\left(\bar{y}, r_M, \frac{(\bar{M} - M_1)\bar{k}_1 \bar{y}}{M_1}\right) = I(r_M),$$

(8I.5)
$$L_2(r_M) = \frac{(\bar{M} - M_1)\bar{k}_1 \bar{y}}{M_1} .$$

(8I.4) is (8I.2) with W replaced by its variable component, M_2/P; M_2 is replaced by $\bar{M} - M_1$, and P by $M_1/\bar{k}_1 \bar{y}$.   (8I.5) is (2D.3), the idle-money supply and demand equality exactly as it appeared in Chapter II-D(1). (8I.4) and (8I.5) together determine the two unknowns, r_M and M_1. Clearly the monetary variables of these two equations, L_2, M, M_1, and k_1, share in the determination of the natural rate. We cannot, however, deduce any simple relationship between changes in these variables and in the equilibrium rate of interest. This requires an examination of the over-all wealth effects of the resulting adjustment process. We shall consider an adjustment to a monetary disturbance, following a specification of the undisturbed growth pattern over time.

As long as realized saving and investment are positive, capital and wealth grow constantly and the saving schedule shifts perpetually to the left. The natural rate is forever above the market rate, though the latter rises as part of a continuing inflationary adjustment. The trend of wealth over time depends on the degree of forced saving. But whatever the rate of growth, the course of wealth cuts across paths that fall with the decline of voluntary saving (cf. pages 278–79). The wealth path therefore tends to be drawn below the undisturbed trend line of Figure 5–12, AD (except in the limiting case in which $\partial I / \partial r_M = 0$ and the wealth effect is absent).[32]

Consider once again an open-market purchase instantaneously carried out. The direct impact of the purchase raises wealth by creating capital gains on securities in the amount of

$$(8I.6) \qquad S'_O(p'' - p') \text{ (see [5B.28])},$$

where S'_O is the total quantity of securities held by households prior to the purchase, p'' is the purchase price (corresponding to r''_M), and p' is the pre-operation price (corresponding to r'_N). In response the saving schedule shifts leftward from

$$(8I.7) \qquad S'[W'(\rho'_K, r'_N)] \text{ to } S''[W''(\rho'_K, r''_M)].$$

Thereafter we shift S only in response to the rate of change of wealth relative to trend. In the absence of the purchase, S and r_M would thus have remained constant at S' and r'_N, respectively.

---

[32] It is *a priori* conceivable that the factors reducing wealth, the rise in the interest rate and the impact of the inflation on real balances, might outweigh those increasing wealth, the rise (if any) in the return to capital and the sum of voluntary and forced saving. Such an occurrence would correspond to movements along the declining portion of the wealth curves of Figure 5–9. If this should occur, saving would shift to the right in response to the net loss of wealth, causing the natural and market rates and the price level all to decline. Wealth would tend to increase as a result of the rising voluntary saving and the increase in real balances on account of the deflation. Saving in turn would decline, and a cyclical pattern of inflation-deflation might characterize the undisturbed growth pattern.

If the ensuing adjustment process generates a wealth path above the trend, S will remain to the left of S'. $S < S'$ will itself interact with the wealth path, causing it to approach the trend. However, if wealth remains above the undisturbed path, the new equilibrium will be characterized by a lower rate of saving and a higher natural rate of interest than that of the pre-disturbance economy.[33] The net increase in wealth is attributable to an excess of forced saving over the reduction in both voluntary saving and m_2, the latter resulting from $\partial L_2 / \partial r_M < 0$. If the adjustment causes wealth to converge with the trend line, S shifts to the right of S'', its post-operation position. The increase in voluntary saving tends to raise wealth, but if it should fall below trend, S will shift to the right of S'. The new equilibrium is one of a greater rate of saving and a lower natural rate of interest.[34] The net decrease in wealth is due to less-than-complete forced saving not offset by the increase in voluntary saving and m_2.

There are several important conclusions to be drawn from the foregoing analysis:

1. A monetary disturbance tends to alter total wealth, the equilibrium rate of saving, and the natural rate of interest via the inverse saving-wealth relation. However, wealth may be increased or decreased relative to trend, depending on the extent of forced saving or investment. Any disturbance, accordingly, may push wealth, saving, and the equilibrium rate of interest in either direction. This is the strongest *a priori* generalization that can be made.

2. The saving-wealth relation does not change the basic stock-flow equilibrating process, as described in Chapter IV. Shifts in S due to changes in wealth change the target rate of interest and, by shifting the excess new security-supply function, the speed with which the equilibrium is reached. But the stock-flow adjustment continues otherwise unabated. The interaction of the new and old excess security-supply (or demand) functions is still the mainspring to the movement of the market rate of interest and the general price level. The reason that (8I.1) does not directly influence prices is that changes in saving are equal and opposite to

---

[33] Stability of the system requires, of course, that the increase in the natural rate is less than that of the market rate over time.

[34] This is the particular conclusion reached by Metzler in "Wealth, Saving, and the Rate of Interest," *Journal of Political Economy,* Vol. LIX (April, 1951), and criticized by Horwich in "Real Assets and the Theory of Interest," *Journal of Political Economy,* Vol. LXX (April, 1962). Cf. p. 220, n. 13.

changes in consumption. A change in saving in response to wealth (or, for that matter, the rate of interest) is a movement between new securities and consumption goods—a diversion of active money from one portion of the income stream to another.[35] Any change in the *quantity* of active money and the price level can only result indirectly from the interaction of non-zero excess security-supply and demand functions.[36]

In the current literature the consumption-wealth relation, the complement of (8I.1), is often interpreted as involving a direct outlay from added monetary wealth. For example, following an open-market purchase, the increase in consumption corresponding to (8I.7) is identified as a direct expenditure—a dishoarding—of the money created by the central bank.[37] However, this interpretation: (*a*) overlooks the complementary relation between consumption and saving, (*b*) ignores the equilibrium in asset holdings implied by a purchase yield, r_M'', at which households are presumably satisfied with the changed quantities of asset money and securities, and (*c*) dubiously makes wealth a short-run dependent as well as an independent variable; i.e., granted that desired saving varies with wealth, why should wealth itself be deliberately altered (via dishoarding) as part of the immediate reaction mechanism? In the present context (*a*) is particularly indefensible, since the behavior of (8I.1) basically involves the desired rate of saving, from which simultaneous consumption changes cannot be dissociated.[38] The consumption behavior is both implied and financed by the change in saving; recourse to additional funds supplied by the bank, and now held in portfolios, is neither necessary nor consistent with the equilibrium of the existing-asset market.

---

[35] For a similar analysis see p. 103, where the response of saving to interest-rate changes is discussed, and Part B(1) of this chapter, where an autonomous shift in saving is described.

[36] The above should be qualified for the case in which S_m (saving applied to idle balances) is positive (Part H[1]). In this event a decrease in saving, for example, in response to an increase in wealth, would result in the hoarding of fewer active balances out of current saving. The inflationary (or better, non-deflationary) effect of the reduced saving is thus immediate and direct.

[37] See D. M. Wright, "Professor Metzler and the Rate of Interest," *Journal of Political Economy*, Vol. LX (June, 1952), pp. 247–49; Metzler, "A Reply," *Journal of Political Economy*, Vol. LX (June, 1952), p. 251; Patinkin, *Money, Interest, and Prices* (Evanston, Ill.: Row, Peterson & Co., 1956), pp. 158–62. Cf. also the discussion in Horwich, "Real Assets and the Theory of Interest," *op. cit.*, pp. 168–69.

[38] See the references cited on p. 305, n. 31. See also the contribution by James Tobin, "Asset Holdings and Spending Decisions," *American Economic Review*, Vol. XLII (May, 1952), pp. 109–23, which clarifies a number of issues in the saving-wealth relation.

Given a wealth change, the fundamental issue is whether changes in the rate of saving-consumption over time are an adequate means of restoring the desired wealth, and whether direct dishoarding must be resorted to. The issue can only be resolved with empirical evidence, but our assumption that wealth changes are accomplished by changes in the rate of saving, and do not stimulate direct outlays between idle and active balances, has the following advantages:

1. It assumes that the widely accepted saving-wealth relation, involving direct movements between consumption and current saving, is an adequate and general means of altering wealth that need not be supplemented by direct dishoarding.

2. It is a *uniform* assumption which applies to all wealth changes, whatever their form or underlying cause. Thus we do not, on the one hand, allow households to dishoard directly balances received via an open-market purchase on wealth account, while, on the other hand, assuming (as we might be prone to do) that a change in *security* value is absorbed entirely by existing-asset demands.

3. It is a *symmetrical* assumption, in the sense that changes in saving-consumption are equally applicable to wealth increases as to wealth decreases. But direct outlays of idle to active balances in response to added monetary wealth do not have a counterpart running from active to idle balances. Consider a loss of idle funds via an open-market sale. Both money and total wealth are reduced. Given the saving-wealth relation, as we interpret it, saving will increase at the expense of consumption, and that is all. Now suppose that there is an additional response in the form of a direct outlay from active to idle balances. But such hoarding cannot be separated from the given volume of saving, which constrains and finances it. In this case a direct outlay simply implies that S_m, the portion of current saving added periodically to idle balances (Section H[1]), is positive and inversely related to wealth. As such, it is already included in our generalization of the saving function. Thus, while an effort to lower wealth by reducing saving may be supplemented by directly *dishoarding* monetary wealth, an increase in saving aimed at raising wealth cannot be *supplemented* by direct *hoarding*, since the latter can only originate in the act of saving itself.

4. It is a completely *effective* assumption, in the sense that efforts to alter wealth by changing the rate of saving will always suc-

ceed, subject, of course, to qualifications as to forced saving or investment or changes in output and employment. However, suppose that forced saving increases the value of securities, inducing households to reduce wealth by a direct liquidation of existing securities, followed by dishoarding. Part G has demonstrated that such a sequence of asset-demand shifts is completely self-defeating.

Nevertheless, as an empirical matter households may not behave uniformly, symmetrically, or effectively! It is particularly tempting to acknowledge the possibility of a direct outlay from M_2 to M_1 when the disturbance is a cash bounty not part of a security transaction. An example would be a temporary fiscal expenditure paid as a subsidy to incomes, such as the veterans' bonus of 1936. The problem here is less one of evaluating the response than one of interpreting the disturbance—is it income or wealth? If the former, we regard it as a direct addition to active balances which will be turned over at the going finite rate of active velocity via expenditure on consumption and saving. But if the recipient treats the monetary increase as a once-for-all wealth gain, we expect him to apply it forthwith to idle balances and existing-asset demands, while reducing his future rate of saving—if he wishes.[39] Monetary changes in the twilight zone between income and wealth are probably rare—households generally will know whether or not a monetary increment represents a permanent change in income to which income (flow) responses are appropriate. However, if, for any reason, households react to wealth changes, or to changes that are not definitely wealth or income, by directly dishoarding, our analysis of the adjustment process must be qualified. For example, when m_2 increases as the price level falls in the deflationary adjustment, households might reduce wealth by transferring M_2 balances directly to the income stream. This slows the deflationary process and offsets the negative wealth effect on interest. If forced saving in inflation should raise S_{VO}, households may reduce wealth immediately by dishoarding idle balances. Provided that the balances are not secured through an instantaneous sale of securities

---

[39] It is basically the *speed* of the reaction that differentiates a wealth (stock) from an income (flow) response. If the new balances are applied instantaneously to, say, security demand, the movement is an increase in M_2 and D_{VO} that must lower the rate of interest. If the expenditure is stretched out over time and applied both to goods and securities, there is some point at which we treat it as an increase in M_1, consumption, and current saving (D_{VN}) which cannot (except perhaps temporarily) lower r_M, since all money values, including investment, are assumed to rise equally in an inflationary process. Cf. Horwich, "Money, Prices and the Theory of Interest Determination," *op. cit.*, p. 639, n. 3.

(Part G), the dishoarding will accelerate the inflation and, by creating a positive wealth effect on interest, speed the return of the interest rate to equilibrium. In general, direct outlays will retard or accelerate the adjustment process. Like the saving-consumption response to wealth, they are not inherently equilibrating.

2. Variable Output

In the event that output varies, saving will change in the same direction (see [2C.19]). Output may change over the course of the business cycle owing to the unemployment or re-employment of given resources, or it may increase as part of the growth process. We shall indicate briefly the result of income changes during growth.

For a given labor force, the growth of income over time is represented by the production function,

$$(8I.8) \qquad y = y(K), \quad \text{where} \quad \frac{\partial y}{\partial K} > 0,$$

and during any interval,

$$(8I.9) \qquad \Delta K = K + I, \quad \text{where} \quad I > 0 \text{ is ex post investment}.$$

Saving increases responsively:

$$(8I.10) \qquad \frac{\partial S}{\partial y} > 0 \quad ([2C.19]).$$

The static stock-flow equilibrium summarized by (2D.1) is not altered, since the growth of output involves a time dimension. The dynamic equilibrium is essentially the converse of that created by (8I.1), in which S shifts perpetually to the left. In view of (8I.8)–(8I.10), S shifts constantly to the right. A continuing deflation is imposed on the system, both because the market rate exceeds the natural rate, and the increased output lowers prices directly (see [2C.1]). The interest rates constantly fall, and wealth pursues a path determined by the extent of forced investment. Since voluntary saving is rising, wealth moves upward across paths such as those of Figures 6–8 and 6–11. For our present purpose the paths of these diagrams should be modified by eliminating the capital gains and losses on government securities. The series will then differ from each other in equilibrium purely because of differences in the capital stock. Changes in capital are, of course, the only source of income changes which are the subject of this section.

The impact of an open-market purchase on saving and the natural rate of interest depends on the sum of voluntary and forced saving relative to capital of the undisturbed economy (the value of idle balances, though a component of wealth, is, of course irrelevant to the growth of income). If forced saving is adequate and $\partial S/\partial r_M$ is above some minimum value, equilibrium income and saving will both exceed the undisturbed values, and the natural rate will be lower. The increase in saving will truncate the adjustment process, the natural rate falling to meet the rising market rate at an intermediate level. While the increase in voluntary saving tends to increase capital, income, and saving itself, it tends to lower these variables somewhat by shortening the adjustment and reducing the transfer of idle balances and the possible degree of forced saving. If voluntary and forced saving are below the undisturbed growth rate, saving shifts to the left of the original schedule, S', producing an equilibrium at a higher natural rate of interest. The leftward movement of S reduces voluntary saving, reinforcing the relative capital decline, but simultaneously it raises the possible amount of forced saving, countering in part the reduction of capital.

A system in which the saving-wealth and saving-income relations both prevail would witness counterveiling forces on the saving function. For example, when capital and wealth increase relative to trend, saving will shift to the left in response to wealth, and to the right in response to income. Theoretical analysis on the level of this volume must be allowed to indulge an inner (though frivolous) desire that the net effect is to stabilize the S schedule; while at the same time the growth which depresses the marginal product of capital and hence, the rate of investment, is exactly countered by an increase of labor and/or innovation that fixes the I schedule as well!

J. COMMERCIAL BANKING

1. An Expanded Money Supply

We shall enlarge the system now by adding a sector of privately owned commercial banks. The banks are profit-maximizing business firms, whose rate of return is described by the general marginal efficiency schedule, and whose net worth, represented by the value of outstanding bank shares held by households, is included in the aggregate S_{vo} function. The unique feature of banks is that their liabilities serve as a medium of exchange, for which only pocket currency is a substitute. As a store of value, the liabilities of banks, like currency, are imperfectly substitutable for non-cash assets (securities), though the rate of substitution varies inversely with the interest rate.

The liabilities of commercial banks are demand deposits (checking accounts) only. Their earning assets are exclusively our equity securities, of which there is a single variety. The banks are subject to a fractional reserve requirement, expressed as a ratio of reserves to deposits, r_r. Their excess reserves (including vault cash) are a constant fraction of deposits, r_e. The non-banking private sector holds pocket currency which is a constant ratio, r_p, of its demand deposits. The total money supply, which excludes bank holdings, is thus

$$(8J.1) \qquad\qquad M = D(1 + r_p),$$

where D is the total volume of deposits. The relationship between total deposits and c, the volume of currency available for use as pocket money and bank reserves is,

$$(8J.2) \qquad\qquad D = \frac{c}{r_r + r_e + r_p},$$

or simply

$$(8J.3) \qquad\qquad D = \frac{c}{r_\Sigma}, \text{ where } r_\Sigma = r_r + r_e + r_p.$$

c, as used in these equations, is referred to as the "currency base." If we substitute (8J.3) for D in (8J.1), then

$$(8J.4) \qquad\qquad M = \frac{c}{r_\Sigma}(1 + r_p) = \left(\frac{1 + r_p}{r_\Sigma}\right)c$$

relates the money supply to the currency base and all of the currency uses, each expressed as a fraction of deposits. Given c and the terms in r_Σ, the money supply is thus determinate. We assume that the allocation of money between idle and active uses is independent of the division between currency and demand deposits. If idle balances were 30 percent of total money, and currency were 40 percent, idle currency holdings would be $(.30 \times .40) = .12$ or 12 percent, and active currency, $(.70 \times .40) = .28$ or 28 percent, of total money. Thus, with given output and active velocity, the introduction of commercial banks merely raises total money and prices proportionately, without affecting M_1/M_2, V, M_1/P, or M_2/P in equilibrium.

An instantaneous open-market purchase by the central bank increases idle money of households and the currency base of the economy by the same amount. We can assume that the new idle money is taken as bank deposits only, or as currency and deposits in the pre-existing ratio. But in either case the central bank increases the total supply of currency available for all uses by the magnitude of the purchase. Given additional reserves, bankers will increase the money supply further to the level given by (8J.4). We can express the total increase in M by differentiating (8J.4) with respect to c:

$$(8J.5) \qquad \frac{\partial M}{\partial c} = \frac{1 + r_p}{r_\Sigma},$$

which we may regard as the "currency multiplier." if Δc is the magnitude of the purchase and the initial increase in the supply of money and the currency base, the total increase in M due to the combined action of the central and commercial banks is the product of Δc and (8J.5):

$$(8J.6) \qquad \Delta M = \Delta c\left(\frac{1 + r_p}{r_\Sigma}\right).$$

We can multiply (8J.5) by Δc for any value of the latter since the relationship between M and c in (8J.4) is linear. While the central bank's contribution to ΔM is Δc, the commercial banks are responsible for

$$\Delta M - \Delta c = \Delta c\left(\frac{1 + r_p}{r_\Sigma}\right) - \Delta c$$

or, upon collecting terms,

$$(8J.7) \qquad \Delta c\left(\frac{1 + r_p}{r_\Sigma} - 1\right).$$

The (8J.7) addition to the money supply occurs as soon as commercial bankers invest the reserves furnished them by the open-market purchase. If, like the central bank, the commercial banks acquire their earning assets instantaneously, then all of ΔM in (8J.6) will be an increase in idle balances only. In effect the commercial banks carry out an open-market purchase on their own level, depressing the interest rate further and adding to the supply of idle money. The magnitude of the collective commercial bank purchase will exceed that of the central bank if (8J.7) $> \Delta c$. Upon substituting the terms of (8J.7), this inequality is

$$\Delta c\left(\frac{1 + r_p}{r_\Sigma} - 1\right) > \Delta c,$$

$$r_p - 2r_\Sigma > -1.$$

If we substitute for r_Σ, we obtain

(8J.8) $2r_r + 2r_e + r_p < 1.$

The lower are r_p and particularly, r_r and r_e, the more likely will the inequality be satisfied.

Equation (8J.4) makes explicit that any given change in the money supply can be achieved by altering c or by changing the r_r term in r_Σ. When M is increased by increasing c, the central bank raises its security holdings by Δc and the commercial banks increase their securities by (8J.7). If the same increase in M is brought about by a reduction in r_r, then the volume of securities acquired by the central and commercial banks in the previous case now go entirely to the commercial banks. In general, we can say that any bank-induced change in M is accompanied by an equal change in the security holdings of the entire banking system. When the central bank participates in the monetary change through open-market operations, it shares in the acquisition or liquidation of securities. When r_r is altered, the given security change is allocated wholly to commercial bank portfolios, with a consequently greater impact on commercial bank earnings.[40]

The (8J.7) increase in money will typically lag behind the central bank's purchase, depending on the rapidity of response of commercial bankers to reserve changes.[41] As long as there is some lag between the action of the central and commercial banks, the latter will increase money balances during the course of the inflationary adjustment already stimulated by the central bank. If all the currency demands are exercised concurrently with changes in deposits, then the commercial banks will raise the money supply directly by the quantity given in (8J.7). However, if r_p, which measures the

---

[40] David A. and Charlotte P. Alhadeff recognize this in their paper, "An Integrated Model for Commercial Banks," *Journal of Finance*, Vol. XII (March, 1957), pp. 24–43, esp. p. 42. The same point is made forcefully in an unpublished statement by Beryl W. Sprinkel, "Reply to Monetary Questions Asked by Mr. Wm. McC. Martin, Jr., Chairman of the Board of Governors of the Federal Reserve System," 1956, p. 8.

[41] See G. Horwich, "Elements of Timing and Response in the Balance Sheet of Banking, 1953–55," *Journal of Finance*, Vol. XII (May, 1957), pp. 238–55.

"internal drain," were exercised with a lag, then the banks would raise deposits initially by

$$(8J.9) \qquad \Delta c\left(\frac{1}{r_\Sigma} - 1\right) = \Delta c\left(\frac{1}{r_r + r_e} - 1\right),$$

which is obtained by substituting $r_p = 0$ in (8J.7). Then, as pocket requirements are gradually met at the expense of bank reserves, the net increment in total deposits and currency would fall to the lower level given by (8J.7). The initial expansion of securities and deposits by the commercial banks is thus partially offset by a later contraction stimulated by the internal drain.

2. The Preceding Analysis Qualified

Any monetary disturbance that changes the currency base of the economy must take account of the reaction of the commercial banks. Shifts of saving and investment or existing-asset demand, or a government budgetary imbalance not involving the creation or destruction of money need not be qualified for the presence of private banks and demand deposits. But a fiscal deficit or surplus entailing a change in the money supply will induce a secondary-level response by the banking system. Consider a temporary deficit financed by borrowing from the central bank (Part C[1]a). Ordinarily, this increases active balances directly and raises the interest rate by reducing the real value of idle balances (see page 282). But as commercial banks receive and respond to their new reserves, there will be a direct nominal increase in idle balances and a reduction in the interest rate. Whether the adjustment in the wake of the deficit is inflationary or deflationary depends on whether the increase in m_2 exceeds, equals, or falls below the value decrease. In any case the adjustment will restore m_2 and M_1/M_2 to their predisturbance values. In the absence of commercial banks a continuing real deficit creates a market rate of interest above the natural (page 283). But if commercial banks are present, the dynamic equilibrium might entail $r_M \gtreqless r'_N$, depending on the magnitude of the currency multiplier ([8J.5]) relative to the impact of the deficit on m_2. The greater the multiplier, the greater is the *continuing* purchase of securities by commercial banks, which is analogous in its effects to that of the central bank (see Part A[2]). The reduction in m_2 on account of the deficit is thus merely an offset to the increase due to the banks. But whatever the net effect on m_2 and r_M, the price level rises continuously in response both to the deficit and the purchase of *new* securities by the banking system. The analysis of combined monetary and fiscal policy in Part D need not be qualified for the presence of commercial banks, since the policy produces no net change in bank reserves or the currency base. If, for any reason, the banking system constantly receives additions to its reserves, or experiences downward adjustments in the required reserve ratio, the normal long-run equilibrium of the economy would be that produced by a perpetual open-market purchase (see Part A[1] and [2]).

We have been assuming that the impact of central and commercial banking operations is essentially identical. However, the reader will recall that the central bank's security transactions were always followed by a subsidy or tax designed to offset the change in total security earnings of households (see Chapter III-B[2]). This was done in order to maintain the stock of money and the flow of income at their given levels. In the case of commercial bank operations, this is unnecessary. The banks are privately owned, and earnings on their security holdings represent a payment of money and income from non-banking firms to the owners of banks, who are members of households. On a first approximation the purchase of new or old securities by commercial banks creates an equal increase in their total capitalized value and thus their net worth.[42] Transactions between households and banks in existing securities do not, accordingly, represent a net change in private security holdings. In this sense the action of commercial banks is more analogous to the changes in L_2 and D_{VO}, described in Part F, than to an open-market operation by the central bank. However, since the security operations of commercial banks create and destroy money, as we have defined it, we find it more useful to classify their actions with those of the central bank. But we shall assume that the initial movement in S_{VO} produced by a transaction between a household and a commercial bank is followed immediately by an opposite change that returns S_{VO} to its previous position. D_{VO} will respond equally, leaving the interest rate and the price of securities intact.[43] While this procedure is somewhat

---

[42] The increase in the capitalized value of the bank should in fact be reduced by the cost of acquiring the security, plus the cost of servicing additional deposits created at the same time. I am indebted to my colleague, Professor R. G. Thomas, for an opportunity to discuss this point with him.

[43] The assumption that S_{VO} returns to its prior position following a commercial-bank security transaction corresponds to the case in Chapter III-B(2) in which the central bank offsets its security earnings by subsidizing security income. The only difference is that S_{VO} is restored by an increase in ρ_s, following the central-bank purchase, and by an increase in S_O, after a commercial-bank operation (see p. 72, n. 12).

artificial, the alternative of classifying the operations of commercial banks with shifts in L_2 is even more awkward. The latter procedure requires that bank reserves be included in m_2, and that bankers' attitudes be incorporated with those of households in L_2 (in the present model the bankers' component of L_2 would be interest-inelastic). This is hardly in accord with accepted definitions of these variables.

3. Idle versus Active Balances: A Digression

It is clear enough in our equities non-commercial-bank model that instantaneous operations by the central bank alter idle balances only, and that the equilibrium ratio of idle to active money is independent of the nominal quantity of money. But it is often assumed that analogous propositions are not applicable to the world of commercial banks, who extend loans and invest in bonds rather than in equities. It is claimed that commercial bank bond purchases, for example, raise idle balances, and that bank loans raise active balances, and that these are enduring effects.[44] The implied evidence is that loan recipients obviously borrow to spend, not to hold the new money, and conversely for the sellers of bonds. However, at best this is a partial analysis. In general, the *direct* allocation of new money between M_1 and M_2 depends on the offerings of excess new and old securities, respectively, during the banks' presence in the money market (see Chapter III-A). This holds whether the "securities" in question are bonds, stocks, or direct customer loans in the form of I.O.U.'s or promissory notes. Only if the bank remains in the market for an extended period is it likely to purchase many excess new securities and increase active balances directly (see Part A). As for the *ultimate* distribution between idle and active money, this is determined by the non-banking sector, and remains invariant for given asset preferences and given natural rates of interest. Nevertheless, how can this be reconciled with the apparent increase in active balances only, when banks extend loans even over the briefest interval of time? There are two ways in which this phenomenon can be explained:

1. The increase in bank loans may coincide with an increase in the I schedule. The loans increase because bankers switch out of investments, the money supply is elastic (see Section 4 below), or

---

[44] Cf. Warren L. Smith, "On the Effectiveness of Monetary Policy," *American Economic Review,* Vol. XLVI (September, 1956), pp. 601–2 and 604–6.

simply because bankers coincidentally respond to increased reserves while the demand for loanable funds is rising. In all events the loan stands an improved chance of being taken as active money —within a very brief period, if not immediately. Moreover, the loan balances will remain active, not because of the action of the bank, but because of the concurrent rise in the natural rate of interest.

The shift from investments to loans is a particularly important aspect of banking policy in an investment boom. In his outstanding work, *Modern Banking,*[45] R. S. Sayers describes how bankers activate idle money by selling bonds to the holders of "Savings" (idle) deposits, applying the proceeds to loans, which are taken as "Cash" (active) deposits. We can rationalize this increased velocity effect, within our own framework, in the following way. We assume that the investment demand schedule, including *both* the supply of new bonds and new loan instruments, increases. Hence when bankers sell bonds, they obtain idle balances while simultaneously driving the bond rate toward its higher natural level.[46] There is thus no tendency for the greater market rate to lead to a subsequent transfer of active to idle money via the bond market (on a first approximation we may assume that the market rate is raised exactly to the higher natural rate, leaving the bond market in perfect equilibrium). Then bankers extend new loan balances, which sooner or later fill the investment-saving gap in that market. While the additional loan demand would ordinarily activate idle funds directly, it does so instead through the intermediary role of commercial banks. The banks act as a catalyst, facilitating the financing of the investment boom in the way best suited to their own portfolios. They curtail excess investment in the bond market by reducing idle balances, and finance excess investment in the loan market by raising active balances.

In terms of the present discussion the crucial point, which Sayers himself stresses, is that bankers are fundamentally passive in the activating process. The additional bank loans are a *dependent* re-

---

[45] London: Oxford University Press, 1951, chap. x, "The Distribution of Deposits."

[46] Even if the bond sales persist over time, bankers cannot effectively reduce active money. This is because they are operating in a market in which the market rate is below the natural. At most they can raise the market rate and reduce the excess investment, but they are unlikely to generate excess *saving*, from which active balances are obtained. Though bankers may in fact sell some bonds to savers, this would merely raise the supply of excess new securities, thereby causing an equal and offsetting decrease in idle balances via the transfer effect.

sponse to an increased loan demand, which the bankers accommodate in the manner described. An independent, active effort by banks to raise loans would manifestly have no permanent effect on the velocity of money. A shift in the marginal efficiency schedule in a liquidity-preference economy promises to have just such an effect, even in the absence of banks.[47]

2. A general explanation of the way in which loans *appear* to increase M_1 balances must assume that the I schedule is fixed. Let us suppose, therefore, that new bank loans are extended instantaneously at the initiative of bankers by lowering the rate of interest. In a zero time interval, there is no opportunity for new investment and current saving to respond to the lower interest rate. Yet the new loan balances, as always, give every indication of being earmarked for expenditure in the income stream. However, in response to the lower interest rate, firms will want to retire debt owed outside the banking system so as to take advantage of the bankers' more favorable terms. On our assumptions, the entire loan proceeds, or an equivalent amount of current receipts can be spent, if at all, only for this retirement operation. When so applied, the loan balances are deactivated. The process by which the lower rate of interest spreads through the market thereby nullifies the apparent increase in M_1 resulting from the bank loan. Though seeming to make new loans that go directly to the income stream, bankers are in fact acquiring pre-existing loans through the substitution operation carried out by the borrowers themselves. Our general proposition that the increase in M_1 is limited to the current saving-investment gap is still applicable.

In the new equilibrium we expect M_1 and M_2 to recover their pre-disturbance ratio, no matter what form the initial monetary increments take. This applies equally to balances created by bond purchases and loan extensions.

Notice that whether the additional money created by the banks is initially active or idle is immaterial to the limits of money expansion. If an individual bank holding excess reserves created an equivalent amount of active money, which is soon spent and deposited elsewhere, then other banks carry out the remaining possible expansion. But if new money is idle, and is neither spent nor

---

[47] The only velocity effects that can clearly be attributed to bankers are those associated with a *perpetual* change in the money supply (Part A). If commercial banks constantly raise M and maintain the market rate below the natural rate, real idle balances are increased and over-all velocity *reduced* to a permanently lower level (cf. p. 275).

redeposited elsewhere, then the individual bank will behave as a "monopoly," creating money by a multiple of its excess reserve holdings. However, given the parameters of currency use, the equilibrium as expressed by (8J.7) is the same whether the expansion is accomplished by one bank or many.

4. An Elastic Money Supply

An interesting modification of the commercial banking model is to drop the assumption that r_e, the ratio of excess reserves to deposits, is a constant. We assume, instead, that r_e is an inverse function of the rate of interest. The result is that the money supply is no longer fixed, but increases with r_M. The relationship between M and c in (8J.4) is thus rewritten

$$(8J.10) \qquad M = \left(\frac{1 + r_p}{r_r + r_e(r_M) + r_p} \right) c,$$

where the terms in the denominator are the components of r_Σ, and $r_e(r_M)$ expresses the functional relationship between r_e and r_M for which

$$(8J.11) \qquad \frac{\partial r_e}{\partial r_M} < 0.$$

An increase in the rate of interest due to a security sale will thus lower the excess reserve ratio and increase the total money stock supported by a given currency base. Assuming that commercial bankers buy or sell securities instantaneously, $r_e(r_M)$ imparts positive interest elasticity to the supply of idle balances. In the equation summary of the existing-asset market (Chapter II-B[5]), (2B.31), the fixed money stock, is thus replaced by

$$(8J.12) \qquad M_2 = M_2(r_M), \text{ where } \frac{\partial M_2}{\partial r_M} > 0.$$

In the stock-flow static equilibrium of Chapter II-D(1), (2D.3) is replaced by two equations,

$$(8J.13) \qquad L_2(r_N) = \frac{(M - M_1)\bar{k}_1 \bar{y}}{M_1},$$

$$M = M_2(r_N) + M_1,$$

which determine M_1 and M.

The market for idle balances is diagramed in Figure 8–8, where

$$(8J.14) \qquad m_{2S} = \frac{M_2(r_M)}{P}$$

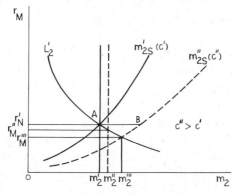

FIGURE 8-8
An Elastic Money Supply Based on a Variable
Excess-Reserve Ratio

denotes the supply schedule of idle money. The fact that we measure idle balances created by bankers in real terms reflects the attitudes of asset holders, rather than any concern by bankers with the price level and real magnitudes. The initial supply schedule is m'_{2S}, based on c'. It intersects L'_2 at m'_2 and r'_N, the natural rate of interest. The positive slope of m'_{2S} indicates that $m_2 \gtrless m'_2$ when $r_M \gtrless r'_N$. Now let the central bank purchase existing securities, raising m_2 to m''_2 and lowering r_M to r''_M. The price level is, and remains temporarily, P'. The currency base increases by $P'(m''_2 - m'_2)$ to c'', shifting the entire m_2 supply schedule to m''_{2S}. m_{2S} shifts more at higher than at lower interest rates since the same currency multipliers applied to a different currency base will raise m_2 by a constant *relative* amount. The action of the commercial banks, presumed to follow the open-market purchase without lag, raises m_2 further to m'''_2 and reduces r_M to r'''_M. The implication of the elastic money supply is that commercial banks raise idle balances less than they would if their excess reserves were insensitive to the rate of interest. For if $\partial r_e/\partial r_M = 0$, then r_e and the currency multiplier would be the same at $r_M < r'_N$ as they are at r'_N. In this event idle balances would undergo a total increase of AB, as indicated in the diagram. But when $\partial r_e/\partial r_M < 0$, the lowering of the interest rate by the central bank and the commercial banks themselves raises r_e and lowers the currency multiplier. On net, m_2 rises by $m'''_2 - m'_2 < AB$.

In the subsequent adjustment process each period produces an interest rate at which

(8J.15) $$I - S = m_{2S} - L_2,$$

where m_{2S} replaces m_2 in the previous analysis. Thus, in addition to absorbing existing idle balances, the excess new securities stimulate the creation of new money (both currency and deposits) by the banks as the rate of interest rises. All funds, both new and old, tapped by excess issues are transferred immediately to the income stream and activated. At the close of each period the upward-sloping m_{2S} schedule is redrawn parallel and to the left through the higher interest rate and lower quantity of idle balances remaining, as given by a point on L_2'. When the price level rises, the entire m_{2S} schedule again shifts leftward, passing through a higher point on L_2. A given shift in an upward-sloping curve will, of course, meet L_2 at a lower interest rate than would a vertical schedule shifting by the same horizontal distance. This is merely the geometrical counterpart of the willingness of bankers to expand the money supply and check the upward movement in r_M as the latter rises in response to the transfer and wealth effects. In the final equilibrium at r_N', m_2 is again m_2', reflecting the same propensity of bankers to create money as preceded the disturbance. Thus, even though the adjustment increases the total money supply, it merely compensates for the earlier tendency of bankers to reduce their utilization of reserves provided by the central bank at a lower interest rate.

An increase in investment, in the face of an elastic money supply, will raise both velocity and the supply of money as it raises the rate of interest. In a contractionary adjustment following a decrease in investment or an open-market sale, savers will purchase existing securities held both by bankers and households. Active money received by the latter will be held idle; that received by bankers is destroyed. In general, any disturbance that entails a temporary or permanent change in the market rate of interest will create a similar change in the money supply by changing the currency multiplier.

The elastic money supply is roughly equivalent to introducing greater interest elasticity in L_2 while leaving m_2 constant. That is, the impact of m_{2S} on r_M, M_1, and the price level could also be brought about by flattening out L_2. In this event changes in total velocity would replace those in the money stock created by the variable excess-reserve ratio. However, our reasons for avoiding this formulation of commercial banking, stated in Section 2, are equally relevant to the elastic money supply.

Notice that the positive slope of m_{2S} does not directly alter the shape of the static wealth function, which continues to be the sum of the given S_{VO} schedule and a *fixed* stock of idle balances. The changes in m_2 implied by m_{2S} are achieved by purchases and sales of securities by commercial banks in response to outside disturbances. The banks stand ready to buy or sell securities in the value amounts and yields indicated by a movement along m_{2S}. In effect the banks passively and automatically carry out open-market operations—buying when the yield rises, and selling when it falls—so that the changes in total wealth implied by m_{2S} are those already described in Chapter III-B(1). When interest falls, the banks sell securities and destroy money. Initially, $S_{VO}(1/r_M)$ rotates clockwise and m_2 shifts to the left along the locus of r_M–m_2 points given by m_{2S}. $W(1/r_M)$, unchanged from its previous formulation, rotates clockwise through the new interest-reciprocal. A moment later S_{VO} returns to its pre-disturbance position, reflecting the fact that bank-held securities are considered to be in household portfolios (page 318). On net, W has its previous slope, but is greater by the addition to idle balances.

K. SUMMARY

This is the first of two chapters that will generalize the analysis by considering additional disturbances, altering assumptions as to the form of functions, and adding new sectors.

The central bank carries out a repeated open-market purchase aimed at fixing the market rate of interest below the natural rate. Each period the bank must buy securities equal in real value to the reduction in idle balances due to the transfer and wealth effects. For given stock and flow functions, the periodic equilibrating reduction in real idle balances is constant, as is therefore the real magnitude of the purchase. The money supply and the price level rise by increasing amounts. A policy of raising the money supply by a constant nominal increment allows the market rate to approach the natural rate asymptotically. If the bank remains in the market continuously, the policy of pegging the interest rate requires a greater purchase and monetary injection than in the case of a repeated (discontinuous) operation. In the dynamic equilibrium of the continuous purchase, the bank buys new securities and sends money directly into the income stream. The velocity of money is constant at a reduced level. The real security price paid by the bank in fixing the interest rate depends on the degree of forced saving. If the latter is complete and immediate, the purchase price approaches the pre-disturbance price. Changing income, technology, and expectations are likely to alter the system during the time period of a continuous disturbance. The burden of the bank in fixing the interest rate varies inversely with the investment-saving gap and the excess-supply function of idle money.

An independent shift to the left of the saving schedule raises the natural rate above the market. An inflationary process, identical to that stimulated by an open-market purchase, is set in motion. Excess new securities raise the market rate and transfer idle money to the income stream. The rise in the price level lowers the value of idle balances and raises the interest rate further. In equilibrium the velocity of money is lower. The real changes in capital and wealth, described for the expansionary adjustment, are applicable to the decrease of saving with minor qualifications. An increase of saving lowers the natural rate below the market, and stimulates a deflationary process broadly analogous to the real and financial adjustment of an open-market sale. An increase in investment is comparable to a decrease in saving, and a decrease in investment to an increase in saving, except that the growth rates tend to move in opposite directions.

The federal government incurs a one-period fiscal deficit, financed by printing new money. The money is received as an addition to incomes and thus active balances. Money consumption, saving, investment, and the price level rise proportionately. But the inflation reduces the value of idle money, thereby raising the market rate above the natural. Saving exceeds investment, and active balances are sent to the idle realm as part of a deflationary adjustment. In equilibrium the market rate is again equal to the natural rate, and the ratio of active to idle money is restored to the pre-disturbance value. The price level has risen in proportion to the over-all increase in money. Though the deficit is inflationary, the wealth and capital changes are essentially those of a deflationary process. If the government maintains the deficit, introducing the same real quantity of money repeatedly, a dynamic equilibrium is reached in which the market rate is constant at a level above the natural rate, saving exceeds investment, and the price level rises by increasing amounts over time.

A one-period fiscal deficit, financed by borrowing from households, raises the interest rate directly and activates idle balances. The inflation raises the market rate further, but the bank departs, allowing the interest rate to fall to the natural level, while prices and idle balances are also restored. The wealth effects are those generated by an open-market sale and an excess of saving over investment. A permanent government deficit, financed by households, is like an increase in investment in raising the price level and the equilibrium interest rate. But the impact on capital and wealth is that of a contractionary adjustment. In equilibrium the growth rate is lower.

A combination of monetary and fiscal policy occurs when the monetary authority conducts a perpetual open-market purchase and a continuing budgetary surplus. The surplus reduces the money supply which, on net, is constant. The dynamic equilibrium is one of a lower interest rate, a constant excess of investment over saving, and a stable price level. The policy aims at raising the growth rate, but since any increase in ex post investment entails forced saving, we are led to question its effectiveness.

An increase in the velocity of active money creates a higher equilibrium price level. The transition to the new equilibrium is essentially the same as that stimulated by a one-period government deficit financed with new money. The adjustment reduces the quantity of active balances, offsetting somewhat the increase in active velocity. The "balanced-budget multiplier," created by an equal increase in government revenues and expenditures, may be based upon an increase in the velocity of active money, or a decrease in saving because of a reduction in private disposable income.

Shifts in the existing-asset demand schedules alter the system in a manner identical with that of open-market operations, except that the initiating disturbance involves the demand, rather than the supply of securities, and velocity changes replace the changes in the money supply.

An autonomous dishoarding of idle balances entails an equal reduction in the demand for, and the idle-balance portion of, wealth. There is no direct effect on the rate of interest. The price level rises, raising the market rate and causing some of the balances to be deactivated. The equilibrium price level and velocity are higher. The wealth effects are a combination of those generated both by inflationary and deflationary processes. If a movement from idle to active balances is financed by an initial shift out of securities, the process is shown to be completely neutralizing. There is no net change in the demand for money and the price level.

A system in which saving is applied both to security purchases and additional idle balances, while investment is entirely a supply of new securities, experiences a constantly declining price level and a higher interest rate than if savers buy securities only. The interest rate tends toward the intersection of new-security supply and demand. Though total saving exceeds total investment, the wealth changes are a mixture of inflationary and deflationary tendencies. If investment is financed both by issuing securities and dishoarding idle balances, while saving goes exclusively into securities, the price level rises constantly and the interest rate moves to a lower level near the intersection of new-security supply and demand. Total investment exceeds total saving. When saving and investment both have a dual financial character, the price level may move in either direction or not at all. Total saving and investment may stand in any relation to each other.

The inverse saving-wealth relation renders the natural rate of interest dependent upon both stock and flow variables, including the supply and demand for all assets. However, there is no simple or predictable relation between changes in the asset variables— including the money supply—and the natural rate of interest. Monetary changes may drive wealth, saving, and the rate of interest in any direction, depending on the degree of forced saving and investment. The saving-wealth relation does not alter the basic stock-flow process by which the market rate of interest and the price level are determined. This is because changes in saving are opposite and equal to changes in consumption, and do not entail direct dishoarding of idle balances. The common assumption that an open-market purchase leads to a direct outlay of balances received by households is shown to be independent of the saving-wealth relation, and inconsistent with the equilibrium of the existing-asset market. Moreover, it carries wealth implications that lack uniformity, symmetry, and, on occasion, effectiveness. However, if households in fact respond to wealth changes with direct outlays, the adjustment process will be extended or shortened, as the case may be.

The positive saving-income relation is opposite to the saving-wealth relation in its effects on saving and the natural rate of interest. The static equilibrium cannot be affected by the dynamic growth of income, but a disturbance that changes the stock of capital and income relative to trend will shift saving in the same direction, and the natural rate of interest in the opposite direction.

A system of privately owned commercial banks raises the money supply to a level determined by the product of the currency base and a multiplier equal to a function of all the parameters of currency use. An open-market purchase by the central bank raises bank reserves and creates an essentially identical second-order purchase by the commercial banks. Any monetary disturbance that changes bank reserves will induce a monetary expansion on that level. Thus a fiscal deficit financed with new money will simultaneously raise active and idle balances and raise and lower the interest rate. In the first instance commercial and central-bank operations are identical, but since commercial banks are privately owned, changes in their security holdings are assumed to be followed by equal spontaneous changes in the security-holdings of households. The common assumption that a commercial-bank loan extension creates active balances, while a bond purchase creates idle balances, is not supported by the analytical framework of this study. An inverse relation between excess bank reserves and the market rate of interest imparts a positive relation to interest and the total supply of money. Thus any disturbance that causes a temporary or permanent change in the interest rate changes the money supply by altering the currency multiplier.

CHAPTER IX

The Generalization Continued

A. FINANCIAL INTERMEDIARIES[1]

1. A Two-Security System

We turn now to a model in which household saving is channeled into investment partly through the mediation of non-bank financial institutions. These institutions, known as financial intermediaries, raise funds by issuing a claim on themselves, and then apply the proceeds to the purchase of the common-stock shares issued by firms throughout the economy. In order to distinguish between the two securities, those issued by firms for direct expenditure on capital goods are designated *primary securities*, while those issued by intermediaries for reinvestment in primary securities are *intermediary* or *i-securities*. Households now have the alternative of buying and holding primary securities directly, or indirectly through the purchase of intermediary issues. Through intermediaries, households reap the benefits of experienced and specialized investment skills. For performing this function, intermediaries and their employees receive the going rate of return on capital and labor. Some of the outstanding primary securities will, of course, represent investment in the intermediaries themselves; i.e., intermediaries, like all firms, finance investment in their own plant and

---

[1] Much of the terminology and many of the ideas discussed in this section are based upon the original work of J. G. Gurley and E. S. Shaw in "Financial Aspects of Economic Growth," *American Economic Review*, Vol. XLV (September, 1955), pp. 515–38; "Financial Intermediaries and the Saving-Investment Process," *Journal of Finance*, Vol. XI (May, 1956), pp. 257–76; and *Money in a Theory of Finance* (Washington, D.C.: The Brookings Institution, 1960), esp. chap. vi. See also the contributions by J. M. Culbertson, "Intermediaries and Monetary Theory," *American Economic Review*, Vol. XLVIII (March, 1958), pp. 119–31; Gurley and Shaw, "Reply," *American Economic Review*, Vol. XLVIII (March, 1958), pp. 132–8; and Warren L. Smith, "Financial Intermediaries and Monetary Controls," *Quarterly Journal of Economics*, Vol. LXIII (November, 1959), pp. 533–53.

equipment by issuing primary securities. Funds raised from i-securities are used only for investment in other firms. The intermediary portfolio consists entirely of primary securities; there are no idle balances in it, and no independent movements by intermediaries between assets. To household savers and wealth holders, primary and intermediary securities are imperfect substitutes, their relative attractiveness varying with their yields. The world of intermediaries is thus a special case of the two-security model developed in Chapter VII. In keeping with the spirit of that chapter the intermediary securities will also be equity-type common stocks, whose real value is independent of the price level. Intermediary securities are thus analogous to the ownership shares of an open-end investment company, except that they are not redeemable.[2]

The framework of Chapter VII is applied to intermediaries in a highly abbreviated form. Only the most essential elements of a two-security system are referred to. The intermediaries are added to the two-sector model, households and firms, as set forth in Chapter II-D. There are no commercial banks, all saving and investment are a demand and supply of securities only, and aggregate output is fixed under conditions of full employment (except in Section 4[c]). Intermediaries will be treated as business firms whose costs vary with their level of activity. Within these constraints we wish to trace the impact of intermediaries on aggregate saving, the price level, and the structure of interest rates. After describing the general intermediary model in Section 2, several disturbances are analyzed in Section 3. Section 4 considers three limiting cases: household saving directed at i-securities is infinitely elastic at the going intermediary yield; intermediaries have constant costs, resulting in an infinitely elastic supply schedule of i-securities; and households consider i-securities and idle balances to be perfect substitutes.

2. The Structure of the Model

We employ the following symbols in describing the stock-flow system of households, firms, and financial intermediaries:

S_1 = "direct" household saving; i.e., household saving applied directly to the purchase of primary securities per unit of time.

---

[2]Cf. Boehmler, Robinson, Gane, and Farwell, *Financial Institutions* (Homewood, Ill.: Richard D. Irwin, Inc., 1956), pp. 390–97.

S_2 = "indirect" household saving; i.e., household saving applied to the purchase of intermediary securities per unit of time.

I_2 = supply of new intermediary securities per unit of time.

F = demand by intermediaries for primary securities per unit of time.

S = "aggregate saving"; i.e., total demand, originating in household saving and intermediaries, for primary securities per unit of time.

I = real investment and supply of new primary securities per unit of time.

r_1 = rate of interest on primary securities.

r_2 = rate of interest on intermediary securities.

m_{12} = real idle balances held as an alternative to primary securities.

m_{22} = real idle balances held as an alternative to intermediary securities.

L_{12} = demand for m_{12}.

L_{22} = demand for m_{22}.

The flow functions are expressed in real-value (q_c) units. I is identical to the I schedule of our previous system. S corresponds to the previous saving function in which S_m (hoarding out of current income) is zero, except that part of saving and the demand for primary securities is channeled through intermediaries. r_1 corresponds to r_M, the market rate of interest on securities issued by firms-in-general. The intermediary model is summarized by the following equations:

(9A.1) $$S_1 = S_1(y, r_1, r_2), \text{ where } \frac{\partial S_1}{\partial y} > 0, \frac{\partial S_1}{\partial r_1} > 0, \frac{\partial S_1}{\partial r_2} < 0,$$

(9A.2) $$S_2 = S_2(y, r_1, r_2), \text{ where } \frac{\partial S_2}{\partial y} > 0, \frac{\partial S_2}{\partial r_1} < 0, \frac{\partial S_2}{\partial r_2} > 0,$$

(9A.3) $$I_2 = I_2(r_1, r_2), \text{ where } \frac{\partial I_2}{\partial r_1} > 0, \frac{\partial I_2}{\partial r_2} < 0,$$

(9A.4) $$S_2 = I_2,$$

(9A.5) $$I_2 = F,$$

(9A.6) $$S = S_1 + F,$$

(9A.7) $$\rho_K = \rho_K(I),$$

(9A.8) $$\rho_K = r_1,$$

(9A.9) $$S = I,$$

(9A.10) $$y = \bar{y},$$

(9A.11) $$L_1 = k_1 Y,$$

$$(9A.12) \qquad k_1 = \bar{k}_1,$$

$$(9A.13) \qquad Y = Py,$$

$$(9A.14) \qquad M_1 = M - (M_{12} + M_{22}),$$

$$(9A.15) \qquad M = \bar{M},$$

$$(9A.16) \qquad L_1 = M_1,$$

$$(9A.17) \qquad m_2 = m_{12} + m_{22},$$

$$(9A.18) \qquad m_{12} = \frac{M_{12}}{P},$$

$$(9A.19) \qquad m_{22} = \frac{M_{22}}{P},$$

$$(9A.20) \qquad L_2 = L_{12} + L_{22},$$

$$(9A.21) \qquad L_{12} = L_{12}(r_1), \text{ where } \frac{\partial L_{12}}{\partial r_1} < 0,$$

$$(9A.22) \qquad L_{22} = L_{22}(r_2), \text{ where } \frac{\partial L_{22}}{\partial r_2} < 0,$$

$$(9A.23) \qquad L_{12} = m_{12},$$

$$(9A.24) \qquad L_{22} = m_{22}.$$

(9A.1) and (9A.2), household saving directed at the primary and substitute intermediary security, respectively, are self-explanatory. As in Chapter VII-B(2) the saving components are substitutes both with respect to each other and consumption. In (9A.3) $\partial I_2/\partial r_2 < 0$ follows from the fact that r_2 is a cost to intermediaries. For example, if r_2 decreases, the net return to intermediaries increases and stimulates a greater level of operations as reflected in the supply of i-securities. More specifically, a given drop in r_2 causes the supply of i-securities to be extended to the point at which the return to intermediaries equals the return to business generally. We assume that the number of financial intermediaries is fixed, so that increasing activity encounters rising marginal costs in the short run. Hence, as the number of i-securities issued and the level of intermediary activity rises, incremental costs increase and the net return falls. The relation, $\partial I_2/\partial r_1 > 0$, derives from the fact that r_1 is the rate of earnings on expenditure by intermediaries on primary securities. Thus a drop in r_1 causes a decline in the profitability of each activity level, reducing thereby the supply of i-securities. The precise response is again determined by the marginal cost function. Intermediary activity and marginal costs will fall until the net return has been raised to the going rate.

(9A.4) is an equilibrium condition for the supply and demand for i-securities, while (9A.5) expresses the automatic channeling of all funds received by intermediaries to the demand side of the market for primary securities. (9A.6), an identity, is the sum of the household and intermediary demand for primary securities. The rest of the equations have previously been encountered in the same form in either the one- or two-security model.

There are 24 variables in the system, (9A.1)–(9A.24):

$$S_1, y, r_1, r_2, S_2, I_2, F, S, \rho_K, I, L_1, k_1, Y,$$

$$P, M_1, M, M_{12}, M_{22}, m_2, m_{12}, m_{22}, L_2, L_{12}, L_{22}.$$

To simplify the presentation, no reference is made to security prices, quantities, or income; existing-security supply and demand, total wealth, the stock of capital, consumption, and financial-substitution functions. Some of these variables are present implicitly. Thus existing-security supply and demand are complementary to the idle-balance functions, consumption is residual to saving, and the financial-substitution functions underlie any system of related commodities. However, the essence of financial intermediation, if not all its static and dynamic properties, can be adequately described within the equations (9A.1)–(9A.24).

The flow equations, (9A.1)–(9A.10), together determine the 10 variables,

$$S_1, S_2, I_2, F, I, S, r_1, r_2, \rho_K, y.$$

This is shown by consolidating the 10 equations into the two saving-investment equalities, (9A.4) and (9A.9):

(9A.25) $$S_2(\bar{y}, r_1, r_2) = I_2(r_1, r_2),$$

$$S_1(\bar{y}, r_1, r_2) + I_2(r_1, r_2) = I(r_1),$$

which are two equations in two unknowns, r_1 and r_2. The remainder of the system, (9A.11)–(9A.24), is summarized by consolidation into the equality of supply and demand for active money, (9A.16):

(9A.26) $$\bar{k}_1 P \bar{y} = \bar{M} - [PL_{12}(r_1') + PL_{22}(r_2')],$$

where r_1' and r_2' are the interest rates given by (9A.25). (9A.26) determines the single unknown, P. The entire system, and all 24 variables, are thus determined.

While (9A.25) determines all of the flow variables, it does not explicitly show us how the intermediary and primary markets achieve a mutually consistent equilibrium. Nor does it give us a total saving function, incorporating the demand for primary securities by intermediaries and households, and expressed in terms of both interest rates. We shall derive both the joint equilibrium and aggregate saving using a diagrammatic representation of the system.

Figure 9–1 presents the flow market for intermediary securities. S_2 and I_2 are drawn as rising and falling, respectively, in r_2 (cf. [9A.2] and [9A.3]). They are also constructed with r_1 as a parameter. The initial schedules, at which the market is in equilibrium

FIGURE 9–1
The Flow Market for Intermediary Securities

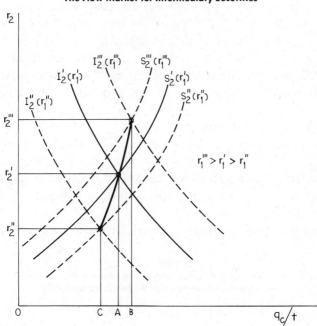

at r_2', are $S_2'(r_1')$ and $I_2'(r_1')$. If r_1 should fall from r_1' to r_1'', S_2 will increase from S_2' to S_2'', reflecting a movement by savers from primary to intermediary securities. At the same time I_2 shifts to the left from I_2' to I_2''. An increase in r_1 from r_1' to r_1''' shifts S_2 to the left and I_2 to the right. In the diagram the positive response of I_2 to r_1 is greater than the negative reaction of S_2. As a result, the intersection points of the two schedules trace an upward path in r_2, as indicated by the connected points. *A priori*, the path might also be downward or perfectly vertical. The upward path tends to occur when: (*a*) savers do not regard the two securities as close substitutes, causing S_2 to move relatively little in response to r_1; (*b*) saving is relatively responsive to changes in r_2; the flatter is S_2, the greater will be the horizontal distance created by a shift in I_2, and the less the distance traced by a movement in S_2 along a given I_2 schedule; (*c*) intermediary marginal costs are relatively horizontal, causing a considerable shift of I_2 when r_1 changes; and (*d*) in spite of a flat marginal cost function, I_2 is relatively insensitive to r_2, since r_2 is only one of many operating costs; as a result, I_2 tends to be vertical, which increases the horizontal movement along S_2 when I_2 shifts and decreases the horizontal distance along I_2 when S_2 shifts.

The relationship between r_1 and r_2 derived from Figure 9–1 is in any case positive, and is plotted as the straight line, s'_{2N}, in Figure 9–2. s'_{2N} indicates the equilibrium value of r_2 produced by each value of r_1 in the new market for intermediary securities. Since r_2 is one of several costs to intermediaries, it cannot be as great as r_1, which tends to equality with ρ_K, the net return to general business enterprise. Thus s'_{2N} will lie below a 45-degree line passing through the origin of Figure 9–2.

The flow market for primary securities is diagramed in Figure 9–3. I' (see [9A.7] and [9A.8]) is the marginal efficiency schedule. S_1, drawn with r_2 as a parameter, rises with r_1 ([9A.1]). A decrease in r_2 to r''_2 will shift S_1 to the right, and an increase to r'''_2 will shift S_1 to the left.

The new demand for primary securities is not complete until we

FIGURE 9–2
The Locus of Primary and Intermediary Yields
Consistent with Equilibrium in the Intermediary Market

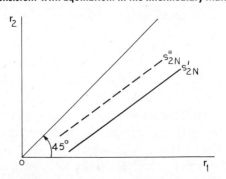

FIGURE 9-3
The Flow Market for Primary Securities,
Incorporating Saving through Intermediaries

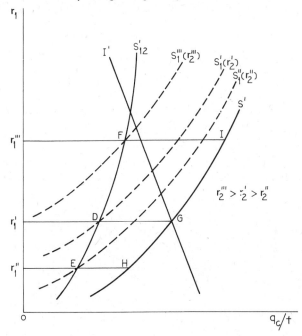

add to S_1 the demand channeled through financial intermediaries. In performing this summation, the interest rates underlying and resulting from the equilibrium in Figure 9–3 must be consistent with those of Figure 9–1, summarized by the s'_{2N} function in Figure 9–2. Hence our first step is to derive the locus of points on the S_1 schedules of Figure 9–3 which reflect the equilibrium yields of Figure 9–1. We do this as follows. Suppose in Figure 9–1 that the primary yield is r'_1. This determines I'_2 and S'_2 and produces an equilibrium intermediary yield, r'_2. In Figure 9–3, r'_2 determines the saving schedule, S'_1. But the only point on S'_1 consistent with the pair of interest rates involved in the equilibrium of the intermediary market is at the ordinate, r'_1. The point is labeled D. Consider now in Figure 9–1 a primary yield, $r''_1 < r'_1$. The relevant schedules are S''_2 and I''_2, and the equilibrium yield is r''_2. In Figure 9–3, r''_2 fixes S_1 at S''_1. But the only admissible point on S''_1 is at the height, r''_1; it is labeled E. A third point is derived in the same manner for $r_1 = r'''_1$. The corresponding intermediary-security schedules are I'''_2 and S'''_2, for which the equilibrium is r'''_2. In turn, r'''_2 determines S'''_1, whose value at r'''_1 is labeled F. F,

D, and E are connected by the curve, S'_{12}, which is the locus of points on S_1 schedules consistent with the interest rates determining and determined by every equilibrium of the intermediary market.

S'_{12} happens to be a rising function of r_1. The conditions favorable to this outcome are: $(a)'$ r_2 in the intermediary market changes relatively little in response to a change in r_1; $(b)'$ S_1 is relatively unresponsive to r_2, and $(c)'$ S_1, as a function of r_1, is a relatively flat schedule, thereby minimizing its horizontal movement when it shifts. $(a)'$ is served by the same conditions, (a) and (b), that produced an upward path of intersection points in Figure 9–1. $(b)'$ is identical to (a), and $(c)'$ is an analogous requirement to (b). The (c) and (d) conditions tend to work against $(a)'$, though given (a) and (b), their perverse influence is dampened.

The next step in deriving the total demand for primary securities is to add to the S'_{12} function the demand channeled through intermediaries. At any r_1 this requires that we add to S'_{12} the corresponding equilibrium *quantities* of the intermediary market. Thus at r'_1 we add to point D on S'_{12} the quantity, OA, the equilibrium in Figure 9–1 for r'_1 and r'_2. This gives us at r'_1 point G, our first value on the curve, S', the *total* demand for primary securities.[3] At r''_1 we add to point E on S'_{12} the quantity, OC, the equilibrium flow of funds through intermediaries for the combination of interest rates, r''_1 and r''_2. This produces point H on S'. Finally, at r'''_1, OB, the equilibrium quantity in Figure 9–1, is added to point F on S'_{12} in Figure 9–3 to yield point I on S'. The curve, S', is the path traced by H, G, I, and similarly derived intermediate points. Since the equilibrium quantities in Figure 9–1 increase with r_1, S' and S'_{12} will be closer together at lower levels of r_1. This reflects the relative reactions of I_2 and S_2 to r_1, and is not a necessary result. S' and I' happen to intersect at G, for which $r_1 = r'_1$, and this is the equilibrium primary yield consistent with equilibrium in the intermediary market and the direct demand of households.

$S(r_1)$ tends to be a rising function, as drawn, when S_{12} is rising, and the intersection points in the intermediary market trace an upward path. The circumstances favorable to *both* of these requirements are the conditions common to (a)–(d) and $(a)'$–$(c)'$ above: savers regard the two securities as poor substitutes, and each household saving component is relatively responsive to its own interest

---

[3]To conserve space, the horizontal axis in Figure 9–3 is condensed relative to that of Figure 9–1. Thus the distance, DG, in the former diagram, is much smaller than OA in the latter diagram even though they are numerically equal.

rate. Conditions involving the cost function of intermediaries (cf. [c] and [d]) do not tend to influence the slope of S in any clear or unambiguous way.

The equilibrium in the primary market is thus arrived at jointly with that of the intermediary market. Unlike our previous analysis of a two-security model, we have not derived an independent r_1 $-r_2$ relationship from the primary market, s'_{1N}, which would interact with s'_{2N} to determine each interest rate (cf. Chapter VII-D[1]). This is because the demand for primary securities is compounded of both household and intermediary-demand elements. Our total demand, S', reflects simultaneously the substitutability reactions of households and the demand channeled through intermediaries, while incorporating a consistent relationship between both interest rates for all suppliers and demanders.

Stock-flow equilibrium in both markets is shown below in Figure 9–4 by the schedules (solid-line) and variables with single primes. Each existing-asset market, represented by the idle-balance schedules, adapts to the interest rates determined in the flow markets by an appropriate price level and distribution of idle money ([9A.26]).

The general effect of introducing financial intermediation is doubtless to increase the flow of saving and thus the rate of growth.[4] The impact on the price level depends on a number of factors. The opportunity to *buy* i-securities periodically may reduce S_m, the portion of current saving added continuously to idle balances (cf. Chapter VIII-H[1]). Thus would a continuing deflationary force be mitigated. The opportunity to *hold* i-securities may cause a once-for-all leftward shift of the demand schedule for idle money, raising the equilibrium price level.[5] Finally, the increase in saving lowers the primary yield and increases thereby the quantity of idle money held along a given L_{12} schedule. This, of course, is deflationary.

3. Monetary Disturbances

How will various schedule shifts affect the system? We shall consider an open-market operation, an increase in the supply of i-securities, and increases in investment and saving.

---

[4] Cf. Gurley and Shaw, *Money in a Theory of Finance*, p. 195.

[5] See Gurley and Shaw, "Financial Aspects of Economic Growth," *op. cit.*, p. 528, esp. n. 16; *Money in a Theory of Finance*, pp. 214–16; and Gurley, "Liquidity and Financial Institutions in the Postwar Economy," U.S. Congress, Joint Economic Committee, *Study of Employment, Growth, and Price Levels* (January, 1960), pp. 3–57, esp. pp. 7–8 (reprinted by The Brookings Institution as Reprint No. 39).

a) An Open-Market Operation

An open-market purchase of primary securities lowers r_1 and raises m_{12}. Suppose that this corresponds in Figure 9–3 to the reduction of r_1 from r_1' to r_1''. The reduced yield creates $I > S$ and, by shifting I_2 in Figure 9–1 leftward to I_2'' and S_2 rightward to S_2'', $S_2 > I_2$. In Figure 9–3 desired investment increases along the I' schedule. But desired aggregate saving will be at a point to the left of the initial schedule, S'. This is because r_2, for the moment, is unchanged at r_2'. Thus direct household saving falls along the $S_1'(r_2')$ schedule, rather than S_{12}'. Moreover, the intermediary market is out of equilibrium, so that the quantities added to S_1' to obtain aggregate saving are not the equilibrium amounts that separate S_{12}' and S'. Instead, at r_2' in Figure 9–1 the *reduced* quantity, $I_2''(r_2')$, is added in Figure 9–3 to $S_1'(r_2')$ at r_1''. On both counts, then, the saving total is to the left of point H.

$I > S$, an excess supply of new primary securities, raises r_1 and transfers m_{12} to the income stream. $S_2 > I_2$, an excess demand for i-securities, lowers r_2 and transfers active balances to m_{22}. As r_1 rises and r_2 falls, direct household saving moves upward along rightward-shifting S_1 schedules. Aggregate saving moves up and toward the S' function. The increase in r_1 causes I_2 and S_2 to shift toward their original positions, I_2' and S_2'. Assuming that

$$\text{(9A.27)} \qquad\qquad I - S > S_2 - I_2,$$

idle balances on net are activated, and the price level rises.[6] The inflation reduces m_{12} and m_{22}, and raises both r_1 and r_2 via a wealth effect. In the final equilibrium the interest rates are restored to r_1' and r_2', real idle balances are again m_{12}' and m_{22}' (though the nominal quantities are greater), and the price level is higher in proportion to the monetary increase. The wealth effects of the adjustment are those attributable to an excess supply of primary securities and some degree of resulting forced saving.[7] Notice that while

---

[6] The requirement that the price level rise directly following the purchase is, upon substituting for S in (9A.27):

$$I - (S_1 + I_2) > S_2 - I_2,$$
$$I > S_1 + S_2.$$

In words, desired investment must exceed the sum of ex ante household direct and indirect saving at the lower primary yield. This is comparable to the requirement of $I > S$ at interest rates below the natural in the general one-security model.

[7] However, in the event that $\partial S/\partial r_1 < 0$, voluntary saving *increases* during the adjustment process. This raises the inflationary wealth curves as drawn in Chapter V.

the rate of supply of i-securities is temporarily reduced, their ultimate earnings and real value depend entirely on the capital formation of the economy.

b) An Increase in the Supply of Intermediary Securities

Suppose that an increase in the supply schedule of i-securities occurs because of a technological advance in financial intermediation. This is represented in Figure 9–4(a) as a rightward shift from I_2' to I_2''. To a smaller extent, I, showing the net return to business in general, will also shift to the right. But this is assumed to be imperceptible, and is not drawn. In response to the shift of I_2, the s_{2N} schedule in Figure 9–2 moves upward to s_{2N}', indicating that in the intermediary market every r_1 is now associated with a higher equilibrium r_2. In particular, r_1' in Figure 9–4(a) now corresponds to $r_2'' > r_2'$. At the same time S_{12} in Figure 9–4(c) will

FIGURE 9–4
The Impact of an Increase in the Supply of New Intermediary Securities

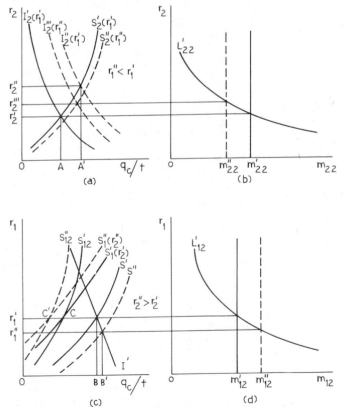

shift leftward to S_{12}'', since at every r_1 the relevant S_1 curve is now drawn for a higher value of r_2, and lies to the left of its previous position. An example is given at r_1' where $S_1''(r_2'')$ replaces $S_1'(r_2')$. Finally, at each r_1 we add to S_{12}'' the *increased* equilibrium quantities now prevailing in the intermediary market. Thus, for r_1' in Figure 9–4(a), the flow of funds through intermediaries rises from OA to OA'; at r_1' in Figure 9–4(c), OA' is added to S_{12}'' to yield a point on S'', the new total demand for primary securities. The new primary equilibrium occurs at the intersection of S'' and I' at a lower interest rate, $r_1'' < r_1'$, and higher quantity, $OB' > OB$. $r_1'' < r_1'$ is reflected back in the intermediary market in lower schedules, I_2''' and S_2'', intersecting at $r_2''' < r_2''$. On net, the intermediary yield is higher and the primary yield is lower.

The most significant feature of the new flow equilibrium is that S'' lies to the right of the initial schedule, S', indicating a net increase in total saving. Direct household saving decreases in response to the increase in r_2. This is the meaning of the leftward shift in S_{12}. But it is more than compensated for by the greater equilibrium quantities in the intermediary market (exemplified by $OA' > OA$), which on net shift S to the right. This result occurs because of substitution between indirect saving and consumption. Accordingly, the increase in indirect saving due to the rise of r_2 is financed not only by a decrease in direct saving, but by a reduction in consumption as well. The greater equilibrium quantities in the intermediary market thereby constitute a net increase in aggregate saving.[8]

The impact on the price level depends on the interest changes and the slopes of the demand schedules for idle balances. In the final equilibrium in Figure 9–4(b), we have at $r_2''' > r_2'$, $m_{22}'' < m_{22}'$, and in Figure 9–4(d) at $r_1'' < r_1'$, $m_{12}'' > m_{12}'$. The real value of *total* idle-money balances, m_2, increases, remains constant, or decreases

---

[8]These relationships appear in Figure 9–4 in the following way. When r_2 rises to r_2', the increase along $S_2'(r_1')$ is shown in Figure 9–4(a) as the distance, AA'. In part, this increase is financed by the leftward shift from $S_1'(r_2')$ to $S_1''(r_2'')$ at the height, r_1', corresponding in Figure 9–4(c) to the distance, CC'. Now, if $AA' = CC'$, this would indicate that indirect saving increases only at the expense of direct saving, consumption remaining constant. As a result, the greater equilibrium quantities added to S_{12}'' would exactly compensate for the decrease of direct saving, and S' would continue to be the total saving schedule. The increase in I_2 would have succeeded only in raising r_2 and redirecting a given rate of saving toward intermediaries. However, since indirect saving is in fact assumed to increase at the expense of both consumption and direct saving, we have $AA' > CC'$ and a net rightward shift of S.

depending on whether

$$(m_{22}' - m_{22}'') \lessgtr (m_{12}'' - m_{12}').$$

If m_2 on net is constant, the loss of idle balances in the intermediary market is exactly offset by the gain in the primary market, and the price level is constant. If m_2 rises, there is net deflation; if it falls, net inflation.[9] The change in the price level cannot be predicted *a priori*. One may speculate that L_{22} is likely to be flatter than L_{12}, since wealth holders regard idle balances as a closer substitute for intermediary than primary securities. In response to given interest changes, this would tend to create a greater reduction than gain in the value of idle balances and a net rise in the price level. However, if r_2 rises little because of a relatively flat S_2 schedule, while r_1 falls considerably due to a rather steep I function, net deflation might in any case result.[10]

The *process* leading to the new equilibrium is roughly as follows. At the beginning intermediary yield, r_2', the increase in I_2 creates $I_2'' > S_2'$ which raises r_2 by luring m_{22} balances into the excess i-securities. The idle money so obtained, plus funds provided by S_2 savers, is added to the flow demand for primary securities, creating at r_1', $S > I$. This depresses r_1 by adding to the quantity of m_{12} balances via a deflationary adjustment. Not only does the fall in r_1 reduce $S - I$, but it reduces $I_2 - S_2$ by lowering each of those schedules. In equilibrium we again have $I_2 = S_2$ and $S = I$. Any of the m_{22} balances applied by intermediaries to the primary market, and not added to the m_{12} supply, become active balances via

---

[9] The relation between the m_2 components and P is given by (9A.26), where $L_{12}(r_1')$ and $L_{22}(r_2')$ are equal to m_{12} and m_{22}, respectively. Writing P as the dependent variable in that equation we obtain

$$P = \frac{\overline{M}}{\overline{k}_1 \overline{y} + L_{12}(r_1') + L_{22}(r_2')}.$$

The relation between the price level and the idle-balance inequality above is thus readily derived by reference to this expression.

[10] Any evaluation of the inflationary impact of financial intermediation must also consider that the availability of i-securities may be a deterrent to hoarding out of current income, S_m. Whether this inflationary—or rather, non-deflationary—tendency is relevant to the analysis of the present disturbance depends on whether the substitution between S_m and S_{2s}, indirect saving constituting a demand for i-securities, varies with r_2. Thus, following an increase in I_2 and r_2, the resulting rise of S_{2s} might be financed at the expense of direct saving, consumption, and hoarding out of income. The increase in r_2 would thereby contribute to inflation by reducing savers' periodic additions to m_{22}, as well as by lowering the desired quantity of m_{22} on any given L_{22} schedule.

expenditure on new investment.[11] The net allocation of money between idle and active uses determines the movement of the price level, as described in the preceding paragraph. The wealth effects of the adjustment are those of $S > I$ and a contractionary adjustment, as outlined in Chapter VI, except that the price level and total idle balances may move in either direction.[12]

c) Changes in Investment and Saving

Consider next an increase in the I schedule. Since the other functions in the primary flow market are independent of I, they remain intact. Hence r_1 rises. This causes I_2 in the intermediary market to shift to the right and S_2 to the left, raising r_2. Both m_{12} and m_{22} decrease, and the price level must rise. The rate of growth increases if $\partial S/\partial r_1 > 0$. The flow of funds through intermediaries increases if r_1 stimulates an upward path of intersection points in that market.

Let I and I_2 increase simultaneously. Since the movement of I_2 shifts S to the right, the new rate of growth is greater, and the change in r_1 is less than if either I or I_2 alone increased.

A spontaneous increase in either S_1 or S_2 will shift S_{12} and S to the right. In the final equilibrium r_1 and r_2 are lower, and both the direct and indirect flow of saving is greater. m_{12} and m_{22} increase, and the price level falls.

4. Three Limiting Cases

A more complete assessment of the role of financial intermediaries is possible if we consider three extreme cases: (a) S_2 is infinitely elastic at a given r_2; i.e., savers respond to a reduction in r_2 to the maximum possible extent; (b) I_2 is infinitely elastic at a given

---

[11] However, it does not follow that m_{12} balances can be increased only by direct transfer of m_{22} balances. Consider, as a counter example, an adjustment in which the intermediary market approaches its equilibrium rapidly, owing to a relatively steep L_{22} function, while the primary market adjusts slowly because of a flat L_{12} schedule. In this case r_2 may rise quickly enough to equate I_2 and S_2, even while the primary yield is still falling. The level reached by r_2 in such a temporary equilibrium would be below r_2' and above r_2''. Meanwhile, we still have $S > I$ which now causes a direct transfer of *active* balances to the m_{12} holdings. There is no necessary identification, and no dependence of the balances transferred to m_{12} upon those withdrawn from m_{22}. In fact, in our hypothetical example the remainder of the adjustment, following the temporary equilibrium in the i-market, would be characterized by falling I_2 and S_2 schedules in response to the continuing reduction in r_1. This causes $I_2 < S_2$ and a simultaneous addition to m_{22} and m_{12} balances.

[12] In the event that $\partial S/\partial r_1 < 0$, the wealth time series of Chapter VI are further modified. In the contractionary adjustment the wealth curves are lowered by the *reduction* in voluntary saving.

r_2; i.e., intermediaries have constant marginal costs, and a drop in r_2 will lead to an infinite supply of i-securities; (c) L_{22} is infinitely elastic at a given r_2; i.e., idle balances and i-securities are perfect existing-asset substitutes. We shall consider each in turn.

a) Indirect Household Saving Infinitely Elastic

When S_2 is infinitely elastic at some intermediary yield, r_2', the equation,

(9A.28) $$r_2 = r_2',$$

replaces (9A.2) and (9A.4). The equation summarizing the flow equilibrium is, in place of (9A.25),

(9A.29) $$S_1(\overline{y}, r_1, r_2') + I_2(r_1, r_2') = I(r_1),$$

which determines the single unknown, r_1.

The flow markets of the system are diagramed in Figure 9-5. In the intermediary market in Figure 9-5(a), S_2 is perfectly horizontal

FIGURE 9-5
The Intermediary and Primary-Security Flow Markets—
The New Demand for Intermediary Securities Infinitely Elastic

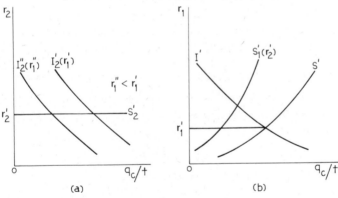

at the height, r_2'. A decrease in r_1 from r_1' to r_1'' shifts I_2 leftward, while S_2 remains S_2'. Changes in r_1 thus change (in the same direction) the flow of funds through intermediaries to a greater degree than in the case pictured in Figure 9-1. In effect the upward path of intersection points in the latter diagram has completely flattened out. In the primary market in Figure 9-5(b), there is only one relevant S_1 schedule, $S_1'(r_2')$, which replaces the steeper S_{12}' curve of Figure 9-3. S', finally, is derived by adding to S_1' in Figure 9-5(b) the greater equilibrium quantities of the intermediary market. S' is thus invariably flatter than S'_1 in the same diagram or S' in Figure 9–3.

An independent increase in I_2 in this system increases the equilibrium quantities in the intermediary market without raising r_2. Thus S shifts rightward to a greater extent than in the previous system. r_1 again falls. Since r_1 is lower while r_2 is constant, the price level falls.

An increase in I will raise r_1 less and the rate of saving—both direct and indirect—more than in the general case of $\partial S_2 / \partial r_2 < \infty$. As r_1 increases, the sympathetic increase in I_2 cannot raise r_2. Thus there is no dishoarding of m_{22} balances; the inflationary impact of the rise in I is limited to the reduction in m_{12} balances.

When $\partial S_2 / \partial r_2 = \infty$, savers are taking the most favorable possible attitude toward investment through intermediaries. S_2 in this case affords the greatest possible increase in the rate of growth in response to increases in I_2 and I. At the same time S_2 introduces a stabilizing tendency in the price level by (*a*) fixing r_2, which removes the need for changing m_{22} balances when the equilibrium r_2 changes; and (*b*) flattening out the S schedule and thereby dampening the changes in the equilibrium r_1, and thus m_{12}, in response to various disturbances. In general, we can say that the more interest-elastic is S_2, the greater is the contribution of intermediaries to the rate of growth, and the less are the fluctuations in the price level.

b) The Supply of Intermediary Securities Infinitely Elastic

Suppose that intermediaries have constant marginal costs.[13] Equation (9A.28) now replaces (9A.3), (9A.4), and (9A.5), while for (9A.6) we substitute

(9A.30) $S = S_1 + S_2.$

The flow equilibrium is summarized by

(9A.31) $S_1(\bar{y}, r_1, r'_2) + S_2(\bar{y}, r_1, r'_2) = I(r_1),$

where r'_2 is the constant cost of issuing i-securities, and r_1 is the single unknown.

The system is diagramed in Figure 9–6. In Figure 9–6(*a*) a decrease in r_1 shifts S_2 to the right, while I_2 is fixed in the horizontal position. The equilibrium quantities are thus invariably inverse with respect to r_1. In Figure 9–6(*b*) only one S_1 schedule, $S'_1(r'_2)$, again is relevant, replacing the steeper S'_{12} schedule of Figure 9–3.

---

[13] See Gurley and Shaw, *Money in a Theory of Finance*, p. 205.

FIGURE 9–6

The Intermediary and Primary-Security Flow Markets—
The Supply of Intermediary Securities Infinitely Elastic

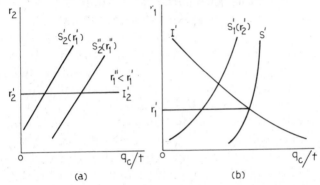

(a)   (b)

But in forming S' we add to S_1' quantities that decrease with r_1. Thus S' on net may have the same slope as in the general system in which $\partial I_2 / \partial r_2 < \infty$. We cannot, in fact, rule out $\partial S / \partial r_1 < 0$.

An increase in I raises r_1 and, if $\partial S / \partial r_1 > 0$, the rate of growth. Even if aggregate saving increases, the increase in r_1 reduces the flow through intermediaries. Since r_2 is fixed, the impact on the price level is once more attributable only to the influence of r_1 on m_{12} balances. An independent increase in S_1 or S_2 will shift S to the right, lowering r_1 and P, raising the rate of growth, and increasing both direct and indirect household saving.

In general, $\partial I_2 / \partial r_2 = \infty$ stabilizes the price level by stabilizing r_2, but not necessarily by increasing the elasticity of S. Since quantities only can change in the i-market, the yield remaining constant, changes in saving create greater changes (in the same direction) in the flow of funds through intermediaries than in the general system. However, changes in investment produce opposite changes in the rate of saving through intermediaries.

c) Idle Balances and Intermediary Securities Perfect Substitutes

The last extreme example is one in which asset holders consider idle money and i-securities to be perfect substitutes. This might be the consequence of governmental insurance covering the face value of the intermediary security. At some intermediary yield, r_2', the demand for idle balances held as an alternative to i-securities, L_{22}, is thus infinitely elastic. (9A.28) now replaces (9A.22) and (9A.24), and (9A.20) is dropped from the system. On net, we have lost two equations and two variables, L_{22} and L_2, leaving the system ostensibly determinate. But the difficulty is that r_2', given by the existing-asset market, may not be the same as the "natural" intermediary yield independently determined by the I_2, S_2, S_1, and I functions. Ordinarily the existing-asset market adapts to the latter yield by appropriate variations in m_{22} and P. But this mechanism is no longer effective, since (9A.28) has replaced (9A.22) and (9A.24). What is now required is that the flow functions be permitted to vary so as to create an equilibrium consistent with (9A.28). In accordance with the traditional solution to this kind of problem,[14] we replace (9A.10) by an equation in which output is variable. Since household saving varies directly with output, both variables will assume values compatible with (9A.28). The precise mechanism, or the time required for y to vary is not germane to this analysis. It is only important that y have the capacity to change through short or longer-run variations in the stock of capital or the employment of labor. However, in order to complete the equation system, we shall assume that labor is unemployed and subject to "money illusion." That is, labor supply varies directly with the money wage rate. An equi-proportionate increase in the price level and money wages increases labor supply and, via the production function, output.[15] Hence (9A.10) is replaced by

$$(9A.32) \qquad y = y(P), \text{ where } \frac{\partial y}{\partial P} > 0.$$

The consolidated system is now:

$$(9A.33) \qquad S_2(y,r_1,r_2') = I_2(r_1,r_2'),$$

$$S_1(y,r_1,r_2') + I_2(r_1,r_2') = I(r_1),$$

$$y = y(P),$$

$$\overline{k}_1 Py = \overline{M} - [PL_{12}(r_1) + M_{12}],$$

which together determine the four unknowns, y, r_1, P, and M_{12}.

The equilibrium is illustrated graphically in Figures 9–7 and 9–8. In Figure 9–7, S_2', based on r_1' and y', meets $I_2'(r_1')$ at the required equilibrium yield, r_2'. The corresponding quantity is OA. The equilibrium in the intermediary market implies a rising relationship

[14] Cf. Modigliani, "Liquidity Preference and the Theory of Interest and Money," *Econometrica*, Vol. XII (January, 1944), p. 74.

[15] See O. H. Brownlee, "The Theory of Employment and Stabilization Policy," *Journal of Political Economy*, Vol. LVIII (October, 1950), pp. 415–16; Jacob Marschak, *Income, Employment, and the Price Level* (New York: Augustus M. Kelley, Inc., 1951), Lectures 19 and 20 and Supplementary Lectures II and III; J. P. McKenna, *Aggregate Economic Analysis* (New York: The Dryden Press, Inc., 1955), chap. xii.

FIGURE 9-7
The Flow Market for Intermediary Securities—
The Demand for Idle Balances Infinitely Elastic

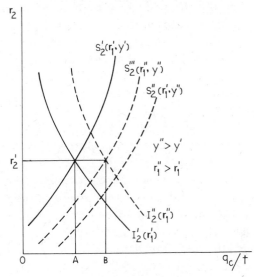

between y and r_1. Thus suppose y were $y'' > y'$, r_1 remaining r_1'. S_2 shifts to S_2''. But the equilibrium at r_2' can only be restored if r_1 is also increased. Given y'', there is some value, $r_1'' > r_1'$, at which S_2 moves leftward and I_2 moves rightward until the two schedules intersect exactly at r_2'. At r_1'' the equilibrium is achieved by S_2''' and I_2'', which meet at $OB > OA$. In the primary market in Figure 9-8, S_1 is drawn for the given value, r_2', and for several levels of output. At r_1', there is only one output, y', that satisfies the intermediary

FIGURE 9-8
The Flow Market for Primary Securities—
Output an Equilibrating Variable

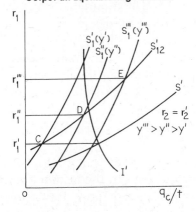

market. Thus $S_1'(y')$ is the only relevant direct-saving schedule, and point C at the ordinate, r_1', its only point consistent with intermediary-market equilibrium. At r_1'' the i-market requires a higher output, y'', which determines a greater schedule, $S_1''(y'')$. Point D at the height, r_1'', is the only point on S_1'' compatible with the i-market. At r_1''' the admissible S_1 schedule is $S_1'''(y''')$, and E its only relevant point. S_{12}' connects C, D, E, and similarly obtained points. S_{12}' corresponds to the schedule of the same label in Figure 9–3, but differs from it by employing y, instead of r_2, as a second variable. Moreover, since $\partial S_1/\partial y > 0$, whereas $\partial S_1/\partial r_2 < 0$, S_{12}' in Figure 9–8 cuts across S_1 schedules that shift to the right, instead of to the left, as r_1 increases. As a result, S_{12}' in the present model is now flatter than the S_1 schedules, where previously it was steeper.

At each ordinate we add to S_{12}' the corresponding equilibrium quantities of the intermediary market. At r_1' in Figure 9–8 we add to point C a distance equal to OA in Figure 9–7. This provides an initial point on S', the total flow demand for primary securities. At r_1'' we add to point D a quantity, $OB > OA$, for a second point on S'. And so on until the entire S' schedule is formed. Like its predecessor, S' incorporates a consistent relationship between all variables of the intermediary and primary markets. However, S' will tend to be a flatter schedule than previously, both because S_{12}' is flatter and because the equilibrium quantities in the i-market necessarily increase with r_1, causing S_{12}' and S' to diverge at higher values of r_1. Equilibrium in the primary market occurs at the intersection of I' and S', for which the interest rate is r_1' and output is y'.

This system exhibits some unusual properties in response to disturbances. An open-market purchase of primary securities creates the usual reduction in r_1 and increase in m_{12}. As previously (Part 3[a]), the lower primary yield stimulates $I > S$, which activates m_{12} balances, and $S_2 > I_2$, which transfers active money to m_{22}. But the changes in idle balances must offset each other, for otherwise prices and output will change. The latter cannot occur, since the equilibrium of the system depends on a unique output level which is not altered by the operation. This result is reminiscent of the "Keynesian" system, described in Part E, in which open-market operations cannot, even in the first instance, cause changes in prices and output.

An increase in I_2 means that at each r_1 a higher output is required to equilibrate S_2 and I_2. Thus in the primary market, the S_1 schedule relevant to any value of r_1 is now drawn for a greater output,

and lies farther to the right. This produces a general rightward shift
of S_{12} and, since the equilibrium quantities in the i-market have increased, an even greater movement in the same direction of S. An
example of these shifts is drawn in Figure 9-9. At r_1' the relevant S_1
schedule is $S_1''(y'')$, which determines at that height a point on the

FIGURE 9-9
**The Impact on the Primary Flow Market of an Increase in the Supply of
Intermediary Securities—Output an Equilibrating Variable**

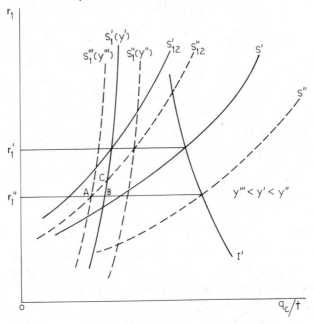

new S_{12} curve, S_{12}''. The new total-saving schedule is S'' which
creates a greater equilibrium rate of investment and a lower primary yield, r_1''.

An interesting feature of the equilibrium caused by an increase
in I_2 is that the price level and output may increase *or* decrease. P
and y will tend to fall the greater is the reduction in the equilibrium
value of r_1. This may be seen with reference to Figure 9-9. At the
lower equilibrium interest rate, r_1'', direct household saving lies on
the new schedule, S_{12}'', at the point labeled A. Point A is determined
by the underlying direct-saving schedule, $S_1'''(y''')$. Now at r_1'' the
pre-disturbance direct-saving rate was given by $S_1'(y')$, or at a point
B to the right of A. From this we infer that $y''' < y'$. Hence, even
though at any r_1 the required outputs are raised by the disturbance,
r_1 has fallen so much as to elicit a lower rate of direct saving based,

as it must be, on a reduced output (the increase in aggregate saving in the new equilibrium is due to a net increase in indirect saving). Clearly this would not have occurred if the equilibrium r_1 were anywhere above the height of point C, the intersection of $S_1'(y')$ and S_{12}''.

An increase in the I schedule meets the given S' schedule at a higher primary yield, for which the growth rate is greater. Since the path to equilibrium is along the given S_{12}' schedule, output, prices, and both direct and indirect saving must increase.

For given output, the system in which i-securities and idle balances are perfect substitutes promises to increase the flow of saving through intermediaries and to make the total saving schedule more elastic. This stimulates the rate of growth. However, the attainment of equilibrium requires that output in fact be a short-run variable. This in turn may be based on substantial and continuing unemployment. If the short-run output changes are not adequate, then the system may require a great deal of time to reach an equilibrium.

B. STATIONARY AND REGRESSIVE ECONOMIES

1. General Characteristics

Let us recast our analysis in terms of an economy that is not growing. Either through design or accidental shifting of the S and I functions, the two schedules meet at a positive rate of interest, but a zero or negative quantity:

$$(9B.1) \qquad\qquad r_M > 0, I \text{ and } S \leq 0.$$

The static equilibrium of Chapter II-D(1) is unaltered; saving and investment, whether positive, zero, or negative, still determine a natural rate of interest to which the existing-asset market adapts. An example is shown in Figure 9–10, where S' and I' meet on the vertical axis at $r_N' = \rho_K'$. The economy is perfectly stationary, production taking the form of consumption and investment for replacement only. New securities are neither supplied nor demanded, entrepreneurs financing replacement expenditures out of revenues, and households allocating their entire incomes to consumption. Thus, while the dynamic equilibrium of Chapter II-D(2) is unchanged in principle, it is modified by the fact that existing-security supply and demand and total wealth are constant.[16]

---

[16] In a diagram of the securities market the total schedules will meet at the intersection of the existing schedules.

FIGURE 9–10
Stock-Flow Equilibrium of the Stationary State

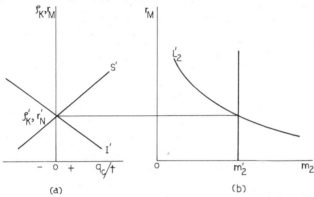

(a)   (b)

Given that S' and I' are both zero in equilibrium, it is natural to consider the meaning of negative values, which either schedule readily assumes as it is extended into the neighboring second quadrant. At $r_M > r'_N$, $I' < 0$ implies that entrepreneurs realize a corresponding return, $\rho_K > \rho'_K$, by *dis*investing at the rates indicated by the I schedule. The act of disinvesting releases resources from replacement-goods investment industries. This reduces the marginal cost of capital production, and lowers both the price of new capital and the periodic depreciation charges on existing capital. On both counts the net return to the remaining stock of capital rises.[17] The financial behavior underlying $I < 0$ is a desire to retire outstanding securities with funds (i.e., depreciation allowances) ordinarily allocated to replacement expenditure. In this way the reduction of the capital stock is matched by an equal-value reduction in the stock of existing securities.

Negative values of S' at $r_M < r'_N$ imply that households want to *dis*save, or add to their consumption, to which all of income at $S'(r'_N)$ is already devoted. Savers finance this additional consumption by selling existing securities. Thus $S < 0$ is a flow supply of existing securities. Were S and I to meet in the second quadrant, the purchase and retirement of outstanding securities by entrepreneurs would equal the sale of securities by savers.[18] Active balances

---

[17] See pp. 40–42.
[18] It is entirely possible that households might dissave by dishoarding idle balances, rather than selling existing securities, and firms might disinvest by adding depreciation allowances to idle balances, instead of retiring outstanding securities. Thus saving a supply, and investment a demand for m_2 is the regressive-state analogue to the case in the growing economy in which saving is a demand and investment a supply of idle money (see Chapter VIII-H).

ordinarily spent on replacement goods would finance a greater level
of consumption by dissavers. The capital stock would constantly
diminish, and the wealth function would rotate counterclockwise as
securities are removed from portfolios and extinguished. Presumably D_{VO} would follow the movement of S_{VO}, and S_O and D_O would
shift parallel and to the left, continuing to meet at the given rate of
interest.

A diagram of all the stock and flow value schedules of a regressive economy is presented in Figure 9–11. The market is drawn for

FIGURE 9–11
Stock-Flow Equilibrium of a Regressive Economy

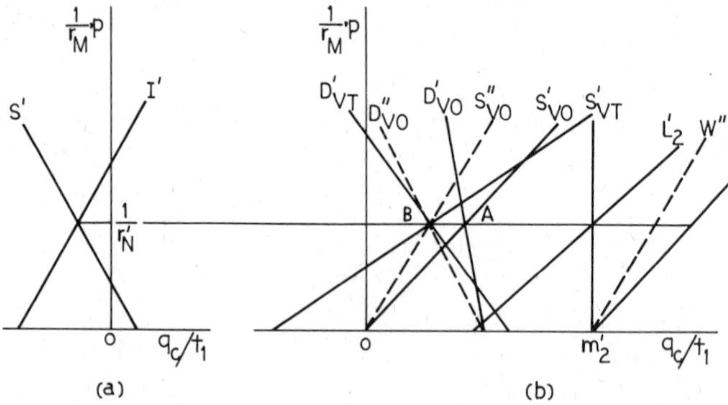

an interval, t_1. $1/r_M$ and p appear on the vertical axes. The total
value of securities supplied and demanded during t_1 are, respectively,

(9B.2) $S'_{VT} = S'_{VO} + I'$ and $D'_{VT} = D'_{VO} + S'.$

The range of interest rates for which $S'_{VT} < S'_{VO}$ reflects $I' < 0$,
while $D'_{VT} < D'_{VO}$ is due to $S' < 0$. The stock and flow markets are
individually in equilibrium at r'_N, as is the total market. Since S'
and I' meet at a negative quantity, S'_{VT} and D'_{VT} meet at point B,
which is to the left of the starting equilibrium at A defined by the
intersection of S'_{VO} and D'_{VO}. The closing security schedules are
S''_{VO} and D''_{VO}, passing through point B. The wealth function is

(9B.3) $W'' = S''_{VO} + m'_2 < W'.$

We shall find it instructive to trace the process leading to zero
and negative-growth equilibria in response to both inflationary and
deflationary disturbances. We shall analyze, in order, a decrease of
saving, a decrease of investment, and an open-market purchase. In
each case we begin with an economy initially in a stationary state.

2. Three Disturbances

a) A Decrease in Saving

In Figure 9–12 the pre-disturbance schedules of a stationary economy are S' and I', which determine r'_N, and S'_{VO}, D'_{VO}, m'_2, L'_2, and $W' = S'_{VO} + m'_2$. At the opening of an interval, t_1, S shifts leftward to S'', raising the equilibrium interest rate to r''_N, at which the growth rate is negative, and idle balances are $L'_2(r''_N) < m'_2$. During t_1 the total security schedules,

(9B.4) $$S'_{VT} = S'_{VO} + I' \text{ and } D'_{VT} = D'_{VO} + S'',$$

meet at $r''_M > r'_N$. $S'_{VT} = D'_{VT}$ implies

(9B.5) $$I' - S'' = D'_{VO} - S'_{VO},$$

corresponding in Figure 9–12 to the distances, $BC = DE$. The left side of (9B.5) is an algebraic excess of negative investment over negative saving. In absolute values, desired dissaving exceeds intended disinvestment. In financial terms, savers want to dissave by selling more existing securities than entrepreneurs are willing to buy for retirement purposes. However, the right side of (9B.5) indicates that at r''_M existing-asset holders will buy exactly the number of existing securities that savers cannot sell to entrepreneurs. Payment for the latter securities is made, of course, with idle balances which, when received by dissavers, is spent forthwith on consumption goods and activated. The loss of idle

FIGURE 9–12
The Impact of a Decrease in Saving in the Stationary State

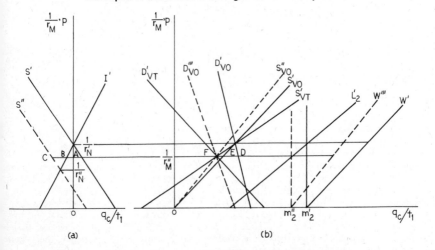

(a)   (b)

balances is

(9B.6) $\qquad D'_{VO}(r''_M) - S'_{VO}(r''_M) = m'_2 - L'_2(r''_M) = m'_2 - m''_2.$

The essence of the adjustment process is thus the sale of excess *existing* securities by savers to existing-asset holders who, at an appropriately higher rate of interest, buy the excess issues in exchange for idle balances. A diagraming of these events only would show at the close of t_1

(9B.7) $\qquad\qquad D''_{VO} = D'_{VO} + (m''_2 - m'_2),$

which is parallel to D'_{VO} and passing through point E; m''_2, as indicated;

(9B.8) $\qquad\qquad W'' = S'_{VO} + m''_2,$

which is parallel to W', and originating on the horizontal axis at m''_2; and S_{VO} and L_2 unchanged at S'_{VO} and L'_2, respectively. In a word, the equilibrating action of savers is an equal leftward shift in D_{VO}, m_2, and W. This is the same action described on page 296—an autonomous movement from idle to active balances, financed by the sale of existing securities—except that it originates with savers, who stand ready to carry it out perpetually.[19]

The closing market actually diagramed in Figure 9–12(b) shows a reduced security-value function, S''_{VO}, passing through the intersection of S'_{VT} and D'_{VT}. The difference,

(9B.9) $\qquad\qquad S'_{VO}(r''_M) - S''_{VO}(r''_M) = EF,$

corresponds to that portion of disinvestment matched by an equal amount of dissaving—the quantity, AB, in Figure 9–12(a). Total wealth is

(9B.10) $\qquad\qquad W''' = S''_{VO} + m''_2,$

parallel to S''_{VO}. Security demand is

(9B.11)

$$D'''_{VO} = D'_{VO} + (W''' - W') = D'_{VO} + (S''_{VO} - S'_{VO}) + (m''_2 - m'_2).$$

---

[19] The detailed analysis on p. 296 indicates that a shift from idle to active balances financed by selling existing securities is preceded by a rightward shift of L_2 (see Figure 8–5[b]), offsetting the simultaneous decrease in D_{VO}. When the idle balances so obtained are activated, this is reflected in a return of L_2 to its former position, D_{VO} remaining to the left of its original location. In Figure 9–12(b), which diagrams a similar movement, only the net shift in D_{VO} is shown; the offsetting movements in L_2 are omitted from the diagram. On p. 296 the asset-demand movements were also shown to be self-neutralizing, in the sense that real idle balances and the price level eventually return to their pre-disturbance values. In the present circumstances, however, the impact of the asset-demand movements persists because they are part of an equilibrating process propelling the system to a new equilibrium interest rate and price level.

The activation of idle balances by dissavers raises the price level and the interest rate by the wealth effect. The latter is reflected in further leftward and parallel movements in m_2, W, and D_{VO}. Thus the entire adjustment, brought about through a sequence of n intervals by the somewhat modified transfer effect and the wealth effect, consists of equal leftward shifts of m_2, W, and D_{VO}. L_2 is fixed by assumption, and S_{VO} is simply not affected by the equilibrating mechanisms. All of this bears a strong resemblance to the contractionary adjustment of the growing economy (Chapter VI-B). In that process savers *purchased* existing securities and raised idle balances. The adjustment consisted of equal rightward and parallel movements in m_2, W, and D_{VO} in response to both the transfer and wealth effects. S_{VO} again was constant in the face of the equilibrating forces. In the inflationary adjustment just reviewed—that of an economy passing from a stationary to a regressive equilibrium—savers *sell* existing securities and reduce idle balances. The process is opposite and symmetrical.

If the rate of ex post disinvestment is AB, as determined by the I schedule, the real adjustment is one of "zero forced disinvestment." A moment's reflection will indicate that the expressions of Chapter VI-D, the analysis of a zero forced-investment contractionary process, are applicable to the present disturbance, except that the capital, security, and idle-balance increments are negative instead of positive. Also, since we are dealing with a change in saving, rather than an open-market operation, there is no limiting first interval to initiate the adjustment. The wealth time series, now originating at, and drawn relative to a horizontal trend, are in fact the inverted mirror images (in relation to trend) of those generated by an *increase* in saving and a zero forced-investment adjustment.[20]

---

[20]Cf. p. 279. Contrary to expectation, however, the inclusion of voluntary disinvestment causes a net *increase* in real security prices each interval, just as in the contractionary growing adjustment of zero forced investment. In the present regressive inflationary adjustment, the relation between the ending and opening price of a typical interval is $p^5 > p'''$ (we are adapting the symbolism of pp. 196–97), or, upon substitution:

$$\frac{K'' - \Delta K''}{S_P'' - \Delta S_I''} > \frac{K''}{S_P''},$$

$$\frac{\Delta K''}{\Delta S_I''} < \frac{K''}{S_P''},$$

$$p^4 < p''',$$

where $-\Delta K''$ and $-\Delta S_I''$ are the voluntary reductions in capital and securities, respectively. The last inequality is the given fact that p^4, the transfer price, is below p''', the opening price. Thus if government securities, whose value is dependent on security prices, are included in portfolios, the symmetry between wealth in a deflationary zero forced-investment process (Chapter VI-D) and the present inflationary adjustment is somewhat qualified.

If the rate of ex post disinvestment is AC, as determined by dissavers, the real adjustment is one of "complete forced disinvestment." The relevant expressions, with signs changed, are those of Chapter VI-E, the account of a complete forced-investment contraction. The wealth and security-price changes occurring during or immediately after an open-market sale are again inapplicable. The wealth time series are the inverted mirror images of those created by an increase in saving and a complete forced-investment adjustment.

b) A Decrease in Investment

Let us turn now to the deflationary adjustment of an economy initially stationary. Suppose that I shifts to the left, meeting S at a lower rate of interest and a negative growth rate. Any interval of the adjustment process is characterized by an (algebraic) excess of intended dissaving over intended disinvestment. In financial terms entrepreneurs want to buy more existing securities for retirement than savers want to sell to finance additional consumption. At an appropriately lower market rate of interest, the excess purchases of entrepreneurs are met by an equal desire of existing-asset holders to relinquish securities. Funds earmarked for the retirement of securities are thus spent directly on existing issues, the sellers of which take the proceeds as idle balances. S_{VO} rotates counterclockwise, both in response to the purchase of excess entrepreneurial demanders, and to that portion of intended disinvestment equal to intended dissaving. The price level falls in response to the increase in idle balances, creating a further decline in the market rate of interest.

The above is essentially equal and opposite to the inflationary adjustment of a growing economy—in particular, to the process stimulated by an increase in investment. Whereas in Chapters IV-B and VIII-B(2), entrepreneurs reduced m_2 and increased the stock of securities by excess new issues, in the present case they raise m_2 and decrease securities by a purchase and retirement in excess of the offerings of dissavers. Where previously the equilibrating process raised S_{VO} and rotated $W(1/r_M)$ clockwise, the deflationary adjustment of an economy passing from a stationary to a declining equilibrium witnesses reductions in S_{VO} and counterclockwise rotations of $W(1/r_M)$. The real phenomena, ranging from zero to complete forced dissaving, are the inverted mirror images of zero and complete forced saving, respectively, of the growing inflationary process.

c) An Open-Market Purchase

If the disturbance to a stationary state is an open-market purchase, the adjustment is a mixture of net increases in S_{VO}, as in the growing economy, plus decreases in D_{VO}, as in the adjustment of Section a. The purchase creates the direct impact described in Chapter III(see Figure 3–3): S_{VO} decreases, m_2 increases, W and D_{VO} rotate counterclockwise through r_M'', the purchase yield. In Figure 9–13(b) the immediate post-operation market is represented

FIGURE 9–13
An Open-Market Purchase in the Stationary State

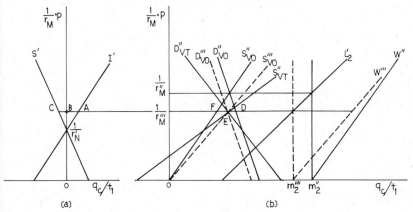

by the double-primed schedules and L_2', which is invariant. During the first adjustment interval, t_1, the total security schedules are

$$(9B.12) \qquad S_{VT}'' = S_{VO}'' + I' \quad \text{and} \quad D_{VT}'' = D_{VO}'' + S',$$

which intersect at r_M''', at which

$$(9B.13) \qquad I' - S' = D_{VO}'' - S_{VO}'',$$

shown as the distances, $AC = DF$. $I' - S'$ is made up of $I' = BA$, a supply of new securities by entrepreneurs, plus $S' = BC$, a supply of existing securities by savers. The total excess supply of securities is $AC = BA + BC$, consisting thus of the total supply of new securities and the total supply of existing securities offered by savers. As r_M rises during t_1 existing-asset holders purchase the entire supply of excess securities—both new and old. At r_M''', $D_{VO}'' - S_{VO}''$ accordingly breaks down into $FE = BA$, an addition of excess new securities to the existing stock, plus $DE = BC$, a reduction in existing-security demand by dissavers. The resulting schedules are

$$(9B.14) \qquad S_{VO}''' = S_{VO}'' + \Delta S_E' p \quad \text{and} \quad D_{VO}''' = D_{VO}'' + S'(r_M'''),$$

where $\Delta S_E'$ is the number of new securities issued at r_M'''.

The FE component of $D_{VO}'' - S_{VO}''$ is the same kind of mechanism encountered in the inflationary adjustment of a growing economy, while the DE component arose in the inflationary adjustment of an economy passing from a stationary to a regressive equilibrium (Section a). Both components reduce the supply of idle balances, which fall by $m_2'' - m_2''' = FD$. Since I' and S' are both a supply of securities, there can be no equal subcomponents; hence, all of I' and S' contribute to the equilibrating process. The final wealth function of the interval is

$$(9B.15) \qquad\qquad W''' = S_{VO}''' + m_2'''.$$

The adjustment continues for n intervals, after which r_N' is again the market rate at which $S' = I' = 0$. If any of the positive investment demand generated during the adjustment is realized, S_{VO}^n will lie to the right of S_{VO}''. On the other hand, if dissavers govern the allocation of resources, $S_{VO}^n < S_{VO}''$. The wealth paths are hybrids of inflationary and deflationary processes.[21]

C. THE CLASSICAL MODEL

An important change in the basic model occurs when the supply and demand for idle balances are zero. The L_2 function is assumed to have the form shown in Figures 2–5 and 2–6. At some high rate of interest, r_M''', and above, L_2 is zero. Interest rates at and above r_M''' can prevail only if m_2 is in fact zero. We take this to be the case. Wealth thus consists of securities only, all of which households are willing to hold at any price and yield, so long as the latter remains above r_M'''. S_{VO}, W, and D_{VO} are *identical* functions, and S_O and D_O are coinciding vertical lines.

The system resulting from $L_2 = m_2 = 0$ is designated the "classical" model. Its identifying characteristic is that it assigns to money a medium-of-exchange function only, eliminating the role of money as an asset. The model is called "classical" since its properties seem to epitomize the thinking of pre-Keynesian writers on various issues of controversy with Keynes.[22] Its empirical relevance would

---

[21] A mixed adjustment process, consisting of increases in S_{VO} and decreases in D_{VO}, might also occur in the inflationary adjustment of a *growing* economy, if the disturbance reduces the equilibrium rate of growth. For example, if S shifts to the left, the new S schedule may assume negative values at interest rates just above the old equilibrium, though not in the new. At the close of some of the earlier intervals of the adjustment process, we would expect to find temporary equilibria characterized by $S < 0$, as in Figure 9–13.

[22] See Modigliani, "Liquidity Preference and the Theory of Interest and Money," *op. cit.*, p. 75; J. Tobin, "Liquidity Preference and Monetary Policy," *Review of Economics and Sta-*

be limited to economies in which the capital stock was so low and ρ_K and r_M so high as to discourage completely the holding of money for asset purposes. An example might be nineteenth-century America, or any contemporary underdeveloped economy. Even the present American economy might approach the classical model during the high interest-rate periods of business upswing.[23] But our interest in the classical model is based only in part on its direct empirical usefulness. Analytically, the model provides an accurate description of some of the longer-run properties of the general system in which $m_2 > 0$ and $\partial L_2 / \partial r_M < 0$.

In terms of the static summary of Chapter II-D(1), the classical model is identical to the general system in the determination of the natural rate of interest. Given the level of output, saving and investment again fix an equilibrium interest rate which is independent of any other variables subsequently determined by the system (cf. [2D.1]). However, the equations involving M_2, m_2, and L_2 are now missing, so there is no need for the existing-asset market to adapt to the natural rate by allocating funds between idle and active uses. Since all money is active, the subscript, 1, can be dropped in equations (2C.26), (2C.27), and (2C.30), which determine the price level via a simple Cambridge or equation-of-exchange route. k or V is constant and independent of the rate of interest. As noted above, the equations (or identities) involving W, S_{VO}, and D_{VO} reduce to simple identities between these three variables.

The dynamic stock-flow equilibrium, described in Chapter II-D(2), is a simplified process in which S_N and D_N are added each period to a single vertical line, $S_O \equiv D_O$, to form the total security demand and supply functions. At the close of each interval a new vertical line, denoting both S_O and D_O, is drawn through the intersection of the total schedules. In real-value units, S and I are added to a single function emanating from the origin, $S_{VO} \equiv D_{VO}$. At the close of any period a new existing-security schedule

tistics, Vol. XXIX (May, 1947), pp. 124–31; and G. Ackley, *Macroeconomic Theory* (New York: The Macmillan Co., 1961), Part Two. The essential properties of the classical model are also achieved when m_2 and L_2 are positive, but coinciding functions; i.e., L_2, though positive, is interest-inelastic. See pp. 27–28, including n. 12.

[23] See L. S. Ritter, "Income Velocity and Anti-Inflationary Monetary Policy," *American Economic Review,* Vol. XLIX (March, 1959), pp. 120–29, esp. p. 128; J. H. Wood, "Aggregate Liquidity Preference Functions for the United States, 1919–1960," Purdue University, Institute for Quantitative Research in Economics and Management, Institute Paper No. 16, p. 27.

is drawn from the origin through the total intersection so determined.

If the stock of money is fixed, saving and investment are thus the only demand and supply schedules relevant to the short or long-run course of the interest rate. Not only do they determine the natural rate of interest, as previously, but they also determine the interest rate on a day-to-day basis, since there are no other markets in which supply or demand is interest-elastic. Given the money supply, the natural rate and the market rate at all times are one. A shift in saving or investment thus creates an unimpeded, immediate movement in the market rate of interest to the new natural level. An increase in I, for example, raises the supply of new securities which instantaneously fall in price and raise at once the market rate of interest and the rate of saving to their higher equilibrium levels. Asset holders no longer inhibit the movement of security prices by spending idle balances on new securities which, at the price so maintained, are in excess of the number purchased by savers. While in the classical, as in any model, there may be impediments to an immediate price adjustment, those furnished by the existing stocks of assets are absent. At the same time the absence of idle balances and the sale of new securities exclusively to savers prevent the increase in investment from raising the commodity price level.[24] Granted that the new equilibrium is reached instantaneously, security prices will return to their pre-disturbance level. Though the increase in I raises r_M by lowering p, the increase in ex post saving and investment to the new equilibrium level raises ρ_K to the higher natural rate of interest. With ρ_K and r_M again equal, p is restored to its previous value, K'/S'_O, both terms of which are essentially unchanged by the shift in I.

An independent increase in saving will immediately raise security prices and lower the yield to the point at which a greater supply of new securities meets the increased rate of saving. The security-price adjustment will be sufficient, and will occur rapidly enough to maintain constant equality between intended saving and investment. There will be neither an excess security demand by savers,

---

[24] However, any interest elasticity in the money supply will produce effects in the classical model essentially the same as those created by idle money (see Chapter VIII-J[4]). The variable money supply is a basic postulate underlying the celebrated Wicksellian analysis (Wicksell, *Lectures on Political Economy,* Vol. II [London: Routledge and Kegan Paul, Ltd., 1935], chap. iv., esp. pp. 193–94). See also Ackley, *Macroeconomic Theory*, pp. 149–50, and "Liquidity Preference and Loanable Fund Theories," *American Economic Review,* Vol. XLVII (September, 1957), pp. 662–73, esp. p. 668.

nor an excess supply of existing securities to lure savings into idle balances. In the new equilibrium, ρ_K and r_M are again equal, and p is unchanged from its pre-disturbance level.

Since existing-security holders are completely insensitive to the interest rate, the central bank can carry out an open-market operation only in the new securities market over an interval of time. A purchase is diagramed in Figure 9–14 as an addition to the

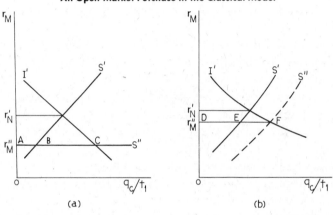

FIGURE 9–14
An Open-Market Purchase in the Classical Model

household saving schedule during a period, t_1. If the bank sets a fixed yield, $r_M'' < r_N'$, and buys all securities forthcoming, the effective demand for securities is shown in Figure 9–14(a) as a horizontal line, S''.[25] At r_M'' the value of new securities supplied during t_1 is AC, AB going to private savers, and BC to the bank. BC is also the real value of the monetary injection, which is added directly to household incomes through investment expenditure. The price level rises immediately. Since there are no holdings of idle money, the inflation has no impact on the value of assets or the rate of interest (the real value of money balances is, of course, constant). For every subsequent period of length, t_1, the bank may continue to obtain new securities at the rate, BC, given the purchase yield, r_M''. When the bank leaves the market, S' is once again the ruling security demand. S', a flow schedule, reasserts itself the instant following the bank's departure, and the interest rate rises immediately to the previous equilibrium at r_N'. The bank's purchase in no way alters S', I', or their equilibrium,

---

[25] Cf. p. 59.

which is re-established without an intervening process of adjustment.[26]

If the policy of the bank is to fix the real value of its purchase, regardless of the resulting interest rate, its action produces a parallel shift in the prevailing saving schedule. In Figure 9–14(b) S'' represents the sum of the private and bank demand for securities. At the lower equilibrium yield, r_M'', the value of new securities supplied is DF, of which DE goes to households and EF to the bank. Immediately following the bank's departure from the market, S' and r_N' are again the ruling demand and yield, respectively.

The wealth changes attributable to the purchase are essentially those described for the inflationary adjustment in Chapter V, except that (a) they are contemporaneous with the purchase, and (b) the disturbance does not involve an initial change in existing securities, or a change in idle balances initially or at any other time. In describing the wealth changes of the classical model, it is also convenient to assume that the purchase has been carried out by the commercial banking system, rather than the central bank. We have previously argued (Chapter V-B[1]) that for wealth analysis the central bank should be limited to the purchase of government securities. In the present context this requires that saving and investment be divided into private and government components—a complicating step that we prefer to avoid. The essence of the classical wealth changes can be described quite adequately with reference to a commercial bank operation.

The purchase of securities by commercial banks was shown in Chapter VIII-J(2) to entail a creation of money without an offsetting change in the security holdings of households; i.e., securities purchased and held by commercial banks are considered to be in household portfolios. Hence if the real adjustment is one of complete and immediate forced saving, the bank purchase would initially raise wealth by raising security prices, but the induced fall in ρ_K to the purchase yield would restore real security prices and wealth to the pre-disturbance level. In Figure 5–12 wealth would move instantaneously along the vertical axis from A to B and back to A. Thereafter, with ρ_K and r_M equal, and idle balances absent, $W = K$ and the path of wealth is that of the capital stock. If, in Figure 9–14(a), the bank's real expenditure, AC, is

[26] See Wicksell, *Lectures on Political Economy,* Vol. II, chap. iv., and D. H. Robertson, "Some Notes on Mr. Keynes' General Theory of Employment," *Quarterly Journal of Economics,* Vol. LI (November, 1936), p. 178.

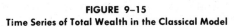

FIGURE 9–15
Time Series of Total Wealth in the Classical Model

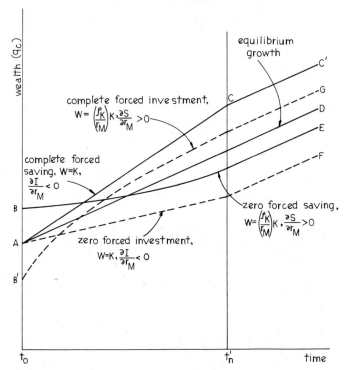

fully and immediately realized in ex post investment, capital and wealth would grow at a rate above that of the previous equilibrium. Thus in Figure 9–15, which reproduces points A and B and the AD equilibrium-growth path of Figure 5–12, wealth would pursue a course like that of ACC'. The segment, AC, terminating at t'_n, results from the increased growth of capital and wealth during the bank's presence in the money market. At t'_n the bank ceases its purchase, and the capital stock again grows at the pre-disturbance rate. In the limiting case of $\partial I/\partial r_M = 0$, wealth would coincide with the AD line, which is the minimum wealth path for complete forced saving.[27] If forced saving is zero, ρ_K remains above r_M and

---

[27] In the general analysis, as summarized by Figure 5–12, the lower bound of wealth for complete forced saving is again produced by $\partial I/\partial r_M = 0$, but it is *below* the AD equilibrium-growth path by the value of securities sold to the bank. However, the bank in that context was the *central* bank, whose assets are not included in household wealth. Notice also that while maximum wealth in Figure 5–12 is generated by $\partial S/\partial r_M = 0$, there is no effective maximum in the classical model, the growth rate simply increasing without limit as the absolute value of $\partial I/\partial r_M$ increases. In the general model, on the other hand, voluntary saving places an upper limit on wealth since forced saving is offset by an equal reduction in the value of idle balances.

$W = (\rho_K/r_M)K$ might follow a path such as BE. Whether wealth lies on or below AD at t_n' depends on whether $\partial S/\partial r_M \gtreqless 0$.[28]

In the classical model an open-market sale is an increase in the supply of securities over time. If the bank sets an offer price at which the yield is r_M'', and provides purchasers with the desired number of securities, its action is represented in Figure 9–16(a) by a horizontal schedule, I''. I'' is the sum of the private and bank

FIGURE 9–16
An Open-Market Sale in the Classical Model

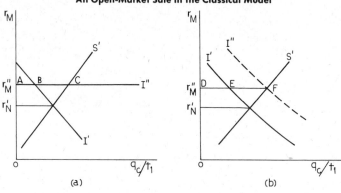

supply of securities during t_1. At r_M'' savers purchase AC in securities, of which AB are new ones supplied by entrepreneurs, and BC are furnished by the bank. BC is also the real value of funds withdrawn from the income stream, creating a proportionate and immediate decline in the price level. At r_M'' the bank can, if it wishes, draw BC from the spending stream in every interval of length t_1. A sale of a given real amount of securities is diagramed in Figure 9–16(b). The bank's action shifts I to I'' and raises r_M to r_M''. Total saving is DF, DE going into new securities and investment, while EF is drained from the system by expenditure on bank-provided issues.

---

[28] In Figure 5–7 wealth at most is *below* the undisturbed path by the value of securities sold to the bank. This is generated by $\partial S/\partial r_M = 0$. But again, it is the central, rather than a commercial, bank which is referred to in that diagram.

Taking account of both complete and zero forced saving, the wealth paths of the inflationary disturbance thus straddle the undisturbed trend line symmetrically. For example, there is always a saving schedule which, in the event of zero forced saving, produces a capital-wealth path below trend which is the mirror image of a path above trend generated by a given I schedule and complete forced saving. We can now see more clearly why the general model, as summarized in Chapter VI-F(2), produces inflationary paths that are concentrated below the trend line. The entire family of curves, symmetrical to the trend, are *lowered* by a constant—the value of securities purchased by the central bank. Moreover, the loss in idle balances during the adjustment places an upper limit on the complete forced-saving curves. Cf. p. 219 and n.27 above.

The deflationary wealth changes are again analyzed on the assumption that the security sale is conducted by a commercial, rather than the central bank. Securities sold by the bank are thus merely transferred from one group of households (those who own bank shares) to another. If forced investment is zero, ex post investment proceeding at the rate, AB, in Figure 9–16(a), the capital-wealth path would appear as AF in Figure 9–15. Wealth initially falls to B' as security prices are lowered, but returns to A when ρ_K rises to the level of the sale yield. Wealth and growth are maximized and coincide with AD when $\partial I/\partial r_M = 0$. A complete forced-investment path, for which periodic growth in Figure 9–16(a) is AC, is illustrated in Figure 9–15 by $B'G$. Wealth is $(\rho_K/r_M)K$, where $\rho_K < r_M$. The minimum path, produced by $\partial S/\partial r_M = 0$, again coincides with AD.[29] If S' and I' are vertical mirror images, then, for equal displacements of the interest rate above and below r'_N, the deflationary and inflationary wealth paths are horizontal mirror images of each other, relative to the undisturbed trend line—complete and zero forced investment corresponding to zero and complete forced saving, respectively.

The essential characteristic of the classical model is that all monetary changes fall directly on the income stream. Whether money is altered through fiscal policy or changes in central or commercial-bank credit, the direct impact is on transactions balances and the commodity price level. In the case of banking policy, monetary changes no longer occur initially in the existing-asset market, reaching the income stream only after a delayed transfer. The classical model telescopes the entire adjustment by making the direct action of the bank identical with the transfer process. Thus the impact on real variables—ex post investment and the rate of growth—is also simultaneous with the action of the bank, rather than occurring as part of a later adjustment between stocks and flows.

Since idle balances are nil, disturbances or adjustments which center on idle money are accordingly absent from the classical model. We have already noted that shifts in saving and investment thus impinge only on the interest rate, and not the price level. A

---

[29] The contractionary wealth curves of Figures 6–8 and 6–11 exceed those of the classical model because a security sale by the central bank—the disturbance of Chapter VI—creates a net increase in household wealth. The curves of Chapter VI also include a component representing capital gains or losses on government securities, which is not relevant to the present analysis.

movement in M via fiscal policy (Chapter VIII-C[1]) changed the rate of interest by changing prices and the value of idle money. The wealth-induced interest change served as a mechanism for transferring balances between idle and active uses in order to restore the pre-disturbance ratio. But with idle balances zero, the need for this transfer disappears, and the wealth effect is not missed. Without the wealth effect, an increase in velocity due to independent action by households, or an increase in a balanced government budget (Chapter VIII-E), will have no secondary deflationary repercussions; the impact is confined to the direct and indirect inflationary effects. The disturbances dealing with shifts in existing-asset demand (Chapter VIII-F) and autonomous movements between idle and active balances (Chapter VIII-G and H) are ruled out in the absence of idle-money holdings. Thus with money no longer serving as an asset, savers are committed to purchasing securities, and entrepreneurs to raising funds by security issues only. To allow households to finance out of saving a continuing increase in the ratio of average balances held to money income, or entrepreneurs to finance investment by perpetually drawing down previously accumulated funds, is to acknowledge that money has an asset function. This the classical model precludes.

D. A NON-DICHOTOMIZED MONEY SUPPLY: THE DEMAND FOR MONEY REINTERPRETED

1. An Undifferentiated Stock of Money

In this section we shall describe the monetary system without use of the assumption that money is divided into idle and active portions. The dichotomy of the money supply, which may or may not accurately describe reality, has been indispensable in helping us to understand and distinguish between the stock (asset) and flow (transactions) demand for money. But we are now sufficiently familiar with these two demand components to proceed without the view that the money supply itself is divided into corresponding stock (idle) and flow (active) portions. The resulting *non-dichotomized* monetary system will retain the essential features of the dichotomized world, while differing in one important respect: the wealth effect on interest is absent in the former model. This will be deduced from the response of the non-dichotomized system to various disturbances.

The supply of money, M, is again defined as the total quantity of all things usable as a medium of exchange. Since the quantity of money held varies during the income period of each household, the latter's holdings are defined as the average quantity on hand during the income interval. The money stock consists of undifferentiated units, all of which perform two basic functions: first, to serve as a medium of exchange, and second, to serve as a store of value. In the former use, money serves the transactions motive, providing a medium for the receipt and expenditure of income. As a store of value, money serves as an asset, an alternative to holding securities. It is in this role that for each household the average quantity of money enters the existing-asset market. But the crucial point is that every unit of money actively performs the asset and transactions function *simultaneously*. There is no specialization of function among units of the money supply, as in our basic model. Nor is there a failure of the money stock to perform one of the functions, as in the classical model, where the asset role is absent (see Part C). Instead, all dollars at any instant serve as both transactions and asset balances. In a sense, the non-dichotomized model resembles the classical in that idle-money holdings are zero in each case. But in the non-dichotomized system the functions of idle money have been taken over by an undifferentiated "active" supply of money.

Once more we distinguish between L_1, the transactions demand, and L_2, the demand for money in its role as an asset. However, L_1 and L_2 are not thereby additive components of a total demand for money. Rather, they represent different kinds of decisions made simultaneously with respect to the same total stock of money. This is shown explicitly now by writing the relevant equations of the non-dichotomized model. The system remains as summarized in Chapter II-B(5) and C(3), except that the equations of supply and demand for money, (2B.28)–(2B.31), (2B.37), (2B.38), (2C.26), (2C.27), and (2C.30), are now written as follows:

(9D.1) $$W = S_{VO} + m,$$

(9D.2) $$m = \frac{M}{P},$$

(9D.3) $$M = \overline{M},$$

(9D.4) $$L = L(y, r_M), \quad \text{where } \frac{\partial L}{\partial y} > 0, \ \frac{\partial L}{\partial r_M} < 0,$$

(9D.5) $L = m$,

(9D.6) $L_2 = L(\bar{y}, r_M)$,

(9D.7) $L_1 = PL(y, \bar{r}_M)$,

(9D.8) $L_1 = kY$,

(9D.9) $Y = P\bar{y}$.

The general demand equation for money is (9D.4), where L, in real terms, varies directly with income and inversely with interest. L_2 is defined in (9D.6) as L with y held constant. L_1, expressed in nominal units, is defined in (9D.7) as the product of P and L, the latter with r_M held constant. L_1 is thus a function of money income, and is accordingly written in (9D.8) as a fraction, k, of Y. (9D.9) is the money-income identity, incorporating (2C.29). The equilibrium condition for L is (9D.5). For L_1 and L_2 the conditions are

(9D.10) $L_1 = M$ and $L_2 = m$,

respectively. The natural rate of interest is determined, as previously, by real saving and investment ([2D.1]). Thus (9D.2)–(9D.5) and (2C.29) yield

$$L(\bar{y}, r'_N) = \frac{M}{P},$$

which sets the general price level,

(9D.11) $P' = \dfrac{M}{L(\bar{y}, r'_N)}$.

We solve for k by substitution in (9D.8), writing k as the dependent variable. The equality is carried back to the original demand function, L:

(9D.12) $k' = \dfrac{L_1}{Y} = \dfrac{M}{P'\bar{y}} = \dfrac{P'L}{P'\bar{y}} = \dfrac{L(\bar{y}, r'_N)}{\bar{y}}$.

Given the level of output, the natural rate of interest, and the stock of money, the price level thus follows directly from the real demand for money. k, the ratio of money to money income, is also determined.

L_1 and L_2 are thus particular forms of a general multi-variate demand function, L. They are obviously interdependent, since they depend on the same variables. However, each represents different behavior with respect to the money supply. The decision made by L_1 is the *turnover* of M against current output. L_1 is the active or *efficient* cause of Y, even though the numerical value of Y must be consistent with forces originating in L_2. The L_2 decision, based on the rate of interest and the existing stock of wealth, allocates wealth between cash and non-cash assets. Disturbances originating with L_2 are instantaneous shifts between money and securities. We shall see more plainly the inter-relatedness of L_1 and L_2, as well as their separate character, by considering the adjustment to various disturbances. Before doing so, we note that the equation of exchange is now written simply as

(9D.13) $M'V' = Y'$, where $V' = \dfrac{1}{k'}$ and $Y' = P'y'$.

Primes are used to designate the initially given values of all variables. The price level is

(9D.14) $$P' = \frac{M'V'}{y'}.$$

A diagram of the monetary equilibrium, involving L_1, is presented in Figure 9–17. L_1', the beginning schedule, is a rectangular hyperbola for which the area of any inscribed rectangle is k'. Thus at the initial equilibrium point, A, whose coordinates are M' and $1/Y'$, the area of such a rectangle is $M' \times 1/Y' = k'$. The prevailing natural rate of interest, r_N', is entered as a parameter for L_1'. The stock-flow equilibrium, involving L_2, is diagramed in Figure 9–18. r_N' equates both S' and I' and L_2' and $m' = M'/P'$, the real value of the total stock of money. By implication, the supply and demand for existing securities are also equal at r_N'.

FIGURE 9–17
The Transactions Demand for Money in a Non-dichotomized System

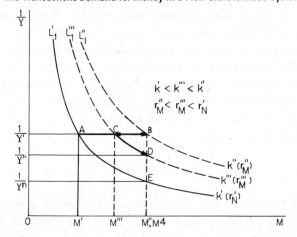

FIGURE 9–18
The Asset Demand for Money and the Saving-Investment Equilibrium
in a Non-dichotomized System

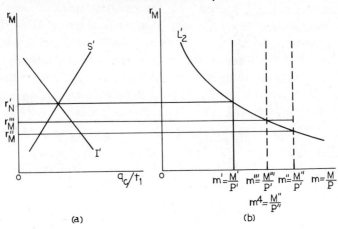

(a)   (b)

2. An Open-Market Purchase

We shall describe the direct impact and financial adjustment
stimulated by an open-market purchase. The central bank carries
out an instantaneous operation by bidding up security prices and
lowering the market rate of interest from r'_N to r''_M. In a zero time
interval households sell existing securities only, the alternative to
which is money in its store-of-value function. Thus at the lower
rate of interest, shown in Figure 9–18(b), the proceeds of the sale
are permitted to raise m from $m' = L'_2(r'_N)$ to

$$L'_2(r''_M) = m'' = \frac{M''}{P'},$$

where M'' is the increased quantity of money. Simultaneously L_1
rises from $L'_1(r'_N)$ to $L''_1(r''_M)$ and k increases from k' to $k'' = M''/$
Y'. There is, of course, no desired change on the part of households in the total level of spending; i.e., the operation involves
the private sector in a *portfolio* adjustment in which the desired
ratio of cash to *given* money expenditures is raised. As a result,
the velocity of money is reduced from V' to $V'' = Y'/M''$. The
price level is thus written

(9D.15) $$P' = \frac{M'' V''}{y'}.$$

The direct impact of the operation is diagramed in Figure 9–17
with reference to the L_1 schedule. The purchase is shown as

shifting L_1 rightward to L_1'', whose parameter is r_M''. The direct impact is indicated by a movement along the horizontal vector from A to B, the coordinates of which are M'' and $1/Y'$.

During a subsequent interval of length, t_1, the adjustment proceeds in the usual manner. At r_M'', $I' > S'$ takes the form of an excess supply of new securities. Security prices drop and r_M rises until at r_M''', reached at the close of the interval, existing-asset holders are willing to buy the reduced quantity of excess new issues. This is shown in Figure 9–18 by the equality between $I' - S'$ and $m'' - L_2'$ at r_M'''. Since the cash balances held momentarily by entrepreneurs are not part of households' balances, the events of t_1 constitute a partial reversal of the open-market operation; i.e., the interest rate rises, lowering both the desired and *de facto* holdings of real balances to

$$L_2'(r_M''') = m''' = \frac{M'''}{P'},$$

$M'' - M'''$ having been transferred to entrepreneurs. Once again the adjustment involves existing assets only, and has no direct effect on the price level or the level of expenditures. By implication L_1 falls to $L_1''' = M'''$, based on the higher interest rate, r_M''', and k falls to $k''' = M'''/Y'$. In Figure 9–17 L_1 shifts leftward to L_1''', and the prevailing equilibrium point moves along a horizontal vector from B to C. The coordinates of C are M''' and $1/Y'$, the balances held by households and the reciprocal of the unchanged expenditures level, respectively. The velocity of money corresponding to k''' is $V''' = Y'/M''' > V''$. The price level can be expressed at this stage as

(9D.16) $$P' = \frac{M''' V'''}{y'}.$$

Entrepreneurs are, of course, committed to spending balances obtained through security sales, and we assume that they do so in the next instant. A quantity of money, $M'' - M'''$, is therefore spent on investment projects, raising the stock of money held by households to M^4. Since the new funds are received on income account, they are turned over at the rate appropriate to balances earmarked for expenditure, V''', and the price level rises proportionately to

(9D.17) $$P'' = \frac{M^4 V'''}{y'}.$$

The net effect of transferring money from households to entrepreneurs and thence back to households is, of course, to leave the
money supply fixed at its post-operation level, M''; i.e.,

$$M^4 = M''' + (M'' - M''') = M''.$$

Thus we can write

(9D.18) $$P'' = \frac{M'' V'''}{y'}.$$

In Figure 9–17 the entrepreneurial expenditure is shown as a movement along L_1''' from C to D, at which the stock of money held by
households is again M'', and $Y'' > Y'$ (where $Y'' = P''y'$) maintains the still desired ratio, $k''' = M''/Y''$.

From the viewpoint of the interest rate, the crucial aspect of the
expenditure is that it produces no change in households' *real* cash
balances, the numerator and denominator of which rise by equal
relative amounts.   The entrepreneurial expenditure is entirely
analogous to a fiscal deficit, financed by printing new money that
raises M and P equally, leaving M/P unchanged.   In our particular example equality between $m''' = M'''/P'$ and $m^4 = M''/
P''$, the value of money directly before and after the entre-
preneurial injection, can be proved by substituting for P ([9D.16]
and [9D.18]) in each expression:

$$\frac{M'''}{P'} = \frac{M''}{P''}$$

$$M'''\left(\frac{y'}{M'''V'''}\right) = M''\left(\frac{y'}{M''V'''}\right)$$

$$\frac{y'}{V'''} = \frac{y'}{V'''}.$$

Since the inflation is not accompanied by a change in the real value
of cash balances, it has no effect on the rate of interest which
remains at the transfer level, r_M'''.[30]

---

[30] The following numerical example illustrates the direct impact of a purchase and the
response in the first adjustment interval in the non-dichotomized model. The data are
initially:

$$M' = \$100, \ V' = 3, \ k' = \frac{1}{V'} = 0.33, \ y' = 300,$$

$$P' = \frac{M'V'}{y'} = \$1.00, \ Y' = P'y' = \$300, m' = \frac{M'}{P'} = \frac{100}{1.00} = 100.$$

The events of the first interval are repeated in every subsequent interval of the adjustment process. Each period excess new securities raise the interest rate, which reduces the desired holdings of real cash balances and the ratio of money to money income. Entrepreneurs immediately spend funds transferred to them, raising the price level by the velocity appropriate to the transfer yield. The increase in the price level has no impact on the market rate of interest. In Figure 9–17 the return to equilibrium consists of a series of movements, such as that from B to C along a leftward-shifting L_1 schedule, followed by a downward movement along a fixed schedule, such as that from C to D. The latter movement will always terminate at the abscissa value, M'', the given post-operation stock of money. Since the equilibrium natural rate of interest remains r'_N, the final equilibrium is at point E, which lies on L'_1, the transactions demand determined by r'_N. The coordinates of E are M'' and Y^n, the final level of money income, where $M''/Y^n = k'$, the pre-operation value of k. With the equilibrium interest rate restored purely by excess new securities, and with L_2 invariant in the face of wealth changes, the total real value of excess issues is equal to the magnitude of the operation, $m'' - m'$.

The central bank purchases \$50 of existing securities by lowering the interest rate. The variables are now:

$$M'' = 150, \quad V'' = \frac{Y'}{M''} = \frac{300}{150} = 2, \quad k'' = \frac{1}{V''} = 0.50, \quad m'' = \frac{150}{1.00} = 150.$$

Say that during the first adjustment interval, t_1, excess investment, equal—at a higher interest rate—to the excess supply of cash balances, is \$30. This amount is transferred to, and held momentarily by entrepreneurs, creating for households the following values:

$$M''' = 120, \quad V''' = \frac{Y'}{M'''} = \frac{300}{120} = 2.5, \quad k''' = \frac{1}{V'''} = 0.40,$$

$$m''' = \frac{120}{1.00} = 120.$$

Notice that given money expenditures of \$300 are supported by successive money stocks of \$100 before the purchase, \$150 directly after the operation, and \$120 after the first adjustment interval. The velocity corresponding to the final stock of money is 2.5, and it is this rate at which the \$30 held by entrepreneurs are turned over when restored to households via investment expenditures. This occurs at the close of t_1, generating new values:

$$M^4 = M'' = 150, \quad V^4 = V''' = 2.5, \quad k^4 = \frac{1}{V^4} = 0.40,$$

$$P'' = \frac{M^4 V^4}{y'} = \frac{150 \times 2.5}{300} = 1.25, \quad Y'' = P''y' = 1.25 \times 300 = 375,$$

$$m^4 = \frac{150}{1.25} = 120 = m'''.$$

In the event of complete forced saving, $m'' - m'$ is also the increase in the real stock of capital attributable to the adjustment process. In general, the entire real analysis of Chapter V is applicable to the non-dichotomized system, with the single qualification that the wealth effect on interest is absent; the financial adjustment in all cases is accomplished by excess new securities only.[31]

3. *The Dichotomized Model Once Again*

In order to see more clearly why the inflation fails to raise the interest rate when money is not dichotomized, let us reconsider the adjustment in the dichotomized model, comparing it at each stage with the non-dichotomized system.

If money is divided into idle and active components, the beginning equation of exchange can be written either as

$$M_1' V_1' = P'y' \quad \text{or} \quad M'V' = P'y', \quad \text{where} \quad M' = M_1' + M_2',$$

$$\text{and} \quad V' = \left(\frac{M_1'}{M'}\right) V_1'.$$

The real value of idle balances is M_2'/P', and the real value of the total stock of money is $(M_1' + M_2')/P'$. Although we customarily include only idle balances in individual and community wealth, there is nothing in the following argument that requires active money to be excluded. Hence we shall calculate both idle and total real balances at each stage.

An instantaneous open-market purchase lowers the interest rate and raises idle balances only. M_2 is now M_2'', the real value of which is M_2''/P'. The total stock of money is

$$M'' = M_1' + M_2'',$$

and real total balances are M''/P'. The velocity of the total supply of money is

$$V'' = \left(\frac{M_1'}{M''}\right) V_1' < V',$$

and the price level, as yet unchanged, can be expressed as

$$P' = \frac{M_1' V_1'}{y'} = \frac{M'' V''}{y'}.$$

---

[31] Thus all the expressions of Chapter V, other than those dealing with the wealth effect, can be applied to the non-dichotomized adjustment by simply replacing m_2 by m.

At this point, there is no substantive difference between the dichotomized and non-dichotomized models. In each case the purchase lowers total velocity or equivalently, raises the ratio of total money to money income, the latter remaining constant. It is immaterial whether the new balances are designated "idle," or instead treated as an undifferentiated increment that raises the ratio of M to Y and has no effect on spending.

An initial transfer raises the market rate of interest by the exchange of excess new securities for idle balances. M_2 is reduced by $\Delta M_2'$ to M_2''' and total money of households is down to

$$M''' = M_1' + M_2'''.$$

Desired real idle and total money holdings are M_2'''/P' and M'''/P', respectively. The higher interest rate has partially reversed the impact of the operation. Total velocity has been raised to

$$V''' = \left(\frac{M_1'}{M'''}\right) V_1' = \frac{P'y'}{M'''} > V'',$$

and the given price level can be written

$$P' = \frac{M'''V'''}{y'}.$$

There is still no real difference between the models—the results are identical whether entrepreneurs secure "idle" balances, or instead induce households to finance unchanged expenditures with a lower undifferentiated stock of money.

Entrepreneurs spend idle money transferred to them on investment projects. M held by households is restored to M'', M_1 rises to

$$M_1'' = M_1' + \Delta M_2',$$

and P rises in proportion to the active increment. $\Delta M_2'$, like all of M_1, is turned over at the rate, V_1'. Hence

$$P'' = \frac{(M_1' + \Delta M_2')V_1'}{y'} = \frac{M_1''V_1'}{y'} = \frac{M''V^4}{y'}.$$

Total velocity in the last expression is

$$V^4 = \left(\frac{M_1''}{M''}\right) V_1'.$$

We can show that $V^4 > V'''$ by substituting in successive terms:

$$V^4 > V'''$$

$$\left(\frac{M_1''}{M''}\right) V_1' > \left(\frac{M_1'}{M'''}\right) V_1'$$

$$\frac{M_1' + \Delta M_2'}{M''' + \Delta M_2'} > \frac{M_1'}{M'''}$$

$$M''' > M_1'$$

$$M_2''' > 0.$$

In the post-interval equilibrium, real idle money is $M_2''/P'' < M_2'''/P'$, and total real balances are M''/P''. We can show that $M''/P'' < M'''/P'$ by substituting $M''V^4/y'$ for P'' and $M'''V'''/y'$ for P':

$$M''\left(\frac{y'}{M''V^4}\right) < M'''\left(\frac{y'}{M'''V'''}\right)$$

$$V''' < V^4.$$

Suppose, as in the non-dichotomized model, that the money transferred to entrepreneurs had been turned over at the velocity of the *total* money supply, rather than that of the active component. The relevant value of V would be V'''', created by the transfer yield. P would then rise in proportion to $\Delta M_2'/M'''$, reaching the level

$$P'' = \frac{(M''' + \Delta M_2')V'''}{y'} = \frac{M''V'''}{y'},$$

and M/P would be unchanged at the value, $M''/P'' = M'''/P'$ (see the proof of this on page 374). But in the dichotomized model, P in fact rises in proportion to $\Delta M_2'/M_1' > \Delta M_2'/M'''$, $\Delta M_2'$ being spent at the rate, $V_1' > V'''$. Since the velocity of the monetary increment is greater than that of the total money supply, V rises and M/P falls. *It is this excess of the marginal over the average velocity of money, resting on the functional specialization of the money supply, that creates the change in real balances and the wealth effect on interest.*[32]

---

[32] Consider a numerical example, in which the aggregate monetary data are the same as those of n. 30 above:

$$M_1' = 50, \ M_2' = 50, \ M' = 100, \ V_1' = 6, \ V' = \left(\frac{M_1'}{M'}\right) V_1' = 3,$$

$$y' = 300, \ P' = \frac{M_1'V_1'}{y'} = 1.00, \ m_2' = \frac{M_2'}{P'} = 50, \ m' = \left(\frac{M'}{P'}\right) = 100.$$

Whether households in fact dichotomize their cash balances is, of course, an empirical question. But it is relevant to consider that only *one* dichotomizing household is sufficient for the presence of the wealth effect and effective dichotomization of the total supply of money.

4. An Open-Market Sale: Is There a Wealth Effect on Interest?

Since there are elements of asymmetry between the inflationary and deflationary adjustments (see Chapter VI), we shall find it fruitful to examine the response to an open-market sale in the non-dichotomized model. We shall do so with particular reference to

---

After an open-market purchase on wealth account of $50:

$$M_1' = 50, \ M_2'' = 100, \ M'' = 150, \ V'' = \left(\frac{M_1'}{M''}\right) V_1' = 2,$$

$$m_2'' = \frac{100}{1.00} = 100, \ m'' = \frac{150}{1.00} = 150.$$

Notice the essential similarity thus far between this example and that of the non-dichotomized system in n. 30. Now, during t_1, $30 are again taken from wealth holders by entrepreneurs. At this instant, which precedes the entrepreneurial expenditure, the variables (from the viewpoint of households) are:

$$M_1' = 50, \ M_2''' = 70, \ M''' = 120, \ V''' = \left(\frac{M_1'}{M'''}\right) V_1' = 2.5,$$

$$m_2''' = \frac{70}{1.00} = 70, \ m''' = \frac{120}{1.00} = 120.$$

A moment later entrepreneurs spend transferred funds on capital projects, activating them. The active increment is spent at the prevailing active velocity, $V_1' = 6$:

$$M_1'' = 80, \ M_2''' = 70, \ M^4 = M'' = 150, \ V^4 = \left(\frac{M_1'}{M^4}\right) V_1' = 3.2,$$

$$P'' = \frac{M_1'' V_1'}{y'} = \frac{80 \times 6}{300} = 1.60, \ m_2^4 = \frac{M_2'''}{P''} = \frac{70}{1.60} = 43.75,$$

$$m^4 = \frac{M^4}{P''} = \frac{150}{1.60} = 93.75.$$

We have both $m_2^4 < m_2'''$ and $m^4 < m'''$. However, if the $30 transfer had instead been turned over at the prevailing (most recent) *total* velocity, $V''' = 2.5$, the variables following the entrepreneurial expenditure would be:

$$M_1'' = 80, \ M_2''' = 70, \ M^4 = M'' = 150, \ V^4 = V''' = 2.5,$$

$$P'' = \frac{M^4 V^4}{y'} = 1.25, \ m_2^4 = \frac{M_2'''}{P''} = \frac{70}{1.25} = 56.00,$$

$$m^4 = \frac{M^4}{P''} = \frac{150}{1.25} = 120 = m'''.$$

Even though $m_2^4 < m_2''$, $m_1 = M_1/P$ increases owing to a relatively greater increase in the numerator than in the denominator. As a result, $m^4 = m'''$.

the question of whether the wealth effect on interest is present in the non-dichotomized deflationary adjustment.

The initial impact of an open-market sale, occurring wholly on wealth account, is to raise the market rate of interest from r'_N to r''_M by increasing securities and reducing the stock of money to M'' $< M'$. Since expenditures are unaltered, k is $k'' = M''/P'y' < k'$, and velocity is $V'' > V'$. Figure 9–19 diagrams the operation in

FIGURE 9–19
The Impact of an Open-Market Sale in Terms of the Transactions Demand for Money—The Money Supply Non-dichotomized

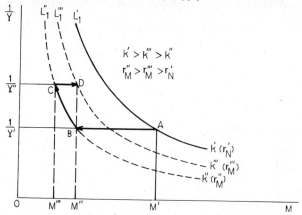

terms of the L_1 schedule. The direct impact is a movement from A at $L'_1(1/Y')$ to B at $L''_1(1/Y'_1)$. In the next non-zero interval the higher rate of interest stimulates an excess rate of saving over investment, which takes the form of an excess flow demand for securities. Security prices rise and interest falls until an equal excess supply of existing securities meets the excess demand of savers. The lower interest rate increases the asset demand for money at the expense of the existing demand for securities. Savers' balances received by the sellers of existing securities are thus permitted to raise the ratio of money to money income, and the price level falls responsively.

In order to see the process more clearly, the excess saving may be compared to a fiscal surplus which reduces the undifferentiated stock of money and the price level *pari passu*. The corresponding movement in Figure 9–19 is from B to C along L''_1. The supply of money held by households (excluding temporarily the holdings of savers) falls momentarily from M'' to M''', but the price level falls proportionately from P' to P'', and $M'''/P'' = M''/P'$.[33] An instant later savers' balances are restored to portfolios by a purchase of existing securities, lowering the rate of interest. This is the movement from C to D, which lies on L_1'' at the coordinates, M'' and $1/Y'' = 1/P''y'$. This view of the adjustment is somewhat artificial, but it serves to highlight the role of the price level and the consequent wealth changes. Along the BC path, the fall in prices raises the value of the money stock, excluding savers' holdings, to the level preceding the adjustment interval. Thus the fall in the price level merely compensates for the "loss" of savers' balances, and prevents the remaining household wealth from falling. Now, it is true that the deflation also increases the value of funds held by excess savers. This enhances the latter's ability to purchase existing securities and lower the market rate of interest, as reflected in the length of the CD path. But the fall in prices cannot properly be regarded as creating a wealth effect on interest. A genuine (downward) wealth effect would take the form of a security purchase not originating in the income stream, but induced instead by an unintended increase in wealth holdings. In the non-dichotomized adjustment the deflation produces a net increase only in the value of balances already earmarked by savers for security purchases. Even though the subsequent fall in the interest rate is thereby augmented, the result cannot be attributed in any way to a general purchase on wealth account. Thus, in both the inflationary and deflationary non-dichotomized adjustment, the change in real balances is deprived of any independent wealth-changing power. To wealth holders, the change in real balances is always a transfer of *nominal* balances—*to* entrepreneurs in the inflationary adjustment, *from* savers in the deflationary case—under terms mutually agreeable to suppliers and demanders. At the same time the movement in the price level is neutral in that it leaves unchanged the value of the relevant total money supply.[34]

---

[33] In order to show that $M'''/P'' = M''/P'$, substitute $M'''V''/y'$ for P'', and $M''V''/y'$ for P'. In the dichotomized model (Part 3), the velocity term in the expression for P'' would be replaced by $V_1' > V''$. Hence we would have $M'''/P'' > M''/P'$.

[34] Let the initial data of n. 30 be altered by an open-market sale of \$50, following which we have:

$$M'' = 50, \quad V'' = \frac{Y'}{M''} = \frac{300}{50} = 6, \quad k'' = \frac{1}{V''} = 0.17, \quad m'' = \frac{50}{1.00} = 50.$$

In the first adjustment interval \$30 of excess saving is generated. Prior to its expenditure on existing securities, but following its withdrawal from money incomes, the data (excluding excess savers' balances) are:

5. Generalization to Other Disturbances

The only real difference between the dichotomized and non-dichotomized models is the absence in the latter system of a wealth effect on interest in the adjustment to monetary change. All of our previous analysis of the basic framework, real and monetary elements of the adjustment to an open-market operation, and the dynamics of the interest structure is unaltered except for the absence of the wealth effect.[35] Wherever a change in the "supply of idle balances" is mentioned, we now refer to a change in the quantity of total money demanded for asset purposes. However, a little further work is required to indicate how disturbances other than a once-for-all open-market operation are treated by the non-dichotomized model.

a) Changes in the Supply of Money

The analysis of continuing open-market activity (Chapter VIII-A) merely extends over time the one-period operation. Since the wealth effect in the dichotomized model is only supplemental to the transfer effect, continuing operations in either system produce similar results. When money is not dichotomized, the absence of the wealth effect eases the burden of the monetary authority, whose continuing activity is aimed at offsetting only the direct

$$M'' = 20, \quad V''' = V'' = 6, \quad k''' = \frac{1}{V'''} = 0.17, \quad P'' = \frac{M''V'''}{y'} = \frac{20 \times 6}{300} = 0.40,$$

$$Y'' = P''y' = 0.40 \times 300 = 120, \quad m''' = \frac{20}{0.40} = 50 = m''.$$

Thus the reduction of the price level has no effect on the value of remaining balances of households. The value of balances held momentarily by excess savers rises from $30/1.00 = 30$ to $30/0.40 = 75$. When the excess saving is finally applied to existing securities, it lowers the desired ratio of given money expenditures to cash balances:

$$M^4 = M'' = 50, \quad V^4 = \frac{Y''}{M^4} = \frac{120}{50} = 2.4, \quad k^4 = \frac{1}{V^4} = 0.42,$$

$$m^4 = \frac{50}{0.40} = 125.$$

$m^4 > m'''$, but this merely reflects the transfer of excess savers' balances to asset holders in exchange for existing securities. It is not attributable to the fall in the price level.

[35] In Chapter VII the undifferentiated stock of money would still be divided into separate components held as alternatives to each of the two securities. The corresponding asset demand-for-money functions would again be designated L_{12} and L_{22}. However, the money supplies remain unspecialized with respect to asset and medium-of-exchange functions, the aggregate money stock being controlled simultaneously by a single L_1 demand. The basic analysis of Chapter VII is thus unchanged, except that those portions dealing with the wealth effect on interest may be omitted (in Part E and in the appendix the transfer effect remains the only force acting on the interest rate and the substitution functions).

effect of excess saving or investment on the interest rate. In Chapter VIII-B independent shifts in saving and investment are seen as minor variants of the one-period open-market operation. Once again the non-dichotomized adjustment will consist only of the transfer effect. In the case of government budgetary policy (Chapter VIII-C), the absence of the wealth effect simplifies the adjustment process. In a one-period budgetary imbalance (Part C[1]), any resulting change in the money supply is turned over at the velocity of the undifferentiated total stock. There is accordingly no change at any time in M/P, wealth, or the rate of interest.[36] In a diagram of L_1, the monetary increment is shown as a parallel shift in the money-supply line, followed by a movement along the given L_1 curve to the new equilibrium. In the L_2 diagram, no changes appear, since neither the demand nor the supply of real balances has been altered. Since in the dichotomized model the wealth effect is the initial force acting on interest following a budgetary disturbance, the adjustment described on page 282 is ruled out. The function of that adjustment is to allocate the monetary increment between M_1 and M_2 so as to restore the pre-disturbance ratio and thereby the velocity of the total money supply. In the non-dichotomized model, the equality between the average and marginal velocity of money precludes the need for an adjustment that brings total velocity to its pre-disturbance level. A continuing budgetary disturbance entailing a changing money supply will again fail to influence the interest rate in the non-dichotomized system. Contrary to the analysis on pages 283–84, the interest rate remains over time at its natural level.[37]

b) A Decrease in L_2

Changes in active velocity and existing-asset demand are somewhat more difficult to translate into the non-dichotomized system. We shall do so by a detailed description of a reduction in the asset demand for money in favor of securities, followed by an account of a reduction in the transactions demand for money, both on the assumption of unspecialized money balances.

In Figure 9–20(a) a decision to reallocate wealth by moving out

---

[36] The impact of the deficit is identical to that of the classical model (see p. 368).

[37] In a government deficit financed by borrowing from households (pp. 284–85), the interest rate would rise to r_M'' in response to the borrowing operation, but would be unaffected by the increase in the price level. In a surplus applied to the retirement of privately held government debt (pp. 286–88), the interest rate would fall only in direct response to the retirement operation.

FIGURE 9–20
A Decrease in the Asset Demand for Money in a Non-dichotomized System

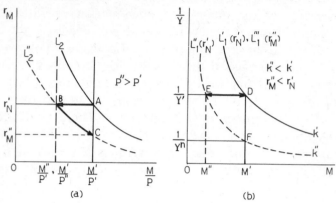

(a)   (b)

of money into securities is shown as a leftward shift in L_2, the asset demand for money. At r'_N, the prevailing equilibrium interest rate, desired cash balances decrease from A to B. Since households can act only on their *nominal* holdings of cash, taking the price level as a given parameter, the desired quantity at B is shown initially as M''/P', where $M'' < M'$, the actual stock of money. The disturbance is basically a decision to reduce cash in its store-of-value function, but households, by implication, are also reducing the desired ratio of money to money income. It is precisely because the community is reshuffling assets without changing commodity expenditures that the shift in L_2 entails simultaneously a decrease in the numerator of k, $L_1 = M$. At the given income level, desired k falls from $k' = M'/Y'$ to $k'' = M''/Y'$. This is shown in Figure 9–20(b) as a movement at the ordinate, $1/Y'$, from D on $L'_1(r'_N)$ to E on $L''_1(r'_N)$. At the prevailing interest and income levels, the shifts in L_1 and L_2, expressed in the same units, are, of course, equal. The desired quantity at point E is thus M''.[38] Now, any change in asset demand is assumed to occur instantaneously. Hence the movement into securities is limited to existing ones, and succeeds only in lowering their yield until the community is willing to hold

---

[38] One cannot require that L_1 and L_2 shift by the same absolute distance for *all* interest and income levels without risking violation of the assumption that L_1 is a rectangular hyperbola. Thus, while we require that the shift in L_2 at r'_N and L_1 at $1/Y'$ be equal (when expressed in the same units), we cannot place any other restrictions on L''_1 relative to L'_1. The D-to-E shift in going from L'_1 to L''_1 completely determines the latter schedule, given its rectangular-hyperbola form. One consequence of the mathematical character postulated for L'_1 and L''_1 is that the horizontal distance between them increases as the ordinate value decreases.

the actual quantity of money. In the left diagram the path to exist-ing-asset market equilibrium is along L_2'' from B to C, the coor-dinates of which are M'/P' and $r_M'' < r_N'$. The renewed willingness to hold the existing quantity of money is reflected in Figure 9–20(b) as a return movement from E to D, which lies on a new schedule, $L_1'''(r_M'')$. L_1''' coincides with L_1' because the lowering of the interest rate has reconciled the community to holding the given stock of money in relation to the given income at the previous and still-prevailing ratio, k'.

The reduced interest rate stimulates the usual $I > S$ inflationary adjustment. The process is identical to that following an open-market purchase, as described in Part 2. From point C in Figure 9–20(a), there is an upward movement along L_2''. From point D in Figure 9–20(b), there is an initial leftward movement in response to the transfer-induced rise in the interest rate. This corresponds in Figure 9–17 to the movement from B to C. The subsequent entrepreneurial expenditure creates a downward path, such as that from C to D in the latter diagram, except that the terminal point is now at M'. This fails to create a wealth effect on interest for the reasons noted in Part 2. The final equilibrium in Figure 9–20(b) is at point F, the intersection of the given money stock, M', with $L_1''(r_N')$. The ratio of money to income is k'', the level *desired* at the equilibrium interest rate, r_N'. Money income is $Y^n > Y'$, ac-complished by an increase in the price level to P''. In Figure 9–20(a) the equilibrium is on L_2'' at point B, for which real bal-ances are $M'/P'' = M''/P'$; i.e., inflation produces the reduction in real balances that households sought initially by an outlay of nominal balances on securities.[39]

c) A Decrease in L_1

Suppose that the initiating disturbance is an independent reduc-tion in L_1, the transactions demand for money. Households choose to lower the ratio of money to income and expenditures by a once-for-all direct increase in spending on goods and services. In Figure 9–21(a), L_1 shifts leftward from L_1' to L_1''. Since individual house-holds can neither plan nor expect to change the permanent level of expenditures by a single act of dishoarding, the movement is drawn from A to B at the given ordinate, $1/Y'$. At B the quantity of money demanded in relation to Y' is $M'' < M'$. Once again the

---

[39] In order to show that $M'/P'' = M''/P'$, we divide each term by y'. Each side of the resulting equality, $M'/P''y' = M''/P'y'$, is equal to k''.

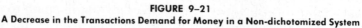

FIGURE 9–21
A Decrease in the Transactions Demand for Money in a Non-dichotomized System

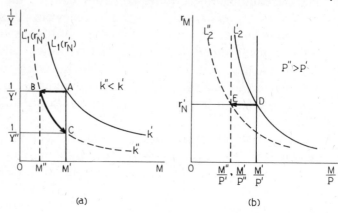

(a)   (b)

asset demand for money, directed at the undifferentiated stock, must shift consistently with the transactions demand. The decision to lower k from $k' = M'/Y'$ to $k'' = M''/Y'$ is reflected in Figure 9–21(b) as a simultaneous leftward shift in L_2 from L_2' to L_2''. At the prevailing interest rate, asset holders reduce their demand for real balances from M'/P' to M''/P'. The movement is from D to E. Unlike the previous disturbance, the direct effect is now on commodity, rather than security prices. As the price level and money income rise, the transactions demand for money increases until M' is again the desired quantity. This is the movement along L_1'' from B to C, at which money income is Y'' and the *de facto* k is $k'' = M'/Y''$. In Figure 9–21(b) the resulting reduction in the aggregate value of real balances from M'/P' to $M'/P'' = M''/P'$ fulfills the desired movement from D to E and has no independent effect on wealth or the rate of interest.

A disturbance that fits within the framework of a reduction in L_1 is an increment in a balanced government budget which forcibly reduces the ratio of money to money income (cf. Chapter VIII-E). But in the non-dichotomized model, there is no secondary (deflationary) impact on the price level via the wealth effect on interest. The secondary inflationary effect, which occurs when the higher price level reduces household disposable income and saving, remains. A disturbance that cannot be categorized as primarily an increase in L_1 or L_2 alone is a desire of savers to add to balances, rather than buy securities over time. Each period in which savers add to balances, expenditures fall below income, and L_1 and k increase. At the same time L_2 shifts constantly to the right, accompanied by an equal increase in real balances due to the fall in prices. As indicated in Chapter VIII-H, the natural rate of interest is determined under these circumstances by S_s and I_s, rather than the whole of saving and investment. In the non-dichotomized model, however, the price level cannot, via a wealth effect, maintain the market rate below the natural rate.[40]

In the non-dichotomized system, there is no distinction between changes in L_1 financed by adjusting the turnover of transactions balances versus changes financed by adding to or subtracting from asset balances. Thus the disturbances described separately in Parts E (a change in active velocity) and G (autonomous shifts between idle and active balances) of Chapter VIII are treated as undifferentiated changes in L_1 in the non-dichotomized model (in either case L_1 and L_2 shift simultaneously). However, a decrease in L_1 preceded by a movement out of existing securities at the expense of asset demand, is again completely neutral with respect to the price level (cf. page 296). Initially L_2 and L_1 shift to the right, the former movement raising the rate of interest. But then the originally desired reduction in L_1 occurs, accompanied by a leftward shift in L_2. Both schedules return to their pre-disturbance locations.

d) Variable Output

In this final section we shall indicate the way in which the non-dichotomized model handles output as a variable. Suppose that output rises spontaneously owing to an increased labor force or a technological innovation. Assume initially that saving is fixed. For a given money supply and L_1, the price level falls, money income (and k) remaining constant. But by (9D.4) L and thus L_2 increase responsively. This is to say that L_2 shifts to the right, maintaining equality with real balances at the going rate of interest. Thus while the increase in output raises real balances, there is no resultant wealth effect on interest. The increase in L_2 is rationalized by the altered relationship between Y and M/P. Though any given Y still requires the same *nominal* quantity of money for transactions (i.e., k is constant), the offsetting changes in y and P mean that the

---

[40] The relevant wealth changes are thus those in Chapter VIII-H based on the assumption that the wealth effect on interest is non-operative (see p. 299). A more detailed mathematical description of the entire process of hoarding out of income is presented in the appendix to Chapter X. This is done both for the dichotomized and non-dichotomized models as part of a reformulation of the Hicks *IS-LM* system.

associated *real* balances are greater than previously. Hence L_2 increases sympathetically.

Now let saving rise in response to the growth of output. This lowers the natural rate and creates an excess of saving over investment. Real balances increase net of demand, as the market rate falls toward the natural rate. This component of the decline in prices is a direct result of the excess saving and does not add further to the downward movement of the market rate (cf. Section 4).

E. THREE KEYNESIAN CASES

This section will describe three extreme models, one in which the demand for idle balances is perfectly horizontal, one in which the supply of money is infinitely elastic, and one in which saving and investment are both completely insensitive to the interest rate. The models are referred to as "Keynesian" cases, since many of the so-called "Keynesian" conclusions seem to require the assumptions of these models.

1. The Demand for Idle Balances Infinitely Elastic

A great many post-Keynesian writers have argued that at a sufficiently low, but positive rate of interest the differences between asset money and securities disappear. The two assets become perfect substitutes, and L_2 is a horizontal line (see Figures 2–5 and 2–6).[41] Keynes himself mentions such a possibility, but denies that it characterizes his own view of the world.[42] Nevertheless, the wide use of Keynesian "income-expenditures" models (often diagramed with the aid of a 45-degree line), in which the interest rate is not explicitly accounted for, is justified if the interest rate is fixed by a "liquidity-trap" (horizontal L_2) function.

We have already encountered a horizontal demand-for-money schedule in Part A(4)c of this chapter. The general analysis of that section is applicable here. In the general model, summarized in Chapter II-D(1), the demand and supply equations of idle balances, (2B.37) and (2B.38), are replaced by

$$(9E.1) \qquad\qquad r_M = r'_M,$$

---

[41] See J. R. Hicks, "Mr. Keynes and the 'Classics'; A Suggested Interpretation," *Econometrica*, Vol. V (April, 1937), pp. 154–55; and Modigliani, "Liquidity Preference and the Theory of Interest and Money," *op. cit.*, pp. 53 and 74.

[42] Keynes, *The General Theory of Employment, Interest and Money* (New York: Harcourt, Brace & Co., 1936), p. 207.

the low interest rate at which L_2 becomes horizontal. The equation for existing-security demand, (2B.39), is written

(9E.2) $$D_{VO} = W - m_2.$$

Thus, on net we have dropped on equation and one variable, L_2. But in order to ensure that the interest rate determined by (2D.1), the saving-investment equilibrium, is the same as (9E.1), output must appear as a variable to which saving responds positively ([2C.19]). Then if the natural rate should be unequal to (9E.1), output and saving will vary until $r_N = r'_M$. We again assume that output varies through "money illusion" in the labor market (see page 348), and is thus a function of the price level. Hence (2C.29) is replaced by

(9E.3) $$y = y(P), \text{ where } \frac{\partial y}{\partial P} > 0.$$

In place of (2D.1) and (2D.3) we now have (cf. [9A.33]):

(9E.4) $$S(y, r'_M) = I(r'_M),$$
$$y = y(P),$$
$$\overline{k}_1 Py = \overline{M} - M_2,$$

which together determine y, P, and M_2.

The Keynesian model reacts to the basic disturbances as follows:

1. Changes in the money supply by central or commercial-bank operations can have no effect on the rate of interest or the level of expenditures, output, and prices. Since money and securities are perfect substitutes, they are exchangeable for one another in any quantity (as long as idle balances or existing securities are not exhausted) at the going price and yield of securities. An open-market purchase, for example, would merely raise m_2, while reducing securities. Since r_M is unaltered by the operation, there is no ensuing adjustment process characterized by $I > S$.

2. Disturbances that previously changed the equilibrium natural rate of interest now stimulate an adjustment in output, the market and natural rates of interest remaining at r'_M. Consider an increase in I. The resulting excess of I over S takes the usual form of an excess supply of new securities. However, the excess issues are now interchangeable with idle balances at the going security price—the transfer fails to lower p or raise r_M. Equilibrium is achieved only when the resulting increase in active balances and output raises S sufficiently to meet the greater I schedule at r'_M. The simultaneous

increase in the commodity price level will lower m_2, but again fail to alter the prevailing rate of interest. The ratio of the increase in output, so described, to the increase in investment is, of course, the Keynesian multiplier.

3. Let there be a one-period government budgetary deficit financed by money creation. As output rises in response to the increase in M_1 and P, real saving increases. Since r_M is fixed, the entire increment in saving is, and remains, in excess of investment. The increase in saving is thus channeled into existing securities and raises the holdings of idle money equally. In fact, the system is out of equilibrium until the total excess saving generated is equal to the magnitude of the deficit; i.e., until excess saving transfers all of the active money created by the deficit to hoards. At this point, output will have returned to its pre-disturbance level which, for the given S and I *functions*, is the only level at which the latter are equal. The rise of the price level merely prolongs the adjustment, while failing to influence the interest rate. We conclude that any once-for-all change in the money supply, whether originating on wealth or income account, affects only idle balances in the Keynesian model. However, if the deficit financed by new money is carried out perpetually, an equilibrium in which excess saving equals the deficit, but output is higher, might be reached. Only if real saving responded so vigorously in the first period as to transfer the entire monetary increment to the idle balances would output fail to rise at all.[43]

4. Shifts in existing-asset demand are comparable in their effects to open-market operations or federal budget imbalances. Thus an instantaneous shift by asset holders between money and securities has no effect on the rate of interest or the level of spending. A once-for-all autonomous shift from idle to active balances raises spending and income, but only until excess saving has deactivated dishoarded funds. An increase in a balanced government budget,

---

[43] Ordinarily we expect real saving in any period to rise by a fraction of the increase in M_1:

$$\Delta S = \Delta y - \Delta C = \frac{\Delta M_1 V_1}{P} - \Delta C,$$

where ΔS and ΔC are the increments in real saving and consumption, respectively. However, if ΔC is sufficiently small and/or V_1 is quite large, it is possible for $\Delta S \geqq \Delta M_1/P$. In that event, all of ΔM_1 will go into hoards. Notice that any tendency of the price level to rise increases money saving and investment equally, without altering the difference between them at the going rate of interest. Thus it is only increases in *real* saving that constitute an excess over investment and a source, thereby, for transfers to the idle realm.

whether it raises V_1 or not, reduces household disposable income and saving. The resulting excess investment activates idle balances and raises real household income until it has recovered its pre-disturbance level. The multiplier is unity (cf. page 292, note 20). The wealth effect on interest is again absent from the adjustment.

A fundamental feature of the Keynesian model concerns the financial character of saving and investment. Previously we have drawn a sharp distinction between S and I that constituted a demand and supply of securities as opposed to idle balances (pages 38–39 and Chapter VIII-H). We did so because the influence of saving, for example, on the price level, the interest rate, and the rate of growth is much different if savers buy securities than if they build up idle balances each period. But in the present Keynesian model the impact of saving and investment does not depend on whether they are a demand and supply of securities or money. Consider an example in which saving, a demand for securities only, is suddenly divided between security purchases and additions to idle balances. Investment continues to be a supply of securities only. In terms of our previous notation (see page 38),

(9E.5) $$S = S_s + S_m, \quad I = I_s.$$

We assume that S_s and S_m each responds positively to output. Figure 9–22 shows the stock and flow markets before and after the introduction of hoarding by savers. Initially $S' = S'_s$ and $I' = I'_s$ are equal at r'_M, as determined by the flat schedule, L'_2. Idle balances are m'_2. During an interval, t_1, the given aggregate saving, S', is divided between S'_s and S'_m. The quantity, S'_m, is added both

FIGURE 9–22
The Division of Saving between Securities and Hoards in the Keynesian Model

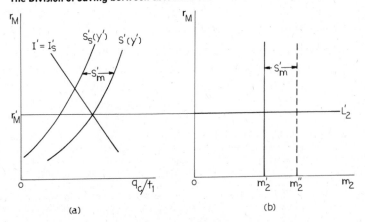

(a) (b)

to L_2' and m_2', the latter becoming m_2''. But since L_2' is already drawn indefinitely to the right, it cannot shift further. Meanwhile, at r_M' the hoarding of savers creates an excess supply of new securities, equal in value to

$$(9E.6) \qquad\qquad I'(r_M') - S_s'(r_M') = S_m'.$$

Since L_2' is perfectly elastic, this quantity of excess securities succeeds in transferring an equal quantity of idle balances to the income stream with no change in the interest rate. At the close of t_1, m_2 is thus again m_2', and there is no net change in active balances, output, or prices. There is no perceptible impact of the hoarding decision on the system, which remains in aggregate saving-investment equilibrium at r_M'. In Chapter VIII-H(1) the same disturbance in the general model was seen to create a new equilibrium of a higher interest rate, an excess of S over I, and a constantly falling price level.

It is thus the fixity of the market rate of interest that enables entrepreneurs to recoup the entire hoardings of savers by selling all excess issues to asset holders. By the same token, any tendency of investment to by-pass the securities market will be equally immaterial to the equilibrium. When $I_m > 0$, we have periodic leftward shifts in L_2 and m_2. The infinite elasticity of L_2 again obscures any tendency for the schedule to shift. If dishoarding by entrepreneurs produces $S_s > I_s$, savers purchase existing securities and raise m_2 by the amount entrepreneurs reduce it. As long as *aggregate* saving and investment are equal, as they will be in this model, the increases and decreases in m_2 on account of S_m and I_m balance out, and the system proceeds in stock-flow equilibrium at a stable price level and output.

2. The Supply of Money Infinitely Elastic

An interesting, and perhaps empirically more relevant variant of the liquidity-trap model, is when L_2 resumes its normal appearance $(\partial L_2/\partial r_M < 0)$, but the money supply is infinitely elastic at the going interest rate.[44] This may be a limiting case of the commercial-

---

[44] My empirical study, "Member Bank Effective Reserves and Earning Assets in the Thirties," summarized in *Econometrica*, Vol. XXVI (October, 1958), pp. 602–3, lends strong support to this characterization of the monetary system during the depression of the 1930's. The whole period of the Federal Reserve's bond support policy (1941–51) is also one in which the interest rates are fixed by an infinitely elastic money supply. However, there is reason to believe that in the latter period the fixed yields were occasionally above those determined by natural market forces. The evidence for this is the very small

banking model described in Chapter VIII-J(4), or the result of central-bank policy. Assuming instantaneous security transactions by the banking system, the perfectly elastic money supply is diagramed in Figure 9–23(b) as a horizontal m_2 supply line, m'_{2s}, at the ordinate, r'_M. Again the rate of interest is effectively fixed at that level, output and real saving making the necessary adjustment for

FIGURE 9–23
The Keynesian Model as Created by an Infinitely Elastic Supply of Money

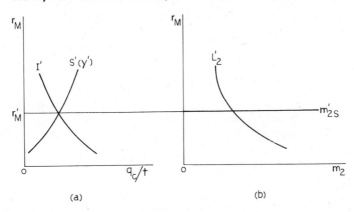

(a)   (b)

equilibrium. In terms of the equation system, (9E.1) is again entered, though now it replaces (2B.29) and (2B.31), along with (2B.38). (2B.28) is written

(9E.7)
$$W = S_{VO} + L_2,$$

while (2B.30) is replaced by

(9E.8)
$$M_1 = M - L_2.$$

There is a net loss of two equations and two variables, m_2 and M_2. The last equation of (9E.4) is replaced by

(9E.9)
$$\bar{k}_1 Py = M - L_2(r'_M).$$

The three summary equations thus determine y, P, and M.

The implication of the infinitely elastic m_{2s} schedule is that the banking system has given up its control of the money supply, instead fixing the interest rate at r'_M by buying and selling securities

number of transactions in government securities undertaken by the Federal Reserve during the late forties (cf. J. Kareken, "Monetary Policy and the Public Debt: An Appraisal of Post-War Developments in the U.S.A.," *Kyklos*, Vol X[1957], pp. 401–31). At such times the horizontal money-supply line would not be operative.

in whatever amounts are necessary to that end. Consider the impact of an increase in the I schedule. The excess supply of new securities would ordinarily fall in price, luring idle balances into the active circulation. But in this model the banking system buys all of the excess issues at the going yield. This sends new money directly into the income stream, the nominal supply of idle balances remaining constant. The subsequent rise in the price level lowers m_2 and ordinarily would stimulate a liquidation of existing securities and a further rise of the interest rate. But again the banks support the market by purchasing securities offered by asset holders. This prevents m_2 from falling and r_M from rising on that account. Notice that the outcome would be identical if, instead of selling securities to finance the additional investment, entrepreneurs each period had themselves dishoarded previously accumulated idle money. L_2 and m_2 would both shift to the left, though the shift in a horizontal m_{2S} schedule is, of course, imperceptible. Active balances and expenditures would rise exactly as before, without benefit of a prior increase in the interest rate. The only difference between the two cases is in the quantity of idle balances and overall velocity in the new equilibrium. When entrepreneurs reduce idle balances directly, the latter remain at the lower level. The increase in total velocity caused by raising M_1 at the expense of M_2 is greater than that due to an increase in M_1 while M_2 is constant.

A central bank that creates an infinitely elastic money supply cannot engage in independent monetary policy. Thus open-market operations, as described in previous sections and chapters, cannot be undertaken. If the commercial banks are responsible for the horizontal money-supply line, then central-bank operations will simply result in equal and opposite changes in the security holdings of commercial banks, the supply of money and the rate of interest remaining constant. The impact of fiscal policy is the same, whether the interest rate is fixed by infinitely elastic demand or supply of money. We have already noted that an increase in investment produces the general outcome observed in the infinitely elastic L_2 model. Moreover, the impact was independent of the means by which the investment was financed. We conclude that the Keynesian results are achieved equally well by a horizontal m_2 demand or supply schedule. The only difference is in the total supply of money, which in the latter model is variable. This dampens the impact of disturbances on total velocity.

3. Saving and Investment Interest-Inelastic

An assumption of the *General Theory*, as well as many earlier works, is that saving (or consumption) has little, if any, interest elasticity.[45] Keynesians have typically regarded the investment schedule as responding weakly to interest changes in depression periods.[46] This section will explore the limiting model in which both saving and investment have zero interest elasticity.

The saving and investment equations, (2C.32), (2C.34), and (2C.35), are now replaced by

$$(9E.10) \qquad S = S(y),$$

$$(9E.11) \qquad I = \overline{I},$$

where r_M has been dropped from the saving function, and a given level of investment replaces the Keynes-Lerner-Robertson investment activity. (2C.29) is again replaced by (9E.3). In this model saving, investment, and the production function together determine output and the price level. We add (9E.3) to the saving-investment equality:

$$(9E.12) \qquad S(y) = \overline{I},$$

$$y = y(P);$$

i.e., there is some price level and resulting output at which saving is equal to the fixed level of investment. The determination of y and P determine the demand and supply of active balances:

$$(9E.13) \qquad \overline{k}_1 P'y' = M_1,$$

where the variables on the left have been substituted for L_1. The primed variables are those determined by (9E.12). Finally, we subtract the active balances from the given stock of money to determine idle balances. The latter, together with the known price level and L_2, determines r_M:

$$(9E.14) \qquad L_2(r_M) = \frac{\overline{M} - M_1'}{P'},$$

where M_1' is given by (9E.13).

Open-market operations in this system create the usual changes in idle balances and the interest rate. But there are no repercussions on saving, investment, the supply of active money, and money

---

[45] *The General Theory of Employment, Interest and Money*, pp. 93–94.

[46] A. H. Hansen, *Monetary Theory and Fiscal Policy* (New York: McGraw-Hill Book Co., Inc., 1949), p. 79.

income. An increase in investment creates an excess supply of new securities which raises the interest rate by reducing the supply of idle balances. However, the excess investment is itself independent of the interest rate, and is eliminated only as saving increases in response to a rise of output. The latter occurs when the idle balances are activated. A once-for-all government deficit financed with new money creates excess saving which is removed only when the additional balances have been added to hoards. The interest rate is lower, but output and prices are unchanged.

In essential details this system parallels the other two Keynesian cases. While the interest rate is now variable, its fluctuations have no influence on spending, income, or prices. The financial character of saving and investment again has no significant effect on the equilibrium. If all of saving, for example, were hoarded, shifting L_2 and m_2 to the right, entrepreneurs could recoup the entire amount by selling all of their securities to asset holders. The interest rate would rise, but this would neither diminish the supply of new securities nor alter the equilibrium income level. If all of both saving and investment by-passed the securities market—i.e., $S = S_m$ and $I = I_m$—the analysis would not be changed. Open-market operations would affect only the interest rate, and shifts in S and I would create new equilibrium income levels by *directly* adding to, or subtracting from, the supply of active balances.

F. SUMMARY

The system is enlarged by a network of financial intermediaries through which a portion of household saving ("indirect" saving) is channeled. These institutions issue an equity claim on themselves, known as intermediary or i-securities, and apply the entire proceeds of such issues to the purchases of the equity ("primary") securities issued by firms for investment expenditure. A portion of household saving ("direct" saving) continues to be spent directly on primary securities. Household savers and asset holders regard intermediary and primary securities as less-than-perfect substitutes. Indirect saving thus varies positively with the intermediary yield, and inversely with the primary yield. The supply of i-securities varies inversely with the intermediary yield and positively with the primary yield (the former yield is a cost to intermediaries, while the latter is the earnings rate on intermediary expenditures). Depending on the relative response of each schedule to the primary yield, the equilibrium flow of funds through intermediaries will be a rising, falling, or vertical function of the primary rate of interest. In the primary market, direct saving varies positively with the primary yield and inversely with the intermediary yield. In order to derive the aggregate saving function, we add to the direct-saving schedule at each primary yield the corresponding equilibrium quantity of the intermediary market. The relevant direct-saving schedule at each primary yield is the one consistent with the equilibrium intermediary yield resulting from the given primary rate of interest. The aggregate saving schedule, so derived, may be a rising, vertical, or downward function of the primary yield. The expected rising schedule results when the two securities are poor substitutes, and direct and indirect saving are relatively elastic with respect to their respective interest rates. The flow equilibrium, established by aggregate saving and investment, determines both interest rates and the rate of direct and indirect saving. The existing-asset markets of each security adapt to the flow equilibrium by an appropriate division between idle and active money. Intermediaries doubtless raise total saving, which tends to lower the equilibrium price level. However, intermediaries may raise prices by reducing the demand schedule for money and by discouraging continuous hoarding out of income.

An open-market purchase of primary securities lowers the primary yield and raises idle balances. The resulting excess of investment over aggregate saving activates idle balances, but the fall in the primary yield causes an excess new demand for i-securities which lowers the intermediary yield and increases idle money. The latter effect offsets somewhat the inflationary pressure. In equilibrium the interest rates have returned to their pre-disturbance values, and the price level is higher. The real adjustment entails more or less forced saving. An increase in the supply of i-securities creates a new equilibrium in which the intermediary yield is higher and the primary yield is lower. Direct saving is less, but indirect and aggregate saving are both greater. Total saving is greater because the rise of indirect saving is financed by a reduction in consumption as well as direct saving. The price level may increase, decrease, or remain constant, depending on the movements of the interest rates and the elasticities of the demand for idle balances with respect to the two yields. In any case the adjustment is characterized by an excess of aggregate saving over investment and the basic wealth changes of a contractionary process. An increase in investment raises both interest rates and the price level. An increase in either saving component lowers the interest rates and the price level.

When indirect saving is infinitely elastic, aggregate saving is more elastic and the flow of funds through intermediaries is greater. Movements in the price level are dampened. Constant intermediary costs, creating an infinitely elastic supply of i-securities, has no predictable influence on the elasticity of total saving. The flow of funds through intermediaries varies inversely with changes in investment, and positively with changes in saving. The price level is again stabilized, though less than in the case of infinitely elastic indirect saving. If i-securities and idle balances are perfect substitutes, output must be variable in order to equilibrate the intermediary flow market at the interest rate determined by intermediary asset holders. Aggregate saving tends to be more elastic and, for given output, saving through intermediaries is greater than in the general model. Open-market operations in this system cannot create a net change in interest, active money, output, or the price level. An increase in the supply of i-securities will raise total saving and lower the primary yield. Output and prices may move in either direction. An increase in investment raises total saving, the primary yield, output, and the price level.

A stationary economy is one in which the rate of interest is positive, but saving and investment are zero. The stock of securities and total wealth are constant. A regressive economy is one in which saving and investment are both negative. Entrepreneurs are failing to maintain the entire capital stock, applying some of their depreciation allowances to the retirement of existing securities. In equilibrium their security purchases are exactly equal to the sale of existing securities by dissavers, who thereby finance a level of consumption above current income. Capital, securities, and wealth constantly diminish. A decrease in saving disturbs a stationary state. In the new equilibrium the interest rate is higher, while saving and investment are negative. In a typical adjustment interval the interest rate rises until the absolute value of desired dissaving exceeds desired disinvestment exactly by the excess existing demand for securities. This is to say that excess dissaving can be financed by the sale of existing securities by savers to asset holders. The latter pay with idle balances which are received and activated by savers. The price level rises. The essence of the equilibrating process is thus equal reductions in existing-security

demand and idle balances—the opposite of the deflationary adjustment of a growing economy. The real adjustment will range from
zero to complete "forced disinvestment," which is shown to be
algebraically opposite and equal to zero and forced investment,
respectively, of the growing contractionary adjustment. A decrease
in investment in a stationary state produces a regressive equilibrium
at a lower interest rate. The adjustment is one of an absolute excess
of intended disinvestment over desired dissaving or, in financial
terms, an excess entrepreneurial demand for existing securities to be
retired. At a lower yield the excess demand is matched by an excess
supply of existing securities, the proceeds from the sale of which
are held idle. The price level falls. The adjustment is thus one
of an increase in idle balances and a decrease in existing securities,
which is opposite to the inflationary adjustment of the growing
economy. An open-market purchase in the stationary state stimulates an adjustment which is a mixture of elements of the two
just described.

In the classical model the supply and demand for idle balances
are zero. Existing-security supply and demand and total wealth are
identically equal. If the money supply is fixed, both the natural
and market rates of interest are determined by saving and investment. Changes in the latter schedules cause immediate equilibrating changes in the interest rate, with no change in the price level.
Central or commercial-bank credit operations can now be carried
out only in the new securities market. A security purchase by the
banks is an addition to the household saving schedule. The interest
rate is lowered and new securities are obtained, sending money
directly into the expenditures stream. At the close of the operation,
the interest rate returns immediately to the natural level. The wealth
changes, contemporaneous with the purchase, are equal to the
changes in the capital stock on account of voluntary and forced
saving. A security sale is an addition to the investment schedule,
raising the interest rate and withdrawing money directly from the
stream of spending. The wealth changes of the inflationary and deflationary disturbances are mirror images of each other relative to the trend line. In the absence of idle balances, there is no
wealth effect on interest. Thus there are no secondary repercussions following an increase in money via fiscal policy, or after an
increase in velocity due to a balanced government budget. In the
classical model, saving and investment must be defined as a demand
and supply respectively, of securities.

In the non-dichotomized monetary system all units of money simultaneously perform the asset and transactions functions. We continue to distinguish between a stock (asset) and flow (transactions) demand. But the demands are directed simultaneously at the same stock of money, and are non-additive. An appropriate price level creates the real balances desired by asset holders at the natural rate of interest. The direct impact of an open-market purchase raises the ratio of money held by households to given expenditures by lowering the interest rate. This entails a movement along the asset demand, but a shift to the right of the transactions demand for money, for which the interest rate is a parameter. The excess securities and transfer of the first adjustment interval create a partial reversal of these movements, including that of the interest rate. When balances transferred to entrepreneurs are then spent on capital projects, these funds are turned over at the prevailing velocity of the undifferentiated stock of money. Accordingly, household balances and the price level rise equally. Real balances are unaltered, and there is no wealth effect on interest; the adjustment is accomplished entirely by excess new securities. This is the only substantive difference between the non-dichotomized and dichotomized models. In the latter system idle money transferred to entrepreneurs is turned over at the velocity of active money, which exceeds the average velocity of all money. Thus entrepreneurial expenditures raise household balances and the price level disproportionately, causing a net reduction in the value of money and a wealth effect on interest. In spite of various asymmetries, the absence of the wealth effect is shown to hold in the non-dichotomized deflationary adjustment as well. The entire previous analysis is translated into the non-dichotomized model by simply deleting the wealth effect. Changes in either demand component are shown to involve sympathetic movements of the other. Variability of output underscores the fact that output enters as a parameter in the asset demand.

Three "Keynesian" models are introduced. The first is characterized by an infinitely elastic demand for idle money. Equilibrium requires variability of output, which brings saving to equality with investment at the existing-asset market rate of interest. Once-for-all changes in the money supply, whether caused by open-market operations or fiscal deficits, result in equal changes in idle balances only; active balances and money income are not altered. Shifts in saving and investment react on output and prices, but not on the rate of interest. Whether saving and investment are a demand and supply of securities or idle balances is shown to be completely immaterial to the equilibrium of the system, which in any case is characterized by aggregate saving-investment equality. In the second Keynesian model the demand for idle money is downward sloping, but the supply is now infinitely elastic. This model is virtually identical to the first one in regard to the impact of monetary disturbances. In the final model both saving and investment are totally insensitive to the interest rate; the supply and demand for idle balances resume their normal form. The latter functions determine the market rate of interest, but a unique output again equilibrates saving and investment. While the interest rate is now variable, the response to disturbances is fundamentally the same as that of the other two Keynesian systems.

CHAPTER X

The Theory of Interest and Prices: A Restatement and a Critique

This chapter will summarize the theory of interest and prices developed throughout the book. The summary is followed by a critical review of alternative theories of Patinkin and Keynes, the latter as represented in both the *Treatise* and the *General Theory*. We then re-evaluate the debate between Keynes and Pigou on the existence of underemployment equilibrium. The chapter concludes with a survey of policy implications of the analysis.

A. INTEREST AND PRICES: A RECAPITULATION

The rate of interest is the yield on securities and is determined by the aggregate supply and demand for securities. Supply and demand are the sum of the flow variables—namely, that portion of saving and investment which are a (new) demand and supply, respectively, of securities, plus the existing-security components. In a zero interval production, saving, and investment are non-existent, and the existing-asset schedules are the sole determinants of the interest rate. Thus at any instant the existing-asset market is always in equilibrium. With the passage of time all security components contribute to the determination of interest—in accordance with their relative size and elasticity. In any period, the interest rate moves to a level midway between the equilibrium yields given independently by the flow and the opening stock schedules. If the flow equilibrium is above the stock, a net excess supply of new securities is added to the existing schedules, and the rate of interest rises. If the flow equilibrium is below the stock, a net excess new demand is added to the existing schedules, and the rate of interest falls.

We assume initially that the real saving and investment functions are constant. Saving and investment vary only with the interest rate and are independent of all other variables, including prices and the value of assets. Output is assumed to be fixed. For the present, we also assume that saving and investment are wholly a demand and supply of securities. This, together with constant output, will maintain a stable equilibrium price level. The invariant saving and investment schedules accordingly determine an equilibrium or "natural" rate of interest toward which the market rate continually moves. Dynamic equilibrium is characterized by a constant rate of interest at which the stock and flow security markets are in balance, both individually and in the aggregate.

Each of the security functions also has a monetary (or, less precisely, a "loanable-funds") counterpart: saving and investment are, respectively, a supply of active balances (i.e., funds originating in the flow of income), and a demand to use balances actively (by payment as income); the complement of existing-security supply and demand is the supply and demand for idle balances. When the securities market is in stock-flow equilibrium, the supply and demand for both active and idle balances are thus also in equilibrium. In disequilibrium, the temporary imbalance between new-security supply and demand is manifested in a net desire to change the supply of active balances. At the same time the movement of the interest rate changes the quantity of idle balances demanded. The changes in the quantities of active and idle balances are equal and complementary. For example, when the interest rate is below the natural, excess new securities raise the rate of interest and dislodge idle balances, which are then activated. If the interest rate is above the natural, excess new-security demand lowers the rate and supplies active balances to meet the induced increase in the quantity of idle balances demanded. Equilibrium is thus characterized by an interest rate equal to the natural, and a division of cash balances between idle and active uses at which all supplies and demands are equal. The distribution of balances determines the price level.

Granted that the equilibrium interest rate is determined by new-security supply and demand, it is not surprising that the equilibrating force acting on a non-equilibrium yield is *excess* new-security supply or demand. Whether the price level, which is involved in the monetary equilibrium, is also a dynamic force propelling the market rate of interest, depends on whether the money supply is dichotomized into idle and active uses. It is, in fact, widely assumed that the price level, through its impact on real balances and the existing demand for securities, creates equilibrating movements in the rate of interest. But a rigorous analysis of the stock-flow interaction reveals that the price level may be quite neutral in this respect. This is precisely the result of interpreting the idle-active relationships as changes in the demand for a non-dichotomized money supply, the asset demand for which is interest-elastic. The fundamental point is that to asset holders a change in real balances is always, in the first instance, a transfer of *nominal* balances: *to* entrepreneurs in exchange for *excess new securities*, in the inflationary adjustment; *from* savers in exchange for *excess existing securities*, in the deflationary process. The changes in nominal balances and securities are equal and offsetting. Since the security change, originating in the investment-saving gap, is the initiating force, it is improper to attribute to the concomitant change in real balances a supplementary influence on the interest rate. However, when the price level responds sympathetically to the transfer of nominal balances, asset holders *may* experience a further change in real balances which reacts independently on the rate of interest. This will occur if, and only if, there is a functional distinction between idle and active money. For then the movement of the price level, in proportion to the active increment, leaves the value of active money constant while causing a net change in the value of idle holdings that are isolated from the income stream. The net change in real balances is a change in wealth which reacts on the existing demand for securities and the market rate of interest. But if money is not dichotomized, prices and asset-holder balances move proportionately, without altering the value of the undifferentiated total stock of money.

From this it follows that any net tendency of savers to by-pass securities and accumulate cash balances, or of firms to finance investment by directly dishoarding, will cause the price level constantly to fall or rise and the interest rate, in the dichotomized system, to move away from the natural rate at the intersection of new-security supply and demand. If savers cause a continuing net addition to idle money and a fall in the price level, real idle balances increase and the interest rate falls. Given real responses, a dynamic equilibrium is reached in which the market rate is constant at a level below the natural rate; the excess new-security supply is balanced by an excess existing-security demand generated by the increase in real balances. Aggregate saving exceeds aggregate investment. If entrepreneurs cause net dishoarding, the price level continually rises and the market rate is stabilized above the natural rate; the excess new-security demand is matched by a constant excess existing-security supply. Aggregate saving is below aggregate investment. But in the non-dichotomized system the change in the price level and real balances can have no such effect on the interest rate, which remains at the natural level. Aggregate saving and investment again are unequal.

The equilibrium price level, or rate of change of prices, thus depends on saving and investment. The new-security demand and supply components determine the natural rate of interest. In the first instance the existing-asset market adapts to this by an appropriate division between idle and active balances, which determines the level of prices. The remainder of saving and investment, a demand and supply of idle balances, causes prices to diverge from their equilibrium at some constant rate of change over time. In the dichotomized system this stabilizes the interest rate above or below the natural rate. But in general, the causal relationship runs from interest to prices—both in the sense of equilibrium quantities, and of increments in each variable—and is not reciprocal. Under the present assumptions, there is no route by which the price *level*, in response to monetary or other changes, can influence saving, investment, and the natural rate of interest. However, *movements* in prices, and thus real balances, cause *movements* in the interest rate if money is dichotomized. There is, of course, no consideration here of changing expectations generated by the price level on the demand for assets; the prices of a given period are expected to prevail indefinitely.

This entire relationship between the price level and the rate of interest is due to the interest elasticity of the demand for money. This is readily apparent when we consider the classical model, in which the supply and demand for idle balances are zero, or—avoiding the dichotomy—the asset demand has zero interest elasticity. The existing supply and demand for securities are thus identically equal. The natural rate is again determined independently by saving and investment. But now the existing-asset market need not be reconciled to this rate through changes in security supply or demand, in idle and active balances (if the distinction exists), and in the price level. Instead, prices are determined via a simple quantity-theory or Cambridge equation in which all money is active, and V or k is independent of the rate of interest. In the absence of outside disturbances, the interest rate in this system cannot depart even momentarily from the level set by saving and investment. Shifts in either function lead instantaneously to the new natural rate. There is no idle money (or interest-elastic asset demand) which will finance a discrepancy between saving and investment, impede the movement of the interest rate to the natural level, and cause prices to change. There can also be no rationalization for saving to be permanently directed at anything other than securities, or investment to be financed other then by issuing securities, since money has lost its asset function. The price level is thus constant over time.

No meaningful analysis of new and old securities can disregard the "real" variables that determine the value of these assets: the capital stock and its rate of return. Only a genuine exchange economy, in which security flows are absent and all stocks are constant, can legitimately avoid explicit reference to capital. Even a stationary state, in which any displacement of the interest rate stimulates positive or negative flows, must support its financial analysis with an account of ex post investment. We have shown that if the real demand for money is relatively insensitive to autonomous wealth changes, the "financial" explanation of interest and prices—i.e., the account of money and security stocks and flows—is entirely adequate. Any changes in the value of securities occasioned by capital will then stimulate approximately equal changes in the existing demand for securities. There is thus no effect on the market rate of interest, the saving-investment gap, and the price level. However, if the demand for money is relatively responsive to wealth, the existing-security equilibrium and the entire money-security interaction depend critically on the degree of capital accumulation. The *a priori* likelihood that in adjustment processes the "real" variables will cause unanticipated changes in security value is almost certain. These variables alter security value by creating changes in the income (dividend) per share. The latter is the product of the return to capital and the capital-security ratio. For given saving and investment functions, the return to capital is constant only if ex post investment, impervious to the efforts of both households and firms to change it, remains at its pre-disturbance level. The capital-security ratio moves in accordance with capital and security increments whose ratio is a function of the real price of securities. Security prices, in turn, are subject to constant fluctuations owing to variability of the return to capital, the market rate of interest, and the degree of capital formation. The latter may range from zero to complete forced saving or investment; the exact amount which maintains stability of security income is itself highly variable over the course of the adjustment process.

Whether the behavior of capital is a crucial constituent, or merely a descriptive supplement to the financial adjustment, it serves as the foundation for the theory of wealth. The latter may be of interest on its own account, or because of the inverse saving-wealth relation, the analysis of which can now be carried out rigorously. This relation, invoked by Pigou as a reply to the Keynesian underemployment doctrine, has typically involved real balances only. Since Metzler, securities are now also included in theoretical models, but the only security changes considered are those caused by external disturbances. As a rule, no serious reckoning is made of security changes generated by the internal adaptive mechanism. As we have seen, such security analysis cannot be separated from the theory of capital.

The saving-wealth relation creates an equilibrium in which saving and new-security demand constantly decrease in response to the growth of capital. The natural rate and the market rate both rise, though the former is above the latter. This stimulates a perpetually rising price level, which reduces real balances and retards the growth of wealth and the increase in the natural rate. The inflation may or may not add to the movement of the market rate. The general relevance of the saving-wealth relation to the theory of interest and prices is that the natural rate is dependent on both stock and flow variables. Among the stock variables are real balances. But the relationship between money, saving, and the natural rate is complex. A given monetary change may raise or lower saving (relative to trend), thereby lowering or raising the natural rate. The outcome depends on the degree of forced saving or investment in the adjustment process, and the interest elasticities of saving and investment. In any case the relation between interest and the monetary variables is now two-way, in the sense that prices determine the value of money, which conditions saving and the natural rate. The determination of the nominal stock of money influences capital and the value of securities, which also react on saving and the natural rate.

If we relax the assumption of fixed output, saving and the flow equilibrium are again determined by a stock variable—this time, the capital stock only. The growth of output lowers prices directly. Indirectly, it adds to the deflation by increasing saving and new-security demand. This causes the natural and the market rate both to fall, the former leading the latter. The price level may or may not accelerate the decline of the market rate. Monetary changes, by altering the stock of capital, again share in the determination of the natural rate.

What is most important for dynamic analysis is that the basic character of the stock-flow interaction of money and securities is independent of the saving-wealth and saving-output relations. The latter shift the excess new-security supply or demand functions, altering the final equilibrium and the speed with which it is reached following a disturbance. But nothing in the essential nature of the process is changed. The ability of the price level to act as an equilibrator of the interest rate again depends only on whether money is dichotomized.

We turn now to alternative explanations of the adjustment process and the dynamic determinants of interest and prices. I shall argue that alternative explanations spring less from a genuinely different view of the monetary process than from a failure to see clearly the main macroeconomic relationships. In general, alternative or opposing views (1) deny that saving and investment can act directly on the market rate of interest, (2) fail to consider that money serves as a medium of exchange against current output, (3) fail to consider that money serves as a store of value.

B. PATINKIN AND THE REAL-BALANCE EFFECT

The most serious challenge of recent years to the type of stock-flow analysis advanced in this book is that of Patinkin in *Money, Interest, and Prices*. It is difficult in a limited space to summarize his monetary theory, capturing the breadth and imagination that characterize his entire work. Nevertheless, I shall try to outline the elements of his analysis that are most directly relevant to the framework of this study.[1]

---

[1] See also the summary and the references cited by Harry G. Johnson in "Monetary Theory and Policy," *American Economic Review*, Vol. LII (June, 1962), pp. 337–41.

In the early chapters of his book Patinkin analyzes the equilibrium of an exchange economy consisting of money, commodities, and bonds. Real balances, like other assets, are held for their utility. An increase in real balances lowers their utility, relative to other assets, and stimulates a money expenditure on goods and bonds[2] until their money values have increased proportionately. This assumes, of course, the absence of distribution effects and of money illusion (the "homogeneity postulate"). The impact of the change in money is named the "real-balance effect," which "measures the influence on demand of a change in real balances, other things being held constant" (page 21). Patinkin adds, "...the assumption that there exists a real-balance effect...is the *sine qua non* of monetary theory. For...in the absence of this effect the absolute level of money prices...is indeterminate."[3] Patinkin generalizes his system to a production economy (Chapter IV), though this entails little more than extending the instantaneous (or one-week) equilibrium over time. Commodities are now reproduced and consumed, and new lending and borrowing generate additional bonds. But the picture of equilibrium is essentially unchanged, and the features of the exchange economy that Patinkin regards as important ("the invariance of relative prices and the rate of interest under a change in the amount of money" [page 60]) are retained. Patinkin himself stresses the great generality of the analysis of the exchange economy.[4] In fact, a number of passages in the first five chapters seem to indicate that he is not greatly concerned in distinguishing between the two systems at any time. In Chapter II, an analysis of an exchange economy consisting of money and commodities only, he refers to the

---

[2] Patinkin assumes that *real* bond holdings are constant, the nominal supply being increased along with money balances (*Money, Interest, and Prices* [Evanston, Ill.: Row, Peterson & Co., 1956], p. 58). In the macroeconomic analysis (Part II), he assumes that the supply of bonds is automatically varied so that "the nominal amount of bonds outstanding can always be kept equal to the current value of the firms' assets" (*ibid.*, p. 141, n. 13). The bonds thereby take on the essential characteristics of our equity security.

[3] *Ibid.*, p. 22. This particular quotation refers to an exchange economy consisting of money and commodities only. It thus has reference to a real-balance effect on commodities. However, as Patinkin soon makes clear, the statement is fully applicable to a production economy containing money, commodities, and bonds. Technically, it is only necessary that there be a real-balance effect with respect to commodities or bonds, not both (*ibid.*, p. 22, n. 13). But Patinkin argues that the real-balance effect on commodities is both empirically and theoretically defensible, even though not logically essential.

[4] *Ibid.*, pp. 60–61. On p. 61, n. 25, he writes: "These paragraphs make clear the untenability of the position—recently endorsed by D. H. Robertson—that there are, from the viewpoint of monetary theory, intrinsic differences between an exchange and a production economy." He then refers to Robertson's, "More Notes on the Rate of Interest," *Review of Economic Studies*, Vol. XXI(1953–54), pp. 136–37, to which we also refer!

real value of the latter as "*real income*" (page 19; italics mine). He begins Chapter IV, the extension to a production economy, by writing, ". . . the value of any week's endowment of commodities is analogous to the *income* of that week" (page 47; italics mine). Finally, on page 69, "Assume now that the individual's money income *or* initial holdings of money are increased . . ." (italics mine). In describing the formal properties of the model, Patinkin clearly is not deeply interested in differentiating between money holdings, assets, and income as such. By his own statement, Patinkin asserts that the real-balance effect—the influence of money balances on expenditure—is *identical* with the saving (or consumption)-real-balance relation of Pigou (page 21, note 11). For the latter the real-balance influence on spending was in fact that of a supplemental *wealth* variable, as distinguished from other variables, including the flow of income.[5] For Patinkin the real-balance effect is really much more universal—it provides a "systematic dynamic analysis" of the way in which the economy is "propelled" from one equilibrium to another, following a monetary increase (page 100), and it is a force "stabilizing the economy at this new position once it is reached" (page 101).

Patinkin is thus entirely consistent when he attacks the traditional dichotomy between the real and monetary sectors; namely, a commodity sector in which supply and demand depend only upon, and determine, relative prices; and a monetary sector which determines the absolute level of prices (page 107). In his own words:

For to say that the demand functions of the real sector are not affected by changes in the absolute price level—that is, to assert that they satisfy the "homogeneity postulate"[6]—is to imply that they are not affected by changes in the real value of cash balances. But it is precisely on this real-balance effect that the quantity theory depends for the inflationary impact of a monetary increase!

. . . More generally, if the function of monetary theory is to explain the determination of the absolute price level, then the "homogeneity postulate"—or, equivalently, absence of "money illusion" in the sense of the

---

[5] See the references cited on p. 305, n. 31 above, including the paper by Patinkin himself. Patinkin's misuse of the saving-wealth relationship is noted clearly in the interesting article by E. J. Mishan, "A Fallacy in the Interpretation of the Cash Balance Effect," *Economica*, N.S., Vol. XXV (May, 1958), pp. 106–18.

[6] Patinkin is using the term, "homogeneity postulate," in the sense of the real-monetary dichotomy, which he considers to be invalid. His own use of that term is with reference to the "absence of money illusion as insensitivity to changes in the absolute level of *accounting*—and not *money*—prices . . ." (*Money, Interest, and Prices*, p. 107, n. 32).

foregoing dichotomy—is the antithesis of all monetary theory. For let the assumptions of the dichotomy obtain. Assume now that an initial position of equilibrium is disturbed in such a way as to cause an equi-proportionate change in all money prices. Since this does not change relative prices, the "homogeneity postulate" implies that none of the demand functions in the real sector are thereby affected. Hence, since the commodity markets of this sector were initially in equilibrium, they must continue to be so. By Walras' Law, so must the money market. Thus the equi-proportionate departure of money prices from any given equilibrium level creates no market forces—that is, creates no amounts of excess demand anywhere in the system—which might cause money prices to return to their initial level. Hence if any set of money prices is an equilibrium set, any multiple of this set must also be an equilibrium set. The absolute price level is indeterminate.[7]

If we are to take seriously Patinkin's own ready identification of commodities and income, then a change in the absolute price level is a change in money income. I cannot imagine Cantabrigian Man or his American counterpart, Fisherian Man, taking this lying down—under any circumstances! Obviously his expenditures will respond positively to the changed income, thereby restoring the absolute level of prices and the desired ratio of money to money income and expenditures. The price level is entirely determinate. Patinkin may reply that we are really employing a "real-balance" effect. But we are definitely not invoking the relation between money and other *assets* defined for an exchange economy (an existing-asset market), or the saving-wealth relation of Pigou. Instead, we are viewing money as the medium of exchange against current output. What is involved is the positive *income*-consumption-saving relation, stressed by Robertson, Pigou, and Keynes, and dismissed by Patinkin as mechanical and incomplete (page 98). One may argue that *empirically* the consumption function is incomplete, and should be supplemented by inclusion of assets.[8] But *logically* it is an entirely adequate explanation of why households spend and save.

---

[7] *Ibid.*, pp. 107–8.

[8] Judging by the success of recent investigators in refining the income concept and measuring the consumption function, the weight of evidence would appear to support income rather than wealth as the best predictor of expenditures. See, for example, Milton Friedman, *A Theory of the Consumption Function* (Princeton, N. J.: Princeton University Press, 1957); and Modigliani and Brumberg, "Utility Analysis and the Consumption Function: An Interpretation of Cross-Section Data," in *Post-Keynesian Economics* (New Brunswick, N. J.: Rutgers University Press, 1954), pp. 388–436. For a summary of the empirical evidence on the consumption-wealth relation, see Ackley, *Macroeconomic Theory* (New York: The Macmillan Co., 1961), pp. 269–82.

The most revealing differences between Patinkin's analysis and my own arise in his discussion of Say's Identity and the financial character of saving and investment. Patinkin correctly observes that, empirically, saving is a demand both for securities and additional cash balances, and investment is financed both by issuing securities and drawing down cash balances (page 188). However, he finds that this dual financial character of saving and investment is also logically necessary for determinacy of the price level:

> Indeed, the very existence of a money economy precludes the simultaneous identity of savings with the demand for bonds, and investment with their supply. For we have already seen that the excess of investment over savings is necessarily equal to the excess of commodities demanded over supply. Hence if this simultaneous identity were to hold, the excess demand for commodities would then necessarily equal the excess supply of bonds. That is, individuals would always plan to finance the additional purchase of commodities by the sale of bonds, and vice versa. Accordingly, they would never plan to change the level of their cash balances; that is, their excess demand for these balances would be identically zero; or, in still other words, Say's Identity would hold. But then... this would mean that any arbitrary departure of prices from their equilibrium level would not create any excess demand or supply of money, and hence would not generate any corrective market forces to return the economy to its original equilibrium position. Hence the equilibrium level of money prices would be indeterminate....[9]

A sharp distinction between stock and flow variables will restore the determinacy of the price level. Consider an increase in saving, which is directed wholly at securities. Security prices are bid up, and the interest rate is lowered. As we have seen (Chapter VIII-B[1]), this stimulates a supply of new *and* old securities. The excess old-security supply is the complement of the excess demand for idle balances (or for money in its store-of-value function). Thus even though savers themselves acquire securities, as they intended, the reduction in the rate of interest has dislodged *existing* securities and increased the demand for cash balances by the sellers of these issues. The lower interest rate raises the demand for money in the sense of a movement *along* the liquidity-preference schedule.[10] By

---

[9] *Money, Interest, and Prices,* p. 188. Patinkin offers a definition of Say's Identity on p. 119.

[10] We use the term "liquidity preference" to mean the demand for money as a function of the interest rate, expressed in real-value units. It corresponds to the "bearishness" function of Keynes' *Treatise,* and the L_2 schedule of the *General Theory.* Haberler was the first to limit the use of "liquidity preference" to this component of the demand for money (*Prosperity and Depression* [Cambridge, Mass.: Harvard University Press, 1958], p. 210).

the same token, "any arbitrary departure of prices from their equilibrium" in a bond model would change the value of cash balances, creating an excess supply or demand for money. This we know is the counterpart of an excess existing-demand or supply of securities, which changes the interest rate and thereby the price level. To Patinkin prices are indeterminate because he fails to distinguish between the flow demand for securities, the alternative to which is consumption, and the stock demand for securities, to which the demand for money is indeed the alternative. In any disequilibrium situation it is impossible to prevent the stock and flow variables from interacting and reacting on each other. Hence all are relevant.[11]

In view of his casual treatment of variables in regard to their stock and flow properties, it is no surprise that Patinkin's dynamic analysis of monetary change does not depend critically on the way in which the change is brought about. Whether it is a fiscal deficit or an open-market purchase that raises the supply of money, the resulting process relies exclusively on the equilibrating force of the real-balance effect. Thus if the government increases its commodity expenditures for one period, financing them with new money, any inflation following its departure is due entirely to the impact of the additional real balances (pages 159–60). The latter raise private expenditures on goods and bonds. The resulting increase in bond prices lowers the yield and stimulates investment spending. The ensuing inflation reduces real balances, causing the increase in expenditures to taper off. "In brief, as the rising price level eliminates the initial increase in the *real* quantity of money in the economy, it also eliminates the excess demand for bonds (excess supply of loans) which temporarily depressed the rate of interest" (pages 161–62). Patinkin himself underscores the basic similarity of all monetary processes by explicitly comparing the behavior of the interest rate—falling at first, and then rising—to the Wicksellian analysis (page 160). But Wicksell is concerned with monetary changes originating in the banking system, and not at all with unbalanced government budgets.

---

[11] Patinkin's rejection of the distinction between stock and flow functions reaches a zenith in his discussion of the infinitely elastic demand for money (*Money, Interest, and Prices*, pp. 146–49 and 245–49). He refuses to acknowledge the possibility that liquidity preference may in fact become perfectly flat at a low rate of interest. In the name of "general-equilibrium" analysis he mixes stocks and flows to the point where the liquidity-preference schedule, horizontal or otherwise, is completely overwhelmed by varied and sundry other functions. I consider this analysis to be a denial of the validity of the entire Hicksian *IS-LL* (or *LM*, as it is more commonly designated now) framework.

Our own account of the fiscal deficit is quite different (see Chapter VIII-C[1]*a*). The new money is received as current income, and this is the force that stimulates additional spending at the going turnover rate of transactions balances. If the money supply is non-dichotomized, as it is for Patinkin, that is all there is to it. The interest rate will not change, granted that money saving and investment (or rather, that part which is a demand and supply of new securities) rise equally and synchronously during the inflation. At this level of analysis I would consider this a reasonable, if not a necessary, assumption. However, I have noted the possibility of a temporary excess of money saving over investment during inflation owing to delays in price adjustments (pages 108–9). This would cause a temporary decline in the interest rate. For Patinkin the reduction in interest is inescapable, since the supply of bonds available to purchasers has all the attributes of a fixed stock. At no time does he consider the possibility that the supply or value of securities might increase *pari passu* with the demand.[12] Curiously, the demand for bonds in the last quotation is identified with the supply of loans—which has all the flavor of a flow.

Patinkin's account of the process generated by an open-market purchase (pages 208 and 231–32) or an increase in bank credit (page 162) is very nearly the same as that of the deficit. In this case the initial impact is on the rate of interest, which is reduced. But with new balances in the economy, the process proceeds as before. The rise in the price level again lowers real balances and raises the rate of interest. But now we must ask Patinkin whether the banks purchase new or old securities. If new ones, then this is the classical or Wicksellian version of credit expansion (see Chapter IX-C). The market rate remains below the natural rate only while the bank is actually purchasing securities or extending loans. The interest rate subsequently rises, not because of the rise in the price level and the reduction in real balances, but because the bank ends its purchase activities. And the price level rises, not because of a real-balance effect, but because the purchase of new securities sends money directly into capital expenditures, which augment the *incomes* and spending of the factors of production.

On the other hand, if the banks acquire old securities, then this is a purchase on wealth account. The increase in real balances

---

[12]On p. 145 he writes, "As in the case of bonds, the demand and supply . . . are for a stock and not a flow."

and the decrease in interest entail a downward movement *along* the liquidity-preference function. The subsequent rise in interest and prices is due to an excess of investment over saving which in some degree is an excess supply of new securities. This is exchanged for idle (or asset-money) balances at a lower price and higher yield. The released funds are spent on capital projects, raising money income and commodity prices. Since Patinkin's money supply is not dichotomized, the inflation has no further effect on real balances of asset holders and thus on the rate of interest.

I would argue that Patinkin's model, which includes a stock-supply and demand for bonds and a liquidity-preference function, commits his banks to a purchase of existing securities. As such, the sense in which real balances stimulate expenditures and the rise in the price level is obscure. If Patinkin really has reference to the saving-wealth relation of Pigou and others, then the real-balance effect does not change the basic nature of the adjustment process (see Chapter VIII-I[1]). If Patinkin instead has reference to direct outlays—i.e., a direct expenditure of the new balances on commodities, by-passing the securities market—then there are new difficulties. These are described in Chapter VIII (pages 309–12). From Patinkin's point of view, not the least difficulty is that a direct outlay, following a purchase on wealth account, implies a reduction in the real demand for cash balances. This will have the effect of raising prices proportionately more than money, destroying the proportionality that he so frequently refers to.[13] Another problem, analytically more serious, is that a reduction in the demand for real balances leads to an equal reduction in supply, given a non-dichotomized stock of money (see Chapter IX-D[5]*b*). There is no route by which the inflation can raise the rate of interest. The market rate remains permanently below the natural rate, and equilibrium is unattainable.[14]

In describing open-market operations, Patinkin carefully notes wealth effects that occur here, as opposed to other types of monetary change (pages 208 and 231–32). In a purchase, for example, the community loses securities to the central bank. Since the inflation tends to reduce real balances to their pre-disturbance value, there is a net wealth loss that raises saving and lowers the equi-

---

[13]See, for example, *Money, Interest, and Prices*, p. 180. See also above pp. 112–14, including n. 17.

[14]Cf. Horwich, "Real Assets and the Theory of Interest," *Journal of Political Economy*, Vol. LXX (April, 1962), p. 168.

librium rate of interest. At no point does Patinkin consider that the adaptive process might to some extent generate new securities to replace those purchased by the bank.[15] Though occasionally he refers to changes in the supply of bonds, it is never clear whether these are new or old ones. In any case, if they are new ones, they are unaccounted for in the new equilibrium. His very explicit assumption that the capital stock is fixed (page 126) is, of course, incompatible with any change in the real value of outstanding bonds (other than through interest movements) as a result of the adjustment process.

C. THE *TREATISE*: THE PREPONDERANCE OF EXISTING SECURITIES

A number of outstanding writers have cited the relatively great magnitude of existing securities as their reason for ignoring saving and investment as dynamic determinants of interest. This explanation seems to originate in Volume I of the *Treatise on Money*. Thus Keynes writes:

But the volume of trading in financial instruments, *i.e.* the *activity* of financial business, is not only highly variable but has no close connection with the volume of output whether of capital-goods or of consumption-goods; for the current output of fixed capital is small compared with the existing stock of wealth, which in the present context we will call the volume of *securities* (excluding from this liquid claims on cash); and the activity with which these securities are being passed round from hand to hand does not depend on the rate at which they are being added to. Thus in a modern Stock-Exchange-equipped community the turnover of currently produced fixed capital is quite a small proportion of the total turnover of securities.

Nor does the price of existing securities depend at all closely over short periods either on the cost of production or on the price of new fixed capital. For existing securities largely consist of properties which cannot be quickly reproduced, of natural resources which cannot be reproduced at all, and of the capitalised value of future income anticipated from the possession of quasi-monopolies or peculiar advantages of one kind or another.[16]

---

[15] I have detailed my views on this issue in "Real Assets and the Theory of Interest," *op. cit.*

[16] Keynes, *A Treatise on Money*, Vol. I (London: Macmillan & Co., Ltd., 1950), pp. 248–49. For a similar point of view see also: Hugh Townshend, "Liquidity-Premium and the Theory of Value," *Economic Journal*, Vol. XLVII (March, 1937), pp. 157–69; T. Scitovsky, "A Study of Interest and Capital," *Economica*, N.S., Vol. VII (August, 1940), pp. 296 and 301; L. R. Klein, *The Keynesian Revolution* (New York: The Macmillan Co., 1947), p. 123; B. F. Haley, "Value and Distribution," in *A Survey of Contemporary Economics*, Vol. I, ed. by H. S. Ellis (Philadelphia: The Blakiston Co., 1948), p. 41; L. A. Metzler, "Wealth, Saving, and the Rate of Interest," *Journal of Political Economy*, Vol. LIX

One may differ with Keynes about the uniqueness of existing investments. In fact, in other passages he himself sees ample opportunity to reproduce existing capital.[17] Nevertheless, he adheres consistently to the position that security prices and interest are not directly influenced by new-security demand and supply originating in saving and investment. This is perhaps even clearer in an earlier passage:

> But the decision as to holding bank-deposits or securities relates, not only to the current increment to the wealth of individuals, but also to the whole block of their existing capital. Indeed, since the current increment is but a trifling proportion of the block of existing wealth, it is but a minor element in the matter.[18]

In the *Treatise,* as in the *General Theory,* Keynes views the interest rate (or the price of securities) as determined by the supply and demand for idle balances ("savings-deposits"[19]) or, alternatively, the supply and demand for existing securities:

> The price-level of investments as a whole, and hence of new investments, is that price-level at which the desire of the public to hold savings-deposits is equal to the amount of savings-deposits which the banking system is willing and able to create.[20]

However, Keynes earlier had defined equilibrium as involving equality between the market and the natural rate of interest. The market rate is the rate "which actually prevails," while "...the natural-rate of interest is the rate at which saving and the value of investment are exactly balanced."[21]   But only movements in the

---

(April, 1951), pp. 102 and 115; H. G. Johnson, "Some Cambridge Controversies in Monetary Theory," *Review of Economic Studies,* Vol. XIX, No. 2 (1951–52), p. 92; and T. Balogh, "Dangers of the New Orthodoxy," *The Banker,* June, 1956, p. 351.

[17] *A Treatise on Money,* Vol. I, pp. 211–12, 257, and 302.

[18] *Ibid.,* p. 141.

[19] Keynes has a three-way classification of money: income, business, and savings-deposits (see *ibid.,* pp. 35–6 and 149–50). The latter have the attributes of idle money, as we define it, while the former are clearly active balances. Business-deposits are an intermediate category. They are held by firms for contingencies, though they are readily used for factor payments, and thereby activated, if the interest rate should be reduced (*ibid.,* p. 266). The price level of consumption goods and of output as a whole is the product only of income-deposits and their velocity (*ibid.,* pp. 149–50).

[20] *Ibid.,* p. 143. Keynes uses the terms, "investments," "investment-goods," and "securities," interchangeably, though occasionally he distinguishes between them. Thus he writes on p. 253, "On the other hand, when security-prices are rising, this is likely—in general but not necessarily—to stimulate a rise in P', the price-level of *new* investment, and when security-prices are falling, the opposite is likely to be the case." He clearly has not made up his mind whether it is worth distinguishing between the capital stock and claims to the stock, which are in fact held by asset holders. His ambiguity on this is in large measure due to his observation that real security prices and investment *commodity* prices tend to move together—at least in the first instance.

[21] *Ibid.,* p. 155.

supply and demand for money can act directly on the market rate of interest. Thus in a boom sparked by an independent increase in the propensity to invest (Chapter 18),[22] the needed finance is provided by "a unanimity of bull sentiment leading to a decrease of the 'bear' position" (page 285). In other words, the funds are provided by a simultaneous independent decrease in the demand schedule for savings-deposits. Keynes does not impute to the increase in investment a direct impact on the market rate of interest, which releases idle balances.[23] At the same time, "a slight rise in bank-rate ...may serve to increase monetary facilities...either by increasing the velocities of circulation as a result of the enhanced cost of maintaining balances...or...by attracting gold from abroad" (pages 285–86). The increase in interest and the termination of the inflation are brought about when "...'bear' views...develop, with the result of augmenting the demand for money in the Financial Circulation and so reducing the supply of money for the Industrial Circulation" (page 290). This is an unambiguous rightward shift of liquidity preference. The upper turning point is also characterized by a further increase in bank-rate (page 291).

In describing the "*modus operandi*" of bank-induced changes in the money supply (Chapters 13 and 17), Keynes seems to alternate between a Wicksellian classical explanation and one that takes account of stocks as well as flows. The monetary change itself will be allocated both to idle and active balances. For example, a bank loan (Chapter 17) will go directly to business deposits, which, strictly speaking, are "idle" in the sense of being outside the income stream. Then,

Some part of this addition to the Business-deposits will probably find its way, more or less directly, into the hands of entrepreneurs, who are encouraged by the easier terms of borrowing, to be used by them to meet an increased earnings-bill $M_1 V_1$.... Thus a part of the new money will quickly find its way from M_2 into M_1, the Income-deposits....

The rest of the addition to the Business-deposits—which may conceivably amount in the first instance to the whole of the additional money—

---

[22] See, in particular, the description of the disturbance, *ibid.*, p. 282.

[23] Though avowedly writing in the spirit of the *Treatise*, R. S. Sayers does not hesitate to attribute to an increase in investment a direct effect on the rate of interest, which activates savings deposits (Sayers, *Modern Banking* [London: Oxford University Press, 1951], chap. x). First published in 1938, the monetary dynamics in this portion of the book are far superior to that of the *Treatise*. Unfortunately, Sayers has dropped the original Chapter 10 ("The Distribution of Deposits") from editions after 1951. For a similar and more detailed analysis see also the excellent account by Hayek in *The Pure Theory of Capital* (London: Routledge and Kegan Paul, Ltd., 1941), chaps. xxvi and xxvii, esp. pp. 356–73.

will fall into the hands of speculators and financiers, *i.e.* of persons who wish to buy commodities or securities with borrowed money. This will raise the price of securities, and the boom in securities thus brought about will probably increase the Stock Exchange turnover. Thus a part, but usually a very small part, of the new money will have to be retained in the Business-deposits B to look after the increased money-turnover of securities. Now for every buyer of a security (or commodity) there must be a seller. The seller may use the proceeds to buy some other security, in which case the rise in price of securities will spread from one category to another. But as the price of securities continues to rise, one or other of two things must, sooner or later, happen. It may be that this price-rise will furnish windfall profits to the producers of *new* investments, with the result that, *via* the new issue market or otherwise, increased funds will reach the hands of entrepreneurs for the purpose of increasing, or endeavouring to increase, the output of investments.[24]

This is a superb account of the stock-flow transfer of money from idle to active uses. But Keynes says nothing in this chapter about the forces returning the interest rate to its equilibrium. In fact, his view on this, as far as can be gathered from Chapter 13 ("The 'Modus Operandi' of Bank-Rate"), is entirely Wicksellian; namely, the market rate is controlled exclusively by saving, investment, and the direct action of the banking system:

> ...This means, in general, that the market-rate of interest cannot be continually held even a little below the natural-rate unless the volume of bank-money is being continually increased.[25]

Though Keynes has a good sense of the stock-flow money transfer, he does not see the simultaneous merger of new and old security markets and their impact on the interest rate. Indeed, his position regarding the relatively small magnitude of new issues prevents him from acknowledging it. Thus while transfers from

---

[24] *A Treatise on Money*, Vol. I, pp. 266–67. The other alternative referred to is the development of a net "bear" or "bull" sentiment regarding the further movement of security prices. For a similar account of the *modus operandi* of monetary change, see the essay of Joan Robinson, "The Rate of Interest," *Econometrica*, Vol. XIX (April, 1951), pp. 92–111, esp. 97–104 (reprinted in *The Rate of Interest and Other Essays* [London: Macmillan & Co., Ltd., 1952], pp. 3–30).

[25] *A Treatise on Money*, Vol. I, p. 198. I must add that I much prefer Wicksell's own account (*Lectures on Political Economy*, Vol. II [London: Routledge and Kegan Paul, Ltd., 1935], chap. iv) to Keynes' in Chapter 13 of the *Treatise*, "The 'Modus Operandi' of Bank-Rate." Though some passages in the latter are perfect gems in regard to the relation between monetary change, the rate of interest, and saving and investment, there are others in which Keynes is unclear about the connection between these variables. On p. 216 he points out that a change in bank rate "must be associated . . . by *some* alteration in the quantity of bank-money." But on pp. 219–20 he seems to equivocate on this point.

idle to active balances occur, they have the aura of direct and
deliberate movements (Chapter VIII-G), rather than the automatic
character of the transfer effect as we have described it (Chapter
IV-B). Keynes' direct transfers are mentioned explicitly in his
account of the investment boom, quoted above. There are other
passages, regarding movements from the financial to the industrial
circulation, that lend themselves to the same interpretation.[26]

The *Treatise* was a serious and brilliant contribution to the
development of stock-flow monetary theory. Where Wicksell gave
us the definitive analysis of flows,[27] Keynes went beyond this to take
account of the existing-asset market: existing securities and money
as a store of value, the demand for which depends upon the rate of
interest.[28] The introduction of an asset demand for money merely
recognizes the conditions of a developed economy: the capital stock
is so great, and both the return to capital and the rate of interest
are reduced to the point where the willingness to *hold* that stock
is interest-elastic. Keynes defines and differentiates between stock
and flow variables with rigor and clarity. At times he integrates
them, but not completely. He perceives the transfer of money
between wealth and income account. But his theory of interest is
inadequate. In his own framework the equilibrium interest rate,

---

[26] For example, *A Treatise on Money*, pp. 252–54. In this section Keynes describes
shifts in the liquidity-preference schedule and their impact on the price level.

[27] This is not to say that Wicksell does not occasionally hint at stock-flow relations.
Thus in *Interest and Prices* (London: Macmillan & Co., Ltd., 1936), first published in 1898,
Wicksell describes a bank loan in which "the money is used for durable investment"
(*ibid.*, p. 95). The bank-induced fall in interest initially causes a sympathetic increase in
"the value of all permanent capital goods, for instance of dwelling-houses . . ." (*ibid.*,
p. 96). This price increase "is based on the assumption that the net earnings of houses
(in particular rents) remain unaltered in the future" (*ibid.*, p. 96). The "inflation," up
to this point, is thus merely a reflection of the lower interest rate as it spreads throughout
the existing capital-goods market. Then, "wages, . . . rents will rise . . . . This will
bring about a further rise in the price of houses . . . and so indirectly a further rise in
the prices of everything else" (*ibid.*, p. 96). The cause of this inflation is presumably,
though not explicitly, the monetary increase itself. Following this is an unmistakable
flow response: "An abnormally *large* amount of investment will now probably be devoted
to durable goods" (*ibid.*, p. 96).

[28] The point is frequently made that Cambridge economists, long before Keynes,
recognized that the demand for money depends upon the rate of interest. See, for example,
Marshall, *Money, Credit and Commerce* (London: Macmillan & Co., Ltd., 1923), pp.
44–45, and Lavington, *The English Capital Market* (London: Methuen and Co., 1921), p. 30.
However, I think it is fair to say that Keynes was the first to explore systematically the
static and dynamic implications of that relationship. There is certainly little in Marshall's
treatment of interest and prices that does not conform to the "classical" or Wicksellian
model. Robertson, of course, was well aware that money might be hoarded, and that the
demand for money depends on the rate of interest (cf. *Money* [London: Nisbet and Co.,
1946], p. 36). But his dynamic analysis of hoarding does not involve an interest-elastic
demand for money (cf. *Banking Policy and the Price Level* [London: Staples Press, Ltd.,
1949]).

determined by the supply and demand for money, must also equal the natural rate. But the explanation of the *process* by which the market and natural rates are brought together is unsatisfactory. In the investment boom the market rate is brought to the higher natural rate by *coincidental* shifts in the supply and demand for money. The demand shift reflects a changed psychological state on the part of asset holders. It also furnishes the funds to finance the increased investment. In the case of monetary change emanating from the banking system, Keynes reverts to the earlier—and for his purposes, inappropriate—Wicksellian model.

A modern writer, remarkably in the tradition of the *Treatise*, is Metzler.[29] His perception of the distinction between stocks and flows is not less than that of Keynes. But like Keynes, he, too, balks at their complete integration. His grounds are the same:

> I assume...that the securities market is dominated by transactions in old securities rather than by supply-and-demand conditions in the new-securities market. Specifically, I assume that security prices tend to rise whenever asset-holders on balance attempt to shift from money to securities and that security prices fall when asset-holders attempt a shift in the opposite direction.[30]

Metzler boldly identifies equilibrium of saving and investment with equality of the demand and supply of new securities.[31] He recognizes that the alternative to holding money is existing securities.[32] Moreover, he sees the commodity price level as the variable linking the market and the natural rates of interest: given the stock of money, there is some level of prices at which *real* balances and the demand for money are equal at the natural rate.[33] Now consider an increase in the supply of money through an open-market purchase. According to Metzler, this initially creates a new temporary equilibrium in private holdings of cash and securities. The money supply and the rate of interest move down along the

---

[29] "Wealth, Saving, and the Rate of Interest," *op. cit.*

[30] *Ibid.*, p. 115. See also p. 102 where Metzler asserts that new securities are "an exceedingly small fraction of the value of previously issued, or old, securities."

[31] *Ibid.*, p. 102. Metzler's specific statement is, ". . . in the absence of hoarding, equality between saving and investment implies equality between the supply of and the demand for new securities." The qualification in regard to hoarding would seem to be superfluous, for nowhere does Metzler indicate that net hoarding, reflected in constant shifts in the demand for money, characterizes his system in or out of equilibrium.

[32] *Ibid.*, pp. 102–4.

[33] *Ibid.*, p. 104. A major point of Metzler's article is, of course, that the natural rate is not entirely independent of the quantity of money. Thus there is a mutual determination between the two interest rates. However, this result, which depends on the saving-wealth relation (see Chapter VIII-I[1]), is not relevant to the present discussion.

prevailing liquidity-preference schedule.[34]   By implication, the added balances replace *existing* securities. The lower market rate then stimulates an excess of investment over saving which raises the commodity price level. The inflation causes real balances to fall below demand at the current market rate. In an effort to replenish their balances, asset holders sell existing securities. But the only result is that security prices fall, and the interest rate rises, until the community is willing to hold the reduced quantity of real balances.[35]

Metzler has apparently resolved the difficulty confronting Keynes: to explain the dynamic force returning the market rate to the natural level, while denying a direct impact to saving and investment on the market rate. For both Keynes and Metzler the investment-saving gap is the proximate cause of the rise in prices. But Metzler employs the price level itself, through its impact on real balances and the existing demand for securities, as the equilibrator of the interest rate. The price level is a much more reliable force—a built-in mechanism, in fact—as compared with Keynes' coincidental shifts in the demand schedule for money.

But Metzler has resolved one dilemma only to create another. His view that saving and investment are a demand and supply of new securities, an imbalance between which causes a rise in the price level but not the interest rate, fails to account for the *financing* of the inflation. Given the temporary equilibrium created by the direct impact of the purchase, inflation can occur only in response to a shift in the demand schedule for money, or a movement along the schedule because of a higher interest rate. In Metzler's

---

[34] *Ibid.*, p. 110. Metzler shifts the liquidity-preference schedule to the left as part of the direct impact of the open-market purchase (*ibid.*, p. 107 and pp. 109–10). It has never been clear to me why Metzler felt that this shift was necessary. He cites as the basis for it a desire of asset holders to maintain at each interest rate a fixed ratio of money to securities. Hence, upon losing securities to the bank, the demand-for-money schedule drops proportionately. But this is a questionable response. Metzler is arguing that the open-market purchase stimulates a decrease in *total* desired wealth, as reflected in the uncompensated movement of the liquidity-demand curve. Hence the desired allocation between assets takes aggregate wealth as a dependent variable, rather than an independently given restraint. This is reminiscent of Keynes' downward shift of the same function at the start of the investment boom (p. 418). As noted, this shift was a means of financing the investment. Since Metzler himself is faced with the problem of providing finance for inflation (pp. 422–23), his motivation for the shift may be the same as Keynes'.

[35] *Ibid.*, pp. 105, 110. Metzler does not spell out the dynamics of this quite as fully as I have here. But I have no serious doubt that this is the relationship he intended between the inflation, real balances, and the rate of interest. The process is, of course, entirely analogous to our own wealth effect on interest. However, we qualify it by recognizing the partially offsetting shift of the liquidity-demand schedule, and by limiting it to a dichotomized money supply. Metzler's balances are non-dichotomized. Cf. n. 39 below.

model an excess of investment over saving can only be interpreted as an excess supply of new securities; this clearly is not a shift in the demand for money. And since Metzler has denied that new securities can act directly on the interest rate, we are left without any wherewithal by which prices can be raised. In the absence of monetary changes of some kind actively contributing to and supporting it, we are even led to doubt that an *excess* of investment over saving can exist.[36]

Thus while Keynes is able, in some sense, to finance his inflationary process, Metzler is not. In these terms it is understandable why Metzler[37] readily conceded a criticism made by Wright;[38] namely, that the inflation is characterized not only by an excess of investment over saving, but also by direct monetary outlays on commodities. I take this to mean a reduction in the demand schedule for money. While this supplies a missing link in Metzler's inflationary process, it is not consistent with his earlier statement that the purchase creates a temporary equilibrium in the existing-asset market. There is no mechanism in the model to explain a subsequent direct shift from money into goods. Though analytically convenient, it is purely arbitrary. And it also undermines Metzler's dynamic interest theory; there can be no movement in the interest rate in response to equal reductions in the supply *and* demand for real balances.[39]

I submit that there is no resolution of the difficulties in the Keynes-Metzler dynamics short of imputing to saving and invest-

---

[36] There are occasional passages in the *Treatise* in which Keynes also seems to treat a saving-investment gap as a sufficient cause of price-level movements, *independently* of simultaneous changes in the quantity of money supplied or demanded. Thus in Vol. I, p. 185, he writes, "Bank-rate . . . is the instrument by which a disturbance is set up or equilibrium restored between the rates of saving and investment; for to raise it stimulates the one and retards the other, and conversely if it is reduced." Then in the succeeding sentence is the significant remark, "This does not preclude it from having secondary effects on other elements in the Fundamental Equations, in particular on the quantity of bank-money, the velocities of circulation, and the proportion of savings-deposits." Again on p. 191 is the statement, "But how far previous writers have perceived that to discourage investment relatively to saving is *in itself* calculated to reduce prices is more difficult to say." The italics are Keynes'.

[37] "A Reply," *Journal of Political Economy*, Vol. LX (June, 1952), p. 251.

[38] "Professor Metzler and the Rate of Interest," *Journal of Political Economy*, Vol. LX (June, 1952), pp. 247–48.

[39] Metzler's money supply, like Patinkin's, is not dichotomized into idle and active portions. Thus there is no opportunity for the inflation to reduce real *idle* balances, raising the market rate through that route (see Chapter VIII-G). Notice the similarity between the above discussion and our effort to rationalize Patinkin's real-balance effect on p. 415. I am indebted to R. W. Clower for pointing out to me the possible similarity between Patinkin's real-balance effect and Wright's direct outlays.

ment a direct impact on the market rate of interest. For both writers this dynamic force will explain the movement of both the interest rate and the price level in a manner that is completely effective, internally consistent, and implicitly contained in the structure of their models. The argument that the old securities market, by dint of superior size, dominates new-security flows and the market rate is itself internally contradictory. Both Keynes and Metzler attribute movements in the interest rate to movements in the old-securities schedules *or* their complements, the supply and demand for cash balances. We have seen repeatedly that the opposite side of the coin of excess *new*-security increments is changes in the supply of money as a store of value. Keynes and Metzler cannot deny to new securities power to act directly on the market rate without calling into question their own liquidity-preference theory of interest!

If excess new-security flows in fact exert only a feeble influence on interest, then by the same token, changes in real balances are equally inconsequential. This applies to increments in real balances due either to external or the adaptive internal forces, since the increments are related, if not actually equal in magnitude. For example, a given increase in nominal balances stimulates an inflation which decreases the value of these funds by an approximately equal amount. The value reduction is, of course, a function of the quantity of excess new-security flotations. One may wish to argue that the value changes take considerable *time*,[40] but they cannot in any case be discounted, or dissociated from the new-securities market.

The quantitative comparison between new and old security mar-

---

[40] Thomas Mayer estimates the time lag in monetary change to be from several months to almost a year ("The Inflexibility of Monetary Policy," *Review of Economics and Statistics*, Vol. XL [November, 1958], pp. 358–74). Let us hazard a guess on this important issue in terms of our own framework. In the first quarter of 1962 the annual rate of net private domestic investment was approximately 30 billion dollars (calculated from tables in the *Federal Reserve Bulletin*, July, 1962, pp. 898–99). If only 40 percent of this amount were financed by security issues, the monthly flow of new-security supply and demand would be one billion dollars. If, further, the absolute arc elasticity of each security-value schedule were unity, a 4 percent reduction in interest (e.g., from a level of 5.0 percent to 4.8 percent) would reduce demand to 960 million and raise supply to 1,040 million dollars. The gap, and thus the activation of balances, is 80 million dollars per month. Consider a monetary increase of 500 million dollars, which goes initially to idle balances and reduces interest by 4 percent (in the sense noted). If equilibrium is restored when, say, half of that amount is activated, the adjustment—on the assumption of a constant nominal transfer—will last just over three months. In fact, the rise in the interest rate will reduce the nominal transfer, while the rise in the price level will tend (though not invariably) to raise it (see Chapter IV-B[1] and D[2]).

kets is, in fact, an unreliable indication of the direct ability of either market to dominate the interest rate in a given period. For once the two-sidedness of the stock-flow adjustment is recognized, it is possible, through quantitative comparisons, to derive conflicting impressions as to the likely impact of saving and investment on the rate of interest. Consider an increase in saving. In any period this generates excess new-security demand which is added both to existing-security demand and the stock of idle or asset-money balances. Thus the direct effect of the saving increment on interest may be gauged by reference *either* to the stock of existing securities or of money. If the supply of money is dwarfed by the stock of securities (which represents all of capital), the excess saving is quantitatively much more impressive when compared with cash balances than with existing securities.[41] Even though the saving increment were relatively an infinitesimal addition to the securities market, it might at the same time be a substantial fraction of the existing supply and demand for money. Hence the comparison of market sizes yields contradictory evidence on the direct importance of saving and investment to the interest rate.

There is no question, in terms of the logical structure of a stock-flow model, that saving and investment must react directly on the market rate of interest. Nevertheless, can the apparently opposite impressions of their impact in any given period, such as we have just observed, be reconciled? They can by considering the absolute *slope* of the existing-security demand schedule. The Keynesian in this whole argument has limited his security-market comparisons to supply quantities, to the exclusion of demand elasticities. But the interest impact of a new-security increment to supply or demand— whatever its size—depends equally on the *slope* of the existing-demand schedule. The more steeply inclined is that schedule, the more effective is any increment in altering the rate of interest. And it is precisely under the circumstances posited; namely, that the supply of money is a small fraction of securities, that existing-security demand tends to have a very substantial slope. The evi-

---

[41] The total money supply, defined as currency outside banks and adjusted demand deposits, was 144 billion dollars on June 1, 1962 (*Federal Reserve Bulletin, op. cit.*, p. 853). Total tangible assets of the United States are estimated by Goldsmith at approximately $1,700 billion in current prices. See R. W. Goldsmith, *The National Wealth of the United States in the Postwar Period* (Princeton, N. J.: Princeton University Press, 1962), p. 117. If we take this figure as a first approximation to the value of existing securities, the ratio of money to securities is thus under 9 percent.

dence for this is as follows. We know that the demands for existing securities and for money are wealth-complements, their slopes tending to mirror each other.[42] Moreover, we have empirical evidence that the slope of L_2 is entirely appropriate to a market the size of m_2 (or total balances, if money is not dichotomized) rather than existing securities.[43] Granted, then, that m_2 is small relative to existing securities, and L_2 is not highly elastic, the complementary security-demand schedule will have an inappropriate slope—much greater (in absolute value) than one might expect in a market of such considerable magnitude. *The freedom to move between cash and securities is limited, as it were, by the preponderance of securities held.* A given demand or supply increment is thus added to, or traced along, a security demand schedule of sizable slope, and the opportunity for altering the interest rate is significantly enhanced.

D. THE *GENERAL THEORY*: LIQUIDITY PREFERENCE AND THE "INCOME" THEORY OF INTEREST

In the *General Theory* Keynes sought to introduce employment and output as important short-run variables. The *Treatise* occasionally had considered fluctuations in each of them. But Keynes now offered a detailed account of the general equilibrium of a variable-output system. His analysis in the new book is much more that of comparative statics, as compared with the dynamics-orientation of the *Treatise*. Nevertheless, there are several references in the *General Theory* to dynamic relationships that bear on the theme of the present volume.[44]

---

[42] The complementarity refers, of course, to liquidity preference and existing-security demand in *value* units (cf. Chapter II-B[2]). However, the slopes of the existing security-value and security-quantity demand curves are related, and it is immaterial to this discussion whether the schedule is expressed in one unit or the other. We have seen that a very flat downward-sloping value schedule, D_{VO}, implies a similar (highly elastic) quantity curve, D_O, and conversely for a steeply inclined value function (which may be downward or upward sloping). On these relationships see Chapter II-B(3).

[43] All of the empirical studies of the liquidity-preference schedule indicate that it is not highly interest-elastic over the greater range of interest rates. See James Tobin, "Liquidity Preference and Monetary Policy," *Review of Economics and Statistics*, Vol. XXIX (May, 1947), pp. 130–31, and "Monetary Velocity and Monetary Policy: A Rejoinder," *Review of Economics and Statistics*, Vol. XXX (November, 1948), pp. 314–17; L. S. Ritter, "Income Velocity and Anti-inflationary Monetary Policy," *American Economic Review*, Vol. XLIX (March, 1959); Martin Bronfenbrenner and Thomas Mayer, "Liquidity Functions in the American Economy," *Econometrica*, Vol. XXVIII (October, 1960), pp. 810–34; and J. H. Wood, "Aggregate Liquidity Preference Functions for the United States, 1919–1960," Purdue University, Institute for Quantitative Research in Economics and Management, Institute Paper No. 16, 1961. See also the references cited by Wood, pp. 2–4.

[44] On this whole question of Keynes' contribution in both the *Treatise* and the *General Theory* see the stimulating papers by J. A. Schumpeter, "Keynes, the Economist," in *The*

The rate of interest in the *General Theory* is determined simply by the supply and demand for money.[45] Though Keynes no longer uses the language of the "market" and the "natural" rate of interest, he grants that in equilibrium, saving and investment are equal at the going rate of interest:

> All these points of agreement can be summed up in a proposition which the classical school would accept and I should not dispute; namely, that, if the level of income is assumed to be given, we can infer that the current rate of interest must lie at the point where the demand curve for capital corresponding to different rates of interest cuts the curve of the amounts saved out of the given income corresponding to different rates of interest.[46]

However, Keynes stresses the impact of saving and investment on the level of income, rather than their relation to the rate of interest. But let us examine the route by which he arrives at the liquidity-preference theory. In Chapter 13, "The General Theory of Interest," he writes:

> It should be obvious that the rate of interest cannot be a return to saving or waiting as such. For if a man hoards his savings in cash, he earns no interest, though he saves just as much as before. On the contrary, the mere definition of the rate of interest tells us in so many words that the rate of interest is the reward for parting with liquidity for a specified period. For the rate of interest is, in itself, nothing more than the inverse proportion between a sum of money and what can be obtained for parting with control over the money in exchange for a debt for a stated period of time.
>
> Thus the rate of interest at any time, being the reward for parting with liquidity, is a measure of the unwillingness of those who possess money to part with their liquid control over it. The rate of interest is not the "price" which brings into equilibrium the demand for resources to invest

---

New Economics, ed. by S. E. Harris (New York: Alfred A. Knopf, Inc., 1948), chap. ix, and H. G. Johnson, "The *General Theory* after Twenty-Five Years," *American Economic Review*, Vol. LI (May, 1961), pp. 1–17. See also the useful critique of the *General Theory* by James R. Schlesinger, "After Twenty Years: The General Theory," *Quarterly Journal of Economics*, Vol. LXX (November, 1956), pp. 581–602.

[45] *The General Theory of Employment, Interest and Money* (New York: Harcourt, Brace & Co., 1936), chap. xiii, esp. pp. 167–68.

[46] *The General Theory*, p. 178. Keynes, of course, had a great deal of difficulty with his concepts of saving and investment. At times they are identical, at other times income must change to bring them to equality. See Robertson, "Mr. Keynes and the Rate of Interest," *Essays in Monetary Theory* (London: Staples Press, Ltd., 1940), pp. 5–7; and R. G. Hawtrey, *Capital and Employment* (London: Longmans, Green & Co., 1937), chap. vii, esp. pp. 174 and 194–95. We shall continue to use saving and investment as they are defined in Chapter II-C, and assume that Keynes also would agree to the widely accepted "ex ante–ex post" distinction.

with the readiness to abstain from present consumption. It is the "price" which equilibrates the desire to hold wealth in the form of cash with the available quantity of cash.... If this explanation is correct, the quantity of money is the other factor, which, in conjunction with liquidity-preference, determines the actual rate of interest in given circumstances.[47]

Keynes begins with the accurate observation that savings may or may not be hoarded. The rate of interest, he recognizes, is the reward to savers who do not hoard—who, by implication, buy securities. But from here Keynes falls into a stock-flow confusion that, in an historical perspective, is monumental. Granted that the financial disposition of saving is critical to the determination of interest, he leaps to the conclusion that the "desire to *hold wealth* in the form of cash" (italics mine) is the demand determinant of interest. The critical missing term in this statement is the word, "additional," or "incremental," which should be inserted between "hold" and "wealth." This modifier, the hallmark of a growing economy, will convert "the desire to hold cash" from a stock to a flow magnitude, which, in the context, is all that it is entitled to be. When savers hoard, there is a *continuing* rightward shift in the demand schedule for money, accompanied by an equal movement in the real value of balances. Whether the equilibrium interest rate is determined by this pair of constantly shifting schedules, of which the complements are the demand and supply of *new* securities, or by the timeless demand for money financed out of existing wealth and by the existing stock of money, the complements of which are the *existing* demand and supply of securities, is and remains at this point an open question. Keynes has only begun to define the issue, and has thrown no light on the answer. His progression from a class-room explanation of interest as involving a present and a future "sum of money" to a stock-of-money theory of interest is unfortunate. His denial that the rate of interest equilibrates investment and saving is contradicted 11 pages later, as noted in the initial quotation of this section.

By his own implicit and explicit statements, Keynes' "general" theory of interest is incomplete, since income both determines the demand for money (liquidity preference) and is determined by the resulting rate of interest.[48] The efforts to describe the joint determination of interest and income by saving, investment, and the

---

[47] *The General Theory*, pp. 166–68. Several footnotes in the original passage are omitted.

[48] E.g., pp. 171–72, 199, 248–49, 298. Keynes uses the term "liquidity preference" to mean the *total* demand for money, including transactions, precautionary, and speculative motives.

supply and demand for money are well known, and will not be re-peated here.[49] But it is ironical that the "integrators" of Keynes and the classics failed to incorporate the very thing that led Keynes to his liquidity-preference doctrine: the division of saving between securities and cash balances. The universal employment of the Hicksian *IS-LM* diagram makes no allowance for the dual financial character of the saving function. As we have seen, it is only that portion of saving and investment constituting a demand and sup-ply of securities that determines the natural rate of interest. *IS*, the relation between the natural rate and income, should be so quali-fied. At the same time *LM* must shift constantly in response to the perpetual monetary changes originating in that part of saving and investment which is a demand and supply of cash balances. If the money supply is dichotomized, the movement of *LM* is due to a continuing net transfer of funds between idle and active uses. If money is not dichotomized, *LM* responds to a net change in the de-mand for real balances over time. The *IS* schedule should thus be more narrowly defined and the *LM* curve more broadly interpreted than is presently the rule. Moreover, there should be recognition of the general interdependence between the functions; a shift of *IS* is very likely to be accompanied by a shift in the rate of change of *LM*.

Since Keynes himself does not derive the mutual determination of interest and income, the "integrators" interpreted the *General Theory* as assuming an infinitely elastic demand for money. In a "liquidity trap" the rate of interest is, of course, fixed and inde-pendent of income. Keynes' expression for the investment multi-plier (page 115) and his failure to define explicitly the financial character of saving and investment are also consistent with such a system.[50] However, his analysis of monetary disturbance assumes the interest rate to be variable.

Keynes treats monetary changes as being invariably transmitted through the rate of interest, even when the disturbance originates outside the banking system. Thus on page 200 he describes a

---

[49] See Hicks, "Mr. Keynes and the 'Classics';' A Suggested Interpretation," *Econometrica*, Vol. V (April, 1937); and Oscar Lange, "The Rate of Interest and the Optimum Propensity to Consume," *Economica*, N.S., Vol. V (February, 1938), pp. 12–32. A detailed reformula-tion of the Hicksian *IS-LM* framework, along the lines indicated in this paragraph, is presented in the appendix to this chapter.

[50] Cf. pp. 391–92. Though Keynes himself denies that the "virtually absolute" liquidity preference is empirically relevant (*The General Theory*, p. 207), he refers to it from time to time as a distinct *possibility*. See, e.g., *ibid.*, pp. 172, 219, and 233.

monetary increase due to an influx of gold, which he compares also to a government fiscal deficit:

> In this case changes in M are, in the first instance, directly associated with changes in Y, since the new gold accrues as someone's income. Exactly the same conditions hold if changes in M are due to the Government printing money wherewith to meet its current expenditures;—in this case also the new money accrues as someone's income. The new level of income, however, will not continue sufficiently high for the requirements of M_1 to absorb the whole of the increase in M; and some portion of the money will seek an outlet in buying securities or other assets until r has fallen so as to bring about an increase in the magnitude of M_2 and at the same time to stimulate a rise in Y to such an extent that the new money is absorbed either in M_2 or in the M_1 which corresponds to the rise in Y caused by the fall in r. Thus at one remove this case comes to the same thing as the alternative case, where the new money can only be issued in the first instance by a relaxation of the conditions of credit by the banking system, so as to induce someone to sell the banks a debt or a bond in exchange for the new cash.
>
> It will, therefore, be safe for us to take the latter case as typical. A change in M can be assumed to operate by changing r, and a change in r will lead to a new equilibrium partly by changing M_2 and partly by changing Y and therefore M_1. The division of the increment of cash between M_1 and M_2 in the new position of equilibrium will depend on the responses of investment to a reduction in the rate of interest and of income to an increase in investment. Since Y partly depends on r, it follows that a given change in M has to cause a sufficient change in r for the resultant changes in M_1 and M_2 respectively to add up to the given change in M.[51]

Since Keynes' money supply is dichotomized, he is quite right to allocate an increment to both active and idle balances in the new equilibrium. But his process of reaching the equilibrium is unsatisfactory. The statement that the higher income induced directly by the disturbance will not absorb all of the new money is unexplained. Ordinarily, we expect income to rise in accordance with the prevailing velocity of active money, whereupon all of any additional funds are "required." But for Keynes there are funds which are excessive, relative to income, and are thus diverted to the securities market where they lower the rate of interest.[52] The

---

[51] *Ibid.*, pp. 200–201. See also p. 298, where Keynes asserts, "The primary effect of a change in the quantity of money on the quantity of effective demand is through its influence on the rate of interest."

[52] This view that additional money balances are in "excess" of demand has had a deep and continuing influence on the monetary literature. It was expounded in the paper by

reduced yield stimulates a rise in income which this time is sustained. He then goes on to say that the case of bank-credit expansion is typical, and we may "assume" that changes in money "operate by changing *r*." Clearly there is a permanence in monetary and income changes associated with private spending, as stimulated by the rate of interest, that Keynes is unwilling to impute to governmental expenditures, including gold purchases. This is an odd distinction to make, particularly for a Keynesian!

A more consistent explanation of the process is as follows. We assume that output and employment are variable, as they would be for Keynes. The government expenditure raises money income by the product of the entire monetary increment and active velocity. The rise in real income causes saving to rise above investment. Excess saving, which we assume to be a demand for securities, is

---

Tobin, "Liquidity Preference and Monetary Policy," *op. cit.*, p. 125, and by Hansen, *Monetary Theory and Fiscal Policy* (New York: McGraw-Hill Book Co., Inc., 1949), p.47. Both writers describe credit expansion in the framework of the "simplified" quantity theory as entailing an increase in balances that initially are "unwanted." The cash is thus spent, raising income and prices until the new money becomes "needed" and "desired." A "sophisticated" version channels the money through the securities market, as Keynes suggested.

A numerical example might serve to clarify the quantity-theory mechanism for changes in money on income account. Suppose that Cantabrigian Man, who is the reciprocal of Fisherian Man, is paid an income of $7 once a week. He spends $1 a day, and the average size of his money balances is (apart from discontinuities in expenditures) equal to one half of a week's income. Now, an addition of 70 cents to his weekly earnings will be spent at the rate of 10 cents a day, so that the old relationship between his average balances and money income is maintained *from the beginning*. Even though immediately following the injection, Marshallian k is above its previous value, it does not follow that any individual spending unit has more cash than it wants or needs.

The "superfluity" theory can be traced to earlier, and even pre-Keynesian writers. The pedagogically influential book by L. V. Chandler, *Introduction to Monetary Theory* (New York: Harper & Bros., 1940), refers to monetary increments as "excess" (pp. 49 and 81). See also Ludwig von Mises (cited by Chandler), *The Theory of Money and Credit* (London: Jonathan Cape, 1952), p. 139. This book was originally published in 1912. Von Mises (*ibid.*, p. 140), Hansen (*Monetary Theory and Fiscal Policy*, p. 48), Wicksell (*Lectures*, Vol. II, pp. 160–61), and others attribute to Hume these non-behavioral mechanistic versions of the quantity theory. Hume was fond of illustrating a point by supposing the quantity of money to be miraculously changed overnight (see *David Hume: Writings on Economics*, ed. by Eugene Rotwein [Madison: University of Wisconsin Press, 1955], pp. 51, 62–63, 192, 197–98). But in each of these passages Hume was merely describing in a comparative-statics vein the implications of a changed price level for the balance of trade or the rate of interest. When he is actually concerned with the dynamic process stimulated by a gold or silver inflow, his analysis refers to greater industrial activity, increased factor payments, and only, as an aftermath, increased prices (*ibid.*, pp. 37–38). On Hume's general contribution to monetary dynamics, see Douglas Vickers, *Studies in the Theory of Money 1690–1776* (Philadelphia: Chilton Co.—Book Division, 1959), chap. xi, esp. pp. 226–36.

For a recent view that monetary changes can work only through the interest rate, see Edward Nevin, *The Mechanism of Cheap Money* (Cardiff, Wales: University of Wales Press, 1955), p. 38.

expended on existing securities. This reduces active balances, raises idle balances, and lowers the rate of interest. The decrease in active balances reduces income and saving, or, rather, moderates their increase. This, together with the fall in interest, closes the saving-investment gap.[53] In the new equilibrium, income is higher and interest is lower. The essential differences between this account and Keynes' are: (a) the increase in active balances is a sufficient cause of the increase in income, and (b) the reduction in interest is a dependent response to an excess of saving over investment, and has no subsequent independent influence on the level of income.[54]

As in the *Treatise*, Keynes will not acknowledge that saving and investment may react directly on the market rate of interest.[55] This led, immediately following publication of the *General Theory*, to the "income" theory of interest. In this formulation an increase, say, in investment, first raises income and then "liquidity preference." The increase in the latter schedule raises the rate of interest. Hansen describes the process vividly:

It is clear that productivity and thrift have very much to do with the rate of interest. A change in thrift will affect the consumption function and in this way influence the level of income; and the level of income will in turn affect liquidity preference and so the rate of interest. It is not true that an increase in the marginal efficiency of capital (caused, for example, by a higher level of technique) will have no effect on the rate of interest. An upward shift in the marginal efficiency schedule will affect the rate of interest through its effect on income, which in turn will affect the liquidity preference schedule and so the rate of interest.[56]

---

[53] If the increase in money income entails a rise in prices also, then the reduction in real balances would, via the wealth effect, contribute to the rise in the interest rate. However, Keynes generally expresses his speculative (idle) balances in nominal units, so this avenue of equilibration is closed off.

[54] However, it is true that if the interest rate were fixed by a horizontal liquidity preference, real income could not be changed by the quantity of money. Equilibrium following the deficit would be restored only when all of the active balances had spilled over into the hoards. The decrease in interest is thus a correlate of the higher equilibrium income. Cf. Chapter IX-E(1).

[55] *The General Theory*, p. 177. The specific statement is: "Similarly—and this is an even more general belief, even to-day—each additional act of investment will necessarily raise the rate of interest, if it is not offset by a change in the readiness to save.... Now the analysis of the previous chapters will have made it plain that this account of the matter must be erroneous." Keynes goes on to say that an increase in investment raises income, and this is the variable that brings saving to the level of investment (*ibid.*, p. 184). On p. 185 he urges us to consider saving and investment as determinants of employment and *not* interest.

[56] A. H. Hansen, *Monetary Theory and Fiscal Policy*, pp. 81–82. The quotation omits a footnote in the original passage.

To my knowledge Keynes himself does not recount such a sequence in the *General Theory*. At most he asserts that an increase in income raises liquidity preference.[57] He does not add that the rate of interest rises responsively. However, in reply to Robertson's prodding,[58] he acknowledged that the sequence, as described by Hansen, was indeed implied by his analysis.[59]

Here again is the detachment of money income from the quantity of money noted in Keynes' account of the gold flow. We have argued that an increase in investment, not immediately matched by saving, raises income *by* raising the quantity of active balances. For each individual an increment to money income is thus *ipso facto* an increase in active balances received. To bring average money holdings to the appropriate higher level, the receiving units need only continue to spend at the prevailing turnover rate of active money. There is no further independent action that needs to be taken with respect to either active or idle balances. *The additional transactions demand for cash is provided for by the rise in income that motivates it,* and apart from the price level, there is no mechanism remaining for a direct effect on the rate of interest.[60]

The interest rate can rise only in response to an excess supply of securities. Since the movement of income *per se* does not generate such a force,[61] we must turn to the investment itself. If investment is not financed out of existing cash balances, it is an excess supply of new securities that raises the interest rate directly and

---

[57] E.g., pp. 171–72 and 248.

[58] Robertson, "Some Notes on Mr. Keynes' General Theory of Employment," *Quarterly Journal of Economics*, Vol. LI (November, 1936), pp. 180–83 and 187–88.

[59] Keynes, "The General Theory of Employment," *Quarterly Journal of Economics*, Vol. LI (February, 1937), p. 210. See also Keynes, "The 'Ex-Ante' Theory of the Rate of Interest," *Economic Journal,* Vol. XLVII (December, 1937), p. 667, where he avers, "Just as an increase in actual activity must (as I have always explained) raise the rate of interest unless either the banks or the rest of the public become more willing to release cash . . . ."

[60] See the numerical example in n. 52 above. The rise in transactions demand is a movement *along* the demand curve for M_1, expressed as a function of money income (see Figure 2–9). This is completely analogous to the simple case of an increase in the supply of a commodity which, through lowering price (in our case, raising money income), induces a movement along the fixed demand schedule. The Keynesian interprets the disturbance as causing a *shift* of the commodity demand curve.

[61] It is true that certain types of borrowing, such as consumer credit, are tied to income. But this is not the source of general interest movement implied by the income theory. Occasionally a writer will refer to the increased *money* investment demand occasioned by the rise in prices (e.g., Patinkin, *Money, Interest, and Prices*, p. 430, and Hayek, *The Pure Theory of Capital,* pp. 390–91). This is said to raise the rate of interest. However, such a movement in the I schedule will impinge on the interest rate only if money saving rises by a lesser amount. This is never shown to be the case (cf. the discussion on p. 414 above). Still another possible link between money income and interest is the wealth effect, as applied to a liquidity-preference schedule expressed in nominal units. That is, the increase in money

frees idle funds for expenditure. Accordingly, the rise in the supply of active money is not a consequence of the rise in income, but is rather its cause, and this is the fundamental difference between the Keynesian version and our own. For the clear implication of the "income" theory is that the rise in income occurs, somehow, independently of the quantity of money. The increase in income generates a greater (transactions) demand for cash, which in turn raises the interest rate and only then depletes idle balances. The sequence is thus from higher income to higher active balances—rather than the other way around. Admittedly, productive activity may anticipate the actual receipt of cash,[62] but any impact on interest occurring thereby is only temporary, pending monetary payment. In his eagerness to elevate the role of money as a store of value, the Keynesian has lost sight of the fact that money is also the medium of exchange.[63]

Shortly after the publication of the *General Theory* Keynes offered another explanation of the movement of interest rates. An increase in investment, he wrote, would be preceded by an increase in the liquidity preference of the entrepreneur himself. Quotations from two articles will illustrate his point:

Planned investment—*i.e.* investment *ex ante*—may have to secure "financial provision" *before* the investment takes place; that is to say, be-

---

income entails a rise in prices, shifting the asset demand for money to the right. The increased nominal demand corresponds to the decrease in the real value of the supply of idle balances in our own formulation. In either version the rate of interest rises (cf. Chapter IV, n. 19 above). However, there is no suggestion in the income theory that the "income" changes refer to changes in prices only and not in real income as well.

[62] Cf. G. Ackley, "The Multiplier Time Period," *American Economic Review*, Vol. XLI (June, 1951), pp. 350–68.

[63] Other writers who at one time or another have espoused the income theory are: Lange, "The Rate of Interest and the Optimum Propensity to Consume," *op. cit.*, pp. 17–18; Scitovsky, "A Study of Interest and Capital," *op. cit.*, pp. 302–3; A. P. Lerner, "Interest Theory—Supply and Demand for Loans or Supply and Demand for Cash?" *Review of Economic Statistics*, Vol. XXVI (May, 1944), p. 91; Mable F. Timlin, *Keynesian Economics* (Toronto, Canada: University of Toronto Press, 1942), p. 156; Tobin, "Liquidity Preference and Monetary Theory," *op. cit.*, p. 126; G. Haberler, *Prosperity and Depression*, p. 211; Nevin, *The Mechanism of Cheap Money*, pp. 61, 78, 103; A. C. L. Day, *Outline of Monetary Economics* (Oxford: Oxford University Press, 1957), pp. 85–87, 95; and W. T. Newlyn, *Theory of Money* (Oxford: Oxford University Press, 1962), pp. 107–8.

Robertson was the first to formulate the theory (see n. 58), and he repeats it in "Comments on Mr. Johnson's Notes," *Review of Economic Studies*, Vol. XIX, No. 2 (1951–52), p. 108, where he seems to grant logical, if not empirical, plausability to it. However, he is also the first to offer the correct alternative to the Keynesian account ("Some Notes," *op. cit.*, pp. 187–89, and "Mr. Keynes and the Rate of Interest," *op. cit.*, pp. 18–19). His description of the way in which increased thrift lowers both the interest rate and income *directly* through the purchase of existing securities is unsurpassed in the stock-flow literature.

fore the corresponding saving has taken place. . . . There has, therefore, to be a technique to bridge this gap between the time when the *decision* to invest is taken and the time when the correlative investment and saving actually occur.

This service may be provided either by the new issue market or by the banks. . . . But if he [the entrepreneur] accumulates a cash balance beforehand (which is more likely to occur if he is financing himself by a new market-issue than if he is depending on his bank), then an accumulation of unexecuted or incompletely executed investment-decisions may occasion for the time being an extra special demand for cash . . . let us call this advance provision of cash the "finance" required by the current decisions to invest . . . if decisions to invest are (*e.g.*) increasing, the extra finance involved will constitute an additional demand for money.[64]

It follows that, if the liquidity-preferences of the public (as distinct from the entrepreneurial investors) and of the banks are unchanged, an excess in the finance required by current ex-ante output (it is not necessary to write "investment", since the same is true of *any* output which has to be planned ahead) over the finance released by current ex-post output will lead to a rise in the rate of interest; and a decrease will lead to a fall.[65]

Keynes has described a shift by entrepreneurs from existing securities into idle balances, followed by direct dishoarding of these balances via investment spending. The liquidity-preference schedule shifts first to the right, raising the rate of interest, and then to the left to its original position. The latter movement is accompanied by an equal decrease in liquidity supply. This is a perfectly consistent sequence of events. But it exhibits the usual Keynesian bias against new securities, which at no point enter into the dynamic process. Keynes allows the sale of existing securities to raise the rate of interest, but he will not grant the same for an *equal* volume of excess new securities! Surely he did not believe that temporary "finance" is not also provided by net additional borrowing, as well as by the liquidation of existing assets. The implication of his analysis is that new issues are equal to, and perfectly synchronized with, current saving. This seems to be less of an effort to describe reality than to retain consistency with an inadequate theory of interest.

I believe that the monetary dynamics contained explicitly or implicitly in the *General Theory* are not only incorrect, but they

---

[64] "Alternative Theories of the Rate of Interest," *Economic Journal*, Vol. XLVII (June, 1937), pp. 246–47.
[65] "The 'Ex-Ante' Theory of the Rate of Interest," *op. cit.*, p. 667.

are a disservice to the book in that they obscure its main contribution. No one of the variables in the *General Theory*—consumption, investment, employment, output, or liquidity preference—was new to the monetary and business-cycle literature. Nevertheless, the variables were combined in a way that was really quite novel. The Keynesian insistence that saving and investment are invariably determinants of income was certainly not a commonplace before 1936. It is true that previous writers had established links between saving and investment and money income, but these were always dependent upon an elastic money supply or on deliberate acts of hoarding and dishoarding by the participants.[66] The novelty of the *General Theory* is that changes in saving and investment react on income even if they are entirely a demand and supply of securities, and the supply and demand for money are fixed. The existence of an interest-elastic demand for money requires that all changes in the natural rate be traced along it, resulting in *automatic* and essentially *unintended* changes in idle balances and money income. If at the same time money wages are inflexible, a change in money income may entail a change in employment and real income as well. Both Keynes and his followers minimized this important relationship, first by denying that saving and investment act directly on interest, and then by interpreting dynamic processes as always involving *shifts* in the liquidity-preference schedule. Certainly there is no novelty in changes in the demand for money—or for that matter, the supply—as a source of monetary instability. But the great novelty and generality of the Keynesian system is that *its* instability holds even when the demand and supply of money are constant. This is especially evident in Keynes' general-equilibrium analysis of money-wage cuts.[67] The novelty of this penetrating discussion is again the insight into the critical role of the liquidity-preference schedule—stable, and not shifting![68]

---

[66] Robertson's *Banking Policy and the Price Level,* first published in 1926, describes discrepancies between saving and investment as created by deliberate movements in or out of cash balances. See also his paper, "Saving and Hoarding," *Economic Journal,* Vol. XLIII (September, 1933), pp. 399–413 (reprinted in *Essays in Monetary Theory* as Chapter IV).

[67] *The General Theory,* chap. xix, esp. pp. 263–67.

[68] It is true that Keynes refers to a shift in the schedule of liquidity preference, following a wage cut (*The General Theory,* p. 263), but he is referring to the demand for money in nominal units. This is made clear by his statement that the wage reduction raises the real value of the supply of money (*ibid.,* p. 266).

I cannot therefore agree with those who place variables other than liquidity preference at the core of Keynesian underemployment. Modigliani, after surveying alternative models, found that wage rigidity was an indispensable condition for unemployment. Moreover,

> It is usually considered as one of the most important achievements of the Keynesian theory that it explains the consistency of economic equilibrium with the presence of involuntary unemployment. It is, however, not sufficiently recognized that, except in a limiting case to be considered later, this result is due entirely to the assumption of "rigid wages" and not to the Keynesian liquidity preference.[69]

In the same vein, "The liquidity-preference theory is neither necessary nor sufficient to explain the dependence of the rate of interest on the quantity of money. This dependence is explained only by the assumption of rigid wages."[70] Finally, Modigliani will not in general attribute underemployment to a "reduced level of investment." "It is true instead that the low level of investment and employment are both the effect of the same cause, namely a basic maladjustment between the quantity of money and the wage rate."[71] Pigou also refuses to impute causal significance to low investment, liquidity preference, or to any other simple combination of variables.[72] But what Modigliani in particular has overlooked is that while rigid wages are necessary, they are not *sufficient* to explain unemployment. The mere introduction of downward inflexibility in money wages does not itself bring on a depressed level of activity. Some kind of disturbance, requiring a reduction in money income, has to be invoked. Then wage rigidity will extend the necessary decline in money income to real income and employment.[73] This is precisely the role of liquidity preference, which imposes price-level and income adjustments following a decline in investment or consumption, where otherwise a simple interest adjustment would suffice. Similarly, one good possible reason why the quantity of money is inadequate relative to the wage rate is that a decline in investment occurred earlier. This created a lower natural rate of

---

[69] Modigliani, "Liquidity Preference and the Theory of Interest and Money," *Econometrica*, Vol. XII (January, 1944), p. 65 (footnote in the original passage is omitted).
   [70] *Ibid.*, p. 76.
   [71] *Ibid.*, pp. 76–77.
   [72] *Keynes's 'General Theory'* (London: Macmillan & Co., Ltd., 1952), pp. 26–27.
   [73] On the *stability* of the resulting equilibrium, see below Part E.

interest in return for which the existing-asset market demanded and received a higher real quantity of money.[74]

E. KEYNES AND PIGOU: UNEMPLOYMENT
EQUILIBRIUM REVISITED

Keynes advanced as the central thesis of the *General Theory* the insufficiency of demand at full-employment income: saving exceeds investment at all positive rates of interest.[75] The economy thus tends to an "equilibrium" income below full employment, at which consumption and saving are both less, and saving and investment are equal. The now classic reply of Pigou was that Keynes' results depended upon two special assumptions: the existence of price rigidities, and the absence of the inverse saving-wealth relation.[76] Pigou contended that under price and wage flexibility the full-employment saving-investment gap would lower the price level, raise the real value of cash balances, and thereby reduce saving until it meets investment at a positive rate of interest. An adjustment of prices and wealth thus replaces the Keynesian income and employment fluctuation, and full employment remains theoretically an automatically attainable goal.[77]

This section will re-examine the Pigovian position in light of our own concepts of wealth and the dynamic adjustment process. Then

---

[74] I think it is fair to ask what would be left of the *General Theory* if liquidity preference—an interest-elastic demand for money—were removed from the system. We might then praise the book as having clarified and deepened our understanding of consumption, investment, and the non-competitive labor market (the investment multiplier is, of course, gone). But then we must also ask what the book contains that was not already covered—more rigorously and at times much more fully—by the earlier writings of Wicksell (*Lectures*), Robertson (*Banking Policy and the Price Level*), and Pigou (*The Theory of Unemployment* [London: Macmillan & Co., Ltd., 1933]).

[75] *The General Theory*, pp. 28 and 30–31. This proposition does not *per se* imply the existence of a liquidity-preference function, which we referred to in Part D as the fundamental Keynesian assumption. However, given the excess of full-employment saving over investment at all positive interest rates, a liquidity-preference schedule will soon enter the system as an active variable, and thereafter play the important role we have attributed to it. Suppose, for example, that the demand for money is initially interest-inelastic (as in the "classical" model). The excess saving will drive the interest rate instantaneously to its minimum positive level, at which the demand for money is not only interest-elastic, but infinitely so. See below p. 440.

[76] Pigou, "The Classical Stationary State," *Economic Journal*, Vol. LIII (December, 1943), pp. 342–51; "Economic Progress in a Stable Environment," *Economica*, N.S., Vol. XIV (August, 1947), pp. 180–88; *Employment and Equilibrium* (London: Macmillan & Co., Ltd., 1949), chap. ix, esp. pp. 130–34; and *Keynes's 'General Theory'*, pp. 33–38.

[77] Pigou did not, of course, propose deflation as a policy measure to maintain full employment (see "Economic Progress in a Stable Environment," *op. cit.*, pp. 187–88). His only purpose was to indicate the importance of price and wage rigidities to Keynes' conclusions.

we shall return to Keynes and re-evaluate the significance of his central argument.

Figure 10-1 diagrams the Keynesian saving and investment functions prevailing at full-employment output, y'.[78] Assume that an instant earlier the two schedules had intersected at a positive equilibrium interest rate, r'_N, on either S' or I'. The circumstance pictured in the diagram is accordingly the result of a spontaneous

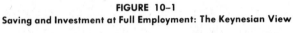

FIGURE 10-1
Saving and Investment at Full Employment: The Keynesian View

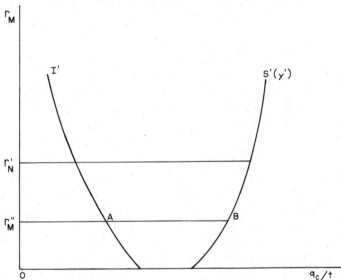

decrease in investment or an increase in saving, respectively. Assume also, for the present, that ex ante saving and investment are, respectively, a demand and supply of securities only. Finally, let the demand for money be a downward function of the rate of interest, as Keynes would have it. The excess saving is thus an excess flow demand for securities which raises security prices, evokes an excess supply of existing securities, and leads to a transfer of active balances from savers to the holders of idle balances. Following Pigou's assumption, prices are perfectly flexible, and

---

[78] The diagram is essentially a duplication of Patinkin's Figure 4 in "Price Flexibility and Full Employment," *American Economic Review*, Vol. XXXVIII (September, 1948), p. 548, and Klein's Figure 4 in *The Keynesian Revolution*, p. 85. The fact that saving is positive at zero and negative rates of interest reflects the desire to save for the "amenity value," in addition to the income (interest) received (see Pigou, "The Classical Stationary State," *op. cit.*, p. 346, and "Economic Progress," *op. cit.*, p. 184).

they fall proportionately to the loss of active money. Full-employment output continues. This deflationary adjustment is identical to the process stimulated by an increase in saving or a decrease in investment, described in Chapter VIII-B. The only novelty in the present analysis is that the equilibrium natural rate is negative. But the market rate cannot in practice be negative, since existing-asset holders have the alternative of holding money at a zero cost. Hence at some low interest rate which just covers the expense of purchasing securities, the demand for money is absolute. L_2 is assumed to be perfectly flat at the yield indicated in the diagram, r_M''. The interest rate accordingly falls until it reaches r_M'', whereupon it is constant. Assuming for the moment that the saving schedule is fixed at S', the dynamic equilibrium is one in which real saving exceeds investment by the quantity, AB; the price level falls by diminishing amounts;[79] and output remains at full employment.

The course of wealth under the moving deflationary "equilibrium" is diagramed in Figure 6-8 or 6-11, depending on whether realized investment is equal to intended investment or intended saving, respectively. Since the curves in these diagrams are based upon an open-market sale, for which the S and I schedules are fixed, the paths will tend to be higher or lower in the present case in which the initiating disturbance is an increase in saving or a decrease in investment, respectively. The generalization of wealth to include securities, as well as money, thus seriously undermines Pigou's belief that wealth necessarily increases during the deflationary process. When S and I are fixed, as in the pure case of monetary contraction, wealth rises and remains above the trend line, except under exceptional circumstances.[80] If the deflation is sparked by an increase in saving, wealth tends to rise even further. In both cases, then, the introduction of the saving-wealth relation would, but for one extreme possibility, cause the S schedule in Figure 10-1 to shift gradually to the left until it meets I' at point A. The system is thereafter in full-employment equilibrium at a stable price level. However, if the deflation is due to a decrease in investment, the family of wealth curves is reduced, quite possibly below trend. In the latter event saving would increase in response to the net loss of wealth, enlarging the deflationary gap.

Equally detrimental to Pigou's position is that the increase in

---

[79] The transfer of active to idle balances is constant in real terms; hence, since the price level is falling, the *nominal* transfer itself falls over time, reducing the periodic decline in the price level.

[80] See pp. 209–10, especially (6E.40).

securities during the adjustment is associated with growth of the capital stock. *Full-employment output is thus itself a variable quantity.* If the deflation is caused by an increase in saving, and I is a downward function of the interest rate, the minimum growth rate of capital in the adjustment is $I'(r''_M)$, which is above the pre-disturbance rate, $I'(r'_N)$. Hence in response to the *net* rise of capital and income, saving will shift to the right, countering more or less any leftward impulses due to wealth. If the deflation is instigated by a decrease in investment, the possibility that capital and income will increase, relative to trend, still exists, but it is not inevitable. In all events the assurance that the "Pigou effect" will restore saving-investment equality is lost in a sea of qualifications involving the growth of wealth, capital, and capacity output, and the response of saving to income and wealth, respectively.[81]

Was Pigou actually unmindful of these basic dynamic considerations qualifying his rebuttal to Keynes? Technically he was not, for Pigou's analysis of deflation—of the insufficiency of aggregate demand—always explicitly assumed the existence of a stationary state and zero net investment.[82] In a moment I shall question whether, in an adjustment process, the former assumption necessarily implies the latter. But is the stationary state under any circumstances a relevant model within which to frame an answer to Keynes? Keynes himself was not unconcerned with the stationary state, for he believed that declining investment opportunities might terminate growth "within a single generation."[83] Nevertheless, Keynes was *in general* preoccupied with a growing economy. Pigou himself reminds us of this:

Thus short-period flow equilibrium, while it can never actually exist unless there is also the long-period flow equilibrium of a stationary state, is a condition to which close approximation can be made. In using the concept, what we do in effect is to postulate all the conditions implicit

---

[81] Martin Bailey makes the interesting point that real cash balances are a factor of production, and yield an imputed stream of services (roughly equal to the return on non-monetary assets) that should be included in consumption and the national income (*National Income and the Price Level* [New York: McGraw-Hill Book Co., Inc., 1962], pp. 59–61). Hence, when deflation raises the value of money, imputed income and consumption also rise, lessening the possibility of still further consumption and reduced saving implied by the Pigovian analysis (*ibid.*, pp. 185–87).

[82] See the references cited in n.76.

[83] *The General Theory*, p. 220. See also p. 221. One might also point out that the low level unemployment equilibrium that Keynes envisioned as the normal state of affairs did not promise to be one of high investment—particularly if investment were a direct function of the level of consumption, as Keynes believed (*ibid.*, p. 106). However, the relevant growth rate in this discussion is that of the *full*-employment deflationary process, to which Pigou addressed himself.

in long-period flow equilibrium, save only that, instead of taking the rate of investment to be nil, we take it to be positive and constant; and we then ignore the reactions which the existence of this positive rate of investment evokes in the other parts of the system—reactions which are in fact trifling in respect of periods that are very short, and which can, of course, be ignored, if we so choose, in respect of periods of any length. This sort of equilibrium is the subject matter of Keynes' *General Theory;* for this is concerned, as he expressly states, with "*the equilibrium level* [my italics] of employment, *i.e.* the level at which there is no inducement to employers as a whole either to expand or to contract employment."[84]

If Pigou wished to show that Keynes' full-employment *dis*equilibrium had within it a self-corrective mechanism, he was obliged to do so in the context of the growing "short-period flow equilibrium" that both writers normally adopted in their analysis of employment. The schedules pictured in Figure 10–1 embody the sufficient and *general* conditions for Keynes' central argument: intended full-employment saving exceeds investment, and both are positive, at all attainable interest rates. Qualifying the functions further only reduces the force and generality of the Keynesian case. Strictly speaking, the first difference in capital—the absolute level of saving-investment—determines only the trend, and is irrelevant to the issue here. It is the first difference, with trend removed, to which saving responds, and this depends only on the saving and investment *slopes* and the realized *excess* of saving over investment. The cumulative saving-investment gap in turn determines the magnitude of the change in real balances of the adjustment process. One cannot therefore legitimately focus on changes in monetary wealth to the exclusion of capital changes stimulated (or not, as the case may be) by the excess flow demand for securities, arguing that one is large and the other is small. While in some respects a given change or rate of change in capital may indeed be "trifling" (e.g., in its impact on the aggregate marginal product of capital), it cannot, as a source of either additional wealth or capacity output, be so regarded *relative* to the magnitude of short-period monetary changes.

Figure 10–2 depicts the full-employment stationary-state disequilibrium that Pigou named "Keynes' Day of Judgment." The return

---

[84] Pigou, *Employment and Equilibrium*, pp. 43–44. All italics are Pigou's. The quotation ends with a citation to p. 27 of *The General Theory*. Keynes' assumption of positive net investment is made very explicit on pp. 27 and 28—more so than Pigou's particular choice of a quotation from these two pages seems to indicate.

FIGURE 10–2
Pigou's "Keynesian Day of Judgment"

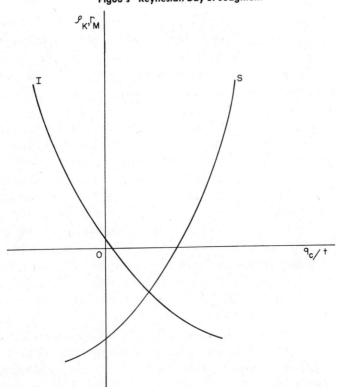

to investment is negative at positive rates of investment, and infinitesimally above zero when $I = 0$.[85] Saving is positive over a range
of positive, zero, and even negative interest rates.[86] The demand for
money is infinitely elastic at the interest rate for which $I = 0$.[87]
Pigou contended that when the economy reaches such a state, the
price level falls in the manner indicated, raising real balances and
shifting S to the left until it meets I on the vertical axis. In the new
equilibrium, capital and income are the same as they were when the
deflation began.[88] But this implicitly assumes that ex ante and ex
post investment are always equal; the indeterminacy in the rate of
growth created by unequal saving and investment flows is resolved
ex post in favor of the investing entrepreneurs. While this assump-

---

[85] *Employment and Equilibrium*, pp. 127–28.
[86] *Ibid.*, p. 129.
[87] *Ibid.*, p. 128.
[88] Pigou, "Economic Progress," *op. cit.*, p. 187.

tion (or presumption) is indeed widespread, I know of no empirical or *a priori* justification for it.

Let us now drop the assumption that intended saving and investment are a demand and supply of securities only. While in this volume we have found it a useful and, at times, a necessary assumption, neither Keynes nor Pigou advances it as his own. Keynes, in particular, explicitly asserts that saving may be allocated both to cash balances and securities.[89] Such a saving schedule is diagramed in Figure 10–3. S_m, the portion which is hoarded each period, is drawn as a downward function of the rate of interest. S_s, the component directed to securities, rises with interest, as does aggregate saving, S, the horizontal sum of S_m and S_s. In order to simplify the analysis and the diagram, investment is taken to be wholly a supply of new securities; i.e., $I = I_s$. Now, we have seen that in general the market rate of interest will lie between r_N'', the intersection of I_s and S_s, and r_M'', the rate at which $S = I$. When the money supply is dichotomized, the prevailing interest rate is below r_N'' and above r_M'' (pages 299–300); when money is not dichotomized, the rate is equal to r_N'' (pages 386–87). In both cases the "equilibrium" of the system is one of an excess of aggregate saving over investment, and constantly falling prices. The only exception to this (assuming interest-elastic saving or investment functions) is the model in which the demand for, or the supply of, money is infinitely elastic at a given rate of interest (Chapter IX-E). Such an interest rate will prevail as the equilibrium rate of the system, and the

---

[89] See above pp. 427–28. Keynes in the *Treatise* also stresses the dual financial character of saving—i.e., as a demand for "securities" and a demand for additional "bank deposits" (*Treatise*, Vol. I, pp. 140–41). To my knowledge the earliest identification of saving and investment as a demand and supply of securities only in the post-*General Theory* literature was made by Metzler in "Wealth, Saving, and the Rate of Interest," *op. cit.*, p. 102. For another early treatment, recognizing the role of this assumption as an equilibrium condition, see E. T. Weiler, *The Economic System* (New York: The Macmillan Co., 1952), chap. xviii (Weiler also employs real balances as an equilibrating variable which acts upon the saving function). Most writers are simply non-committal on the financial aspects of S and I. (For two recent exceptions see T. F. Dernburg and D. M. McDougall, *Macro-Economics* [New York: McGraw-Hill Book Co., Inc., 1960], chap. xiv; and Ackley, *Macroeconomic Theory*, p. 141). Modigliani, in "Liquidity Preference and the Theory of Interest and Money," *op. cit.*, p. 71, explicitly denies that the saving and investment schedules are a demand and supply of securities. Yet on p. 61 he describes an increase in saving as lowering the rate of interest by raising the supply of idle balances. At the prevailing rate of interest, he argues, the extra supply of M_2 is not wanted and so is spent on securities. But if saving is not a demand for securities, then within Modigliani's own model it can only be a demand for idle money. In that event the additional supply of M_2 is met by an equal shift to the right in L_2, and there is no mechanism for a direct effect on the rate of interest (see Chapter VIII-H[1]). The possible later influence of the wealth effect on interest is ruled out for Modigliani since it is nominal rather than real idle balances that are held in his system.

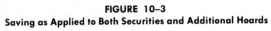

FIGURE 10-3
Saving as Applied to Both Securities and Additional Hoards

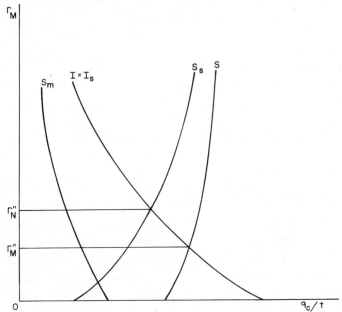

traditional aggregate equilibrium condition, $S = I$, will also obtain. Suppose in Figure 10–3 that r_M'' is such a liquidity-trap yield. Then even though at this rate, $I_s > S_s$, the resulting excess supply of new securities activates, and thereby offsets, the entire hoardings of savers at the going rate of interest.[90]

Manifestly, since Keynes is concerned with a growing economy, he must rest his case for aggregate saving-investment equality—at or below full employment—on the existence of a liquidity trap. For otherwise, as long as some part of current ex ante saving is hoarded (or investment is financed by dishoarding), the ex ante equality of total saving and investment is unattainable. Starting from a position of full employment, as pictured in Figure 10–1, income and employment will contract endlessly until such time as savers may cease to hoard or the stationary state itself is reached. Keynes, as we have noted (page 429), is unwilling to attribute empirical relevance to the liquidity trap (nor does he believe that both saving and investment are completely interest-inelastic). This,

---

[90] Cf. (9E.6), p. 392.

together with his emphasis on hoarding by savers, destroys the foundation of his unemployment "equilibrium."[91]

The ability to achieve aggregate saving-investment equality is thus independent of income, employment, interest, or wealth, except for a particular combination of these variables that might produce a liquidity trap or a stationary state. If savers hoard, as Keynes believed they do, money income will fall perpetually, even though real income has fallen to the point where total saving and investment *could* be equated at a positive rate of interest. Keynes' central argument that full-employment saving and investment meet at a negative interest rate is thus only a special case of their inequality under most circumstances. The villain-at-large is hoarding out of current income, for which there is no apparent eradicator other than coincidental equal dishoarding by entrepreneurs.

In this perspective Keynes' thesis that full employment may require a negative equilibrium interest rate reduces to the proposition that the deflationary forces operating at full employment are greater than at levels of unemployment. But even granting the full-employment negative interest rate, the proposition cannot be accepted without empirical evidence on the hoarding of savers as related to income, wealth, and the rate of interest. A truly general evaluation of inherent deflationary tendencies should also relax the common assumption that the output of a growing economy is constant, and assess the direct deflationary impact of growth itself. We have now come full circle, from Keynes' proclamation that full employment is unattainable, to the far less menacing deflationary character of a rising output! And yet in principle they are the same. As Pigou readily noted, Keynes' saving-investment disequilibrium would, with flexible prices and stable expectations, generate a moving deflationary equilibrium of full employment.[92] Pigou argued that wealth changes would eventually stabilize the price level, and we have questioned this. But the essential point here is that Keynes' analysis, while serious in its implications, is no more than the analysis of deflation, and no more than we might *a priori* expect at other levels of employment, and in growing economies at all levels of employment. The viewpoint of many writers that

---

[91] We have argued that in the "classical" model, in which no idle balances are held, all of saving will be directed to securities (p. 368). However, the high interest rates at which L_2 might go to zero are not attainable, since the interest rate is constantly declining in the deflationary process.

[92] "Economic Progress," *op. cit.,* p. 186.

the Keynesian full-employment system was in some sense "over-determined,"[93] the price level being in "neutral equilibrium,"[94] simply reflects an unwillingness to see the price level as a dynamically changing variable. And this downward tendency of prices is, basically, all that Keynes could claim about full employment. This is not to say that deflation is socially desirable or even tolerable. But it places Keynes' attack on capitalism in a proper perspective.

F. SOME IMPLICATIONS FOR POLICY

It is not easy to draw together the strands of our analysis that are relevant to monetary policy. In many important respects the analysis is *a priori*, and needs to be supplemented by empirical knowledge. For example, we have taken no stand on the actual degree of forced saving or investment in adjustment processes. We have entered this phenomenon, of obvious interest to policy makers, as a variable in the model. But our analysis embraces the whole range of possible cases, leaving it to empirical research to furnish specific information. Nevertheless, the recognition of capital formation as a variable in monetary adjustment influences the questions that policy makers will ask. It is in this sense and on this level that we turn to the main policy implications of the book.

Any policy calculus needs an organizing framework, and there is none better for this purpose than the equation of exchange. Though an identity ex post, the equation can provide a rich and ready summary of ex ante causal relationships.[95] The earliest and best known is the quantity theory, according to which prices are determined by, and vary proportionately with, the quantity of money. It is a short and obvious step to allow the other variables, velocity and transactions, to vary. In this discussion we shall limit transactions to the narrower category of final output, to which income velocity corresponds. But these additional variables need not fluctuate in such a way as to violate what I consider the basic premise of the quantity theory: left-side to right-side causality. In other words, a generalized or "modern" quantity theory might

---

[93] Cf. Modigliani, "Liquidity Preference and the Theory of Interest and Money," *op. cit.,* p. 74.

[94] *Ibid.*

[95] See the essay by Sidney Weintraub, "The Equation of Exchange and the Theory of the Price Level," chap. iv in *Classical Keynesianism, Monetary Theory, and the Price Level* (Philadelphia: Chilton Co.—Book Division, 1961).

be phrased as follows: the product, MV (total expenditures), is the cause of the product, Py (total income receipts or money income). The transmission is from M or V to P or y in any combination. This is not to say that a change in M or V is necessarily transmitted to the right side. A change in M may be offset by a temporary or even permanent change in V. But the modern quantity theory holds that independent changes in P or y are necessarily offsetting; they cannot be transmitted to the left side. An example would be the classic crop failure, which results in higher prices without changing M or V.

At the opposite pole of the modern quantity theory is the view that Py determines MV. For example, a totally monopolized product economy might independently determine both output and prices. An acquiescent monetary authority then provides the amount of money which, together with the prevailing velocity, supports the resulting money income. I regard the various "cost-push" theories as falling largely within right-to-left causality. Thus prices might be determined independently by a national wage agreement (as in a highly socialized country). The monetary authority again supplies the appropriate quantity of money, preventing output from responding dependently to the wage-price negotiation. The cost-push theorist need not, and probably as a rule does not, deny the possibility of left-to-right causation. His main purpose is to call attention to the opposite relationship.

Much of the analysis in this book, by virtue of its assumptions, adheres to the framework of the modern quantity theory. Since output is generally fixed, we have been primarily occupied in describing changes in M and V, both independently of each other in the form of initiating disturbances, and dependently in the context of adjustment processes. Apart from monetary changes in the Keynesian model, the left-side changes are carried over only to the price level. But even on our simple assumptions, there is some reciprocal influence of prices via the wealth effect. This equilibrator of the interest rate helps to determine the saving-investment gap and thereby the time path of velocity. The final equilibrium velocity is also conditioned by the right side through the impact of transitional wealth changes on the demand for money. A primary source of wealth fluctuations is capital formation. Since the capital stock is one of the variables underlying output, it provides a right-to-left direction of influence.

The more general the model becomes, the more numerous are right-side sources of causality. When wealth is a determinant of saving, capital bears on velocity by sharing in the determination of the natural rate of interest. Once output becomes a variable, then, like wealth, it influences velocity by its impact on the natural rate. If there is interest elasticity in the supply of money, the right-side variables will share in the determination of both M and V.

Though we have not dealt with cost-push disturbances as such, our analysis of monetary change is applicable to them. Thus open-market operations can be interpreted equally well as initiating a change in the price level, or as responding to a set of prices implicit in a wage-price negotiation currently in progress. There is no commitment in our analysis to the underlying causes of disturbances.

I regard a successful monetary policy as one that has a lively sense of all the possible inter-relationships of the equation of exchange. Though they cannot all be equally pertinent in every institutional setting, an adequate policy should be prepared to consider the whole variety of possible disturbances, behavioral responses, and particular techniques to achieve its goals. I do not feel that at this stage of our knowledge a simple set of "rules" regarding both the guideposts and the instruments of policy, as opposed to "authorities," is practicable. Nevertheless, there are certain specific implications of the study relevant to the formulation of policy, and they are as follows:

1. Given a secularly increasing commercial banking system, the money supply will grow at some relative rate over time. *Ceteris paribus*, this causes the market rate (or rates) to be permanently below the natural rate (or rates) of interest. A change in the supply of money, for policy purposes, may thus entail a change in the rate of increase of M, which changes (rather than creates) the discrepancy between the market and the natural rate.

2. *Ceteris paribus*, changes in one or more market rates of interest due to once-for-all changes in the money supply are reversed, more or less, by the stock-flow adjustment process. A permanent change in interest rates through monetary action requires *continuing real* changes in the supply of money.

3. In all likelihood monetary policy must take for granted both cyclical and secular changes in velocity. In the liquidity-preference economy any change in the equilibrium interest rate creates a corresponding change in velocity. If any part of saving or invest-

ment is on net hoarded, or financed by dishoarding, respectively, velocity will change constantly over time. In the classical model interest changes will not affect velocity, but they can produce similar results through changes in an interest-elastic money supply. A change in the *balanced* government budget, whether it be state, local, or federal, will change velocity in *any* economy if the budget alters transactions velocity.

4. A *ceteris paribus* increase in M via the banking system operates by stimulating excess new securities and capital formation which may or may not represent a net increase in the rate of growth of these variables.[96] However, if the economy is in a recession because of an over-rapid rate of investment (for example, in inventories), the monetary authority may want to weigh the prudence of banking policy as the particular instrument of revival. A fiscal deficit designed to raise consumption may in fact be a much preferred action. The deficit may or may not raise the money supply. In either case, if money is dichotomized the deficit will tend to raise interest rates and thereby possibly to reduce ex post private investment. If money is not dichotomized, only a deficit financed by borrowing from the private sector will have this particular inhibiting effect on investment. If the economy is one of the extreme "Keynesian" cases, monetary increase should be avoided, since new money from any source is sooner or later hoarded, or destroyed by the commercial banks. Properly designed, a deficit may thus accelerate the recovery, while banking policy may aggravate the causes of the recession.

5. The analysis of monetary policy should not assume that the actions are invariably of the *ceteris paribus* variety. In practice this means that open-market activity, for example, may coincide with internal disturbances that also operate through the interest rate. An open-market purchase may thus coincide with a decrease in the propensity to invest or an increase in the desire to save, both of which are mediated through the securities market. In each case the purchase raises idle (or asset-money) balances and lowers the interest rate directly, obviating the need for an internal adjustment that accomplishes both of these changes through deflation.

---

[96] Thus an open-market purchase of Treasury bills may lead, through the substitution process, to higher prices and increased production of all the asset-substitutes for bills. The substitutes may include traders' inventories and apartment houses. On this subject see the author's account of the channels of monetary policy in "Moneyflows and Monetary Theory," *Proceedings of the Business and Economics Section of the American Statistical Association, 1955–56,* pp. 49–51.

Monetary policy thereby stabilizes the economy by *preventing* prices and income from falling, rather than endeavoring to raise these variables following a decline, as implied by the action of (4). In a word, monetary policy, through once-for-all transactions in the open market, facilitates changes in the market rate occasioned by changes in the natural rate.[97] In terms of the equation of exchange, changes in M are substituted for changes in V, which thereby are quashed. This "preventive" aspect of policy was stressed both by Keynes[98] and Mints.[99] If this is an accurate model of policy—and I believe that it has been in this country on a number of occasions during the fifties—then the question of the lag in policy is to this extent irrelevant. For if the policy is effective, it is effective immediately. Moreover, if the policy is in error, it is easily reversed. Suppose that an open-market sale designed to raise the market rate to a higher natural level were inappropriate. This would be revealed by deflationary tendencies in the economy. But the presence of a lag in this circumstance would itself give the authority time to discover its error and to reverse its policy before the ill effects were widespread.

6. The policy goal of price-level stabilization is perfectly compatible with the analysis of this study. However, I would not insist that a price index be the sole guidepost to this end. It is conceivable that an authority acting in the framework of (5) might wish to anticipate price-level fluctuations by reference to events in the securities market. An increase in the marginal efficiency of investment, as reflected in new security flotations and rising capital expenditures, might justify monetary contraction and a higher market rate of interest in advance of actual recorded inflation.

---

[97] Monetary policy in this context fosters the illusion that the monetary authority itself is responsible for the changed interest rate. It is undeniably true that in responding, say, to a higher natural rate, the authority raises the market rate. But if the market rate remains at its higher level following a *once-for-all* transaction by the authority, then it is the private sector which has "caused" the higher interest rate. The authority has merely served as a catalyst for an increase which would have occurred in any event. The literature on monetary policy rarely indicates an awareness of this possibility.

[98] *A Treatise on Money*, Vol. I, p. 273, and Vol. II, chap. xxxvii, esp. pp. 351–52, 362. For a modern treatment in the same spirit see Bailey, *National Income and the Price Level*, pp. 156–57.

[99] *Monetary Policy for a Competitive Society* (New York: McGraw-Hill Book Co., Inc., 1950), chap. ix, esp. pp. 196–97 and 206. Mints emphasizes the immediate stabilizing impact of monetary policy on expectations, rather than on the market rate of interest. He believes that most internal monetary disturbances take the form of direct movements between goods and money (*ibid.*, chap. iii, esp. pp. 29–36, and p. 70). In this respect he is closer to Robertson of *Banking Policy and the Price Level* than to Keynes of the *Treatise*.

Non-linear Security-Value Functions

This appendix will extend the analysis of Parts B(3) and C(2) by considering non-linear D_{VO}, D_{VN}, and S_{VN} functions. Our interest in each case is in the slope of the underlying security-quantity schedule. We shall find that in several instances D_O, D_N, and S_N do not have the customary slopes of demand and supply curves.

1. Non-linear D_{VO} Functions

As long as $\partial D_{VO}/\partial p \leq 0$ (see Figure 2–7[a] and [b]), the associated D_O schedule is also downward sloping, with $\eta \leq -1$. Clearly this must be true whether D_{VO} is linear or not.[1] However, the case of $\partial D_{VO}/\partial p > 0$ is less plain. In the linear case, shown in Figure 2–7(c), vectors from the origin, the p-axis slopes of which are equal to D_O, established that D_O was downward sloping (page 31). But consider the two non-linear cases drawn in Figure 2A–1. In the left diagram, in which D_{VO} is concave to the vertical axis, the slope of vectors from the origin to the curve falls monotonically with p. D_O is thus downward sloping with $\eta > -1$. In Figure 2A–1(b), D_{VO} is rising and convex to the vertical axis. As a result, the slope of vectors from the origin diminishes as p rises only until a vector, shown as a dashed line, meets D_{VO} at a tangency point. Thereafter the vectors increase in slope as p increases. Hence D_O is downward sloping and inelastic below p'', the ordinate of the tangency point, but upward sloping above p''.

---

[1] The case in which D_{VO} assumes the limiting forms shown in Figure 2–5 implies a downward-sloping D_O curve, except at the price and yield at which D_{VO} is horizontal. At that price D_O will coincide with the horizontal portion of D_{VO}. The horizontal segment of D_O will extend beyond that of D_{VO}, or terminate earlier, depending on whether the unity price is above or below the price of the horizontal segment. D_O approaches the horizontal axis asymptotically. Its elasticity is $-\infty$ over the horizontal range, but η increases gradually until it is greater than -1 (i.e., D_O is inelastic) for prices at which $D_{VO} = W$.

FIGURE 2A-1
The Existing Security-Quantity Demand Schedule Corresponding to
Two Upward-Sloping, Non-linear Security-Value Demand Functions

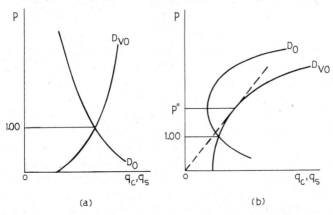

(a)   (b)

The entire existing-asset market that gives rise to an upward-sloping D_O schedule is diagramed in Figure 2A-2. It is clear geometrically that S_{VO} must intersect D_{VO} at a price, p', below p'', the height at which a vector from the origin is tangent to D_{VO}. Thus D_O becomes upward sloping at a price above the equilibrium. Notice that D_O intersects D_{VO} at the unity price, which happens to lie between p' and p''. Since D_{VO} is convex to the p-axis, L_2 must be concave (see page 28, note 13), as in Figure 2A-2. With L_2 in this form, there is some security price at which D_{VO} not only increases with p, but does so by increasing amounts. Initially this causes D_O, still downward sloping at p infinitesimally above p', to become *increasingly* inelastic. But eventually, at $p = p''$, D_O is brought to a per-

FIGURE 2A-2
The Existing-Asset Market for Which Security Demand Becomes
an Upward-Sloping Function of Price

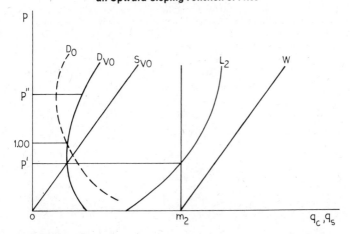

fectly vertical (zero-elastic) position. Thereafter D_O changes direction and becomes upward sloping. What has happened is that L_2, concave toward the p-axis, fails increasingly to keep up with the linear appreciation of wealth due to higher security prices. This leaves a real quantity of wealth for embodiment in securities that ultimately grows at an increasing rate. A point is finally reached at which the capital gains, relative to the demand for money, are so great that the community chooses to hold more, rather than fewer, securities at higher prices. A positive wealth effect swamps the negative price effect on the existing demand for securities.[2]

Let us summarize our findings with regard to $\partial D_O/\partial p$ here and in Part B(3): $\partial D_O/\partial p < 0$ at all prices if D_{VO}, consistent with stability, is either linear or concave to the vertical axis. $\partial D_O/\partial p > 0$ at prices above the equilibrium when and only when D_{VO} is rising and convex to the vertical axis. L_2 in this case is concave to the p-axis.[3] Since in all cases D_O is downward sloping in the range of the equilibrium price, its possible upward slope at higher prices has no effect on the equilibrium-growth process described in Part D(2).

A function, D'_O, that becomes upward sloping is drawn in Figure 2A–3 together with a supply schedule of existing securities, S'_O. There is no possibility that D'_O and S'_O will intersect at a second point above p', for such an intersection would imply that there are also two intersections for D_{VO} and S_{VO} and L_2 and m_2. But we have drawn L_2 so that it has only one intersection with m_2; therefore, both D_{VO} and S_{VO} and D_O and S_O must themselves have a unique intersection. Hence D'_O will have an inflection point in its rising range, above which it is concave to the vertical axis. D'_O is so constructed in Figure 2A–3.

In spite of the foregoing argument, the reader may still be disturbed by the geometric implication of Figure 2A–3 that a sufficient leftward shift in S_O will lead to a double intersection with D'_O. But movements in S_O

---

[2] See below Appendix B(1), p. 460 for an indifference-curve treatment of this subject.

[3] It is of some interest that when $L_2(r_M)$ is either linear or concave downward, $L_2(1/r_M)$ is concave upward, ensuring that $\partial D_O/\partial p$ eventually becomes positive. To show this, we define two functions,

$$y = f(x) \quad \text{and} \quad z = f\left(\frac{1}{x}\right).$$

Then

$$\frac{\partial z}{\partial x} = f'\left(\frac{1}{x}\right)\left(-\frac{1}{x^2}\right) \quad \text{and} \quad \frac{\partial^2 z}{\partial x^2} = f''\left(\frac{1}{x}\right)\left(\frac{1}{x^4}\right) + \frac{2}{x^2} f'\left(\frac{1}{x}\right).$$

Let

$$y = z = L_2 \quad \text{and} \quad \frac{1}{x} = r_M.$$

It follows that when $f'(r_M) < 0$ and $f''(r_M) \leqq 0$, $\partial^2 L_2/\partial(1/r_M)^2 < 0$. If $f''(r_M) > 0$, as it is ordinarily drawn, $\partial^2 L_2/\partial(1/r_M)^2 \gtreqless 0$.

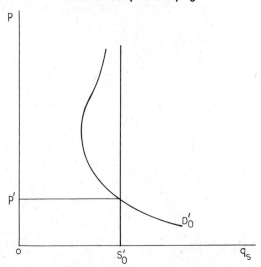

FIGURE 2A–3
The Existing Security-Quantity Market in Which a Portion
of Demand is Upward Sloping

can only be analyzed in a dynamic context. This is done in Chapter III. On page 64, note 4, the *process* by which the double intersection is avoided is described.

2. Non-linear D_{VN} and S_{VN} Functions

Since D_{VN} is downward sloping (see Figure 2–10), it is clear that whether it is linear, concave, or convex to the vertical axis, the slope of vectors drawn from the origin must decrease with p. Hence D_N is invariably an inverse function of price. S_{VN}, the investment function, is upward sloping.

FIGURE 2A–4
The New Security-Quantity Supply Schedule Corresponding to Two Non-linear
Security-Value Supply Functions

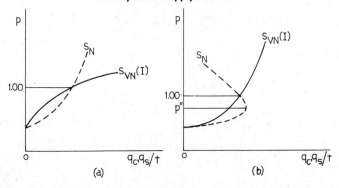

S_N also has the expected upward slope if S_{VN} is linear, as in Figure 2–10, or convex to the p-axis, as in Figure 2A–4(a). But in Figure 2A–4(b), where S_{VN} is concave to the vertical axis, the slope of vectors increases only until p'', the ordinate of the tangency point, is reached. At $p > p''$, the vector slopes and thus, S_N, decrease.[4]

There is no particular significance to a downward-sloping S_N function. From the viewpoint of stability, the only requirement is that the excess demand, $D_N - S_N$, vary inversely with p. This will occur if the excess value demand, $D_{VN} - S_{VN}$, is inverse, since $D_N - S_N$ differs from it only by the factor, p.

---

[4] If $I(r_M)$ is linear or concave downward, $I(1/r_M)$ is concave upward, as in Figure 2A–4. This is proved by reference to n. 3 (above), letting $I = L_2$.

An Indifference-Curve Analysis of the Existing-Asset Market

This appendix will describe the demand responses of the existing-asset market in terms of the underlying indifference curves. We shall consider two cases: (1) the supply components are fixed, and demand varies as a function of the security price; and (2) autonomous wealth changes occur, causing shifts in the demand schedules.

1. Fixed Supply

Figure 2B–1 presents a community indifference curve with respect to security quantities, S_O, and idle balances, m_2.[1] The budget line, or line of attainable combinations, is based on a given stock of wealth,

$$(2B.1)' \qquad\qquad W'_1 = S'_O p' + m'_2 ,$$

where W'_1 is a specific point on the wealth function,

$$(2B.2)' \qquad\qquad W' = S'_O p + m'_2 ,$$

S'_O and m'_2 are the existing quantities of securities and real idle balances, respectively, and p' is the given price of securities. The commodity price

---

[1] For a summary of the difficulties involved in the construction of community indifference curves, see Paul A. Samuelson, "Social Indifference Curves," *Quarterly Journal of Economics*, Vol. LXX (February, 1956), pp. 1–22. Even though there is no commonly accepted resolution of these difficulties, I feel that the exposition of this appendix enlarges our understanding of the existing-asset market. At the least, the development of the budget line throws light on the supply and demand inter-relationships of the market. Whether the indifference curves are conceptually possible is not entirely germane to this point. I am willing to suggest as one basis for the validity of the curves that they be treated as aggregates of individual indifference curves, all of which are identical (cf. *ibid.*, p. 3).

FIGURE 2B–1

FIGURE 2B–1
The Indifference-Curve Equilibrium of the Existing-Asset Market

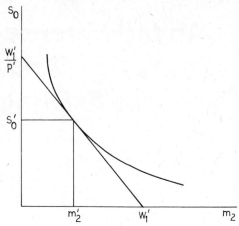

level is taken as given. The system is in equilibrium, since at p' the desired quantities of S_O and m_2, as evidenced by the intersection of the budget line and the highest attainable indifference curve, are equal to the existing supplies of each.

The equation of the budget line is obtained from (2B.1)′ by replacing the specific quantities, S'_O and m'_2, by general variables, S_O and m_2, and solving for S_O:

(2B.3)′ $$S_O = \frac{W'_1 - m_2}{p'} = \frac{W'_1}{p'} - \left(\frac{1}{p'}\right) m_2.$$

Hence the vertical-axis intercept is W'_1/p', the maximum obtainable quantity of securities, and the slope of the line is

(2B.4)′ $$\frac{\partial S_O}{\partial m_2} = -\frac{1}{p'}.$$

The horizontal intercept is simply the total stock of wealth, W'_1, since m_2 and W are measured in the same units (q_c).

Consider the effect on the budget line of an increase in the price of securities. This tends directly to reduce the community's ability to finance the holding of securities, but by raising total wealth, it tends to increase the ability to hold all assets, including securities. However, we can show that the negative price effect on securities predominates over the positive wealth effect, causing the vertical intercept of the budget line to fall. The general expression for the vertical intercept is obtained from (2B.2)′:

(2B.5)′ $$\frac{W'}{p} = S'_O + \frac{m'_2}{p}.$$

The derivative of (2B.5)' with respect to p is

(2B.6)'
$$\frac{\partial\left(\dfrac{W'}{p}\right)}{\partial p} = -\frac{m_2'}{p^2}.$$

Thus in Figure 2B–2 the vertical intercept corresponding to a price, $p'' > p'$, is

(2B.7)'
$$\frac{W_2'}{p''} < \frac{W_1'}{p'}, \text{ where } W_2' = S_O'p'' + m_2' .$$

FIGURE 2B–2

**The Effect of an Increase in the Price of Securities
on Desired Holdings of Securities and Idle Money**

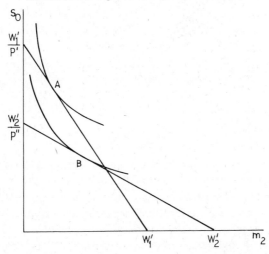

The horizontal intercept is equal to the increased stock of wealth, W_2'. The movement in the horizontal intercept for a unit change in price is the derivative of (2B.2)':

(2B.8)'
$$\frac{\partial W'}{\partial p} = S_O' .$$

The ability to hold idle balances varies directly and equally with the change in wealth, S_O'.

Given that $\partial L_2/\partial p > 0$, the new tangency point will entail an increased quantity of idle balances. If $\partial D_O/\partial p < 0$, the desired quantity of securities will be less. Thus the new tangency point, B, will be southeast of the old one, A. This is the case pictured in Figure 2B–2.

The expansion path created by raising p will have the appearance of the downward vector in Figure 2B–3. Starting at $p = 0$, the vector is asymptotic to the vertical axis. As p increases, it moves downward and to the

FIGURE 2B-3
The Expansion Path as a Function of the Price of Securities

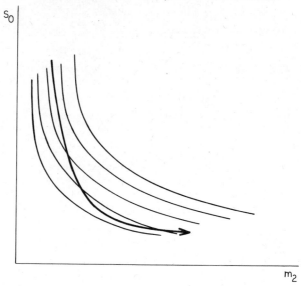

right. But its rate of descent diminishes, because constant price increments raise the abscissa of the budget line by constant amounts (see
[2B.8]'), and the ordinate by decreasing amounts (see [2B.6]'). The net effect is to draw the tangency points increasingly to the right. This is
to say that the wealth effect of an increased price on the budget line,
which tends to raise both intercepts, increases relative to the negative effect of the higher price on the ordinate. In the event that L_2 increases with
p at a sufficiently low rate, the expansion path will eventually turn upward. This is the case of $\partial D_O / \partial p > 0$ (see Appendix A[1]).

One of the characteristics of the expansion path in Figure 2B-3 is that
initially it cuts across successively lower indifference curves. This is also
true of the movement in Figure 2B-2; the new budget line lies below the
indifference curve of the beginning equilibrium at every point. Hence the
new equilibrium involves a tangency point with a lower curve. However,
as the path in Figure 2B-3 levels out, it moves across higher curves. This
pattern of moving first across decreasing, and later, increasing satisfaction
levels as price increases is not inevitable. One may conceive of indifference maps in which the expansion path cuts across successively higher or
lower curves throughout its range.[2] But the lack of a uniform relationship
between security-price movements and community welfare is clear.

---

[2] When $\partial D_O / \partial p > 0$, the expansion path turns upward and must, of course, cut
across successively higher curves over this range of price.

2. Supply Changes

This section will describe the demand response to autonomous wealth changes, using the framework of indifference curves. The analysis amplifies the discussion of Part B(4).

In Figure 2B–4 the existing-asset market equilibrium is disturbed by a subsidy of idle balances. The initial quantities of the assets are designated

FIGURE 2B–4
The Impact of a Subsidy of Idle Balances on the Existing-Asset Market

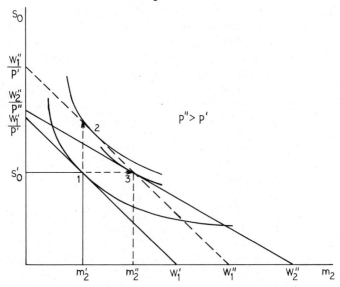

by point 1. Following the subsidy, the quantities are at point 3, the abscissa of which is m_2'', the new supply of idle money. When security prices are allowed to adjust sufficiently, point 2 will become the new equilibrium position. For the moment, however we hold p fixed at p', and consider the shift in the budget line and the desired holdings of each asset. When m_2 increases to m_2'', wealth becomes

$$(2B.9)' \qquad W_1'' = S_O'p' + m_2'',$$

where W_1'' is the point at p' on the new wealth function,

$$(2B.10)' \qquad W'' = S_O'p + m_2''.$$

The line of attainable combinations corresponding to W_1'' is

$$(2B.11)' \qquad S_O = \frac{W_1''}{p'} - \left(\frac{1}{p'}\right)m_2,$$

whose vertical intercept, W_1''/p', exceeds that of the previous line, $(2B.3)'$, by

$$\frac{W_1''}{p'} - \frac{W_1'}{p'} = \frac{m_2'' - m_2'}{p'}.$$

The horizontal intercept of the new line is W_1'', which is greater than the previous intercept by

$$W_1'' - W_1' = m_2'' - m_2',$$

the wealth subsidy. Since p is still p', the lines are parallel.

In view of our assumptions in Part B(4), the tangency point will lie along the new budget line between the two vectors drawn from point 1; i.e., desired holdings of *both* assets will increase ([2B.26]). However, in view of (2B.27) and the comments following, the new point, 2, is located nearer to the vertical than the horizontal vector.

The effect of the subsidy is to raise p, except in the limiting case in which point 2 coincides with point 3 in the first instance. As p increases, the budget line rotates counterclockwise through point 3 (see Figure 2B–4). At $p'' > p'$, we have

$(2B.12)'$ $$W_2'' \doteq S_O' p'' + m_2'',$$

FIGURE 2B–5
The Impact of a Subsidy of Securities on the
Existing-Asset Market

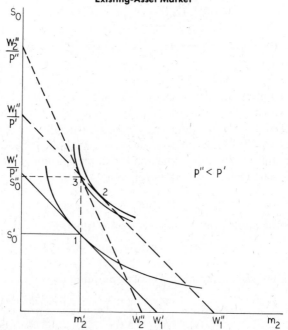

and a budget line,

$$(2B.13)' \qquad S_O = \frac{W_2''}{p''} - \left(\frac{1}{p''}\right)m_2 .$$

Point 3 is common to both budget lines since at any price, the budget based on the wealth function, W'', is exhaustible between the underlying *de facto* quantities, S_O' and m_2''. If p'' is high enough to equate demand to the existing supplies, this will be reflected in a tangency at point 3. This is the case shown in the diagram. Notice that point 3 lies on a lower indifference curve than does point 2. This will invariably be true.[3]

A subsidy of securities is diagramed in Figure 2B–5. The increase in securities to S_O'' shifts the supply point from 1 to 3, and the budget line to

$$(2B.14)' \qquad S_O = \frac{W_1''}{p'} - \left(\frac{1}{p'}\right)m_2, \quad \text{where} \quad W_1'' = S_O''p' + m_2'.$$

With p fixed at p', the initial effect is to create a tangency at point 2. However, p will tend to fall, causing the budget line to rotate clockwise through point 3. This continues until the tangency occurs at point 3, which represents a lower satisfaction level than does point 2.

---

[3] The vertical intercept of the final budget line, W_2''/p'', is shown in Figure 2B-4 to be greater than the intercept of the initial line, W_1'/p'. There is, in fact, no necessary relationship between these intercepts. We may observe

$$\frac{W_2''}{p''} \gtreqless \frac{W_1'}{p'} .$$

Upon substitution, this inequality is

$$\frac{S_O'p'' + m_2''}{p''} \gtreqless \frac{S_O''p' + m_2'}{p'} ,$$

$$\frac{m_2''}{p''} \gtreqless \frac{m_2'}{p'} .$$

Clearly, there is no necessity that the final ratios bear any particular relationship to each other.

A Quantitative Comparison of the Transfer and Wealth Effects

Our purpose here is to assess the general relative importance of the transfer and wealth effects to the adjustment process. We want to know what part of the return of the interest rate to equilibrium is attributable to each equilibrating mechanism. We provide a first approximation to the influences acting on r_M by isolating their relative impact on the value of idle money. Specifically, we determine upper and lower limits for that part of the total decline in m_2 during the adjustment process accomplished by the transfer and wealth effects, respectively. We can focus on idle balances for this analysis since they are the medium through which the whole trio of forces altering the interest rate acts: the initial disturbance, which is an open-market purchase, is an assumed increase in idle balances only; the transfer effect is a depletion of idle funds in favor of the active circulation; and the wealth effect is a devaluation of m_2 on account of the increased price level. Moreover, whatever changes occur later in the stock of capital and the real value of securities have no impact on the quantity or value of idle balances. Ideally, the change in r_M resulting from changes in m_2 would be measured along a specific L_2 schedule, taking account of its shifts and rotations during the transition to the new equilibrium. But if we are willing to assume that the change in r_M is proportional to the change in m_2, whatever its source, the following analysis will provide a rough and ready approximation to the importance of each equilibrating mechanism.

The extent to which the transfer and wealth effects individually lower m_2 and raise r_M depends on the timing of the transfers relative to the movement of the price level. We can show that the nominal transfers of

M_2 will diminish M_2/P more the lower is the general price level:

(4A.1)'
$$\frac{\partial\left(\dfrac{M_2}{P}\right)}{\partial M_2} = \frac{1}{P}.$$

On the other hand, a rise in the price level will produce a greater reduction in M_2/P the greater is M_2 and the less is P:

(4A.2)'
$$\frac{\partial\left(\dfrac{M_2}{P}\right)}{\partial P} = -\frac{M_2}{P^2}.$$

Thus the transfers and the inflation will exercise a maximum impact on m_2 the sooner they occur relative to each other. Our procedure, accordingly, will be to express the portion of the total required change in m_2 attributable to an equilibrating mechanism, assuming, first, that it completely leads, and then completely lags the alternative mechanism. We can illustrate the procedure by applying it to the numerical example of Part D(1). The task of the equilibrating mechanisms there was to reduce m_2 from $65/2 = 32.50$, its value immediately following an open-market purchase occurring entirely on wealth account, to 25.00, its new equilibrium value on the assumption that m_2 returns to its pre-operation level. This was accomplished by transferring $10 in idle balances to the income stream, following which the price level increased to $2.2, and m_2 was $55/2.2 = 25.00$, the required value. If the entire $10 transfer occurs prior to any change in the price level, and ceases when P starts to rise, the transfer effect lowers m_2 from 32.50 to $55/2 = 27.50$, accomplishing

$$\frac{32.50 - 27.50}{32.50 - 25.00} = \frac{5.00}{7.50} \text{ or 67 percent}$$

of the total required movement in m_2. Then the rise in P lowers m_2 from 27.50 to $55/2.2 = 25.00$, accounting for the remaining 33 percent of the reduction. At the opposite and, of course, impossible extreme, a rise in P to 2.2 prior to any transfer would lower m_2 from 32.50 to $65/2.2 = 29.55$, accomplishing

$$\frac{32.50 - 29.55}{32.50 - 25.00} = \frac{2.95}{7.50} \text{ or 39 percent}$$

of the movement in m_2. The transfers would then lower an idle-money supply initially valued at $65/2.2 = 29.55$ to 25.00, accounting for 61 percent of the total decline in m_2. The adjustment process is characterized, of course, by simultaneous transfers and movements of the price level. The relative contribution of the transfer effect to the total reduction of m_2 will therefore lie between 61 percent and 67 percent, and that of the wealth effect, between 33 percent and 39 percent. The greater percentage in each case will be approached the sooner the equilibrating mechanism operates, and thus the greater the value of M_2/P^2 confronting the price level, and $1/P$ facing the transfers, at the time m_2 is acted upon. But since an initial transfer must precede any movement in P, the contribution of the transfer effect will tend to exceed 61 percent, and that of the wealth effect to fall below 39 percent.

The general factors determining the upper and lower limits are derived as follows. We drop the assumption that m_2 in the new equilibrium, m_2^n, is necessarily the same as before the operation, m_2'. The monetary magnitudes prior to the operation are as given in Part D(1):

$$M' = M_1' + M_2', V_1', y', P' = \frac{M_1' V_1'}{y'}.$$

The purchase raises the money supply to

$$M^n = M' + \Delta M^n, \text{ where } \Delta M^n = \Delta M_1^n + \Delta M_2^n.$$

The Δ-terms are, in order, the total magnitude of the purchase, the total portion transferred to the income stream during the adjustment, and the total addition to idle balances remaining in the new equilibrium. The new equilibrium variables are

$$M_1^n = M_1' + \Delta M_1^n, M_2^n = M_2' + \Delta M_2^n, \text{ and } P^n = \frac{M_1^n V_1'}{y'}.$$

Since the purchase occurs entirely on wealth account, the value of idle money immediately following the operation is

$$(4A.3)' \qquad\qquad m_2'' = \frac{M_2' + \Delta M^n}{P'}.$$

In the final equilibrium, m_2 is

$$(4A.4)' \qquad\qquad m_2^n = \frac{M_2^n}{P^n}.$$

The total required reduction in m_2 during the adjustment is thus

$$(4A.5)' \qquad m_2'' - m_2^n = (4A.3)' - (4A.4)' = \frac{M^n \Delta M_1^n}{M_1^n P'}.$$

Assume that the transfer of idle to active balances is completed before any rise in the price level occurs. The impact of the transfer on m_2 and r_M will thus be maximized, and that of the price level minimized. Under these circumstances the transfer reduces m_2 to

$$(4A.6)' \qquad\qquad m_2''' = \frac{M_2^n}{P'}.$$

The subsequent rise in the price level lowers m_2 to its new equilibrium value, m_2^n ([4A.4]'). Denote by $\bar{t}$ the maximum possible reduction in m_2 created by the transfer:

$$(4A.7)' \qquad \bar{t} = m_2'' - m_2''' = (4A.3)' - (4A.6)' = \frac{\Delta M_1^n}{P'},$$

which is the value of the transfer when $P = P'$. Let $\underline{w}$ be the minimum possible reduction in m_2 created by the rise in the price level:

$$(4A.8)' \qquad \underline{w} = m_2''' - m_2^n = (4A.6)' - (4A.4)' = \frac{M_2^n \Delta M_1^n}{M_1^n P'}.$$

The *relative* part of the total required movement in m_2 attributable to the maximum transfer is

$$(4A.9)' \qquad \frac{\bar{t}}{m_2'' - m_2^n} = \frac{(4A.7)'}{(4A.5)'} = \frac{M_1^n}{M^n},$$

the ratio of active to total money balances in the new equilibrium. The *relative* part of the total required movement in m_2 created by the delayed rise in the price level is

$$(4A.10)' \qquad \frac{\underline{w}}{m_2'' - m_2^n} = \frac{(4A.8)'}{(4A.5)'} = \frac{M_2^n}{M^n},$$

the ratio of idle to total money in the post-operation equilibrium. In the numerical example

$$\frac{\bar{t}}{m_2'' - m_2^n} = \frac{M_1^n}{M^n} = \frac{110}{165} = .67,$$

and

$$\frac{\underline{w}}{m_2'' - m_2^n} = \frac{M_2^n}{M^n} = \frac{55}{165} = .33.$$

Suppose, alternatively, that the price level rises to P'' before any part of the transfer is executed. In this event the inflation reduces m_2 from $m_2''([4A.3]')$ to

$$(4A.11)' \qquad m_2''' = \frac{M_2' + \Delta M^n}{P''},$$

and the transfer reduces m_2 from this value to m_2^n ([4A.4]'). Thus when the increase in the price level precedes the transfer, we have the maximum possible wealth effect on m_2,

$$(4A.12)' \qquad \bar{w} = m_2'' - m_2''' = (4A.3)' - (4A.11)' = \frac{(M_2' + \Delta M^n)\Delta M_1^n}{M_1^n P'}.$$

The minimum impact of the transfer on m_2 is

$$(4A.13)' \qquad \underline{t} = m_2''' - m_2^n = (4A.11)' - (4A.4)' = \frac{\Delta M_1^n}{P''},$$

the value of the transfer when $P = P''$. The relative movement in m_2 created by the minimum transfer is

$$(4A.14)' \qquad \frac{t}{m_2'' - m_2^n} = \frac{(4A.13)'}{(4A.5)'} = \frac{M_1'}{M''},$$

the ratio of the pre-operation quantity of active money to the post-operation total money supply. The relative movement in m_2 due to the price level that leads the transfer is

$$(4A.15)' \qquad \frac{\overline{w}}{m_2'' - m_2^n} = \frac{(4A.12)'}{(4A.5)'} = \frac{M_2' + \Delta M''}{M''},$$

the ratio of pre-operation idle balances plus the entire magnitude of the operation to total money following the purchase. In the numerical example

$$\frac{t}{m_2'' - m_2^n} = \frac{M_1'}{M''} = \frac{100}{165} = .61,$$

and

$$\frac{\overline{w}}{m_2'' - m_2^n} = \frac{M_2' + \Delta M''}{M''} = \frac{65}{165} = .39.$$

If the open-market operation creates increments to active and idle balances that are relatively very small, or that in any case do not seriously disturb the pre-existing ratio, then both (4A.9)' and (4A.14)', which express the relative contribution of the transfer to the total equilibrating change in m_2, approach M_1'/M', the pre-operation ratio of active to total balances. Under the same circumstances the relative contribution of the price level, as given by (4A.10)' and (4A.15)', approaches M_2'/M', the ratio of idle to total money prior to the purchase.

We can enlarge our understanding of these results by constructing two additional numerical examples, differing essentially in their ratio of active to idle balances. The relevent monetary data for each are presented below, before and after an open-market purchase that raises the total money supply of $M' = 100$ by $\Delta M'' = 10$. m_2 is computed in each example at four stages: m_2' is the pre-disturbance value, m_2'' is the immediate post-operation value on the assumption that only idle balances are raised initially, m_2''' is computed directly after a transfer that occurs before the price level rises, and m_2^n is the new equilibrium value following the increase in the price level. The assumption is made that the pre- and post-operation equilibrium ratio of active to total balances is the same. Thus

$$m_2^n = m_2' \quad \text{and} \quad \Delta M_1^n = \left(\frac{M_1'}{M'}\right) \Delta M''.$$

The relative contribution of the transfer and wealth effects to the total movement in m_2 during the adjustment process, $m_2'' - m_2^n$, is computed, and all four values of m_2 are plotted on diagrams of the L_2 function in Figures 4A-1 and 4A-2. L_2 is constructed as a fixed schedule, abstracting from its shifts and rotations during the period of adjustment. In each diagram r_N' is the equilibrium interest rate, r_M'' is the bank's purchase yield, and r_M''' is the yield remaining after the transfers and sales of excess new securities.

Example (a)

$$\frac{M_1'}{M'} = 0.20,\ M' = 100,\ M_1' = 20,\ M_2' = 80,\ V_1' = 2,\ y' = 100.$$

$$P' = \frac{M_1' V_1'}{y'} = \frac{20 \times 2}{100} = 0.4.$$

$$\Delta M_1'' = \frac{M_1'}{M'}\Delta M'' = \frac{20}{100} \times 10 = 2,\ \Delta M_2'' = \Delta M'' - \Delta M_1'' = 10 - 2 = 8.$$

$$P'' = \frac{(M_1' + \Delta M_1'')V_1'}{y'} = \frac{(20 + 2) \times 2}{100} = 0.44.$$

$$m_2' = \frac{M_2'}{P'} = \frac{80}{0.4} = 200.$$

$$m_2'' = \frac{M_2' + \Delta M''}{P'} = \frac{90}{0.4} = 225.$$

$$m_2''' = \frac{M_2' + \Delta M_2''}{P'} = \frac{88}{0.4} = 220.$$

$$m_2^n = \frac{M_2' + \Delta M_2''}{P''} = \frac{88}{0.44} = 200.$$

$$\frac{t}{m_2'' - m_2^n} = \frac{m_2'' - m_2'''}{m_2'' - m_2^n} = \frac{225 - 220}{225 - 200} = \frac{5}{25} = 0.20.$$

$$\frac{w}{m_2'' - m_2^n} = \frac{m_2''' - m_2^n}{m_2'' - m_2^n} = \frac{220 - 200}{225 - 200} = \frac{20}{25} = 0.80.$$

(See Figure 4A-1)

Example (b)

$$\frac{M_1'}{M'} = 0.80,\ M' = 100,\ M_1' = 80,\ M_2' = 20,\ V_1' = 2,\ y' = 100.$$

$$P' = \frac{M_1' V_1'}{y'} = \frac{80 \times 2}{100} = 1.6.$$

$$\Delta M_1'' = \frac{M_1'}{M'}\Delta M'' = \frac{80}{100} \times 10 = 8,\ \Delta M_2'' = \Delta M'' - \Delta M_1'' = 10 - 8 = 2.$$

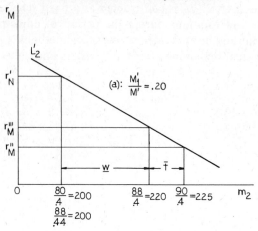

FIGURE 4A–1
The Impact of Each Equilibrating Mechanism on the
Value of Idle Money and the Rate of Interest When
Idle Balances Are Relatively Numerous

$$P'' = \frac{(M_1' + \Delta M_1'')V_1'}{y'} = \frac{(80 + 8)2}{100} = 1.76 .$$

$$m_2' = \frac{M_2'}{P'} = \frac{20}{1.6} = 12.50 .$$

$$m_2'' = \frac{M_2' + \Delta M''}{P'} = \frac{30}{1.6} = 18.75 .$$

$$m_2''' = \frac{M_2' + \Delta M_2''}{P'} = \frac{22}{1.6} = 13.75 .$$

$$m_2^n = \frac{M_2' + \Delta M_2''}{P''} = \frac{22}{1.76} = 12.50 .$$

$$\frac{\bar{t}}{m_2'' - m_2^n} = \frac{m_2'' - m_2'''}{m_2'' - m_2^n} = \frac{18.75 - 13.75}{18.75 - 12.50} = \frac{5.00}{6.25} = 0.80 .$$

$$\frac{w}{m_2'' - m_2^n} = \frac{m_2''' - m_2^n}{m_2'' - m_2^n} = \frac{13.75 - 12.50}{18.75 - 12.50} = \frac{1.25}{6.25} = 0.20 .$$

(See Figure 4A–2)

$M_1'/M' = .20$ in Example (a) and $.80$ in Example (b). The transfer, carried out under conditions most favorable to it, is $\Delta M_1'' = 2$ in (a) and $\Delta M_1'' = 8$ in (b), and its relative contribution to the decline in m_2 in (a) is .20, and in (b), .80. Each of these ratios is equal to $M_1'/M' = M_1''/M''$ ([4A.9]'). The wealth effect lowers m_2 in (a) by

$$m_2''' - m_2^n = 220 - 200 = 20,$$

and in (b) by

$$13.75 - 12.50 = 1.25.$$

The corresponding relative reductions in m_2 are .80 in (a), and .20 in (b), both of which are equal to M'_2/M' (cf. [4A.10]'). Thus, when M'_1/M' is small, as in (a), the price level predominates over the impact of the transfer on m_2. This is because most of the funds introduced by a purchase tend to remain idle balances, in accordance with the pre-operation ratio, while a relatively small amount is transferred to the income stream. But even a relatively small transfer is substantial relative to the existing quantity of active balances. Since M_2 is large, the resulting increase in P creates a large relative decline in real idle balances. If M'_1/M' is large, as in (b), the transfer accounts for more of the change in m_2 than does the inflation. In this case most of a monetary injection tends to be transferred to the active circulation. But transfers are small in comparison with existing active balances, and, in fact, create the same relative increase in the price level (10 percent) that occurred in (a). This, together with the fact that the quantity of idle balances is not great, means that the inflation creates a small part of the total reduction in m_2.

The monetary systems of Examples (a) and (b) differ not only in the ratio of idle to active balances, but also in the implied slope of the demand schedule for idle balances. If the interest movement created by the purchase, r'_N to r''_M, is the same for each example, then, for a given interest increment, L_2 in (a) is drawn over an increase of real idle balances of $225 - 200 = 25$, compared with L_2 in (b), where the increase is just one fourth as great, $18.75 - 12.50 = 6.25$. L_2 is thus much flatter in (a) than

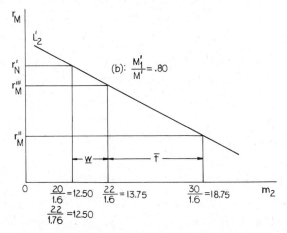

FIGURE 4A–2
The Impact of Each Equilibrating Mechanism on the Value of Idle Money and the Rate of Interest When Idle Balances Are Relatively Scarce

in (b). This is a reasonable difference between the two systems, since, other things equal, one would expect a flatter, more elastic demand schedule to be associated with a greater idle-money supply. The greater quantity of idle balances in (a), with the resulting lower price level, is also the reason that a purchase of \$10 has a much greater real magnitude in (a)—25—compared with 6.25 in (b). However, the difference between the magnitude of the purchase in each example is of no importance, since the relative roles of the transfer and wealth effects depend only on the ratio of idle to active balances and would be the same for any magnitude of purchase.

Security Prices and Quantities: Quantitative Limits

In this appendix we shall derive upper and lower quantitative limits for the final security price, the average price, and the number of securities—both excess and savers' purchases—floated during the adjustment process. Four pairs of limits—one each for p^n, p_a, $\sum_n \Delta S_E$, and $\sum_n \Delta S_S$—are derived for zero and complete forced saving in the context of the growing economy as described in Parts C(6) and D(6). The individual limits are presented in a sequence dictated by analytical requirements. Thus, while we start with $p^n(U)$, the upper limit for the final price, $p^n(L)$, the lower limit, cannot be found until limits for all of the other variables are known. We begin with the zero forced-saving adjustment.

1. Zero Forced Saving

a) $p^n(U)$

$p^n(U)$ is an upper bound for the real security price of the zero forced-saving equilibrium. It is derived by induction from the analysis of the first interval of the growing economy (Part C[6]a). We assume that ρ_K is constant at ρ_K', and the wealth effect on interest is zero. The closing price of the first interval is

$$p^4 = \frac{\rho_s^4}{r_M'''}, \quad \text{where} \quad \rho_s^4 = \frac{\rho_K'(K' + \Delta K')}{(S_P' + \Delta S_E' + \Delta S_S')}.$$

Accordingly, $p^4(U) = \rho_s^4(U)/r_M'''$. Replacing ΔK by $\Delta S_S' p'''$ ([5C.33]),

$$\rho_s^4(U) = \lim \left(\frac{\rho_K'(K' + \Delta S_S' p''')}{S_P' + \Delta S_E' + \Delta S_S'} \right) = \rho_K' p''.$$

$$\Delta S_S' \to \infty$$

$$\Delta S_E' \to 0$$

$$p''' \to p''$$

The limit is taken for $\Delta S_S' = \infty$ and $\Delta S_E' = 0$, since voluntary saving raises ρ_s ([5C.40]), while excess securities lower it (page 129–30).[1] p'', the opening price, is an upper limit for p''', the transfer price. Substituting $\rho_s^4(U)$,

$$p^4(U) = \left(\frac{\rho_K'}{r_M'''}\right)p'', \quad \text{where} \quad \frac{\rho_K'}{r_M'''} > 1.$$

At the close of the second interval, the upper bound for ρ_s, based on the same kind of limit taken for the first interval, is

$$\rho_s^5(U) = \rho_K' p^4(U) = \left(\frac{(\rho_K')^2}{r_M'''}\right)p''.$$

After n intervals,

$$\rho_s^n(U) = \left(\frac{(\rho_K')^n}{\prod\limits^{n-1} r_M}\right)p'',$$

where the denominator is the product over $n - 1$ intervals of the interest rates between r_M''' and r_M^{n-1}, the yield of the penultimate interval. The upper limit for the final security price is

$$p^n(U) = \frac{\rho_s^n(U)}{r_N'} = \left(\frac{(\rho_K')^n}{r_N'\prod\limits^{n-1} r_M}\right)p'' = \left(\frac{(\rho_K')^{n-1}}{\prod\limits^{n-1} r_M}\right)p'',$$

where the coefficient of p'' is greater than one. Hence

(5A.1)′
$$p^n < \left(\frac{(\rho_K')^{n-1}}{\prod\limits^{n-1} r_M}\right)p''.$$

We avoid entering an equality sign in (5A.1)′ since some of the limiting assumptions—namely, that $\Delta S_E = 0$ and $p''' = p''$ in the first interval, cannot actually be achieved.

If the wealth effect on interest is present, security prices, including p^n, tend to be raised (page 149 and Part C[5]). However, (5A.1)′ is still the upper limit for p^n, since it incorporates the assumption that ΔS_E of each interval approaches zero, the condition most favorable to the wealth effect. If the wealth effect were in fact the *only* equilibrating mechanism, the adjustment would be instantaneous and p^n would be at most $\rho_K' K'/r_N' S_P' = p'$, which is less than (5A.1)′.

If ρ_K should rise, $p^n(U)$ may rise above (5A.1)′. The rise in ρ_K raises

---

[1] Given $\Delta K' = \Delta S_S' p'''$ and $p''' > 0$, $\Delta S_S' = \infty$ is incompatible with our assumption that the maximum rate of voluntary saving is a finite amount, $\Delta K' = \hat{\Delta}K'$, which occurs when $\partial S/\partial r_M = 0$. However, the limit may be regarded as a maximum maximorum, applicable to any system, however great its rate of equilibrium growth.

p^n by raising the average security price, which lowers the security quantities without affecting the other terms in p^n. The highest final price produced by variability of ρ_K is

$$p^n(U) = \lim \frac{K' + \sum_n \Delta K}{S'_P + \sum_n \Delta S_E + \sum_n \Delta S_S} = \frac{K' + n\hat{\Delta}K'}{S'_P} = p' + \frac{n\hat{\Delta}K'}{S'_P}.$$

$$\sum_n \Delta S_E \to 0,$$

$$\sum_n \Delta S_S \to 0,$$

$$\sum_n \Delta K \to n\hat{\Delta}K'$$

p^n in this case is maximized by taking the highest possible value of $\sum_n \Delta K$, $n\hat{\Delta}K'$, the growth of the undisturbed economy. Thus a possible alternative to (5A.1)' is

(5A.2)' $$p^n < p' + \frac{n\hat{\Delta}K'}{S'_P}.$$

 b) $p_a(U)$

p_a, the mean real security price over the entire adjustment, is the average of prices between p'' and p^n, the opening and final price, respectively. We know that even with ρ_K constant, the closing price of any interval may exceed the opening price, starting with p'' (Part C[2]). Since $p^n(U)$, as given by (5A.1)', was generated by closing prices that are above each opening price, p_a may itself exceed p''. In general, the most we can say about the upper limit for p_a is

(5A.3)' $$p_a < p(\text{max.}),$$

where p (max.) is the highest possible individual price during the adjustment. p (max.) is equal to (5A.1)' if ρ_K is constant, and possibly to (5A.2)' otherwise.

 c) $\sum_n \Delta S_E(L)$

$\sum_n \Delta S_E$, the total quantity of excess new securities, can be expressed as a function of S'_B. If Δw is the absolute total reduction in m_2 created by the inflation, then

$$\sum_n \Delta S_E p_a = (m''_2 - m'_2) - \Delta w,$$

and by (5B.22),

(5A.4)' $$\sum_n \Delta S_E = \frac{S'_B p'' - \Delta w}{p_a}.$$

Assume for the moment that $\Delta w = 0$ (i.e., that the wealth effect on interest is absent). Then, $\sum_n \Delta S_E \gtreqless S'_B$ when $p_a \lesseqgtr p''$. Let us start with the lower limit for $\sum_n \Delta S_E$. Is there any assurance that $\sum_n \Delta S_E \gtreqless S'_B$? This would require $p_a \lesseqgtr p''$. But we have just noted that even if ρ_K is constant at ρ'_K, p_a may exceed p''(Section b), resulting in $\sum_n \Delta S_E < S'_B$. ρ_K, of course, may rise temporarily during the adjustment, raising p_a and reducing $\sum_n \Delta S_E$ to zero in the limit. Finally, we know that the wealth effect tends to reduce $\sum_n \Delta S_E$—directly, by leaving fewer idle balances available for transfer, and indirectly by raising p_a (Part C[5]). In the limiting case in which Δw approaches $S'_B p''$, $\sum_n \Delta S_E$ goes to zero. The only certain lower limit that can be assigned to $\sum_n \Delta S_E$ is thus

(5A.5)′ $$\sum_n \Delta S_E > 0.$$

(5A.5)′ omits an equality sign since the adjustment requires that some excess securities be floated.

d) $\sum_n \Delta S_E(U)$

The upper limit for $\sum_n \Delta S_E$ is derived by reconsidering the adjustment process in terms of the existing security-quantity schedules. Since we are seeking the upper limit, we consider the most favorable case in which ρ_K is constant at ρ'_K and $\Delta w = 0$. In Figure 5A–1, S'_O and D'_O are the predisturbance existing supply and demand for securities. The purchase re-

FIGURE 5A–1
Rotations of the Security-Quantity Demand Schedule
during the Zero Forced-Saving Adjustment

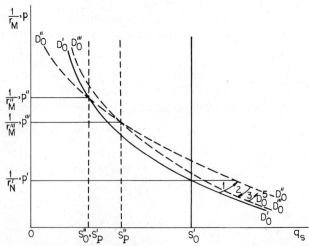

duces S_O to $S_O'' = S_P'$ and r_M to r_M'', through the reciprocal of which D_O rotates counterclockwise to the position of D_O''. The direction of this and subsequent rotations is indicated by small arrows in the diagram. The numbers above the arrows indicate their order of occurrence over time. During the first adjustment interval the interest rate is raised to r_M''' by excess securities of $\Delta S_E' = D_O''(r_M''') - S_P'$. This raises the security total to S_P''. The resulting clockwise rotation through $1/r_M'''$ brings D_O to D_O'''. At the same time, however, savers also purchase new securities. This is reflected in a further increase to S_P'''. But since this increment is accompanied by an equal parallel movement in D_O to D_O^4, it is omitted from the diagram. Our conclusions regarding $\sum_n \Delta S_E$ depend only on movements in D_O relative to S_O, and are in no way qualified by equal parallel shifts in the two schedules.

At the close of the interval ρ_s changes spontaneously in response to the increase in capital due to voluntary saving, and the stock watering due to $\Delta S_E'$. If ρ_s rises, D_O rotates clockwise through $1/r_M'''$ (Chapter III-B[2]b), falling even farther to the left of $D_O''(r_N')$. If ρ_s falls, the rotation in D_O is counterclockwise, carrying it toward $D_O''(r_N')$, as indicated by the arrow. However, we can prove that at r_N', the fall in ρ_s cannot bring the final schedule, D_O^5 (not diagramed), as far to the right as D_O''. The proof of $D_O^5(r_N') < D_O''(r_N')$ is presented in Section e, which also generalizes this result for the over-all adjustment; i.e., at r_N', the closing demand schedule of any subsequent interval lies to the left of D_O''. Since at r_N', D_O'' is a right boundary to all demand schedules generated during the adjustment, we take as the upper limit for excess securities,

$$\sum_n \Delta S_E = D_O''(r_N') - S_P'.$$

Upon further substitution (see Figure 5A–1),

$$\sum_n \Delta S_E = S_O' - S_P' + [D_O''(r_N') - S_O'] = S_B' + [D_O''(r_N') - S_O'].$$

With reference to (3B.6), incorporating the assumption that D_{VO} absorbs the entire wealth increment,

$$D_O''(r_N') - S_O' = \frac{S_B'(p'' - p')}{p'}.$$

Hence

$$\sum_n \Delta S_E = S_B'\left(1 + \frac{p'' - p'}{p'}\right) = S_B'\left(\frac{p''}{p'}\right).$$

Combining this result with (5A.5)′, we conclude:

(5A.6)′ $$0 < \sum_n \Delta S_E < S_B'\left(\frac{p''}{p'}\right).$$

Since none of the demand schedules can ever quite reach D_O'' at r_N', we omit the equality sign in the upper limit.

e) Proof of $D_O^s(r_N') < D_O''(r_N')$

We wish to prove that during the first interval of zero forced saving, the final security demand schedule, D_O^s, is to the left of the opening schedule, D_O'', at the equilibrium interest rate, r_N'; i.e., $D_O^s(r_N') < D_O''(r_N')$. The proof is carried out with reference to the existing value schedules, which are drawn in Figure 5A-2. The initial schedules are S_{VO}'' and D_{VO}'', which meet at $1/r_M''$. $\partial D_{VO}''/\partial p = 0$. Following the transfer of $D_{VO}''(r_M''') - S_{VO}''(r_M''') = AB$ in idle balances, S_{VO}''' and D_{VO}''', reflecting a clockwise rotation through $1/r_M'''$, prevail. These are the same schedules drawn in Figure 5-6, except that we are omitting those produced by voluntary saving.

FIGURE 5A–2
The Security-Value Schedules
during the First Interval of Zero Forced Saving

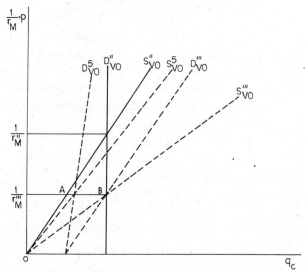

Now, if ρ_s should fall at the close of the interval, the movement from S_{VO}'' to S_{VO}''' will tend to be reversed. However, we can show that the movement cannot be completely reversed, and the final schedule incorporating the excess securities only, S_{VO}^s, will lie to the right of S_{VO}''. $S_{VO}^s > S_{VO}''$ is

$$(S_P' + \Delta S_E')\left(\frac{\rho_s^4}{r_M}\right) > S_P'\left(\frac{\rho_s'''}{r_M}\right),$$

$$(S_P' + \Delta S_E')\left(\frac{\rho_K'(K' + \Delta K')}{r_M(S_P' + \Delta S_E' + \Delta S_S')}\right) > S_P'\left(\frac{\rho_K'K'}{r_M S_P'}\right),$$

which, upon expansion and collection of terms, is

$$\frac{\Delta K'}{\Delta S'_S} > \frac{K'}{S'_P + \Delta S'_E}.$$

Since $\Delta K'/\Delta S'_S = p'''$ ([5C.33]), the inequality is

$$p''' > \frac{K'}{S'_P + \Delta S'_E},$$

$$\left(\frac{\rho'_K}{r'''_M}\right)\left(\frac{K'}{S'_P}\right) > \frac{K'}{S'_P + \Delta S'_E},$$

where $\rho'_K/r'''_M > 1$. Both factors on the left are greater than the single term on the right, establishing the inequality.

S^5_{VO} is accordingly drawn to the right of S''_{VO} in Figure 5A–2. D_{VO} moves equally to

$$D^5_{VO} = D''_{VO} - [AB + (S^5_{VO} - S''_{VO})].$$

Since $S^5_{VO} - S''_{VO}$ increases with p, $D''_{VO} - D^5_{VO}$ decreases; i.e., the latter schedules converge. The corresponding quantity demand schedules are

$$D''_O = \frac{D''_{VO}}{\left(\dfrac{\rho'_s}{r_M}\right)} \quad \text{and} \quad D^5_O = \frac{D^5_{VO}}{\left(\dfrac{\rho^4_s}{r_M}\right)}.$$

Their ratio is

$$\frac{D''_O}{D^5_O} = \left(\frac{D''_{VO}}{D^5_{VO}}\right)\left(\frac{\rho^4_s}{\rho'''_s}\right), \quad \text{where } \rho'''_s = \rho'_s.$$

But

$$\frac{S^5_{VO}}{S'''_{VO}} = \frac{(S'_P + \Delta S'_E)\left(\dfrac{\rho^4_s}{r_M}\right)}{(S'_P + \Delta S'_E)\left(\dfrac{\rho'''_s}{r_M}\right)} = \frac{\rho^4_s}{\rho'''_s}, \quad \text{a constant.}$$

Hence

(5A.7)′ $$\frac{D''_O}{D^5_O} = \left(\frac{D''_{VO}}{D^5_{VO}}\right)\left(\frac{S^5_{VO}}{S'''_{VO}}\right).$$

In Figure 5A–2 at r'''_M, $D^5_{VO} = S^5_{VO}$ and $D''_{VO} = S'''_{VO}$. At this yield the shifts from D''_{VO} to D^5_{VO} and S'''_{VO} to S^5_{VO} are thus equal absolute and relative movements, and by (5A.7)′, $D''_O/D^5_O = 1$. But at $r_M < r'''_M$, D''_{VO}/D^5_{VO} has decreased, since D''_{VO}, a constant, is divided by a greater denominator. Since S^5_{VO}/S'''_{VO} is constant, $D''_O/D^5_O < 1$. At $r_M > r'''_M$, D''_{VO}/D^5_{VO} has increased, and $D''_O/D^5_O > 1$. To summarize:

(5A.8)′ $$\frac{D_O''}{D_O^s} \gtreqless 1 \quad \text{when} \quad r_M \gtreqless r_M'''.$$

If, alternatively, the interval had begun with $\partial D_{VO}''/\partial p \gtrless 0$, (5A.7)′ would still hold. If $\partial D_{VO}''/\partial p > 0$, then $\partial D_{VO}^s/\partial p > 0$, since D_{VO}'' and D_{VO}^s converge as p increases. (5A.8)′ continues to hold since D_{VO}'' increases less rapidly than does D_{VO}^s as r_M falls. If $\partial D_{VO}''/\partial p < 0$, convergence provides that $\partial D_{VO}^s/\partial p \gtrless 0$. If, in this case, $\partial D_{VO}^s/\partial p < 0$, (5A.8)′ holds since D_{VO}'' falls more rapidly than does D_{VO}^s as r_M decreases. If, alternatively, $\partial D_{VO}^s/\partial p > 0$, D_{VO}'' falls while D_{VO}^s increases. In all cases, then, D_O^s represents a net clockwise rotation relative to D_O'', and $D_O^s(r_N') < D_O''(r_N')$.

The events of the first interval can be extrapolated to any subsequent interval. The transfer will cause a clockwise rotation that exceeds any counterclockwise movement in the event that ρ_s falls. At r_N', which exceeds the transfer yield, the closing demand curve is to the left of the opening one. This will occur, whatever the slope of the opening D_{VO} schedule. D_O'', produced directly by the purchase, is therefore a right boundary at r_N' to all subsequent D_O curves, abstracting from increments due to voluntary saving.

f) $p_a(L)$

The results of Section d are the basis of a lower limit for p_a. Since the conditions that maximize $\sum_n \Delta S_E$ are also those that minimize p_a, we assume $\Delta w = 0$ and ρ_K constant at ρ_K'. (5A.4)′ will thus yield

$$p_a = p'' \left(\frac{S_B'}{\sum_n \Delta S_E} \right).$$

If we substitute on the right side of this expression, $S_B'/\sum_n \Delta S_E > p'/p''$, derived from (5A.6)′, we obtain a lower limit,

(5A.9)′ $$p_a > p'.$$

Combining (5A.9)′ with (5A.3)′:

(5A.10)′ $$p' < p_a < p(\text{max.}).$$

g) $\sum_n \Delta S_S(U)$ and (L)

$\sum_n \Delta S_S$, the number of securities purchased by savers during the adjustment, will be expressed as a function of $\sum_n \Delta \hat{S}_S = n\Delta \hat{S}_S'$, the number purchased during a comparable period of equilibrium growth. Since $\sum_n \Delta S_S = \sum_n \Delta K/p_a$ and $n\Delta \hat{S}_S' = n\Delta \hat{K}'/p'$,

$$\frac{\sum_n \Delta S_S}{n\Delta \hat{S}_S'} = \left(\frac{\sum_n \Delta K}{n\Delta \hat{K}'} \right) \left(\frac{p'}{p_a} \right).$$

If $\sum_n \Delta K = n\hat{\Delta}K'$,

$$\sum_n \Delta S_S = n\hat{\Delta}S_S'\left(\frac{p'}{p_a}\right).$$

But $p_a > p'$ ([5A.9]'), yielding an upper limit,

(5A.11)' $$\sum_n \Delta S_S < n\hat{\Delta}S_S'.$$

If, in view of $\partial S/\partial r_M > 0$, $\sum_n \Delta K < n\hat{\Delta}K'$, $\sum_n \Delta S_S$ falls even farther below $n\hat{\Delta}S_S'$. Given higher values of p_a (up to p [max.]), and lower values of $\sum_n \Delta K$ (down to zero), the lower limit is simply $\sum_n \Delta S_S \geqq 0$. Hence

(5A.12)' $$0 \lesseqgtr \sum_n \Delta S_S < n\hat{\Delta}S_S'.$$

h) $p^n(L)$

A lower bound for the final price is $p^n(L) = \rho_s^n(L)/r_N'$. The lower limit of p^n is thus

$$\lim\left(\frac{\rho_s^n}{r_N'}\right) = \lim\frac{\rho_K'(K' + \sum_n \Delta S_S p_a)}{r_N'(S_P' + \sum_n \Delta S_E + \sum_n \Delta S_S)} = \frac{K'}{S_P' + S_B'\left(\dfrac{p''}{p'}\right)}.$$

$$\sum_n \Delta S_S \to 0$$

$$\sum_n \Delta S_E \to S_B'\left(\frac{p''}{p'}\right)$$

Accordingly,

(5A.13)' $$p^n > \frac{K'}{S_P' + S_B'\left(\dfrac{p''}{p'}\right)}.$$

In ρ_s^n, $\sum_n \Delta K$ has been replaced by $\sum_n \Delta S_S p_a$. Since voluntary saving tends to raise ρ_s and p, the limit is taken as $\sum_n \Delta S_S$ goes to zero. The limit is also taken for the maximum possible value of $\sum_n \Delta S_E$, $S_B'(p''/p')$ ([5A.6]'). Notice that (5A.13)' corresponds to p^n produced by a zero forced-saving adjustment in abstraction from voluntary saving ([5C.23]). (5A.13)' and (5A.1)', which assumes ρ_K to be constant, together yield

(5A.14)' $$\frac{K'}{S_P' + S_B'\left(\dfrac{p''}{p'}\right)} < p^n < \left(\frac{(\rho_K')^{n-1}}{\prod^{n-1} r_M}\right)p''.$$

There is no equality sign in the lower limit since $\sum_n \Delta S_E$ cannot actually reach $S_B'(p''/p')$.

2. Complete Forced Saving

a) $p^n(U)$

The adjustment starts at p'', the purchase price, but the limiting first interval reduces p immediately to $p''' = p'$ (Part D[2]). Thereafter the net movement of p is downward, in direct proportion to the amount of voluntary and forced saving (pages 154 and 162). The upper limit is thus $p^n(U) = \rho_s^n(U)/r_N'$ or

$$\lim \frac{\rho_K'[K' + (m_2'' - m_2') + \sum_n \Delta K]}{r_N'(S_P' + \sum_n \Delta S_E + \sum_n \Delta S_S)} = \frac{K'}{S_P'} = p'.$$

$$(m_2'' - m_2') \to 0$$

$$\sum_n \Delta K \to 0$$

$$\sum_n \Delta S_E \to 0$$

$$\sum_n \Delta S_S \to 0$$

Since all security issues lead to capital formation, the limit is taken as both securities and capital go to zero. Thus

$$(5A.15)' \qquad\qquad\qquad p^n < p'.$$

p^n cannot, of course, equal p', since neither $m_2'' - m_2'$ nor $\sum_n \Delta S_E$ can actually be zero.

A positive wealth effect tends to raise ρ_s and p by reducing forced saving (Part D[5]), but this is already accounted for in (5A.15)' since the limit is taken for zero values of $m_2'' - m_2'$ (as capital stock) and $\sum_n \Delta S_E$.

b) $p_a(U)$

p_a is effectively the average of prices between p' and $p^n < p'$ (Section *a*). An upper bound for p_a is thus simply

$$(5A.16)' \qquad\qquad\qquad p_a < p'.$$

c) $\sum_n \Delta S_E(L)$

With reference to (5A.4)': if $\Delta w = 0$, $\sum_n \Delta S_E \gtreqless S_B'$ when $p \lesseqgtr p''$. But $p_a < p'$ ([5A.16]'). Substituting (5A.16)' for p_a in (5A.4)', where $\Delta w = 0$, a lower limit is

$$(5A.17)' \qquad\qquad \sum_n \Delta S_E > S_B'\left(\frac{p''}{p'}\right),$$

which is the same as the upper limit for $\sum_n \Delta S_E$ in zero forced saving ([5A.6]'). However, as Δw approaches $S_B'p''$, $\sum_n \Delta S_E$ approaches zero.

Thus a general lower limit is

$$(5A.18)' \qquad \sum_n \Delta S_E > 0.$$

d) $\sum_n \Delta S_E(U)$

The upper limit for excess securities is derived on the assumption that $\Delta w = 0$, since this maximizes $\sum_n \Delta S_E$. The analysis is carried out with the aid of Figure 5A–3. Following the counterclockwise rotation from D'_O to D''_O due to the direct impact of the purchase, the limiting first interval lowers ρ_K to ρ''_K and ρ_s to ρ'''_s. The drop in ρ_s creates a further counterclockwise rotation in D_O through the reciprocal of the purchase yield, producing D'''_O. Abstracting from the equal parallel shifts in S_O and D_O due to voluntary saving, all of the subsequent movements in D_O are clockwise rotations through the successively higher interest rates.

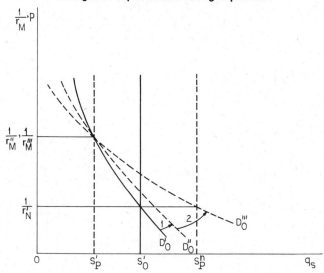

FIGURE 5A–3

Rotations of the Security-Quantity Demand Schedule during the Complete Forced-Saving Adjustment

In any interval, there is first the clockwise rotation due to the exchange of idle balances for excess securities. Following this, forced saving raises ρ_s, causing a further clockwise movement through the prevailing interest rate. At the height, $1/r'_N$, D_O thus moves constantly to the left until equilibrium is reached. D'''_O is accordingly a right boundary at r'_N to all of the D_O schedules of the adjustment process. An upper limit for $\sum_n \Delta S_E$ is thereby

$$\sum_n \Delta S_E = D'''_O(r'_N) - S'_P.$$

A convenient expression for the latter is obtained as follows:

$$D_O''' - S_P' = \frac{D_{VO}'''}{p} - S_P',$$

$$= \frac{D_{VO}'' + (S_{VO}''' - S_{VO}'')}{p} - S_P',$$

$$= \frac{D_O''\left(\frac{\rho_s'}{r_M}\right) + S_P'\left(\frac{\rho_s'''}{r_M}\right) - S_P'\left(\frac{\rho_s'}{r_M}\right)}{\frac{\rho_s'''}{r_M}} - S_P',$$

$$= D_O''\left(\frac{\rho_s'}{\rho_s'''}\right) + S_P' - S_P'\left(\frac{\rho_s'}{\rho_s'''}\right) - S_P',$$

$$= \left(\frac{\rho_s'}{\rho_s'''}\right)(D_O'' - S_P').$$

Upon successive substitutions,

$$\frac{\rho_s'}{\rho_s'''} = \frac{p' r_N'}{p' r_M''} = \frac{r_N'}{r_M''} = \frac{\frac{\rho_s'}{p'}}{\frac{\rho_s'}{p''}} = \frac{p''}{p'}.$$

With reference to the diagram and (3B.6), at r_N'

$$D_O'' - S_P' = (D_O'' - D_O') + (D_O' - S_P')$$

$$= S_B'(p'' - p') + S_B'.$$

Thus

$$D_O''' - S_P' = \left(\frac{p''}{p'}\right)S_B'(p'' - p' + 1),$$

and our upper limit is

(5A.19)' $$\sum_n \Delta S_E < S_B'\left(\frac{p''}{p'}\right)(p'' - p' + 1).$$

$\sum_n \Delta S_E$ cannot, of course, actually equal its upper limit, since the demand schedules move constantly to the left of $D_O'''(r_N')$.

A more useful form of the right side of (5A.19)' results from expanding and rearranging its last two terms:

$$\frac{p''}{p'}(p'' - p' + 1) = \frac{(p'')^2}{p'} - p'' + \frac{p''}{p'} = \frac{p''}{p'} + p''\left(\frac{p''}{p'} - 1\right),$$

where the parenthetical term is the relative increment between p' and p''. Combining the rearranged upper limit with (5A.17)', for which Δw also is zero,

$$(5A.20)' \qquad S'_B\left(\frac{p''}{p'}\right) < \sum_n \Delta S_E < S'_B\left[\frac{p''}{p'} + p''\left(\frac{p''}{p'} - 1\right)\right].$$

Notice that if $p' = 1$, the lower and upper limits are $S'_B p''$ and $S'_B(p'')^2$, respectively. In the general case in which $\Delta w > 0$, we combine (5A.18)' with (5A.19)':

$$(5A.21)' \qquad 0 < \sum_n \Delta S_E < S'_B\left(\frac{p''}{p'}\right)(p'' - p' + 1).$$

e) $p_a(L)$

A lower limit for p_a is obtained by substituting (5A.19)' in (5A.4)', letting $\Delta w = 0$:

$$(5A.22)' \qquad p_a > \frac{p'}{p'' - p' + 1}.$$

Together with (5A.16)':

$$(5A.23)' \qquad \frac{p'}{p'' - p' + 1} < p_a < p'.$$

f) $\sum_n \Delta S_S(U)$ *and* (L)

During complete forced saving, savers purchase a quantity of securities, $\sum_n \Delta S_S = \sum_n \Delta K / p_a$. Their purchases in the undisturbed equilibrium-growth sequence were $n\widehat{\Delta S'_S} = n\widehat{\Delta K'}/p'$, yielding

$$\frac{\sum_n \Delta S_S}{n\widehat{\Delta S'_S}} = \frac{\sum_n \Delta K}{n\widehat{\Delta K'}}\left(\frac{p'}{p_a}\right),$$

or simply p'/p_a if $\sum_n \Delta K = n\widehat{\Delta K'}$. However, $p_a < p'([5A.16]')$, causing $\sum_n \Delta S_S > n\widehat{\Delta S'_S}$. In the extreme case in which $p_a = p'/(p'' - p' + 1)$ ([5A.22]'),

$$\sum_n \Delta S_S = n\widehat{\Delta S'_S}(p'' - p' + 1),$$

an upper limit. The minimum for $\sum_n \Delta S_S$ occurs when $\sum_n \Delta K$ goes to zero: $\sum_n \Delta S_S = 0$. Accordingly,

$$(5A.24)' \qquad 0 \leqq \sum_n \Delta S_S < n\widehat{\Delta S'_S}(p'' - p' + 1).$$

g) $p^n(L)$

A lower limit for p^n is

$$\lim\left(\frac{\rho^n_s}{r^n_N}\right) = \lim \frac{\rho'_K(K' + m''_2 - m'_2 + \sum_n \Delta K)}{r'_N(S'_P + \sum_n \Delta S_E + \sum_n \Delta S_S)},$$

$$\sum_n \Delta K \rightarrow n \hat{\Delta} K'$$

$$\sum_n \Delta S_S \rightarrow n \hat{\Delta} S'_S (p'' - p' + 1)$$

$$\sum_n \Delta S_E \rightarrow S'_B \left(\frac{p''}{p'} \right) (p'' - p' + 1)$$

which is

(5A.25)′
$$\frac{K' + m''_2 - m'_2 + n\hat{\Delta}K'}{S'_P + S'_B \left(\dfrac{p''}{p'} \right)(p'' - p' + 1) + n\hat{\Delta}S'_S(p'' - p' + 1)}.$$

Since voluntary saving tends to reduce ρ_s and p, the limit is taken for the maximum value of $\sum_n \Delta K, n\hat{\Delta}K'$, the rate produced by $\partial S/\partial r_M = 0$. Both $\sum_n \Delta S_S$ and $\sum_n \Delta S_E$ in the denominator are also at their maximum values ([5A.24]′) and ([5A.19]′). Combining (5A.25)′ with (5A.15)′, we obtain

(5A.26)′
$$\left(\frac{K' + m''_2 - m'_2 + n\hat{\Delta}K'}{S'_P + S'_B \left(\dfrac{p''}{p'} \right)(p'' - p' + 1) + n\hat{\Delta}S'_S(p'' - p' + 1)} \right)$$

$$< p^n < p'.$$

3. Summary

A summary of the security price and quantity limits follows. The corresponding zero and complete forced-saving limits are paired. To facilitate comparison, the symbol, $\sim$, placed above a variable indicates that it is generated during the zero forced-saving adjustment; the symbol, $*$, identifies the variable as belonging to the complete forced-saving adjustment.

(5A.14)′
$$\frac{K'}{S'_P + S'_B \left(\dfrac{p''}{p'} \right)} < \tilde{p}^n < \left(\frac{(\rho'_K)^{n-1}}{\prod_{n-1} r_M} \right) p''.$$

(5A.26)′
$$\frac{K' + m''_2 - m'_2 + n\hat{\Delta}K'}{S'_P + S'_B \left(\dfrac{p''}{p'} \right)(p'' - p' + 1) + n\hat{\Delta}S'_S(p'' - p' + 1)} < \overset{*}{p}{}^n < p'.$$

(5A.10)′
$$p' < \tilde{p}_a < p \text{ (max.)}.$$

(5A.23)′
$$\frac{p'}{p'' - p' + 1} < \overset{*}{p}_a < p'.$$

(5A.6)′
$$0 < \sum_n \tilde{\Delta} S_E < S'_B \left(\frac{p''}{p'} \right).$$

$$(5A.21)' \qquad 0 < \sum_n \overset{*}{\Delta} S_E < S'_B\left(\frac{p''}{p'}\right)(p'' - p' + 1).$$

$$(5A.12)' \qquad 0 \lesseqgtr \sum_n \Delta \tilde{S}_S < n\hat{\Delta} S'_S.$$

$$(5A.24)' \qquad 0 \lesseqgtr \sum_n \overset{*}{\Delta} S_S < n\hat{\Delta} S'_S(p'' - p' + 1).$$

Where more than one limit is available, the most general was selected. $(5A.14)'$ contains the only limit based on a special assumption. $\tilde{p}^n(U)$ takes ρ_K to be constant; if ρ_K rises, $\tilde{p}^n(U)$ may be greater (cf. $[5A.2]'$).

A clear pattern emerging from the first four equations is that, despite some overlap, real security prices tend to be higher for zero than complete forced saving. For example, $(5A.10)'$ and $(5A.23)'$ indicate that $\tilde{p}_a(L) > \overset{*}{p}_a(U)$ (p' is the common boundary, which neither limit quite reaches). Thus $\tilde{p}_a > \overset{*}{p}_a$. This may seem paradoxical, in view of the stock-watering aspect of zero forced saving. But we have already noted that in the latter adjustment $\rho_K/r_M > 1$ exerts an upward tendency on p which varies directly with the rate of voluntary saving. Meanwhile, in complete forced saving the downward tendency of p is unrelenting—and greater for increased levels of voluntary saving. However, if the stock-watering effect on prices is sufficiently dominant over the influence of voluntary saving, then $\tilde{p}^n(L) < \overset{*}{p}^n(L)$ is a distinct possibility. An example of this would be if in $\overset{*}{p}^n(L)$ ($[5A.26]'$) the ratio of the numerator, excluding K', to the denominator, excluding S'_P, were at its maximum, $\overset{*}{p}_a = p'$ ($[5A.23]'$). Then since $K'/S'_P = p'$, $\overset{*}{p}^n(L)$ itself would be p', which is clearly above $\tilde{p}^n(L)$. Since $\tilde{p}^n(U) > \overset{*}{p}^n(U)$ ($[5A.14]'$ and $[5A.26]'$), our general conclusion is that security prices, including the final one, have a greater range for zero than complete forced saving. Since the range overlaps, $\tilde{p}^n$ may be above or below $\overset{*}{p}^n$, but in any case, $\tilde{p}_a > \overset{*}{p}_a$.

The upper limits for security quantities are in all cases greater for complete forced saving. Given $\tilde{p}_a > \overset{*}{p}_a$, this is the expected result. The lower limits are all zero, but there are more avenues for approaching them in the case of zero than complete forced saving. In the former adjustment a positive wealth effect and a variable ρ_K will both reduce the security quantities, but only the wealth effect may contribute to this end in complete forced saving.

For partial forced saving, the limits would encompass the entire possible range afforded by zero and complete forced saving together. Thus for a small degree of partial forced saving, $p^n(U)$ would approach $\tilde{p}^n(U)$ ($[5A.14]'$), while a greater degree might bring on $\overset{*}{p}^n(U)$ ($[5A.26]'$). Similarly, p_a may range from p (max.) ($[5A.10]'$) at the upper bound to $p'/(p'' - p' + 1)$ ($[5A.23]'$) at the lower. If ρ_K and thus ρ_s should fall sufficiently, $\sum_n \Delta S_E(U)$ will approach $\sum_n \overset{*}{\Delta} S_E(U)$ ($[5A.21]'$). By the same token, a sufficiently low p_a will generate $\sum_n \overset{*}{\Delta} S_S(U)$ ($[5A.24]'$), rather than $\sum_n \Delta \tilde{S}_S(U)$ ($[5A.12]'$).

The "λ-Model"

1. A Single-Security System

The model of Chapter V will be modified in this appendix by assuming, once again, that there is a single equity security in the economy held both by households and the central bank. Each security represents a proportionate claim to the private stock of capital. The total stock of existing securities is

$$(5B.1)' \qquad S_\tau = S_O + S_B,$$

where S_O is the quantity held by households, and S_B the quantity of the same kind of security held by the central bank. The ratio of privately held to total securities is

$$(5B.2)' \qquad \lambda = \frac{S_O}{S_\tau}.$$

The return per share and the share price are

$$(5B.3)' \qquad \rho_s = \frac{\rho_K K}{S_\tau} \text{ and } p = \frac{\rho_s}{r_M} = \frac{\rho_K K}{r_M S_\tau},$$

respectively. The value of securities held by households is

$$(5B.4)' \qquad S_{VO} = S_O p = S_O\left(\frac{\rho_s}{r_M}\right) = \left(\frac{S_O}{S_\tau}\right)\left(\frac{\rho_K K}{r_M}\right) = \lambda\left(\frac{\rho_K}{r_M}\right)K.$$

Total household wealth is

$$(5B.5)' \qquad W = S_{VO} + m_2 = \lambda\left(\frac{\rho_K}{r_M}\right)K + m_2.$$

In equilibrium, when $\rho_K = r_M$,

$$(5B.6)' \qquad W = \lambda K + m_2.$$

All saving and investment entail the purchase and sale, respectively, of the single equity security, which is also the only alternative to the holding of idle balances.

Though the model is basically simpler in that it consists of one, instead of two securities, it exhibits some interesting complications in regard to household wealth during an adjustment process. These arise from the fact that households share their ownership of capital with an outside agency. Nothing else in Chapter V is altered by reverting to a single security. Since the governmental issue was so closely tied to the private security in regard to ρ_s, p, and r_M, the existence of a single private security will in no way change the analysis of those three variables, as presented in Chapter V.

Our interest in the "λ-model" is due partly to its empirical relevance. It is obviously applicable to an economy in which households share the ownership of private industry with the central bank or government. It may also be useful in international trade in describing the wealth of a nation, part of whose capital is owned by another country or an international agency. A second reason for exploring the λ-model is that it seems to embody the basic wealth postulates of Metzler, whose 1951 work[1] has stimulated a number of papers on the "saving-wealth relation."[2]

We begin by examining the extent to which the undisturbed equilibrium-growth process must be qualified when some of the outstanding securities are held by the central bank. Following an open-market purchase, we shall then analyze the wealth impact of $\lambda < 1$ in the zero and complete forced-saving adjustments.

2. Equilibrium Growth

Consider an interval of equilibrium growth. The initial data are:

$$(5B.7)' \qquad K', \rho_K' = r_N' = r_M', S_\tau' = S_O' + S_B', \rho_s' = \frac{\rho_K' K'}{S_\tau'},$$

$$p' = \frac{\rho_s'}{r_N'}, \quad \lambda' = \frac{S_O'}{S_\tau'}, m_2'.$$

[1] "Wealth, Saving, and the Rate of Interest," *op. cit.*

[2] See V. Lutz, "Real and Monetary Factors in the Determination of Employment Levels," *Quarterly Journal of Economics*, Vol. LXVI (May, 1952), pp. 251–72; Gottfried Haberler, "The Pigou Effect Once More," *Journal of Political Economy*, Vol. LX (June, 1952), pp. 240–46 (reprinted in Haberler, *Prosperity and Depression* [4th ed.; Cambridge, Mass.: Harvard University Press, 1958], Part III, Appendix II); Louis Hough, "An Asset Influence in the Labor Market," *Journal of Political Economy*, Vol. LXIII (June, 1955), pp. 202–15; Warren L. Smith, "A Graphical Exposition of the Complete Keynesian System," *Southern Economic Journal*, Vol. XXIII (October, 1956), pp. 119–20; James R. Schlesinger, "After Twenty Years: The General Theory," *Quarterly Journal of Economics*, Vol. LXX (November, 1956), pp. 594–95; Sidney Weintraub, "The Theory of Open Market Operations: A Comment," *Review of Economics and Statistics*, Vol. XLI (August, 1959), p. 308; Arnold Collery, "A Note on the Saving-Wealth Relation and the Rate of Interest," *Journal of Political Economy*, Vol. LXVIII (October, 1960), pp. 509–10; and Robert A. Mundell, "The Public Debt, Corporate Income Taxes, and the Rate of Interest," *Journal of Political Economy*, Vol. LXVIII (December, 1960), pp. 622–26. See Also D. Patinkin, *Money, Interest, and Prices*, Part II, "Macroeconomics"; and J. W. Conard, *Introduction to the Theory of Interest* (Berkely, Calif.: University of California Press, 1959), chap. xiii, esp. pp. 255 and 269–70.

The value of securities is

$$(5B.8)' \qquad S'_{VO}(\rho'_K, r'_N) = S'_O p' = \lambda' K',$$

and total wealth is

$$(5B.9)' \qquad W'(\rho'_K, r'_N) = S'_{VO}(\rho'_K, r'_N) + m'_2 = \lambda' K' + m'_2.$$

The bank's holdings, which were acquired at some earlier time, are assumed to remain constant at S'_B. During the interval

$$(5B.10)' \qquad \hat{S}'(r'_N) = \hat{I}'(r'_N) = \hat{\Delta K}',$$

and $\hat{\Delta S}'_S = \hat{\Delta K}'/\hat{p}'$ is the number of securities issued. At the close of the interval

$$(5B.11)' \qquad \hat{K}' = K' + \hat{\Delta K}', \hat{S}'_\tau = S'_\tau + \hat{\Delta S}'_S, \hat{S}'_O = S'_O + \hat{\Delta S}'_S, \hat{\lambda}' = \frac{\hat{S}'_O}{\hat{S}'_\tau}$$

$$= \frac{S'_O + \hat{\Delta S}'_S}{S'_\tau + \hat{\Delta S}'_S}, \text{ and } \hat{m}'_2 = m'_2.$$

Security value is

$$(5B.12)' \qquad \hat{S}'_{VO}(\rho'_K, r'_N) = \hat{S}'_O \hat{p}' = \hat{\lambda}' \hat{K}', \text{ where } \hat{p}' = p',$$

and total wealth is

$$(5B.13)' \qquad \hat{W}'(\rho'_K, r'_N) = \hat{S}'_{VO}(\rho'_K, r'_N) + \hat{m}'_2 = \hat{\lambda}'(K' + \hat{\Delta K}') + m'_2.$$

Even though households share the earnings of capital with the central bank (i.e., λ is < 1), we can show that a capital *increment* is reflected fully and equally in the value of privately held securities. We wish to prove that during the interval,

$$(5B.14)' \qquad \hat{S}'_{VO} - S'_{VO} = \hat{K}' - K'.$$

The λ terms appear when we substitute $\hat{\lambda}' \hat{K}'$ for $\hat{S}'_{VO}$ and $\lambda' K'$ for S'_{VO}:

$$\hat{\lambda}' \hat{K}' - \lambda' K' = \hat{K}' - K'.$$

Since

$$\hat{\lambda}' = \frac{\hat{S}'_O}{\hat{S}'_\tau}, \quad \lambda' = \frac{S'_O}{S'_\tau}, \text{ and } \frac{\hat{K}'}{\hat{S}'_\tau} = \frac{K'}{S'_\tau} = p',$$

we can write

$$\left(\frac{\hat{S}'_O}{\hat{S}'_\tau}\right)\hat{K}' - \left(\frac{S'_O}{S'_\tau}\right)K' = \hat{K}' - K'$$

$$\hat{S}'_O p' - S'_O p' = \hat{K}' - K'$$

$$(\hat{S}'_O - S'_O) p' = \hat{K}' - K'$$

$$\hat{\Delta S}'_S p' = \hat{\Delta K}'.$$

The last expression, which is a given fact, tells us what we need to know. The increase in capital, $\hat{\Delta K}'$, is equal to $\hat{\Delta S}'_S p'$, the product of the number of securities sold to households and their price. As long as the bank's holdings remain constant, the entire growth of capital is financed by new security sales to households, to whom all of $\hat{\Delta K}'$ accrues as additional security value, $\hat{\Delta S}'_S p'$. The increase in λ during equilibrium growth will invariably maintain this relationship. The crucial element in the proof is that p remains constant at p', both during and after the security sale; as a result, the additional securities continue to be valued by the increment in capital they financed. In equilibrium growth, p is constant at p' since we add to the numerator and denominator of K/S_τ, the expression for p, increments whose ratio, $\Delta K/\Delta S_S$, is also equal to p'. With S, I, ρ_K, and r_M constant, p' itself is perpetuated as a constant over time. Our account of the equilibrium-growth process in Chapter II-D(2) does not, therefore, need to be qualified for the presence of the bank as a claimant to the earnings of capital. It is still true that S_{VO}, W, and D_{VO} increase each period by the full $S = I$ addition to the existing stock of capital.

Total wealth after n intervals of undisturbed growth is obtained by extending the results of the first interval. The bank's holdings continue to be fixed at S'_B, saving and investment per interval are constant at $\hat{S}'$ and $\hat{I}'$, respectively, the periodic increments to capital are $\hat{\Delta K}'$ ([5B.10]'), and $\hat{\Delta S}'_S$ in new securities at a price p' are issued each period. After n intervals,

$$\hat{W}^n(\rho'_K, r'_N) = \hat{S}^n_{VO}(\rho'_K, r'_N) + \hat{m}^n_2$$
$$= \hat{\lambda}^n \hat{K}^n + \hat{m}^n_2$$
$$= \left(\frac{\hat{S}^n_O}{\hat{S}^n_\tau}\right)\hat{K}^n + m'_2.$$

Hence

(5B.15)'

$$\hat{W}^n(\rho'_K, r'_N) = \frac{(S'_O + n\hat{\Delta S}'_S)}{(S'_\tau + S'_B + n\hat{\Delta S}'_S)}(K' + n\hat{\Delta K}') + m'_2.$$

3. The Purchase

The open-market purchase occurs in the usual way by bidding up security prices to p'' and lowering interest to r''_M. The bank obtains existing securities only, the quantity of which is now designated S''_B. The entire purchase creates an addition to idle balances,

(5B.16)' $$m''_2 - m'_2 = S''_B p''.$$

Households are left with a quantity of securities,

(5B.17)' $$S''_O = S'_O - S''_B,$$

and λ is

$$(5B.18)' \qquad \lambda'' = \frac{S''_O}{S'_\tau} = \frac{S''_O}{S''_O + S'_B + S''_B}.$$

ρ_s is constant at $\rho'_s = \rho'_K K'/S'_\tau$. Security value and total wealth are

$$(5B.19)' \qquad S''_{VO} = S''_O\left(\frac{\rho'_s}{r_M}\right) \text{ and } W'' = S''_{VO} + m''_2,$$

respectively. The bank restores household income by subsidizing personal incomes. The events up to this point are indistinguishable from those described in Chapter V-B(3). The single and double-primed schedules in Figure 5–1 are equally representative of the present disturbance.

4. Zero Forced Saving

Consider first the zero forced-saving adjustment in abstraction from voluntary saving. The initial interval begins as described in Part C(2) and in Figure 5–2. ρ_K is assumed constant at ρ'_K, and the price level is fixed. The expressions for ρ_s and p are fully applicable to the present case, if we substitute S'_τ for S'_P. However, in the λ-model, the final S_{VO} function produced by the stock watering is

$$(5B.20)' \qquad S^4_{VO} = S'''_O\left(\frac{\rho^4_s}{r_M}\right)$$

$$= (S''_O + \Delta S'_E)\left(\frac{\rho'_K K'}{r_M(S'_\tau + \Delta S'_E)}\right)$$

$$= \lambda'''\left(\frac{\rho'_K K'}{r_M}\right).$$

Even though the excess securities fail to finance an increase in the stock of capital, they raise λ, preventing S_{VO} from returning completely to S''_{VO} at the close of the interval. The proof of $S^4_{VO} > S''_{VO}$ is, upon substitution:

$$\lambda'''\left(\frac{\rho'_K K'}{r_M}\right) > \lambda''\left(\frac{\rho'_K K'}{r_M}\right),$$

$$\lambda''' > \lambda'',$$

$$\frac{S''_O + \Delta S'_E}{S'_\tau + \Delta S'_E} > \frac{S''_O}{S'_\tau},$$

$$S'_\tau \Delta S'_E > \Delta S'_E S''_O,$$

$$S'_O + S'_B > S'_O - S''_B,$$

$$S'_B + S''_B > 0,$$

which is satisfied as long as the bank holds any securities. For the λ-model we would thus rotate S_{VO}^4, W^4, and D_{VO}^4 in Figure 5–2 somewhat to the right of their indicated positions. But while the λ-effect produces $S_{VO}^4 > S_{VO}''$, it cannot prevent wealth from falling during the interval. We have:

$$W^4(\rho_K', r_M''') < W''(\rho_K', r_M''),$$

$$S_{VO}^4(\rho_K', r_M''') + m_2''' < S_{VO}''(\rho_K', r_M'') + m_2'',$$

$$S_O'''p^4 + m_2''' < \overline{S_O''p'' + m_2''},$$

$$S_O'''p^4 - S_O''p'' < m_2'' - m_2''',$$

$$S_O'''p^4 - S_O''p'' < (S_O''' - S_O'')p'''.$$

Expansion and rearrangement yield

$$\frac{S_O'''}{S_O''} > \frac{p'' - p'''}{p^4 - p'''}.$$

Since $p'' > p''' > p^4$, $p'' - p''' > 0$ and $p^4 - p''' < 0$. Hence the inequality has changed direction in the final step, and is readily satisfied.

The remainder of the adjustment process follows the description in Chapter V-C(3), with the qualification that S_{VO} rises each interval as excess securities dilute the bank's claim to the fixed stock of capital. In Figure 5–3 the curve, BC, is still an accurate time portrayal of wealth, given $\partial S/\partial r_M = 0$ and a zero wealth effect, except that the terminus, C, is not necessarily below the height of point A, the beginning wealth total. The presence of λ in the wealth equation introduces some flexibility in the relationship between $W''(\rho_K', r_N')$ and $W'(\rho_K', r_N')$. The conditions underlying $W'' > W'$ follow after substitution of the individual terms:

$$S_{VO}''(\rho_K', r_N') + m_2'' > S_{VO}'(\rho_K', r_N') + m_2',$$

$$\lambda''\left(\frac{\rho_K' K'}{r_N'}\right) + m_2'' > \lambda'\left(\frac{\rho_K' K'}{r_N'}\right) + m_2',$$

$$\lambda'' > \lambda',$$

$$\frac{S_O''}{S_O'' + S_B' + S_B''} > \frac{S_O'}{S_O' + S_B'},$$

$$S_O'' S_B' > S_O' S_B' + S_O' S_B''.$$

We replace S_O'' by $S_O' + \sum_n \Delta S_E = S_O' - S_B'' + \sum_n \Delta S_E$:

$$(S_O' - S_B'' + \sum_n \Delta S_E)S_B' > S_O' S_B' + S_O' S_B'',$$

$$\sum_n \Delta S_E S_B' > S_O' S_B'' + S_B'' S_B'.$$

Dividing each side by $S_B'' S_B'$ produces

(5B.21)'
$$\frac{\sum_n \Delta S_E}{S_B''} > \frac{S_O' + S_B'}{S_B'}.$$

The right side of the inequality, which cannot be less than unity, will be very large for an economy in which the central bank holds a small fraction of total securities. In Appendix A, we have seen that the left side cannot exceed p''/p', and may even fall below unity (cf. [5A.6]').[3] p''/p' does not promise to be greatly in excess of unity, given that the magnitude of the purchase is small relative to the existing quantity of money. For the likely scale of open-market activity in the modern economy, there is thus little *a priori* ground for expecting (5B.21)' to be satisfied; i.e., the increase in λ in the zero forced-saving adjustment is unlikely to restore the value of securities to its pre-operation level.

A simple numerical example will indicate intuitively why λ would fail to recover its original value. Suppose that

$$S_O' = 90, \; S_B' = 10, \; S_B'' = 5, \; \text{and} \; \frac{\sum_n \Delta S_E}{S_B''} = 1.20.$$

$$\sum_n \Delta S_E = 1.20 \times 5 = 6, \; \lambda' = \frac{90}{100} = .9000, \; \lambda'' = \frac{85}{100} = .8500,$$

$$\lambda^n = \frac{91}{106} = .8585.$$

The reduction from λ' to λ'' due to the purchase entails a reduction in the numerator only, the total number of securities remaining constant. The subsequent issue of excess new securities increases the numerator and denominator equally. Since λ is < 1, the adjustment will not raise the ratio as much as the purchase lowered it, unless $\sum_n \Delta S_E$ is many times greater than S_B''. But consider an alternative example that might characterize an underdeveloped economy:

$$S_O' = 10, \; S_B' = 90, \; S_B'' = 5, \; \frac{\sum_n \Delta S_E}{S_B''} = 1.20, \; \sum_n \Delta S_E = 1.20 \times 5 = 6.$$

$$\lambda' = \frac{10}{100} = .1000, \; \lambda'' = \frac{5}{100} = .0500, \; \lambda^n = \frac{11}{106} = .1038 > \lambda'.$$

In terms of (5B.21)' the inequality is $1.20 > (10 + 90)/90 = 1.11$.[4]

---

[3] The results of Appendix A are completely applicable to the λ-model. Symbolically, S_B' and S_P' in that appendix correspond to S_B'' and S_O'', respectively, in this one. In Appendix A (*e*) the proof of $S_{VO}^5 > S_{VO}''$ is strengthened by entering λ''' and λ'', where $\lambda''' > \lambda''$, as coefficients of S_{VO}' and S_{VO}'', respectively. Nothing else in that appendix, the results of which are based on movements in ρ_s and p, is altered by the introduction of λ.

[4] The example is characterized by a small value of λ. While this facilitates (5B.21)', it is, strictly speaking, neither necessary nor sufficient.

Whereas the temporary increase in ρ_K when $\partial S / \partial r_M > 0$ previously had no influence on the final wealth total (Section C[4]), it lowers wealth in the λ-model by reducing $\sum_n \Delta S_E$ (page 135). Formerly, the only relevance of security quantities was to the level of security prices, but now both λ and wealth are dependent on $\sum_n \Delta S_E$. In Figure 5–3 the terminus of the path, DE, for which $\partial S / \partial r_M > 0$, must be drawn below the height of C. By the same token, the tendency of the wealth effect to reduce $\sum_n \Delta S_E$ (Section C[5]) also lowers the increase in λ and the level of wealth in the new equilibrium. BF, in Figure 5–3, must also be extended below the height of C.

In the total growth process the presence of λ provides an additional stimulus to wealth increases during the adjustment. In (5C.41), which compares ending and beginning wealth of the initial interval, λ''' and λ'', where $\lambda''' > \lambda''$, would be added as coefficients of the capital stock on the left and right side, respectively. While none of the wealth lines in Figures 5–7 and 5–9 could lie above the undisturbed path, AC, in equilibrium, appropriate (though perhaps unlikely) values of λ will now result in $W^n(\rho_K', r_N') > \hat{W}^n(\rho_K', r_N')$. The latter inequality is

$$S_{VO}^n(\rho_K', r_N') + m_2^n > \hat{S}_{VO}^n(\rho_K', r_N') + \hat{m}_2',$$

$$\lambda^n \left(\frac{\rho_K' K^n}{r_N'} \right) + m_2' > \hat{\lambda}^n \left(\frac{\rho_K' \hat{K}^n}{r_N'} \right) + m_2'.$$

In the case of $\partial S / \partial r_M = 0$, the circumstance most favorable to wealth of the adjustment process, $K^n = \hat{K}^n$, reducing the inequality to

$$\lambda^n > \hat{\lambda}^n,$$

$$\frac{S_O' - S_B'' + \sum_n \Delta S_S + \sum_n \Delta S_E}{S_O' + S_B' + \sum_n \Delta S_S + \sum_n \Delta S_E} > \frac{S_O' + n \hat{\Delta} S_S'}{S_O' + S_B' + n \hat{\Delta} S_S'}.$$

Letting $a = S_O' + \sum_n \Delta S_S + \sum_n \Delta S_E$ and $b = S_O' + n \hat{\Delta} S_S'$ yields

$$\frac{a - S_B''}{a + S_B'} > \frac{b}{b + S_B'}$$

or, upon expansion and rearrangement,

$$\frac{a - b}{S_B''} > \frac{b + S_B'}{S_B'}.$$

Substituting for a and b, we obtain

$$(5B.22)' \qquad \frac{\sum_n \Delta S_E + \left(\sum_n \Delta S_S - n \hat{\Delta} S_S' \right)}{S_B''} > \frac{S_O' + S_B' + n \hat{\Delta} S_S'}{S_B'}.$$

(5B.22)′ bears a strong resemblance to (5B.21)′, which expresses the same inequality in the absence of voluntary saving (in [5B.21]′ $n\hat{\Delta S}'_S = \sum_n \Delta S_S$ = 0). The same empirical circumstances that prevailed against (5B.21)′ are relevant to (5B.22)′. In addition, (5B.22)′ has $n\hat{\Delta S}'_S > 0$, which raises the right side, and, in view of (5A.11)′, $\sum_n \Delta S_S - n\hat{\Delta S}'_S < 0$, which reduces the left side.[5] Thus the addition of voluntary saving makes (5B.22)′ even more difficult to satisfy than (5B.21)′.

5. Complete Forced Saving

The limiting first interval is the same for the λ-model as the previous one. The only effective movement is the reduction in ρ_K to $\rho_K''' = r_M'''$ = r_M''. In the present context, wealth is reduced to

$$(5B.23)'\quad W'''(\rho_K''', r_M''') = S_{VO}'''(\rho_K''', r_M''') + m_2'''$$

$$= \lambda'''\left(\frac{\rho_K''' K''}{r_M'''}\right) + m_2''' = \lambda'' K' + m_2''.$$

As earlier, wealth is still above the pre-disturbance level:

$$W'''(\rho_K''', r_M''') - W'(\rho_K', r_N')$$

$$= \lambda'' K' + m_2'' - (\lambda' K' + m_2')$$

$$= K'(\lambda'' - \lambda') + m_2'' - m_2'$$

$$= K'\left(\frac{S_O''}{S_\tau'} - \frac{S_O'}{S_\tau'}\right) + m_2'' - m_2'$$

$$= \frac{K'}{S_\tau'}(S_O'' - S_O') + m_2'' - m_2'$$

$$= p'(-S_B'') + S_B'' p''$$

$$= S_B''(p'' - p'),$$

which is exactly the result of the previous model ([5D.33]), except that S_B'' replaces $S_B' = S_G'$.

In the second interval, abstracting from voluntary saving, wealth in Chapter V-D(3) remained constant. $\lambda < 1$, however, makes for a net increase in wealth. We now have:

$$W^5(\rho_K^4, r_M^4) > W'''(\rho_K''', r_M'''),$$

$$S_{VO}^5(\rho_K^4, r_M^4) + m_2^4 > S_{VO}'''(\rho_K''', r_M''') + m_2''',$$

---

[5] Since voluntary saving tends to raise ρ_s and p (Part C[6]a), we would expect $\sum_n \Delta S_E$ to be lower than in abstraction from the total growth process. This would be an additional factor reducing the left side of (5B.22)′ relative to that of (5B.21)′.

$$S_{VO}^5(\rho_K^4, r_M^4) - S_{VO}'''(\rho_K''', r_M''') > m_2''' - m_2^4,$$

$$\lambda^4 \left(\frac{\rho_K^4 K'''}{r_M^4}\right) - \lambda''' \left(\frac{\rho_K''' K''}{r_M'''}\right) > K''' - K'',$$

$$\lambda^4 K''' - \lambda''' K'' > K''' - K'',$$

$$K'''(\lambda^4 - 1) > K'' (\lambda''' - 1),$$

$$K'''\left(\frac{S_O^4}{S_\tau^4} - 1\right) > K''\left(\frac{S_O'''}{S_\tau'''} - 1\right),$$

$$K'''\left(\frac{S_O^4 - S_\tau^4}{S_\tau^4}\right) > K''\left(\frac{S_O''' - S_\tau'''}{S_\tau'''}\right),$$

$$K''' \left(\frac{S_\tau^4 - S_O^4}{S_\tau^4}\right) < K''\left(\frac{S_\tau''' - S_O'''}{S_\tau'''}\right)$$

Since $S_\tau^4 - S_O^4$ and $S_\tau''' - S_O'''$, the difference between total and household security holdings, is in each case equal to the bank's given holdings, $S_B' + S_B''$, we have

$$K'''\left(\frac{S_B' + S_B''}{S_\tau^4}\right) < K''\left(\frac{S_B' + S_B''}{S_\tau'''}\right),$$

$$\frac{K'''}{S_\tau^4} < \frac{K''}{S_\tau'''},$$

$$p^5 < p'''.$$

The reader is referred to page 154 for the proof of $p^5 < p'''$.

In Figure 5–10 the wealth increment would be reflected in point G lying to the right of point E. In Figure 5–11 the path from B to C is unchanged, but the c vector would now slope down and to the right. A positive wealth effect in the λ-model would reduce wealth not only by curtailing the increase in capital financed by idle balances, but also by reducing security issues and the rise in λ.

In the growing economy $\lambda < 1$ again serves to raise the wealth increments. In the wealth totals of the typical interval described on page 162, λ^4 and λ''' would appear as coefficients of the capital stock underlying S_{VO}^5 and S_{VO}''', respectively. In the adjustment for which $\partial S/\partial r_M = 0$ and the wealth effect is absent, $W''(\rho_K', r_N')$ will exceed $\hat{W}''(\rho_K', r_N')$ by a greater amount than it would have with $\lambda = 1$ throughout. In fact, $\lambda < 1$ results in

$$(5B.24)' \qquad W''(\rho_K', r_N') - \hat{W}''(\rho_K', r_N') > W'''(\rho_K''', r_M''') - W'(\rho_K', r_N').$$

In terms of Figure 5–12, this is to say that the distance between CE and AD is greater at t_n' than at t_0. The right side of (5B.24)' already has been calculated to be S_B'' $(p'' - p')$ (page 496). For $W''(\rho_K', r_N')$

$- \hat{W}^n(\rho'_K, r'_N)$ we have

$$S^n_{VO}(\rho'_K, r'_N) + m^n_2 - [\hat{S}^n_{VO}(\rho'_K, r'_N) + \hat{m}^n_2]$$

$$= \lambda^n \left(\frac{\rho'_K K^n}{r'_N} \right) + m'_2 - \left\{ \hat{\lambda}^n \left(\frac{\rho'_K \hat{K}^n}{r'_N} \right) + m'_2 \right\}$$

Since $\partial S / \partial r_M = 0$ and the wealth effect on interest is zero,

$$K^n = \hat{K}^n + (m''_2 - m'_2) = \hat{K}^n + S''_B p''.$$

Upon substituting and cancelling,

$$W^n - \hat{W}^n = \lambda^n(\hat{K}^n + S''_B p'') - \hat{\lambda}^n \hat{K}^n$$

$$= \left(\frac{S'_O + \sum_n \Delta S_S + \sum_n \Delta S_E - S''_B}{S'_O + \sum_n \Delta S_S + S'_B + \sum_n \Delta S_E} \right) (\hat{K}^n + S''_B p'')$$

$$- (S'_O + n\hat{\Delta S'_S}) \left(\frac{\hat{K}^n}{S'_O + n\hat{\Delta S'_S} + S'_B} \right),$$

where $\hat{K}^n / (S'_O + n\hat{\Delta S'_S} + S'_B)$, the ratio of total capital to total securities after n intervals of equilibrium growth, is p'. In order to simplify this expression further, we let $\sum_n \Delta S_S = n\hat{\Delta S'_S}$ and $\sum_n \Delta S_E = S''_B(p''/p')$. In fact, we know that $\sum_n \Delta S_S > n\hat{\Delta S'_S}$ (cf. [5A.24]') and $\sum_n \Delta S_E > S''_B (p''/p')$ ([5A.17]'). The simplifying assumptions therefore entail subtracting $\sum_n \Delta S_S - n\hat{\Delta S'_S} > 0$ and $\sum_n \Delta S_E - S''_B > 0$ from both the numerator and denominator of $\lambda^n_{\wedge} < 1$. This has the effect of lowering λ^n, W^n, and the difference, $W^n - \hat{W}^n$. Next if we let

$$a = S'_O + n\hat{\Delta S'_S} = S'_O + \sum_n \Delta S_S \text{ and } b = a + S'_B,$$

$W^n - \hat{W}^n$ becomes

$$\frac{a + \left\{ S''_B \left(\frac{p''}{p'} \right) - S''_B \right\}}{b + S''_B \left(\frac{p''}{p'} \right)} (\hat{K}^n + S''_B p'') - ap'.$$

Expansion and collection of terms in the numerator and denominator of the first term yields

$$\left(\frac{ap' + S''_B p'' - S''_B p'}{bp' + S''_B p''} \right) (\hat{K}^n + S''_B p'') - ap'.$$

Since

$$bp' = (S'_O + n\hat{\Delta S'_S} + S'_B) \left(\frac{\hat{K}^n}{S'_O + n\hat{\Delta S'_S} + S'_B} \right) = \hat{K}^n,$$

$W^n - \hat{W}^n$ is

$$\left(\frac{ap' + S_B'' p'' - S_B'' p'}{\hat{K}^n + S_B'' p''}\right)(\hat{K}^n + S_B'' p'') - ap'$$

$$= ap' + S_B'' p'' - S_B'' p' - ap'$$

$$= S_B''(p'' - p').$$

This is equal to $W'''(\rho_K''', r_M''') - W'(\rho_K', r_N')$ (page 496), shown as the distance in Figure 5–12 between points C and A. However, since $W^n - \hat{W}^n$ was obtained through simplifying assumptions that reduced λ^n and W^n below their *de facto* values, $W^n - \hat{W}^n > W''' - W'$. The wealth curve corresponding to CE would be rising and concave downward, becoming parallel to AD at t_n'.

Relaxation of the assumptions that $\partial S/\partial r_M = 0$ and the wealth effect is absent would again tend to produce the other configurations shown in Figure 5–12. But $\lambda < 1$ raises the slopes of the curves and their heights in equilibrium. Any smaller amount of capital due to $\partial S/\partial r_M > 0$, a positive wealth effect, or partial forced saving may be compensated for by a sufficient increase in λ. The conditions necessary for $\lambda^n > \hat{\lambda}^n$ are given by (5B.22)′.

CHAPTER VII

Paths to Equilibrium

This appendix will describe the possible paths to equilibrium in the two-security model following an open-market purchase. The analytical framework is the system of Hicksian substitution functions developed in Part D. The appendix is essentially a more detailed treatment of the financial adjustment outlined in Part E. The specific task is to endeavor to show that the transfer and wealth effects will sooner or later bring the market rates of interest to equality with the equilibrium natural rates. This is to say that the dynamic process will one way or another carry the old and total s-schedules to their pre-operation intersection with s_{1N} and s_{2N}. To establish this result we assume that all shifts in the s-functions are parallel, and that s_{1N} and s_{2N} are fixed throughout the adjustment. Whenever the equilibrating mechanisms contribute opposite tendencies to the movement of an s-schedule, we assume that first one and then the other force predominates, and finally that they neutralize each other. After tracing through the consequences on each assumption, we emerge with conclusions which are thus perfectly general.

"Point 1" will designate the constant intersection of s_{1N} and s_{2N}, whose coordinates are the equilibrium natural rates of interest. "Point 2" will be the moving intersection of s_{1T} and s_{2T}, whose coordinates are the market rates of interest. Our objective is to show whether, and by what route, point 2 approaches point 1. Since they add nothing to this particular analysis, we omit reference to s_{1O} and s_{2O}, and describe the dynamic paths purely in terms of the s_N and s_T s-functions. Illustrative diagrams are included in the description. The directional impulse on the s_T schedules provided by the transfer and wealth effects will be designated by small arrows labeled "t" and "w," respectively.

In Section 1 we take as given the general stability condition—that the horizontal-axis slope of any s_2 s-schedule is greater than that of the corresponding s_1 schedule—and assume that the stable price-level line, PP', is a downward function. Section 1 will establish that the market rates of interest will meet directly at the equilibrium natural rates, or on PP', from which they proceed to the equilibrium. We shall isolate seven general cases with regard to the combined action of the transfer and wealth effects on the movement of the s-functions. Of the seven cases, three (referred to as Cases 1, 2, and 7) represent starting positions, in the sense that they are possible market situations created by the direct impact of the operation. All seven cases, however, including these three, may arise at one time or another during the process of adjustment. After describing the seven basic cases, we shall discuss the movement from a point on PP' to the equilibrium.

Section 2 will treat the case of a rising PP' schedule, and that of an unstable pair of s_{1N} and s_{2N} functions in combination with stable s_{1T} and s_{2T} schedules. The failure to reach equilibrium will be established as a possibility in the first case, and a necessity in the second.

1. The General Analysis

Case 1. Point 1 is within the lower vertical angle of s_{1T} and s_{2T}.

Point 2 is within the upper vertical angle of s_{1N} and s_{2N}.

The wealth effect is equilibrating with respect to both s_{1T} and s_{2T}. The transfer effect is equilibrating with respect to both s_{1T} and s_{2T}. Depending on the slopes of the total schedules relative to those of the new, and the relative speed with which each total schedule moves in response to the equilibrating forces, Case 1 will develop into one of the following four cases, which are described below:

a) If $\dfrac{\partial s_{2T}}{\partial p_2} > \dfrac{\partial s_{2N}}{\partial p_2}$ (see Figure 7A–1[b]), and s_{2T} moves leftward with
   sufficient speed, Case 1 merges into Case 2.

FIGURE 7A–1

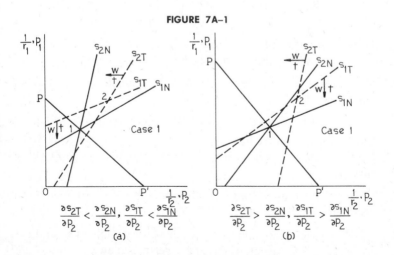

(a)

$$\frac{\partial s_{2T}}{\partial p_2} < \frac{\partial s_{2N}}{\partial p_2}, \ \frac{\partial s_{1T}}{\partial p_2} < \frac{\partial s_{1N}}{\partial p_2}$$

(b)

$$\frac{\partial s_{2T}}{\partial p_2} > \frac{\partial s_{2N}}{\partial p_2}, \ \frac{\partial s_{1T}}{\partial p_2} > \frac{\partial s_{1N}}{\partial p_2}$$

b) If $\frac{\partial s_{2T}}{\partial p_2} < \frac{\partial s_{2N}}{\partial p_2}$ (see Figure 7A-1[a]), and s_{2T} moves leftward with sufficient speed, Case 1 merges into Case 4.

c) If $\frac{\partial s_{1T}}{\partial p_2} > \frac{\partial s_{1N}}{\partial p_2}$ (see Figure 7A-1[b]), and s_{1T} moves down with sufficient speed, Case 1 merges into Case 5.

d) If $\frac{\partial s_{1T}}{\partial p_2} < \frac{\partial s_{1N}}{\partial p_2}$ (see Figure 7A-1[a]), and s_{1T} moves down with sufficient speed, Case 1 merges into Case 7.

Case 2.   Point 1 is within the lower vertical angle of s_{1T} and s_{2T}.
           Point 2 is to the left of the upper vertical angle of s_{1N} and s_{2N}.

     A necessary condition for Case 2 is $\partial s_{2T}/\partial p_2 > \partial s_{2N}/\partial p_2$, as in Figure 7A-2. The wealth effect is equilibrating with respect to both s_{1T} and s_{2T}. The transfer effect is equilibrating with respect to s_{1T}, and non-equilibrating with respect to s_{2T} (it exerts a rightward push on s_{2T}). Depending on

FIGURE 7A-2

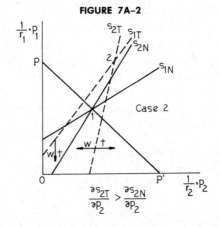

the relative strength of the two opposing tendencies acting on s_{2T}, Case 2 will develop into one of the following cases:

a) If the wealth effect on s_{2T} neutralizes the transfer effect, leaving s_{2T} fixed, Case 2 merges into Case 1.

b) If the wealth effect on s_{2T} predominates over the transfer effect, Case 2 merges either into Case 1, when s_{1T} moves down with sufficient speed, or Case 3, when s_{2T} shifts to the left with sufficient speed.

c) If the transfer effect on s_{2T} predominates over the wealth effect, Case 2 merges into Case 1.

Case 3.   Point 1 is to the right of the lower vertical angle of s_{1T} and s_{2T}.
           Point 2 is to the left of the upper vertical angle of s_{1N} and s_{2N}.

There are two subcases of Case 3, one for which $\partial s_{2T}/\partial p_2 > \partial s_{2N}/\partial p_2$ (see Figure 7A–3[a]), and the other when $\partial s_{2T}/\partial p_2 < \partial s_{2N}/\partial p_2$ (see Figure 7A–3[b]). In both cases, the wealth effect is equilibrating with respect to s_{1T}, but non-equilibrating with respect to s_{2T} (it exerts a leftward push on

FIGURE 7A–3

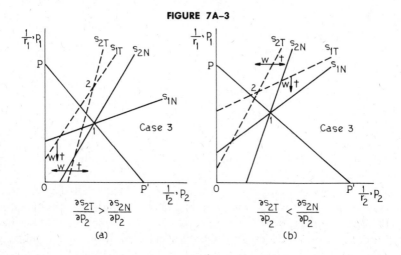

(a) $\dfrac{\partial s_{2T}}{\partial p_2} > \dfrac{\partial s_{2N}}{\partial p_2}$

(b) $\dfrac{\partial s_{2T}}{\partial p_2} < \dfrac{\partial s_{2N}}{\partial p_2}$

s_{2T}). The transfer effect is equilibrating with respect to both s_{1T} and s_{2T}. Depending on the comparative strength of the two opposing forces on s_{2T}, Case 3 develops as follows:

a) Whatever the relative slopes of s_{2T} and s_{2N}, if the wealth effect on s_{2T} neutralizes the transfer effect, Case 3 leads to an intersection of s_{1T} and s_{2T} on PP' above point 1.

b) Whatever the relative slopes of s_{2T} and s_{2N}, if the wealth effect on s_{2T} predominates over the transfer effect, Case 3 leads to an intersection of s_{1T} and s_{2T} on PP' above point 1.

c) If the transfer effect on s_{2T} predominates over the wealth effect, Case 3 merges either into Case 2, when $\dfrac{\partial s_{2T}}{\partial p_2} > \dfrac{\partial s_{2N}}{\partial p_2}$, or Case 4, when $\dfrac{\partial s_{2T}}{\partial p_2} < \dfrac{\partial s_{2N}}{\partial p_2}$.

Case 4. Point 1 is to the right of the lower vertical angle of s_{1T} and s_{2T}. Point 2 is within the upper vertical angle of s_{1N} and s_{2N}.

A necessary condition for Case 4 is $\partial s_{2T}/\partial p_2 < \partial s_{2N}/\partial p_2$, as in Figure 7A–4. The wealth effect is equilibrating with respect to s_{1T}, but non-equilibrating with respect to s_{2T} (it exerts a leftward push on s_{2T}). The transfer effect is equilibrating with respect to s_{1T}, but non-equilibrating with respect to s_{2T} (it exerts a leftward push on s_{2T}). If s_{1T} shifts down rapidly enough, Case 4 will lead directly to an intersection of s_{1T} and s_{2T}

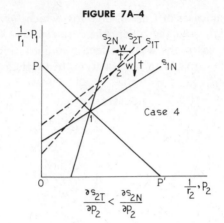

FIGURE 7A–4

on PP' above point 1. If s_{2T} moves leftward with sufficient speed, Case 4 leads to Case 3.

Let us summarize the paths to equilibrium thus far. Of the first four cases, only Cases 1 and 2 represent possible starting positions, created by the direct impact of the operation. Cases 3 and 4 are ruled out, since the direct impact produces a counterclockwise rotation in s_{2T}, shifting it to the right of point 1, as in Figure 7–17.

Starting with Case 1, we get four possible movements:

$$1\text{-}2, \quad 1\text{-}4, \quad 1\text{-}5, \quad 1\text{-}7.$$

From 1–2 we can get 2–1 or 2–3, and having arrived at 3 via 2, we can get either an intersection of s_{1T} and s_{2T} on PP' above point 1, or 3–2. Thus, possible movements are 1–2, 2–1, 2–3, 3–2, and any internally consistent combination of these. However, after each transition from one case to another, point 2 will be closer to PP'. This is because there is always at least one schedule moving unambiguously toward the equilibrium. Eventually point 2 will converge on PP' at or above point 1.

From 1–4, we can get a direct intersection of s_{1T} and s_{2T} on PP', or 4–3. Having arrived at 3 via 4, we can get a direct meeting of s_{1T} and s_{2T} on PP' above point 1, or 4–3. But continued movements between 3 and 4 must lead eventually to an intersection of s_{1T} and s_{2T} on PP' above point 1. Notice that the path, 1–4, is irreversible.

Starting with Case 2, we can get 2–1 or 2–3. Having arrived at 1 via 2, we can get 1–2 and either a direct landing of point 2 on PP' above point 1, or 1–5. Having arrived at 3 via 2, we can get a meeting of s_{1T} and s_{2T} on PP' above point 1, or a return movement, 3–2. Continued movements involving possible combinations of 2–1, 1–2, 2–3, 3–2 must eventually lead to an intersection of s_{1T} and s_{2T} on PP' above point 1.

We shall discuss the movements, 1–5, 1–7, and 2–1 followed by 1–5, as soon as we have described the remaining cases.

Case 5. Point 1 is to the left of the lower vertical angle of s_{1T} and s_{2T}.

Point 2 is within the upper vertical angle of s_{1N} and s_{2N}.

A necessary condition for Case 5 is $\partial s_{1T}/\partial p_2 > \partial s_{1N}/\partial p_2$, as in Figure 7A–5. The wealth effect is non-equilibrating with respect to s_{1T} (it exerts a downward push), but equilibrating with respect to s_{2T}. The transfer

FIGURE 7A–5

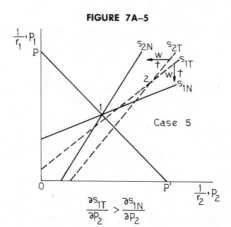

effect is non-equilibrating with respect to s_{1T} (it exerts a downward push), but equilibrating with respect to s_{2T}. If s_{2T} shifts leftward rapidly enough, Case 5 will lead directly to an intersection of s_{1T} and s_{2T} on PP' below point 1. If s_{1T} shifts down with sufficient speed, Case 5 leads to Case 6.

Case 6. Point 1 is above the lower vertical angle of s_{1T} and s_{2T}.

Point 2 is below the upper vertical angle of s_{1N} and s_{2N}.

There are two subcases of Case 6, one for which $\partial s_{1T}/\partial p_2 > \partial s_{1N}/\partial p_2$ (see Figure 7A–6[a]), and the other when $\partial s_{1T}/\partial p_2 < \partial s_{1N}/\partial p_2$ (see Figure

FIGURE 7A–6

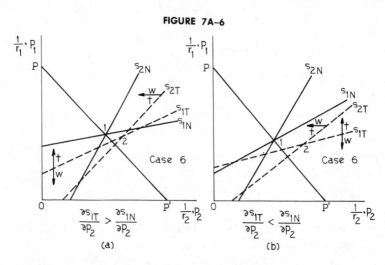

7A–6[b]). In both cases, the wealth effect is non-equilibrating with respect to s_{1T} (it exerts a downward push), but equilibrating with respect to s_{2T}. The transfer effect is equilibrating with respect to both s_{1T} and s_{2T}. Depending on the comparative force of the two opposing effects on s_{1T}, Case 6 develops as follows:

a) Whatever the relative slopes of s_{1T} and s_{1N}, if the wealth effect on s_{1T} neutralizes the transfer effect, Case 6 leads to an intersection of s_{1T} and s_{2T} on PP' below point 1.

b) Whatever the relative slopes of s_{1T} and s_{1N}, if the wealth effect on s_{1T} predominates over the transfer effect, Case 6 leads to an intersection of s_{1T} and s_{2T} on PP' below point 1.

c) If the transfer effect on s_{1T} predominates over the wealth effect, Case 6 merges either into Case 5, if $\dfrac{\partial s_{1T}}{\partial p_2} > \dfrac{\partial s_{1N}}{\partial p_2}$, or Case 7, if $\dfrac{\partial s_{1T}}{\partial p_2} < \dfrac{\partial s_{1N}}{\partial p_2}$.

Case 7. Point 1 is within the lower vertical angle of s_{1T} and s_{2T}.
Point 2 is to the right of the upper vertical angle of s_{1N} and s_{2N}.

A necessary condition for Case 7 is $\partial s_{1T}/\partial p_2 < \partial s_{1N}/\partial p_2$, as in Figure 7A–7. The wealth effect is equilibrating with respect to both s_{1T} and s_{2T}.

FIGURE 7A–7

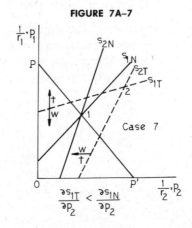

The transfer effect is non-equilibrating with respect to s_{1T} (it exerts an upward push), but equilibrating with respect to s_{2T}. Depending on the relative strength of the two opposing tendencies acting on s_{1T}, Case 7 will develop into one of the following cases:

a) If the wealth effect on s_{1T} neutralizes the transfer effect, Case 7 merges into Case 1.

b) If the wealth effect on s_{1T} predominates over the transfer effect, Case 7 merges either into Case 1, when s_{2T} moves leftward with sufficient speed, or Case 6, when s_{1T} shifts down with sufficient speed.

c) If the transfer effect on s_{1T} predominates over the wealth effect, Case 7 merges into Case 1.

We complete our summary of the equilibrium paths as follows. Starting with Case 1, two possibilities remained: 1–5 and 1–7. From 1–5, we get a direct intersection of s_{1T} and s_{2T} on PP' below point 1, or 5–6. Having arrived at 6 via 5, we can get a direct intersection on PP' below point 1, or 6–5. But, continued shifts between 5 and 6 must lead eventually to an intersection of s_{1T} and s_{2T} on PP' below point 1. Notice that the path, 1–5, is irreversible.

From 1–7, we can get 7–1 or 7–6, and having arrived at 6 via 7, we can get either an intersection of s_{1T} and s_{2T} on PP' below point 1, or 6–7. Thus, possible movements are 1–7, 7–1, 7–6, 6–7, and any self-consistent combination of these. However, such continued movements must lead eventually to a convergence of point 2 on PP' at or below point 1.

Starting with Case 2, one possibility was unexplored: 2–1, 1–5. The 1–5 movement just described is also relevant here.

Of Cases 5, 6, and 7, only Case 7 represents a possible starting position. This is because the direct impact of the purchase raises s_{1T} above point 1, as in Figure 7–16. In Cases 5 and 6, s_{1T} lies below point 1. Starting, thus, with Case 7, we can get 7–1 or 7–6. Having arrived at 1 or 6 via 7, we can get 1–7, and either a direct landing of point 2 on PP' below point 1, or 6–7. But, continued movements involving possible combinations of 7–1, 1–7, 7–6, 6–7 must in time lead to an intersection of s_{1T} and s_{2T} on PP' below point 1.

Our assumption that s_{1T} and s_{2T} shift parallel to themselves will not necessarily hold in practice. If the slopes change sufficiently during the adjustment process so as to alter the slope of an s_T s-schedule relative to that of the corresponding s_N schedule, the possible paths to equilibrium are enlarged. For example, a 1–7, 7–6, 6–7 path, for which $\partial s_{1T}/\partial p_2 < \partial s_{1N}/\partial p_2$, could in an extreme case, merge into the 1–5, 5–6, 6–5 combinations, for which $\partial s_{1T}/\partial p_2 > \partial s_{1N}/\partial p_2$. However, this does not qualify our general conclusion that s_{1T} and s_{2T} will finally intersect somewhere on PP'.

Having once landed on PP', what is the further course of the interest rates to equilibrium? If s_{1T} and s_{2T} meet on PP' above point 1, the price level is momentarily stable, and the transfer effect lowers s_{1T} and shifts s_{2T} to the right. Since at their intersection the schedules are equidistant from point 1, they will tend to shift equally, tracing out a southeast path for point 2. If this path coincides with PP', the price level remains stable, and point 2 moves to a direct meeting with point 1. If point 2 falls along a path that is less steep than PP', the schedules conform to a Case 3 configuration, and the inflation is resumed. But point 2 continues on its way to point 1 via the paths to equilibrium outlined under Case 3. If point 2 drops from PP' along a path steeper than PP', the interest rates fall into the deflationary zone below that function, as in Figure 7A–8. The transfer

FIGURE 7A–8

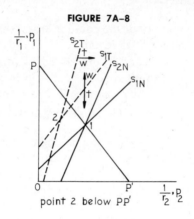

point 2 below PP'

effect continues lowering s_{1T} and shifting s_{2T} rightward. But the wealth effect raises s_{1T}, while moving s_{2T} farther to the right. If the transfer effect on s_{1T} neutralizes the wealth effect, s_{1T} is stationary, and point 2 must return to PP' above point 1. If the wealth effect on s_{1T} predominates over the transfer effect, s_{1T} rises, and again point 2 returns to PP'. However, if the transfer effect on s_{1T} predominates over the wealth effect, s_{1T} falls, and point 2 conceivably may fall away from PP'. With two opposing forces acting on s_{1T}, its downward movement would appear to be less than the rightward shift in s_{2T}, thereby enabling point 2 to fall toward PP'. But assume, for the sake of argument, that point 2 tends to move away from PP', farther into the deflationary zone. As this occurs, the net deflationary gap increases, and the price level falls more rapidly. Thus the upward force acting on s_{1T} is strengthened. At the same time, s_{1T}, in falling, approaches s_{1N}, thereby ameliorating the pressure tending to pull s_{1T} downward. The forces acting on s_{1T} are thus gradually brought into balance, reducing its rate of fall to zero. When s_{1T} begins falling less rapidly than s_{2T} is shifting to the right, point 2 moves directly to PP'. Thus, whether the price level remains stable or oscillates during these final adjustments, the continued movement of point 2 to point 1 is assured. An analogous argument will establish this result if point 2 reaches PP' below point 1.

2. Alternative Assumptions

a) A Rising Stable Price-Level Line

Suppose that PP' is positively sloped. How will this affect the paths to equilibrium? Of the seven basic cases, only those for which the market rates of interest lie outside the upper vertical angle of s_{1N} and s_{2N} are concerned with the slope or location of PP'. This is because PP', whether positively or negatively inclined, cannot pass through the angles defined by s_{1N} and s_{2N}, which are areas of inflation or deflation in both markets. However, Cases 2 and 3, in which point 2 lies to the left of the upper vertical angle of s_{1N} and s_{2N}, might encounter a positively sloped PP' function lying just to the left of s_{2N}. Cases 6 and 7, in which point 2 lies to the right of the upper vertical angle of s_{1N} and s_{2N}, could encounter a positively sloped PP' function passing just below s_{1N}. Let us analyze the influence of the rising PP' schedule by considering the impact in Case 2, which is one of the possible starting positions created by the purchase.

Suppose, in Figure 7A–9, that the direct impact of the purchase creates a Case 2 configuration in which point 2, the market rates of interest, lies to the left of the rising PP' line drawn in the diagram. The equilibrium of the system still requires that s_{1T} and s_{2T} join s_{1N} and s_{2N} in a common intersection at point 1. But, initially, the deflationary tendency

FIGURE 7A–9

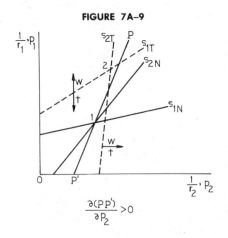

$$\frac{\partial (PP')}{\partial P_2} > 0$$

in the s_2 market exceeds the inflationary impulse in s_1, and the price level drops. The deflationary wealth effect shifts s_{1T} upward and s_{2T} to the right. Meanwhile, the transfer effect shifts s_{1T} downward and s_{2T} again to the right. If the transfer effect on s_{1T} neutralizes the wealth effect, s_{1T} and s_{2T} will meet on PP' above point 1. If the transfer effect on s_{1T} predominates over the wealth effect, s_{1T} falls, and point 2 will again land on PP' above point 1. But if the wealth effect on s_{1T} predominates over the transfer effect, s_{1T} rises, and in a limiting case point 2 could rise away from PP'. Since the point will also be moving away from s_{1N}, the strength of both equilibrating forces grows. But there is no *a priori* reason for the strength of one to increase more rapidly than the other. Point 2 conceivably may drift away from the equilibrium.

In the event that point 2 lands on the PP' schedule of Figure 7A–9, the price level is momentarily fixed. The transfer effect continues to lower

s_{1T} and shift s_{2T} to the right. Point 2 moves in a southeast direction to the inflationary side of PP'. Thereafter, the analysis follows the equilibrium paths for Case 2 above, with this qualification: it is now possible for Case 2 to create a direct intersection of s_{1T} and s_{2T} on PP' above point 1. If point 2 meets PP' without passing to the left of it, point 2 will be returned to the inflationary zone along a southeast path. Then, if the leftward tendency in s_{2T} predominates over the rightward force (see Case 2[b]), point 2 may again meet PP', though at a lower point. Again point 2 will be driven along a southeast path. In this way Case 2 may lead point 2 along a positively inclined zig-zag course directly to equilibrium. The movement of point 2 is the same if, in the interim, Case 2 merges into Case 3. The direction of movement in s_{1T} and s_{2T} is the same in both cases.

The analysis is completely analogous if we start with Case 7 and point 2 lying below a positively sloped PP' line. Once more point 2 may sooner or later return to the line, but not invariably. If it does, point 2 will be propelled along a southwest path into the inflationary zone. Thereafter, point 2 could pursue a zig-zag path, just to the left of PP', directly to equilibrium. The path would not be altered if, in the interim, Case 7 merged into Case 6.

b) Unstable New Substitution Functions

We shall examine the adjustment process for a system in which s_{1N} and s_{2N} are unstable, though the total schedules, s_{1T} and s_{2T}, meet the stability requirement. This is to say that $\partial s_{1N}/\partial p_2 > \partial s_{2N}/\partial p_2$ and $\partial s_{2T}/\partial p_2 > \partial s_{1T}/\partial p_2$. The characteristic of such a system is that, despite the new-market instability, the interest rates pursue a convergent path over time to the intersection of the total s-functions (see page 251). However, in the context of an adjustment process involving the total system, equilibrium is shown to be unattainable. Point 2, at the intersection of s_{1T} and s_{2T}, moves constantly away from the equilibrium natural rates at point 1. PP' is again assumed to be a downward function. The reader will recall that in this model the deflationary zone is to the right of PP', and the inflationary to the left (see page 257, note 13).

The three possible configurations produced by the direct impact of the purchase are drawn in Figure 7A–10. In the (a) graph, point 2 is to the left of the upper vertical angle of s_{1N} and s_{2N}, while point 1 is within the lower vertical angle of s_{1T} and s_{2T}. The induced movements of the total schedules are indicated by the usual labeled arrows. Clearly point 2 may remain to the left of s_{1N} and drift away from point 1, or it may drift rightward into the upper vertical angle of s_{1N} and s_{2N}. The latter possibility is illustrated by the (b) drawing, in which point 2 may drift up and away from point 1, or rightward until it is to the right of s_{2N}. The latter case is illustrated by the (c) drawing, in which point 2 may drift away from point 1 on a rightward path, or it may move back into the upper vertical

FIGURE 7A-10

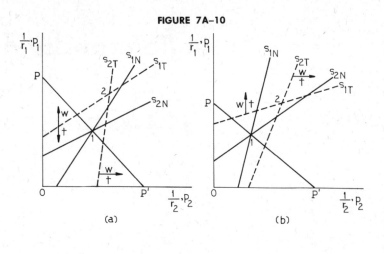

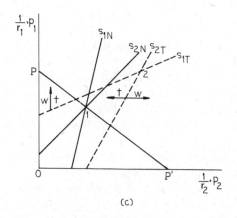

angle of s_{1N} and s_{2N}. To summarize, point 2 may either move away from point 1 in the first instance, or it may oscillate between the upper vertical angle of s_{1N} and s_{2N} and the area to the right of that angle. Since one of the schedules is always moving unambiguously away from equilibrium, such continued oscillations will drive point 2 farther away from point 1. In no case do the market rates tend to approach PP' or the equilibrium natural rates.

Minor variants of the three cases presented in Figure 7A–10 can be drawn. For example, while in (a) $\partial s_{1T}/\partial p_2 < \partial s_{1N}/\partial p_2$, the same general pattern can be constructed with $\partial s_{1T}/\partial p_2 > \partial s_{1N}/\partial p_2$. The reader may verify that such differences will not alter the general conclusion that equilibrium cannot be reached.

A Reformulation
of the Hicks
IS-LM Diagram

1. Introduction

The *IS-LM* diagram of Hicks was originally offered as a generalization of the theory of interest and income implicit in Keynes' *General Theory*.[1] Today the diagram is still a valuable device for showing the joint determination of these variables and the price level by saving, investment, the supply and demand for money, and the supply of output. But saving and investment are invariably employed in the Hicksian framework without regard to their *financial* character. Whether ex ante saving is applied to the purchase of securities or the holding of additional cash balances, and whether ex ante investment is financed by the issuance of securities or the drawing down of cash balances, is a consideration that has not been allowed to encumber the almost universal application of the *IS-LM* system.[2]

This appendix will generalize the Hicksian framework by assuming that saving and investment each have a dual financial character. The analysis is carried out in terms of a simplified version of our general stock-flow model. There is one commodity, usable as a capital or a consumption good, and two financial assets, money and interest-bearing equity securities. As we have noted in the text, only that portion of saving and investment constituting a demand and supply of securities is relevant to the construction of the *IS* curve; the net hoarding or dishoarding of savers and investors causes the *LM* curve to be in constant motion; and *IS* and

---

[1] Hicks, "Mr. Keynes and the 'Classics'; A Suggested Interpretation," *op. cit.* A virtually identical analysis was presented by Lange in "The Rate of Interest and the Optimum Propensity to Consume," *op. cit.* Cf. also Robertson, "Some Notes on Mr. Keynes' General Theory of Employment," *op. cit.*

[2] The only writer who has specifically noted several of the limitations of the *IS-LM* framework discussed here is Hugh Rose in "Liquidity Preference and Loanable Funds," *Review of Economic Studies,* Vol. XXIV (February, 1957), p. 119.

LM are, in general, interdependent functions. We shall derive the modified *IS-LM* system by first writing the dynamic equations for models in which saving and investment are a demand and supply of securities only, saving is a demand for both securities and additional cash balances, investment is financed both by supplying new securities and dishoarding cash balances, and saving and investment each have the dual financial character. We shall assume initially that the money supply is non-dichotomized; i.e., the several functions of money are performed simultaneously by an undifferentiated stock of money. A later section will introduce a dichotomized (idle-active) monetary system. After applying these models to the *IS-LM* diagram, we shall describe the impact of variations in output. A final section will describe the basic stock-flow adjustment process in terms of the diagram, and discuss the concept of income underlying the Hicksian tools.[3]

2. Saving and Investment: A Demand and Supply of Securities Only

We shall describe this model by assuming initially an infinitesimal time period. On this assumption we can safely ignore the impact of saving and investment on the existing-asset market. The model is summarized by 13 equations:

$(10A.1)'$ $\qquad S = S(y, r_M)$, where $\dfrac{\partial S}{\partial y} > 0, \dfrac{\partial S}{\partial r_M} > 0,$

$(10A.2)'$ $\qquad I = I(r_M)$, where $\dfrac{\partial I}{\partial r_M} < 0,$

$(10A.3)'$ $\qquad S = S_s + S_m,$

$(10A.4)'$ $\qquad I = I_s + I_m,$

$(10A.5)'$ $\qquad S_s = I_s,$

$(10A.6)'$ $\qquad S_m = 0,$

$(10A.7)'$ $\qquad I_m = 0,$

$(10A.8)'$ $\qquad y = \bar{y},$

$(10A.9)'$ $\qquad m = \dfrac{M}{P},$

$(10A.10)'$ $\qquad L = L(y, r_M)$, where $\dfrac{\partial L}{\partial y} > 0, \dfrac{\partial L}{\partial r_M} < 0,$

$(10A.11)'$ $\qquad L = m,$

---

[3] The material that follows is intended to be more or less self-contained. To some extent this entails repeating or restating the analysis of earlier chapters.

(10A.12)' $M = \overline{M}$,

(10A.13)' $Y = Py$.

S_s is the portion of real intended saving directed each period to the purchase of securities, and S_m is the amount added directly to real cash balances. I_s is the real value of new securities supplied per unit of time, and I_m is that part of I financed by directly and continuously reducing real balances. (10A.5)' is the equilibrium condition in the saving-investment market. (10A.6)' and (10A.7)' are the distinguishing features of this particular model. Equation (10A.8)' asserts that output is fixed, as it would be in a static equilibrium. The fixed output level is one at which resources are fully employed. (10A.9)'–(10A.12)' are the supply and demand equations of the non-dichotomized money supply. S, I, and L are linear and homogeneous in the price level, and prices are assumed to be perfectly flexible. We abstract from the impact of autonomous wealth changes on L.

Equations (10A.1)'–(10A.8)' together determine the equilibrium levels of real saving, investment, the demand and supply of new securities, the rate of interest, and output. Consolidating these equations into (10A.5)', we obtain

(10A.14)' $S(\overline{y}, r_M) = I(r_M)$,

which determines r'_N, the natural rate of interest.

Equations (10A.8)'–(10A.12)' determine real balances and the price level. We consolidate these equations into (10A.11)', substituting r'_N for r_M:

(10A.15)' $L(\overline{y}, r'_N) = \dfrac{M}{P}$,

which sets commodity prices at a level, P'. The system is now fully accounted for, including (10A.13)', the money-income identity.

We now drop the assumption of an infinitesimal period, and consider the model during an unrestricted interval. However, except in Section 8, we describe the dynamic system retaining the assumption of fixed output. We do this to simplify the analysis. Acknowledging the growth of output would introduce a direct deflationary force, raising real balances over time. The increase of output would also constantly increase saving, which lowers the rate of interest and raises the rate of investment.[4] Our aim at this point is to describe the financial disposal of saving and investment independently of these complications.

Given the fixity of output, (10A.1)'–(10A.13)' accurately describe the

---

[4] A more complete saving function would take account of wealth, to which saving is inversely related. As both wealth and output increase over time, the net change in saving cannot therefore be predicted *a priori*. See above p. 313 and below n. 23.

system over any interval of time. In equilibrium growth at r'_N, the variables that change are the stock of capital, wealth, and the supply and demand for existing securities, all of which increase equally by the balanced saving-investment flow. None of these variables is present in the equation system, which accordingly is unchanged.

The significance of this model is that all of saving and investment are relevant to the determination of the natural rate of interest. In the dynamic equilibrium, ex ante saving and investment are equal, and the demand for money, the stock of real balances, and the price level are constant.

3. Saving: A Demand for Both Securities and Money

Let savers allocate their funds both to securities and additional cash balances. Since economic units hold both assets, this hypothesis plausibly asserts that the pattern of current accumulation resembles that of the past. Investment is and continues to be exclusively a supply of securities. Equations (10A.1)′–(10A.8)′ still describe saving, investment, and output, except that (10A.6)′ is replaced by

$$(10A.16)' \qquad S_m = S_m(y), \text{ where } \frac{\partial S_m}{\partial y} > 0.$$

The absence of r_M in (10A.16)′ implies that the interest elasticity of total saving derives solely from the S_s component;[5] however, S_s, as well as S_m, is understood to vary positively with output. In the remainder of the system, which contains the supply and demand equations for money and the money-income identity, we make the dynamic element explicit by entering subscripts, t and $t+1$. The subscript, t, will indicate the value of the variable at the opening instant of the tth period, while $t+1$ applies to the closing instant of t or the opening moment of $t+1$. The only exception to this is the stock of money, M, which is written without subscripts. Like the functions and variables of (10A.1)′–(10A.8)′, M does not change over time, and thus need not be dated. The money and income equations follow:

$$(10A.17)' \qquad m_t = \frac{M}{P_t},$$

$$(10A.18)' \qquad L_t = L_t(y, r_M),$$

$$(10A.19)' \qquad L_t = m_t,$$

$$(10A.20)' \qquad M = \overline{M},$$

---

[5] The omission of r_M in (10A.16)′ is purely for simplicity. *A priori*, hoarding out of current income and consumption might both be expected to vary inversely with the interest rate (cf. Figure 10–3).

(10A.21)′ $Y_t = P_t y,$

(10A.22)′ $m_{t+1} = m_t + S_m,$

(10A.23)′ $L_{t+1} = L_t + S_m,$

(10A.24)′ $Y_{t+1} = P_{t+1} y,$

(10A.25)′ $m_{t+1} = \dfrac{M}{P_{t+1}}.$

Given the level of output, the natural rate of interest is again determined by new-security supply and demand, except that demand is now less than total saving. We consolidate (10A.1)′–(10A.4)′, (10A.7)′, and 10A.8)′ into (10A.5)′:

(10A.26)′ $S_s(\overline{y}, r_M) = I_s(r_M),$

which again determines an equilibrium yield, r'_N. The left side of (10A.26)′ derives from (10A.1)′, (10A.3)′, (10A.8)′, and the understanding, noted above, that S_s adheres to the same relationships posited for total saving. The right side of (10A.26)′ is based upon (10A.2)′, (10A.4)′, and (10A.7)′.

Turning to the monetary equations at t, the opening instant of the period, the natural rate and the given level of output once more determine the demand for money, real balances, the price level, and money income. Upon substituting in (10A.19)′:

(10A.27)′ $L_t(\overline{y}, r'_N) = \dfrac{\dot{M}}{P_t},$

which determines P'_t. In (10A.21)′, $Y'_t = P'_t \overline{y}$.

Equations (10A.22)′–(10A.25)′ describe the monetary impact of the hoarding of savers during the course of the interval. (10A.23)′ indicates that the demand *schedule* for real balances increases by the quantity, S_m. Moreover, since saving is financed out of current income receipts, the transfer of savings to real balances causes a proportionate decline in the price level and an increase in the aggregate *supply* of real balances. The supply increase is governed by, and equal to, the demand increase. Thus in (10A.22)′ m_t is also raised by the amount, S_m. L and m are assumed to increase equally and synchronously during the interval. Since they were equal at the beginning, they are also equal at the end of the period; (10A.22)′ and (10A.23)′ accordingly imply the equality of L_{t+1} and m_{t+1}, which is not explicitly written. (10A.24)′ and (10A.25)′ are the closing identities for money income and real balances.

Since the flows of new-security supply and demand are constant and equal, while the demand and supply of real balances increase equally during the interval, the interest rate remains at the natural level, r'_N. But the price level falls. We solve for P_{t+1} by setting (10A.23)′ equal to

(10A.25)′, and substituting known values for each variable:

(10A.28)′ $$L_t(\bar{y},r'_N) + S_m(\bar{y}) = \frac{\overline{M}}{P_{t+1}}.$$

The difference between P'_{t+1}, which is the solution to (10A.28)′, and P'_t, as derived from (10A.27)′, is

(10A.29)′ $$\Delta P'_t = P'_{t+1} - P'_t = -\frac{\overline{M}S_m(\bar{y})}{[L_t(\bar{y},r'_N) + S_m(\bar{y})][L_t(\bar{y},r'_N)]}.^{6}$$

In (10A.24)′ we have the identity, $Y'_{t+1} = P'_{t+1}\bar{y}.^{7}$

When a portion of ex ante saving is hoarded, the equilibrium interest rate is thus determined by investment and the portion of saving which is a demand for securities. The hoarded savings are converted into a continuing increase in the demand for real balances over time. This raises the supply of real balances equally by lowering the price level. In the moving equilibrium, *total* ex ante saving exceeds desired investment, and the growth of capital may lie anywhere between $I_s(r'_N)$ and $S(\bar{y},r'_N)$. Any capital increment in excess of $I_s(r'_N)$, the equilibrium amount both by firms and savers, is forced investment.

4. Investment: A Supply of Both Securities and Money

Let us assume that entrepreneurs finance investment expenditures both by issuing securities and by continuously drawing down their existing

---

[6] At the opening of the $(t+n)^{\text{th}}$ period the price level will have changed by

$$P'_{t+n} - P'_t = -\frac{n\overline{M}S_m(\bar{y})}{[L_t(\bar{y},r'_N) + nS_m(\bar{y})][L_t(\bar{y},r'_N)]}.$$

[7] We can derive the change in k, the ratio of nominal balances held to money income, as follows. Since L is in real terms,

$$k = \frac{PL}{Y} = \frac{L}{y}.$$

The value of k at time t is

$$k'_t = \frac{L_t(\bar{y},r'_N)}{\bar{y}}.$$

At $t+1$,

$$k'_{t+1} = \frac{L_{t+1}(\bar{y},r'_N) + S_m(\bar{y})}{\bar{y}}.$$

Hence

$$k'_{t+1} - k'_t = \frac{S_m(\bar{y})}{\bar{y}} > 0.$$

holdings of real balances. Saving is once again directed at securities only. The resulting system is opposite and symmetrical to the preceding model. The system is summarized by equations (10A.1)'–(10A.8)' and (10A.17)'–(10A.25)', with the following exceptions. We replace (10A.7)' by

$$(10A.30)' \qquad\qquad I_m = \overline{I}_m,$$

a given constant. In (10A.22)' and (10A.23)', $-I_m$ is substituted for S_m. The natural rate of interest again is determined in the new securities market, in which only a portion of investment expenditures is now financed. Each period the demand for real balances falls in the amount of I_m, and the supply falls equally as the price level rises.[8] Ex ante investment exceeds ex ante saving, and ex post investment depends on the degree of forced saving.

5. Saving: A Demand for Securities and Money; Investment: A Supply of Securities and Money

The most general system is one in which S_s, S_m, I_s, and I_m all are positive. Thus in (10A.1)'–(10A.8)' we drop both (10A.6)' and (10A.7)', replacing them by (10A.16)' and (10A.30)', respectively. We define a new variable,

$$(10A.31)' \qquad\qquad \delta = S_m - I_m,$$

which is substituted for S_m in the system, (10A.17)'–(10A.25)'. When $\delta > 0$, there is a net increase in the demand and supply of real balances, a decline in the price level, and an excess of total desired saving over total investment each period. When $\delta < 0$, the moving equilibrium is an inflationary one, characterized by $I > S$. When $\delta = 0$, hoarding and dishoarding offset each other, real balances and prices are constant, and aggregate desired saving and investment are equal. This final model is essentially the same as the initial one, described in Section 2, except that a part of investment is financed outside of the securities market.

6. A Dichotomized Money Supply

The moving equilibrium assumes a somewhat different character if the money supply is divided into specialized idle and active components. That is, we not only distinguish between two different motives of the demand for money, but we assume that there exist two separable components of the stock of money which meet these demands. One portion is asset or idle money, held on wealth account as the object of liquidity

---

[8] The change in the price level is given by an expression analogous to (10A.29)':

$$P'_{t+1} - P'_t = \frac{\overline{M}\overline{I}_m}{[L_t(\overline{y},r'_N) - \overline{I}_m][L_t(\overline{y},r'_N)]} > 0.$$

preference. The other portion, transactions or active balances, is turned over against current output in accordance with the transactions demand. The significance of this system, as opposed to the non-dichotomized model of Sections 2–5, is that changes in the price level and real balances independently influence the level of the market rate of interest (see Chapter IX-D). This is particularly important in the dynamic equilibrium of hoarded savings and investment.

Our reasons for introducing the dichotomized monetary system here are two-fold. First, it is the model of Keynes in both the *Treatise* and the *General Theory*. Second, while it is not the model of Hicks, it is the model of the vast majority of users of the Hicksian *IS-LM* framework.[9] Our critique of *IS* and *LM* should thus be specifically applicable to the "dichotomizers."

We describe the dichotomized money supply in the context of Section 3, in which saving is applied both to securities and cash balances, while investment is wholly a supply of securities. Saving, investment, and output are summarized by equations (10A.1)′–(10A.4)′, (10A.7)′, (10A.8)′, and (10A.16)′. (10A.5)′, the equality of new-security supply and demand, is replaced by a stock-flow equilibrium condition below, (10A.50)′. The monetary equations follow. The subscripts, 1 and 2, denote active and idle balances, respectively.

(10A.32)′ $$m_{2,t} = \frac{M_{2,t}}{P_t},$$

(10A.33)′ $$L_{2,t} = L_{2,t}(r_M), \text{ where } \frac{\partial L_2}{\partial r_M} < 0,$$

(10A.34)′ $$L_{2,t} = m_{2,t},$$

(10A.35)′ $$M = \bar{M},$$

(10A.36)′ $$M_{2,t} = M - M_{1,t},$$

(10A.37)′ $$Y_t = P_t y,$$

(10A.38)′ $$L_{1,t} = k_1 Y_t, \text{ where } k_1 > 0,$$

(10A.39)′ $$k_1 = \bar{k}_1,$$

(10A.40)′ $$L_{1,t} = M_{1,t},$$

(10A.41)′ $$m_{2,t+1} = m_{2,t} + S_m + \alpha_{t+1},$$

(10A.42)′ $$\alpha_{t+1} = \frac{M_{2,t}}{P_{t+1}} - \frac{M_{2,t}}{P_t},$$

---

[9] The common practice of textbook writers is to resort to the dichotomy in deriving *IS-LM*, but to employ a non-dichotomized money supply otherwise. There is no recognition of the fact that the models are not really identical.

(10A.43)′ $L_{2,t+1} = L_{2,t} + S_m ,$

(10A.44)′ $L_{2,t+1} = m_{2,t+1} ,$

(10A.45)′ $m_{2,t+1} = \dfrac{M_{2,t+1}}{P_{t+1}} ,$

(10A.46)′ $M_{2,t+1} = M - M_{1,t+1} ,$

(10A.47)′ $Y_{t+1} = P_{t+1} y ,$

(10A.48)′ $L_{1,t+1} = k_1 Y_{t+1} ,$

(10A.49)′ $L_{1,t+1} = M_{1,t+1} .$

In this model the hoarding of savers, S_m, appears in (10A.41)′ and (10A.43)′ as equal additions to the initial supply and demand for real *idle* balances. We assume that savers transfer a quantity of active money, taken from current income, directly to the idle realm. Prices fall proportionately, leaving the value of active money intact. But deflation creates a *further* increment in m_2, represented by the α_{t+1} term in (10A.41)′. α_{t+1} is defined in (10A.42)′ as the increase in the value of *pre-existing* idle balances due to the deflation. It is an addition of m_2 over and above the *nominal* increases that savers effect.[10] α_{t+1} is thus a net increase in the value of idle money, which reduces the market rate of interest (cf. Chapter VI-B[2]). In the non-dichotomized model of Sections 2–5 the price level had no such side effect. We may, in fact, reinterpret the hoarding of savers in that system as a "withdrawal" of money from the expenditures stream. But now the undifferentiated *total* stock of money and prices fall

---

[10] We can illustrate the impact of savers' hoarding on m_2 by a numerical example. Suppose the data at time t are:

$M_{1,t} = 100, \overline{V}_1 = 1/k_1 = 2, \overline{y} = 200, P_t = 1.00, M_{2,t} = 50, m_{2,t} = M_{2,t}/P_t = 50 .$

Savers transfer \$10 of M_1 to M_2, reducing the price level to

$$P_{t+1} = \frac{M_{1,t+1}\overline{V}_1}{y} = \frac{90 \times 2}{200} = 0.90 .$$

Thus S_m, valued at the new price level, is $10/0.90 = 11.11$, and this is the quantity added both to m_2 and L_2. But

$$m_{2,t+1} = \frac{M_{2,t+1}}{P_{t+1}} = \frac{60}{0.90} = 66.67 ,$$

and

$$\alpha_{t+1} = m_{2,t+1} - (m_{2,t} + S_m) = 66.67 - (50.00 + 11.11) = 5.56.$$

We may also compute α_{t+1} directly:

$$\alpha_{t+1} = \frac{M_{2,t}}{P_{t+1}} - \frac{M_{2,t}}{P_t} = \frac{50}{0.90} - 50 = 5.56 .$$

proportionately, total real balances (exclusive of savers' hoardings) remaining constant. Then as savers restore *nominal* balances to their portfolios, the supply and demand for real balances rise equally, as we have previously assumed. There is no disturbance to the market rate of interest (cf. Chapter IX-D[4]).[11]

The value of idle balances accordingly rises each period above demand, and the market rate of interest falls. But as this occurs, $I_s - S_s$ increases and tends to offset the decline in the interest rate. This is because $I_s - S_s$ is an excess supply of new securities, while $m_2 - L_2$, the excess supply of idle balances, is simultaneously an excess demand to hold securities. In a period, $t + n$, a rate of interest, r''_M, is reached at which the excess security supply is exactly equal to the excess security demand:

$$(10A.50)' \quad I_s(r''_M) - S_s(r''_M) = m_{2,t+n} - L_{2,t+n}(r''_M) = \alpha'_{t+n} ,$$

and the interest rate thereafter is constant. Apart from savers' direct increases, m_2 itself is constant. This is because the excess supply of new securities is exchanged for a quantity of real idle balances exactly equal to the value increase due to deflation. Idle balances spent on new securities are, of course, activated.[12] In the moving equilibrium, m_2 and L_2 continue to increase equally by

$$(10A.51)' \quad S_m(\bar{y}) = S(\bar{y}, r''_M) - S_s(\bar{y}, r''_M),$$

where $r''_M < r'_N$, the natural rate. The price level falls continuously.[13]

---

[11] Consider a numerical example. The beginning data are

$$M_t = 100, V_t \text{ (velocity)} = 2, \bar{y} = 200, P_t = 1.00 ,$$
$$M_t/P_t = 100/1.00 = 100.00 .$$

Savers transfer \$10 from income to wealth account by a direct act of hoarding. Abstracting momentarily from savers' additional hoards,

$$M_{t+1} = 90, P_{t+1} = \frac{M_{t+1}V_t}{\bar{y}} = \frac{90 \times 2}{200} = 0.90 ,$$
$$M_{t+1}/P_{t+1} = 90/0.90 = 100.00 = M_t/P_t .$$

The hoarding is then manifested in an equal increase in nominal balances held, and the demand to hold these balances, L. The final data are

$$M_{t+1} = 100, M_{t+1}/P_{t+1} = 100/0.90 = 111.11 .$$

[12] Thus $I_s - S_s$ counters the impact of the price level in raising m_2, both by reducing the nominal holdings of idle money, and then by activating these balances and retarding the downward course of the price level.

[13] Between the $(t+n)^{\text{th}}$ and $(t+n+1)^{\text{th}}$ interval the movement of the price level can be shown to be

$$P'_{t+n+1} - P'_{t+n} = - \frac{\bar{M} S_m(\bar{y})}{[\bar{k}_1 \bar{y} + L_{2,t+n}(r''_M) + S_m(\bar{y})][\bar{k}_1 \bar{y} + L_{2,t+n}(r''_M)]} .$$

$(10A.51)'$ is, of course, the gross rather than the net increase in m_2 and L_2. Cf. Figure 8–6.

Should there be net dishoarding of idle balances by investing entrepreneurs, the moving equilibrium is one of constantly rising prices and a constant interest rate above the natural level.

7. The IS-LM Diagram

We now translate our findings to the Hicks *IS-LM* framework. The *IS* curve is the functional relation between interest and output derived from saving-investment equilibrium. More precisely, it is the natural rate of interest, as determined by new-security supply and demand, expressed as a function of output. In equation (10A.26)′ y and r_M are both allowed to vary. An increase in y raises S_s and lowers the equilibrium yield along the given I_s schedule. Thus the functional relation, labeled $I_s S_s$ in Figure 10A–1, is downward sloping.

LM is the relation between y and r_M implied by the monetary equations, with M and P held constant. It is usually derived in straightforward fashion in terms of a dichotomized money supply.[14] Hicks, who does not dichotomize, asserts merely that *LM* is a rising function, "since an increase in income tends to raise the demand for money, and an increase in the rate of interest tends to lower it."[15] In terms of our monetary equations for the non-dichotomized system, (10A.9)′–(10A.11)′, we set $M = \overline{M}$, $P = \overline{P}$, and write

(10A.52)′ $$L(y, r_M) = \frac{\overline{M}}{\overline{P}}.$$

Thus the *LM* relationship implies that L is equal to a constant. In order to maintain the equilibrium as expressed by (10A.52)′, any change in r_M requires a change of the same sign in y. In Figure 10A–1, *LM* is drawn as the familiar rising schedule.

The solid-line schedules of Figure 10A–1 illustrate the "equilibrium" of a non-dichotomized system in which $\delta > 0$ (see Section 3). The vertical

---

[14] To my knowledge Modigliani was the first to do this. See "Liquidity Preference and the Theory of Interest and Money," *op. cit.*, pp. 54–57. In terms of our dichotomized equations, we have the equilibrium condition,

$$L_1 = k_1 Y = M - M_2.$$

After substituting $PL_2(r_M)$ for M_2, $P = \overline{P}$, $M = \overline{M}$, and known values for k_1 and Y, we obtain

$$\overline{k}_1 y + L_2(r_M) = \frac{\overline{M}}{\overline{P}}.$$

Since the right side is a constant, movements in y are associated with movements in the same direction in r_M.

[15] "Mr. Keynes and the 'Classics'," *op. cit.*, p. 153. However, in *A Contribution to the Theory of the Trade Cycle* (London: Oxford University Press, 1950), pp. 140–41, Hicks derives *LM* using the Keynesian dichotomized money supply.

FIGURE 10A-1
The Hicksian Diagram Incorporating Dual-Financial Saving and Investment Behavior

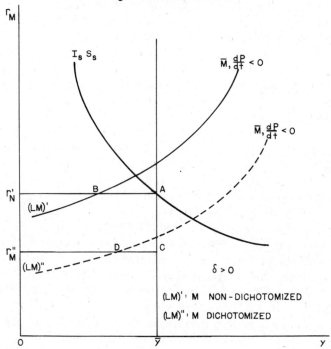

line originating at $\bar{y}$ on the horizontal axis represents the fixed supply of output.[16] If $\delta = 0$ the equilibrium would be at point A, at which $I_s S_s$ and the output line meet.[17] An appropriate price level would then cause LM, a stable function, to pass through A.[18] But with $\delta > 0$ the demand for money increases and LM shifts to the left each period.[19] We

---

[16] Hicks does not enter a supply function on his diagram, nor does he discuss the determination of the price level. It is clear, however, that he considers interest and income to be determined by his flow and stock demand functions, IS and LM (or LL, as he designates it). The only supply function consistent with this procedure is one which is infinitely elastic at a given price level: $P = P$. This is, of course, generally unrealistic. But the assumption might conceivably have validity in a deep depression, such as that of the thirties, during which Keynes and Hicks wrote. Under these circumstances an output increase, for example, might be accomplished by employing additional units of capital and labor, both of which are unemployed in large numbers. The result could be constant marginal costs and thus a constant supply price of output.

[17] When $\delta = 0$, $I_s S_s$ coincides with IS, the functional relation between aggregate saving and investment.

[18] With reference to (10A.52)' a *ceteris paribus* decrease in P raises the level of real balances. This requires that L be raised, which may be accomplished either by increasing y (holding r_M constant) or decreasing r_M (holding y constant). This has the effect of shifting LM downward, or, equivalently, to the right. An increase in P produces an opposite shift of LM.

[19] In terms of (10A.52)' an increase in L, with r_M held constant, requires that y be lowered. This is equivalent to shifting LM to the left.

know that simultaneously the price level falls, and this shifts LM to the right toward an intersection through point A.[20] The schedule, $(LM)'$, in Figure 10A–1 represents a resultant function, midway between the LM curves produced by the leftward and rightward impulses. Point B on $(LM)'$ at the height, r'_N, may be regarded as the effective "demand" for output. $B < A$ attests to the deflationary character of the equilibrium.[21]

When the money supply is dichotomized, the LM schedule is represented by $(LM)''$ (see Section 6). For $\delta > 0$, the equilibrium market rate of interest is $r''_M < r'_N$. The supply point is now C at $(\bar{y}, r''_M)$. The demand point, $D < C$, is the resultant of two pairs of offsetting forces. One pair, a set of horizontal vectors, is the same as that acting on point B. Another pair is a set of vertical vectors that stabilizes the interest rate.

In this broader formulation the IS-LM framework has lost its essential simplicity and probably some of its appeal. Once we acknowledge continuous hoarding or dishoarding by savers or investors, IS is interpreted more narrowly as $I_s S_s$, the locus of new security-market points of equilibrium. LM, a related function, stands on a razor's edge between counterbalancing forces. Where previously an equilibrium of stable prices was represented by a single point common to IS, LM, and the output function, supply and demand are now unequal and the price level is in constant motion. The equilibrium interest rate lies on $I_s S_s$ only if the money supply is not dichotomized. Finally, since $I_s S_s$ and LM are interdependent, they will tend to shift together. Thus an increase in I, raising both I_s and I_m, will raise $I_s S_s$ and increase the length of the vectors acting upon LM. A new resultant LM function will lie to the right of the original one.[22]

8. Variable Output

Consider now the growth of output over time. This is reflected in Figure 10A–1 in constant rightward shifts of the vertical supply line, $\bar{y}$. If $\delta = 0$, the price level will now fall, and LM will shift constantly to the right toward the moving intersection of $I_s S_s$ and the supply line. The

---

[20] See n. 18.

[21] A fuller account of the supply-demand relations of the traditional Hicksian diagram is given in G. Horwich and V. L. Smith, "A Reconsideration of Aggregate General-Equilibrium Theory," Purdue University, Institute for Quantitative Research in Economics and Management, Institute Paper Series, 1959.

[22] We have noted that in "Keynesian" models characterized by an infinitely elastic demand or supply of money (pp. 391–92 and 394), the financial disposition of saving and the form of investment financing are irrelevant to the equilibrium of the system. The traditional aggregate equality, $S = I$, holds, and, for given output, the price level is constant. This is reflected in the Hicksian diagram in an intersection between IS, as determined by aggregate saving and investment, and a horizontal section of LM. Another such case occurs when both S and I are completely interest-inelastic (p. 396). In this event LM is again upward sloping, but IS is a vertical line at the output that equates total saving and investment.

rise in output raises intended saving above investment, and the market rate, as given by a point on LM above and to the left of the supply point, falls in pursuit of the natural rate.[23] If $\delta > 0$, the additional output increases the rate of decline in prices, and LM again shifts to the right. Assuming that the growth of output increases both S_s and S_m, the deflation is further intensified. The market rate follows the natural rate. In Figure 10A–1 the supply path of a non-dichotomized system would fall from point A along I_sS_s. The demand path, originating at point B, would be a southeast vector moving downward at the same rate as the supply point. For a dichotomized money supply, the supply and demand paths would be southeast vectors extending from points C and D, respectively.[24]

9. Further Notes on IS-LM

a) The Stock-Flow Adjustment

This section will indicate briefly the way in which our general stock-flow adjustment process appears on the Hicksian diagram. For this purpose we revert to the model of Section 2 in which $S_m = I_m = 0$ and $y = \bar{y}$. In Figure 10A–2 the system is initially in equilibrium at point A, the intersection of I_sS_s, $(LM)'$, and the supply line, $\bar{y}$. The parameters of $(LM)'$ are a money supply of M' and a price level, P'. The natural rate is r'_N. Consider an open-market purchase, carried out instantaneously by the central bank. The interest rate falls to r''_M, and money increases to M''. The increased money supply lowers LM to $(LM)''$. Since there is no direct impact on commodity prices or output, the action of the central bank appears as a vertical demand vector, a, connecting point A with B, whose coordinates are $(\bar{y}, r''_M)$.

In the first adjustment interval we have at r''_M an excess of investment over saving, which takes the form of an excess supply of new securities. The market rate rises and households transfer balances to entrepreneurs in exchange for the excess securities. Since household expenditures remain constant, while entrepreneurs immediately spend their additional funds, we have, at the prevailing price level, a net increase in the effective demand for output. In terms of the diagram, there is an upward movement along $(LM)''$, reflecting the simultaneous increase in interest and effective demand. The path is indicated by the vector, b.

---

[23] If saving were an inverse function of wealth, the growth of capital and real balances over time would reduce saving at any level of output. This causes I_sS_s to shift constantly upward, countering the tendency of the natural rate to fall.

[24] If output varies because of short-run changes in employment, which in turn are due to money illusion in the labor market, then the supply line shifts with changes in prices (see, e.g., Bailey, *National Income and the Price Level,* pp. 44–47). However, I find the Hicksian diagram less suitable in this connection than the price-output diagram pioneered by Brownlee and Marschak (see Chapter IX, n. 15).

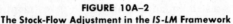

FIGURE 10A–2
The Stock-Flow Adjustment in the *IS-LM* Framework

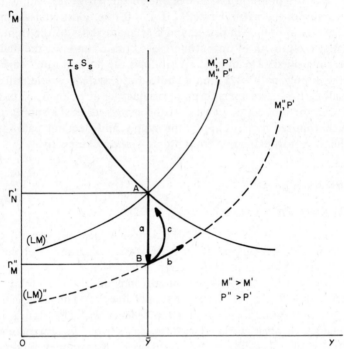

But the supply of output is fixed at $\bar{y}$, and prices rise. The entire *LM* schedule rises responsively, carrying the demand vector with it. A resultant demand path is given by c, which is drawn toward the supply line and the ultimate intersection at point A.

If the money supply were dichotomized, the price rise would add to the increase in interest, causing c to converge more rapidly to A.

Suppose once again that $\delta > 0$. The direct impact of the purchase again causes *LM* to shift rightward, reflecting the increase in the money supply. If diagramed in Figure 10A–1, the initial demand vector would be a downward vertical line from point B to the new *LM* curve. The adjustment again generates northeastern vectors along *LM*. The transfer of money to entrepreneurs counters the inherent deflationary tendency of the system. Prices may not actually rise, but at least their rate of decline is temporarily reduced. This weakens the rightward pressure on *LM* of the declining price level (prior to the disturbance, this pressure was just equal to the leftward force due to savers' hoarding). Thus *LM* moves to the left with each additional round of entrepreneurial spending. Eventually *LM* returns to its original position. Prices decline at the same rate as formerly, but their absolute level at any point in time is greater.

b) The Definition of Income

At the conclusion of his article Hicks warns us that "the concept of 'Income' is worked monstrously hard."[25] He is particularly concerned about the distribution of income. This can, in fact, become a serious problem for the diagram as soon as a governmental sector is introduced. The division of income between households and the government means that IS and LM will in general involve different income concepts. If the government is a taxer, saving is based on disposable income, and this is the variable on the horizontal axis toward which IS (or $I_s S_s$) is directed. On the other hand, the demand for money underlying LM is generally understood to incorporate the behavior of all sectors, including firms and the government, through which the supply of money normally passes. As such, aggregate income—say, net real national product (NNP)—is the relevant income variable for LM.[26]

The introduction of the government can be handled either by using a double scale on the horizontal axis, or by placing NNP alone on the axis while constructing IS as a function of the level of taxes. We shall illustrate the latter procedure, analyzing the impact of a balanced government-budgetary increment.

We assume $S_m = I_m = 0$, the money supply is not dichotomized, $y = \bar{y}$, and the balanced government budget, β, initially is zero. The system is in equilibrium in Figure 10A-3 at point A. Assume that the balanced-budget increment entails a reduction in the demand for money. The government secures balances through taxes and gives them an extra turnover against output, returning them without lag to the expenditures stream. The reduction in L causes LM in Figure 10A-3 to shift to the right.[27] Since households are deprived of these balances only for an instant, the government's expenditure is a net addition to the aggregate demand for output. The direct impact of the disturbance is shown as the vector, a, connecting point A with B on the new LM curve, $(LM)''$. The length of the vector is equal to the magnitude of the expenditure, measured in output units. The vector is horizontal, since there is no immediate impact on the rate of interest. Since output is fixed, prices begin

---

[25] "Mr. Keynes and the 'Classics'," *op. cit.*, p. 158.

[26] It is difficult to find a single concept of aggregate income which is suitable for all purposes. Since we are interested in the determination of the commodity price level, new production has to be supplemented by sales (plus or minus) out of inventories. We have in fact noted the influence of inventory changes on prices in Chapter IV-C(2)b. There is not much basis for choosing between gross and net national product, given our assumption that depreciation is calculated, and maintenance expenditures are made, automatically and uniformly over time. However, if capital were allowed to decline through a reduction in maintenance activity, then GNP would rise, both absolutely and relatively to NNP, and would be the more appropriate output aggregate for the equation of exchange.

[27] See n. 19, where an opposite shift in L and LM is described. The present disturbance is, of course, a once-for-all, rather than a continuing movement in the schedules. If the money supply is dichotomized, the government's action reduces k_1 (see n. 14).

FIGURE 10A-3
The Balanced Government Budget in the *IS-LM* Framework

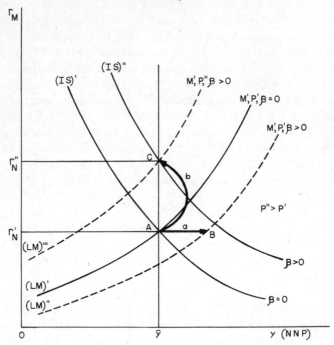

to rise immediately. However, instead of returning on a horizontal path to point *A* along leftward-shifting *LM* curves, the resultant demand vector is a rising curve, *b*. This is because the inflation lowers real private disposable income, which reduces the level of saving at any given *NNP*. Thus *IS* rises to *(IS)''*, creating a new equilibrium with the supply line at point *C*. It is this point, at which prices and the natural rate are higher, and aggregate output is the same, toward which *b* is drawn.

A Glossary of Symbols

The following symbols are listed under the chapter in which they initially appear. Symbols that are used only in footnotes or appendices are not included.

CHAPTER II

$C.$ Total consumption expenditures per unit of time in real-value units.

$D_N.$ The number of securities demanded per unit of time by current savers (the "new" demand).

$D_O.$ The number of securities demanded by existing-wealth holders (the "old" demand).

$D_T.$ The aggregate number of securities demanded per unit of time (the "total" demand).

$D_{VN}.$ The real value of the demand for securities by savers per unit of time.

$D_{VO}.$ The real value of the demand for securities by existing-wealth holders.

$D_{VT}.$ The real value of the aggregate demand for securities per unit of time.

$\eta.$ The (algebraic) price elasticity of the demand for securities.

$I.$ Real ex post (or realized) investment per unit of time; also the real value of funds directed at investment goods per unit of time (intended or ex ante investment).

$I_m.$ The real value of ex ante investment financed by drawing down existing cash balances.

$I_s.$ The real value of ex ante investment financed by issuing new securities (the same as S_{VN}).

$K.$ The number of units of capital stock.

$k_1.$ The ratio of active balances to total money income or expenditures.

$L_1.$ The nominal quantity of active (transactions) balances demanded.

$L_2.$ The real quantity of idle (asset) balances demanded.

$M.$ The nominal quantity of the total supply of money.

$M_1.$ The nominal supply of active balances.

$M_2.$ The nominal supply of idle balances.

$m_2.$ The real value of the supply of idle balances.

$P.$ The unit price of commodities (the "price level").

$\pi.$ The nominal price of a security.

$p.$ The real price of a security.

$q_c.$ The real-value unit of account (output units).

$q_s.$ The number-of-securities unit of account.

$r_M.$ The market rate of interest.

$r_N.$ The natural rate of interest.

$\rho_K.$ The net real annual return or income per unit of capital.

$\rho_s.$ The real annual income (dividend) per security.

$S.$ Total intended or ex ante saving per unit of time in real-value units.

S_m. The real value of ex ante saving applied to the building up of cash balances.

S_N. The number of new securities supplied per unit of time.

S_O. The supply of existing securities.

S_s. The real value of ex ante saving applied to the purchase of securities (the same as D_{VN}).

S_T. The total number of securities supplied per unit of time.

S_{VN}. The real value of the supply of new securities per unit of time.

S_{VO}. The real value of the existing supply of securities.

S_{VT}. The real value of the total supply of securities per unit of time.

t. A unit of time.

V. The velocity of the total stock of money (total or aggregate velocity).

V_1. The velocity of active balances.

V_2. The velocity of idle balances.

W. Total existing wealth in real-value units.

x_K. The net nominal annual return or income per unit of capital.

x_s. The nominal annual income (dividend) per security.

Y. Total annual money income or expenditures.

y. Total annual output of commodities, or real income.

CHAPTER III

E_N. The number of excess new securities supplied per unit of time.

E_O. The excess supply of existing securities in security-quantity units.

E_T. The total number of excess securities supplied per unit of time.

CHAPTER V

ΔS_E. The number of excess new securities issued in an interval.

ΔS_S. The number of securities purchased by savers in an interval.

$\hat{\ }$. A symbol placed over variables generated during an undisturbed equilibrium-growth sequence.

p_G. The real price of government securities.

p_P. The real price of privately issued securities.

$(r_m)_G$. The rate of interest on government securities.

$(r_M)_P$. The rate of interest on privately issued securities.

$(\rho_s)_G$. The real income on a government security.

$(\rho_s)_P$. The real income on a privately issued security.

S_B. The number of existing securities held by the central bank.

S_G. The existing supply of government securities held by households.

S_P. The total existing supply of privately issued securities.

S_τ. The total existing supply of government and private securities.

CHAPTER VI

ΔS_I. The number of new securities issued in an interval.

μ. The capital gains or losses (following the adjustment process) on government securities held by households prior to an open-market sale.

v. The capital gains or losses (following the adjustment process) on government securities sold by the central bank to households.

CHAPTER VII

In this chapter the existing-asset and output markets are divided into submarkets in which each of two substitute securities is held or traded. Most of the variables of Chapter II are now divided into those that apply to the type 1 and type 2 security, respectively. A subscript number, 1 or 2, is used to differentiate the two classes of functions. Thus, S_{10} and S_{20} are the existing supplies of type 1 and type 2 securities, respectively, and D_{10} and D_{20} their corresponding demands. ρ_{s_1} and ρ_{s_2} are the respective incomes per security, r_1 and r_2 the yields, and p_1 and p_2 the prices. m_{12} is the real quantity of idle balances held as an alternative to the type 1 security, and m_{22} as an alternative to the type 2 security. W_1 is a sum that includes the value of the type 1 security and m_{12}. C_1 is the consumption alternative to the purchase of type 1 securities out of S_1 current saving. C_1 and S_1 are components of y_1 real income. Other symbols, not analogous to those of Chapter II, are as follows:

$\Delta D_{1VO} = \Delta_1$. The real value of the substitution demand for type 1 securities by the existing holders of type 2 securities.

$\Delta D_{2VO} = \Delta_2$. The real value of the substitution demand for type 2 securities by the existing holders of type 1 securities.

$\Delta D_{1VN} = \Delta S_1$. The real value of the substitution demand for type 1 securities by saver-purchasers of the type 2 security.

$\Delta D_{2VN} = \Delta S_2$. The real value of the substitution demand for type 2 securities by saver-purchasers of the type 1 security.

PP'. The stable price-level line.

s_1. The type 1 security.

s_2. The type 2 security.

s_{1N}. The Hicksian substitution function derived from the new supply and the demand of saver-purchasers of the type 1 security.

s_{2N}. The Hicksian substitution function derived from the new supply and the demand of saver-purchasers of the type 2 security.

s_{1O}. The Hicksian substitution function derived from the existing supply and the demand of existing holders of the type 1 security.

s_{2O}. The Hicksian substitution function derived from the existing supply and the demand of existing holders of the type 2 security.

s_{1T}. The Hicksian substitution function derived from the total supply and demand for type 1 securities over time.

s_{2T}. The Hicksian substitution function derived from the total supply and demand for type 2 securities over time.

CHAPTER VIII

c. The currency base of the economy.

D. Total commercial bank deposits.

G. Real government expenditures per unit of time.

m_1. The real value of the supply of active balances.

m_{2S}. The supply schedule of real idle balances.

r_e. The ratio of excess bank reserves to total deposits.

r_p. The ratio of pocket currency to deposits.

r_r. The ratio of required reserves to deposits.

r_Σ. The sum of the currency-use ratios: $r_e + r_p + r_r$.

CHAPTER IX

F. The real value of the demand by financial intermediaries for primary securities per unit of time.

I_2. The real value of new intermediary securities supplied per unit of time.

k. The ratio of total money balances to total money income and expenditures.

L. The over-all demand for total real cash balances (Part D only).

L_1. The transactions demand for the total nominal stock of money (Part D only).

L_2. The asset demand for the total real supply of money (Part D only).

L_{12}. The demand for real idle balances held as an alternative to primary securities.

L_{22}. The demand for real idle balances held as an alternative to intermediary securities.

M_{12}. The nominal quantity of idle balances held as an alternative to primary securities.

M_{22}. The nominal quantity of idle balances held as an alternative to intermediary securities.

m. The real value of the total stock of money.

m_{12}. The real value of idle balances held as an alternative to primary securities.

m_{22}. The real value of idle balances held as an alternative to intermediary securities.

r_1. The yield on primary securities.

r_2. The yield on intermediary securities.

S_1. The real value of saving applied directly to the purchase of primary securities per unit of time ("direct" saving).

S_2. The real value of saving applied to the purchase of intermediary securities per unit of time ("indirect" saving).

S_{12}. The locus of points on S_1 schedules consistent with the equilibrium of the intermediary market.

s_{2N}. The Hicksian substitution function derived from the flow intermediary market.

ACKLEY, G. "Liquidity Preference and Loanable Fund Theories of Interest: Comment," *American Economic Review*, Vol. XLVII (September, 1957), pp. 662–73.

————. *Macroeconomic Theory*. New York: The Macmillan Co., 1960.

————. "The Multiplier Time Period," *American Economic Review*, Vol. XLI (June, 1951), pp. 350–68.

ALHADEFF, D. A. and C. P. "An Integrated Model for Commercial Banks," *Journal of Finance*, Vol. XII (March, 1957), pp. 24–43.

ARCHIBALD, G. C., and LIPSEY, R. G. "Monetary and Value Theory: A Critique of Lange and Patinkin," *Review of Economic Studies*, Vol. XXVI (October, 1958), pp. 1–22.

———— and ————. "Monetary and Value Theory: Further Comment," *Review of Economic Studies*, Vol. XXVIII (October, 1960), pp. 50–56.

BAILEY, M. J. *National Income and the Price Level*. New York: McGraw-Hill Book Co., Inc., 1962.

BALL, R. J. and BODKIN, R. "The Real Balance Effect and Orthodox Demand Theory: A Critique of Archibald and Lipsey," *Review of Economic Studies*, Vol. XXVIII (October, 1960), pp. 44–49.

BALOGH, T. "Dangers of the New Orthodoxy," *The Banker* (June, 1956), pp. 347–53.

BOARD OF GOVERNORS OF THE FEDERAL RESERVE SYSTEM. *Forty-Seventh Annual Report*. Washington, D.C., 1961.

————. *The Federal Reserve Bulletin*, July, 1962.

BOEHMLER, ROBINSON, GANE, and FARWELL. *Financial Institutions*. Homewood, Ill.: Richard D. Irwin, Inc., 1956.

BOULDING, K. E. "A Liquidity Preference Theory of Market Prices," *Economica*, N.S., Vol. IX (May, 1944), pp. 55–63.

BRECHLING, F. P. R. "A Note on Bond Holding and the Liquidity Preference Theory of Interest," *Review of Economic Studies*, Vol. XXIV (June, 1957), pp. 190–97.

BRONFENBRENNER, M., and MAYER, T. "Liquidity Functions in the American Economy," *Econometrica*, Vol. XXVIII (October, 1960), pp. 810–34.

BROWNLEE, O. H. "The Theory of Employment and Stabilization Policy," *Journal of Political Economy*, Vol. LVIII (October, 1950), pp. 412–24.

CHANDLER, L. V. *Introduction to Monetary Theory*. New York: Harper & Bros., 1940.

CLOWER, R. W. "An Investigation into the Dynamics of Investment," *American Economic Review*, Vol. XLIV (March, 1954), pp. 64–81.

————. "Productivity, Thrift and the Rate of Interest," *Economic Journal*, Vol. LXIV (March, 1954), pp. 107–15.

COLLERY, A. "A Note on the Saving-Wealth Relation and the Rate of Interest," *Journal of Political Economy*, Vol. LXVIII (October, 1960), pp. 509–10.

CONARD, J. W. *Introduction to the Theory of Interest*. Berkeley, Calif.: University of California Press, 1959.

ERTSON, J. M. "Intermediaries and Monetary Theory: A Criticism of the Gurley-Shaw Theory," *American Economic Review*, Vol. XLVIII (March, 1958), pp. 119–31.

_____. "The Term Structure of Interest Rates," *Quarterly Journal of Economics*, Vol. LXXI (November, 1957), pp. 485–517.

DAVIDSON, SMITH, and WILEY. *Economics: An Analytical Approach*. Homewood, Ill.: Richard D. Irwin, Inc., 1958.

DAVIS, R. M. "Re-Examination of the Speculative Demand for Money," *Quarterly Journal of Economics*, Vol. LXXIII (May, 1959), pp. 326–32.

DAY, A. C. L. *Outline of Monetary Economics*. London: Oxford University Press, 1957.

DERNBURG, T. F., and McDOUGALL, D. M. *Macro-Economics*. New York: McGraw-Hill Book Co., Inc., 1960.

DUNAWAY, W. "A Liquidity Theory of Interest Rates Unfettered by 'Constant' Structure," Unpublished paper, University of Chicago, 1951.

FISHER, I. *The Purchasing Power of Money*. New York: The Macmillan Co., 1925.

FRIEDMAN, M. *A Theory of the Consumption Function*. Princeton, N.J.: Princeton University Press, 1957.

GOLDSMITH, R. W. *The National Wealth of the United States in the Postwar Period*. Princeton, N.J.: Princeton University Press, 1962.

GURLEY, J. G. "Liquidity and Financial Institutions in the Postwar Economy," *Study of Employment, Growth, and Price Levels*. Study Paper 14, U.S. Congress, Joint Economic Committee, January, 1960.

GURLEY, J. G., and SHAW, E. S. "Financial Aspects of Economic Growth," *American Economic Review*, Vol. XLV (September, 1955), pp. 515–38.

_____ and _____. "Financial Intermediaries and the Saving-Investment Process," *Journal of Finance*, Vol. XI (May, 1956), pp. 257–76.

_____ and _____. *Money in a Theory of Finance*. Washington, D.C.: The Brookings Institution, 1960.

_____ and _____. "Reply," *American Economic Review*, Vol. XLVIII (March, 1958), pp. 132–38.

HABERLER, G. *Prosperity and Depression*. Cambridge, Mass.: Harvard University Press, 1958.

_____. "The Pigou Effect Once More," *Journal of Political Economy*, Vol. LX (June, 1952), pp. 240–46.

HALEY, B. F. "Value and Distribution," *A Survey of Contemporary Economics*, Vol. I, ed. by H. S. Ellis. Philadelphia: The Blakiston Co., 1948.

HANSEN, A. H. *Monetary Theory and Fiscal Policy*. New York: McGraw-Hill Book Co., Inc., 1949.

HAWTREY, R. G. *Capital and Employment*. London: Longmans, Green & Co., 1937.

HAYEK, F. A. *The Pure Theory of Capital*. London: Routledge and Kegan Paul, Ltd., 1941.

HICKS, J. R. *A Contribution to the Theory of the Trade Cycle*. London: Oxford University Press, 1950.

_____. "Mr. Keynes and the 'Classics'; A Suggested Interpretation," *Econometrica*, Vol. V (April, 1937), pp. 147–59.

_____. *Value and Capital*. London: Oxford University Press, 1946.

HORWICH, G. "Elements of Timing and Response in the Balance Sheet of Banking, 1953–55," *Journal of Finance*, Vol. XII (May, 1957), pp. 238–55.

_____. "Member Bank Effective Reserves and Earning Assets in the Thirties," *Econometrica*, Vol. XXVI (October, 1958), pp. 602–3.

_____. "Money, Prices and the Theory of Interest Determination," *Economic Journal*, Vol. LXVII (December, 1957), pp. 625–43.

_____. "Moneyflows and Monetary Theory," *Proceedings of the Business and Economics Section of the American Statistical Association*, 1955–56, pp. 49–51.

—————. *Open Market Operations, the Rate of Interest, and the Price Level: An Essay in the Pure Theory of Interest and Money.* University of Chicago dissertation, March, 1954. Summarized in the *Journal of Finance*, Vol. X (December, 1955), pp. 508–9.

—————. "Real Assets and the Theory of Interest," *Journal of Political Economy*, Vol. LXX (April, 1962), pp. 157–69.

—————. "Re-Examination of the Speculative Demand for Money: Comment," *Quarterly Journal of Economics*, Vol. LXIII (November, 1959), pp. 686–91.

HORWICH, G., and SMITH, V. L. "A Reconsideration of Aggregate General-Equilibrium Theory," Purdue University, Institute for Quantitative Research in Economics and Management, Institute Paper Series, 1959.

HOUGH, L. "An Asset Influence in the Labor Market," *Journal of Political Economy*, Vol. LXIII (June, 1955), pp. 202–15.

HUME, D. *Writings on Economics*, ed. by Eugene Rotwein. Madison, Wis.: University of Wisconsin Press, 1955.

JOHNSON, H. G. "Monetary Theory and Policy," *American Economic Review*, Vol. LII (June, 1962), pp. 335–84.

—————. "Some Cambridge Controversies in Monetary Theory," *Review of Economic Studies*, Vol. XIX (1951–52), pp. 90–104.

—————. "The *General Theory* after Twenty-Five Years," *American Economic Review*, Vol. LI (May, 1961), pp. 1–17.

—————. "The Matrix Multiplier and an Ambiguity in the Keynesian Concept of Saving," *Economic Journal*, Vol. LXII (March, 1952), pp. 197–200.

KAREKEN, J. "Monetary Policy and the Public Debt: An Appraisal of Post-War Developments in the U.S.A.," *Kyklos*, Vol. X (1957), pp. 401–31.

KEYNES, J. M. *A Treatise on Money*, Vols. I and II. London: Macmillan & Co., Ltd., 1950.

—————. "Alternative Theories of the Rate of Interest," *Economic Journal*, Vol. XLVII (June, 1937), pp. 241–52.

—————. "The 'Ex-Ante' Theory of the Rate of Interest, *Economic Journal*, Vol. XLVII (December, 1937), pp. 663–69.

—————. "The General Theory of Employment," *Quarterly Journal of Economics*, Vol. LI (February, 1937), pp. 209–23.

—————. *The General Theory of Employment, Interest and Money.* New York: Harcourt, Brace & Co., 1936.

KLEIN, L. R. *The Keynesian Revolution.* New York: The Macmillan Co., 1947.

LANGE, O. "The Rate of Interest and the Optimum Propensity to Consume," *Economica*, N.S., Vol. V (February, 1938), pp. 12–32.

LAVINGTON, F. *The English Capital Market.* London: Methuen and Co., 1921.

LEONTIEF, W. W. "Theoretical Note on Time-Preference, Productivity of Capital, Stagnation and Economic Growth," *American Economic Review*, Vol. XLVIII (March, 1958), pp. 105–11.

LERNER, A. P. "A Note on the Rate of Interest and the Value of Assets," *Economic Journal*, Vol. LXXI (September, 1961), pp. 539–43.

—————. "Interest Theory—Supply and Demand for Loans or Supply and Demand for Cash?" *Review of Economic Statistics*, Vol. XXVI (May, 1944), pp. 88–91.

—————. *The Economics of Control.* New York: The Macmillan Co., 1944.

LUTZ, F. A. "The Structure of Interest Rates," *Quarterly Journal of Economics*, Vol. LV. (November, 1940), pp. 36–63.

LUTZ, V. "Real and Monetary Factors in the Determination of Employment Levels," *Quarterly Journal of Economics*, Vol. LXVI (May, 1952), pp. 251–72.

McKENNA, J. P. *Aggregate Economic Analysis.* New York: The Dryden Press, Inc., 1955.

MARSCHAK, J. *Income, Employment, and the Price Level.* New York: Augustus M. Kelley, Inc., 1951.

MARSHALL, A. *Money, Credit and Commerce.* London: Macmillan & Co., Ltd., 1923.

MAYER, T. "The Inflexibility of Monetary Policy," *Review of Economics and Statistics,* Vol. XL (November, 1958), pp. 358–74.

————. "The Quantity Theory and the Balanced Budget Theorem," *Review of Economics and Statistics,* Vol. XLIII (February, 1961), pp. 88–90.

MEISELMAN, D. *The Term Structure of Interest Rates.* Englewood Cliffs, N.J.: Prentice-Hall, Inc., 1962.

METZLER, L. A. "A Reply," *Journal of Political Economy,* Vol. LX (June, 1952), pp. 249–52.

————. "Wealth, Saving, and the Rate of Interest," *Journal of Political Economy,* Vol. LIX (April, 1951), pp. 93–116.

MINTS, L. W. *Monetary Policy for a Competitive Society.* New York: McGraw-Hill Book Co., Inc., 1950.

MISHAN, E. J. "A Fallacy in the Interpretation of the Cash Balance Effect." *Economica,* N.S., Vol. XXV (May, 1958), pp. 106–18.

MODIGLIANI, F. "Liquidity Preference and the Theory of Interest and Money," *Econometrica,* Vol. XII (January, 1944), pp. 45–88.

————. "Long-Run Implications of Alternative Fiscal Policies and the Burden of the National Debt," *Economic Journal,* Vol. LXXI (December, 1961), pp. 730–55.

MODIGLIANI, F., and BRUMBERG, R. "Utility Analysis and the Consumption Function: An Interpretation of Cross-Section Data," *Post-Keynesian Economics,* ed. by K. Kurihara. New Brunswick, N.J.: Rutgers University Press, 1954.

MODIGLIANI, F., and MILLER, M. H. "The Cost of Capital, Corporation Finance and the Theory of Investment," *American Economic Review,* Vol. XLVIII (June, 1958), pp. 261–97.

MUNDELL, R. A. "The Public Debt, Corporate Income Taxes, and the ate of Interest," *Journal of Political Economy,* Vol. LXVIII (December, 1960), pp. 622–26.

MUSGRAVE, R. A. "Money, Liquidity, and the Valuation of Assets," *Money, Trade, and Economic Growth: Essays in Honor of J. H. Williams.* New York: The Macmillan Co., 1951.

NEVIN, E. *The Mechanism of Cheap Money.* Cardiff, Wales: University of Wales Press, 1955.

NEWLYN, W. T. *Theory of Money.* London: Oxford University Press, 1962.

PATINKIN, D. "Keynesian Economics and the Quantity Theory," *Post-Keynesian Economics,* ed. by K. Kurihara. New Brunswick, N.J.: Rutgers University Press, 1954.

————. *Money, Interest, and Prices.* Evanston, Ill.: Row, Peterson & Co., 1956.

————. "Price Flexibility and Full Employment," *American Economic Review,* Vol. XXXVIII (September, 1948), pp. 543–64.

PIGOU, A. C. "Economic Progress in a Stable Environment," *Economica,* N.S., Vol. XIV (August, 1947), pp. 180–88.

————. *Employment and Equilibrium.* London: Macmillan & Co., Ltd., 1949.

————. *Keynes's 'General Theory.'* London: Macmillan & Co., Ltd., 1952.

————. "The Classical Stationary State," *Economic Journal,* Vol. LIII (December, 1943), pp. 342–51.

————. *The Theory of Unemployment.* London: Macmillan & Co., Ltd., 1933.

RITTER, L. S. "Income Velocity and Anti-Inflationary Monetary Policy," *American Economic Review,* Vol. XLIX (March, 1959), pp. 120–29.

ROBERTSON, D. H. *Banking Policy and the Price Level.* London: Staples Press, Ltd., 1949.

————. "Comments on Mr. Johnson's Notes," *Review of Economic Studies,* Vol. XIX (1951–52), pp. 105–10.

————. *Lectures on Economic Principles,* Vol. II. London: Staples Press, Ltd., 1958.

————. *Money.* London: Nisbet and Co., 1946.

————. "More Notes on the Rate of Interest," *Review of Economic Studies,* Vol. XXI (1953–54), pp. 136–41.

_____. "Mr. Keynes and the Rate of Interest," *Essays in Monetary Theory*. London: Staples Press, Ltd., 1940.

_____. "Saving and Hoarding," *Economic Journal*, Vol. XLIII (September, 1933), pp. 399–413.

_____. "Some Notes on Mr. Keynes' General Theory of Employment," *Quarterly Journal of Economics*, Vol. LI (November, 1936), pp. 168–91.

_____. "Some Notes on the Theory of Interest," *Money, Trade, and Economic Growth: Essays in Honor of J. H. Williams*. New York: The Macmillan Co., 1951.

ROBINSON, J. "The Rate of Interest," *Econometrica*, Vol. XIX (April, 1951), pp. 92–111.

ROSE, H. "Liquidity Preference and Loanable Funds," *Review of Economic Studies*, Vol. XXIV (February, 1957), pp. 111–19.

SAMUELSON, P. A. "Social Indifference Curves," *Quarterly Journal of Economics*, Vol. LXX (February, 1956), pp. 1–22.

_____. "The Simple Mathematics of Income Determination," *Income, Employment and Public Policy: Essays in Honor of A. H. Hansen*. New York: W. W. Norton & Co., Inc., 1948.

SAYERS, R. S. *Modern Banking*. London: Oxford University Press, 1951.

SCHLESINGER, J. R. "After Twenty Years: The General Theory," *Quarterly Journal of Economics*, Vol. LXX (November, 1956), pp. 581–602.

SCHUMPETER, J. A. "Keynes, the Economist," *The New Economics*, ed. by S. E. Harris. New York: Alfred A. Knopf, Inc., 1948.

SCITOVSKY, T. "A Study of Interest and Capital," *Economica*, N.S., Vol. VII (August, 1940), pp. 293–317.

SMITH, W. L. "A Graphical Exposition of the Complete Keynesian System," *Southern Economic Journal*, Vol. XXIII (October, 1956), pp. 115–25.

_____. "Financial Intermediaries and Monetary Controls," *Quarterly Journal of Economics*, Vol. LXIII (November, 1959), pp. 533–53.

_____. "On the Effectiveness of Monetary Policy," *American Economic Review*, Vol. XLVI (September, 1956), pp. 588–606.

SMITHIES, A. "The Quantity of Money and the Rate of Interest," *Review of Economic Statistics*, Vol. XXV (February, 1943), pp. 69–76.

SPRINKEL, B. W. "Reply to Monetary Questions Asked by Mr. Wm. McC. Martin, Jr., Chairman of the Board of Governors of the Federal Reserve System," Unpublished statement, 1956.

STEIN, H. "Price Flexibility and Full Employment: Comment," *American Economic Review*, Vol. XXXIX (June, 1949), pp. 725–26.

TIMLIN, M. F. *Keynesian Economics*. Toronto, Canada: University of Toronto Press, 1942.

TOBIN, J. "A Dynamic Aggregative Model," *Journal of Political Economy*, Vol. LXII (April, 1955), pp. 103–15.

_____. "Asset Holdings and Spending Decisions," *American Economic Review*, Vol. XLII (May, 1952), pp. 109–23.

_____. "Liquidity Preference as Behavior toward Risk," *Review of Economic Studies*, Vol. XXV (February, 1958), pp. 65–86.

_____. "Liquidity Preference and Monetary Policy," *Review of Economics and Statistics*, Vol. XXIX (May, 1947), pp. 124–31.

_____. "Monetary Velocity and Monetary Policy: A Rejoinder," *Review of Economics and Statistics*, Vol. XXX (November, 1948), pp. 314–17.

TOWNSHEND, H. "Liquidity-Premium and the Theory of Value," *Economic Journal*, Vol. XLVII (March, 1937), pp. 157–69.

VICKERS, D. *Studies in the Theory of Money 1690–1776*. Philadelphia: Chilton Co.—Book Division, 1959.

VON MISES, L. *The Theory of Money and Credit*. London: Jonathan Cape, 1952.

WEILER, E. T. *The Economic System*. New York: The Macmillan Co., 1952.

WEINTRAUB, S.   *An Approach to the Theory of Income Distribution.* Philadelphia: Chilton Co.—Book Division, 1958.

—————.   "The Equation of Exchange and the Theory of the Price Level," *Classical Keynesianism, Monetary Theory, and the Price Level.* Philadelphia: Chilton Co.—Book Division, 1961.

—————.   "The Theory of Open Market Operations: A Comment," *Review of Economics and Statistics,* Vol. XLI (August, 1959), pp. 308–12.

WICKSELL, K.   *Interest and Prices.* London: Macmillan & Co., Ltd., 1936.

—————.   *Lectures on Political Economy*, Vol. II (*Money*). London: Routledge and Kegan Paul, Ltd., 1935.

WOOD, J. H.   "Aggregate Liquidity Preference Functions for the United States, 1919–60," Purdue University, Institute for Quantitative Research in Economics and Management, Institute Paper No. 16, 1961.

—————,   *The Term Structure of Interest Rates: A Theoretical and Empirical Study.* Purdue University dissertation, June, 1962.

WORCESTER, D. A., JR.,   "Monetary versus Fiscal Policy at Full Employment," *Journal of Finance*, Vol. XII (March, 1957), pp. 1–15.

WRIGHT, D. M.   "Professor Metzler and the Rate of Interest," *Journal of Political Economy,* Vol. LX (June, 1952), pp. 247–49.

Subject Index

(An italicized page number refers to a diagram.)

Name Index

*This book has been set by Photon in 11
point Times New Roman, leaded 2 points.
Chapter numbers and titles are in 14 and 24
point Techno Bold. The size of the type page
is 27 by 46½ picas.*